Frommer's®

New Orleans
2010

by Mary Herczog

WILEY

Wiley Publishing, Inc.

ABOUT THE AUTHOR

Mary Herczog remains a proud New Orleans homeowner. In addition to this book, she writes *Frommer's Las Vegas, California For Dummies,* and other Frommer's titles. She has also written about Bali for *Frommer's Dream Vacations* and *Frommer's Southeast Asia.* She is the author of the young adult novel *Figures of Echo,* the basis for the recent Lifetime movie *Custody.*

Published by:

WILEY PUBLISHING, INC.

111 River St.
Hoboken, NJ 07030-5774

ISBN 978-0-470-50471-0
Editor: Michael Kelly, with Cate Latting
Production Editor: Jonathan Scott
Cartographer: Guy Ruggiero
Photo Editor: Richard Fox
Production by Wiley Indianapolis Composition Services

Front cover photo: Local zydeco musician Anthony Dopsie ©Cheryl Gerber Photography
Back cover photo: A balcony in the French Quarter ©Uripos Photography / eStock Photo

For information on our other products and services or to obtain technical support, please contact our Customer Care Department within the U.S. at 877/762-2974, outside the U.S. at 317/572-3993 or fax 317/572-4002.

Wiley also publishes its books in a variety of electronic formats. Some content that appears in print may not be available in electronic formats.

Manufactured in the United States of America

5 4 3 2 1

CONTENTS

5 SUGGESTED NEW ORLEANS ITINERARIES 66

6 WHERE TO STAY 82

7 WHERE TO DINE 116

8 SIGHTS TO SEE & PLACES TO BE 167

LIST OF MAPS

ACKNOWLEDGMENTS

Thank you to the city of New Orleans and its greatest asset, its people. Thank you to Frommer's and Cate Latting, for their continued support of the city, and me, through difficult times. Thank you to the Metropolitan Convention and Visitor's Bureau for help with arrangements. Thanks to the Fat Pack (Chuck, Wesly, Diana, Robin, Dave, Nettie, John, and Fiona) for valuable pork-based research. This year's Stunt Stomachs (Caroline, Jean, and Debi) did their parts with gusto. I love the North Rendon All Stars and I love our house, even the parts that have to be fixed all the time. Nothing can fix Steve Hochman because he is perfect.

HOW TO CONTACT US

In researching this book, we discovered many wonderful places—hotels, restaurants, shops, and more. We're sure you'll find others. Please tell us about them, so we can share the information with your fellow travelers in upcoming editions. If you were disappointed with a recommendation, we'd love to know that, too. Please write to:

Frommer's New Orleans 2010
Wiley Publishing, Inc. • 111 River St. • Hoboken, NJ 07030-5774

AN ADDITIONAL NOTE

Please be advised that travel information is subject to change at any time—and this is especially true of prices. We therefore suggest that you write or call ahead for confirmation when making your travel plans. The authors, editors, and publisher cannot be held responsible for the experiences of readers while traveling. Your safety is important to us, however, so we encourage you to stay alert and be aware of your surroundings. Keep a close eye on cameras, purses, and wallets, all favorite targets of thieves and pickpockets.

FROMMER'S STAR RATINGS, ICONS & ABBREVIATIONS

Every hotel, restaurant, and attraction listing in this guide has been ranked for quality, value, service, amenities, and special features using a **star-rating system.** In country, state, and regional guides, we also rate towns and regions to help you narrow down your choices and budget your time accordingly. Hotels and restaurants are rated on a scale of zero (recommended) to three stars (exceptional). Attractions, shopping, nightlife, towns, and regions are rated according to the following scale: zero stars (recommended), one star (highly recommended), two stars (very highly recommended), and three stars (must-see).

In addition to the star-rating system, we also use **seven feature icons** that point you to the great deals, in-the-know advice, and unique experiences that separate travelers from tourists. Throughout the book, look for:

Finds	Special finds—those places only insiders know about
Fun Facts	Fun facts—details that make travelers more informed and their trips more fun
Kids	Best bets for kids and advice for the whole family
Moments	Special moments—those experiences that memories are made of
Overrated	Places or experiences not worth your time or money
Tips	Insider tips—great ways to save time and money
Value	Great values—where to get the best deals

The following **abbreviations** are used for credit cards:

AE	American Express	DISC	Discover	V	Visa
DC	Diners Club	MC	MasterCard		

TRAVEL RESOURCES AT FROMMERS.COM

Frommer's travel resources don't end with this guide. Frommer's website, **www.frommers. com**, has travel information on more than 4,000 destinations. We update features regularly, giving you access to the most current trip-planning information and the best airfare, lodging, and car-rental bargains. You can also listen to podcasts, connect with other Frommers.com members through our active-reader forums, share your travel photos, read blogs from guidebook editors and fellow travelers, and much more.

The Best of New Orleans

New Orleans should come with a warning label.

No, no, not about hurricanes. Forget that. That's like solely identifying San Francisco and Los Angeles with earthquakes. No, this is about the city itself. See, there's this group of residents whom locals call the "never lefts." They are the people who came to New Orleans as tourists: came for Mardi Gras, came for Jazz Fest, or just came. And the city worked its magic on them. They listened to street musicians around Jackson Square. They danced to brass bands in clubs at night. They gazed at lush tropical courtyards hidden behind unassuming building fronts. They strolled down streets time seemed to have forgotten. They kissed beneath flickering gas lamps. They ate incredible meals and topped them off with beignets at 3am at the Café du Monde while watching the passing human parade. They found themselves perusing newspaper ads for houses and apartments, because as their trip's scheduled end date came and went, they were still in New Orleans. They came for Mardi Gras, came for Jazz Fest, just came—and *never left*.

New Orleans does that to people.

It's a remarkable thing, but even with the thick layer of catastrophic damage around it, the core of New Orleans remains as magical and seductive as ever. It should be cliché to use those words, but when even news anchors and relief workers who have never been to the city before find themselves falling into local ways and going to efforts to return again and again, you know there is something powerful about the place. The visual delights of the remarkable French Quarter and Garden District remain. Once again music flows from random doorways or is played right in the street. Jazz, Cajun, blues, whatever—you'll find yourself moving to a rhythm and wondering if the streets really are dancing along with you. There are delicious smells in the moist, honeyed air, which seems to carry a whiff of the Caribbean while caressing your skin, almost as if it were alive.

And then there's the food. Don't get us started on the food.

The best way to get inside New Orleans is to plunge right in. Don't just go for the obvious. Sure, we've met people who never left Bourbon Street and had a terrific time, but the city has so much more to offer. We've also met people who went for recognizable names and quick and easy decisions and then were disappointed that their experiences were no more than adequate.

Look over the advice that follows, here and in the hotel and dining chapters, and you should be able to sidestep the inevitable tourist traps. We want you to go home having passed a real good time, as the locals say. If you want to get your hands dirty and help with some of the ongoing work, thank you. But if all your dirt comes from the powdered sugar on a beignet, then you did your trip right, too. You came. That matters a lot. Maybe you will even come back again.

That is, assuming you do go home. Remember: We warned you, so don't blame us if you come to New Orleans and one day discover that you never left.

1 THE BEST FIRST-TIME NEW ORLEANS EXPERIENCES

- **Beignets & Café au Lait at Café du Monde:** Sit on the crowded patio gazing at the action on Decatur Street and Jackson Square. Gorge on hot French-style doughnuts liberally coated in powdered sugar (everyone will know what you've been doing from the sprinkles on your shirt) and washed down with potent chicory coffee. And do it at any hour of the day—3pm or 3am. It's open 24 hours! See p. 163.

- **Jazz at Preservation Hall:** Drop your eight bucks in the hat and squeeze into one of the country's time-honored jazz institutions. Your feet will be moving and your ears will be happy, even if they never knew they liked jazz before. See p. 258.

- **A Crowded Night at the Maple Leaf:** The Maple Leaf is a very "New Orleans" club and a terrific place to hang out. On nights when popular bands fill the place to hot, sweaty capacity and the crowd spills over into the street and dances right on the sidewalk, it's sublime. See p. 264.

- **Dinner at Commander's Palace:** It took over a year after Katrina for this legendary restaurant to reopen, thanks to massive reconstruction requirements. It's romantic, gracious, attentive, and delicious. See p. 155.

- **A Cemetery Tour:** New Orleans's above-the-ground tombs are hard to forget once you've seen them, and touring these ghostly cities of the dead provides you with a unique look into the history and culture of the city. See p. 196.

- **A Stroll Through the Garden District:** These elegant (not flashy) old homes, nestled among lush trees, are wonderful to gaze at and covet. At the right time of day, you might have the streets largely to yourself and feel you've slipped back in time—or into an Anne Rice novel. See p. 221.

- **A Stroll Along St. John's Bayou:** Most tourists don't get much beyond the Quarter or they speed past this low-slung body of water as they head for City Park. Slow down local-style, finally away from the hordes as you meander along the bayou and admire the less high-profile but no less romantic neighborhood around it. See p. 226.

- **Bourbon Street After Dark:** Even if you end up hating it, you have to see it at least once. Music spurts and oozes out of windows and doors, drinkers reign supreme, and sex is widely available—on paper, on stage, and on video. It's wild, disgusting, and strangely exhilarating. See chapter 11.

- **Club Hopping in the Frenchmen Section:** This portion of the Faubourg Marigny (the neighborhood that borders the French Quarter to the north and east) features at least a dozen clubs and several bars, each with its own personality and charm. Stroll from one to the other, dipping in for a bit or just listening to the music pouring out the doors before moving on to sample something farther down the street. See chapter 11.

- **Dancing to the ReBirth Brass Band, John Boutte, and/or Kermit Ruffins:** Dancing to three of the best musical acts New Orleans has to offer (a brass band, an astonishing soul crooner, and a jazz musician in the tradition of Louis Armstrong, respectively) is the physical manifestation of the word *fun*—and the truest spirit of New Orleans. See chapter 11.

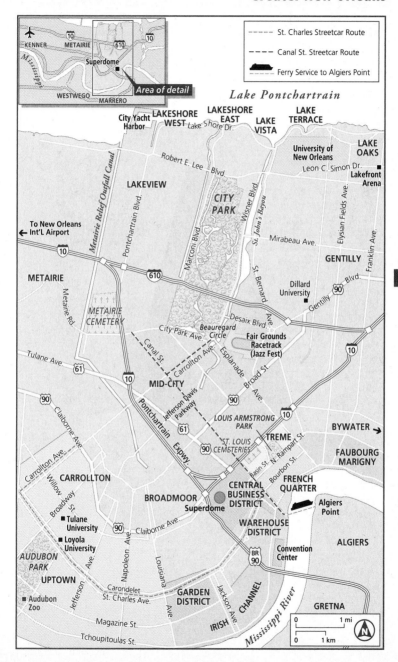

2 THE BEST TRIP MEMENTOS

The following are just a few suggestions for New Orleans souvenirs beyond the T-shirts and snow globes, and more welcome than a couple of extra pounds around your hips.

- **A Book from Faulkner House,** 624 Pirates Alley (© **504/524-2940**): In chapter 2, we've listed a portion of the many books inspired by this city, and you should consider picking up a couple from this jewel of that vanishing species, the independent bookstore. Tucked into the bottom floor of the house where William Faulkner lived long enough to write two novels (*Mosquitoes* and *Soldiers' Pay*), this charming shop's centerpiece is a table crammed with New Orleans– and Louisiana-related literature, novels, nonfiction, poetry, and art books, with still more on the surrounding shelves (ask the staff to point you in the right direction). Many an author has tried, with varying success, to capture New Orleans on the page, and you may find their efforts will help you get a little fix back home when you begin to know what it means to miss New Orleans. And where better to buy it than at a local institution with a literary history? See p. 237.

- **A Photo or Art Book from A Gallery for Fine Photography,** 241 Chartres St. (© **504/568-1313**): The owner calls his impressive shop "the only museum where you can buy the art." Always feeling free to spend your money, we do admit we are talking about a bigger investment than a poster. Many famous photographers are represented here, but for our purposes at this moment, you will want to concentrate on the local artists' works such as E. J. Bellocq's famous Storyville photos, or possibly more affordably, atmospheric cemetery images from Sandra Russell

Clark, Michael P. Smith's locally beloved moments of New Orleans color and custom (Jazz Fest photos from throughout the festival's 30-year history, jazz funerals, Mardi Gras Indians, and much more), or even photos of the New Orleans World Fair taken by owner Joshua Mann Pailet. If an original is still out of your financial reach, they also carry a range of photo art books. See p. 235.

- **A Southern Scent from Hove,** 824 Royal St. (© **504/525-7827**): A perfumery since the 1930s, Hove not only creates their own unique perfumes (like Bayou D'Amor and Creole Days) but also carries some traditional scents. We got hooked on their version of vetiver, which was described by one Virginia-native-turned-Louisiana-resident as "smelling like the South" (Creoles used it to freshen up stuffy closets). Locals also adore the tea olive (made from the indigenous sweet olive). The scents come in perfume drams, as cologne, and some in soaps, while they also sell dried vetiver for your own closet. And they have scents for men, too! See p. 237.

- **A CD from the Louisiana Music Factory,** 210 Decatur St. (© **504/586-1094**): A visitor might first think of the sights or tastes of New Orleans as his or her primary sensory experience, but take away the music and you just have another pretty, aging city. Bring some of it home with you, courtesy of an independent store that doesn't just hold the best selection of New Orleans music but embodies its funky spirit. We've listed a number of possibilities to consider in chapter 2, "New Orleans in Depth," and you can always ask the salespeople as well. See p. 244.

- **Mardi Gras Beads:** Here's an interesting phenomenon: You go to New Orleans, especially around Mardi Gras time, and you get saturated by beads. They are like leaves on the ground—valueless by reason of their ubiquity and seasonal expiration date. But hand a friend at home a few strands, and watch her face light up with pleasure. Even the beads that you know are the cheap, crappy ones will delight, because outside of the parade setting, they are novel.

Don't buy beads (unless it's just a strand or two) in shops around the Quarter, where you can pay 10 times what the beads cost at the source, **Accent Annex,** 1009 McDermott Rd., Metairie (✆ **888/ 394-5537** or 504/391-3900). Sadly, they no longer have a Quarter outlet, but the money you'll save on beads will make driving to their store in Metairie worth it, especially if you intend to buy in bulk. The smaller antiques stores on Esplanade near Decatur often have bags of used beads, which can produce some curious variations, and in those same shops and the like on Magazine you can often find antique Czech glass beads, though even those cost about three times what they did some years ago. Finally, you can go to the headquarters for the Zulu Krewe, known for the coolest beads of any krewe. You will have to pay a bit more for them, but all the money goes back to the krewe: Zulu Social Aid & Pleasure Club, 732 N. Broad St. (✆ **504/827-1661**).

- **Christmas Tree Ornaments and Other Handicrafts:** The Poor Claire nuns make everything in their little gift shop, from handmade rosaries and ceramic statues (look for the glazed nativity scenes) to, best of all, Sr. Olivia's amazing Christmas tree ornaments. Various iconic New Orleans landmarks (from the Cabildo to the Cathedral, from a Lucky Dog cart to Mardi Gras floats) are meticulously re-created in architecturally accurate and scaled detail, and then hand-painted on balsa wood. Locals collect them all (there are some standards, but she also introduces new designs each year). The prices are so low it feels sinful. Buy a lot, to ease your conscience. (**Monastery Gift Shop,** 720 Henry Clay Ave.; ✆ **504/895-2019;** go to the sliding window when you enter the building, and ring the bell. The nun on duty that day will open the gift shop for you.)

- **Glasswork from Studio Inferno:** This art gallery/shop features playful New Orleans–inspired glass pieces—cocktail glasses with a fleur-de-lis in the stem, "milagros" with flames shooting out of them (a sacred heart for faithfulness, a torso for good health), spicy-looking peppers on cords to wear as a necklace—at prices that will allow you to fill up your whole gift list. 3000 Royal St. (✆ **504/945-1878**).

3 THE BEST NEW ORLEANS DRINKS

Keep this in mind: Hurricanes are for tourists; Sazeracs are for natives.

This is a town that knows its booze, for sure, and it has contributed a few cocktails to the pantheon. You can drink beer anywhere. Why not try a few indigenous cocktails? That said, there's nothing wrong with a Hurricane every now and again,

even for natives. (We'd like to thank Chuck Taggart, who regularly reports on New Orleans and other cocktails at www. gumbopages.com, for this list.)

- **Sazerac:** The quintessential New Orleans cocktail, one of the first, and perhaps the greatest ever. The combination of rye whiskey (or cognac), Peychaud's Bitters, a touch of sugar, a hint of Herbsaint anise liqueur, and a breath of lemon oil create a symphony of flavor, and it plays new movements as the drink warms up.

- **Ramos Gin Fizz:** There was a time when there were 35 barback boys shaking gin fizzes behind the bar at Henry C. Ramos' Stag Saloon, and Huey P. Long took his favorite bartender from the Roosevelt Hotel to Washington with him so that he would never be deprived of his beloved gin fizz. What's in it? Gin, egg whites, orange flower water, lemon and lime juice, soda water, and cream. It might be hard to find these days. (The Old Absinthe House still makes it.) Ask for it, and make the local bartenders learn about their own history.
- **Vieux Carré Cocktail:** Unjustly forgotten except for a growing number of cocktailians and the bartenders at the Hotel Monteleone, this wonderful creation was given to us by Walter Bergeron, head bartender at the hotel in the 1930s. He put together rye whiskey, cognac, sweet vermouth, Benedictine D.O.M., and two kinds of bitters, and we thank him.

- **The Brandy Crusta:** Created at Santina's Saloon in New Orleans in the 1880s, this drink was the first to combine a base spirit, liqueur, and citrus juice, plus a dash of bitters. This makes it the father of the Sidecar, the margarita, and all of their descendants in a category of drinks that author and cocktailian Gary Regan calls "New Orleans Sours." It's a beautiful drink, with a beautiful garnish—the rim is frosted with sugar, and a wide piece of lemon peel encircles the mouth of the glass; you sip the drink over the lemon peel.
- **Hurricane:** Okay, okay, so we dissed the Hurricane before, but really, it's a fruity delight, a deviously stealthy drink (as you can't really taste the alcohol). But Pat O'Brien's is actually a nice, fun bar and worth going to (unless you have to wait in a long line of tourists to get in). What you get these days is a far cry from what Charlie Cantrell first concocted out of rum, passion fruit, and other ingredients back in the 1940s; what we get today is made from a bottled and/or powdered premix. Still, everybody needs to knock back a Hurricane once in a while.

4 THE BEST BARS BEYOND BOURBON

So now that you've read the above, you want to branch out with your drinking environment as well as your choice of drinks. There are many fine bars in this city, but here's a sampling for those looking for something more interesting than the watering holes of the frat variety.

- **French 75 Bar at Arnaud's,** 813 Bienville St. (© **504/523-5433**): Beautiful room, beautiful bar, with enthusiastic, friendly bartenders who now keep a copy of Ted "Dr. Cocktail" Haigh's

book *Vintage Spirits and Forgotten Cocktails* behind the bar. (Haigh is the curator of the Museum of the American Cocktail.) See p. 268.
- **Napoleon House,** 500 Chartres St. (© **504/524-9752**): One of the most civilized drinking spaces in the world. It looks its age (over a century), classical and jazz music play gently, and they serve really good Sazeracs along with their house cocktail (the Pimm's Cup, garnished with a cucumber spear), plus warm muffulettas to boot. See p. 269.

- **Carousel Bar at the Monteleone Hotel,** 214 Royal St. (© **504/523-3341**): No, you're not drunk. The bar is actually spinning; the stools rotate around the central hub of the Carousel Bar. Ask for the Vieux Carré Cocktail, their signature drink for nearly 75 years. See p. 266.
- **The Columns,** 3811 St. Charles Ave. (© **504/899-9308**): The interior substituted for the brothel in the movie *Pretty Baby,* which is reason enough to come here, but truly, it's the wide, deep veranda that will inspire your Southern, warm summer night, mint-julep-sipping fantasies. See p. 270.
- **Ralph's on the Park,** 900 City Park Ave. (© **504/488-1000**): The newest venue on our list, once the site of a tavern frequented by the ladies of Storyville, though in being spiffed up it's lost that particular ooh-la-la flavor. Still, who cares? Look how gorgeous that bar is! A grown-up but not stuffy place to drink, with a gorgeous view of the oak trees at City Park, plus real Sazerac rye to make their Sazeracs! See p. 145.
- **Swizzle Stick Bar at Café Adelaide,** 300 Poydras St., in the Loews Hotel (© **504/595-3305**): Classy and sassy, with its own self-named signature cocktail. Get the cocktail sampler, which comes with shots of the Swizzle (made with New Orleans silver rum, lime juice, bitters, a splash of club soda, and a secret ingredient), or sometimes additionally Sidecars and Sazeracs. See p. 273.
- **Orleans Grapevine Wine Bar & Bistro,** 720 Orleans Ave. (© **504/523-1930**): A wonderfully intimate venue, dark and cool, and surprisingly quiet so close to the bustle of Bourbon Street. There's a staggeringly extensive wine list and a small but delightful seasonal dining menu. See p. 269.

2

New Orleans in Depth

Throughout this book, we'll talk about the mystique of New Orleans and its ineffable essence. But first, it's time for some hard-core stats. The largest city in Louisiana (pre-Katrina) and one of the chief cities of the South, New Orleans is nearly 100 miles above the mouth of the Mississippi River system and stretches along a strip of land 5 to 8 miles wide between the Mississippi and Lake Pontchartrain to the north. This is a city surrounded by water—a gulf, a river, and a lake—and it's all largely under sea level. The highest natural point is in City Park, a whole 35 feet above sea level. That brings us to grimmer, more recent facts. There are 350 miles of levee systems, designed to keep the city dry. Breeches in at least three main levees, plus more in the Mississippi River Gulf Outlet, caused flooding in 80% of the city shortly after August 29, 2005. The flooding ranged in depth from mere inches to well over 12 feet, resulting in billions of dollars in damage. Recovery will be ongoing for decades.

1   HISTORY 101

IN THE BEGINNING

Two French-Canadian brothers found this spot at the turn of the 18th century. Pierre Le Moyne, Sieur d'Iberville, led an expedition from France to rediscover the mouth of the Mississippi in 1699. René Robert Cavelier, Sieur de la Salle, had claimed the region for France in 1682. (He was murdered in Texas in 1687 by his own party because his lack of navigational and leadership skills risked many of their lives.) Iberville's expedition succeeded, and he planted a cross at a dramatic bend in the river near where La Salle had stopped almost 2 decades before. On his voyage, Iberville also established a fort at Biloxi, naming it the capital of France's new and uncharted territory. His brother, 18-year-old Jean Baptiste Le Moyne, Sieur de Bienville, stayed behind in Biloxi and quickly became commanding officer of the territory. For the next 20 years, he harbored thoughts of returning up the river and establishing a new capital city at the spot where he and his brother had stopped.

In 1718 Bienville got his chance. The previous year, Louisiana had been entrusted to the Company of the West (also known as Company of the Indies or the Mississippi Company) for development as a populated colony. The company was headed by John Law, a Scottish entrepreneur who had convinced the French monarch and many stockholders in his company that fortunes were to be had in the new land. The company authorized Bienville to find a suitable location for a settlement on the river at a spot that would also protect France's holdings in the New World from British expansion.

Bienville quickly settled on high ground at the site he had previously seen, and not only because the bend in the river would be relatively easy to defend: Although it was some 100 miles inland along the river from the Gulf of Mexico, the site was near St. John's Bayou, which provided easy water transportation directly into Lake Pontchartrain. It was convenient from a military standpoint—providing a "back door" for defense or escape should the fortunes of war turn against the French—and it gave the site great potential as a trade route because it would allow relatively easy access to the Gulf.

The new town was named New Orleans in honor of the duc d'Orléans, then the regent of France. Following the plan of a late French medieval town, a central square (the Place d'Armes) was laid out with streets forming a grid around it. A church, government office, priest's house, and official residences fronted the square, and earthen ramparts dotted with forts were built around the perimeter. A tiny wooden levee was raised against the river, which still flooded periodically and turned the streets into rivers of mud. Today this area of original settlement is known as the Vieux Carré ("old square") and the Place d'Armes as Jackson Square.

A MELTING POT

In its first few years, New Orleans was a community of French officials, adventurers, merchants, slaves, soldiers, and convicts from French prisons, all living in rude huts of cypress, moss, and clay. These were the first ingredients of New Orleans's population gumbo. The city's commerce was mainly limited to trade with native tribes and to beginning agricultural production.

To supply people and capital to the colony, John Law's company began what was essentially the first real estate scam in the New World. The territory and the city were marketed on the continent as Heaven on Earth, full of immediate and boundless opportunities for wealth and luxury. The value of real estate in the territory rose dramatically with the spreading of these lies as wealthy Europeans, aristocrats, merchants, exiles, soldiers, and a large contingent of German farmers arrived—to find only mosquitoes, a raw frontier existence, and swampy land. Ultimately, the company's scheme nearly bankrupted the French nation. It did succeed, however, in swelling the population of the territory and of New Orleans; in 1723, the city replaced Biloxi as the capital of the Louisiana territory.

In 1724 Bienville approved the *Code Noir*, which set forth the laws under which African slaves were to be treated and established Catholicism as the territory's official religion. While it codified slavery and banished Jews from Louisiana, the code did provide slaves recognition and a degree of protection under the law.

One significant natural barrier to development of the population and society in Louisiana remained: a lack of potential wives. In 1727 a small contingent of Ursuline nuns arrived in the city and set about establishing a convent. While they weren't exactly eligible, they did provide a temporary home and education to many shiploads of *les filles à la cassette*. The "cassette girls" or "casket girls"—named for the

DATELINE

- **1682** Sieur de la Salle stops near the present site while traveling down the Mississippi River from the Great Lakes region and plants a cross claiming the territory for Louis XIV.
- **1699** Pierre Le Moyne, Sieur d'Iberville, rediscovers and secures the mouth of the Mississippi—on Mardi Gras day, appropriately.

- **1718** The first governor of Louisiana, Iberville's brother, Jean-Baptiste Le Moyne, Sieur de Bienville, founds New Orleans.
- **1723** New Orleans replaces Biloxi as the capital of Louisiana.
- **1726** Capuchin monastery erected.
- **1752** Ursuline Convent completed.
- **1762** Louis XV secretly cedes New Orleans and all of Louisiana west of the Mississippi to Spain.

- **1768** French residents in New Orleans banish Spanish commissioner Don Antonio de Ulloa, proclaiming independence from Spain.
- **1769** The Spanish return.
- **1783** Treaty of Paris confirms Spanish possession.
- **1788, 1794** Fires destroy much of the city; new brick buildings replace wood.

continues

government-issue *cassettes* or casketlike trunks in which they carried their possessions—were young women of appropriate character sent to Louisiana by the French government to be courted and married by the colonists. (If we're to believe the current residents of the city, the plan was remarkably successful: Nearly everyone in New Orleans claims descent from the casket girls or from Spanish or French nobility, which makes one wonder at the terrible infertility of the colony's earlier population of convicts and "fallen women.")

John Law's company relinquished its governance of Louisiana in 1731, and the French monarch regained direct control of the territory. In the following decades, a number of planters established estates up and down the river from New Orleans. In the city, wealthier society began to develop a courtly atmosphere on the French model. In the midst of the rough-and-tumble frontier, families competed to see who could throw the most elegant and opulent parties.

Farther afield, westward along the Gulf of Mexico, other French speakers were creating a very different kind of society in a decidedly more rural mode. During the 18th century, many French colonists, displaced by British rule from Acadia, Nova Scotia, formed an outpost on the new French territory along the coastland. Today you'll find the Acadians' descendants living

a little to the west of New Orleans, still engaged in farming and trapping, some still speaking their unique brand of French, and proudly calling themselves "Cajuns."

New Orleans experienced only modest commercial development in its first decades, in large part due to trading restrictions imposed by France: The colony could trade only with the mother country. Colonists quickly found ways around the restrictions, however, and smugglers and pirates provided alternative markets and transportation for the region's agricultural products, furs, bricks, and tar.

Despite the awkward relationship with France, New Orleanians were greatly disturbed to learn in 1764 that 2 years earlier (news traveled right slow back then) Louis XV had given their city and all of Louisiana west of the Mississippi to his cousin, Charles III of Spain, in the secret Treaty of Fontainebleau. The Spanish, in turn, took 2 more years to send a governor, Don Antonio de Ulloa, who made few friends among local residents. By 1768 a large number of French residents of New Orleans and outlying areas assembled to demand Ulloa's removal. Some proposed the formation of a Louisiana republic. Ulloa was sent packing, and for nearly 2 years, New Orleans and Louisiana were effectively independent of any foreign power. This episode ended in 1769 when

- **1794** Planter Etienne de Boré granulates sugar from cane for the first time, spawning a boom in the industry.
- **1795** Treaty of Madrid opens port to Americans; trade thrives.
- **1800** Louisiana again becomes a French possession.
- **1803** France officially takes possession of the territory.

United States then purchases it and takes possession.
- **1805** New Orleans incorporates as a city; first elections are held.
- **1812** The New Orleans, the first steam vessel to travel the Mississippi, arrives from Pittsburgh. Louisiana admitted as a U.S. state.
- **1815** Battle of New Orleans.
- **1831** The first (horse-drawn) railway west of the

Alleghenies is completed, linking New Orleans and Milneburg.
- **1832–33** Yellow fever and cholera epidemic kills 10,000 people in 2 years.
- **1834** Medical College of Louisiana (forerunner of Tulane University) founded.
- **1837** First newspaper coverage of a Mardi Gras parade.
- **1840** Antoine Alciatore, founder of Antoine's restaurant, arrives from Marseille.

Don Alexander O'Reilly (known as "Bloody O'Reilly") and 3,000 soldiers arrived in the city, dispatched by the Spanish Crown. What had been a relatively peaceful rebellion was extinguished, its leaders were executed, and Spanish rule was reimposed. With a Gallic shrug, French aristocracy mingled with Spanish nobility, intermarried, and helped to create a new "Creole" culture.

Devastating fires struck in 1788 (when more than 850 buildings were destroyed) and again in 1794 in the midst of rebuilding. From the ashes emerged a new architecture dominated by the proud Spanish style of brick-and-plaster buildings replete with arches, courtyards, balconies, and, of course, attached slave quarters. Even today you'll see tile markers giving Spanish street names at every corner in the French Quarter.

The city of New Orleans was coveted by the English and the Americans—and the French, though the trade to Spain was partly motivated because the unsuccessful colony was costing them money and they could no longer afford it. The Spanish imposed the same kind of trade restrictions on the city that the French had, with even less success (these were boom years for pirates and buccaneers like the infamous Jean Lafitte and his brother Pierre). This being a period of intense imperial conflict and maneuvering, Spain did allow

some American revolutionaries to trade through the city in support of the colonists' fight against Britain. France regained possession of the territory in 1800 with a surprisingly quiet transfer of ownership and held on for 3 years while Napoleon negotiated the Louisiana Purchase with the United States for the paltry (as it turned out) sum of $15 million. For Creole society, the return to French rule was unpleasant enough because France had long been facing serious financial troubles, but a sale to America was anathema. To their minds, it meant the end of a European lifestyle in the Vieux Carré.

Thus, when Americans arrived in the city, the upper classes made it known that they were welcome to settle—but across Canal Street (so named because a drainage canal was once planned along its route, although it was never constructed), away from the old city and Creole society. And so it was that New Orleans came to be two parallel cities. The American section spread outward from Canal Street along St. Charles Avenue; business and cultural institutions centered in the Central Business District, and mansions rose in what is now the Garden District, which was a separate, incorporated city until 1852. French and Creole society dominated the Quarter for the rest of the 19th century, extending toward the lake along Esplanade Avenue. Soon, however, the Americans

New Orleans is the fourth-largest city in the United States and is second only to New York as a port.
- **1849** The Place d'Armes renamed Jackson Square.
- **1850** Booming commerce totals $200 million; cotton accounts for 45% of total trade. City becomes largest slave market in the country.
- **1852** Consolidation of municipal government; New

Orleans annexes city of Lafayette.
- **1853–55** Yellow fever epidemic during the summer; 12% of the population killed in 1853 in roughly 2 months.
- **1861–62** Louisiana secedes from the Union; city captured by Adm. David Farragut. Gen. Benjamin Butler assumes command of the city and earns a reputation for harsh and unfriendly governance.

- **1865–77** Reconstruction; "carpetbaggers" swarm into the city, and tensions climax in clashes between the Crescent White League and government forces.
- **1870** Algiers and Jefferson City annexed.
- **1872** Carrollton annexed.
- **1884–85** Cotton Centennial Exposition (World's Fair) held at the present site of Audubon Park.

continues

(crass though they may have seemed) brought commercial success to the city, which quickly warmed relations—the Americans sought the vitality of downtown society, and the Creoles sought the profit of American business. They also had occasion to join forces against hurricanes, yellow-fever epidemics, and floods.

FROM THE BATTLE OF NEW ORLEANS TO THE CIVIL WAR

Perhaps nothing helped to cement a sense of community more than the Battle of New Orleans, during the War of 1812. The great turning point in Creole-American relations was the cooperation of Andrew Jackson and Jean Lafitte. To save the city, Jackson set aside his disdain for the pirate, and Lafitte turned down offers to fight for the British, instead supplying the Americans with cannons and ammunition that helped swing the battle in their favor. When Jackson called for volunteers, some 5,000 citizens from both sides of Canal Street responded. Battle was joined on January 8, 1815, in a field a few miles downstream from the city, and approximately 2,000 British troops and 20 Americans were killed or wounded. The dramatic battle made a local and national hero of Jackson. Ironically, though, neither Jackson nor the British had been aware that a treaty concluding the war had been signed a full 2 weeks before, on December 24, 1814.

From then until the Civil War, New Orleans was a boomtown. Colonial trade restrictions had evaporated with the Louisiana Purchase, and more importantly, the era of steam-powered river travel arrived in 1812 with the first riverboat, the aptly named *New Orleans,* delivered from a Pittsburgh shipyard. River commerce exploded, peaking in the 1840s and putting New Orleans's port on par with New York's. Cotton and sugar made many fortunes in New Orleans and its environs; wealthy planters joined the city merchants in building luxurious town houses and attending festivals, opera, theater, banquets, parades, and spectacular balls (including "Quadroon Balls," where beautiful mulatto girls were displayed to the male gentry as possible mistresses). As always, politics and gambling were dominant pastimes of these citizens and visitors.

By the middle of the century, cotton-related business was responsible for nearly half of the total commerce in New Orleans, so it's no surprise that the city housed one of the nation's largest and most ruthless slave markets. Paradoxically, New Orleans also had one of the most extended and established populations of "free men (and women) of color" in the American South. Furthermore, racial distinctions within the

- **1890** Jelly Roll Morton born.
- **1890** Creole of color Homer Plessy gets arrested riding a train recently segregated by Jim Crow laws. He sues the state, an effort that culminates in the landmark U.S. Supreme Court decision *Plessy v. Ferguson.*
- **1892** First electric streetcar operates along St. Charles Avenue.
- **1897** Sidney Bechet born. Storyville established.

- **1901** Louis Armstrong born in New Orleans.
- **1911** Razzy Dazzy Spasm Band performs in New York, where its name is changed to Razzy Dazzy Jazz Band.
- **1917** Original Dixieland Jazz Band attains height of popularity.
- **1921** Inner-Harbor Navigational Canal built, connecting Lake Pontchartrain and the Mississippi.

- **1928** Colorful Huey P. Long elected governor of Louisiana; 4 years later he is elected to U.S. Senate.
- **1935** Long is shot dead.
- **1938** Tennessee Williams arrives in New Orleans; Huey P. Long Bridge built over Mississippi River.
- **1939** French Quarter Residents Association formed as an agent for preservation.

city increasingly became difficult to determine; people could often trace their ancestry back to two or even three different continents. Adding to the diversity, waves of Irish and German immigrants arrived in New Orleans during this period, supplying important sources of labor to support the city's growth.

This growth—upriver and downriver from the original center and away from the river toward Lake Pontchartrain—required extensive drainage of swamps and the construction of a system of canals and levees. The only major impediments to the development of the city in these decades were occasional yellow-fever epidemics, which killed thousands of residents and visitors. Despite the clearing of swampland, the mosquito-borne disease persisted until the final decades of the 19th century.

RECONSTRUCTION & BEYOND

The boom era ended rather abruptly with the Civil War and Louisiana's secession from the United States in 1861. Federal troops marched into the city in 1862 and stayed until 1877, through the bitter Reconstruction period. As was the case elsewhere in the South, this period saw violent clashes between armed white groups and the state's Reconstruction forces.

After the war the city went about the business of rebuilding its economic life—this time without slavery. By 1880 a number of annexations had rounded out the city limits, port activity had begun to pick up, and railroads were establishing their importance to the local and national economies. Also, a new group of immigrants, Italians this time, came to put their unique mark on the city. Through it all, an undiminished enthusiasm for fun survived. Gambling again thrived in more than 80 establishments, there were almost 800 saloons, and scores of "bawdy houses" engaged in prostitution, which was illegal but uncontrolled. New Orleans was earning an international reputation for open vice, much to the chagrin of the city's polite society.

In 1897 Alderman Sidney Story thought he had figured out how to improve the city's tarnishing image. He moved all illegal (but highly profitable) activities into a restricted district along Basin Street, next door to the French Quarter. Quickly nicknamed Storyville, the district boasted fancy "sporting palaces" with elaborate decor, musical entertainment, and a wide variety of ladies of pleasure. Visitors and residents could purchase a directory (the *Blue Book*) that listed alphabetically the names, addresses, and races of more than 700 prostitutes, ranging from those in the "palaces" to the poorer inhabitants of wretched, decaying

- **1956** Lake Pontchartrain Causeway, world's longest bridge, completed.
- **1960** The city's public schools integrated.
- **1973** Parades banned in the Vieux Carré, changing the character of the city's observance of Mardi Gras.
- **1975** Superdome opens.
- **1977** Ernest N. "Dutch" Morial becomes first African-American mayor.
- **1984** Louisiana World Expo draws disappointing crowds but spurs redevelopment of the riverside area between Canal and Poydras streets.
- **1988** Anne Rice moves back to New Orleans, which has enormous impact on the city.
- **1999** Harrah's opens new casino.
- **2000** The National World War II Museum opens along

with Jazzland, a new theme park just outside the city. Mardi Gras 2000 draws record crowds.
- **2005** Hurricane Katrina hits August 29.

shacks (called "cribs") on the blocks behind Basin Street. Black musicians such as Jelly Roll Morton played the earliest form of jazz in some of Basin Street's ornate bordellos. Although jazz predates Storyville, here it gained popularity before moving upriver and into record collections everywhere. When the secretary of the navy decreed in 1917 that armed forces should not be exposed to so much open vice, Storyville closed down and disappeared without a trace. None of the fancy sporting houses remains.

THE 20TH CENTURY

The 20th century found the city's port becoming the largest in the United States and the second-busiest in the world (after Amsterdam), with goods coming in by barge and rail. Drainage problems were conquered by means of high levees, canals, pumping stations, and great spillways, which are opened to direct floodwater away from the city. Bridges were built across the Mississippi River, including the Huey P. Long Bridge, named after Louisiana's famous politician and demagogue. New Orleans's emergence as a regional financial center, with more than 50 commercial banks, led to the construction of soaring office buildings, mostly in the Central Business District.

As in most other American cities, the city's population spread outward through the 20th century, filling suburbs and nearby municipalities. Unlike other cities, however, New Orleans has been able to preserve its original town center and much of its historic architecture.

HURRICANE KATRINA

This rich, complex, maddening city had 300 years of history before August 29, 2005, and yet that single day will come to define New Orleans for certainly its next century. The third-strongest hurricane to make landfall in U.S. history, it was "only" a Category 3 when it hit the coast, about 63 miles to the southeast of New Orleans,

with winds of 125 mph. However, the time spent out in the Gulf as a Category 5 (175-mph winds) caused the storm surge that inflicted the worst damage. Despite the ferocious wind, New Orleans escaped major problems from the storm itself and initially felt it had "dodged the bullet." But the surge was too much for the poorly constructed levee system (since the disaster, it has been revealed that the Army Corps of Engineers, who constructed the system in the first place, had not done the job properly), and several levees, most notably ones at the 17th Street Canal, Industrial Canal, and London Canal, were breached, along with breaks in the Mississippi River Gulf Outlet, a little-used shipping lane. These failures caused flooding in 80% of the city, though the best-known areas, including the French Quarter and the Garden District, did not flood at all. While Mayor Ray Nagin ordered mandatory evacuations on August 28, there were no plans in place to enforce this, nor were provisions made to enable the city's poorest people, a large demographic, as many as 112,000 of whom were without cars or other transportation, to do so. The Superdome was designated as a "shelter of last resort," and somewhere around 28,000 people took refuge there. With inadequate facilities and some roof loss during the storm, plus no additional aid nor rescue for 5 days following the storm, the former grand sports arena became a scene of suffering and misery. Images of residents stranded on rooftops as their houses flooded, or at the Convention Center awaiting rescue, were broadcast around the world. Overnight New Orleans was transformed from a quaint historical relic and/or party destination to a brutal wake-up call about poverty and class limitations in America. It took weeks for the floodwaters to be pumped out—months, in the case of the worst-hit Lower 9th Ward—and it will take decades for the city to recover. But at 4 years and counting, it is well on its way.

BOOKS

You can fill many bookcases with New Orleans literature and authors, so the following list is just considered a starter kit. Get more recommendations at **Faulkner House Books,** 624 Pirates Alley (© **504/ 524-2940**), or the **Garden District Book Shop,** 2727 Prytania St. (© **504/895- 2266**).

General Fiction

There are many examples of early fiction that give a good flavor of old-time New Orleans life. George Washington Cable's stories and novels are revealing and colorful; the collection to read is *Old Creole Days* (1879). Grace King answered Cable's not-always-flattering portrait of the Creoles in her short stories and in her novel *The Pleasant Ways of St. Médard* (1916). Perhaps the best writer to touch on the lives of the earliest Creoles is Kate Chopin, who lived in Louisiana for only 14 years in the late 19th century, first in New Orleans and later in Cloutierville. Many of her short stories and novels, the most famous of which is *The Awakening,* are set in the region or involve characters from here.

Frances Parkinson Keyes lived on Chartres Street for more than 25 years. Her most famous works are *Dinner at Antoine's* and *Madame Castel's Lodger,* and each has curious descriptions of life in the city at that time, along with excellent descriptions of food.

Ellen Gilchrist is a nationally recognized contemporary fiction writer with roots in the city. *In the Land of Dreamy Dreams,* a collection of her short stories, portrays life in wealthy uptown New Orleans. Sheila Bosworth's wonderful tragicomedies perfectly sum up the city and its collection of characters—check out *Almost Innocent* or *Slow Poison,* two of our all-time favorite books. Valerie Martin's *The Great Divorce* is a retelling of *Dr. Jekyll and Mr. Hyde* set in the streets of antebellum New Orleans. Other possibilities are Nancy Levin's delightful *Lives of the Saints* and John Gregory Brown's critically acclaimed *Decorations in a Ruined Cemetery.* Michael Ondaatje's controversial *Coming Through Slaughter* is a fictionalized account of Buddy Bolden and the early New Orleans jazz era.

Poppy Z. Brite, a New Orleans native who originally gained fame via horror tales, has since turned her talents to a series of comic novels set in the New Orleans restaurant world. Stuffed full of NOLA (and the chef biz) verisimilitude, *Liquor, Prime,* and *Soul Kitchen* (with at least two more to come) are hilarious odes to an eccentric town and the people who work very hard to help us eat so well there.

Many of the recent books by poet and essayist Andrei Codrescu contain pieces about his adopted city of New Orleans. Codrescu has captured the city's appeal better than anyone else in recent times. Start with *New Orleans, Mon Amour* and go from there.

And then, of course, there is the cottage industry known as Anne Rice. Whatever you might think of her writing skills, she loves her native city and does an arguably underrated job of capturing its essence. (More than one person has come to New Orleans just because he or she fell in love with it from one of Rice's books.) Her *Vampire Chronicles,* set in New Orleans, are her best-known works, but the city plays a significant (and seductive) role in *The Witching Hour* and is the backdrop for a historical novel, the well-researched *Feast of All Saints,* about the free people of color in 19th-century New Orleans.

History

Lyle Saxon's *Fabulous New Orleans* is the most charming place to start learning about the city's past. (Saxon was director of the writer's program under the WPA.) From there, move on to his collaboration with Edward Dreyer and Robert Tallant, *Gumbo Ya-Ya.* Roark Bradford's Civil War novel, *Kingdom Coming,* contains a lot of information about voodoo. Mark Twain visited the city often in his riverboat days, and his *Life on the Mississippi* has a good number of tales about New Orleans and its riverfront life. *The WPA Guide to New Orleans* also contains some excellent social and historical background and provides a fascinating picture of the city in 1938. *Beautiful Crescent,* by Joan Garvey and Mary Lou Widmer, is a readable reference book on the history of New Orleans. Those who loved *Gangs of New York* will be pleased to learn Herbert Asbury gave the same (which is to say, highly entertaining and not terribly factual) treatment to New Orleans in *The French Quarter: An Informal History of the New Orleans Underworld.* New Orleans's favorite patroness, the Baroness de Pontalba, gets the biography treatment in Christina Vella's *Intimate Enemies.*

There are many guides to Mardi Gras. The definitive account is Henri Schindler's *Mardi Gras New Orleans.* Schindler produced balls and parades for Mardi Gras for 20 years and is considered carnival's foremost historian. *Mardi Gras in New Orleans: An Illustrated History* is a concise history of the celebration from ancient times to 2001. It was produced by *Mardi Gras Guide* publisher Arthur Hardy.

Literature

William Faulkner came to New Orleans, lived on Pirates Alley, and penned *Soldiers' Pay.* Several other Faulkner novels and short stories are set in New Orleans. Tennessee Williams became a devoted New Orleans fan, living in the city on and off for many years. It inspired him to write *A Streetcar Named Desire,* one of the best-known New Orleans tales. He also set *The Rose Tattoo* in the city.

Other notable New Orleans writers include Walker Percy and Shirley Ann Grau. Percy's novels, including *The Moviegoer* and *Love in the Ruins,* are classic portrayals of the idiosyncrasies of New Orleans and its residents. Grau's most famous novel, *The Keepers of the House,* won the Pulitzer Prize in 1964. John Kennedy Toole also received a Pulitzer, but he wasn't around to know about it, having committed suicide years before. At the time of his death, none of his works had even been published. Toole's *A Confederacy of Dunces* is a timeless New Orleans tragicomedy that'll have you laughing out loud.

Robert Penn Warren's classic novel *All the King's Men,* an exceedingly loose telling of the story of Huey P. Long, makes the list because it's so good, because it gives a portrait of the performance art known as Louisiana politics, and because the 2006 movie adaptation was mostly shot in New Orleans.

A further notable modern writer is Robert Olen Butler, who won the Pulitzer in 1993 for his collection of stories, *A Good Scent from a Strange Mountain,* set primarily in New Orleans's Vietnamese community.

Post-Katrina Literature

It's become a cottage industry already, but just because books have appeared quickly doesn't mean they were produced in haste. There are so many, but the following help give a picture of pre- and post-flood New Orleans, in direct response to the disaster. Tom Piazza's *Why New Orleans Matters* (Regan Books, 2005) is a love letter to and about the city, reminding all who love it why they do and encouraging a similar love in novices. Rosemary James, of Faulkner House Books, edited *My New Orleans* (Touchstone, 2006), a collection of essays by locals ranging from writers to restaurateurs and raconteurs, attempting to pin down just what it is about this place that keeps them here, come hell or high water. Local historian Douglas Brinkley's meticulous *The Great Deluge* (William Morrow, 2006) may not end up the definitive post-mortem examination of Katrina, but it will be hard to top. *Times-Picayune* columnist

Chris Rose collected his heartbreaking personal essays, written as he and his colleagues covered their flooded city, in *1 Dead in Attic* (CR Books, 2006).

Books About Music

We highly recommend Ann Allen Savoy's *Cajun Music Vol. 1* (Bluebird Press, 1984), a combination songbook and oral history. It features previously untranscribed Cajun music with lyrics in French (including a pronunciation guide) and English. A labor of many years, it's an invaluable resource.

For a look at specific time periods, people, and places in the history of New Orleans jazz, you have a number of choices. They include William Carter's *Preservation Hall* (Norton, 1991); John Chilton's *Sidney Bechet: The Wizard of Jazz* (Oxford University Press, 1988); Gunther Schuller's *Early Jazz: Its Roots and Musical Development* (Oxford University Press, 1968); *Jazz, New Orleans, 1885–1963* (Da Capo Press, 1983), by Samuel Charters; *New Orleans Jazz: A Revised History*, by R. Collins (Vantage Press, 1996); *Music in New Orleans* (Louisiana State University Press, 1966), by Henry Kmen; *In Search of Buddy Bolden* (Louisiana State University Press, 1978), by Donald Marquis; *New Orleans Jazz: A Family Album* (Louisiana State University Press, 1967), by Al Rose and Edmond Souchon; *New Orleans Style*, by Bill Russell (Jazzology Press, 1994); and *Jazz Masters of New Orleans*, by Martin Williams (Da Capo Press, 1979). Al Rose's *Storyville, New Orleans* (University of Alabama Press, 1974) is an excellent source of information about the very beginnings of jazz.

If you prefer primary sources, read Louis Armstrong's *Satchmo: My Life in New Orleans* (Da Capo Press, 1986) and Sidney Bechet's *Treat It Gentle* (Da Capo Press, 1960).

RECORDINGS

The selections listed below should give you a good start; if you want advice or recommendations on recently released recordings, drop by or call the **Louisiana Music Factory,** 210 Decatur St. (Ⓒ **504/586-1094**), in New Orleans, or **Floyd's Record Shop,** 434 E. Main St., Ville Platte (Ⓒ **337/363-2138**). (Floyd's is about 3 hr. from New Orleans, so be sure to call before heading out if you're making a special trip—see chapter 12, "Plantation Homes & Cajun Country: Side Trips from New Orleans," for more info.)

Anthologies

There are many collections and anthologies of various New Orleans and Louisiana music available, including such series as the Alligator Stomp CDs put out in the 1990s by Rhino Records. But the most comprehensive and best considered is *Doctors, Professors, Kings & Queens: The Big Ol' Box of New Orleans*, a four-disc package released in 2004 by Shout! Factory. Critically acclaimed, it really is the one collection that touches all the bases of the diverse musical gumbo that is the Crescent City.

Post-Katrina Recordings

Among the most prominent projects to emerge in the wake of the flood were benefit collaborations, including *Our New Orleans,* with all-new recordings by Allen Toussaint, Dr. John, Randy Newman, and others (Nonesuch Records, 2005), and *Sing Me Back Home,* by the New Orleans Social Club (a "supergroup" of Crescent City funksters with featured vocalists including Dr. John, Irma Thomas, Cyril Neville, and Ivan Neville, the latter on a searing version of Creedence Clearwater Revival's "Fortunate Son"; Burgundy Records/Sony BMG, 2006). Irma Thomas made one of the strongest albums of her long career with the earthy *After the Rain* (Rounder Records, 2006). The Dirty Dozen Brass Band found release via an entire reinterpretation of Marvin Gaye's ever-more-pertinent 1971 *What's Going On* album (Shout! Factory, 2006). Toussaint and Elvis Costello teamed up for the spectacular *The River in Reverse* (Verve/Forecast, 2006), collaborating on new songs and a few Toussaint classics. *A Tale of God's Will (A Requiem for Katrina)* (Blue Note, 2006) is Terence Blanchard's Grammy-winning haunting suite drawn from his score for the Spike Lee–directed Katrina documentary *When the Levees Broke.*

Jazz

Most of Louis Armstrong's recordings are in print and can be found in many record stores. The same is true for Jelly Roll Morton, Wynton Marsalis, Harry Connick, Jr., and trumpeter Nicholas Payton—we particularly recommend his Grammy-winning collaboration with now-deceased veteran Doc Cheatham, *Doc Cheatham & Nicholas Payton* (Verve, 1994), and his stunning modern-jazz reimaginings of Louis Armstrong material, *Dear Louis* (Verve, 2001). The rising stars of the scene are without question brothers James and Troy Andrews, playing trumpet and trombone, respectively. They've made several albums each, but check out their collaboration *12 & Shorty* (Keep Swingin' Records, 2004).

For the sound of early jazz, the following are recommended: *Streets and Scenes of New Orleans* (Good Time Jazz), by the Silver Leaf Jazz Band; *New Orleans Rhythm Kings* (Milestone); *King Oliver with Louis Armstrong* (Milestone); and the anthologies *New Orleans* (Atlantic Jazz), *Recorded in New Orleans Volumes 1 and 2* (Good Time Jazz), and *New Orleans Jazz* (Arhoolie). Don't miss a series of CDs being put out by the essential traditional jazz club, Preservation Hall. Also, don't overlook the crucial Crescent City/Caribbean cross-pollinations, explored by the vibrant ensemble Los Hombres Calientes.

Brass Bands

The tradition of brass-oriented street bands predates Louis Armstrong but underwent a spectacular revival in the 1980s and 1990s with the revitalization of such long-term presences as the Olympia Brass Band and the arrival of such newcomers as the Dirty Dozen Brass Band, who took the sound global and collaborated with stars ranging from Dizzy Gillespie to Elvis Costello and Norah Jones. The anthology, *This Is the Dirty Dozen Brass Band* (Shout! Factory, 2005), spans 25 years of recordings. The Dirty Dozen in turn inspired an even younger and funkier generation, with the ReBirth Brass Band, the New Birth Brass Band, the Hot 8, and the Soul Rebels, the best of the crowd. The ReBirth's *Kickin' It Live* (Rounder, 1991), recorded when the members were in their teens, and later *The Main Event: Live at the Maple Leaf* (Louisiana Red Hot, 1999), and New Birth's *New Birth Family* (Fat Back Records, 2004), a moving tribute to late co-founder Tuba Fats, are irresistible.

Rhythm & Blues

Don't miss Dr. John's *Gris-Gris* (Atco, 1968), *Gumbo* (Atco, 1972), and *Mos Scocious: The Dr. John Anthology* (Rhino, 1993). Also try the Wild Tchoupitoulas' (or Mardi Gras Indians) *The Wild Tchoupitoulas* (Antilles, 1976), and the Meters' *Cissy Strut* (Island, 1975) and *Rejuvenation* (Reprise, 1974). You can't go wrong with hometown heroes the Neville Brothers' *Yellow Moon* (A&M, 1989) and *Treacherous: A History of the Neville Brothers, 1955–1985* (Rhino, 1986), or producer/writer Allen Toussaint's *The Complete 'Tousan' Sessions* (Bear Family Records, 1992). He's a legend for a reason. We can't overlook Professor Longhair's *New Orleans Piano* (Atco, 1953) and *'Fess: The Professor Longhair Anthology* (Rhino, 1993). Worthwhile anthologies include *The Best of New Orleans Rhythm & Blues Volumes 1 and 2* (Rhino, 1988) and *The Mardi Gras Indians Super Sunday Showdown* (Rounder, 1992).

3

Mardi Gras, Jazz Fest & Other Festivals

New Orleans is a city that really loves a good party. Never was that more evident than a couple weeks after Katrina, when the stubborn residents who had refused to evacuate threw a jazz funeral in order to mourn their many losses, and to celebrate their own survival and commitment to renewal. And what happens when a party gets too big? It becomes a festival. That's what happened over the years to the Jazz & Heritage Festival—it evolved from an event where people were literally begged to take free tickets into a hugely crowded, multiday affair that has, relatively speaking, not that much to do with jazz (but is no less fun for it).

New Orleanians know what makes a great party: really good food and music, and lots of it. That's what you will find at any festival in Louisiana—regardless of what it is ostensibly celebrating. Anything is an excuse for a party here; you can experience festivals centered around swamps, gumbo, crawfish, frogs, tomatoes, architecture, and more.

This chapter covers some of the largest festivals in New Orleans and the outlying areas; others are listed in the "Calendar of Events" in chapter 4, "Planning Your Trip to New Orleans."

You can get information on many of the events mentioned in both chapters by contacting the **New Orleans Metropolitan Convention and Visitors Bureau,** 2020 St. Charles Ave., New Orleans, LA 70130 (© **800/672-6124** or 504/566-5011; www.neworleanscvb.com).

1 MARDI GRAS

Obviously, the granddaddy of all New Orleans celebrations is Mardi Gras. Thanks to sensational media accounts that zero in on the salacious aspects of this carnival, its rep has it as nothing more than a version of spring break, *Girls Gone Wild*–style, while the accounts have attracted more and more participants looking for decadent X-rated action rather than tradition. But despite what you may have heard, Mardi Gras remains one of the most exciting times to visit New Orleans. The truth of the matter is that you can spend several days admiring and reveling in the city's traditions and never even venture into the frat-party atmosphere of Bourbon Street.

A great deal of speculation was cast about whether New Orleans should cancel Mardi Gras 2006, the first after Katrina—whether it was appropriate to hold the traditional massive celebration at such a somber time. The opposition failed to take into account several things: Because it is a holiday separate from any observation of it, one can no more "cancel" Mardi Gras than one can cancel Christmas. Secondly, Mardi Gras celebrations—that is, parades and parties—are all privately funded and operated, so it's not really a city decision (though city permits are required for parades and city funds are needed for security and cleanup). And finally, for a town that tends to throw a party just because it's a day with a *y* in it, the response to any suggestions that official celebrations should be postponed for a year or two was "Fine. Then we will load up little red wagons with a bunch of beads, and walk down the streets and do it ourselves."

It didn't come to that. Six months to the virtual day after Katrina, Zulu and Rex paraded as usual, along with the other krewes who march earlier. Some parades were a little shorter, but the beads and throws were even more plentiful. (Tourists who opted not to go really missed out!) The crowds may not have been as thick as usual (though conversely, Sun night may have set a record for attendance), but that wasn't unexpected, given the decrease in local population. More to the point, the spirit was immeasurably high, as New Orleanians and lovers of the city alike turned out in their most glittery or satirical costumes, screaming for beads, engaging in other traditions, and generally exalting in a moment that not that long before seemed like it would never come again. They had survived, and they were filled with hope that their city would, too. That there has not been this same focus on Katrina during subsequent Mardi Gras is a good sign; it means the city and its loyal residents are moving into the future that has brought along the best, not the worst, of the past.

Forget media reports that tend to focus on the wanton action. There is a lot more to Carnival than that. Knowledge of some of the long and fascinating history of Mardi Gras may help put matters in perspective. First of all, it's not a festival, it's a *carnival,* which is from a Latin word roughly meaning "farewell to flesh." Mardi Gras is both a day and a time period. It's French for "Fat Tuesday," the day before Ash Wednesday, when Lent begins, and it historically refers to the 5- to 8-week stretch from Twelfth Night (Jan 6) to Mardi Gras Day (which can fall as late as Mar 9). With Lent comes fasting and deprivation. The idea was that good Christians would take the opportunity to eat as much as they could in preparation for their impending denial.

The party's origins can be traced to that Roman excuse for an orgy, the **Lupercalia festival.** It will sound strangely familiar to today's Mardi Gras participant: 2 days when all sexual and social order disappeared, cross-dressing was mandatory, and the population ran riot. The early Christian church was naturally appalled by this but was unable to stop it (as someone later said about Storyville and prostitution, you can make it illegal but you can't make it unpopular). Grafting Lupercalia to the beginning of Lent may have been a compromise to bribe everyone into observing Lent, and they may have needed those 40 days to recover!

Carnival, with lavish masked balls and other revels, became popular in Italy and France, and so naturally, the tradition followed the Creoles to New Orleans. The first Carnival balls occurred in 1743, but the first detailed accounts of Mardi Gras–specific festivities showed up in 1824. Informal parades and masked revelers cavorting in the streets characterized the celebrations. By the mid-1800s, Mardi Gras mischief had grown so ugly (the habit of tossing flour on revelers gradually turned into throwing bricks at them) that everyone predicted the end of the tradition. (The more things change, the more they stay the same.)

THE BIRTH OF THE KREWES Everything changed in 1856. Tired of being left out of the Creoles' Mardi Gras, a group of Americans who belonged to a secret society called Cowbellians formed the Mystick Krewe of Comus (named after the hero of a John Milton poem). On Mardi Gras evening, they presented a torchlit parade, seemingly out of nowhere, that was breathtaking in its design, effects, and imagination. A new tradition was born. Every Mardi Gras night thereafter (with some exceptions) climaxed with the appearance of Comus, each time grander and more astounding.

And so the new standard was set. Mardi Gras societies became known as **krewes,** and most were made up of prominent society types or businessmen; the event marked the height of the social season. The next krewe to emerge was that of Rex, the King of Carnival. Rex paraded in the morning and later paid public homage to Comus. Their meeting became the high point of Mardi Gras.

Rex was born in part to celebrate the Mardi Gras appearance of the grand duke of Russia, Alexis Alexandrovich Romanov, who had followed the actress Lydia Thompson from New York when she came to star in *Bluebeard.* The city went all out to welcome him, and when it was learned that his favorite song was Lydia's burlesque tune "If Ever I Cease to Love," every band in the Rex parade was asked to play it. That sprightly melody is now the official song of Mardi Gras, and the **royal colors**—purple for justice, green for faith, and gold for power—were adopted as the festival's official colors. More krewes, such as Momus and Proteus, came into being, each throwing a lavish ball along with its parade and each with an exclusive membership.

The Civil War put a temporary halt to things, but Comus was parading again by 1866. In 1870 the Twelfth Night Revelers krewe was founded and added two new customs that still endure. Members threw trinkets to onlookers (the first thrower was dressed as Santa Claus), and a "queen" reigned over their ball.

As a classic elite Old South institution, Mardi Gras was not exactly at the forefront of promoting racial equality or harmony. Throughout the 19th century, the city's African Americans participated in parades only by carrying torches to illuminate the route (the *flambeaux,* as the torches are known, are still around, a welcome, atmospheric Mardi Gras tradition). In 1909, a black man named William Storey mocked the elaborately garbed Rex by prancing after his float wearing a lard can for a crown. Storey was promptly dubbed "King Zulu." By 1916, his followers had so grown in number that they formed the Krewe of Zulu (officially the Zulu Social Aid and Pleasure Club), developing a parody of Rex and making a mockery of racial stereotypes. The Zulu parade quickly became one of the most popular aspects of Mardi Gras. The most famous King Zulu was Louis Armstrong, who reigned in 1949.

Unfortunately, most krewes remained notable for their lack of blacks, Jews, and women, and as times changed, the public, which was not permitted to join the krewes but was supposed to be happy to pay taxes for post-parade cleanup, demanded equality. It was not considered enough that some krewes had begun (grudgingly) inviting blacks to their balls. An ordinance passed in 1992 denies a parade permit to any group that discriminates on the basis of race or religion. (Krewes are still not required to integrate along gender lines, a choice of the all-female krewes as much as the male, though men in drag are a hallmark of Mardi Gras.) Rex acceded to the new regulations, but mighty Comus, in a move that many still feel marked the beginning of the end of classic Mardi Gras, canceled its parade. Proteus and Momus soon followed suit.

Some say the flavor of Mardi Gras had already changed long before the 1992 ordinance.

SPECTACLE & BEAUTY   Parades were always things of spectacle and beauty with literally antique floats: 19th-century caissons with wooden wheels. But the processions had become so big over the years that they had to be taken out of the Quarter. The old krewes were gradually replaced by "superkrewes" like Orpheus (founded by musician Harry Connick, Jr., because he loves Mardi Gras so much), Bacchus, and Endymion, whose memberships were nonexclusive. One of their floats was as big as an entire Comus parade. The largest parades can have more than 20 floats, celebrity guests, marching bands, dancing groups, motorcycle squads, and a total of many thousands of participants. Celebrities are often the superkrewes' kings; recent Bacchus kings include Larry King, Elijah Wood, Nicolas Cage, and James Gandolfini. In 1998 the Krewe of the Americas, completely made up of non–New Orleans residents, paraded for the first time, on Mardi Gras afternoon itself, a sacrilege to natives who long considered this Comus's day.

The trinkets known as **throws** fly thick and fast from the floats of these superkrewes, but they lack the tradition of the old krewes. In the 1880s Rex began throwing trinkets to parade-watchers, a forerunner of the Rex doubloon, which was introduced in 1960. Other krewes eventually followed suit, and now throws are mandatory. The ubiquitous beads were originally glass (often from Czechoslovakia) but now are of less expensive plastic. **Doubloons** are another popular souvenir. Usually made of aluminum, these oversize coins show the krewe's coat of arms on one side and the year's parade theme on the other. They are collector's items for natives, many of whom have every krewe's doubloons from many different years. Other throws include **stuffed animals, plastic krewe cups,** and especially the highly prized, hand-painted **Zulu coconuts.**

Alas, the traditional cry of "Throw me something, Mister!" to obtain a trinket has gradually turned into the request/demand, "Show me your tits!" But though it seems Mardi Gras is moving ever further away from its traditions, remember that Comus has in the past disappeared for several years and always risen again. Indeed, Proteus returned for Mardi Gras 2000 to cries of "Welcome back!"

KICKIN' UP YOUR HEELS: MARDI GRAS ACTIVITIES

Mardi Gras can be whatever you want. Don't be suckered by media reports that focus only on the exhibitionism and drunken orgies. Sure, some of Mardi Gras is becoming more and more like spring break as college kids pour into town, eager to have license to do anything. Thankfully, that kind of activity is largely confined to Bourbon Street. If that's what you want, go there. But if you avoid Bourbon Street, you will find an entirely different Mardi Gras experience.

THE SEASON   The date of Fat Tuesday is different each year, but Carnival season always starts on **Twelfth Night,** January 6, as much as 2 months before Mardi Gras. On that night the Phunny Phorty Phellows kick off the season with a streetcar ride from Carrollton Avenue to Canal Street and back.

Over the following weeks, the city celebrates Mardi Gras in its own inimitable fashion. For most people, this means attending a string of **King Cake parties.** The traditional King Cake is a round, braided coffeecake-like confection, dusted with Mardi Gras purple-, green-, and gold-colored sugar, into which a plastic baby is baked; getting the piece with the baby can be a good omen or can mean you have to throw the next King Cake party. For the high-society crowd, the season brings the year's best parties, some of which hark back to the grand masked balls of the 19th century. Each krewe throws a ball, ostensibly to introduce its royalty for the year. There are dozens of these parties between Twelfth Night and Mardi Gras, but most are not traditional masked balls. (By the way, don't expect to be invited—they are quite exclusive.)

Two or 3 weeks before Mardi Gras itself, parades begin chugging through the streets with increasing frequency. There are also plenty of parodies, such as the adorable parade of the **Mystick Krewe of Barkus** and the **Krewe du Vieux**'s yearly expression of decidedly funny and decidedly un-family-friendly decadence (open to the public). Barkus is, as you might guess, a krewe for pets that parades through the Quarter (some of the dogs get quite gussied up) and is a total hoot, while Krewe du Vieux are humans just having a wild time, preening in outrageous costumes.

If you want to experience Mardi Gras but don't want to face the full force of craziness, consider coming for the weekend 10 days before Fat Tuesday (the season officially begins the Fri of this weekend). You can count on 10 to 15 parades during the weekend by lesser-known krewes such as Cleopatra, Pontchartrain, Sparta, and Camelot. The crowds are more manageable than the ones you'll find just a week later. You should probably check to make sure those krewes have returned post-Katrina, as some were not able to for some post-Katrina Mardi Gras.

The following weekend there are another 15 parades—the biggies. The parades are bigger, the crowds are bigger—everything's bigger. By this point, the city has succumbed to Carnival fever. After a day of screaming for beads, you'll probably find yourself heading somewhere to get a drink or three. The French Quarter will be the center of late-night revelry; all of the larger bars will be packed. If you travel uptown or to Mid-City to see a parade, however, you might consider staying put and spending your evening at one of the joints nearby. The last parade each day (on both weekends) usually ends around 9:30pm or later; you might be exhausted by the time you get back to the hotel.

LUNDI GRAS   In the 19th century, Rex's **King of Carnival** arrived downtown from the Mississippi River on this night, the Monday before Fat Tuesday. Over the years, the day gradually lost its special significance, becoming just another day of parades. In the 1980s, however, Rex revived Lundi Gras, the old tradition of arriving on the Mississippi.

These days, festivities at the riverfront begin in the afternoon with lots of drink and live music leading up to the king's arrival at around 6pm. Down the levee a few hundred feet at Woldenberg Park, Zulu has its own Lundi Gras celebration with the king arriving at around 5pm. (In 1999, for the first time, King Zulu met up with Rex in an impressive ceremony.) That night the **Krewe of Orpheus** holds their parade. It's one of the biggest and most popular parades, thanks to the generosity of the krewe's throws. And although it's a recent addition to the Mardi Gras scene (it began in 1994), it holds fast to old Mardi Gras traditions, including floats designed by master float creator Henri Schindler. For Mardi Gras 2000, venerable Proteus returned to parading, right before Orpheus.

Because Lent begins the following night at midnight, Monday is the final dusk-to-dawn night of Mardi Gras. A good portion of the city forgoes sleep so as not to waste the occasion—which only adds to the craziness.

MARDI GRAS   The day begins early, starting with the two biggest parades, **Zulu** and **Rex,** which run back to back. Zulu starts near the Central Business District at 8:30am; Rex starts uptown at 10am.

Throughout the early morning, in between the parades, you can also see the elaborately costumed Mardi Gras **"walking clubs,"** such as the Jefferson City Buzzards, the Pete Fountain Half Fast, and the Mondo Kayo Social and Marching Club (identifiable by their tropical/banana theme). They walk, they drink, they're usually accompanied by marching bands, and because they probably didn't sleep the night before, they don't move very fast. You can catch these "marchers" anywhere along their St. Charles Avenue route (btw. Poydras St. and Washington Ave.). Keep your eyes open also for the unofficial marching club, the Julus, which includes members of the New Orleans Klezmer All-Stars and tends to follow the Zulu parade, throwing not coconuts but painted bagels.

It will be early afternoon when Rex spills into the Central Business District. Nearby at about this time, you may be able to find some of the most elusive New Orleans figures, the **Mardi Gras Indians.** The "tribes" of New Orleans are small communities of African Americans and black Creoles (some of whom have Native American ancestors), mostly from the inner city. Their elaborate (and that's an understatement) beaded and feathered costumes, rivaling Bob Mackie Vegas headdresses in outrageousness and size, are entirely made by hand. The men begin working on them on Ash Wednesday, the day after Mardi Gras, to get them ready in time for the next year. Traditionally, throughout the day, tribes of Indians from all over town converge along the median of Claiborne Avenue, underneath the interstate, where a large crowd of locals is always milling around to see the spectacle. If two tribes meet on the median or back in their neighborhoods, they'll stage a mock confrontation, resettling their territory and common borders. Because the Indians lived in particularly flood-ravaged neighborhoods, not that many were able to come back for Mardi Gras 2006 or 2007. Many suits were destroyed in the flood (a painful loss for them considering the time, effort, and pride that goes into the construction), though some tribes, such as Fi-Yi-Yi, were able to sew new ones post-storm. You can see some tribes gather around St. Augustine's school in Treme, and also uptown. This unique cultural tradition is in considerable jeopardy thanks to the New Orleans diaspora, and it may be harder than ever for a tourist to spot them on Mardi Gras. Ask locals for rumors about times and intersections, and then bike, walk, or drive around (it's probably the only time a car is useful on Mardi Gras), keeping eyes and ears open for feathers and drums. (If you're lucky, you can sometimes catch these confrontations during other times of the year if the Indians are out to celebrate something else, like Jazz Fest or the mayor's inauguration.)

After the parades, the action picks up in the Quarter. En route, you'll see that Mardi Gras is still very much a family tradition, with whole families dressing up in similar costumes. Marvel at how an entire city has shut down so that every citizen can join in the celebrations. Some people don't bother hitting the streets; instead, they hang out on their balconies, watching the action below, or have barbecues in their courtyards. If you are lucky and seem like the right sort, you might well get invited in.

In the Quarter the frat-party action is largely confined to Bourbon Street. The more interesting activity is in the lower Quarter and the Frenchmen section of the Faubourg Marigny (just east of the Quarter), where the artists and gay community really know how to celebrate. The costumes are elaborate works of art, some the products of months of work. Although the people may be (okay, probably *will* be) drunk, they are boisterous and enthusiastic, not (for the most part) obnoxious.

As you make your way through the streets, keep your eyes peeled for members of the legendary **Krewe of Comus.** They will be men dressed in tuxes with brooms over their shoulders, holding cowbells. Ask them if they are Comus, and they will deny it, insisting they are Cowbellians. But then they might hand you a vintage Comus doubloon, and the truth will be out.

If you can, try to stay until midnight when the police come through the Quarter, officially shutting down Mardi Gras.

PLANNING A VISIT DURING MARDI GRAS

LODGING   You can't just drop in on Mardi Gras. Accommodations in the city and the nearby suburbs are booked solid, *so make your plans well ahead and book a room as early as possible.* Many people plan a year or more in advance. Prices are usually much higher during Mardi Gras, and most hotels and guesthouses impose minimum-stay requirements.

Tips **Save the Date**

You can always figure out the **date of Mardi Gras** because it falls exactly 47 days before Easter. If you can't find your calendar or just can't be bothered with the math, here are the next 5 years for you: February 16, 2010; March 8, 2011; February 21, 2012; February 12, 2013; and March 4, 2014.

CLOTHING   As with anything in New Orleans, you must join in if you want to have the best time—simply being a spectator is not enough. And that means a **costume** and **mask** (anything goes). Once you are masked and dressed up, you are automatically part of it all. (Tellingly, the Bourbon St. participants usually do not wear costumes.) A mask tends to bring out the extrovert in everyone. It makes it much easier to talk to strangers or simply to jump up and down begging for beads. It's so simple—a $1.50 piece of plastic will make you part of the spectacle rather than a spectator. As far as costumes go, you need not do anything fancy—an old loud suit or dress from a thrift shop plus that mask will do. You can't possibly compete with those residents who spend all year and thousands of dollars on their costumes, but don't feel bad. If anything, feel morally superior to those who don't bother dressing up at all. They aren't in the Carnival spirit, but you are.

If you've come unprepared, several shops in town specialize in Mardi Gras costumes and masks. (See p. 239 for more listings.) You might also try the secondhand stores along Magazine Street that have a large inventory of costumes from the year before—you can usually pick up something quite snazzy for not very much money there.

DINING   If you want to eat at a restaurant during Mardi Gras, make reservations as early as possible. And pay very close attention to **parade routes** (map on p. 27), because if there is one between you and your restaurant, you may not be able to cross the street, and you can kiss your dinner goodbye. For those of you who don't plan in advance, this might work to your advantage; restaurants often have a high no-show rate during Mardi Gras for this reason, so a well-timed drop-in may work.

PARKING   Remember that even though the huge crowds you'll find everywhere add to the general merriment, they also grind traffic to a halt all over town. So our admonition against ever renting a car is even stronger during Mardi Gras. ***Don't drive.*** Instead, relax and take a cab or walk. Go with the flow. Don't get irritated. Remember, the fun is everywhere, so you don't really have to go anywhere. Parking along any parade route is not allowed 2 hours before and 2 hours after the parade. In addition, although you'll see people leaving their cars on *neutral ground* (the median strip), it's illegal to park there, and chances are good that you'll be towed. Traffic in New Orleans is never worse than ***in the hour after a parade. Note:*** Streetcars and buses do run during Mardi Gras (if they can), but they may have radically altered routes during that time (you won't find anything running on St. Charles Ave.). Contact the Regional Transit Authority (RTA; ✆ **504/ 248-3900;** www.norta.com) for more information.

SAFETY   Many, many cops are out, making the walk from uptown to downtown safer than at other times of year, but not surprisingly, the streets of New Orleans are a haven for pickpockets during Mardi Gras. Take precautions.

> **Tips** **For More Information . . .**
>
> You'll enjoy Mardi Gras more if you've done a little homework before your trip. Contact the **New Orleans Metropolitan Convention and Visitors Bureau,** 2020 St. Charles Ave., New Orleans, LA 70130 (② **800/672-6124** or 504/566-5011; www.neworleanscvb.com), and ask for current Mardi Gras info.
>
> You'll also want to get your hands on the latest edition of **Arthur Hardy's Mardi Gras Guide.** This will tell you which krewes are parading where and when, among much other useful information. Your best bet is to contact the magazine directly through its website, www.mardigrasneworleans.com/arthur. This valuable guide is sold all over town and is full of history, tips, and maps of the parade routes.

HOW TO SPEND THE BIG DAY

While the national media focuses only on the Bourbon Street zoo, there are plenty of traditions and family-friendly fun that can be had elsewhere. What you come away with will depend on where you go and whom you hang out with. Indeed, you need never see nudity if you plan your day correctly. Basically, there are three ways of doing it: nice, naughty, and nasty. See below for examples of each kind of Mardi Gras experience. Us? We prefer a mix of the first two.

NICE　Hang out exclusively uptown with the families. Find a spot on St. Charles Avenue, which is entirely closed for the day, and camp out with a blanket, a picnic lunch, and some kids if you can find any, and spend the day there. After **Rex** there are countless smaller parades (with trucks acting as floats) put on by the Elks and other groups. (Zulu, alas, doesn't go through Uptown.) Dressed-up families are all around. One side of St. Charles is for the parades and the other is open only to foot traffic, so you can wander about and admire the costumes, with **walking groups** (groups who make their own ad hoc parades) and everyone just milling about on the street. You might well get asked to join in a group barbecue or balcony party. New Orleans kids assure us that Mardi Gras is more fun than Halloween, and we can see why.

NAUGHTY　In the morning, around the start of Zulu, head to Jackson Avenue or Claiborne Avenue and the neighborhoods around those main thoroughfares and look for the **Mardi Gras Indians.** It's a hit-or-miss proposition; the Indians themselves never know when they are going to start or where they are going to be, but running across them on their own turf is one of the great sights and experiences of Mardi Gras. Play it cool, however—this is not your neighborhood. Consider not bringing your camera; this is not an attraction put on for your benefit, and the Indians do not like being treated like a sideshow carnival act. By early to midafternoon, they often gather at Indian ground zero, on Claiborne under the freeway, where a festival of sorts takes place. Post-Katrina, that traditional gathering has not taken place; it may return in some form as time passes.

At noon try to be around the corner of Burgundy and St. Ann streets for the **Bourbon Street** awards. You may not get close enough to actually see the judging, but the participants are all around you so that you can gawk up close and personal at their sometimes R- and X-rated costumes. As you wander the Quarter, keep an eye out (or ask around) for the **Krewe of Kosmic Debris** and the **Society of St. Anne,** marvelously costumed

CITY PARK

Endymion starts here

City Park Avenue

Esplanade Ave.

Fair Grounds Racetrack (Jazz Fest)

Lake Pontchartrain

CITY PARK

610

Fair Grounds Racetrack

Superdome

Area of detail

Mississippi

MID-CITY

S. Carrollton Ave.

Orleans Ave.

Bienville

Jefferson Parkway

Canal

Tulane Ave.

Pontchartrain Expressway

N. Broad Ave.

N. Galvez

Zulu ends here

LOUIS ARMSTRONG PARK

N. Rampart

Bourbon St.

FRENCH QUARTER

Duncan Plaza Civic Center

Endymion ends here

Superdome

Girod

Julia

Superdome Union Passenger Terminal

Loyola Ave.

Girod

Julia

Howard

Poydras

Magazine St.

Rex ends here

Iris ends here

World Trade Center

M. L. King Blvd.

BROADMOOR

Toledano

Lousiana Pkwy.

Zulu starts here

S. Claiborne Ave.

Jackson Ave.

Melpomene Ave.

Washington Ave.

LaSalle St.

Lee Circle

CENTRAL BUSINESS DISTRICT

Orpheus & Bacchus end here

Iris starts here

Rex starts here

Napoleon Ave.

Loyola Ave.

St. Charles

BR 90

Baronne

Prytania

St. Charles

GARDEN DISTRICT

Jackson Ave.

Felicity

Magazine St.

Mississippi River

Orpheus & Bacchus start here

0   1/4 mi
0   0.25 km

N

Prime Bead Catching Area

■— Endymion Parade Route

●····· Other Routes

revelers without floats. After the awards (about midafternoon), head over to the Frenchmen section, where everyone is in costume, dancing in the street to tribal drums, drinking, and generally celebrating Carnival as it should be, often well into the night.

NASTY Stay strictly on **Bourbon Street.** Yep, it's every bit as crowded, vulgar, and obscene as you've heard (and you can't even see the floats from here). The street is full of drunks (and the occasional bewildered soul), few (if any) in costume, with balconies full of more drunks, dangling expensive beads (some with X-rated anatomical features on them), which they will hand over in exchange for a glimpse of flesh. Sometimes they show flesh themselves (and they are never the people who ought to be exposing themselves). This is the "anything goes" attitude of Carnival taken to an unimaginative extreme, and while it might be worth getting a quick peep at, it grows boring more quickly than you might think. The city has tried to keep this sort of thing confined just to Bourbon Street, and efforts seem to have paid off. Astonishingly, a mere one street over is like another world. Dauphine Street, just above Bourbon, is largely empty, while Royal Street, below, is full of naughty, not nasty, Mardi Gras participants.

PARADE WATCH

A Mardi Gras parade works a spell on people. There's no other way to explain why thousands of otherwise rational men and women scream, plead, and sometimes expose themselves for no more reward than a plastic bead necklace, a plastic cup, or a little aluminum medallion. Today's parades have become bloated affairs: Natives seem to be unimpressed with a parade of fewer than 20 major floats—and if your parade has 20 floats, it'll need many high-school marching bands, the Shriners and their ilk, and a few thousand other participants just to balance it out. Krewe members and guests drop tons of trinkets off their floats in the course of a parade, leaving a trail of trash that is truly astounding. Trees on parade routes have beads hanging in their branches all year long.

In your zeal to catch beads, don't forget to actually look at the parades, where considerable effort goes into the floats. Unfortunately, it's getting more and more common for bead-lust-blinded paradegoers to pay little attention to what is actually passing before their eyes (besides the beads), which is really too bad as they are missing some amazing creations. (When the nighttime floats are lit by flambeaux, it is easy for revelers to be suddenly flung back to a time when Mardi Gras meant mystery and magic.) Floats aren't drawn by mules anymore (tractors instead), but the Rex floats come on the same antique wagons the krewe has been using since the 19th century.

There are two environments for viewing each parade. You can choose to stay downtown in the thick of the action, or you can walk out into the neighborhood the parade will traverse (see the map of major parade routes on p. 27). There are still crowds uptown and in Mid-City (though some of these parades have moved to Uptown for the time being), but they're not as large or as rowdy as those farther downtown—and they're much more family oriented. In fact, a good portion of the crowd lined up for a parade on St. Charles Avenue and Canal Street will be local children and families.

Generally, the best place to watch parades on St. Charles Avenue is between Napoleon and Jackson avenues, where the crowds are somewhat smaller and consist mostly of local families and college students. Frankly, we wouldn't attend a Mardi Gras parade (if we can help it) without children—their delight increases your enjoyment considerably. Don't forget to bring a bag to hold any throws you catch and consider bringing moist towelettes (your hands get dirty), drinks, a blanket or chair to sit on, and a picnic.

Tips

Catch Them If You Can: Tips on Getting the Best Throws

So float riders throw beads. "So what?" you think. That's because you've never been in the middle of a Mardi Gras mob before. Trust us, you're going to go crazy for beads, plastic cups, aluminum coins, and other "throws."

First, you stand there passively. All around you, the strands fly thick and fast. You catch a few. "Hmm," you think, "they look kind of good around my neck." Timidly you hold up one hand. You catch a few more. Then you notice the guy next to you/cute college girl in front of you/kid on ladder behind you is getting a lot of beads. A lot more than you. You reach more aggressively for the strands as they fly overhead. "Wait, that guy/cute girl/kid got a really good strand! And another! I want one like that! How come I'm not getting any like that?!?"

Now you find yourself shrieking, "Throw me something, Mister!" with everyone else. You jump. You wail. You plead. You knock over a kid. You are completely consumed by bead lust. You think, "This is stupid. It's a 5¢-piece of plastic—oh, look, a really glittery strand! I want it, I want it, I want it! Please, *mistah!!!*"

And that's not even discussing Zulu coconuts.

Now, if there's a trick to bead catching, we're darned if we know it. One sure-fire way is to be a small child or a cute college girl (or even better, a cute college girl sitting on a tall person's shoulders). If you are none of these, you must plead and beg and whine like everybody else. Local pros stand on ladders, which puts them almost at eye level with float riders. Others bring umbrellas or nets, challenging float riders to hone their aim. Direct eye contact with a float rider also works. Sob stories invoking real and fictional ailments and family members can't hurt—if you can make yourself heard above the din of everyone else's tales of woe.

Personally, we find the popular pastime of flashing body parts in exchange for beads tacky. So does the city of New Orleans, which, in an effort to reclaim Mardi Gras from the party-hearty types, has sternly asked float riders not to throw to exhibitionists. This tactic hasn't entirely worked, but hopes are that this will largely be confined to Bourbon Street.

But if you really want to score, try positioning yourself at the end of a parade route, particularly for one of the generous superkrewes like Orpheus. Throws are of no use to float riders once the parade is over, and toward the end of the ride, they often shovel out their excess inventory in great amounts (even heaving whole packages of beads overboard). By accidentally ending up at the very last block of Zulu, we scored no fewer than two of the highly prized Zulu coconuts, and a man near us got three.

Note: When beads land on the ground, put your foot over them to claim them; if you reach for them with your hands, you might well get your fingers broken by someone else stepping on them. If you get lucky and are tossed a whole package of beads, don't be greedy—share with your neighbors, who might well trade you a nifty strand in exchange.

These are just a few of the major parades of the last days of Carnival. (Times and dates are subject to change; some parade routes have been altered for recent Mardi Gras, and severe weather can reschedule parades, so check with your concierge or online if you plan to attend.)

- **Iris** (founded 1917): This women's krewe follows traditional Carnival rules of costume and behavior. It parades on the Saturday afternoon before Mardi Gras along Napoleon Avenue to St. Charles Avenue to Canal Street, and then along Convention Center Boulevard.
- **Endymion** (founded 1967): This became one of the early "superkrewes" in the 1970s by featuring a glut of floats and celebrity guests such as Alice Cooper, Charo, Tom Jones, Dolly Parton, John Goodman, Chuck Norris, and 2008's grand marshall, Kevin Costner. Returned to its original Mid-City route, it runs Saturday evening down Canal Street to St. Charles Avenue, then on to Howard and Girod streets and into the Superdome for a big party.
- **Bacchus** (founded 1968): The original "superkrewe," Bacchus was the first to host international celebrities, especially as grand marshalls. It traditionally runs the Sunday before Mardi Gras from Napoleon Avenue to St. Charles Avenue to Canal Street, then along Tchoupitoulas Street and into the convention center.
- **Orpheus** (founded 1994): One of the youngest krewes, it was founded by a group that includes Harry Connick, Jr., and tries to adhere to classic krewe traditions. It is popular for its many amazing floats and for the generosity of its throws. The parade is on the evening of Lundi Gras and follows the same route as Bacchus.
- **Zulu** (founded 1916): Zulu is the liveliest parade, with float riders decked out in woolly wigs and blackface. They carry the most prized of Mardi Gras souvenirs: gold-and-black-painted coconuts. (Each of these coconuts is hand-decorated—some more nicely than others—with glitter and paint, so they look phenomenal. But that's not the only reason people want them. These distinctive coconuts are a rarity of sorts— they are made and given out only by Zulu as opposed to the beads that you can get at any parade, so they have become a bit of a status symbol.) The parade runs on Mardi Gras morning from Claiborne Avenue to Jackson Avenue to St. Charles Avenue to Canal Street, and then along Galvez and Orleans streets to Armstrong Park.
- **Rex** (founded 1872): Rex, the original Mardi Gras parade, follows Zulu down St. Charles. It features the King of Carnival and some of the classic floats of Carnival. Various independent walking clubs often precede the parade along its route.

MARDI GRAS MEMORIES: RIDING A FLOAT

Sure, it's fun to watch a Mardi Gras parade, but we all yearn to actually be in one, to ride one of those glorious floats in a fabulous, shiny costume, wearing a mask, tossing beads to an adoring public. Even lifelong New Orleanians almost never get to have that experience, as only a few krewes invite outsiders to ride. So when the krewe of Orpheus generously offered to let me join their 1999 Mardi Gras parade, I didn't hesitate.

The theme was "Premieres of the French Opera," an homage to the beloved building that burned down in the 1920s. The floats were conceived by master float designer Henri Schindler. I would be riding on *Le Cid* (an opera by Jules Massenet). I had to send in measurements for my costume (float riders must be masked and costumed throughout the parade) and purchase beads to throw. Many, many beads. How many? "Oh, about 50 or 60 gross."

"That's more than 7,000 strands!" I said, calculating that this was going to set me back several hundred bucks.

"Yeah, you're right—you might want to get a few more."

Orpheus parades on Lundi Gras night, starting at 6pm. I show up at 10am at the convention center to load my beads on the float. Several other float riders do the same, and before long, we are surrounded by little fortresses of beads and other throws. My neighbors, noticing my thrifty (read: cheap) beads (the better-quality beads cost a lot more, especially for 7,000 of them), graciously share a few good strands with me so I may bestow them on especially worthy people. I resolve to throw only to people who don't have many beads, who've been overlooked by other float riders, who aren't cute college girls—in short, people like me. (I'd been frustrated all week by float riders who seemed to find me invisible.)

I try on my costume, which is vaguely knightlike (that is, if knights wore shiny metallic fabric and orange polyester). I look like a big pumpkin. The sleeves hang down 4 inches past my fingers. Good thing they had my measurements—imagine if they hadn't!

We finally get on the floats at 3:30pm, ready to head to the parade route. My husband, in mandatory tux, will meet me at the finish line near the convention center, home of the Orpheus Ball.

4pm: The floats start to move toward the starting point on Tchoupitoulas.

4:30pm: Our float stops. The float in front of us has a flat tire.

4:31pm: Everyone around me starts drinking.

5pm: Float starts to move again.

5:20pm: Float stops moving.

5:45pm: Pizzas (dinner) are delivered to the float. Only in New Orleans.

6pm: Parade starts. It doesn't really affect us. We are float 24, and it's a long, long time until we hit the starting line.

6:05 to 7:35pm: People still drinking.

7:35pm: Float starts to move again.

7:37pm: Float stops.

8pm: Float starts again. We can see the starting point.

8:05pm: So much for moving.

8:30pm: Everyone is deeply, crushingly bored.

9pm: Even the drinkers have stopped drinking.

9:17pm: I think of my husband at the ball and wonder if I will ever see him again.

9:30pm: Here we go! And it's mayhem. Thousands of people, waving hands, screaming, shrieking, pleading, crying, "Please, Mister, throw me something; throw me something, Mister!" I start to grin and don't stop for hours. I throw beads, feeling, at last, like a queen tossing largesse to the populace. I am sparing in my generosity, however, minding advice not to go overboard too early, lest I run out of beads. I discover my aim isn't bad, and from my upper-level vantage point, I can throw quite far out, to specific people in the back. I also learn that from atop the float, you can see everybody, no matter how small, so if it seems like float riders are ignoring you, it's because they are.

9:35pm: One heavily endowed young woman flashes me and looks expectant, but I say, "Put those away!"

10pm: As we turn onto St. Charles, I hear someone shout my name. It's my cousin's son, a Tulane med student whom I've never actually met before. Of course, since I'm masked and costumed, he still doesn't know what I look like.

10:15pm: Orpheus is known for its generosity, so by now every paradegoer's neck is already thickly covered in beads. There is no bead-challenged person to throw to. Worse, because so many floats have already gone by, everyone only wants the really good beads, not the utilitarian stuff I'm throwing. Oh, dear.

10:45pm: I notice how my friend Ann is really good at taunting the crowd with the good beads. She holds out long, thick strands, shows them off, whips the crowd into a frenzy, then shakes her head sadly and puts them away to await more worthy types.

11pm: The crowd's impatience is high whenever the float comes to a halt—that's when riders supposedly throw the really good stuff. The crowd threatens to turn ugly when I don't. The occasional good strand given by a sympathetic co-rider means I can then appease the angry mob. Lacking a worthy target, I choose to turn my back and throw blindly. Meanwhile, my neat fortress of beads is now in shambles, and I slip and slide on loose strands, frantically trying to get some to throw before revelers scale the float to rip them from me.

11:04pm: I never want to see another bead as long as I live.

11:05pm: Oh, goody, only about halfway there!

11:06pm to 12:35am: Pleasemisterthrowmesomethingpleasemisterpleasemister c'monmisterheymisterpleasemisterpleasemisterpleasepleaseplease*mistaaaahhh!*

12:40am: I make a horrifying discovery. With less than one-third of the parade to go, I still have several thousand beads left. These are worthless once the parade is over (particularly my crappy cheap beads), so as we hit Canal Street, I start to heave them at a great rate, by the dozen, and sometimes entire packages of several dozen. Suddenly, I am *very* popular. Especially fun is throwing the packages into knots of frat boys and watching them pummel each other for it.

1:30am: We arrive at the convention center. Although these people have been watching floats arrive for at least 3 hours, they are still surprisingly fresh and enthusiastic. This howling mob of gowned women and tuxedoed men stands on chairs and tables and shrieks for beads. Among them is my husband, who catches the camera I toss him, so he can take a picture of my dirty, bedraggled self.

1:35am: I descend from the float and proceed to the party. "How was it?" my husband's new friends (he's been sitting there a long time) inquire. "Ask me tomorrow," I say.

2 CAJUN MARDI GRAS

If Mardi Gras in New Orleans sounds like too much for you no matter how low-key you keep it, consider driving out to Cajun Country, where Mardi Gras traditions are just as strong but considerably more, er, wholesome. **Lafayette,** the capital of French Acadiana, celebrates Carnival in a different manner, one that really reflects the Cajun heritage and spirit. Activities beginning Friday night lead up to Cajun Mardi Gras, making it second in size only to New Orleans's celebration. There's one *big* difference, though: Their final pageant and ball are open to the general public. Don your formal wear and join right in!

Instead of Rex and his queen, the Lafayette festivities are ruled by King Gabriel and Queen Evangeline. They are the fictional hero and heroine of Henry Wadsworth Longfellow's epic poem *Evangeline,* which was based on real-life lovers who were separated during the British expulsion of Acadians from Nova Scotia around the time of the French and Indian War. Their story is still very much alive here among the descendants of those who shared their wanderings.

Things get off to a joyous start with a Friday night parade and then kick into high gear with the **Children's Krewe** and **Krewe of Bonaparte** parades and ball, held on the Saturday before Mardi Gras, following a full day of celebration at Cajun Field. On Monday night Queen Evangeline is honored at the **Queen's Parade.** The **King's Parade,** held the following morning, honors King Gabriel and opens a full day of merriment. Lafayette's African-American community stages the **Parade of King Toussaint L'Ouverture** and **Queen Suzanne Simonne** at about noon, just after the King's Parade. Then the **Krewe of Lafayette** invites everyone to get into the act as its parade winds through the streets. Krewe participants trot along on foot or ride in the vehicle of their choice—some very imaginative modes of transportation turn up every year. The Mardi Gras climax, a formal ball presided over by the king and queen and their royal court, takes place that night. Everything stops promptly at midnight, as Cajuns and visitors alike depart to begin their observance of Lent.

MASKED MEN & A BIG GUMBO   In the Cajun countryside that surrounds Lafayette, there's yet another form of Mardi Gras celebration, one tied to the rural lifestyle. Cajuns firmly believe in sharing, so you're welcome to come along. The celebration goes like this: Bands of masked men dressed in raggedy patchwork costumes (unlike the New Orleans costumes, which are heavy on glitter and shine) and peaked hats known as *capichons* set off on Mardi Gras morning on horseback (but don't count on getting a horse—instead, plan on walking or hitching a ride in a car), led by their *capitaine.* They ride from farm to farm, asking at each, *"Voulez-vous reçevoir le Mardi Gras?"* ("Will you receive the Mardi Gras?") and dismounting as the invariable *"Oui"* comes in reply. Each farmyard then becomes a miniature festival as the revelers *faire le macaque* ("make monkeyshines") with song and dance, much drinking of beer, and other antics loosely labeled "entertainment." As payment for their show, they demand, and get, "a fat little chicken to make a big gumbo" (or sometimes a bag of rice or other ingredients).

When each band has visited its allotted farmyards, they all head back to town where everyone else has already begun the general festivities. There'll be dancing in the streets, rowdy card games, storytelling, and the like until the wee hours, and you can be sure that all those fat little chickens go into the *"gumbo gros"* pot to make a very big gumbo indeed.

You can write or call ahead for particulars on both the urban (Lafayette) and rural (the rest of Cajun Country) Mardi Gras celebrations. For the latter, the towns of **Eunice** and **Mamou** stage some of the most enjoyable celebrations. Contact the **Lafayette Parish Convention and Visitors Commission,** P.O. Box 52066, Lafayette, LA 70505 (© **800/ 346-1958** in the U.S., 800/543-5340 in Canada, or 337/232-3737; www.lafayettetravel. com), for more information.

3 NEW ORLEANS JAZZ & HERITAGE FESTIVAL

What began in 1969 as a small gathering in a public park to celebrate the music of New Orleans now ranks as one of the best attended, most respected, and most musically comprehensive festivals in the world. Although people call it Jazz Fest, the full name is New Orleans Jazz & Heritage Festival, and the heritage is about as broad as it can get. Stand in the right place and, depending on which way the wind's blowing, you can catch as many as 10 musical styles from several continents, smell the tantalizing aromas of a dozen or so different food offerings, and meet a UN-like spectrum of fellow festgoers all at once.

In the days following Katrina, one of the things lovers of the city wondered about was the fate of Fest. It seems like a trivial thing to focus on, but it wasn't. The music festival is one of the city's two largest draws (Mardi Gras being the other one), and much of the local economy (particularly hotels and restaurants) relies on it. But it goes deeper than that: Over its lifespan, Jazz Fest has come to encompass everything the city has to offer, in terms of music, food, and culture. That, and it's a hell of a party. When its return was announced (thanks in part to Shell Oil, the festival's first corporate underwriters—a necessary step under the circumstances), it was seen as a sign that the city really would survive after all. Jazz Fest 2006, the first after Katrina, was a moment of resurrection for the city, as crowded as any year, with virtually the same amount of music and food, and highlighted by an emotional and resonant set by Bruce Springsteen and his Seeger Sessions band. The traditional songs about hard times and hope, coupled with Springsteen's own ire about the state of a city he loved, in front of tens of thousands who had endured much in the previous months, was a confluence of artist, material, time, and place like no other.

And yet, you don't need a star to have musical and emotional epiphanies at Fest. While such headliners as Stevie Wonder, Van Morrison, Dave Matthews, Bob Dylan, Sting, and Paul Simon have drawn record-setting crowds in recent years, serious Jazz Fest aficionados savor the lesser-known acts. They range from Mardi Gras Indians to old-time bluesmen who have never played outside the Delta, from Dixieland to avant-garde, from African artists making rare U.S. appearances to the top names in Cajun, zydeco, and, of course, jazz.

Gone are the days when the event was held in Congo Square and only a few hundred people came. Now filling the infield of the Fair Grounds horse-racing track up near City Park, the festival covers the last weekend in April and the first in May. It's set up about as well as such an event can be. When the crowds get big, though—the second Saturday, traditionally, is the busiest—it can be tough to move around, especially if the grounds are muddy from rain. And the lines at the most popular of the several dozen food booths can be frustratingly long. However, the crowds are remarkably well behaved—to make a sweeping generalization, these are not the same types who come for Mardi Gras. Tellingly, there are few, if any, arrests during Jazz Fest.

Attending Jazz Fest means making a few decisions. Hotel and restaurant reservations, not to mention choice flights, fill up months (if not a year) in advance, but the schedule is not announced until a couple of months before the event. That may mean scheduling your visit around your own availability, not an appearance by a particular band (unless you go each weekend). Just about every day at Jazz Fest is a good day, however, so this is not a hardship.

The second Saturday does attract some of the top acts, and each year it sets a record for single-day attendance. But we feel the fun tends to diminish with that many people. The Thursday before the second weekend is traditionally targeted to locals, with more local bands and generally smaller crowds because fewer tourists are around than on the weekends. It's a great time to hit the best food booths and to check out the crafts areas. The day has been left off the schedule post-Katrina as part of hard choices needed to make Fest viable, but it may be added back at some point. Whenever you decide to go, contact **New Orleans Jazz & Heritage Festival,** 1205 N. Rampart St., New Orleans, LA 70116 (© **504/410-4100;** www.nojazzfest.com), to get the schedule for each weekend and information about other Jazz Fest–related shows around town.

Of course, going to Jazz Fest means marathon endurance. With so many stages and musical choices, your mind can almost freeze. The festival's main feature, the Louisiana Heritage Fair, offers music on as many as 12 stages. You can plot out your day or just wander from stage to stage, catching a few songs by just about everyone. There is something to be said for the latter approach; some of the best Jazz Fest experiences come from discovering a hitherto unknown (at least to you) band or otherwise stumbling across a gem of a musical moment. Or you can camp out at just one stage—from the big ones, which feature famous headliners, to the gospel tent, where magical moments seem to happen several times a day.

Regardless, a typical Jazz Fest day has you arriving sometime after the gates open at 11am and staying until you are pooped or until they close at around 7pm (incredibly, the whole thing usually runs as efficiently as a Swiss train). After you leave the Fair Grounds for the day, get some dinner, and then hit the clubs. Every club in the city has Jazz Fest–related bookings (of special note is the **Ponderosa Stomp,** an event featuring "unsung heroes" of the blues, rockabilly, Swamp Pop, and New Orleans R&B; usually Tues and Wed btw. Fest weekends). Bouncing from one club to another can keep you out until dawn. Then you get up and start all over again. This is part of the reason we think Jazz Fest is so fun.

There are also many nonmusical aspects of Jazz Fest to distract you, particularly the crafts. Local craftspeople and imported artisans fill a sizable section of the Fair Grounds with displays of their products during the festival. Many of them offer demonstrations. You might get to see Louisiana Native American basket making; Cajun accordion, fiddle, and triangle making; and/or Mardi Gras Indian beading and costume making. Contemporary arts and crafts—such as jewelry, handblown glass, and painting—are also featured. In addition, you'll find an open marketplace at Congo Square filled with contemporary and traditional African (and African-influenced) crafts and performing artists.

And then, as always in New Orleans, there's the food. The heck with the music—when we dream of Jazz Fest, we are often thinking more about those 50-plus food booths filled with some of the best goodies we've ever tasted. We have friends who, at the end of every Jazz Fest, buy tickets for the very popular soft-shell crab po' boy stand *for next year* so that they won't suffer a moment's delay in getting their mouths around one of the best sandwiches they've ever tasted.

The food ranges from local standbys—red beans and rice, jambalaya, étouffée, and gumbo—to more interesting choices such as oyster sacks, the hugely popular sausage bread, *cochon de lait* (a mouthwatering roast-pig sandwich), andouille *calas* (fried rice fritters), and quail and pheasant gumbo. There's crawfish every way, including crawfish sushi, crawfish beignets, and the divine crawfish Monica (a white-cream sauce over pasta). And that's not even discussing the various Caribbean, African, Spanish, and even vegetarian dishes available. And how about dessert? Fresh strawberry shortbread, Italian ice cream, Key lime tarts, chocolate snoballs with condensed milk on them—oh, my! There's plenty of cold beer available, too, although you'll have to wait in some mighty long lines to get to it.

But there is even more to the Fest than food, music, and crafts. A number of cultural presentations on a wealth of topics (for starters, folklore or local food, complete with tastes!) are held daily throughout the fairgrounds. These little jewels are easily overlooked or missed altogether. We encourage you to either buy a program (which lists everything

(Tips) More Fun on the Bayou

A possible alternative to Jazz Fest is the **Festival International de Louisiane.** This multiday celebration of the music and art of southern Louisiana and its French-speaking cousins around the world is held on the blocked-off streets of Lafayette. It usually runs through the last weekend in April. Between the considerably smaller crowds and even smaller price (it's free!), it makes for a nice change of pace from Jazz Fest, with which it overlaps. For information, call or write the Festival International de Louisiane, 735 Jefferson St., Ste. 205, Lafayette, LA 70501 (✆ **337/232-8086;** www.festivalinternational.com).

being offered) or drop by one of the information booths scattered around the grounds to look over the listings.

Experienced Fest-goers also know that the Grandstand is the best-kept secret; it's air-conditioned, for one thing, and full of art and photography exhibits, and cooking demonstrations by the city's best chefs. Upstairs in the Grandstand is the Heritage Stage, which features interviews and short performances by some of the acts. This is a chance to perhaps see someone very popular in a more intimate setting, with often unpredictable and wild results. We once saw Elvis Costello and Allen Toussaint with only a handful of people, compared with the thousands who struggled to see their full set later in the day.

Try to purchase tickets as early as February if possible, when they are the cheapest. They're available by mail through **Ticketmaster** (✆ **504/522-5555;** www.ticketmaster. com). To order tickets by phone or to get ticket information, call **New Orleans Jazz & Heritage Festival** (✆ **504/410-4100;** www.nojazzfest.com). Admission for adults is $40 to $50, depending on when you buy them in advance (Ticketmaster charges a large per-ticket handling fee) and $50 at the gate; $5 for children. Evening events and concerts (order tickets in advance for these events as well) may be attended at an additional cost. The good news is that Fest tickets are always available at the gate (there is no sellout). The bad news is that tickets are always available at the gate, which can lead to severe overcrowding.

Note: No outside beverages (apart from water) are allowed at Jazz Fest. Though there are seats at some of the stages (two jazz tents and the gospel tent, and some at Fais Do Do) and some bleachers at another stage, people either sit on the ground, stand, or bring folding chairs or small blankets.

JAZZ FEST PARKING & TRANSPORTATION Parking at the Fair Grounds is extremely limited, mostly just for people with disabilities at $50 a day. It must be purchased in advance. We strongly recommend that you take public transportation or one of the available shuttles. The **Regional Transit Authority** operates bus routes from various pickup points to the Fair Grounds. For schedules, contact ✆ **504/248-3900** (www. norta.com). Taxis, though probably scarce, will also take you to the Fair Grounds at a special-event rate of $5 per person (or the meter reading if it's higher). We recommend **United Cabs** (✆ **504/524-9606**). **New Orleans Jazz & Heritage Festival** (✆ **800/488-5252** for Ticketmaster outside Louisiana, or **504/522-5555** locally; **504/410-4100** for the Fest office itself; www.nojazzfest.com) has information about shuttle transportation, which is not included in the ticket price.

Note: The **Canal Street streetcar line** runs up Canal from the Quarter all the way to 37
City Park Avenue (right to the cemeteries there), with a branch going down Carrollton
to close by the City Park entrance at the top of Esplanade.

PACKAGE DEALS **Festival Tours International,** 15237 Sunset Blvd., Ste. 17, Pacific
Palisades, CA 90272 (✆ **310/454-4080;** www.gumbopages.com/festivaltours), designs
tour packages that include not just accommodations and tickets for Jazz Fest but also a
visit to Cajun Country for unique personal encounters with local musicians.

If you're flying to New Orleans specifically for the Jazz & Heritage Festival, visit **www.
nojazzfest.com** to get a Jazz Fest promotional code from a list of airlines that offer special
fares during the event.

4 OTHER TOP FESTIVALS

THE FRENCH QUARTER FESTIVAL

The 3-day French Quarter Festival in early April is a celebration of the ingredients of
French Quarter life. Although the diversity of music is nowhere near as great as that
found at Jazz Fest, this is rapidly growing as an alternative to what many feel has become
too sprawling, massive, and expensive. There are scores of free outdoor concerts, art
shows, and children's activities. Most of the music is of the traditional jazz, brass band,
Cajun/zydeco, or funk variety. Stages are set throughout the Quarter (making it easy to
return to your hotel room for a rest), along Bourbon, Royal, and even down by the river,
where the breeze adds to the experience. Jackson Square and Woldenberg Riverfront Park
are transformed into the world's largest jazz brunch, with about 60 leading restaurants
serving Cajun and Creole specialties.

For details, write to **French Quarter Festivals,** 400 N. Peters St., Ste. 205, New
Orleans, LA 70130 (✆ **800/673-5725** or 504/522-5730; www.fqfi.org).

FESTIVALS ACADIENS

This is a Cajun Country celebration—or rather, several celebrations—held during the third
week of September in Lafayette. The festivals, lumped together under the heading Festivals
Acadiens, pay tribute to the culture and heritage of Cajun families who have been here since
the British expelled them from their Nova Scotia homes nearly 250 years ago.

At the **Bayou Food Festival,** you'll be able to taste the cuisine of more than 30 top
Cajun restaurants. Specialties such as stuffed crabs, crawfish étouffée, oysters Bienville,
shrimp de la Teche, catfish *en brochette,* jambalaya, chicken-and-sausage gumbo, smothered quail, and hot *boudin* (sausage) are everyday eating for Cajuns, and this is a rare
opportunity to try them all. The Bayou Food Festival is held in Girard Park, adjacent to
the music festival. Admission is free.

The **Festival de Musique Acadienne** began in 1974 when some Cajun musicians
were engaged to play briefly for visiting French newspaper editors. It was a rainy night,
but some 12,000 Cajun residents showed up to listen. It has become an annual affair
with more than 50,000 visitors usually on hand. Because of the crowds, the festival is
now held outdoors in Girard Park, where fans can listen in grassy comfort. Performed
almost entirely in French, the music covers both traditional and modern Cajun styles,
including zydeco. The music starts early and ends late, and there's no charge to come to
the park and listen.

You'll see native Louisiana artisans demonstrating their skills at the **Louisiana Native Crafts Festival.** All crafts presented must have been practiced before or during the early 1900s, and all materials used must be native to Louisiana. Meeting these criteria are such arts as woodcarving, soap making, and palmetto weaving.

For details on all, contact the **Lafayette Conventions and Visitors Center,** P.O. Box 52066, Lafayette, LA 70505 (© **800/346-1958** in the U.S., 800/543-5340 in Canada, or 337/232-3737; www.lafayettetravel.com).

4

Planning Your Trip to New Orleans

No matter what your idea of the ideal New Orleans trip is, this chapter will give you the information to make informed plans and help point you toward some additional resources. For more help in planning your trip and for more on-the-ground resources in New Orleans, please see chapter 13, "Fast Facts."

1 VISITOR INFORMATION

Even a seasoned traveler should consider writing or calling ahead to the **New Orleans Metropolitan Convention and Visitors Bureau,** 2020 St. Charles Ave., New Orleans, LA 70130 (© **800/672-6124** or 504/566-5011; www.neworleans cvb.com). The staff is extremely friendly and helpful, and you can easily get any information you can't find in this book from them. If you're having trouble making decisions, they can give you good advice; if you have a special interest, they'll help you plan your visit around it—this is definitely one of the most helpful tourist centers in any major city.

Once you've arrived in the city, you also might want to stop by the **Visitor Information Center,** 529 St. Ann St. (© **504/568-5661**), in the French Quarter. The center is open Tuesday to Saturday from 9am to 5pm and has walking- and driving-tour maps and booklets on restaurants, accommodations, sightseeing, special tours, and pretty much anything else you might want to know about. The staff is friendly and knowledgeable about both the city and the state.

NOLA.com is an excellent resource, offering online versions of the *Times-Picayune,* information about nightlife and festivals, and good links.

Among the blogs about New Orleans, try **www.gumbopages.com** for plenty of information about New Orleans–related food and music, plus updates on the native author's many local friends and family. For additional blog action, **www.appetites.us** has excellent NOLA food coverage. The following is a roundup of literate locals, musing (and sometimes ranting) about the state of their beloved city, post-Katrina.

- www.righthandthief.blogspot.com
- www.bloggingneworleans.com
- www.peoplegetready.jockamofeenanay. com
- www.humidcity.com
- www.dapoblog.blogspot.com

2 WHEN TO GO

With the possible exception of July and August (unless you thrive on heat and humidity—and some really exceptional hotel deals!), just about any time is the right time to go to New Orleans. Mardi Gras is, of course, the time of year when it's hardest to get a hotel room, but it can also be difficult during the various music festivals throughout the year, especially the Jazz & Heritage Festival. (See chapter 3.)

It's important to know what's going on when; the city's landscape can change dramatically depending not just on what festival or convention is happening, but also what happens with recovery efforts, and prices can also reflect that. The best time of year, in our opinion, is December, before and during Christmas. The town is gussied up with decorations, there are all kinds of seasonal special events, the weather is nice—but for some reason, tourists become scarce. Hotels, eager to lure any business, lower their rates dramatically, and most restaurants are so empty that you can walk in just about anywhere without a reservation. Take advantage of it.

THE WEATHER

In 2005, weather in New Orleans became international news. Given that the media trumpets about hurricane season (June 1 to some time in Nov, depending on whom you talk to), tourists may be anxious about visiting during those months. Obviously, there are no guarantees, but remember that hurricanes, while unpredictable, don't happen too terribly often.

The average mean temperature in New Orleans is an inviting 70°F (21°C), but it can drop or rise considerably in a single day. (We've experienced 40°F/4°C and rain one day, 80°F/27°C and humidity the next.) Conditions depend primarily on two things: whether it rains and whether there is direct sunlight or cloud cover.

Rain can provide slight and temporary relief on a hot day; for the most part, it hits in sudden (and sometimes dramatically heavy) showers, which disappear as quickly as they arrive. Anytime the sun shines unimpeded, it gets much warmer. The region's high humidity can make even mild warms and colds feel intense. Still, the city's semitropical climate is part of its appeal—a slight bit of moistness makes the air come sensually alive.

New Orleans should be pleasant at almost any time of year except July and August, which can be exceptionally hot and muggy. If you do come during those months, you'll quickly learn to follow the natives' example, staying out of the noon-day sun and ducking from one air-conditioned building to another. Winter is very mild by American standards but is punctuated by an occasional cold snap, when the mercury can drop below the freezing point. Then again, "unpredictable" is the watchword. As one example, August 2004 brought some of the most beautiful summer days in living memory, with temperatures more appropriate to fall. And then October came and brought heat and humidity the likes of which are usually found during the dog days of summer. And Jazz Fest that year? It was cold at night and perfectly balmy every single day. And between hurricanes Katrina and Rita in 2005, not a drop of rain fell.

In the dead of summer, T-shirts and shorts are absolutely acceptable everywhere except the finest restaurants. In the spring and fall, something a little warmer is in order; in the winter, you should plan to carry a lightweight coat or jacket,

New Orleans Average Temperatures & Rainfall

	Jan	Feb	Mar	Apr	May	June	July	Aug	Sept	Oct	Nov	Dec
High (°F)	63	64	72	79	84	90	91	90	88	79	70	64
Low (°F)	43	45	52	59	64	72	73	72	70	59	50	45
High (°C)	17	18	22	26	29	32	33	32	31	26	21	18
Low (°C)	6	7	11	15	18	22	23	22	21	15	10	7
Days of Rainfall	10	9	9	7	8	10	15	13	10	5	7	10

Tips Hot Time in the City

If you can stand it, do consider braving the summer; apart from conventions, the town is often slow, which produces secret hotel bargains. On a recent July visit, high-end hotels were offering rooms from $59 to $129 (way, way below their regular rates), sometimes with additional bargains (like breaks on parking fees) built in. You can also often get upgrades to fancy suites for a song—ask when you check in. The past couple of years local restaurants have run "COOL-inary" specials during August, three-course meals for set fees like $20.10 or $30.10. Yeah, it's hot and humid, though maybe not as much as you might think, but for the most part, you can travel from air-conditioned place to air-conditioned place with minimal discomfort. In fact, the biggest climate problem can sometimes be the overcompensation with air-conditioning that chills restaurants to near–meat locker temps!

though umbrellas and cheap rain jackets are available everywhere for those tourists who inevitably get caught in a sudden, unexpected downpour. Also note that many restaurants are overzealous with air-conditioning, so bring those light wraps along on warm nights just in case.

CALENDAR OF EVENTS

For more information on **Mardi Gras, Jazz Fest, Festivals Acadiens,** and other major area events, see chapter 3, "Mardi Gras, Jazz Fest & Other Festivals." For general information, contact the **New Orleans Metropolitan Convention and Visitors Bureau,** 2020 St. Charles Ave., New Orleans, LA 70130 (© **800/672-6124** or 504/566-5011; www.neworleanscvb.com).

For an exhaustive list of events beyond those listed here, check http://events.frommers.com, where you'll find a searchable, up-to-the-minute roster of what's happening in cities all over the world.

JANUARY

Allstate Sugar Bowl Classic. First held in 1934, this is New Orleans's oldest yearly sporting occasion. Allstate began sponsoring this college football bowl game in 2007, in the triumphantly refurbished, if still tarnished emotionally, Superdome. The football game is the main event, but there are a series of other fan- and visitor-related activities. Fans tend to be really loud, really boisterous, and everywhere during the festivities. For information, contact Allstate Sugar Bowl, 1500 Sugar Bowl Dr., New Orleans, LA 70112 (© **504/828-2440;** www.allstatesugarbowl.org). January 1, 2010.

FEBRUARY

Lundi Gras. This is an old tradition that has been revived in the last decade or so. It's free, it's outdoors (celebrations are at Spanish Plaza), and it features music (including a jazz competition) and the arrival of Rex at 6pm, marking the beginning of Mardi Gras, plus an appearance by the King of Zulu. For more information, contact New Orleans Riverwalk Marketplace, 1 Poydras St.,

New Orleans, LA 70130 (© **504/522-1555**). See also p. 23. Monday before Mardi Gras. February 15, 2010.

Mardi Gras. The culmination of the 2-month-long carnival season, Mardi Gras is the big annual blowout, a citywide party that takes place on Fat Tuesday (the last day before Lent on the Christian calendar). The entire city stops working (sometimes days in advance!) and starts partying in the early morning, and the streets are taken over by some overwhelming parades—which, these days, go through the Central Business District instead of the French Quarter. See chapter 3, "Mardi Gras, Jazz Fest & Other Festivals," for more details. Day before Ash Wednesday. February 16, 2010.

MARCH

St. Patrick's Day Parades. There are two: One takes place in the French Quarter beginning at Molly's at the Market (1107 Decatur St.) on March 14, and the other goes through the Irish Channel neighborhood following a route that begins at Jackson Avenue and Magazine Street, goes over to St. Charles Avenue, turns uptown to Louisiana Avenue, and returns to Jackson Avenue. The parades have the flavor of Mardi Gras, but instead of beads, watchers are pelted with cabbages, carrots, and other veggies. For information on the French Quarter parade, call Molly's at the Market (© **504/525-5169**). The Irish Channel parade takes place in early March. Because there's no organization to contact about this one, you can try the New Orleans Metropolitan Convention and Visitors Bureau (p. 39) for more information.

St. Joseph's Day Parade. Another citycentric festivity that gets little play outside of the area. St. Joseph is the patron saint of families and working men. His veneration was brought to New Orleans

by Italian and Sicilian immigrants. On his saint's day, in addition to the parade, which takes place the weekend around March 19, you may want to visit the altars devoted to St. Joseph, moving and elaborate works of art featuring food, candles, statues, and much more, all of which takes days to construct. You can find them all over the city, at various churches (where you might get fed after services), private homes (where you will likely also get fed), and at the American Italian Museum and Library, 537 S. Peters St. For more information, call © **504/522-7294.**

Super Sunday. This is the annual Mardi Gras Indians showdown, which takes place on the Sunday nearest St. Joseph's Day. This is an incredible but sadly underappreciated event in New Orleans, when the Indians are all in one place; the feathers fly and the chants are ongoing. These days more than ever, it's hard to say who will show. Unfortunately, there are no contact numbers nor firm times or locations for this event (though it's roughly in the Bayou St. John area and uptown, around the corner of LaSalle and Washington), and for that matter, recently the two neighborhoods have been doing their respective things on Sundays 2 weeks apart. For more information, you can try checking with www.nola.com or the Metropolitan Tourism board, or just show up in town and drive into that area and ask around, or just watch for feathers and listen for drums. Usually in mid- to late March.

Tennessee Williams New Orleans Literary Festival. The 24th anniversary of the festival takes place in 2010. A 5-day series celebrating New Orleans's rich literary heritage, this festival includes theatrical performances, readings, discussion panels, master classes, musical events, and literary walking tours dedicated to the playwright. By the way, the focus is not confined to Tennessee Williams. Events take place at venues throughout the city. For info, call ✆ **504/581-1144** or go to www.tennesseewilliams.net. March 24–28, 2010.

Spring Fiesta. The fiesta, which begins with the crowning of the Spring Fiesta queen, is more than half a century old and takes place throughout the city— from the Garden District to the French Quarter to Uptown and beyond. Historical and architectural tours of many of the city's private homes, courtyards, and plantation homes are offered in conjunction with the 5-day event. For the schedule, contact the Spring Fiesta Association (✆ **504/581-1367;** www. springfiesta.com). March 20–28, 2010.

APRIL

The Crescent City Classic. This 6-mile road race, from Jackson Square to Audubon Park, brings an international field of top runners to the city. For more info, call or write the Classic, P.O. Box 13587, New Orleans, LA 70185 (✆ **504/861-8686;** www.ccc10k.com). Saturday before Easter. April 3, 2010.

French Quarter Festival. For hard-core jazz fans, this is rapidly becoming an alternative to Jazz Fest, where actual jazz is becoming less and less prominent. It kicks off with a parade down Bourbon Street. Among other things, you can join people dancing in the streets, learn the history of jazz, visit historic homes, and take a ride on a riverboat. Many local restaurants set up booths in Jackson Square, so the eating is exceptionally good. Events are held all over the French Quarter. For information, call or write French Quarter Festivals, 400 N. Peters St., New Orleans, LA 70130 (✆ **504/522-5730;** www.fqfi.org). Usually mid-April.

New Orleans Jazz & Heritage Festival (Jazz Fest). A 10-day event that draws musicians, music fans, cooks, and craftspeople to celebrate music and life, Jazz Fest rivals Mardi Gras in popularity. Lodgings in the city tend to sell out up to a year ahead, so book early. Events take place at the Fair Grounds Race Track and various venues throughout the city. For information, call or write New Orleans Jazz & Heritage Festival, 1205 N. Rampart St., New Orleans, LA 70116 (✆ **504/410-4100;** www.nojazzfest.com). Look for more information in chapter 3, "Mardi Gras, Jazz Fest & Other Festivals." The last weekend in April and first weekend in May.

MAY

Greek Festival. Located at the Holy Trinity Cathedral's Hellenic Cultural Center, this 3-day festival features Greek folk dancing, specialty foods, crafts, and music. For more information, call or write Holy Trinity Cathedral, 1200 Robert E. Lee Blvd., New Orleans, LA 70122 (✆ **504/282-0259;** www.greekfestnola.com). Last weekend of May.

New Orleans Wine & Food Experience. During this time, antiques shops and art galleries throughout the French Quarter hold wine and food tastings, winemakers and local chefs conduct seminars, and a variety of vintner dinners and grand tastings are held for your gourmandistic pleasure. More than 150 wines and 40 restaurants are featured every day. For information and schedule, call or write Mary Reynolds, P.O. Box 70514, New Orleans, LA 70172 (✆ **504/529-9463;** www.nowfe.com). Five days toward the end May.

JUNE

Creole Tomato Festival. A celebration of tomato diversity, this daylong event features cooking and tastings in the historic French Market. For more info, call or write the French Market, P.O. Box 51749, New Orleans, LA 70151

(© 504/522-2621; www.frenchmarket. org). First Sunday in June.

JULY

Go Fourth on the River. The annual Fourth of July celebration begins in the morning at the riverfront and continues into the night, culminating into a spectacular fireworks display. For details, go to www.go4thontheriver.com or contact the New Orleans Metropolitan Convention and Visitors Bureau at © 800/672-6124. July 4th.

Essence Music Festival. This 3-day event, sponsored by the venerable magazine, is a significant one for the city. Nighttime entertainment brings the top names in African-American entertainment (2009's lineup included Beyoncé, Anita Baker, John Legend, Lionel Richie, and many others). Known as a "party with a purpose," the daytime offers seminars with motivational speakers, crafts and trade fairs, and other activities, not to mention huge crowds. www.essence.com/essence/emf. Early July.

Tales of the Cocktail. The first mixed drink was invented in New Orleans, where they still love to drink (you may have noticed!), and eat, and talk about both those activities. With cocktail tours of local bars; tie-ins with local restaurants; panels featuring local restaurant owners, chefs, drinks specialists, authors; and plenty of clever, quirky events, it's quickly becoming one of the year's top events. For details, go to www.talesofthecocktail.com. Mid-July.

AUGUST

Satchmo Summerfest. Louis Armstrong, hometown boy made very good, is now celebrated with his own festival, held around his real birthday (he claimed to be born on July 4th, but records prove otherwise). It includes the usual local food and music in Satchmo's honor, with the emphasis on jazz entertainment and education, including activities for kids to ensure Satchmo lives on for generations to come. For location updates and information, call or write French Quarter Festivals, 400 N. Peters St., New Orleans, LA 70130 (© 504/522-5730; www.fqfi.org). Early August.

SEPTEMBER

Southern Decadence. The pinnacle of gay New Orleans, where more than 100,000 gay men come to town to flaunt it, whether they got it or not. The multiday party hits its frenzied peak on the Sunday before Labor Day as participants flock to follow a secret parade route, making sure to stop into many bars along the way. People travel from far and wide to be a part of the festivities. There is only an informal organization associated with the festival, and it's hard to get anyone on the phone. For information, try the website **www.southerndecadence.com** or contact *Ambush Magazine* (© 504/522-8047; fax 522-0907). Labor Day weekend.

OCTOBER

Art for Arts' Sake. The arts season begins with gallery openings throughout the city. Julia, Magazine, and Royal streets are where the action is. For more information, contact the Contemporary Arts Center, 900 Camp St., New Orleans, LA 70130 (© 504/523-1216; www.cacno.org). Throughout the month.

Gumbo Festival. This festival showcases one of the region's signature dishes and celebrates Cajun culture to boot. It's 3 days of gumbo-related events (including the presentation of the royal court of King and Miss Creole Gumbo), plus many hours of Cajun music. The festival is held in Bridge City, on the outskirts of New Orleans. For more information, contact the Gumbo Festival, P.O. Box

9069, Bridge City, LA 70096 (© **504/ 436-4712;** www.hgaparish.org/gumbo festival.htm). Second weekend in October.

Festivals Acadiens. This is a series of happenings that celebrate Cajun music, food, crafts, and culture in and near Lafayette, Louisiana. (Most of the events are in Lafayette.) For more information, contact the **Lafayette Convention and Visitors Commission,** P.O. Box 52066, Lafayette, LA 70505 (© **800/346-1958** in the U.S., 800/543-5340 in Canada, or 337/232-3737; www.lafayettetravel. com). Second weekend in October.

New Orleans Film Festival. Canal Place Cinemas and other theaters throughout the city screen award-winning local and international films and host writers, actors, and directors over the course of a week. Admission prices range from $6.25 for NOFF members to $7.25 for general admission. For dates, contact the New Orleans Film Society, 843 Carondelet, No. 1, New Orleans, LA 70130 (© **504/309-6633;** www.neworleans filmfest.com). Midmonth.

Halloween. Rivaling Mardi Gras in terms of costumes, Halloween is certainly celebrated more grandly here than it is in any other American city. After all, New Orleans has a way with ghosts. Events include Boo-at-the-Zoo (end of Oct) for children, costume parties (including a Monster Bash at the Ernest N. Morial Convention Center), haunted houses, formal and informal costume extravaganzas, and much more. Apart from Southern Decadence, it's the biggest magnet for gay and lesbian visitors. You can catch the ghoulish action all over the city—many museums get in on the fun with specially designed tours—but the French Quarter, as always, is the center of the Halloween-night universe. October 31.

Voodoo Music Experience. This 3-day music festival, set in City Park, is the biggest music festival for a younger demographic, pulling in top touring bands and the best the local scene has to offer. Look for everything from hip hop to hard rock, plus a tent featuring some of the stars of the local music scene. In 2009, the eclectic lineup included everything from KISS to Eminem to Eagles of Death Metal, among many others. An increasingly big draw, it really packs its seven stages and even includes artists and craftspeople. Oddly, the food selections are not the greatest, but with the stellar lineup, it's one weekend in New Orleans that doesn't focus on eats (www.voodoomusicfest. com). Last weekend in October.

NOVEMBER

Swamp Festival. Sponsored by the Audubon Institute, the Swamp Festival features long days of live Swamp Music performances (lots of good zydeco here), as well as hands-on contact with Louisiana swamp animals. Admission to the festival is free with zoo admission. For information, call or write the Audubon Nature Institute, 6500 Magazine St., New Orleans, LA 70118 (© **504/861-2537;** www.audubon institute.org). First weekend in November.

The Rayne Frog Festival. Cajuns can always find an excuse to hold a party, and in this case they've turned to the lowly frog as an excuse for a *fais-do-do* (dance) and a waltz contest. Frog races and frog-jumping contests fill the entertainment bill—and if you arrive without your amphibian, there's a Rent-a-Frog service. A lively frog-eating contest winds things up. For dates and full details, contact Lafayette Convention and Visitors Commission, P.O. Box 52066, Lafayette, LA 70505 (© **800/ 346-1958** in the U.S., 800/543-5340 in Canada, or 337/232-3808; www. raynefrogfestival.org). Mid-November.

Words & Music: A Literary Fest in New Orleans. This highly ambitious literary and music conference (originated in large part by the folks behind Faulkner House Books) offers 5 days' worth of roundtable discussions with eminent authors (with varying connections to the city), original drama, poetry readings, and master classes, plus great music and food. For authors seeking guidance and inspiration and for book lovers in general, call ✆ **504/586-1609** or visit their website at **www.words andmusic.org** for exact dates.

DECEMBER

Christmas New Orleans–Style. New Orleans loves to celebrate, so it should be no surprise that they do Christmas really well. The town is decorated to a fare-thee-well, there is an evening of candlelit caroling in Jackson Square, bonfires line the levees along the River Road on Christmas Eve (to guide Papa Noël, his sled drawn by alligators, on his gift-delivering way), restaurants offer specially created multicourse Réveillon dinners, and hotels throughout the city offer "Papa Noël" rates.

Why? Because despite all the fun and the generally nice (read: not hot and humid) weather, tourism goes *waaay* down at this time of year, and hotels are eager to lure you all in with cheaper rates. This is one of the top times to come to town—you can have the city virtually to yourself. For information, contact French Quarter Festivals, 400 N. Peters St., Ste. 205, New Orleans, LA 70130 (✆ **504/522-5730;** www. frenchquarterfestivals.org). All month.

Celebration in the Oaks. Lights and lighted figures designed to illustrate holiday themes bedeck sections of City Park. It's unclear if driving tours, which were suspended post-Katrina, will return. The walking tours, at $6 per person, offer winter wonderment for the whole family. It's simple, nostalgic fun. For information, contact Celebration in the Oaks, 1 Palm Dr., New Orleans, LA 70124 (✆ **544/482-4888;** www.neworleanscitypark.com). Late November to early January.

New Year's Eve. The countdown takes place in Jackson Square and is a big, reliable street party. In the Southern equivalent of New York's Times Square, revelers watch a lighted ball drop from the top of Jackson Brewery. December 31.

3 ENTRY REQUIREMENTS

PASSPORTS

Virtually every traveler (including U.S. citizens) entering the U.S.—by air, land, or sea—is required to present a valid passport. For information on how to obtain a passport, see "Passports" in "Fast Facts: New Orleans," in chapter 13.

VISAS

The U.S. State Department has a **Visa Waiver Program (VWP)** allowing citizens

of the following countries to enter the United States without a visa for stays of up to 90 days: Andorra, Australia, Austria, Belgium, Brunei, Denmark, Finland, France, Germany, Iceland, Ireland, Italy, Japan, Liechtenstein, Luxembourg, Monaco, the Netherlands, New Zealand, Norway, Portugal, San Marino, Singapore, Slovenia, Spain, Sweden, Switzerland, and the United Kingdom. (*Note:* This list was

Cut to the Front of the Airport Security Line As a Registered Traveler

In 2003, the **Transportation Security Administration** (**TSA;** www.tsa.gov) approved a pilot program to help ease the time spent in line for airport security screenings. In exchange for information and a fee, persons can be pre-screened as registered travelers, granting them a front-of-the-line position when they fly. The program is run through private firms—the largest and most well-known is Steven Brill's **Clear** (www.flyclear.com), and it works like this: Travelers complete an online application providing specific points of personal information including name, addresses for the previous 5 years, birth date, social security number, driver's license number, and a valid credit card (you're not charged the **$99 fee** until your application is approved). Print out the completed form and take it, along with proper ID, to an "enrollment station" (this can be found in over 20 participating airports and in a growing number of American Express offices around the country, for example). It's at this point where it gets seemingly sci-fi. At the enrollment station, a Clear representative will record your biometrics necessary for clearance; in this case, your fingerprints and your irises will be digitally recorded.

Once your application has been screened against no-fly lists, outstanding warrants, and other security measures, you'll be issued a clear plastic card that holds a chip containing your information. Each time you fly through participating airports (and the numbers are steadily growing), go to the Clear Pass station located next to the standard TSA screening line. Here you'll insert your card into a slot and place your finger on a scanner to read your print—when the information matches up, you're cleared to cut to the front of the security line. You'll still have to follow all the procedures of the day like removing your shoes and walking through the x-ray machine, but Clear promises to cut 30 minutes off your wait time at the airport.

On a personal note: Each time I've used my Clear Pass, my travel companions are still waiting to go through security while I'm already sitting down, reading the paper and sipping my overpriced smoothie. Granted, registered traveler programs are not for the infrequent traveler, but for those of us who fly on a regular basis, it's a perk I'm willing to pay for.

—David A. Lytle

accurate at press time; for the most up-to-date list of countries in the VWP, consult www.travel.state.gov/visa.) Even though a visa isn't necessary, in an effort to help U.S. officials check travelers against terror watch lists before they arrive at U.S. borders, as of January 12, 2009, visitors from VWP countries must register online before boarding a plane or a boat to the U.S. Travelers will complete an electronic application providing basic personal and travel eligibility information. The Department of Homeland Security recommends filling out the form at least 3 days before traveling. Authorizations will be valid for up to 2 years or until the traveler's passport expires, whichever comes first. Currently, there is no fee for the online application. Canadian citizens may enter the United States without visas; they will need to show passports (if traveling by air) and proof of residence, however. *Note:* Any passport issued on or after October 26, 2006, by a VWP country must be an **e-Passport** for VWP travelers to be eligible to enter the U.S. without a visa. Citizens of these nations also need to present a round-trip air or cruise ticket upon arrival. E-Passports contain computer chips capable of storing biometric information, such as the required digital photograph of the holder. (You can identify an e-Passport by the symbol on the bottom center cover of your passport.) If your passport doesn't have this feature, you can still travel without a visa if it is a valid passport issued before October 26, 2005, and includes a machine-readable zone, or between October 26, 2005, and October 25, 2006, and includes a digital photograph. For more information, go to **www. travel.state.gov/visa**.

Citizens of all other countries must have (1) a valid passport that expires at least 6 months later than the scheduled end of their visit to the U.S., and (2) a tourist visa. To obtain a visa, applicants must schedule an appointment with a U.S. consulate or embassy, fill out the application forms (available from www. travel.state.gov/visa), and pay a $131 fee. Wait times can be lengthy, so it's best to initiate the process as soon as possible.

As of January 2004, many international visitors traveling on visas to the United States will be photographed and finger-printed on arrival at Customs in airports and on cruise ships in a program created by the Department of Homeland Security called **US-VISIT.** Exempt from the extra scrutiny are visitors entering by land or those (mostly in Europe; see p. 324) that don't require a visa for short-term visits. For more information, go to the Homeland Security website at **www.dhs.gov/ dhspublic**.

For specifics on how to get a visa, see "Visas" in "Fast Facts: New Orleans," in chapter 13.

MEDICAL REQUIREMENTS

Unless you're arriving from an area known to be suffering from an epidemic (particularly cholera or yellow fever), inoculations or vaccinations are not required for entry into the United States.

CUSTOMS
What You Can Bring into the U.S.

Every visitor more than 21 years of age may bring in, free of duty, the following: (1) 1 liter of wine or hard liquor; (2) 200 cigarettes, 100 cigars (but not from Cuba), or 3 pounds of smoking tobacco; and (3) $100 worth of gifts. These exemptions are offered to travelers who spend at least 72 hours in the United States and who have not claimed them within the preceding 6 months. It is forbidden to bring into the country almost any meat products (including canned, fresh, and dried meat products such as buillion, soup mixes, and so on). Generally, condiments including vinegars, oils, spices, coffee, tea, and some cheeses and baked goods are permitted. Avoid rice products, as rice can often harbor insects. Bringing fruits and vegetables is not advised, though not prohibited. Customs will allow produce depending on where you got it and where you're going after you arrive in the U.S. Foreign tourists may carry in or out up to $10,000 in U.S. or foreign currency with no formalities; larger sums must be declared to U.S. Customs on entering or leaving, which includes filing form CM 4790. For details regarding U.S. Customs and Border Protection, consult your nearest U.S. embassy or consulate, or **U.S. Customs** (www.customs.ustreas.gov).

What You Can Take Home from New Orleans

U.S. Citizens: For specifics on what you can bring back and the corresponding fees, download the invaluable free pamphlet *Know Before You Go* online at www.cbp.gov. (Click on "Travel," and then click on "Know Before You Go! Online Brochure.") Or contact the U.S. Customs & Border Protection (CBP), 1300 Pennsylvania Ave., NW, Washington, DC 20229 (© 877/ 287-8667) and request the pamphlet.

Canadian Citizens: For a clear summary of Canadian rules, write for the booklet *I Declare,* issued by the Canada Border Services Agency (© **800/461-9999** in Canada, or 204/983-3500; www.cbsa-asfc. gc.ca).

U.K. Citizens: For information, contact **HM Customs & Excise** at © **0845/ 010-9000** (from outside the U.K.,

020/8929-0152), or consult their website at **www.hmce.gov.uk**.

Australian Citizens: A helpful brochure available from Australian consulates or Customs offices is *Know Before You Go.* For more information, call the **Australian Customs Service** at © **1300/363-263,** or log on to **www.customs.gov.au**.

New Zealand Citizens: Most questions are answered in a free pamphlet available at New Zealand consulates and Customs offices: *New Zealand Customs Guide for Travellers, Notice no. 4.* For more information, contact **New Zealand Customs,** The Customhouse, 17–21 Whitmore St., Box 2218, Wellington (© **04/473-6099** or 0800/428-786; **www.customs.govt.nz**).

---

4 GETTING THERE & GETTING AROUND

GETTING TO NEW ORLEANS
By Plane

Among the airlines serving the city's **Louis Armstrong New Orleans International Airport (MSY)** are **America West** (© 800/ 235-9292; www.americawest.com), **American** (© 800/433-7300; www.aa. com), **Continental** (© 800/525-0280 or 504/581-2965; www.continental.com), **Delta** (© 800/221-1212; www.delta. com), **JetBlue** (© 800/538-2583; www. jetblue.com), **Northwest** (© 800/225-2525; www.nwa.com), **Southwest** (© 800/ 435-9792; www.southwest.com), **US Airways** (© 800/428-4322; www.usairways. com), and **United** (© 800/241-6522; www.ual.com).

The airport is 15 miles west of the city, in Kenner. You'll find information booths scattered around the airport and in the baggage claim area, as well as a branch of the **Travelers Aid Society.** For information on getting into New Orleans from the airport, see below.

With the federalization of airport security, security procedures at U.S. airports

are more stable and consistent than ever. Generally, you'll be fine if you arrive at the airport **1 hour** before a domestic flight and **2 hours** before an international flight; if you show up late, tell an airline employee and he or she will probably whisk you to the front of the line.

Bring a **current, government-issued photo ID** such as a driver's license or passport, and if you've got an e-ticket, print out the **official confirmation page;** you'll need to show your confirmation at the security checkpoint, and your ID at the ticket counter or the gate. (Children under 18 do not need photo IDs for domestic flights, but the adults checking in with them need them.)

At press time, the Transportation Security Administration (TSA) recommended practicing the **3-1-1** rule for getting carry-on baggage through security without problems: Liquids or gels must be in a **3**-ounce bottle (or smaller); items must be stored in a **1**-quart clear, plastic zip-top bag; **1** bag per passenger is allowed in the screening bin. Prescription medications, baby formula, and breast milk in amounts greater than 3 ounces may be carried on, but they must be declared. Travelers in the U.S. are allowed one carry-on bag, plus a "personal item" such as a purse, briefcase, or laptop bag. Carry-on hoarders can stuff all sorts of things into a laptop bag; as long as it has a laptop in it, it's still considered a personal item. For more information on restricted and nonrestricted items, check the website for the TSA (**www.tsa.gov**) for details.

In 2003 the TSA phased out **gate check-in** at all U.S. airports. Passengers with e-tickets and without checked bags can still beat the ticket-counter lines by using **electronic kiosks** or even **online check-in.** Ask your airline which alternatives are available, and if you're using a kiosk, bring the credit card you used to book the ticket. If you're checking bags, you will still be able to use most airlines' kiosks; again, call your airline for up-to-date information. **Curbside check-in** is also a good way to avoid lines, though some airlines are now charging for it (around $2–$3). However, a few airlines still ban curbside check-in entirely; call before you go.

At press time, the TSA is also recommending that you **not lock your checked luggage** so screeners can search it by hand if necessary. The agency says to use plastic "zip ties" instead, which can be bought at hardware stores and can be easily cut off.

Arriving at the Airport
IMMIGRATION & CUSTOMS CLEARANCE International visitors arriving by air, no matter what the port of entry, should cultivate patience and resignation before setting foot on U.S. soil. U.S. airports have considerably beefed up security clearances in the years since the terrorist attacks of September 11, and clearing Customs and Immigration can take as long as 2 hours.

Getting Into Town from the Airport
From the airport, you can get to your hotel on the **Airport Shuttle** (✆ **504/522-3500**).

For $15 per person (one-way), the van will take you directly to your hotel. There are Airport Shuttle information desks (staffed 24 hr.) in the airport. Shuttles go to the French Quarter, Garden District, Central Business District, and Faubourg Marigny.

Note: If you plan to take the Airport Shuttle *to* the airport when you depart, you must call a day in advance and let them know what time your flight is leaving. They will then tell you what time they will pick you up. You can also book and pay for a round-trip in advance.

A **taxi** from the airport to most hotels will cost about $29 for one to two people; if there are three or more passengers, the fare is $12 per person plus a $2 gas surcharge.

If you want to ride in style from the airport to your hotel, try **New Orleans Limousine Service** (✆ **504/529-5226**). Express transfer service for a six-passenger limo is $100 plus 20% gratuity.

From the airport, you can reach the **Central Business District** by bus for $1.60 (exact change required). Buses run from 6am to 6:30pm. From 6 to 9am and 3 to 6pm, they leave the airport every 12 to 15 minutes and go to the downtown side of Tulane Avenue between Elks Place and South Saratoga Street; at other times, they leave every 23 minutes. For more information, call the **Regional Transit Authority** (✆ **504/248-3900;** www. norta.com).

Long-Haul Flights: How to Stay Comfortable
- Your choice of airline and airplane will definitely affect your legroom. Find more details about U.S. airlines at **www. seatguru.com**. For international airlines, the research firm Skytrax has posted a list of average seat pitches at **www.airlinequality.com**.
- Emergency exit seats and bulkhead seats typically have the most legroom. Emergency exit seats are usually left unassigned until the day of a flight (to ensure that someone able-bodied fills

the seats); it's worth checking in online at home (if the airline offers that option) or getting to the ticket counter early to snag one of these spots for a long flight. Many passengers find that bulkhead seating offers more legroom, but keep in mind that bulkhead seats have no storage space on the floor in front of you.

- To have two seats for yourself in a three-seat row, try for an aisle seat in a center section toward the back of coach. If you're traveling with a companion, book an aisle and a window seat. Middle seats are usually booked last, so chances are good you'll end up with three seats to yourselves. And in the event that a third passenger is assigned the middle seat, he or she will probably be more than happy to trade for a window or an aisle.

- To sleep, avoid the last row of any section or the row in front of an emergency exit, as these seats are the least likely to recline. Avoid seats near highly trafficked toilet areas. Avoid seats in the back of many jets—these can be narrower than those in the rest of coach. Or reserve a window seat so you can rest your head and avoid being bumped in the aisle.

- Get up, walk around, and stretch every 60 to 90 minutes to keep your blood flowing. This helps avoid **deep vein thrombosis,** or "economy-class syndrome." See the box "Avoiding 'Economy Class Syndrome,'" p. 57.

- Drink water before, during, and after your flight to combat the lack of humidity in airplane cabins. Avoid caffeine and alcohol, which will dehydrate you.

By Car
You can drive to New Orleans via **I-10, I-55, U.S. 90, U.S. 61,** or across the Lake Pontchartrain Causeway on **La. 25.** From any direction, you'll see the city's distinctive and swampy outlying regions; if you can, try to drive in while you can enjoy the

scenery in daylight. For the best roadside views, take U.S. 61 or La. 25, but only if you have time to spare. The larger roads are considerably faster.

It's a good idea to call before you leave home to ask for directions to your hotel. Most hotels have parking facilities (for a hefty daily fee); if they don't, they'll give you the names and addresses of nearby parking lots.

AAA (© 504/367-4095; www.aaa. com) will assist members with trip planning and emergency services.

Driving in New Orleans can be a hassle, and parking is a nightmare. It's a great city for walking, and cabs are plentiful and not too expensive, so you really don't need a car unless you're planning several day trips.

Nevertheless, most major national car-rental companies are represented at the airport. For a listing of the major car rental agencies in New Orleans, see "Airline, Hotel & Car Rental Websites," in chapter 13.

By Train
As with the interstates and highways into New Orleans, the passenger rail lines cut through some beautiful scenery. **Amtrak** (© 800/USA-RAIL [872-7245] or 504/ 528-1610; www.amtrak.com) trains serve the city's **Union Passenger Terminal,** 1001 Loyola Ave.

The New Orleans train station is in the Central Business District. Plenty of taxis wait outside the main entrance to the passenger terminal. Hotels in the French Quarter and the Central Business District are just a short ride away.

GETTING AROUND
By Car
You really don't need to rent a car during your stay in New Orleans. Not only is the town just made for walking (thanks to being so flat—and so darn picturesque), but most places you want to go are also easily accessible on foot or by some form of the largely excellent public transportation system. Indeed, we find a streetcar

ride to be as much entertainment as a practical means of getting around. At night, when you need them most, cabs are easy to come by. Meanwhile, driving and parking in the French Quarter bring grief. The streets are narrow and crowded, and many go only one way. (This is easily the most confusing city we have ever driven around in, and we've driven in Rome.) Street parking is minimal (and likely to attract thieves), and parking lots are fiendishly expensive.

Sure, everything takes a bit longer when you are depending on the kindness of strangers to get around, but driving and parking headaches take time, too, and are not conducive to a pleasant vacation. Besides, you need to walk off all those calories you'll be ingesting!

If you're visiting from abroad and plan to rent a car in the United States, keep in mind that foreign driver's licenses are usually recognized in the U.S., but you should get an international one if your home license is not in English.

If you must have a car, try one of the following car-rental agencies: **Avis,** 2024 Canal St. (© 800/331-1212 or 504/523-4317; www.avis.com); **Budget Rent-A-Car,** 1675 Canal St. (© 800/527-0700 or 504/565-5600; www.budget.com); **Dollar Rent-A-Car,** 1910 Airline Hwy., Kenner (© 800/800-4000 or 504/467-2285; www.dollar.com); **Hertz,** 300 Poydras St. (in the Loews Hotel; © 800/654-3131 or 504/568-1645; www.hertz.com); or **Alamo,** 225 East Airline Hwy., Kenner (© 888/826-6893 or 504/469-0532; www.goalamo.com). Also check out **Breezenet. com,** which offers domestic car-rental discounts with some of the most competitive rates around. Also worth visiting are Orbitz, Hotwire.com, Travelocity, and Priceline.com, all of which offer competitive online car-rental rates. For additional car rental agencies, see "Airline, Hotel & Car Rental Websites," in chapter 13.

Rental rates vary according to the time of your visit and from company to company, so call ahead and do some comparison shopping. Ask lots of questions, try different dates and pickup points, and ask about corporate or organizational discounts (such as AAA or frequent-flier-program memberships). And if you're staying for a week or more, be sure to ask about weekly rates, which are cheaper.

To rent a car in the United States, you need a valid driver's license, a passport, and a major credit card. The minimum age is usually 25, but some companies will rent to younger people and add a surcharge. It's a good idea to buy maximum insurance coverage unless you're positive your own auto or credit card insurance is sufficient. Stick to the major companies because what you might save with smaller companies might not be worth the headache if you have mechanical troubles on the road. Rates vary, so it pays to call around.

By Taxi

Taxis aren't quite as plentiful as they have been in New Orleans, but they can still be hailed easily on the street in the French Quarter and in some parts of the Central Business District, and they are usually lined up at taxi stands at larger hotels. Otherwise, telephone and expect a cab to appear in about 15 minutes. The rate is $4.50 (up thanks to the current high price of gas) when you enter the taxi and $1.60 per mile thereafter. During special events (like Mardi Gras and Jazz Fest), the rate is $5 per person (or the meter rate if it's greater) no matter where you go in the city. It is a $10 fee for transfers between hotels no matter how short the ride.

Most taxis can be hired for a special rate for up to five passengers. It's a hassle-free and economical way for a small group to tour far-flung areas of the city (the lakefront, for example). Within the city you pay an hourly rate; out-of-town trips cost double the amount on the meter.

The city's most reliable company is **United Cabs** (© **504/524-9606;** www.unitedcabs.com).

On Foot

We can't stress this enough: Walking is by far the best way to see New Orleans. There are too many unique and sometimes glorious sights that you can miss if you whiz past them by using other forms of transportation. Slow down. Have a drink to go. Get a snack. Stroll. Take one of our walking tours (see chapter 9, "City Strolls"). Sure, sometimes it's too hot or humid—or raining too hard—to make walking attractive, but there is always a cab or bus nearby. Remember to drink lots of water if it's hot and pay close attention to your surroundings. If you enter an area that seems unsafe, retreat.

By Bike

One of the best ways to see the city is by bike. The terrain is flat, the breeze feels good, and you can cover a whole lot of ground on two wheels. A bike store near the French Quarter rents bikes by the hour, day, or longer. **Bicycle Michael's,** 622 Frenchmen St. (© **504/945-9505;** www. bicyclemichaels.com), rents mountain and hybrid bikes; during Jazz Fest it has a fleet of 100 bikes at the ready. Rates are $7.50 an hour, $20 a day, and $80 for 5 days. The shop requires a credit card deposit.

By Ferry

The Canal Street ferry is one of the city's secrets—and it's free for pedestrians. The ride takes you across the Mississippi River from the foot of Canal to Algiers Point (25-min. round-trip), and it affords great views of downtown New Orleans and the commerce on the river. Once in Algiers, you can walk around the old Algiers Point neighborhood and tour Mardi Gras World (p. 192). At night, with the city's glowing skyline reflecting on the river, a ride on the ferry can be quite romantic. The ferry also carries car traffic (for free), in case you'd like to do some West Bank driving.

By Bus

DISCOUNT PASSES If you won't have a car in New Orleans, we strongly encourage you to invest in a **VisiTour** pass, which entitles you to an unlimited number of rides on all streetcar and bus lines. It costs $5 for 1 day, $12 for 3 days. Many visitors think this was the best tip they got about their New Orleans stay and the finest bargain in town. Passes are available from VisiTour vendors—to find the nearest one, ask at your hotel or guesthouse or contact the **Regional Transit Authority** (RTA; © **504/248-3900;** www.norta.com). You can contact the RTA for information about any part of the city's public transportation system.

BUSES New Orleans has an excellent public bus system, so chances are there's a bus that runs exactly where you want to go. Local fares at press time are $1.25 (you must have exact change in bills or coins), transfers are an extra 25¢, and express buses are $1.25 (or you can use a VisiTour unlimited pass; see above). You can get complete route information by contacting the RTA (© **504/248-3900;** www.norta. com) or by picking up one of the excellent city maps available at the Visitor Information Center, 529 St. Ann St., in the French Quarter.

STREETCARS Besides being a National Historic Landmark, the **St. Charles Avenue streetcar** is also a convenient and fun way to get from downtown to Uptown and back. Badly damaged by Katrina, it is once again running its full 6½-mile length, ending at South Carrollton and South Claiborne avenues. In the meantime, the iconic green cars survived fine and have been transferred temporarily to the newer Canal and riverfront lines (see below). When restored to full service, the streetcars run 24 hours a day at frequent intervals, and the fare is $1.25 each way (you must have exact change in bills or coins). Streetcars can get crowded at rush hour and when school is out for the day. Board at Canal and Carondelet streets (directly across Canal from Bourbon St. in the French Quarter) or anywhere along St.

A Bus Named Desire

"They told me to take a streetcar named Desire and then transfer to one called Cemeteries and ride 6 blocks and get off at Elysian Fields!"

Although Blanche's directions wouldn't actually have gotten her to Stella and Stanley's house (Tennessee Williams fiddled with streetcar lines to make his metaphor work), there were indeed once streetcars called *Desire* and *Cemeteries*. The signs indicated their ultimate destinations—a street and a district, respectively. However, Blanche's later question, "Is that streetcar named Desire still grinding along the tracks?" must now be answered "no." (Unless we are still using that metaphor.)

The streetcar in question, which used to run through the French Quarter along Bourbon and Royal streets, has, like all but two of its brethren, been replaced by buses. That means you can't take a whirl on the legendary streetcar (though *Cemeteries* was revived in 2004!), but you can still ride buses called *Desire*.

Charles Avenue, sit back, and look for landmarks or just enjoy the scenery.

The streetcar line extends beyond the point where St. Charles Avenue bends into Carrollton Avenue. The end of the line is at Palmer Park and Playground at Claiborne Avenue, but you'll want to mount a shopping expedition at the Riverbend shopping area (p. 231). It will cost you another $1.25 for the ride back to Canal Street. It costs 10¢ to transfer from the streetcar to a bus.

The **riverfront streetcar** runs for 2 miles, from the Old Mint across Canal Street to Riverview, with stops along the way. It's a great step saver as you explore the riverfront. The fare is $1.50, and there's wheelchair ramp access (but not on the St. Charles line).

The **Canal Street streetcar** line started running just in time for Jazz Fest 2006.

Naturally, all of the spiffy new air-conditioned bright-red cars flooded, hence the use of the historic green cars on this line, though word at press time is that the red cars should be back soon. Be sure to check the destination sign, because one branch, Cemeteries, only goes there (to several of the older cemeteries, in fact), while the other, labeled either City Park or Beauregard Circle, is the one you want if you are taking it to Mid-City, City Park/the New Orleans Museum of Art, or Jazz Fest. Be prepared for jammed cars during Jazz Fest, because the line runs to within a few blocks of the fairgrounds. If your destination is strictly Canal Street/Carrollton, any of the cars will take you there. One-way fares are $1.25.

5 MONEY & COSTS

Frommer's lists prices in the local currency. The currency conversions quoted on p. 55 were correct at press time. However, rates fluctuate, so before departing, consult a

currency exchange website such as **www. oanda.com/convert/classic** to check up-to-the-minute rates.

US$	Can$	UK £	Euro €	Aus$	NZ$
$1	C$1.19	£0.67	€0.75	A$1.37	NZ$1.76

It's always advisable to bring money in a variety of forms on a vacation: a mix of cash, credit cards, and traveler's checks. You should also exchange enough petty cash to cover airport incidentals, tipping, and transportation to your hotel before you leave home, or withdraw money upon arrival at an airport ATM.

The most common bills are the $1 (a "buck"), $5, $10, and $20 denominations. There are also $2 bills (seldom encountered), $50 bills, and $100 bills. (The last two are usually not welcome as payment for small purchases.)

Coins come in seven denominations: 1¢ (1 cent, or a penny); 5¢ (5 cents, or a nickel); 10¢ (10 cents, or a dime); 25¢ (25 cents, or a quarter); 50¢ (50 cents, or a half-dollar); the gold-colored Sacagawea coin and the presidential coin, both worth $1; and the rare silver dollar.

ATMS

Almost all New Orleans ATMs are linked to a national network that most likely includes your bank at home. **Cirrus** (© 800/424-7787; www.mastercard.com) and **PLUS** (© 800/843-7587; www.visa.com) are the two most popular networks.

Some centrally located ATMs in New Orleans are at the **First National Bank of Commerce,** 240 Royal St.; **Hibernia National Bank,** 701 Poydras St.; and **Whitney National Bank,** 228 St. Charles Ave. There are now ATMs all over the French Quarter, a big change from 10 years ago when there was just one.

Avoid poorly lit or out-of-the-way ATMs, especially at night. Use an indoor machine or one at a well-trafficked, well-lit location. Put your money away discreetly; don't flash it around or count it in a way that attracts unwanted attention.

Note: Many banks impose a fee every time you use a card at another bank's ATM, and that fee is often higher for international transactions (up to $5 or more) than for domestic ones (where they're rarely more than $2). In addition, the bank from which you withdraw cash may charge its own fee. To compare banks' ATM fees within the U.S., use **www.bankrate.com.** Visitors from outside the U.S. should also find out whether their bank assesses a 1% to 3% fee on charges incurred abroad.

CREDIT CARDS & DEBIT CARDS

Credit cards are the most widely used form of payment in the United States: **Visa** (Barclaycard in Britain), **MasterCard** (Eurocard in Europe), **American Express, Diners Club,** and **Discover.** They also provide a convenient record of all your expenses, and offer relatively good exchange rates. You can withdraw cash advances from your credit cards at banks or ATMs, but high fees make credit card cash advances a pricey way to get cash.

It's highly recommended that you travel with at least one major credit card. You must have a credit card to rent a car, and hotels and airlines usually require a credit card imprint as a deposit against expenses.

ATM cards with major credit card backing, known as **"debit cards,"** are now a commonly acceptable form of payment in most stores and restaurants. Debit cards draw money directly from your checking account. Some stores enable you to receive cash back on your debit card purchases as well. The same is true at most U.S. post offices.

PLANNING YOUR TRIP TO NEW ORLEANS

4

MONEY & COSTS

What Things Cost	US$
Taxi from airport to the Quarter	28.00 (for two people)
	12.00 (for each additional person)
Shuttle from airport to the Quarter	15.00 (per person)
Cost of bus/streetcar one-way	1.25
Day pass for bus/streetcar	5.00
Standard room at Ritz-Carlton	169.00–419.00
Standard room at International House	149.00–379.00
Standard room at Drury Inn	109.00
Cup of coffee at Café du Monde	2.00
Order of beignets at Café du Monde	2.00
Dinner at Commander's Palace	70.00 (per person)
Dinner at Irene's Cuisine	50.00 (per person)
Muffuletta sandwich at Central Grocery	13.00
Ticket to a show at Tipitina's	10.00–15.00
Ticket to a show at Preservation Hall	8.00
Cost of a Hurricane at Pat O'Brien's	9.00
Cost of a Ramos Gin Fizz at Napoleon House	9.00

TRAVELER'S CHECKS

Traveler's checks are something of an anachronism from the days before the ATM made cash accessible at any time. But you may want to avoid withdrawal fees and enjoy the security of traveler's checks—provided you don't mind showing identification every time you want to cash one.

You can get traveler's checks at almost any bank. **American Express** offers checks for a service charge ranging from 1% to 4%. You can also get American Express traveler's checks over the phone by calling © **800/221-7282.** Amex gold or platinum cardholders can avoid paying the fee by ordering over the telephone; platinum cardholders can also purchase checks fee-free in person at Amex Travel Service locations. (Check www.americanexpress.com for the office nearest you.)

Visa offers traveler's checks at Citibank locations nationwide, as well as at several other banks. The service charge ranges between 1.5% and 2%; checks come in denominations of $20, $50, $100, $500, and $1,000. Call © **800/732-1322** for information. AAA members can obtain Visa checks for a $9.95 fee (for checks up to $1,500) at most AAA offices or by calling © **866/339-3378. MasterCard** also offers traveler's checks. Call © **800/223-9920** for a location near you.

If you carry traveler's checks, be sure to keep a record of their serial numbers (separate from the checks, of course) so that you're ensured a refund in case they're lost or stolen.

Most hotels will happily cash traveler's checks for you, and many stores and restaurants are equally pleased to accept them (as are even the food booths at Jazz Fest!).

STAYING HEALTHY

Major ill effects of floodwater and mold-related illnesses post-disaster did not materialize (some locals did develop a cough that has become known as "Katrina catarrh"), and travelers should not be concerned along those lines. However, given the still-limited medical facilities (a notable number of hospitals and nursing homes remain closed), if you have a medical condition that may require some form of urgent care, you may wish to take that into consideration before traveling to New Orleans, and make appropriate arrangements.

General Availability of Healthcare

Contact the **International Association for Medical Assistance to Travelers** (**IAMAT;** ✆ **716/754-4883** or, in Canada, 416/652-0137; www.iamat.org) for tips on travel and health concerns in the countries you're visiting, and for lists of local, English-speaking doctors. The United States **Centers for Disease Control and Prevention** (✆ **800/311-3435;** www.cdc.gov) provides up-to-date information on health hazards by region or country and offers tips on food safety. The website **www.tripprep.com,** sponsored by a consortium of travel-medicine practitioners, may also offer helpful advice on traveling abroad. You can find listings of reliable clinics overseas at the **International Society of Travel Medicine** (www. istm.org).

COMMON AILMENTS

BUGS, BITES & OTHER WILDLIFE CONCERNS West Nile Virus is here to stay, and while the mosquitoes aren't too bad in New Orleans, they are present (and are thick outside the city). Bring or buy some repellent, especially during the hot or rainy periods.

What to Do If You Get Sick Away from Home

Hospitals, urgent-care centers, and **emergency numbers** are listed in the section, "Fast Facts: New Orleans," in chapter 13. If your health concerns are less urgent or you're in need of a doctor, try **Ochsner Physician Referral Service** (✆ **504/842-3155** or 842-4106; www.ochsner.org) or Methodist Physician Referral (✆ **504/ 244-5455**).

Avoiding "Economy Class Syndrome"

Deep vein thrombosis, or as it's known in the world of flying, "economy-class syndrome," is a blood clot that develops in a deep vein. It's a potentially deadly condition that can be caused by sitting in cramped conditions—such as an airplane cabin—for too long. During a flight (especially a long-haul flight), get up, walk around, and stretch your legs every 60 to 90 minutes to keep your blood flowing. Other preventative measures include frequent flexing of the legs while sitting, drinking lots of water, and avoiding alcohol and sleeping pills. If you have a history of deep vein thrombosis, heart disease, or another condition that puts you at high risk, some experts recommend wearing compression stockings or taking anticoagulants when you fly; always ask your physician about the best course for you. Symptoms of deep vein thrombosis include leg pain or swelling, or even shortness of breath.

If you suffer from a chronic illness, consult your doctor before your departure. Pack **prescription medications** in your carry-on luggage, and carry them in their original containers, with pharmacy labels—otherwise they won't make it through airport security.

Visitors from outside the U.S. should carry generic names of prescription drugs.

For U.S. travelers, most reliable healthcare plans provide coverage if you get sick away from home. Foreign visitors may have to pay all medical costs upfront and be reimbursed later. See "Medical Insurance," under "Insurance," in the section, "Fast Facts: New Orleans," in chapter 13.

7 SAFETY

New Orleans's crime rate is an area of difficulty. Over the years, it climbed so high the city became the murder capital of the country. Concentrated efforts paid off, and the city became pretty safe again. But even before Katrina, crime was starting to rise, and now after the storm, there are even more problems, thanks to a decreased police force and a low-income population under great stress and frustration. Most of the serious crime is drug-related, and confined to areas where tourists do not go, but once again, we need to urge you to be very cautious about where you go at night.

STREET SMARTS The short version is you should behave with the same savvy you would demonstrate in any big city. The **French Quarter** is fairly safe, especially during the daytime, thanks to the number of people present at any given time, but some areas are better than others. (Rampart and the north part of Esplanade have bad reputations.) On the other hand, anything can happen anywhere, so just pay attention and use basic street smarts. On Bourbon Street be careful when socializing with strangers and in particular be alert to distractions by potential pickpocket teams. Dauphine and Burgundy are in quiet, lovely old parts of the Quarter, but as you near Esplanade, watch out for purse snatchers. At night stay in well-lighted areas with plenty of both street and pedestrian traffic and take cabs down Esplanade and into the **Faubourg Marigny.**

Conventional wisdom holds that one should not go much above Bourbon toward Rampart alone after dark, so it's best to stay in a group (or near one) if you can; and if you feel uncomfortable, consider taking a cab, even if it seems silly, for the (very) short ride. In the **Garden District,** as you get past Magazine toward the river, the neighborhoods can be rough, so exercise caution (more cabs, probably). At all times try to avoid looking distracted or confused. If you appear confident and alert, you will look less like a target. Speaking of which, one way to ensure you will look like a tourist—and thus, a target—is to wear Mardi Gras beads at any time other than Mardi Gras day or right after one of the parades leading up to same. Sorry if we sound like spoilsports, but it's clear that criminals target unseasonal bead-wearers. The reasoning probably goes something like: 1) not local since locals never wear beads out of season, 2) therefore probably has vacation money/other valuables on them, 3) likely to be drunk or otherwise distracted, and honestly, you look kind of dorky wearing them out of season.

TRAVEL SMARTS Don't hang that expensive camera around your neck when it's not in use. Put it out of sight, if you can, in a camera bag or other case. If the bag or case has a shoulder strap, carry it so the bag is on your hip with the strap over the opposite shoulder so that a simple tug won't dislodge it. That goes for purses as well. You might consider using a money belt or other hidden, pickpocket-proof type of travel wallet. Women probably won't want to bring purses to clubs where they plan on dancing. And never leave valuables in the outside pocket of a backpack. Should you stop for a bite to eat,

keep everything within easy reach—of you, not a purse snatcher. If you're traveling in a car, place your belongings in the trunk, not under the seat. It's always a good idea to leave expensive-looking jewelry and other conspicuous valuables at home anyway. And finally, unless it's Mardi Gras, *avoid wearing beads.*

8 SPECIALIZED TRAVEL RESOURCES

Most disabilities shouldn't stop anyone from traveling in the U.S. Thanks to provisions in the Americans with Disabilities Act, most public places are required to comply with disability-friendly regulations. Almost all public establishments (including hotels, restaurants, museums, and so on, but not including certain National Historic Landmarks), and at least some modes of public transportation provide accessible entrances and other facilities for those with disabilities.

Be aware, however, that although New Orleans facilities are mostly accessible (especially in the Quarter), with proprietors being most accommodating (making narrow doors wider to fit wheelchairs and such), you are still dealing with older structures created before thoughts of ease for those with disabilities. Before you book a hotel, **ask questions** based on your needs. If you have mobility issues, you'll probably do best to stay in one of the city's newer hotels, which tend to be more spacious and accommodating. Sidewalks are often bumpy and uneven, and getting on the St. Charles streetcar might be too great a challenge. Streets are better for maneuvering wheelchairs than sidewalks. (Some French Quarter streets are closed for pedestrian traffic only.)

For information about specialized transportation systems, call **LIFT** (© **504/827-7433**).

The **America the Beautiful—National Park and Federal Recreational Lands**

Pass—Access Pass (formerly the **Golden Access Passport**) gives visually impaired or persons with permanent disabilities (regardless of age) free lifetime entrance to federal recreation sites administered by the National Park Service, including the Fish and Wildlife Service, the Forest Service, the Bureau of Land Management, and the Bureau of Reclamation. This may include national parks, monuments, historic sites, recreation areas, and national wildlife refuges.

The America the Beautiful Access Pass can be obtained only in person at any NPS facility that charges an entrance fee. You need to show proof of a medically determined disability. Besides free entry, the pass also offers a 50% discount on some federal-use fees charged for such facilities as camping, swimming, parking, boat launching, and tours. For more information, go to www.nps.gov/fees_passes.htm or call the United States Geological Survey (USGS), which issues the passes, at © **888/275-8747.**

For more on organizations that offer resources to travelers with disabilities, go to www.frommers.com/planning.

GAY & LESBIAN TRAVELERS

New Orleans is a very gay-friendly town with a high-profile homosexual population that contributes much to the color and flavor of the city. You'll find an abundance of establishments serving gay and lesbian interests, from bars to restaurants to community services to certain businesses.

Ambush Magazine, 828-A Bourbon St., New Orleans, LA 70116 (© **504/522-8047;** www.ambushmag.com), is a weekly entertainment and news publication for the Gulf South's gay, lesbian, bisexual, and transgender communities. The website offers plenty of links to other interesting sites. **Grace Fellowship,** 3151 Dauphine St. (© **504/944-9836**), and the **Vieux Carré Metropolitan Community Church,** 1128 St. Roch Ave. (© **504/945-5390**), are religious organizations that serve primarily gay and lesbian congregations. Both invite visitors to attend services.

One useful website is **www.gaynew orleans.com,** which provides information on lodging, dining, arts, and nightlife as well as links to other information on New Orleans gay life.

The **International Gay and Lesbian Travel Association (IGLTA;** © **800/448-8550** or 954/776-2626; www.iglta.org) is the trade association for the gay and lesbian travel industry, and offers an online directory of gay- and lesbian-friendly travel businesses and tour operators.

Gay.com Travel (© **800/929-2268** or 415/644-8044; www.gay.com/travel or www.outandabout.com) is an excellent online successor to the popular *Out & About* print magazine. It provides regularly updated information about gay-owned, gay-oriented, and gay-friendly lodging, dining, sightseeing, nightlife, and shopping establishments in every important destination worldwide. British travelers should click on the "Travel" link at **www.uk.gay. com** for advice and gay-friendly trip ideas.

The Canadian website **GayTraveler** (www.gaytraveler.ca) offers ideas and advice for gay travel all over the world.

For more gay and lesbian travel resources, visit www.frommers.com/planning.

SENIOR TRAVEL

Don't be shy about asking for discounts, but always carry some kind of identification, such as a driver's license, that shows your date of birth, especially if you've kept your youthful glow.

Mention the fact that you're a senior when you make your travel reservations; many hotels still offer discounts for seniors. *Note:* Seniors who show their Medicare card can ride New Orleans streetcars and buses for 40¢.

The U.S. National Park Service offers an **America the Beautiful—National Park and Federal Recreational Lands Pass—Senior Pass** (formerly the **Golden Age Passport**), which gives seniors 62 years or older lifetime entrance to all properties administered by the National Park Service—national parks, monuments, historic sites, recreation areas, and national wildlife refuges—for a one-time processing fee of $10. The pass must be purchased in person at any NPS facility that charges an entrance fee. Besides free entry, the American the Beautiful Senior Pass also offers a 50% discount on some federal-use fees charged for such facilities as camping, swimming, parking, boat launching, and tours. For more information, go to www.nps.gov/fees_passes.htm or call the United States Geological Survey (USGS), who issues the passes, at © **888/275-8747.**

For more information and resources on travel for seniors, see www.frommers.com/planning.

FAMILY TRAVEL

New Orleans doesn't spring to mind as the first place to take a child, but savvy travelers who have done it once are usually eager to do it again. There are plenty of activities, detailed in chapter 8, appropriate for children, who often get a kick out of the city. (Admittedly, they, too, probably dislike the heat, and so summer months may not be the best time to introduce them to the joys of the city.) To locate accommodations, restaurants, and attractions that are particularly kid-friendly, refer to the "Kids" icon throughout this guide.

For a list of more family-friendly travel resources, visit www.frommers.com/planning.

9 SUSTAINABLE TOURISM

Sustainable tourism is conscientious travel. It means being careful with the environments you explore, and respecting the communities you visit. Two overlapping components of sustainable travel are **ecotourism** and **ethical tourism.** The **International Ecotourism Society** (TIES) defines ecotourism as responsible travel to natural areas that conserves the environment and improves the well-being of local people. TIES suggests that ecotourists follow these principles:

- Minimize environmental impact.
- Build environmental and cultural awareness and respect.
- Provide positive experiences for both visitors and hosts.
- Provide direct financial benefits for conservation and for local people.
- Raise sensitivity to host countries' political, environmental, and social climates.
- Support international human rights and labor agreements.

You can find some eco-friendly travel tips and statistics, as well as touring companies and associations—listed by destination under "Travel Choice"—at the **TIES** website, www.ecotourism.org. Also check out **Ecotravel.com,** which lets you search for sustainable touring companies in several categories (water-based, land-based, spiritually oriented, and so on).

While much of the focus of eco-tourism is about reducing impacts on the natural environment, ethical tourism concentrates on ways to preserve and enhance local economies and communities, regardless of location. You can embrace ethical tourism by staying at a locally owned hotel or shopping at a store that employs local workers and sells locally produced goods.

Responsible Travel (www.responsible travel.com) is a great source of sustainable travel ideas; the site is run by a spokesperson for ethical tourism in the travel industry. **Sustainable Travel International**

Frommers.com: The Complete Travel Resource

Planning a trip or just returned? Head to **Frommers.com,** voted Best Travel Site by *PC Magazine*. We think you'll find our site indispensable before, during, and after your travels—with expert advice and tips; independent reviews of hotels, restaurants, attractions, and preferred shopping and nightlife venues; vacation giveaways; and an online booking tool. We publish the complete contents of over 135 travel guides in our **Destinations** section, covering over 4,000 places worldwide. Each weekday, we publish original articles that report on **Deals and News** via our free **Frommers.com Newsletters.** What's more, **Arthur Frommer** himself blogs 5 days a week, with cutting opinions about the state of travel in the modern world. We're betting you'll find our **Events** listings an invaluable resource; it's an up-to-the-minute roster of what's happening in cities everywhere—including concerts, festivals, lectures, and more. We've also added weekly **podcasts, interactive maps,** and hundreds of new images across the site. Finally, don't forget to visit our **Message Boards,** where you can join in conversations with thousands of fellow Frommer's travelers and post your trip report once you return.

ⓣ It's Easy Being Green

Here are a few simple ways you can help conserve fuel and energy when you travel:

- Each time you take a flight or drive a car, greenhouse gases release into the atmosphere. You can help neutralize this danger to the planet through "carbon offsetting"—paying someone to invest your money in programs that reduce your greenhouse gas emissions by the same amount you've added. Before buying carbon offset credits, just make sure that you're using a reputable company, one with a proven program that invests in renewable energy. Reliable carbon offset companies include **Carbonfund** (www.carbonfund.org), **TerraPass** (www.terrapass.org), and **Carbon Neutral** (www.carbonneutral.org).
- Whenever possible, choose nonstop flights; they generally require less fuel than indirect flights that stop and take off again. Try to fly during the day—some scientists estimate that nighttime flights are twice as harmful to the environment. And pack light—each 15 pounds of luggage on a 5,000-mile flight adds up to 50 pounds of carbon dioxide emitted.
- Where you stay during your travels can have a major environmental impact. To determine the green credentials of a property, ask about trash disposal and recycling, water conservation, and energy use; also question if sustainable materials were used in the construction of the property. The website **www.greenhotels.com** recommends green-rated member hotels around the world that fulfill the company's stringent environmental requirements. Also consult **www.environmentallyfriendlyhotels.com** for more green accommodation ratings.
- At hotels, request that your sheets and towels not be changed daily. (Many hotels already have programs like this in place.) Turn off the lights and air-conditioner (or heater) when you leave your room.
- Use public transport where possible—trains, buses, and even taxis are more energy-efficient forms of transport than driving. Even better is to walk or cycle; you'll produce zero emissions and stay fit and healthy on your travels.
- If renting a car is necessary, ask the rental agent for a hybrid, or rent the most fuel-efficient car available. You'll use less gas and save money at the tank.
- Eat at locally owned and operated restaurants that use produce grown in the area. This contributes to the local economy and cuts down on greenhouse gas emissions by supporting restaurants where the food is not flown or trucked in across long distances. Visit **Sustain Lane** (www.sustainlane.org) to find sustainable eating and drinking choices around the U.S.; also check out **www.eatwellguide.org** for tips on eating sustainably in the U.S. and Canada.

(www.sustainabletravelinternational.org) promotes ethical tourism practices, and manages an extensive directory of sustainable properties and tour operators around the world.

In the U.K., **Tourism Concern** (www. tourismconcern.org.uk) works to reduce social and environmental problems connected to tourism. The **Association of Independent Tour Operators** (AITO; www.aito.co.uk) is a group of specialist operators leading the field in making holidays sustainable.

Volunteer travel has become increasingly popular among those who want to venture beyond the standard group-tour experience to learn languages, interact with locals, and make a positive difference while on vacation. Volunteer travel usually doesn't require special skills—just a willingness to

work hard—and programs vary in length from a few days to a number of weeks. Some programs provide free housing and food, but many require volunteers to pay for travel expenses, which can add up quickly.

For general info on volunteer travel, visit **www.volunteerabroad.org** and **www. idealist.org**. Specific volunteer options in New Orleans are listed under "Special-Interest Trips," later in this chapter.

Before you commit to a volunteer program, it's important to make sure any money you're giving is truly going back to the local community, and that the work you'll be doing will be a good fit for you. **Volunteer International** (www.volunteer international.org) has a helpful list of questions to ask to determine the intentions and the nature of a volunteer program.

10 SPECIAL-INTEREST TRIPS

VOLUNTEER & WORKING TRIPS

There are many opportunities to volunteer in New Orleans, as you can imagine, and spending a day or two of your trip lending a hand is something to strongly consider. **Habitat for Humanity,** which is creating the Musicians Village for artists who lost their homes in the flood, is the most recognizable name. Contact them at www. habitat-nola.org, or at 7100 St. Charles

Ave., New Orleans, LA 70118 (ⓒ **504/ 861-2077**). **Volunteer New Orleans,** 127 S. Solomon St., New Orleans, LA 70119 (ⓒ **504/483-3564;** www.volunteernew orleans.com), acts as a kind of clearinghouse of the many other possibilities (from the SPCA to the arts to rebuilding and many more) in the city and has a page on its website where a potential volunteer can be matched with an appropriate-level task on the day(s) available.

11 STAYING CONNECTED

TELEPHONES

Generally, hotel surcharges on long-distance and local calls are astronomical, so you're better off using your **cellphone** or a **public pay telephone.** Many convenience groceries and packaging services sell **prepaid calling cards** in denominations up to $50; for international visitors these can be

the least expensive way to call home. Many public pay phones at airports now accept American Express, MasterCard, and Visa credit cards. **Local calls** made from pay phones in most locales cost either 25¢ or 35¢ (no pennies, please).

Most long-distance and international calls can be dialed directly from any

Tips Hey, Google, Did You Get My Text Message?

It's bound to happen: The day you leave this guidebook back at the hotel for an unencumbered stroll through the Quarter, you'll forget the address of the coffee stop you had earmarked. If you're traveling with a mobile device, send a text message to ✆ **466453 (GOOGLE)** for a lightning-fast response. For instance, type "cafe du monde new orleans" and within 10 seconds you'll receive a text message with the address and phone number. This nifty trick works in a range of search categories: Look up weather ("weather philadelphia"), language translations ("translate goodbye in spanish"), currency conversions ("10 usd in pounds"), and more. If your search results are off, be more specific ("the abbey gay bar west hollywood"). For more tips and search options, see www.google.com/intl/en_us/mobile/sms. Regular text message charges apply.

phone. **For calls within the United States and to Canada,** dial 1 followed by the area code and the seven-digit number. **For other international calls,** dial 011 followed by the country code, city code, and the number you are calling.

Calls to area codes **800, 888, 877,** and **866** are toll-free. However, calls to area codes **700** and **900** (chat lines, bulletin boards, "dating" services, and so on) can be very expensive—usually a charge of 95¢ to $3 or more per minute, and they sometimes have minimum charges that can run as high as $15 or more.

For **reversed-charge or collect calls,** and for person-to-person calls, dial the number 0, then the area code and number; an operator will come on the line, and you should specify whether you are calling collect, person-to-person, or both. If your operator-assisted call is international, ask for the overseas operator.

For **local directory assistance** ("information"), dial ✆ 411; for long-distance information, dial 1, then the appropriate area code and 555-1212.

CELLPHONES

Just because your cellphone works at home doesn't mean it'll work everywhere in the U.S. (thanks to our nation's fragmented cellphone system). It's a good bet that your phone will work in major cities, but take a look at your wireless company's coverage map on its website before heading out; T-Mobile, Sprint, and Nextel are particularly weak in rural areas. If you need to stay in touch at a destination where you know your phone won't work, **rent** a phone that does from **InTouch USA** (✆ **800/872-7626;** www.intouchglobal.com) or a rental-car location, but beware that you'll pay $1 a minute or more for airtime.

If you're not from the U.S., you'll be appalled at the poor reach of the **GSM (Global System for Mobile Communications) wireless network,** which is used by much of the rest of the world. Your phone will probably work in most major U.S. cities; it definitely won't work in many rural areas. To see where GSM phones work in the U.S., check out www.t-mobile.com/coverage. And you may or may not be able to send SMS (text messaging) home.

VOICE OVER INTERNET PROTOCOL (VOIP)

If you have Web access while traveling, consider a broadband-based telephone service (**Voice over Internet protocol,** or **VoIP**) such as Skype (www.skype.com) or Vonage (www.vonage.com), which allow you to make free international calls from your laptop or in a cybercafe. Neither service requires the people you're calling to also have that service (though there are fees if they do not).

INTERNET & E-MAIL
With Your Own Computer

More and more hotels, resorts, airports, cafes, and retailers are going Wi-Fi (wireless fidelity), becoming "hotspots" that offer free high-speed Wi-Fi access or charge a small fee (around $10 a day) for usage. There is free Wi-Fi throughout the city of New Orleans, but it's very slow.

For dial-up access, most business-class hotels in the U.S. offer dataports for laptop modems, and a few thousand hotels in the U.S. and Europe now offer free high-speed Internet access.

Mac owners have their own networking technology, Apple AirPort. **T-Mobile Hotspot** (www.t-mobile.com/hotspot) serves up wireless connections at more than 1,000 Starbucks coffee shops nationwide. **Boingo** (www.boingo.com) and **Wayport** (www.wayport.com) have set up networks in airports and high-class hotel lobbies. iPass providers (see below) also give you access to a few hundred wireless hotel-lobby setups. To locate other hotspots that provide **free wireless networks** in cities around the world, go to **www.personaltelco.net/index.cgi/wireless communities**.

Another resource to find public Wi-Fi hotspots at your destination is **www.jiwire.com;** its Hotspot Finder holds the world's largest directory of public wireless hotspots.

In addition, major Internet service providers (ISPs) have **local access numbers**

around the world, allowing you to go online by placing a local call. The **iPass** network also has dial-up numbers around the world. You'll have to sign up with an iPass provider, who will then tell you how to set up your computer for your destination(s). For a list of iPass providers, go to www.ipass.com and click on "Individuals Buy Now." One solid provider is **i2Roam** (© **866/811-6209** or 920/235-0475; www.i2roam.com).

Wherever you go, bring a **connection kit** of power and phone adapters, a spare phone cord, and a spare Ethernet network cable—or find out whether your hotel supplies them to guests.

For information on electrical currency conversions, see "Fast Facts: New Orleans," in chapter 13.

Without Your Own Computer

There currently is an Internet cafe in the Riverwalk mall.

To find other cybercafes in New Orleans, check **www.cybercaptive.com** and **www.cybercafe.com**.

Aside from formal cybercafes, most **youth hostels** and **public libraries** offer Internet access. Avoid **hotel business centers** unless you're willing to pay exorbitant rates.

Most major airports have **Internet kiosks** that provide basic Web access for a per-minute fee that's usually higher than cybercafe prices. Check out copy shops like FedEx Office (formerly FedEx Kinko's), which offers computer stations with fully loaded software (as well as Wi-Fi).

Suggested New Orleans Itineraries

Unlike other cities, New Orleans doesn't have many specific sights, per se; it's more like one big sight. You could just spend your time wandering aimlessly, and that would be just fine. But there are some quirky spots of interest, curious little nooks you probably shouldn't miss, plus there is always the risk that without direction, you might duck into the nearest club and not be heard from again until your flight home. Not that there would be anything all that wrong with that. All the same, the following may help you to navigate the city and your time in it.

1 THE NEIGHBORHOODS IN BRIEF

"Where y'at?" goes the traditional local greeting. "Where" is easy enough when you are in the French Quarter, the site of the original settlement. A 13-block-long grid between Canal Street and Esplanade Avenue, running from the Mississippi River to North Rampart Street, it's the closest the city comes to a geographic center.

After that, all bets are off. Because of the bend in the river, the streets are laid out at angles and curves that render north, south, east, and west useless. It's time to readjust your thinking: In New Orleans the compass points are *lakeside, riverside, uptown,* and *downtown.* You'll catch on quickly if you keep in mind that North Rampart Street is the *lakeside* boundary of the Quarter and that St. Charles Avenue extends from the French Quarter, *downtown,* to Tulane University, *uptown.*

Canal Street forms the boundary between new and old New Orleans. Street names change when they cross Canal (Bourbon St., for example, becomes Carondelet St.), and addresses begin at 100 on either side of Canal. In the Quarter, street numbers begin at 400 at the river because 4 blocks of numbered buildings were lost to the river before the levee was built.

MAPS Don't think you can get along without one in New Orleans! For a map, call the Convention and Visitors Bureau, 2020 St. Charles Ave., New Orleans, LA 70130 (© 800/672-6124 or 504/566-5011; www.neworleanscvb.com); stop by the Visitor Information Center, 529 St. Ann St. (© 504/568-5661) for a free one; or pay for one at any major bookstore. If you rent a car, be sure to ask for maps of the city—the rental agents have good detailed ones.

STREET NAMES As if the streets themselves weren't colorful enough, there are the street names, from Felicity to the jawbreaker Tchoupitoulas (chop-i-*too*-las). How did they get these fanciful monikers? Well, in some cases, from overeducated city fathers who named streets after Greek muses (Calliope and Terpsichore). Some immortalize long-dead and otherwise forgotten women (Julia was a free woman of color, but who was Felicity?).

Many streets in the French Quarter—Burgundy, Dauphine, Toulouse, and Dumaine—
honor French royalty or nobility, while St. Peter and St. Ann were favorite baptismal names of the Orleans family. The Faubourg Marigny (Faubourg being the local word for *suburb*) neighborhood was once part of the Marigny (say *Mare*-i-nee) family plantation. After scion Bernard squandered his family's fortune (mostly on gambling), he sold off parcels to the city, naming the streets after his favorite things: Desire, Piety, Poets, Duels, Craps, and so forth.

By the way, if pronunciation seems a mystery, try it with a French accent, and you might actually get it right. Unless it's Chartres (*Chart*-ers), that is, or Burgundy (Bur-*gun*-dee) Street. Or Gallier (*Gaul*-ee-er). Or Calliope (Cal-lee-*ope*). Oh, never mind. When in doubt, just ask a local. They're used to it.

CITY LAYOUT

The French Quarter Made up of about 90 square blocks, this section is also known as the *Vieux Carré* ("Old Square") and is enclosed by Canal Street, North Rampart Street, the Mississippi River, and Esplanade Avenue. The Quarter is full of clubs, bars, stores, residences, and museums; its major public area is Jackson Square, bounded by Chartres, Decatur, St. Peter, and St. Ann streets. The most historic and best-preserved area in the city, a survivor of two major fires in the 1700s in addition to Katrina, it's likely to be the focal point of your stay.

Storyville North of the Quarter (just above Rampart St.) is Basin Street, the birthplace of jazz—or, at least, that's the legend. In fact, jazz probably predates the rise of Storyville (the old red-light district along Basin St.) by a good number of years. To give credit where credit is due, however, Storyville's "sporting houses" did provide a place for the music to grab the ear of a wide segment of the public who came to enjoy the houses', uh, services. King Oliver, Jelly Roll Morton, and Louis Armstrong were among the jazz greats who got their start on Basin Street in the brothels between Canal Street and Beauregard Square.

Apart from a couple of nondescript buildings, no trace of the old Storyville survives (and note this is now a dangerous neighborhood, and not any better

since Katrina). A low-income public housing project now sprawls over much of the site, and statues depicting Latin American heroes—Simón Bolívar, Benito Juárez, and General Francisco Morazán—dot the landscape.

Faubourg Marigny This area is east of the French Quarter (on the other side of Esplanade Ave.). Over the past decade, the Marigny has emerged as one of the city's vital centers of activity, and it was fortunate that it did not experience flooding from Katrina. Here, you can still find the outlines of a small Creole suburb, and many old-time residents remain. Younger urban dwellers have moved into the area in significant numbers recently. Today some of the best bars and nightspots in New Orleans are along Frenchmen Street, the Marigny's main drag. Along with the adjacent sections of the French Quarter, the Marigny is also a social center for the city's gay and lesbian communities.

Bywater This riverside neighborhood is past the Faubourg Marigny and is bounded on the east by an industrial canal. It is tempting to misspeak and call it "Backwater" because at first glance it seems like a wasteland of light industry and run-down homes. In fact, Bywater has plenty of nice, modest residential sections. Furthermore, it's home

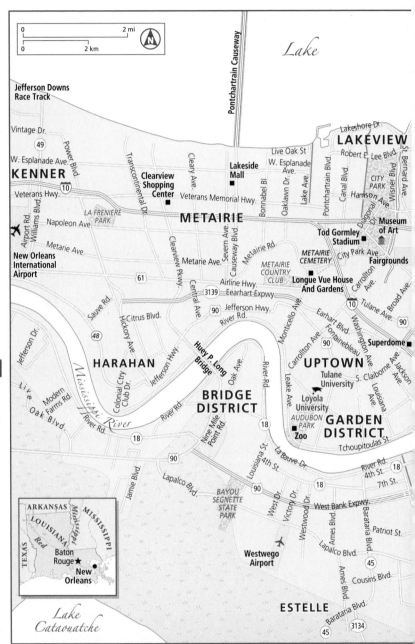

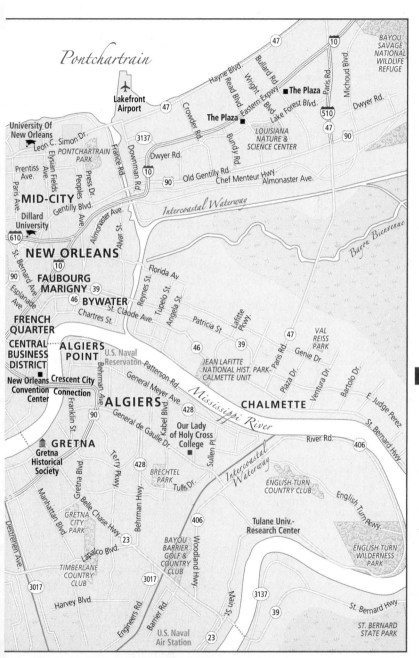

to the city's artists-in-hiding, and many local designers have shops among the urban decay. This is in keeping with the history of the area, which early on was home to artisans as well as communities of immigrants and free people of color. The lower Bywater adjacent to the Marigny suffered relatively little damage and looks pretty good until one travels past St. Claude toward the lake, where there was severe flooding thanks to the breach in the Industrial Canal.

Mid-City/Esplanade Ridge Stretching north from the French Quarter to City Park, Esplanade Ridge hugs either side of Esplanade Avenue. This area encompasses a few distinct neighborhoods, all of which have certain things in common. In the 19th century, Esplanade was the grand avenue of New Orleans's Creole society—the St. Charles Avenue of downriver. Many sections of the avenue and houses along it have seen better days, but there is still evidence of those times, especially in the ancient oak trees forming a canopy above the road. If you drive or stroll toward City Park along Esplanade (see Walking Tour 3, "Esplanade Ridge," in chapter 9, "City Strolls"), you can measure the progress of the avenue's development in the styles of its houses. Because of this relatively high ground, most of the buildings along Esplanade escaped damaging flooding.

The oldest section of Esplanade Ridge, **Faubourg Treme,** is located directly across Rampart Street from the French Quarter. Like the Quarter, it was a dense 19th-century Creole community. Unlike the Quarter, Treme (pronounced Treh-*may*) has remained almost untouched by preservationists (apart from some plucky folks who have beautifully restored a number of turn-of-the-20th-c. and older houses) and so has continued to be an organic residential community. Prior to Katrina, it was

one of the most vibrant African-American neighborhoods in New Orleans, home to more than a few of the city's best brass bands. Despite major community efforts to reclaim the neighborhood, Treme is usually plagued by severe crime and not advisable to walk through at night. Hurricane and flood damage has set back this historic neighborhood, and there is fear that reconstruction may lead to the sort of gentrification that could force out families who have lived here for generations, though so far those fears have gone unrealized.

Central Business District Historically, **Canal Street** has been New Orleans's main street, and in the 19th century it also divided the French and American sections of the city. (By the way, there's no canal—the one that was planned for the spot never came to be.) Parts of the Central Business District (CBD) were relentlessly featured on the news thanks to the looters that targeted the T-shirt and sporting goods stores that line Canal Street, and the Hyatt, which had many windows blown out by Katrina. This may have led to the impression that the area was devastated by the disaster, but it actually bounced back quite quickly. Canal Street itself is still shabby compared to its former days of splendor when it was the center of local shopping, but improvements to the street, including spots for sidewalk cafes, may help lure in some better businesses in addition to the several very fine hotels and restaurants already in place. Admire the streetlights on the neutral ground (as locals call it; you might call it the meridian); they were a gift from France and when they were first lit—none other than Thomas Edison throwing the switch—they made Canal Street the most illuminated street in the world.

The **CBD** is roughly bounded by Canal Street and the elevated Pontchartrain Expressway (Business Rte. U.S.

90) between Loyola Avenue and the Mississippi River. Some of the most elegant luxury hotels are in this area. Most of the district was known as Faubourg St. Mary when Americans began settling here after the Louisiana Purchase. Lafayette Square was the center of life here during the 19th century.

Within the CBD is the **Warehouse District.** More than 20 years ago, this area was full of abandoned warehouses and almost nothing else. With the efforts of some dedicated individuals and institutions, however, it's steadily evolving into a residential neighborhood with some commercial activity. Furthermore, this area also serves as the city's art gallery district, with many of the premier galleries concentrated along **Julia Street** (see chapter 10, "Shopping"). Most of these galleries show the works of local and regional contemporary artists. The Contemporary Arts Center and Louisiana Children's Museum (p. 185 and 210) are also in this area.

Uptown/The Garden District Bounded by St. Charles Avenue (lakeside) and Magazine Street (riverside) between Jackson and Louisiana avenues, the Garden District remains one of the most picturesque areas in the city. Originally the site of a plantation, the area was subdivided and developed as a residential neighborhood for wealthy Americans. Throughout the middle of the 19th century, developers built the Victorian, Italianate, and Greek Revival homes that still line the streets. Most of the homes had elaborate lawns and gardens, but few of those still exist. The Garden District is located uptown (as opposed to the CBD, which is downtown); the neighborhood west of the Garden District is often called Uptown (not to be confused with the directions people often use here: The Garden District is located uptown from both the Quarter and CBD and is *in* what is

collectively referred to as Uptown). Because it did not flood, much of Uptown looks as it always did, although some trees toppled and others look like they were pruned by drunks. (See chapter 9, "City Strolls," for a suggested stroll through this area.)

The Irish Channel The area bounded by Magazine Street and the Mississippi River, Louisiana Avenue, and the Central Business District got its name during the 1800s when more than 100,000 Irish immigrated to New Orleans. As was true elsewhere in the country, the Irish of New Orleans were often considered "expendable" labor, and many were killed while employed at dangerous construction work and other manual labor.

These days, the Channel is significantly less Irish, but it retains its lively spirit and distinctive neighborhood flavor. Much of the area is run-down, but just as much is filled with quiet residential neighborhoods. To get a glimpse of the Irish Channel, go to the antiques-shop district on Magazine Street and stroll between Felicity Street and Jackson Avenue.

Algiers Point Directly across the Mississippi River from the Central Business District and the French Quarter and connected by the Canal Street Ferry, Algiers Point is the old town center of Algiers. It is another of the city's original Creole suburbs but probably the one that has changed the least over the decades. Today you can't see many signs of the area's once-booming railroad and dry-docking industries, but you can see some of the best-preserved small gingerbread and Creole cottages in New Orleans. The neighborhood has recently begun to attract attention as a historic landmark, and it makes for one of the city's most pleasant strolls (see chapter 8, "Sights to See & Places to Be," for tips on how to get here).

How to Make Like the Locals Do

We are so proud of you. Not for you the "I went to New Orleans but I never got off Bourbon Street" refrain. Not for you any old tourist trap, or maybe even any other tourist. You want to make like the locals do. Having said that, by and large this book avoids tourist traps, and while it won't help you avoid tourists, it does feature many a spot that has prompted many a local to say, "You've got that place in there?! No one knows about that!" (Not to blow our own horn or anything.) But here are a few more residents-only suggestions that, in addition to a few specific venues, featured elsewhere in this guide, have their own traditional following. Be aware that making like a local sometimes means heading into areas that will prompt your cabdriver (yes, take a cab if you don't have your own car) to shake his or her head about your foolhardy behavior. Ignore them, though do please be cautious. Here, in no particular order:

Po' Boys at Gene's This is an authentic dive, which, for New Orleans, is about as authentic as it gets. It may be a little *too* local for you, so just plan to get food to go (it's not really eat-in, anyway). Much of the roof was ripped away by Katrina, and they flooded, but a year later, they had bravely reopened. All you get at Gene's are po' boys, but oh, that's all you need. Particularly when the po' boy is the classic house-made Creole hot sausage and cheese (American cheese, please!), fully dressed. Divine. Gene's also offers a roast beef po' boy and a hamburger, but that's it for menu options. No chips, no dessert. One drink comes with your generously sized sandwich. Five dollars total. Don't you feel local already? Gene's is at 1040 Elysian Fields (© **504/943-3861**).

Fried Chicken at McHardy's When beloved friends of ours married, they served fried chicken from McHardy's, 1458 N. Broad St. (© **504/949-0000**), at their wedding reception. And you know what? No fancy-pants expensive, catered extravaganza had better food. It's some of the best fried chicken we've ever eaten—moist, tender, slightly crispy skin, perfectly seasoned, and only 50¢ a piece.

A Real Gospel Brunch Speaking of church, forget the so-called "Gospel Brunch" at the House of Blues. Go see the real thing in a real place of worship, like the **Guiding Light Missionary Baptist Church,** 2012 Washington Ave. (© **504/891-7654**). It's humble, but it's right and true, and the singing of the choir (not to mention the sometimes-fiery preaching) is what it's all about. And boy, do they have things to sing about these days. You may well be the only nonparishioner there, but the congregation is always welcoming. Worship begins at 7am on Sunday, but you don't need to be there before 8:30am. Remember to put some of those dollars you saved by not going to the House of Blues into the collection plate, but also note that said plate is passed early and often, so pace your giving.

For a different musical religious experience, take in Sunday 10am Mass at historic **St. Augustine's.** Located in the heart of the Treme, and the home church for many a famous local musician—Sidney Bechet was a parishioner—St. Augustine's holds frequent jazz Masses, with a number of local high-profile musicians participating. But even the regular weekly Masses are celebrated with New Orleans–related music and cultural color. Call ahead for details, especially to see if charismatic former pastor Fr. LeDoux is making a rare appearance in the pulpit. St. Augustine's is at 1210 Gov. Nichols St. (© **504/525-5934;** www.staugustinecatholicchurch-neworleans.org). See p. 188 for more details on the church and its history.

Crescent City Farmers Markets This is the collective name for the weekly produce (and other foodstuffs) wonderlands in various city locales. It's *the* place to commune with local gourmands. You may not want to cart home fresh produce, though sampling in season is always a pleasure, but you can bring home some powerful Creole cream cheese, fresh breads and biscuits, and other regional treats. Local chefs do demonstrations (crawfish-and-shrimp quesadillas!), and gourmet snacks are on sale as well. The markets are held on Tuesday from 9am to 1pm in the Uptown Square parking lot at 200 Broadway and Saturday from 8am to noon at 700 Magazine St. For more info, go to **www.crescentcityfarmersmarket.org**.

Snake & Jake's Christmas Club Lounge Tiny. Cramped. Full of Christmas twinkle lights and locals drinking and some out-of-towners, also drinking, because they consider it their own local lounge when they come to town. See p. 272.

Kermit Ruffins & the Barbecue Swingers Every Thursday night, Kermit Ruffins, he of the smooth trumpet and gravelly, Satchmo-inspired voice, plays at **Vaughan's Lounge** (p. 260). Because this is his home turf, he feels much freer here, and his sets veer away from tourist-pleasing, conservative performances to looser repertoires. And because his band is called the Barbecue Swingers, and because he loves to cook, he often makes free barbecues before the shows.

Super Sunday All year long the Mardi Gras Indians work on their elaborate suits of hand-sewn beaded mosaics and feathers, creating concoctions that would make even over-the-top designer Bob Mackie burst into tears of helpless envy. And once a year they meet on their home turfs to compete, with chants, drums, and costumes, to prove once and for all which tribe is the most glorious and who is the prettiest. All that work for nothing but honor, pride, and beauty. Watching them parade and square off is one of the great sights of New Orleans, and hardly anyone goes. Perhaps that's because of the location (the Uptown Indians start and end at the corner of Washington Ave. and LaSalle St.; the Mid-City tribes start around Bayou St. John and Orleans Ave.; in both cases, just drive around looking for feathers and listening for drums); perhaps it's because the Indians are supposed to parade on the Sunday closest to St. Joseph's Day (Mar 19), but that's only if the weather is good (rain and wind are hard on feathers: "Ever seen a wet chicken?" one Indian pointed out) and if the Indians feel like it. We don't know what will happen to this tradition, because the Indians were from the neighborhoods worst hit by the flood, so whoever does return is all the more worth celebrating. Take your chances because it's a sight you won't see anywhere else.

2 THE BEST OF NEW ORLEANS IN 1 DAY

If you have only a day in New Orleans, you might as well spend it all in the **French Quarter**—after all, you could easily spend a much longer trip entirely within its confines. (We just won't let you do so if you have the additional time.) But this is a day that will include all the important factors of a New Orleans visit: eating, walking, drinking, eating some more, listening to music, and dancing. *Start: River side of Jackson Square.*

❶ Café du Monde ★★★

Downing a cup of chicory coffee and some beignets is a good way to start a New Orleans day, all hopped up on sugar and caffeine. You can watch this city come to lazy life (most tourists will likely still be sleeping off the previous evening), as the carriage drivers begin to line up across the street. Just don't wear black, unless you want everyone you encounter during the day to know where you had breakfast. See p. 163.

❷ Take a Walking Tour of the Quarter ★★★

You need to get the overall lay of the land before you start branching out. We provide a tour for you in chapter 9, though you can take an official one from Historic New Orleans Tours (p. ###). Ours gives you a bit of history in addition to pointing out individual buildings, and it also helps you slow down and admire the architecture of this unique neighborhood. As you wander, take notice of how the building exteriors, apart from the ironwork (slave-made, originally, most of it), are rather plain. The Creoles believed that because they lived inside, that's where all the beauty should be.

❸ St. Louis Cathedral ★

It's a humdrum ecclesiastical building, but it is the center of spiritual life for a town that is surprisingly devoutly Catholic (it's always a shock to note how many foreheads soberly bear ashes the day after the frantic party antics of Mardi Gras). Go around the back to the little garden (usually locked, but

you might be able to coax someone into letting you in), a serene oasis that legend has it was a favorite haunt of good Catholic Marie Laveau, who went to Mass daily at the cathedral, where the infamous Pere Antoine (sent to New Orleans by none other than the office of the Inquisition) futilely attempted to get his parishioner to forsake her voodoo ways. It lost its sweeping oak trees to Katrina, and the lack is felt, but plans are to re-landscape it to reflect the original early 1800s design. See p. 174.

❹ CENTRAL GROCERY ★★★

Get a muffuletta for lunch at **Central Grocery** (split it with somebody; they're gigantic) and thread your way through the buildings across the street to eat it by the banks of the Mississippi River. 923 Decatur St. ✆ **504/523-1620.** See p. 142.

❺ Stroll the Moonwalk ★★★

Walk off your lunch on a stroll down the Moonwalk, the park and pedestrian walkway that runs along the river, stopping to notice some of the curious public art installations and local cultural monuments planted along the way. Ol' Man River will keep rolling along, and you can watch riverboats, cruise lines, and other ships sail on by, just like they have, minus some modern engineering, ever since there was a New Orleans. See p. 180.

❻ The Cabildo ★★★

The site of the signing of the Louisiana Purchase, one of two buildings erected by the Baroness Pontalba's father, who thus

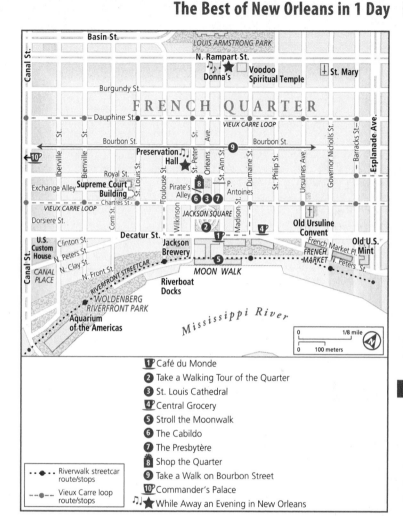

1 Café du Monde
2 Take a Walking Tour of the Quarter
3 St. Louis Cathedral
4 Central Grocery
5 Stroll the Moonwalk
6 The Cabildo
7 The Presbytère
8 Shop the Quarter
9 Take a Walk on Bourbon Street
10 Commander's Palace
♪★ While Away an Evening in New Orleans

- - -●- - - Riverwalk streetcar route/stops
- - -●- - - Vieux Carre loop route/stops

set the tone for the Place D'Armes, as Jackson Square was originally known. It has fine exhibits illustrating New Orleans and Louisiana history and culture. But we love the Napoleon death mask here the best. See p. 177.

❼ The Presbytère ★★★

The former home of the priests who worked at St. Louis Cathedral has been turned into a wonderful Mardi Gras museum that covers in admirable detail all the many aspects of this varied and misunderstood local holiday institution. Take the time to watch the short film on the Mardi Gras Indians and shake your head over the elaborate dresses worn by Mardi Gras queens. And don't miss the section on the Cajun Mardi Gras, especially the video installation that allows you to experience life inside a Cajun house when a bunch of drunks in costumes come around to play tricks and demand a chicken for their gumbo. See p. 180.

❽ Shop the Quarter

You are released from sightseeing and freed up for browsing through some of the curious shops in the Quarter. We suggest starting in nearby Pirate's Alley, at **Faulkner House Books** (p. 237), so you can ease into the whole "not-seeing-the-sights" thing with a glance at the author's former residence. Consider choosing a literary souvenir from the comprehensive selection of New Orleans–related books. Then walk down Royal Street and admire the antiques. Head around the corner and drop in at the new Chartres Street address of **A Gallery for Fine Photography** (p. 235); it's like a museum of photos, many of which relate to local culture and history. Swing by the shops toward the Esplanade Avenue end of Decatur Street, where the objets d'art are a lot cheaper than the goods on Royal Street.

❾ Take a Walk on Bourbon Street

Dusk is the best time to do this; during the day, it's too tame, and once night really falls, it's pretty rowdy. Sure, it's gaudy, loud, and kind of disgusting and comes off as a combination giant T-shirt shop and bar. At the right time of day, when things are starting to heat up but the real obnoxious types aren't too drunk, when different kinds of music pour from every door, and when captivating smells waft from restaurants, it's also seductive and exhilarating. You have to do it once, though probably no more than that. Have a predinner drink at the darkly mysterious **Lafitte's Blacksmith Shop** (the oldest building in town, at the end of the business part of the street; p. 268) or sample a Hurricane at the not-so-dark-but-always-

lively **Pat O'Brien's** (p. 267), or get off Bourbon and go to the darkly romantic **Napoleon House Bar & Café** (p. 269).

🔟 COMMANDER'S PALACE ★★

Food is a very, very important part of your time in New Orleans. Tonight we are forcing you out of the Quarter, just for variety's sake. You could try the deservedly famous and long-lived Commander's Palace, which recovered from severe storm damage to return to serving excellent examples of nouveau Orleans cuisine that have influenced the cooking of many a local chef. 1403 Washington Ave. ℂ **504/ 899-8221.** See p. 155.

⓫ While Away an Evening in New Orleans ★★★

Nightlife is too important a part of this city to leave it off your list. Do not miss hearing some jazz at **Preservation Hall** (p. 258)—it's cheap, and it's the real McCoy. You may also want to navigate Bourbon Street; now that night has fallen, the scene will have truly kicked in. You have to see it once, even if you never want to see it again. For equal fun, less like that found at a frat party, head to the Frenchmen section of the Faubourg Marigny, where at least a dozen clubs and bars are within a few blocks. Wander from one to another, sometimes never even going inside (often the music can be heard outside just as easily), simply mingling with the friendly crowds. You can also drop by **Donna's** (p. 255) for some fine local music. Suddenly feeling hungry again? Grab a dozen oysters at **Acme Oyster House** (p. 139) or **Felix's Restaurant & Oyster Bar** (p. 140). Have you exercised restraint and missed a bar or two? Go now. If you don't collapse exhausted—and full—in your bed, you haven't done your day properly.

Get out of the Quarter, *get out of the Quarter,* **get out of the Quarter.** Are we getting through to you? You can come back; you probably still have serious shopping (if not serious drinking) to do. But today you must begin to see what else New Orleans has to offer. We've constructed this tour so that the sights mentioned follow a logical geographic order, but if you have limited time, just take the streetcar/bus ride/tour, a short stroll through the Garden District, and visit the National World War II Museum. *Start: St. Charles Streetcar line, Canal Street stop.*

❶ St. Charles Avenue Streetcar ★★★

Hop on the oldest continuously operating wooden streetcar in the country—and that means no air-conditioning, so doing this in the cool of the morning is a good idea. Don't forget to have exact change ($1.25). Admire the gorgeous homes along the way (if you are awake enough) and remember which side of the car you rode on so that you can get on the other side for the ride back. See p. 53.

❷ Take a Walking Tour of the Garden District ★★★

Aside from its historical significance and interest, this neighborhood, full of fabulous houses and lush greenery, is just plain beautiful. Recall the plain exteriors of the buildings in the "French" Quarter. Notice how the houses suddenly got big, grand, and ornamental. Are you surprised to learn you are in what was once known as the "American district"? You can use the walking tour we supply in chapter 9 or take a guided tour from Historic New Orleans Tours. See p. 204.

❸ Lafayette Cemetery No. 1

The "little cities of the dead" are part of the iconic landscape of New Orleans. St. Louis No. 1 is older and has more historic graves, and you may well wish to consider going there instead, particularly with a guided tour so you won't miss some of the more significant tombs. But this cemetery, which catered to the Uptown folks, is perhaps prettier, thanks to the foliage and the larger square footage. Notice the

tombs with French or German writing, and notice the four matching mausoleums in the far left corner, which belong to four boyhood friends (one a Civil War vet) who used to play together in that corner of the graveyard. Though tour groups do go through here regularly, exercise caution if you find you have the grounds mostly to yourself. See p. 197.

Take the St. Charles streetcar line (or temporary bus) to the end and transfer to the City Park streetcar line, which ends at the entrance to:

❹ City Park ★★★

City Park is full of all sorts of sights, from the Spanish moss–draped giant live oaks to the **New Orleans Museum of Art,** to the **Sculpture Garden,** to the lake to wander around, to the kids' amusement park and **Storybook Land.** The **Botanical Gardens** include the **Train Gardens,** a sort of melted Dr. Seuss replica of the city in miniature, complete with model trains. There's a lot to do here, and it's rarely as crowded as it deserves to be, except maybe on weekends. It got battered by the storm and flooding, but it's coming back, and its progress is interesting to follow. See p. 194.

❺ St. John's Bayou ★★★

Just outside the gates of City Park lies this former canal turned useless, if scenic, body of water. A stroll here is one of the lesser-known delights of the city. Stand outside the Pitot House (p. 190) and imagine owning one of the surrounding neighborhood's former plantation homes, back in the days when the main entertainment would be sitting on the upper verandas,

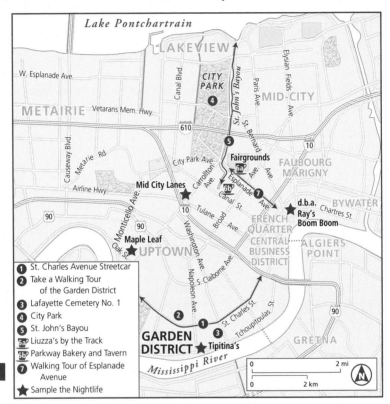

Lake Pontchartrain

LAKEVIEW

CITY PARK ❹

MID-CITY

METAIRIE

FAUBOURG MARIGNY

Fairgrounds ❻ᴬ

Mid City Lanes ★

d.b.a.
Ray's
Boom Boom

BYWATER

FRENCH QUARTER

Maple Leaf ★

UPTOWN

CENTRAL BUSINESS DISTRICT

ALGIERS POINT

❶ St. Charles Avenue Streetcar
❷ Take a Walking Tour
    of the Garden District
❸ Lafayette Cemetery No. 1
❹ City Park
❺ St. John's Bayou
❻ᴬ Liuzza's by the Track
❻ᴮ Parkway Bakery and Tavern
❼ Walking Tour of Esplanade
    Avenue
★ Sample the Nightlife

GARDEN DISTRICT ★ Tipitina's

Mississippi River

GRETNA

0 — 2 mi
0 — 2 km

watching the boats go by. Keep your eyes peeled for herons, pelicans, and other local birds. See p. 181.

❻ᴬ LIUZZA'S BY THE TRACK ★★
Head down Esplanade Avenue and turn left on Lopez to get some lunch at the popular **❻ᴬ Liuzza's by the Track.** You'll find authentic local food—excellent gumbo, wonderful po' boys, but with large, well-constructed salads so vegetarians won't feel left out—but it can get crowded at lunch. 1518 N. Lopez. ☎ **504/218-7888.** See p. 148. Or stay put. Right off the Bayou, **❻ᴮ Parkway Bakery and Tavern** has some of the best po' boys in town in possibly the best atmosphere. 538 Hagan St. ☎ **504/482-3047.** See p. 148.

❼ Walking Tour of Esplanade Avenue
You are here, after all, and we suggest you follow our nice walking tour in chapter 9 (if you do this itinerary in chronological order, follow our walking tour in reverse order). Architecturally similar to the Garden District—again, the post–Louisiana Purchase Americans felt unwelcome among the Creoles of the Vieux Carré and so made their homes outside that tightly knit community—the area does include at least one home with a French connection—the birthplace of Impressionist Edgar Degas's mother and grandmother, and the only studio belonging to the former artist that is open to the public. See p. 226.

❽ Sample the Nightlife

For a dinner recommendation, see chapter 7. Once you've eaten, if you get to **Mid City Lanes,** otherwise known as **Rock 'n' Bowl** (p. 262), by 9pm, you shouldn't have any trouble getting a lane—you can bowl as well as listen to some zydeco and other local music. Or head to **Tipitina's** (p. 265), or the **Maple Leaf Bar** (p. 264), or to Frenchman Street, paying special attention to **Ray's** (p. 263), and **d.b.a.** (p. 262) for more local music. Or all of them if you are up for it. Try to be.

---

4 THE BEST OF NEW ORLEANS IN 3 DAYS

Yes, we are dragging you out of the Quarter again, but we will let you come back later. *Start: Taxi to Algiers Point Ferry Terminal or Canal Streetcar line to Convention Center Boulevard.*

❶ A Ferry Ride to Algiers

Not so much because Algiers is so great, but because it's a free ride across the Mississippi. Wind in your face, visions of Tom and Huck, all that. But once on the other side, you can visit **Blaine Kern's Mardi Gras World** ★★ (shuttles meet each ferry). The neighborhood itself is worth strolling, as it's a more or less undisturbed turn-of-the-20th-century suburb. And the ride back across on the ferry will give you a wonderful view of the New Orleans skyline. See p. 192.

❷ Audubon Aquarium of the Americas ★★★

Here's a fine refuge for a rainy (or for that matter, overly warm) day, and a perfect outing for kids, who will want to see the jellyfish and spend lots of time giggling at the sea otters. Because they had to restock after losing nearly everything during the power outage, their regeneration is an exciting time. Wave to the penguins who survived and got a hurri-cation in Oakland. Get here early to avoid the busloads of schoolchildren. Consider also taking in the excellent new **Audubon Insectarium** ★★★, the largest free-standing museum in the world devoted to creepy-crawly-flutters. See p. 173.

Take the riverboat to Audubon Park.

❸ Audubon Park ★★ **and Audubon Zoo** ★★★

You may or may not want to visit the zoo, which is small but sweetly developed, but if you do and it's a hot day, plan on coming here before any other activity. Animals are smart enough to rest rather than romp in the heat, so if you want to see anything other than a pile of fur snoozing in the shade, you need to be here when the place opens. But even if you don't visit the zoo, you must stroll through Audubon Park. See p. 192.

4A **LILETTE** ★★

Owned by one of the most interesting and creative chefs in town, **4A** **Lilette** is a charming—and popular—spot for lunch. 3637 Magazine St. ☎ **504/895-1636.** See p. 159. If you just want a sweet, sample some of the myriad flavors concocted at **4B** **Creole Creamery,** including lavender honey, red velvet, and pepper. 4924 Prytania St. ☎ **504/894-8680.**

---

❺ Shop Magazine Street

The quirky shops along Magazine (they clump together in pockets here and there, but a good stretch runs from roughly the 3500–4200 blocks) are a mix of some

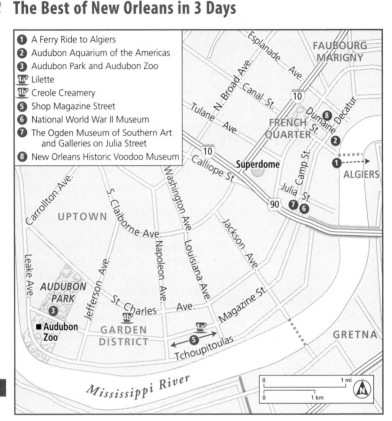

1 A Ferry Ride to Algiers
2 Audubon Aquarium of the Americas
3 Audubon Park and Audubon Zoo
4a Lilette
4b Creole Creamery
5 Shop Magazine Street
6 National World War II Museum
7 The Ogden Museum of Southern Art and Galleries on Julia Street
8 New Orleans Historic Voodoo Museum

affordable antiques and geegaws, shops of no particular theme, and good clothing stores. Part of the very hip Lower Garden District, it makes for a change from the Quarter and it's certainly more affordable. The no. 11 Magazine Street bus line begins at Audubon Park. See p. 231.

6 National World War II Museum ★★★

Begun with an emphasis on D-day, but gradually turning its focus to all of World War II, this was the inspiration of historian (and *Saving Private Ryan* consultant) Stephen Ambrose. A tribute to the extraordinary efforts and sacrifices that marked the turning point in World War II, it is a

world-class museum. D-day vets are often found taking tickets and doing other jobs—say thank you for us, please, and we don't just mean for that day's volunteer work. By afternoon the crowds should be thinner, but if you have a special interest in the subject matter, you should allow at least 3 hours. You can take the no. 11 Magazine Street bus and exit as close to Calliope as you can get. See p. 185.

7 The Ogden Museum of Southern Art ★★★ and the Galleries on Julia Street

The premier collection of Southern art in the country. We gravitate toward outsider art and photos and do appreciate special touches, such as an exhibit of photographs of old blues men that had an appropriate soundtrack. Once you are done seeing the past of Southern art, walk around the corner to the galleries on Julia Street to see its present and future. You can take the no. 11 Magazine Street bus from the Lower Garden District (get off as close to St. Joseph as you can), or walk from the National World War II Museum or in from the Quarter. See p. 186 for the Ogden and p. 233 for the Julia Street galleries.

⑧ New Orleans Historic Voodoo Museum

It's not like you can visit voodoo—it's a religion, not a place—but you can tour the musty and a bit touristy **New Orleans Historic Voodoo Museum** (p. 179), which has some informative exhibits and a staff that should be able to give you a tour if you ask nicely. Combine a visit here with one to the **Voodoo Spiritual Temple** (p. 201) run by Priestess Miriam. A charismatic figure used to delivering talks on her religion to outsiders, she gladly shows people around her place of worship. But it is just that, so please be respectful.

Where to Stay

If you're doing your New Orleans trip right, you shouldn't be doing much sleeping. But you do have to put your change of clothes somewhere. Fortunately, New Orleans is bursting with hotels of every variety (though increasingly of the brand-name chain sort), so you should be able to find something that fits your preferences.

Given a choice, we tend to favor slightly faded, ever-so-faintly decayed, just-this-side-of-elegant locales; a new, sterile chain or even a luxury hotel doesn't seem right for New Orleans, where atmosphere is everything. Slightly tattered lace curtains; faded antiques; mossy courtyards with banana trees and fountains; a musty, Miss Havisham air—to us, it's all part of the fun. We prefer to stay in a Tennessee Williams play, if not an Anne Rice novel (though in summertime, we'll take air-conditioning, thank you very much).

Understandably, this may not appeal to you. It may, in fact, describe your own home, and who wants one's own home on vacation? Meanwhile, here are a few tips. Don't stay on Bourbon Street unless you absolutely have to or don't mind getting no sleep. The open-air frat party that is this thoroughfare does mean a free show below your window, but it is hardly conducive to . . . well, just about anything other than participation in the same. On the other hand, making a night of it on your balcony, people-watching—and people-egging-on— is an activity with its own merits, one enjoyed by a number of happy tourists. If you must stay on Bourbon Street, try to get a room away from the street.

A first-time visitor might also strongly consider not staying in the Quarter at all. Most of your sightseeing will take place there, but you may want to get away from

it all after dinner or simply see a neighborhood whose raison d'être isn't to entertain first-time visitors. Try the beautiful Garden District instead. It's an easy streetcar ride away from the Quarter, and it's close to a number of wonderful clubs and restaurants. Finally, while staying in the Garden District and the Quarter means you can avoid seeing any Katrina damage, staying in the increasingly interesting Mid-City might bring you in proximity, depending on which place you choose. You can decide for yourself if this bothers you.

All the guesthouses in this chapter have their merits. If you want more information, we recommend **PIANO,** the Professional Innkeepers Association of New Orleans. Their website (www.bbnola.com) will provide you with quick descriptions and photos of and quick links to a variety of B&Bs, inns, and more. All members must be licensed by the city and inspected by a state official.

Though tourism is not what it was pre-Katrina, as a general rule, just to be on the safe side, always book ahead in spring and fall. And if your trip will coincide with Mardi Gras or Jazz Fest, book *way* ahead (and we can't stress this enough—*please* look at "Calendar of Events," in chapter 4, to make sure)—up to a year in advance if you want to ensure a room. Sugar Bowl week and other festival times when visitors flood New Orleans also require planning for accommodations, and there's always the chance that a big convention or sports event will be in town, making it difficult to find a room. (Though we have to admit that's often when the maligned anonymous chain hotels do come in handy because they may not be the first choice of regular visitors. If a convention didn't take one over with block booking, there is often an extra room for a decent rate floating around. See the box, "Spending the Night in Chains," later in this chapter.) You might conceivably run across a cancellation and get a last-minute booking, but the chances are remote at best. You should also be aware that rates frequently jump more than a notch or two for Mardi Gras and other festival times (sometimes they even double), and in most cases, there's a 4- or 5-night minimum requirement during those periods.

If you want to miss the crowds and the lodgings squeeze that mark the big festivals, consider coming in the month immediately following Mardi Gras or, if you can stand the heat and humidity, in the summer, when the streets are not nearly as thronged. December, before the Sugar Bowl and New Year's activities, is a good time, too, but perhaps a bit chilly and rainy. In both cases, hotel prices fall dramatically and great deals can be had just about everywhere. (And these prices might not be accounted for in the rack rate quoted in this guide, so you might have a pleasant surprise!)

There are no recommendable inexpensive *hotels* in the French Quarter. If you're on a budget and must stay there, consider a guesthouse. On the whole, however, you'll have a better selection of inexpensive lodgings outside the Quarter. There are also a couple of hostels in New Orleans; check the website **www.hostels.com** for more information.

You'll find a list of our favorite accommodations in a variety of eclectic categories in the first section of this chapter.

The rates we've given in this chapter are for double rooms and do not include the city's 13% hotel tax. You may see some wide ranges of room rates below, which hotels were not eager to break down more specifically for us. Realize that rates often shift according to demand. Unless it includes the caveat "higher rates for special events" (implying higher prices then) or "seasonal rates apply" (implying either higher or lower prices during same), the high end of the range is for popular times such as Mardi Gras and Jazz Fest, and the low end is for quieter periods such as the month of December. *Note:* Some of the hotels listed under "Expensive" have some surprisingly low numbers at said low end of their range. These could indicate certain times of year or even just whim. Therefore, it's worth searching those out and making a call; you might get very lucky!

1 NEW ORLEANS'S BEST HOTEL BETS

Selecting just one hotel in New Orleans is a little like picking your favorite flavor of ice cream—there are just so many great options to choose from.

- **Best for a Romantic Getaway:** Take an old indigo plantation some blocks away from the Quarter, outfit it with some of the nicest furnishings in town, add in a full lavish breakfast, and you've got the **House on Bayou Road,** 2275 Bayou Rd. (© **800/882-2968** or 504/945-0992). See p. 100.
- **Best Basic Hotel:** You know, just a hotel, albeit a hotel that looks sufficiently NOLA-like. It's friendly, it's sweet, and it's better than *basic* allows it to sound—it's the **Maison Dupuy,** 1001 Toulouse St. (© **800/535-9177** or 504/586-8000). See p. 93.
- **Best Fabulous B&B:** You need to see the **Magnolia Mansion** to believe it, from the blood-red entrance hall to the antiques-crammed public rooms to the wonderfully over-the-top accommodations. 2127 Prytania St. (© **504/412-9500**). See p. 110.

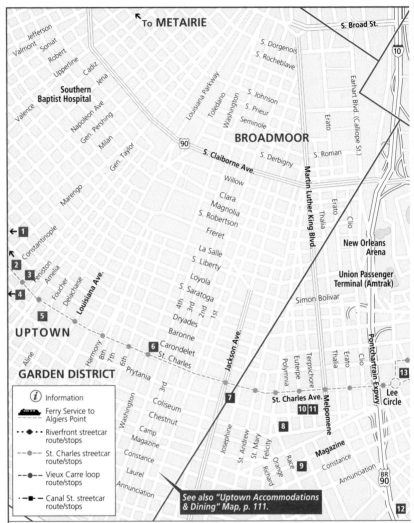

See also "Uptown Accommodations & Dining" Map, p. 111.

Ashtons Bed & Breakfast **45**
B&W Courtyards Bed & Breakfast **48**
Best Western St. Christopher **26**
Chimes B&B **4**
The Columns **3**
Comfort Suites **41**
Cotton Exchange **37**
Country Inn and Suites by Carlson **28**
Courtyard by Marriott **18**
The Depot at Madame Julia's **14**

Drury Inn & Suites **39**
Embassy Suites **17**
The Frenchmen Hotel **47**
The Grand Victorian Bed
   & Breakfast **6**
Hampton Inn and Suites **12**
Hampton Inn Garden District **5**
Harrah's **20**
Hilton New Orleans
   Riverside Hotel **20**

Hilton St. Charles **36**
Holiday Inn Express **38**
Homewood Suites **39**
The House on Bayou Road **44**
Iberville Suites **43**
InterContinental New Orleans **3**
International House **32**
Lafayette Hotel **34**
La Quinta Inn and Suites **33**
Le Cirque **13**

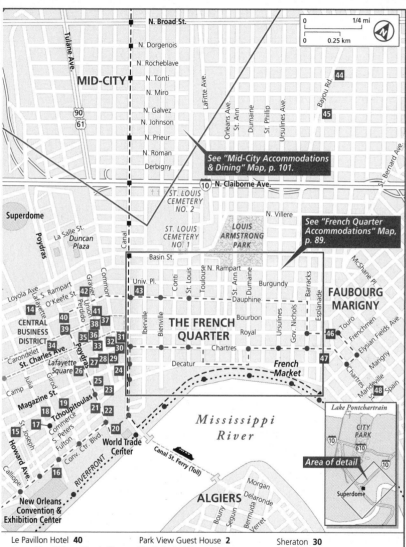

Le Pavillon Hotel **40**
Loews New Orleans Hotel **22**
Loft 523 **29**
Magnolia Mansion **7**
Maison Perrier Bed
  & Breakfast **1**
Marriott **31**
The McKendrick-Breaux
  House **9**

Park View Guest House **2**
The Pelham **24**
Prytania Park Hotel **11**
Quality Inn **42**
Queen Anne **10**
Renaissance Arts Hotel **19**
Residence Inn by Marriott **15**
Ritz-Carlton, New Orleans **43**
Royal Street Inn & R Bar **46**

Sheraton **30**
SpringHill Suites by Marriott **16**
St. Charles Guest House **8**
St. James Hotel **25**
The Whitney—A Wyndham
  Historic Hotel **27**
Windsor Court **23**
W New Orleans **21**

- **Best More Modest B&B: Chimes B&B,** 1146 Constantinople St. (© **504/899-2621**), is a delightful family-owned guesthouse in the Garden District. The charming owners have been operating the B&B for over 20 years, generating loyal return guests. See p. 113.
- **Best Moderately Priced Hotel:** The **Bienville House,** 320 Decatur St. (© **800/535-7836** or 504/529-2345), features amenities befitting somewhat swankier digs. Though not centrally located, you're in easy walking distance from everything in the Quarter. See p. 94.
- **Best for Travelers with Disabilities:** Two of the most accessible and accommodating choices are the **Hotel Monteleone,** 214 Royal St. (© **800/535-9595** or 504/523-3341), and the **Windsor Court,** 300 Gravier St. (© **800/262-2662** or 504/523-6000). See p. 92 and 104.
- **Best Hotel for Hip Executives:** The innovative minimalist style and myriad comforts at the **International House,** 221 Camp St. (© **800/633-5770** or 504/553-9550), have justly made this every film- and record-company dude's (and dudette's) favorite hotel. It's the perfect palate cleanser if you can't stand Victorian frills. See p. 106.
- **Best Health Club:** The hands-down winner is the **Hilton New Orleans Riverside Hotel,** 2 Poydras St. (© **800/445-8667** or 504/561-0500). Its Rivercenter Racquet and Health Club features outdoor and indoor tennis courts, squash and racquetball courts, a rooftop jogging track, tanning beds, massage, a hair salon, and a golf studio. The Mayor works out here! See p. 103.
- **Best Hotel in the Quarter:** The Ritz-Carlton—they know how to do hotels. A top-to-bottom post-K fix-up has only enhanced this already splendid property. And if you want to go even more decadent, stay in the smaller but elegant club-level rooms in their **Maison Orleans** annex. Just say the words "24-hour butler service." You know you want it. 921 Canal St. (© **800/241-3333** or 504/524-1331).
- **Best Funky Little Hotel: The Frenchmen,** 417 Frenchmen St. (© **504/948-2166**), is small but full of pure New Orleans charm. But bear in mind that one person's "funky" may be another person's "dingy," though an excellent post-Katrina makeover has addressed some of those concerns. See p. 99.
- **Best Brand-Name Hotel Addition:** The Loews chain took over an old office building in the Central Business District and not only refurbished the Piazza D'Italia, a silly bit of public art that had long needed a fix-up, but also brought their brand of style and comfort to a city that probably has enough hotels but is always glad to have another swell place to stay. It's **Loews New Orleans Hotel,** 300 Poydras St. (© **800/23-LOEWS** [235-6397] or 504/595-3300). See p. 107.
- **Best Hidden Gem:** Back behind a fence at the start of a so-so neighborhood above the Quarter is an enchanting set of renovated old buildings, a series of suites and rooms full of the sort of impossible romantic details that exist only on the pages of novels about New Orleans. And, of course, at the **Garlands Historic Creole Cottages,** 1129 St. Philip St. (© **800/523-1060** or 504/523-1372). See p. 91.
- **In a Class by Itself:** Of all the hotels in New Orleans, the **Windsor Court,** 300 Gravier St. (© **800/262-2662** or 504/523-6000), stands head and shoulders above the rest. Most guest rooms are suites with Italian marble bathrooms, balconies or bay windows, living rooms, kitchenettes, and dressing rooms. If you choose one of the two-bedroom penthouse suites, you'll have the added luxury of a private library and a terrace that overlooks the mighty Mississippi. See p. 104.

2 THE FRENCH QUARTER

For hotels in this section, see the "French Quarter Accommodations" map on p. 89.

VERY EXPENSIVE

Maison Orleans ★★★ This is for those who say, "I'd stay at the Ritz-Carlton if only it were even nicer and had even better service." *Voilà!* This operates at the Ritz's Club Level, but with, get this, 24-hour butler service. Yes, ring a special button, "ask for the sun" (they say themselves), and your own personal Jeeves will fetch it for you.

The rooms here are gorgeous little classics of NOLA style: wood floors, paneling, and furniture; superb moldings; fireplace facades; and bathrooms containing about the deepest hotel tub and separate shower (rooms whose numbers end with 05s have smaller bathrooms, with tub/shower combinations), quality amenities, and thick bath sheets. You get both local aesthetics *and* modern comforts, though window size can vary. Beds are ultralush, with feather beds, down comforters with soft covers, and a half canopy. All of this doesn't come cheap, to say the least. However, there are also five food servings a day (enough so that you need not eat anywhere else, though that would be a mistake in New Orleans!), and drinks are free. Summertime can bring incredible specials as well.

904 Iberville St., New Orleans, LA 70112. ℂ **504/670-2900.** Fax 504/670-2910. www.ritzcarlton.com. 75 units. $309–$1,199 double and suite. AE, DC, DISC, MC, V. Valet parking $36. **Amenities:** Restaurant; continental breakfast plus daily snacks/meal presentations; babysitting; health club; spa; full access to Ritz-Carlton shops; room service; 24-hr. butler service; special baths drawn by butler. *In room:* A/C, TV, CD and DVD players (and complimentary selections), hair dryer, minibar (stocked according to personal preference), MP3 docking station, robes and slippers, Wi-Fi.

Melrose Mansion ★ A standout even on a street full of mansions in a town full of pampering guesthouses, the Melrose Mansion has long combined luxury resort living with the best guesthouse offerings. Unfortunately, it seems somewhat resting on its laurels, needing some paint touch-ups and the like here and there. Service is still attentive and accommodating, and the continental breakfasts include delicious pastries from La Louisiane. It still remains a charming old mansion, with well-maintained grounds, but it may no longer be justifying its cost (though the prices are better than others in this bracket, especially for a suite) and cancellation policies.

The rooms vary from classic Victorian antiques to lighter country-style decor; we love the bright-yellow Miss Kitty's Room (named for a former tenant and burlesque dancer) and the more classic Burgundy Room. Bathrooms can be small, but fancy linens help. The Parc Henry suite overlooks the year-round heated pool and, between that and its

---

Tips   Staying Safe

There is, of course, considerable concern about personal safety in New Orleans. Your hotel choice, for the most part, need not be influenced by that. Daytime is mostly safe, and at night you will probably be traveling in cabs or, if you're in the French Quarter, in well-populated areas. If you stay above Bourbon Street, closer to Rampart, don't walk back to your hotel alone at night; take a cab or travel in a group.

large dining room and kitchen, seems perfect for entertaining and hanging out. There are some very good rates to be had during the summer.

937 Esplanade Ave., New Orleans, LA 70116. ℭ **800/650-3323** or 504/944-2455. Fax 504/945-1794. www.melrosegroup.com. 14 units. $150–$250 double and suites. Rates include continental breakfast and cocktail hour. AE, MC, V. Private parking $23. **Amenities:** Heated outdoor pool. *In room:* A/C, TV, hair dryer, Wi-Fi.

Ramada Plaza Hotel—The Inn on Bourbon   A too-pricey chain hotel, with modestly good-looking, vaguely Southern decor, plus cottage-cheese ceilings and fluorescent lights in the hallways. The justification for staying here is the location: the former site of the 1859 French Opera House—the first opera house built in the United States (it burned down in 1919). Party animals should note that this means the hotel is right in the middle of the liveliest action on Bourbon, and many rooms (not standards, though) have balconies overlooking the mayhem below. If you have a serious commitment to sleeping, though, choose another place to stay, or at least request an interior room. On the other hand, there are worse ways to spend a N'Awlins evening than having a pizza on your balcony while enjoying the free show on Bourbon Street below. All rooms have king-size or double beds. Bathroom upgrades include marble sinks, nicer fixtures, and new tub/shower combos. The pool is fine but unheated. The **Bourbon Street Cafeteria** serves breakfast and lunch buffets.

541 Bourbon St., New Orleans, LA 70130. ℭ **800/272-6232** or 504/524-7611. Fax 504/568-9427. www. innonbourbon.com. 186 units. $219–$299 double. AE, DC, DISC, MC, V. Valet parking $25. **Amenities:** Bar; concierge; fitness room; outdoor pool; jewelry shop; gift shop; express checkout. *In room:* A/C, TV, hair dryer, minibar, Wi-Fi.

Ritz-Carlton, New Orleans ★★★   Sentimentalists that we are, we were deeply sad to see the venerable Maison Blanche department store go the way of Woolworth's, D. H. Holmes, and other Canal Street shopping landmarks. But for the city's sake, we are pleased to have the Ritz-Carlton take its place, preserving the classic, glazed terra-cotta building and bringing a high-end luxury hotel to the Quarter. Service is sterling. Rooms are light green, purple, and gold in tribute to New Orleans and have lovely beds. King rooms are nicer than doubles, while rooms on the 12th, 14th, and 15th floors are the largest (some ridiculously large). The toiletries are by Bulgari, and they've added a fancy coffee and tea service that comes in a cleverly designed wooden box. The whole effect is most gracious. Consider ponying up for the Club Level over at the Maison Orleans (see above). There are a great many elevators and different levels, so getting around does require some zigzagging to and fro. The spa is by far the nicest and largest in town, and though undeniably expensive, it's gorgeous, and the treatments are utter perfection; the fitness center is open 24 hours. Look for fun site-specific events in the courtyard, like crawfish boils and voodoo ceremonies. The whole hotel is nonsmoking.

921 Canal St., New Orleans, LA 70112. ℭ **800/241-3333** or 504/524-1331. Fax 504/524-7675. www. ritzcarlton.com. 452 units. $169–$419 double; from $569 and way, way up for suites. AE, DC, DISC, MC, V. Valet parking $32. Pets welcome. **Amenities:** Restaurant; 2 bars; babysitting; concierge; top-of-the-line spa (w/brand-new treatment rooms) and health club (w/resistance pool, Jacuzzi, and personal trainers); room service; shops; Wi-Fi. *In room:* A/C, TV, hair dryer, high-speed Internet ($9.95/day), minibar, newspaper delivery, Nintendo, robes and slippers.

Royal Sonesta ★★   The Royal Sonesta brags that it never closed, providing refuge during and after Katrina. (Anderson Cooper stayed here!) As one of the classiest hotels in the Quarter, the contrast between the boisterous hurly-burly of Bourbon Street and the Sonesta's elegant lobby couldn't be greater. Inside, all is quiet and gracious, and if your

Map labels:

Basin St. · LOUIS ARMSTRONG PARK 23 24 · N. Rampart St. · Canal St. · Burgundy St. · Voodoo Spiritual Temple 22 16 · St. Mary · FRENCH QUARTER 31 · Dauphine St. 4 5 · VIEUX CARRE LOOP · 1 2 · 3 6 · Iberville St. · Bienville St. · Bourbon St. 15 17 · St. Peter St. · Orleans Ave. · St. Ann St. 19 · 25 · Ursulines Ave. · Governor Nicholls St. · Barracks St. · Esplanade Ave. · 7 18 · Toulouse St. · Dumaine St. · St. Philip St. · 8 · Royal St. · St. Anthony's Square 20 21 · Exchange Alley 9 Supreme Court Building · St. Louis St. · Pirate's Alley · Antoine · 26 · 28 30 · VIEUX CARRE LOOP 14 · Chartres St. · 10 13 · Conti St. · Wilkinson · JACKSON SQUARE · Madison St. · 27 29 · Old Ursuline Convent · Dorsiere St. · Decatur St. · U.S. Custom House 12 · Clinton St. · N. Peters St. · Jackson Brewery · French Market Pl · Old U.S. Mint · CANAL PLACE · N. Clay St. · N. Front St. · RIVERFRONT STREETCAR · FRENCH MARKET · N. Peters St. · MOON WALK · Riverboat Docks · Mississippi River · WOLDENBERG RIVERFRONT PARK · 11 · Aquarium of the Americas · 0 1/8 mile · 0 100 meters

(i) Information · Riverfront streetcar route/stops · Vieux Carre loop route/stops

WHERE TO STAY · 6 · THE FRENCH QUARTER

room faces the courtyard (complete with a large pool), you are in another world altogether. Big and bustling (a favorite of business travelers, so it always seems busy), this is considered the only acceptable, top-flight Bourbon Street hotel, though noise is still a problem in rooms that face Bourbon (or even the side streets). But because the Sonesta is so large, reaching nearly to Royal Street, unless you do have one of those rooms, you won't believe you are so close to such craziness. Rooms are good if not memorable, except for that enormous combo armoire/TV cabinet—it leaves scant few inches between it and the end of the king-size beds. The bathrooms gleam, but don't try to swing a cat inside one. *Note:* This is the best place in the Quarter to catch a cab; they line up at the corner.

300 Bourbon St., New Orleans, LA 70130. ✆ **800/766-3782** or 504/586-0300. Fax 504/586-0335. www. sonesta.com/royalneworleans. 500 units. $119–$389 double; $400–$1,000 suite. AE, DC, DISC, MC, V. Parking $31 car, $35 oversize. **Amenities:** 2 restaurants; bar; concierge; exercise room; pool; room service. *In room:* A/C, TV, hair dryer, minibar, Wi-Fi.

Soniat House ★★ The recipient of endless tributes from various prestigious travel journals, the wonderful and romantic Soniat House lives up to the hype, though the prices are daunting. Inside the unassuming plain Creole exterior is a perfect little hideaway, an oasis of calm that seems impossible in the Quarter. The beyond-efficient staff spoils guests, and the sweet courtyards, candlelit at night, soothe them. The experience here is gracious and adult.

Rooms do vary, if not in quality then at least in distinction. (Be aware that designations such as "junior suite" just mean a room with a sitting area.) All have antiques, but if you want, say, high ceilings and really grand furniture (room no. 23 has a 17th-c. bed), you are better off in the main house or the suite-filled annex across the street (many of smaller antiques in the rooms are for sale). The rooms in the old kitchen and other buildings are not quite as smashing by comparison. On the main property, bathrooms are small, though some rooms have their own private balconies. Our only real complaint is the extra charge ($13) for the admittedly delicious, but small, breakfast (fresh-squeezed orange juice and fluffy biscuits made to order)—it seems petty given the already high prices, and lack of room service.

1133 Chartres St., New Orleans, LA 70116. ✆ **800/544-8808** or 504/522-0570. Fax 504/522-7208. www. soniathouse.com. 31 units. $195–$325 double; $350–$750 suite. AE, MC, V. Valet parking $25. No children 11 or under. **Amenities:** Concierge; access to nearby health club (for additional charge). *In room:* A/C, TV, hair dryer, robes, Wi-Fi.

W French Quarter ★★ The groovy hip vibe of the W never seemed to fit New Orleans all that well—it's a New York thing, isn't it?—but it was okay if it was safely in the CBD with the rest of the businesspeople hotels. But a rethink of this location post-Katrina cleanup has neatly melded a more subdued version of the brand into a very New Orleans space, and it doesn't feel jarring at all. What it does feel like is the luxury one would want from a more modern hotel, plus the sultry lassitude decadence that comes when hanging out in a courtyard by a (small) pool, or lounging, inside or out, on the W's plush furniture. Rooms (which are grouped around said courtyard and seem to be larger upstairs than down) are done in a more New Orleans–appropriate series of neutrals, and there are the usual winking details plus fancy amenities. If you can get the lower end of the price range, hop on it.

316 Chartres St., New Orleans, LA 70130. ✆ **800/522-6963** or 504/581-1200. Fax 504/523-2910. www. whotels.com. 98 units. $209–$469 double. AE, DC, DISC, MC, V. Valet parking $29 for cars, $32 for SUVs. **Amenities:** Restaurant; bar; concierge; access to Sheraton health club (2 blocks west at 500 Water St.); pool; room service. *In room:* A/C, TV/VCR, CD player, hair dryer, minibar, Wi-Fi ($14).

EXPENSIVE

Chateau LeMoyne—Holiday Inn French Quarter ★ The Chateau LeMoyne is in a good location, just around the corner from Bourbon Street but away from the noise and not far from Canal. It's a nice surprise to find a Holiday Inn housed in century-plus-old buildings, but the ambience stops at your room's threshold. Once inside, matters look pretty much like they do in every Holiday Inn—too bad. Famed architect James Gallier designed one of these 19th-century buildings, and you can still see bits of old brick, old ovens, and exposed cypress beams here and there, along with a graceful curving outdoor staircase. You wish they'd made more of their space, but even the spacious courtyard feels oddly sterile. Maybe it's the new brick, which seems sandblasted free of pesky (but atmospheric) moss.

Suites aren't much different from standard rooms, just with frillier furniture, though the enormous Executive Suite is probably worth budget busting for its four large (if dark) rooms that include a Jacuzzi and sauna.

301 Dauphine St., New Orleans, LA 70112. © **800/447-2830** or 504/581-1303. Fax 504/525-8531. www. hiclneworleanshotelsite.com. 171 units. $89–$309 double; $59–$499 suite, depending on season. Extra person $15 and up depending on season. AE, DC, DISC, MC, V. Valet parking $30; trucks, van, oversize $35. **Amenities:** Restaurant; bar; outdoor pool; room service. *In room:* A/C, TV, hair dryer, Wi-Fi.

Chateau Sonesta Hotel New Orleans ★★   On the site of the former D. H. Holmes Canal Street department store (1849), the Chateau Sonesta Hotel maintains the structure's 1913 facade. Many rooms feature balconies overlooking Bourbon or Dauphine street, which you might want to avoid if you are a light sleeper or request if you want the party action that location encourages. High ceilings and a fairly spacious layout, not to mention that proximity to Bourbon, make this a potentially well-priced (if slightly generic) choice, already popular among business groups for its meeting rooms and location. At the Canal Street entrance is a newly erected statue of Ignatius Reilly, hero of *A Confederacy of Dunces,* whom we first met when he was waiting, as all of New Orleans once did, "under the clock"—the old Holmes clock, now located in the hotel's Clock Bar, was for decades the favored rendezvous point for *tout* New Orleanians.

800 Iberville St., New Orleans, LA 70112. © **800/SONESTA** (766-3782) or 504/586-0800. Fax 504/586-1987. www.chateausonesta.com. 251 units. $99–$350 double; $285–$798 suite. Extra person $20. Children 16 and under stay free in parent's room. AE, DC, DISC, MC, V. Valet parking $28. **Amenities:** Restaurant; bar; babysitting; concierge; gift shop; exercise room; heated outdoor pool; room service. *In room:* A/C, TV w/pay movies, hair dryer, minibar, Wi-Fi.

Dauphine Orleans Hotel ★   On a relatively quiet and peaceful block of the Quarter, the Dauphine Orleans Hotel is relaxed but not unkempt. It's just a block from the action on Bourbon Street, but you wouldn't know it if you were sitting in any of its three secluded courtyards. Guests tend to like the atmosphere a lot. The hotel's buildings have a colorful history: The license a former owner took out to make the place a bordello is proudly displayed in the bar, and its proprietors are happy to admit that ghosts have been sighted on the premises. The hotel's back buildings were once the studio of John James Audubon, and the "patio rooms" across the street from the main building were originally built in 1834 as the home of New Orleans merchant Samuel Herrmann. A thorough room remodel has given the rooms a fresh, clean, and somewhat more modern (previously it was semi-period) feel, with white duvets, plasma TVs, and sleek tubs. The salt-water pool is adequately sized.

415 Dauphine St., New Orleans, LA 70112. © **800/521-7111** or 504/586-1800. Fax 504/586-1409. www. dauphineorleans.com. 111 units. $149–$269 double; $149–$329 patio room; $179–$399 suite. Rates include continental breakfast and welcome wine or beer coupon. Extra person $20. Children 17 and under stay free in parent's room. AE, DC, DISC, MC, V. Valet parking $28, oversize vehicle $32. **Amenities:** Bar; babysitting; small fitness room; Jacuzzi; guest library; outdoor pool. *In room:* A/C, TV, minibar, Wi-Fi (free).

The Garlands Historic Creole Cottages ★★   Here's a hidden gem across a side street from Armstrong Park, which makes it not the best location in town, though the inn itself is completely safe thanks to a good security fence. Please don't let our warning discourage you; this B&B is utterly charming, with some of the nicest accommodations

Impressions

There is something left in this people here that makes them like one another, that leads to constant outbursts of the spirit of play, that keeps them from being too con-foundedly serious about death and the ballot and reform and other less important things in life.

—Sherwood Anderson, *New Orleans and the Double-Dealer*

in the city, set on the grounds of the former Claude Treme plantation. Creole cottages such as the three-room Queen Elizabeth feature big, sexy canopy beds, wide pine-board floors, exposed brick walls, a fireplace, a big oval soaking tub, and good-taste furniture. Some come with kitchens and small living rooms, while other rooms are smaller (since units vary in size, ask when booking), but all are impeccably maintained, and the whole place is set in small delightful Southern gardens. The breakfast includes dishes such as curried eggs with crabmeat on puff pastry, and there are often snacks, such as homemade sweet bread, around. Still, you should exercise some caution coming home at night, and don't plan on venturing deeper into the Treme neighborhood.

1129 St. Philip St., New Orleans, LA 70116. ✆ **800/523-1060** or 504/523-1372. Fax 504/523-1951. www. historicgarlands.com. 15 units. $115–$225 double; $355 2-bedroom cottage. Special events higher. Rates include breakfast. AE, MC, V. Free parking. Pet-friendly (call ahead for specifics about your pet). **Amenities:** Wi-Fi. *In room:* A/C, TV.

Hotel Monteleone ★★   Opened in 1886, the Monteleone is the largest hotel in the French Quarter (and was home to Truman Capote's parents when he was born!), and it seems to keep getting bigger without losing a trace of its trademark charm. Because of its size, you can almost always get a reservation here, even when other places are booked. Everyone who stays here loves it, probably because it's a family hotel whose approach to business is reflected by the staff, among the most helpful in town. One guest who stayed here with a child with disabilities raved about the facilities.

Until recently, the big problem was the inconsistency among the rooms. But all have been freshly renovated (Katrina winds broke windows) and look blandly pretty as a result, though there is still some difference in terms of size and style. Rooms with numbers in the 60s are near the ice machine; rooms with numbers from 56 to 59 are slightly bigger with old high ceilings; rooms with numbers in the 27s have no windows. Executive suites are just big rooms but have the nicest new furniture, including four-poster beds and Jacuzzis. The glass fitness room overlooking the city got nailed by the storm, as you can imagine, but to its benefit, it's now well stocked with the latest elliptical machines.

One of the city's best-kept secrets is the renovated rooftop pool; on a recent visit, we were among a handful of folks lounging on the deck high above the street noise, with unencumbered views of the city and beyond. It's quite a scene, with snacks served there in the evening.

214 Royal St., New Orleans, LA 70130. ✆ **800/535-9595** or 504/523-3341. Fax 504/561-5803. www. hotelmonteleone.com. 570 units. $199–$309 double; $360–$2,500 suite. Extra person $25. Children 17 and under stay free in parent's room. Package rates available. AE, DC, DISC, MC, V. Valet parking $30 car, $35 small SUV and trucks. Pets allowed on the 3rd floor only, for a fee and deposit. **Amenities:** 2 restaurants; 2 bars (Carousel Bar & Lounge, p. 266); babysitting; concierge; fitness center; heated rooftop pool (year-round); room service. *In room:* A/C, TV, hair dryer, minibar, Wi-Fi.

Lafitte Guest House ★   Here you'll find the best of both worlds: antique living just blocks from Bourbon Street mayhem (though the Lafitte's cute little parlor seems almost antithetical to rowdy merriment). The three-story brick building, with wrought-iron balconies on the second and third floors, was constructed in 1849. Each room has its own mostly Victorian flair, with thoughtful touches such as pralines on the pillow and even white-noise machines to handle Bourbon Street ruckus, which is an excellent idea. Some rooms have balconies overlooking Bourbon. Room no. 21 has its own sitting room, while garconerie rooms are smaller and probably best for singles. Room no. 5 is in the old stables in back and has a tiny loft (the ceiling may be a little low for a tall person). It has a wonderful quality, good for a couple wanting a little extra privacy. Breakfast is delivered to wherever you want (your room, your balcony, the courtyard). The owners are committed to supporting their city and now only use products from local vendors. Altogether, a delightful little place, but the prices are a bit steep, considering.

1003 Bourbon St., New Orleans, LA 70116. ℂ **800/331-7971** or 504/581-2678. Fax 504/581-2677. www.lafitteguesthouse.com. 14 units. $179–$269 double. Extra person $25. Rates include continental breakfast. AE, DISC, MC, V. Parking $15. **Amenities:** 24-hr. concierge. *In room:* A/C, TV, fridge (in some rooms), hair dryers available, Wi-Fi.

Maison Dupuy ★   We often forget to recommend this place, but that's a mistake. A little out of the main French Quarter action and a tad closer than some might like to dicey Rampart (though the hotel is entirely safe), the Maison Dupuy, with its seven town houses surrounding a good-size courtyard (and a heated pool), is still warm and inviting. While the rooms aren't remarkable, they are comfortable. Though floor space and balconies (with either courtyard or street views—the former is quieter) vary, the staff is most friendly and helpful, the courtyard of sufficiently pleasing ambience, and the location— a quieter end of the Quarter, near a bar with pool tables (a rarity in town)—puts it right in the middle of the "Oh, they've got rooms available? Why not?" category.

1001 Toulouse St., New Orleans, LA 70112. ℂ **800/535-9177** or 504/586-8000. Fax 504/525-5334. www.maisondupuy.com. 200 units. $99–$269 superior double; $149–$299 deluxe double with balcony; $329–$838 suite. AE, DC, DISC, MC, V. Valet parking $28 for cars, $32 for SUVs and trucks when available. **Amenities:** Restaurant; bar; babysitting; exercise room; heated outdoor saltwater pool; room service. *In room:* A/C, TV, hair dryer, Wi-Fi.

Omni Royal Orleans ★★ (Kids)   Despite being part of a chain, this is an elegant hotel that escapes feeling sterile and generic. This is only proper given that it is on the former site of the venerable 1836 St. Louis Exchange Hotel, one of the country's premier hostelries and a center of New Orleans social life until the final years of the Civil War. The original building was finally destroyed by a 1915 hurricane (it suffered no damage from Katrina), but the Omni, built in 1960, is a worthy successor, enjoying a prime location smack in the center of the Quarter. Truman Capote and William Styron have stayed here, and there is a Tennessee Williams suite. The guest rooms (which are quietly getting paint-and-wallpaper overhauls) have grave good taste, full of muted tones and plush furniture, with windows that let you look dreamily out over the Quarter. Renovations to increase the size of the hotel's smaller rooms began in fall 2009, with "European traditional opulence" somehow reflected in the new furnishings. Suites are vast, making this a good choice for families despite the fancy appearance. Service is swift and conscientious, and there are more amenities available here than in comparable properties. Altogether, an especially worthwhile choice.

621 St. Louis St., New Orleans, LA 70140. ℂ **800/THE-OMNI** (843-6664) in the U.S. and Canada, or 504/529-5333. Fax 504/529-7089. www.omniroyalorleans.com. 346 units. $189–$339 double; $339–$850

suite; $1,200–$1,600 penthouse. Children 17 and under stay free in parent's room. AE, DC, DISC, MC, V. Valet parking $32. **Amenities:** Restaurant; 2 bars; babysitting; concierge; florist; health club; heated outdoor pool; room service; sundries shop and newsstand; emergency mending and pressing; complimentary shoeshine. *In room:* A/C, TV, hair dryer, minibar, newspaper delivery on request, robes, Wi-Fi ($9.95).

St. Louis ★   Right in the heart of the Quarter, the St. Louis is a small hotel that surrounds a lush courtyard with a fountain. But it's somewhat disappointingly dull for what ought to be a charming boutique hotel. Some third-floor rooms have private balconies overlooking Bienville Street, and all open onto the central courtyard. The exterior is looking a little battered, but the standard quality of the rooms seems better than ever thanks to the precipitous drop in price. King rooms are smaller than doubles, and there are far more of the latter (leaving queen-sizes for the single rooms). An additional wing with pricey units featuring parlors and kitchenettes has been added. The otherwise uninteresting bathrooms do have bidets. If the price holds, it's a great deal, especially considering the location.

730 Bienville St., New Orleans, LA 70130. ☎ **800/535-9111** or 504/581-7300. Fax 504/679-5013. www. stlouishotel.com. 96 units. $69–$179 double (seasonal rates higher). Up to 4 people (depending on number of beds) free in room. AE, MC, V. Valet parking $34; self-parking $15–$28. **Amenities:** Restaurant; concierge; newspapers in lobby. *In room:* A/C, TV, hair dryer, Wi-Fi.

Westin New Orleans at Canal Place ★★   At the foot of Canal Street, the Westin is technically *in* the French Quarter—but not quite *of* it. It is literally *above* the Quarter: The grand-scale lobby is on the 11th floor of the Canal Place tower. The views of the Mississippi and French Quarter are unparalleled in the city (and will cost you about $25 more per night; it's worth it!). Rooms are now equipped with the marshmallow delight that is the Westin Heavenly bed. Entirely redone rooms have a boring but clean and fresh contemporary look in neutral colors. Bathrooms are adequately sized, but the tub/shower combo is nothing special, despite the double shower head. The renovated swimming pool has a view of the whole city while the well-equipped gym has up-to-date equipment. It's an easy walk from here to the Convention Center.

100 Iberville St., New Orleans, LA 70130. ☎ **504/566-7006.** Fax 504/553-5120. www.starwood.com/ westin. 438 units. $159–$309 double. Ask about packages and specials. AE, DISC, MC, V. Self-parking $20. **Amenities:** Restaurant; bar; concierge; direct elevator access to Canal Place shopping center w/barbershop, salon, and stores; heated pool; room service. *In room:* A/C, TV, hair dryer, minibar, Wi-Fi ($13/day).

MODERATE

Bienville House ★★   A nice little Quarter hotel, better than most (thanks to a combo of location, price, and room quality), though not as good as some (owing to a lack of specific personality and the odd bit of shabbiness despite a recent overhaul). It's generally sedate, except perhaps during Mardi Gras, when the mad gay revelers take over—as they do everywhere, truth be told. The truly friendly and helpful staff adds a lot of welcoming spirit. If you can score some of the lower-end prices, nab a spot here. Rooms mostly have high ceilings, though some don't have windows, and all have new, comfortable four-poster beds and fresh linens. Some rooms have balconies overlooking the small courtyard that features a pretty saltwater pool (open 24 hr. if guests aren't too rowdy!), and all have the standard amenities of a fine hotel. Note that the Iberville Suite is so large it actually made us laugh out loud—and we mean that in a good way. Also, take note of the excellent restaurant, **Iris** (p. 137).

320 Decatur St., New Orleans, LA 70130. ☎ **800/535-7836** or 504/529-2345. Fax 504/525-6079. www. bienvillehouse.com. 83 units. $99–$189 double; $650 penthouse. Rates include continental breakfast. AE,

Historic Hotel

A lot of hotels claim to be centrally located in the French Quarter, but the **Bourbon Orleans** (review, p. 95) really is. The place takes up an entire block of prime real estate at the intersection of—guess where—Bourbon and Orleans streets. And while many hotels *claim* to have an interesting history, this one actually does: The oldest part of the hotel is the Orleans Ballroom, constructed in 1815 as a venue for the city's masquerade, carnival, and quadroon balls. In 1881 the building was sold to the Sisters of the Holy Family, members of the South's first order of African-American nuns. The sisters converted the ballroom into a school and remained for 80 years until the building was sold to real estate developers from Baton Rouge, who turned it into an apartment hotel.

DC, DISC, MC, V. Parking $20, $25 for SUVs. **Amenities:** Restaurant; afternoon reception w/cookies and punch; outdoor saltwater pool; room service; Wi-Fi (free). *In room:* A/C, TV, hair dryer, Wi-Fi ($9.95).

Bourbon Orleans Hotel ★ This hotel occupies three historic buildings. Ceilings in the rooms feel lower than the frequent high variety found around town, which may be an optical illusion. Beds are too firm while bathrooms are long and narrow with a natty use of stripes and brocades (they feature Golden Door Spa toiletries). Small rooms are cozy but not unbearable, though if occupied by two people, they had better like each other. The rooms for the mobility-impaired are well designed. Some rooms have only armoires, no closets, and some have balconies. Rooms with numbers in the 170s have views up Bourbon Street, but if you want to escape noisy street excitement, ask for an interior room. We are fond of the two-story town house rooms, with exposed brickwork on the walls, and the beds upstairs in a romantic loft. It's classy sexy, good for a multiple-day stay.

717 Orleans St., New Orleans, LA 70116. ✆ **504/523-2222.** Fax 504/525-8166. www.bourbonorleans. com. 218 units. $139–$199 petite queen or twin; $189–$329 deluxe king or double; $239–$489 junior suite; $299–$599 town house suite; $272–$482 town house suite with balcony. Extra person $30. AE, DC, DISC, MC, V. Valet parking $30. **Amenities:** Restaurant (breakfast only); bar; concierge; outdoor pool; room service (breakfast only). *In room:* A/C, TV, fax, hair dryer, Wi-Fi.

Bourgoyne Guest House ⓥ**alue** This is an eccentric place with an owner to match. If you dislike stuffy hotels and will happily take things a little worn at the edges in exchange for a relaxed, hangout atmosphere, come here. Accommodations are arranged around a nicely cluttered courtyard, the right spot to visit and regroup before diving back out onto Bourbon Street (whose main action begins just a few feet away). Studios are adequate little rooms with kitchens and bathrooms that appear grimy but are not (we saw the strong potions housekeeping uses; it's just a result of age). The Green Suite is as big and grand as one would like, with huge, tall rooms, a second smaller bedroom, a bigger bathroom, and a balcony overlooking Bourbon Street. For price and location, it's a heck of a deal, maybe the best in the Quarter. The first floor can suffer from street noise, though that probably depends on the time of year and how far up Bourbon the party travels.

839 Bourbon St., New Orleans, LA 70116. ✆ **504/525-3983** or 524-3621. 5 apts. $93 studio double; La Petite Suite $121 double; Green Suite $131 double, $160 triple, $191 quad. AE, MC, V. *In room:* A/C, unstocked fridge.

Fencing at the Cornstalk Hotel

Thanks to the famous fence out front, the **Cornstalk Hotel,** 915 Royal St. (📞 **800/759-6112** or 504/523-1515; www.cornstalkhotel.com), is a well-known sightseeing stop. It's at least 130 years old (photos indicate it might be even older), is made of cast iron, and looks like cornstalks painted in the appropriate colors. When it was a private home, Harriet Beecher Stowe stayed here— a trip that inspired her to write *Uncle Tom's Cabin.*

Hôtel Provincial ★ Don't mention this to the owners, who are sensitive about it, but word from the ghost tours is that the Provincial is haunted, mostly by soldiers treated here when it was a Civil War hospital. It must not be too much of a problem, though, because guests rave about the hotel and never mention ghostly visitors. With flickering gas lamps, no elevators, no fewer than five patios, and a tranquil setting, this feels less like a hotel than a guesthouse. Both the quiet and the terrific service belie its size, so it seems smaller and more intimate than it is. It's also in a good part of the Quarter on a quiet street off the beaten path. For views of the river (plus higher ceilings), get a room on the third or fourth floor of the back building. Some rooms have half-tester beds (the furniture is a mix of antique and reproductions). Regular rooms are dark but roomy. Finally, with such a pretty pool area, it's a shame there isn't much in the way of lounging or shade.

1024 Chartres St., New Orleans, LA 70116. 📞 **800/535-7922** or 504/581-4995. Fax 504/581-1018. www. hotelprovincial.com. 94 units. $79–$289 double. AE, DC, DISC, MC, V. Valet parking $21. **Amenities:** Restaurant; bar; complimentary continental breakfast; pool. *In room:* A/C, TV, hair dryer, Wi-Fi.

Hotel St. Marie Location, location, location. Just a little above Bourbon Street on an otherwise quiet street, this hotel could be on your list of "clean and safe backup places to stay if my top choices are full." Surrounding a pretty, foliage-and-light-bedecked courtyard with a small pool (which you will bless the heavens for in summer), rooms are generic New Orleans, with dark colors and standard-issue, and mock European hotel furniture. Note that king rooms are more pleasant than doubles, and corner rooms are more spacious, which include the otherwise dinky bathrooms. Some rooms from the original town house have balconies overlooking the street and courtyard. Hallways are not numbered and can be dim, which could make a tipsy late-night return a challenge.

827 Toulouse St., New Orleans, LA 70112. 📞 **800/366-2743** or 504/561-8951. Fax 504/571-2802. www. hotelstmarie.com. 100 units. $49–$199 double, depending on season; higher during special events. AE, DC, DISC, MC, V. Valet parking $25. *In room:* A/C, TV, hair dryer, Wi-Fi.

Hotel Villa Convento ★ Local tour guides say this was the original House of the Rising Sun bordello, so if you have a sense of humor (or theater), be sure to pose in your bathrobe on your balcony so that you can be pointed out to passing tour groups. With its rather small public spaces and the personal attention that its owners and operators, the Campo family, give to their guests, the Villa Convento has the feel of a small European inn or guesthouse and does a lot of repeat business. The building is a Creole town house; some rooms open onto the tropical patio, others to the street, and many have balconies. There is much to be fond of in this place—though parts can be shabbier than one would like and truth be told, it can smell like mold. They now offer free garage parking about 5 blocks away.

616 Ursulines St., New Orleans, LA 70116. (© **800/887-2817** or 504/522-1793. Fax 504/524-1902. www. villaconvento.com. 25 units. $89–$125 double; $125–$165 suite. Extra person $10; no children 9 or under allowed. AE, DC, DISC, MC, V. **Amenities:** Wi-Fi. *In room:* A/C, TV, hair dryer.

Iberville Suites ★★   Part of the sprawling Ritz complex, this can be a heck of a deal, because while the rooms aren't nearly as fancy as at the sister properties, they are still comfortable, and guests get to avail themselves of all the other Ritz amenities for a usually considerably smaller daily rate. By the time you add in the generous continental breakfast and the sparkling service, you are hardly likely to miss the posh factor. Especially during the summer, this may be the best deal in the city, and certainly one to consider for families. Rooms are a tad motel-y, with small but nice bathrooms, but it is good to have a living room with a sleeper sofa and TV. Queen rooms have lighter colors and are prettier.

910 Iberville, New Orleans, LA 70112. (© **866/229-4351** or 504/523-2400. www.ibervillesuites.com. 230 units. $89–$349 double. (Seasonal rates apply.) Rates include continental breakfast. Valet parking $32. Pets welcome with $150 deposit. AE, DC, DISC, MC, V. **Amenities:** 2 restaurants; 2 bars; babysitting; concierge; top-of-the-line spa (w/brand-new treatment rooms) and health club (w/resistance pool, Jacuzzi, and personal trainers; $12 per day); room service. *In room:* A/C, TV, CD player, fridge, Wi-Fi ($13/day).

Lamothe House ★   Somehow, a shiny new hotel doesn't seem quite right for New Orleans. More appropriate is slightly faded, somewhat threadbare elegance, and the Lamothe House neatly fits that bill. The Creole-style plain facade of this 1840s town house hides the atmosphere you are looking for—a mossy, brick-lined courtyard with a fish-filled fountain and banana trees and rooms filled with antiques that are worn in the right places but not shabby. Despite recent interior upgrades, rooms can be dark and small, with clashing decor. Room no. 101 is a grand affair with lots of original plaster frills, though we wish there were good wood floors instead of that carpet. Room no. 117 nearly gets it right in terms of size and style. A continental breakfast is served in a second-floor dining room that just screams faded gentility. It's a short walk to the action in the Quarter and just a couple of blocks to the bustling Frenchmen scene in the Faubourg Marigny.

621 Esplanade Ave., New Orleans, LA 70116. (© **800/367-5858** or 504/947-1161. Fax 504/943-6536. www.lamothehouse.com. 36 units. $65–$199 double. Rates include breakfast. AE, DISC, MC, V. Self-parking $15. **Amenities:** Afternoon brandy; newspaper in lobby; pool. *In room:* A/C, TV, hair dryer, Wi-Fi.

Le Richelieu Hotel ★ (Kids)   First a row mansion, then a macaroni factory, then a hotel, and finally a Katrina victim—this building has seen it all, including part of its roof collapsing. But the latter mess allowed for some new paint (or textured wallpaper), carpet, drapes, and beds, and consequently Le Richelieu looks as good as it ever has (though some rooms still look rather motel-like, thanks to dated mirrored walls). Bathrooms are still the same, only fair, just like any old hotel. Other rooms are standard high-end motel rooms. Many have balconies, and all overlook either the French Quarter or the courtyard. Le Richelieu is good for families (despite the surcharge for children), being away from the adult action and with a nice pool. The McCartney family thought so; Paul, the late Linda, and their kids stayed here for some months long ago while Wings was recording an album. Le Richelieu is the only hotel in the French Quarter with free self-parking on the premises.

1234 Chartres St., New Orleans, LA 70116. (© **800/535-9653** or 504/529-2492. Fax 504/524-8179. www. lerichelieuhotel.com. 86 units. $95–$180 double; $200–$550 suite. Extra person, including children, $15.

Honeymoon and seasonal packages available. AE, DC, DISC, MC, V. Free parking. **Amenities:** Restaurant (breakfast and lunch only); bar; concierge; outdoor pool; room service. *In room:* A/C, TV, unstocked fridge, hair dryer, Wi-Fi.

Place d'Armes Hotel ★ (Kids)   Parts of this hotel seem a bit grim and old, though its quite large courtyard and amoeba-shaped pool are ideal for hanging out and may make up for it. Plus, it's only half a block from the Café du Monde (p. 163)—very convenient when you need a beignet at 3am. This also makes it a favorite for families traveling with kids. Rooms (all nonsmoking) are homey and furnished in traditional style; however, 32 of them do not have windows and can be cell-like—be sure to ask for a room with a window when you reserve. Breakfast is served in a breakfast room, and the location, just off Jackson Square, makes sightseeing a breeze.

625 St. Ann St., New Orleans, LA 70116. ✆ **800/366-2743** or 504/524-4531. Fax 504/571-3803. www. placedarmes.com. 80 units. $59–$219, depending on season. Rates include continental breakfast. AE, DC, DISC, MC, V. Parking $25. **Amenities:** Newspapers; outdoor pool. *In room:* A/C, TV, hair dryer, Wi-Fi.

Prince Conti Hotel ★   This tiny but friendly hotel is in a great location right off Bourbon and not generally noisy. Rooms are decorated with attractive reproduction antiques. They all have high ceilings, some with ceiling fans and exposed brick walls, and are bright and pretty. Flatscreen TVs are a bit incongruous with the antique decor. Bathrooms can be ultra-tiny, with the toilet virtually on top of the sink. Travelers with kids should stay at the hotel's sister location, the Place d'Armes (see above), because it is farther from Bourbon and has a pool.

830 Conti St., New Orleans, LA 70112. ✆ **800/366-2743** or 504/529-4172. Fax 504/636-1046. www. princecontihotel.com. 76 units. $49–$199 double; $119–$299 suite, depending on season. AE, DC, DISC, MC, V. Valet parking $25. **Amenities:** Restaurant; breakfast cafe; piano bar. *In room:* A/C, TV, Wi-Fi (free).

Victorian House ★   This longtime B&B (formerly the Old Victorian Inn, and before that, PJ Holbrook's Old Victorian Inn—and at some point before that, possibly a brothel!) has benefited from some spiffing up by the most recent owners, though longtime clients will recognize many of the furnishings. Set around a mossy brick courtyard, it feels very New Orleans, again in a manner that seems to be disappearing from the city. All rooms have queen-size beds, antiques, elaborate comforters, and deep dark-wood floors. There are claw-foot tubs in all but the Somerset room, the smallest of the accommodations—it's quite wee. The yellow Gentilly room has a romantic balcony overlooking Rampart, and a nice bathroom. Breakfast is simple. We do like the collection of NOLA-related movies, as well as the bikes available for guest use at no charge.

914 N. Rampart, New Orleans, LA 70116. ✆ **866/408-5311** or 504/218-5661. www.victorianhousenola. com. 7 units. $79–$220 double. Rates include continental breakfast. MC, V. Self-parking $15 (at Garlands Inn down Rampart if available). **Amenities:** Computer in lobby; newspapers. *In room:* TV, DVD player, Wi-Fi.

INEXPENSIVE

New Orleans Guest House ★   Run for many years by Ray Cronk and Alvin Payne, this guesthouse is a little off the beaten path (just outside the French Quarter across N. Rampart St.), but it's painted a startling hot, Pepto-Bismol pink, so it's hard to miss. Top floor and back rooms have been redone, mostly to fine, funky, and fun effect, all in a way that is classic NOLA guesthouse, in a manner that is being lost to generic good taste. Main-house rooms are dark colored, sometimes with gaudy new bathrooms, but sweet, and room no. 8 has an outrageous Art Nouveau bedroom suite. The slave quarters are simpler but with interesting antiques and light colors. Some rooms have exposed brick walls, while others open directly on to the green plant-stuffed courtyard, a veritable tropical garden, with some intricately carved old fountains. There is a 24-hour desk clerk and two gray kitties are now in place!

1118 Ursulines St., New Orleans, LA 70116. ℭ **800/562-1177** or 504/566-1177. Fax 504/566-1179. 14 units. $59–$79 double; $69–$99 queen or twin; $89–$109 king or 2 full beds. Rates include continental breakfast. All rooms nonsmoking. Extra person $15. AE, MC, V. Free parking. *In room:* A/C, TV, hair dryers available, Wi-Fi.

3 THE FAUBOURG MARIGNY

The Faubourg Marigny is very distinct from the French Quarter, though they border each other and are just an easy walk apart. This arty and bohemian neighborhood may be better for a younger crowd who wants to be near the French Quarter without actually being in it. If you stay in the farther reaches of it, however, please either take a cab or be very cautious returning at night; the neighborhood has suffered from crime problems lately.

For hotels in this section, see the "New Orleans Accommodations" map on p. 84.

MODERATE

B&W Courtyards Bed & Breakfast ★★   The deceptively simple facade hides a sweet and very hospitable little B&B, complete with two small courtyards and a fountain. It's located in the Faubourg Marigny next to the bustling nighttime Frenchmen scene, a 10-minute walk or short cab ride to the Quarter. Owners Rob Boyd and Kevin Wu went to ingenious lengths to turn six oddly shaped spaces into comfortable rooms. No two rooms are alike—you enter one through its bathroom. Another room is more like a small, two-story apartment with the bedroom upstairs and a virtually full kitchen downstairs. All are carefully and thoughtfully decorated and have recently been given a cosmetic overhaul. Rob (who designs jewelry, some of which has been worn by Mary J. Blige, Kanye West, and Oprah) and Kevin (a trained masseuse who can treat you in your room) are adept at giving advice—and strong opinions—not just about the city but about their own local favorites. Breakfast is light (fruit, homemade granola) but beautifully presented. If you are visiting to volunteer for Habitat for Humanity or the St. Bernard Project, they offer a special rate.

2425 Chartres St., New Orleans, LA 70117. ℭ **800/585-5731** or 504/945-9418. Fax 504/949-3483. www.bandwcourtyards.com. 6 units. $99–$250 double. Rates include continental breakfast. AE, DISC, MC, V. Free parking available on street. **Amenities:** Hot tub. *In room:* A/C, flatscreen TV, hair dryer, MP3 docking station, robes, Wi-Fi.

The Frenchmen Hotel ★   This is seen by some as a small, sweet, and slightly funky inn, very popular with in-the-know regular visitors who think of it as quintessential New Orleans. Some others think it's a total dump. The latter may not be any more pleased by the all-new rooms, but we are. It's just across from the Quarter and a block away from the main drag of the Frenchmen section of the Faubourg Marigny, where all sorts of clubs and happenings make for a lively night scene. Housed in two 19th-century buildings, the rooms vary in size considerably (rooms with two beds are quite large), and some are very small indeed. Each has its own rather eccentric, bright new paint color, plus old-timey prints or paintings, and new mattresses. They are a big improvement. First-floor rooms have tile floors, and some rooms have new large TVs. It still smells a bit musty, though, like old Quarter hotels. There is a small, newly cleaned-up pool and Jacuzzi in the inn's tropical courtyard. They have a carb-heavy (muffins, pastries, bagels, cereals) breakfast.

417 Frenchmen St. (at Esplanade Ave.), New Orleans, LA 70116. ℭ **504/948-2166.** Fax 504/948-2258. www.frenchmenhotel.com. 27 units. $59–$299 double. Rates include breakfast. AE, DISC, MC, V. Parking $15. **Amenities:** Jacuzzi; pool. *In room:* A/C, TV, Wi-Fi.

INEXPENSIVE

Royal Street Inn & R Bar ★★   This is an offbeat, happening little establishment on the edge of the so-happening Frenchmen street scene. It's loose but not disorganized, and there couldn't be a better choice for laid-back travelers. B&B stands for bed-and-*beverage*—the lobby is the highly enjoyable **R Bar** (p. 269), and as a guest, you get two complimentary cocktails.

A long overdue stripped-to-the-walls redo of the rooms (converting them all into sometimes rather wee "suites" with separate sitting areas) gave this place the hip, clever, fresh look it totally deserves coupled with a great New Orleans vibe. Leather couches, exposed brickwork, gorgeous gleaming wood floors, geometric colors—sure, most of the rooms are small, and two open onto the street, but if you are looking for something special in New Orleans, it's hard to beat. Accommodations in the attic is a big room with sloping ceilings, pleasing for those with starving-artist garret fantasies. Couples traveling together may love the smashing suite, with two large bedrooms and its own balcony; it's perfect for those wanting a party with its own accessible bar.

1431 Royal St., New Orleans, LA 70116. ℭ **800/449-5535** or 504/948-7499. Fax 504/943-9880. www.royalstreetinn.com. 5 units. $75–$250 double. Price includes tax; rates include bar beverage. AE, DISC, MC, V. Street parking available—purchase special permit from management. **Amenities:** Bar. *In room:* A/C, TV, DVD player, hair dryer, MP3 docking station, Wi-Fi.

4 MID-CITY/ESPLANADE

For hotels in this section, see the "Mid-City Accommodations & Dining" map on p. 101.

EXPENSIVE

The House on Bayou Road ★★   If you want to stay in a rural and romantic plantation setting but not be far from the action, try what is quite possibly the most smashing guesthouse in town. Just off Esplanade Avenue, this intimate 1700s Creole plantation home, one of the most distinctive accommodations in a city full of curious places to stay, is romantic and peaceful, yet only a few minutes away by car from the Quarter.

Each room has its own charm and is individually decorated to a fare-thee-well—slightly cluttered, not quite fussy but still lovingly done aesthetic. The Bayou St. John Room (the old library) holds a queen-size four-poster bed and a working fireplace; the Bayou Delacroix has the same kind of bed and a wonderfully large bathtub. The large cottage has four rooms that can be rented separately or together (perfect for a large family). The private cottage has been rebuilt post-Katrina, and is even larger and better than before. The unusually extensive grounds are beautifully manicured and there's an outdoor pool, patio, and screened-in porch. Expect a hearty plantation-style breakfast. *Note:* At press time, the property was for sale—thus, anything could change by the time you read this.

2275 Bayou Rd., New Orleans, LA 70119. ℭ **800/882-2968** or 504/945-0992. Fax 504/945-0993. www.houseonbayouroad.com. 8 units, 2 cottages. $155–$305 double, with summer specials available online. Rates include full breakfast. AE, DISC, MC, V. Free off-street parking. Children 13 and older welcome. **Amenities:** Outdoor pool. *In room:* A/C, TV, hair dryer, minibar, robes and slippers, Wi-Fi.

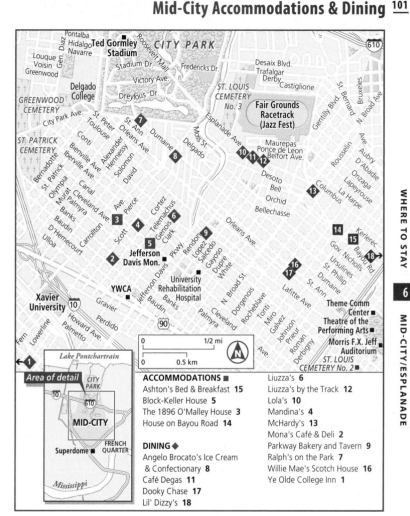

ACCOMMODATIONS ■

Ashton's Bed & Breakfast **15**
Block-Keller House **5**
The 1896 O'Malley House **3**
House on Bayou Road **14**

DINING ◆

Angelo Brocato's Ice Cream
 & Confectionary **8**
Café Degas **11**
Dooky Chase **17**
Lil' Dizzy's **18**

Liuzza's **6**
Liuzza's by the Track **12**
Lola's **10**
Mandina's **4**
McHardy's **13**
Mona's Café & Deli **2**
Parkway Bakery and Tavern **9**
Ralph's on the Park **7**
Willie Mae's Scotch House **16**
Ye Olde College Inn **1**

MODERATE

Ashtons Bed & Breakfast ★★   This charming guesthouse represents one of the gutsiest ventures in the city. Another Katrina victim, their chimney collapsed and 5,000 bricks tore a gaping hole in their top story, causing all kinds of mayhem inside. And yet, it's been fully restored to great beauty and effect, and is a fine and worthy alternative to some of its more costly compatriots. There are pretty custom-paint treatments like shadow striping on top of new molding and chandeliers, and the whole effect is bright, cheerful, and handsome. All the rooms have wide wooden floorboards and inviting beds. Room no. 4's bed has a half canopy, while room no. 1's bathroom is contained in a curtained-off corner. A full breakfast is served, featuring such fun as bananas Foster waffles and sweet-potato-stuffed French toast. They sell artistic glassware (some featured on the breakfast table) and their excellent robes. They worked hard to come back; join them in celebrating.

2023 Esplanade Ave., New Orleans, LA 70116. © **800/725-4131** or 504/942-7048. Fax 504/947-9382. www.ashtonsbb.com. 8 units. $119–$179 double; $179–$209 for Mardi Gras and special events; $229–$259 during Jazz Fest; call for off-season specials. Rates include full breakfast. AE, DISC, MC, V. Free secure parking. **Amenities:** Complimentary soft drinks. *In room:* A/C, TV, hair dryer, robes, Wi-Fi.

Block-Keller House ★★   This inn was extensively restored with an eye toward both guest comfort and preservation of the full Victorian aesthetic. It's a splendid choice for someone who wants both the classic Victorian B&B experience (look for period excess in the front rooms' gorgeous details) but also guiltily wants a room with modern amenities (Berber carpet, Jacuzzi tubs, and the like). If that's you, stay upstairs in the absurdly large top-floor rooms. However, if you do desire traditional surroundings, the ground-floor rooms, with fireplaces and grand old beds, are for you. You'll find comfy communal sitting areas upstairs and in the bottom level. Room nos. 3 and 5 are large, while room no. 4 has a window seat. The gardens are stunning. All in all, this place is perfect in looks, style, and service—plus, it's a block away from Mandina's restaurant (p. 147) and right on the Canal streetcar line, making it an easy hop to either the Quarter or City Park, where the end of the line is just blocks from the racetrack and Jazz Fest. And say hello for us to sweet Milo and Buster, the black and yellow labs.

3620 Canal St., New Orleans, LA 70119. © **877/588-3033** or 504/483-3033. Fax 504/483-3032. www.blockkellerhouse.com. 5 units. $125–$165 double. (Special events higher, seasonal rates lower.) Rates include breakfast. Special packages on website. AE, MC, V. **Amenities:** Coffee and tea service; fridge and microwave access; newspaper. *In room:* A/C, TV, hair dryer, Wi-Fi.

1896 O'Malley House ★★   One of the most smashing B&Bs in the city, just a treasure inside, full of gorgeous antiques and repro furniture. Although it's located on a dull stretch of street and in a neighborhood gradually returning post-flood (though there are increasingly all kinds of newly restored Mid-City options close by), the B&B is also mere minutes from a nice section of Canal and a streetcar ride to the Quarter. Many of the original details, including marvelous tile on the various fireplaces in several of the rooms, are still intact. The handsome, somewhat masculine (as opposed to frilly) rooms are each meticulously decorated, using clever touches such as vintage (at least appearing) oil paintings, Bali puppets, and European art. Second-floor rooms are larger, and most have Jacuzzi tubs. The third floor is a clever use of design and space, with formerly dull wood walls turned most striking by pickling the wood to a lighter color (ask to see the photos of the mysterious science equations found scrawled on one wall). These rooms are smaller and more garretlike, though they pale in desirability only if you really, *really* want that classic high-ceilinged look.

120 S. Pierce St., New Orleans, LA 70119. © **866/226-1896** or 504/488-5896. www.1896omalleyhouse. com. 9 units. $135–$155 double; $200 special events such as Mardi Gras and Jazz Fest; call for special summer rates. Rates include breakfast, complimentary beer, wine, and soft drinks. AE, MC, V. *In room:* A/C, flatscreen TV w/built-in DVD player, hair dryer, Wi-Fi.

5 CENTRAL BUSINESS DISTRICT

At first glance, the CBD seems too generic big city for a proper New Orleans stay. And while it is true that many of its hotels blur together in terms of style, quality is consistent, and you can get very good rates here compared to prices just across Canal. It's an easy walk to the Quarter, but given the increasing number of more moderately priced, and excellent, restaurants in the area, you may not care. For hotels in this section, please see the "New Orleans Accommodations" map on p. 84.

VERY EXPENSIVE

Harrah's ★   If you've had any experience with Vegas hotels, you would know this new (built post-Katrina) property was casino-owned. New Orleans doesn't lack for impressive, grand hotels, but there is something so . . . *big* . . . about the Harrah's lobby that it passes right through grand and into something almost too immense to be truly elegant. Which isn't to knock the place; everyone did a good job. The rooms are sharp, if a touch generic, though photos by local artist Richard Sexton and splashes of Mardi Gras purple and gold help. Rooms are all pretty much the same size, except for the larger corner suites. Those don't offer enough extra to justify the price. Rooms ending in nos. 1 to 10 have romantic river views, while city views aren't anything special. There is an airy gym with a tall ceiling and windows, well stocked with a good mix of aerobic and weight machines. Naturally, it's right across from the casino. *Tip:* Since this is a casino property, special deals are offered to players club members. The on-site restaurant is Ruth's Chris.

228 Poydras St. ℂ **800/VIP-JAZZ** (847-5299) or 504/533-6000. www.harrahs.com. 450 units. $149–$449 double, though can vary depending on events. $30 additional person. AE, DC, DISC, MC, V. Valet and self-parking $34. **Amenities:** Restaurant; 2 bars; babysitting; car service (w/fee); concierge; gym; room service. *In room:* A/C, TV, Web TV, CD player, fridge, hair dryer, newspaper, robes, turndown, umbrellas, Wi-Fi ($12/day).

Hilton New Orleans Riverside Hotel ★ (Kids)   The Hilton is in the neighborhood of the Windsor Court (see below) but in a more central location—right at the riverfront near the New Orleans Convention Center and the aquarium. It's a self-contained complex of nearly a dozen restaurants, bistros, and bars; two gift shops; two pools; a full and exceptional racquet-and-health club; a huge exhibition space; and no fewer than 38 conference rooms. In addition, Harrah's Casino and the Riverwalk Marketplace are accessible from the hotel's lobby, which contains a nine-story atrium. Rooms are spacious (double-bedded rooms are smaller), but a tiny bit dull, though the now completed renovations—adding marble tops to some furniture, new white bedding, and plasma TVs—helped. Parlor rooms have rather awesome versions of Murphy beds with hydraulics lifts! River views (usually with even-numbered rooms) are astonishing, though higher is always better. Given all that, this is a good choice for families—there is much in the way of child-friendly entertainment right in the hotel or within a block or two—but not terrific for those with mobility issues, given the sheer size of the place.

2 Poydras St., New Orleans, LA 70140. ℂ **800/445-8667** or 504/561-0500. Fax 504/568-1721. www. neworleans.hilton.com. 1,600 units. $139–$409 double; $750–$2,500 suite. Special packages and some lower seasonal rates available. AE, DC, DISC, MC, V. Valet parking $35; self-parking $31. **Amenities:** 3 restaurants; 3 bars; airport transportation; concierge; eligibility for membership ($12/day, comped for Hilton club members) in the hotel's Rivercenter Racquet and Health Club; room service. *In room:* A/C, flatscreen TV, hair dryer, minibar, turndown, Wi-Fi ($15/day).

InterContinental New Orleans ★   The red-granite Hotel InterContinental rises from the heart of the Central Business District within walking distance of the French Quarter and the Mississippi River attractions. It's a favorite of groups (including rock groups; the Rolling Stones have stayed here) and conventions. It's an old-fashioned—or what passes for that in this brave new Ian Schrager–ized world—business hotel, clearly targeting a certain kind of traveler who isn't impressed by the hip minimalists springing up everywhere. There is no better place to camp out for Mardi Gras, particularly since the Rex parade stops right in front. Rooms are done in dark-wood furniture (mattresses are nothing special) with similarly woodsy strong golds and reds; bathrooms can be small but dignified. Call it masculine in a slightly frilly way. All the rooms are decently sized, but the doubles (especially corner doubles) are somewhat larger, and "deluxe kings" are larger still, with patio balconies (overlooking office buildings, alas). Some rooms have balconies that overlook the modern and industrial courtyard.

444 St. Charles Ave., New Orleans, LA 70130. ✆ **800/327-0200** or 504/525-5566. Fax 504/585-4350. www.new-orleans.intercontinental.com. 479 units. $200–$429 double; $500–$2,500 suite. AE, DC, DISC, MC, V. Valet parking $29. **Amenities:** Restaurant; Pete's Pub serving lunch daily; coffee, sweets, and sandwich bar; bar; concierge; gift shop; health club; outdoor rooftop pool; room service; Wi-Fi (free) in lobby. *In room:* A/C, TV, hair dryer, minibar, robes.

JW Marriott Hotel New Orleans ★ You can't fault the location on Canal right across from the Quarter (excellent for viewing Mardi Gras parades). But ultimately it's classy but boring—yes, we're spoiled—more for business travelers who don't plan on spending much time in their rooms. New NOLA-specific touches such as local photos and drawings are appreciated, as are the thickly made beds. The public areas are far more grand than the actual rooms. Bathrooms are dinky, though amenities are good. Corner "deluxe" king rooms (usually numbered 04 and 09) have extra windows for an additional view, though higher up is best. The fitness center is decent sized and there is a Don Shula Steakhouse on the property.

614 Canal St., New Orleans, LA 70130. ✆ **888/771-9067** or 504/525-6500. Fax 504/586-1543. www. jwmarriottneworleans.com. 494 units. $189–$355 double; $750–$1,500 suite. AE, DC, DISC, MC, V. Valet parking $32. **Amenities:** Restaurant; 2 bars; concierge; gift shop; health club; heated outdoor pool; room service. *In room:* A/C, TV, hair dryer, minibar, newspaper, Wi-Fi ($15/day).

Loft 523 ★ Located in an old carriage and dry-goods warehouse, each of the 18 lofts is a marvel of modern design, sort of a *Jetsons*-futuristic-meets-NYC-minimalist fantasy. They are sleek and handsome ("superior" and "leisure" are larger than "deluxe" but smaller might be better, given the following), but those wanting plushy and overstuffed will be miserable as soon as they see the concrete floors. Beds are platforms, surprisingly comfortable with Frette linens (but just a chenille throw blanket over that; ask for the down comforters if the night brings a chill). The bathrooms are so big you could fit the entire ReBirth Brass Band inside. (Check out that Agape "spoon" tub.) Yet throughout are reminders of the building's provenance—old wood planks form the floor downstairs, turn-of-the-20th-century tin ceiling tiles outfit the elevators, and columns from the old warehouse decorate the lounge. Note that there may be some room service, but it's spotty—all the food comes from the International House's restaurant, down the street.

523 Gravier St., New Orleans, LA 70130. ✆ **800/633-5770** or 504/200-6523. Fax 504/200-6522. www. loft523.com. 18 units (3 of them penthouses). $259–$359 double; $859–$1,100 suite. Look for way-low online seasonal specials. AE, DC, DISC, MC, V. Valet parking $32, SUVs $38. **Amenities:** Lounge; computer in lobby; health club; newspaper. *In room:* A/C, TV, DVD, hair dryer, MP3 docking stations, remote-control stereo system, Wi-Fi.

Windsor Court ★★ Pre-Katrina, *Condé Nast Traveler* voted the Windsor Court the Best Hotel in North America (and probably did it a disservice—who, after all, could ever live up to such hype?). And post-? It's still mighty fine. There's a reason this remains the center of high New Orleans society, from traditional afternoon tea to fancy dinners before or after some significant society function. It's that kind of place. Two corridors

Spending the Night in Chains

For those of you who prefer the predictability of a chain hotel or are gambling that generic lodgings get overlooked during popular events, there's a perfectly okay **Marriott** ★ at 555 Canal St., at the edge of the Quarter (© 800/654-3990 or 504/581-1000). A **Sheraton** at 500 Canal St. (© 504/525-2500) is also a good bet.

In the Central Business District (CBD), check out the **Holiday Inn Express,** 221 Carondelet St. (© 504/962-0800), or consider the slightly spiffier **Cotton Exchange** next door at 231 Carondelet St. (which is now part of the Holiday Inn), in the historic building of the same name (© 504/962-0700). **Residence Inn by Marriott** ★, 345 St. Joseph St. (© 800/331-3131 or 504/522-1300), and **Courtyard by Marriott** ★, 300 Julia St. (© 888/703-0390 or 504/598-9898), are both a couple of blocks from the convention center. The **Homewood Suites,** at 901 Poydras St., is pretty dazzling, in a cookie-cutter way (© 800/225-4663 or 504/581-5599), while the **Quality Inn,** at 210 O'Keefe Ave., seems clean and fine (© 877/525-6900 or 504/525-6800).

Still need a last-minute emergency reservation? Here's a bunch more, all more or less CBD or adjacent: **Comfort Suites** (346 Baronne St.; © 800/524-1140 or 504/524-1140), **Country Inn and Suites by Carlson** (315 Magazine St.; © 800/456-4000 or 504/324-5400), **Embassy Suites** (315 Julia St.; © 504/525-1993), **Hampton Inn and Suites** (1201 Convention Center Blvd.; © 866/311-1200 or 504/566-9990), **La Quinta Inn and Suites** (301 Camp St.; © 800/531-5900 or 504/598-9977), and **SpringHill Suites by Marriott** (301 St. Joseph St.; © 800/287-9400 or 504/522-3100).

And if all the rooms in town are booked, you might try to see if one of the chains down by the airport has something for you.

downstairs are mini-galleries that display original 17th-, 18th-, and 19th-century art. Everything here is very, very traditional and serene, though not unwarm. It's not too stiff for restless children, though it still feels more like a grown-up hotel. The accommodations, admittedly showing a touch of wear, are exceptionally spacious, with classy, not flashy, decor. Almost all are suites (either really big or downright huge) featuring large bay windows or a private balcony overlooking the river (get a river view if at all possible) or the city, a private foyer, a large living room, a bedroom with French doors, a large marble bathroom with particularly luxe amenities, two dressing rooms, and a "petite" kitchen. Some rooms have flatscreen TVs.

300 Gravier St., New Orleans, LA 70130. © **800/262-2662** or 504/523-6000. Fax 504/596-4749. www. windsorcourthotel.com. 322 units. $149–$520 standard double; $179–$550 junior suite; $199–$600 full suite. Children 16 and under stay free in parent's room. Packages available. AE, DC, DISC, MC, V. Valet parking $30. **Amenities:** Restaurant; lounge; concierge; health club w/resort-size pool; hot tub; suite service (much more than your average room service). *In room:* A/C, TV, hair dryer, minibar, robes, Wi-Fi.

W New Orleans ★★ While we have strong feelings indeed about staying in more New Orleans–appropriate, site-specific accommodations, we cheerfully admit that this is one fun hotel, and what is New Orleans about if not fun? There are certainly no more-playful rooms in town, done up as they are in black, plum, and white—frosty chic, to be sure, but oh, so comfortable, thanks to feather everything (pillows, comforters, beds—and yes, allergy sufferers, they have foam alternatives). There are nifty amenities and gewgaws galore; suites offer little difference from the rooms except more space and, indeed, more of everything (two bigger TVs, two DVD players). Not all rooms have views, but the ones that do, especially those of the river, are outstanding. The ultrachic bar was designed by hip bar/club owner Rande Gerber. We do wish this whole experience wasn't so, well, New York, but then again, we find ourselves having so much fun, it's kinda hard to get all that worked up about it.

333 Poydras St., New Orleans, LA 70130. ☎ **800/522-6963** or 504/525-9444. Fax 504/581-7179. www. whotels.com. 423 units. $179–$469 double. AE, DC, DISC, MC, V. Valet parking $28. **Amenities:** Restaurant; bar; concierge; fitness center; pool; room service. *In room:* A/C, 32-in. flatscreen TV/DVD, CD player, hair dryer, minibar, MP3 docking stations, Wi-Fi ($11/day).

EXPENSIVE

Hilton St. Charles ★   The site of the old Masonic Temple, and the second skyscraper in the city (after the Hypernia building), this establishment was taken over by Hilton in 2007 (it was the Hotel Monaco), and it keeps making improvements and upgrades. It's not as whimsical as in its former hotel incarnation, but it's a lot more memorable than the other Hilton in town. Rooms still have some pizazz in the form of wild prints and designs, plus black marble vanities in the spacious bathrooms (tubs are small, though), fresh new bedding, Lavazza coffee and Crabtree & Evelyn bath products. Corner-room doubles have extra space perfect for non-couple traveling partners. Upgrades to suites start at $60—if that rate's available, go for it. The smashing wood deck that overlooks the city is sure to become a nighttime hot spot, and the wedding chapel (the only hotel-based one in town) still carries its Masonic roots. The terrific restaurant Lüke is reviewed on p. 153.

333 St. Charles Ave., New Orleans, LA 70130. ☎ **504/524-8890.** www.hhneworleansstcharles.com. 250 units. $109–$389 double; $169–$450 suite. AE, DC, DISC, MC, V. Valet parking $32. **Amenities:** Restaurant; bar; babysitter; concierge; health club; indoor pool; room service; wedding chapel; Wi-Fi. *In room:* A/C, TV, hair dryer, MP3 docking station, newspaper.

International House ★★★   The International House sets the local standard for modern hotels with its creative design and meticulous attention to detail. Record-company and film execs love it, but so should anyone who's had enough of Victorian sweetness and needs a palate cleanser. Here, a wonderful old Beaux Arts bank building has been transformed into a modern space that still pays tribute to its locale. Consequently, in the graceful lobby, classical pilasters stand next to modern wrought-iron chandeliers. Interiors are the embodiment of minimalist chic. Rooms are simple with muted, monochromatic (okay, beige) tones, tall ceilings and ceiling fans, up-to-the-minute bathroom fixtures, but also black-and-white photos of local musicians and characters, and other clever decorating touches that anchor the room in its New Orleans setting. The commitment to hip, neat, cool, and groovy means dark corridors and hard-to-read room numbers, and although the big bathrooms boast large tubs or space-age glassed-in showers, they do come off as a bit industrial.

221 Camp St., New Orleans, LA 70130. ☎ **800/633-5770** or 504/553-9550. Fax 504/553-9560. www. ihhotel.com. 117 units. $149–$379 double; $369–$1,799 suite. Look for special deals online. AE, DC, DISC, MC, V. Valet parking $32 cars, $38 SUVs. Hotel is entirely nonsmoking. **Amenities:** Restaurant; bar; concierge; health club; newspaper; room service. *In room:* A/C, TV, CD player, fridge, hair dryer, Wi-Fi.

Le Cirque   A smart, sharp, and chic version of the generic business hotel—sort of like a Crowne Plaza, if it was done up in chartreuse and that new misty gray-blue that's all the rage. Oddly, it's not set up as a business hotel, lacking amenities such as separate dataports and even room service, but it does offer 4,000 square feet of meeting space. Rooms are average size; the ones with king-size beds are a bit cramped thanks to all the furniture jammed in along with the beds (chair, desk, TV). Queen rooms are even smaller. A wine bar with *tapas* and small plates provides a dining option.

936 St. Charles Ave., New Orleans, LA 70130. ℂ **888/211-3447** or 504/962-0900. Fax 504/962-0901. www.neworleansfinehotels.com/hotellecirque. 138 units. $69–$299 double. AE, DC, DISC, MC, V. **Amenities:** Bar; babysitting; concierge. *In room:* A/C, TV, hair dryer, Wi-Fi.

Loews New Orleans Hotel ★★   Swanky. Ooo-la-la. These are the words that spring to mind as you enter the stylish Loews hotel. It's a sharp-dressed combo of modern and *moderne*, with judiciously applied sprinkles of New Orleans flavor. Whatever it is, we are quite smitten. The rooms are all spacious, starting with the "Delux" rooms, at 346 square feet—bright and decorated with art by a local photographer, with goose-down comforters and pillows. Bathrooms are small, but granite and wood vanities make up for the lack of space. "Grand Luxury" rooms and bathrooms are bigger (and more costly, naturally). Views vary from river to partial river plus piazza to New Orleans city skyline, which get better the higher up you go. Note that the hotel's lowest floor is the 11th, so this is not the choice for those with vertigo or other high-floor issues. There is also a steamy indoor pool and a good-size workout room that could use more machines, plus the excellent restaurant Café Adelaide and the Swizzle Stick bar. Possibly best of all: Loews has a company-wide "Loews Loves Pets" policy, which practically encourages Fido to come join in the fun.

300 Poydras St., New Orleans, LA 70130. ℂ **800/23-LOEWS** (235-6397) or 504/595-3300. www.loews hotels.com. 285 units. Delux unit $129–$500; Grand unit $159–$600. AE, DC, DISC, MC, V. Valet parking $29. Pets allowed ($25 pet cleaning fee). **Amenities:** Restaurant; bar; babysitting; concierge; pool; room service; spa; workout room. *In room:* A/C, TV, CD player, hair dryer, minibar, umbrella, video games, Wi-Fi ($13/day).

The Pelham   This small hotel, in a renovated building that dates from the late 1800s, is one of the new wave of boutique hotels. From the outside and in its public areas, the Pelham feels like an upscale apartment building. Centrally located rooms are generally less bright than those on the exterior of the building. Some rooms have sitting areas, some have four-poster kings and old-fashioned art on the walls, most have high ceilings, all have boring bathrooms. The staff is nice, so it's worth considering if you can get the low-end price.

444 Common St., New Orleans, LA 70130. ℂ **888/211-3447** or 504/522-4444. Fax 504/539-9010. www. thepelhamhotel.com. 60 units. $79–$299 double. AE, DC, DISC, MC, V. Valet parking $28. **Amenities:** Restaurant; concierge. *In room:* A/C, TV, hair dryer, Wi-Fi ($4.95/day).

Renaissance Arts Hotel ★   The Arts Hotel is so named because it's at the border of the Arts District and attached to a branch of Arthur Rogers, a well-respected local gallery. Don't expect painters in the lobby, splattering like Pollock or staging suspicious performance-art gags. What "arts" means here is that the designers made a concerted effort to incorporate art, specifically local art, into the decor. On first glance, it just seems like a throwback to 1970s business hotels (thanks to an atrium) with the simple addition of some brightly colored modern art. But the theme gets stronger once you enter the hallways, and comes into stronger focus in the rooms, which are hung with the works of several Louisiana artists (from Lafayette-based Francis Pavy to New Orleans's highly recommended Studio Inferno glassworks). The rooms are well sized (look for a connecting room to get extra square footage) and include down pillows and covers. The hotel has a dull rooftop pool with a view of industrial New Orleans, and a health club with adequate elbowroom.

700 Tchoupitoulas St., New Orleans, LA 70130. ✆ **504/613-2330.** Fax 504/613-2331. www.marriott.com. 217 units. $229–$299 double, call for specials. AE, DC, DISC, MC, V. Valet parking $28. **Amenities:** Restaurant; bar; babysitting; concierge; gift shop; health club; newspaper delivery; pool; room service; Wi-Fi. *In room:* A/C, TV, hair dryer.

St. James Hotel ★ Actually, this is two different buildings, one of which used to be—get this!—the St. James Infirmary, sung about so memorably by many a mournful jazz musician. Either that, or an old coffee and sugar company. (Whichever.) A new semi-Caribbean post-K redo gives the place a touch more style than the fresh white-bed generic look popping up all over town. Look for parrots, palm trees, and even monkey-shaped pull chains on the lamps. Rooms vary in size and style, and a few lack windows. Rooms in the back building have high ceilings. Rooms have either painted texture or, on the top floor, exposed brick and wood. All have feather beds, soft towels, and marble bathrooms. Two suites and a room share a small, private brick courtyard with a fountain—a nice setup for a small group. There is a teeny-weeny pool—you might be forgiven for considering it really just a large puddle with nice tile. The hotel's restaurant is Cuvée, reviewed on p. 151.

330 Magazine St., New Orleans, LA 70130. ✆ **888/211-3447** or 504/304-4000. www.saintjameshotel. com. 86 units. $109–$299 double. AE, DC, DISC, MC, V. Valet parking $25. **Amenities:** Restaurant; concierge; pool. *In room:* A/C, TV, CD player, hair dryer, Wi-Fi.

The Whitney—A Wyndham Historic Hotel ★ A clever and welcome use of space as a grand old bank building has been converted into a fine modern hotel. The unique results include gawk-worthy public spaces; be sure to look up at all the fanciful, wedding-cake-decoration old plasterwork (they don't make 'em like that anymore—pity) and help us wonder how the heck safecrackers got past those thick slabs of doors. Best of all is the imposing lobby, full of stately pillars (doubtless the grandeur intimidated many a loan applicant of yesteryear), now part restaurant but also still part working bank—it puts other swellegant establishments in town to shame.

Rooms are a little too stately to classify as true business efficient, but also a little too generic to make this a proper romantic getaway. The restaurant is currently a branch of local Creole/soul favorite Lil' Dizzy's. Overall, the Whitney has more character than your average upscale chain, so it ultimately gets a positive vote. And if you are a preservationist, you will probably like it a lot.

610 Poydras St., New Orleans, LA 70130 ✆ **504/581-4222.** www.wyndhamneworleanshotels.com. 93 units. $79–$399 double. AE, DC, DISC, MC, V. Valet parking $28. **Amenities:** Private dining room; lobby bar; fitness center. *In room:* A/C, TV, CD player, hair dryer.

MODERATE

Best Western St. Christopher New Orleans by way of a chain hotel—but a good design for all that. Exposed brick walls in rooms help slightly relieve the generic quality. Bathrooms feel new if still cramped. Check out the punning painting in the lobby (there's a visual joke; see if you get it), which is attached to a courtyard-inspired (if indoors) bar that works better than you might think. This is a great location for Mardi Gras celebrations, and easy access to the Quarter, CBD, and Uptown.

114 Magazine St., New Orleans, LA 70130-2421. ✆ **504/648-0444.** Fax 504/648-0445. www.stchristopher
hotel.com. 108 units. $89–$299 double, seasonally. Rates include continental breakfast. AE, DC, DISC, MC,
V. Parking $28. Pet friendly. **Amenities:** Off-site fitness center; newspapers in lobby. *In room:* A/C, TV, hair
dryer, Wi-Fi (free).

Drury Inn & Suites ★ (Value)   This family-owned chain looks all too generic outside,
but inside is a pleasant surprise, with grander-than-expected public spaces and rooms
that are fancier than those in the average chain, not to mention new beds. All have high
ceilings (except for those on the fifth floor) and a decent amount of square footage,
though rooms on the first floor can be dark with zero views. Bathrooms are small (with
sinks in the dressing area). There is a nice little heated rooftop pool plus a small exercise
room. Free popcorn and sodas are offered from 3 to 10pm, and a nachos-and-wine snack
service goes from 5:30 to 7pm, touches that encourage guest socializing. Look for more
specials, like 1 hour of free long-distance calling per night. All that plus a friendly staff
and a generous comp breakfast makes this not a bad little bargain for the area.

820 Poydras St., New Orleans, LA 70112-1016. ✆ **800/DRURY-INN** (378-7946) or 504/529-7800. Fax 504/
581-3328. www.druryhotels.com/properties/neworleans.cfm. 156 units. $109 regular room; $139 suite.
Rates include full breakfast and weekday evening beverages. AE, DC, DISC, MC, V. Parking $15. **Ameni-
ties:** Exercise room; heated pool. *In room:* A/C, TV, fridge, hair dryer, microwave, whirlpool tubs in some
suites, Wi-Fi.

Lafayette Hotel ★   Built as a hotel in 1915, with some of the earliest indoor plumbing and telephones for such an establishment, this is a cute place that is only getting
better as they renovate their rooms. Out is the English botanicals; in is French Regency—
think pale blues and greens, reproduction photos and paintings, and other simple but
thoughtful touches. The new carpets are a bit blah, but the effect of the rest is fresh and
charming. Get a new room, that's the point. The second floor has some balconies, just
right for watching Mardi Gras parades. This is the right place for those who want something more than a B&B but don't quite want the generic quality that comes with a chain
or business-oriented hotel. All rooms are kings except king suites. Suites offer a living
room with foldout couches and some have minibars/fridges.

600 St. Charles Ave., New Orleans, LA 70130. ✆ **504/524-4441.** www.neworleansfinehotels.com/the
lafayettehotel. 44 units. $109–$459 king; $129–$499 king suite. (Seasonal rates apply.) AE, DISC, MC, V.
Amenities: Concierge; newspaper. *In room:* A/C, TV, CD player, hair dryer, robes, Wi-Fi.

Le Pavillon Hotel ★★   Established in 1907 in a prime CBD location, Le Pavillon
was the first hotel in New Orleans to have elevators. It's now a member of Historic Hotels
of America, and it feels like elegant old New Orleans in a way that, sadly, so few places
now do. The lobby is stunning, just what you want in a big, grand hotel, with giant
columns and chandeliers. The standard guest rooms are all rather pretty and have similar
furnishings, but they differ in size. Deluxe rooms have ceiling fans, detailed ceiling painting, and black granite bathrooms. "Bay Rooms" are standard with two double beds and
bay windows. Suites are actually hit-or-miss in terms of decor, with the nadir being the
mind-bogglingly ugly Art Deco Suite. Much better is the Plantation Suite, decorated
in—you guessed it—antiques. The Honeymoon Suite has "Napoleon's" marble bathtub
and is a riot of fantasy hilarity. Note the statues by the pool. Late-night peanut-butter-
and-jelly sandwiches, one of New Orleans's sweetest traditions, are offered in the lobby.
Tip: Covet those suites? If you are staying during a slow period, ask at check-in about
upgrades—they may offer you some incredible deal.

833 Poydras St., New Orleans, LA 70112. ℂ **800/535-9095** or 504/581-3111. Fax 504/522-5543. www.lepavillon.com. 226 units. $149–$319 double; $199–$1,695 suite. AE, DC, DISC, MC, V. Valet parking $28. **Amenities:** Restaurant; bar; babysitting; concierge; fitness center and whirlpool spa; heated outdoor pool; room service; spa service. *In room:* A/C, TV, hair dryer, minibar, robes, Wi-Fi.

INEXPENSIVE

The Depot at Madame Julia's ★ Ⓕinds   A low-budget alternative to more commercial hotels in the Central Business District. Then again, it may be full of volunteer groups helping to rebuild the city when you call. Low prices and a guesthouse environment mean a number of good things—including rooms with character and a proprietor who loves to help guests with all the details of their stay—but it also means shared bathrooms, rooms on the small and cozy side, virtually no amenities, and a location that, although quiet on the weekends, can get noisy in the mornings as the working neighborhood gets going. The neighborhood is hit-or-miss, but more of the former than the latter thanks to artsy Julia Street. A mere 7 blocks (safe in the daytime) from the Quarter, it's a quick walk or a short streetcar/bus ride, which makes it an affordable alternative to the Quarter's much more expensive accommodations. The budget-conscious and those who prefer their hotels with personality will consider this a find.

748 O'Keefe St., New Orleans, LA 70113. ℂ **504/529-2952.** Fax 504/529-1908. 15 units, all with shared bathrooms. $65–$85 double. Rates include continental breakfast. Cash or personal checks only (if paid in advance). Off-street parking available. *In room:* A/C.

6 UPTOWN/THE GARDEN DISTRICT

For hotels in this section, see the "Uptown Accommodations & Dining" map on p. 111 or the "New Orleans Accommodations" map on p. 84.

EXPENSIVE

The Grand Victorian Bed & Breakfast ★★   A former crumbling Queen Anne–style Victorian mansion right on the corner of Washington (2 blocks from Lafayette cemetery and Commander's Palace with a streetcar stop right in front) is now a fine B&B. The location makes its porches and balconies a perfect place to spend Mardi Gras; parade viewing doesn't come any more comfortable or convenient. The stunning rooms are full of antiques (each has an impressive four-poster or wood canopy bed—though a couple are small thanks to their vintage), with the slightly fussy details demanded by big Victorian rooms. Linens, pillows, and towels are ultraplush, and some bathrooms have big Jacuzzi tubs. The largest room—our favorite—overlooks the street corner (and has its own St. Charles–view balcony) and so is potentially noisy. You can always request one toward the back. A generous continental breakfast is served, and friendly owner Bonnie is ready with suggestions on how to spend your time. Though Bonnie does live on the third floor, she is not always there, so as in any B&B, do not expect 24-hour service.

2727 St. Charles Ave., New Orleans, LA 70130. ℂ **800/977-0008** or 504/895-1104. Fax 504/896-8688. www.gvbb.com. 8 units. $150–$300 double. Rates include continental breakfast. AE, DISC, MC, V. *In room:* A/C, TV, hair dryer, Wi-Fi.

Magnolia Mansion ★★   Don't you want to stay in an archetypal big, white Southern mansion? With a large veranda, perfect for sittin' a spell? Sure you do! This hilarious and alluring B&B features huge public rooms splashed with plaster curlicues and Victorian

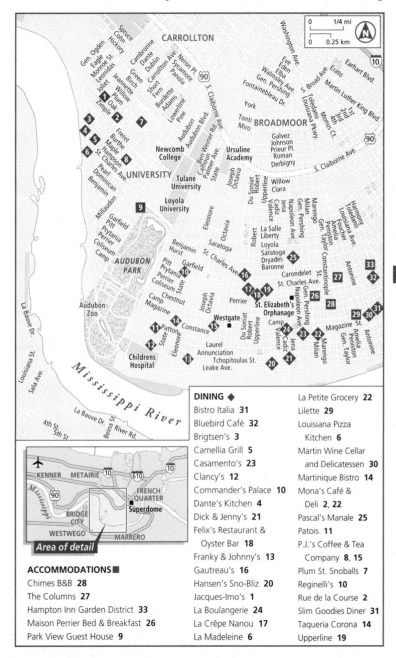

WHERE TO STAY

6

UPTOWN/THE GARDEN DISTRICT

DINING ◆

Bistro Italia **31**
Bluebird Café **32**
Brigtsen's **3**
Camellia Grill **5**
Casamento's **23**
Clancy's **12**
Commander's Palace **10**
Dante's Kitchen **4**
Dick & Jenny's **21**
Felix's Restaurant &
 Oyster Bar **18**
Franky & Johnny's **13**
Gautreau's **16**
Hansen's Sno-Bliz **20**
Jacques-Imo's **1**
La Boulangerie **24**
La Crêpe Nanou **17**
La Madeleine **6**

La Petite Grocery **22**
Lilette **29**
Louisiana Pizza
 Kitchen **6**
Martin Wine Cellar
 and Delicatessen **30**
Martinique Bistro **14**
Mona's Café &
 Deli **2, 22**
Pascal's Manale **25**
Patois **11**
P.J.'s Coffee & Tea
 Company **8, 15**
Plum St. Snoballs **7**
Reginelli's **10**
Rue de la Course **2**
Slim Goodies Diner **31**
Taqueria Corona **14**
Upperline **19**

ACCOMMODATIONS■

Chimes B&B **28**
The Columns **27**
Hampton Inn Garden District **33**
Maison Perrier Bed & Breakfast **26**
Park View Guest House **9**

furniture, while the theatrical guest rooms are the owner's imagination run amok. With the exception of the appropriately named Napoleon's Retreat, downstairs rooms are bigger, with 15-foot ceilings and elaborately explored decor. The black, blood red, and green Vampire's Lair is your Gothic fantasy, while the front bridal room is the largest. Upstairs rooms are smaller and not quite as over-the-top, but are similar bonbons of delight, with their own murals (such as the Storyville room or the Princess room, featuring one Cinderella and her coach), and many have extra twin beds.

2127 Prytania St. (at Jackson), New Orleans, LA 70130. ☎ **504/412-9500.** Fax 504/412-9502. www. magnoliamansion.com. 9 units. $125 and up double, depending on time of year. Rates include breakfast. AE, DISC, MC, V. Guests must be 21 or older; no children. *In room:* A/C, TV w/VCR or DVD, hair dryer, robes.

Maison Perrier Bed & Breakfast ★★ Decorated with art by local artists and run by genuinely friendly folk, the splashy, good-looking rooms feature antique elements and the breakfast room features Abita Amber on tap. It all adds up to very likable accommodations. The rooms have good beds with high-quality linens, well-appointed bathrooms, and nearly all have whirlpool tubs. The Lillian suite is quite spacious and includes a double Jacuzzi tub. The least impressive room is also the cheapest, a modest space just off the kitchen. A hearty cooked breakfast (with delicacies like praline French toast and puff pancakes) is offered by the resident chef, and there is a fully stocked honor bar, along with a weekend wine-and-cheese party and daily snacks like fresh-baked brownies.

4117 Perrier St. (2 blocks riverside from St. Charles Ave., 3 blocks downtown from Napoleon Ave.), New Orleans, LA 70115. ☎ **888/610-1807** or 504/897-1807. Fax 504/897-1399. www.maisonperrier.com. 14 units. $130–$260 double. Rates include tax and breakfast. AE, DISC, MC, V. Parking available on street, free limited on-site parking as well. **Amenities:** Concierge; free parking. *In room:* A/C, TV w/DVD player, CD players, hair dryer, Wi-Fi.

The McKendrick-Breaux House ★★ Each room in this likable B&B is done in impeccable good taste, with high-quality mattresses and pillows, and each has its own style; the ones in the main house have claw-foot tubs and (sadly nonworking) fireplaces. Room no. 36 is the largest but also has the most traffic noise. Third-floor rooms (reached by a steep, narrow staircase) evoke classic garret quarters, with exposed brick walls and less of that traffic noise, thanks perhaps to lower ceilings and fewer windows (we swoon over room no. 38). Rooms in the second building are somewhat larger; the first-floor units are slightly more modern in appearance (but have large bathrooms), which is probably why we like the ones on the second floor (especially the front room, and the deep-purple walls and bright-green bathroom wainscoting of the Clio room). A full breakfast featuring local and farmers market ingredients has been added, and the staff doesn't skimp on suggestions for how to spend your time in the city they love.

1474 Magazine St., New Orleans, LA 70130. ☎ **888/570-1700** or 504/586-1700. Fax 504/522-7134. www. mckendrick-breaux.com. 9 units. $145–$235 double. Rates include tax and breakfast. AE, DC, DISC, MC, V; cash or check preferred. Limited free off-street parking. **Amenities:** Jacuzzi in courtyard. *In room:* A/C, TV, hair dryer, Wi-Fi.

Queen Anne ★ A somewhat different take on lodging from the same folks who bring you the Prytania Park Hotel (see below), this was a one-family home for 130 years. The owners had to pass muster with the mayor, the governor, and the park service when they renovated it, and the result is perhaps the grandest building for a B&B in town. Furnishings are a bit sterile, however—hotel-room furniture masquerading as antique (though mattresses are top-of-the-line). The Queen Anne is not our first choice for decor, but the stately rooms (each of which has some exquisite detail like beautifully tiled nonworking fireplaces or 10–14 ft. ceilings) pull it off. The tiniest room has quite a large bathroom, while the three attic rooms are too conventional to be worth your while. The inn is nicely located near the Mardi Gras parade route. The phones are answered "Prytania Park." **Note:** No children allowed, and you must be over 25 to rent a room here.

1625 Prytania St., New Orleans, LA 70130. Registration is at the Prytania Park Hotel on Terpsichore St. btw. Prytania St. and St. Charles Ave. ✆ **800/862-1984** or 504/524-0427. Fax 504/522-2977. www.thequeen anne.com. 12 units. $99–$129 double; $159–$179 during special events. Rates include continental break-fast. AE, DC, DISC, MC, V. Free self-parking. **Amenities:** Wi-Fi (free). *In room:* A/C, TV, unstocked fridge, hair dryer, microwave.

MODERATE

Chimes B&B ★★★ (Finds) This is a real hidden gem, one that truly allows you to experience the city away from the typical tourist experience. The Chimes is in a less-fashionable but more neighborhood-like portion of the Garden District, just 2 blocks off St. Charles Avenue. Jill and Charles Abbyad have run this B&B for over 20 years, and their experience shows.

Rooms vary in size from a generous L-shape to a two-story loft type (with a very small bathroom) to some that are downright cozy. All have antiques but are so tastefully under-decorated, particularly in contrast to other B&Bs, that they are positively Zen. An ambi-tious continental breakfast is served in the hosts' house. The Chimes has made improvements designed for the business traveler, and all we need to say is laptop + court-yard = working bliss. One recent guest, a veteran of many New Orleans hotels, spent 1 night and proclaimed that on subsequent trips she would stay nowhere else but here.

1146 Constantinople St., New Orleans, LA 70115. ✆ **504/899-2621** or 453-2183 (owner's cell). Fax 504/ 899-9858. www.chimesneworleans.com. 5 units. $130–$160 double in season; $99–$140 double off season; rates can go higher during special events. Rates include breakfast, tax, parking. Look for rates, availability, and featured specials online. AE, MC, V. Limited free off-street parking. Well-behaved pets accepted, with prior approval; please call to discuss. *In room:* A/C, TV, hair dryer, Wi-Fi.

The Columns ★ The Columns interior was used by Louis Malle for his film about Storyville, *Pretty Baby.* Built in 1883, the building is one of the city's greatest examples of a late-19th-century Louisiana residence. The grand, columned porch is a highly popu-lar evening scene thanks to the bar inside. The immediate interior is utterly smashing; we challenge any other hotel to match the grand staircase and stained-glass-window combi-nation. We wish still more had been done to make the upstairs match that smashing downstairs; it's still a bit too dark and the color schemes are not that great. The totally renovated third floor looks more modern, mostly to good and comfortable effect. The Pretty Baby room has no discernable nods to its ostensible theme (nor does the Bellocq), but it does have a nice garret sitting area. We particularly like room no. 16, with its grand furniture and floor-to-ceiling shutters that lead out to a private, second-story porch. The Columns is worth the money if you can get a low rate, but otherwise, come by for a drink. Smoking is not permitted in the rooms.

3811 St. Charles Ave., New Orleans, LA 70115. ✆ **800/445-9308** or 504/899-9308. Fax 504/899-8170. www.thecolumns.com. 20 units. $120–$173 double Mon–Thurs, $160–$230 Fri–Sun. Rates include full breakfast. AE, DISC, MC, V. Parking available on street. Pet friendly (call to make arrangements). **Ameni-ties:** Bar; newspaper. *In room:* A/C, TV, hair dryer, Wi-Fi.

Hampton Inn Garden District This is a top choice for a chain hotel, if you don't mind being a bit out-of-the-way. The public areas are slightly more stylish than those found in other chains, and there are welcome touches like free coffee in the lobby and complimentary cheese and tea served daily from 5 to 7pm. The style does not extend to the rooms, however, which are pretty mundane. But they're not *that* bad (mustard-colored walls excepted). There are all kinds of personality-enhancing details (decent photos for artwork, ever-so-slight arts-and-crafts detailing on furniture, and big TVs) hidden in that bland color scheme.

3626 St. Charles Ave., New Orleans, LA 70115. ✆ **800/426-7866** or 504/899-9990. Fax 504/899-9908. www.neworleanshamptoninns.com. 100 units. $129–$179 double. Rates include continental breakfast with hot items, free local calls, and free incoming faxes. AE, DC, DISC, MC, V. Free parking. **Amenities:** Small outdoor lap pool. *In room:* A/C, TV, fridge, hair dryer, microwave, Wi-Fi (free).

INEXPENSIVE

Park View Guest House ★   Built in the late 1800s as a boardinghouse for the World Cotton Exchange, this is an inn crossed with a B&B, which means a front desk staffed 24/7 and proper public areas. But it's far uptown, so if you can't live without Bourbon Street and bars mere steps from your hotel entrance, then this is not the place for you. Otherwise, the stunning location on St. Charles (with a streetcar stop just opposite, so it's easy to get to and from the Quarter), with views right across to Audubon Park, makes it well worth considering. Still, we wish they were more careful with their decor, a mix of antiques and sometimes truly bad modern furniture—witness no. 19, a spacious room with a balcony, claw-foot tub, and fireplace with glazed tiles, and some god-awful 1980s motel-room furniture. If this sort of aesthetic mistake bothers you, you are better off with no. 9 (two antique wood beds, nice old fireplace, large balcony, new bathroom) or no. 17 (bigger bathroom, better furniture). Most of the rooms are spacious, and those downstairs, while just off the public areas, are grander still. New bathrooms mean only a few shared ones remain.

7004 St. Charles Ave., New Orleans, LA 70118. ✆ **888/533-0746** or 504/861-7564. Fax 504/861-1225. www.parkviewguesthouse.com. 20 units, 19 with private bathroom. $109–$159 double. (Special-event rates higher.) Rates include continental breakfast. Extra person $10. AE, DISC, MC, V. Parking available. **Amenities:** Coffee available throughout the day; newspaper in dining room. *In room:* A/C, TV, hair dryers available, Wi-Fi.

Prytania Park Hotel   This 1840s building (which once housed Huey Long's girlfriend) is now equal parts motel and funky simulated Quarter digs. Rooms vary: Some have been redone to the owner's pride (adding darker wood tones and four-poster beds plus bathrooms that still have a Holiday Inn feel), but we kind of prefer the older section with its pine furniture, tall ceilings, and nonworking fireplaces. All rooms have lots of good reading lights. Some units have balconies or loft bedrooms (accessible by spiral staircases). Those without the loft can be small, and the dark-wood furniture makes it a bit ponderous. The hotel is currently remodeling all of the rooms; new paint, curtains, furnishings, and mattresses will be the result. Rooms closer to the lobby have better Wi-Fi reception.

1525 Prytania St. (enter off Terpsichore St.), New Orleans, LA 70130. ✆ **800/862-1984** or 504/524-0427. Fax 504/522-2977. www.prytaniaparkhotel.com. 62 units. $79–$90 double, depending on season. Extra person $10. Rates include continental breakfast. Children 18 and under stay free in parent's room, must be 21 to check-in. Seasonal rates and special packages available. AE, DC, DISC, MC, V. Off-street free parking available. *In room:* A/C, TV, fridge, microwave, Wi-Fi.

St. Charles Guest House ★   Our first choice for budget travelers or the less-than-picky folks who have spent time in European pensions and aren't looking for the spick-and-span hotel experience. You can't beat the quiet, pretty location, simply because it gets you out of the engulfing Quarter and into a different part of town. Rooms are plain and vary wildly in size—from reasonably spacious to "small and spartan" (the management's words)—and also range from low-end backpacker with no air-conditioning to larger chambers with air-conditioning and private bathrooms. Room no. A-5, with twin beds in a separate room, is perfect for a family. A bonus is the banana-tree-lined courtyard with a pool. While it's still a little musty smelling, here you can pay very little for a good-size room with a mix of antiques and new furnishings and humble bathrooms with bright green or yellow tile. It's a little crumbly in places, but it's still one of the best values in town.

1748 Prytania St., New Orleans, LA 70130. ℭ **504/523-6556.** Fax 504/522-6340. www.stcharlesguest house.com. 35 units, 23 with private bathroom. $45–$95 double. Rates include continental breakfast. No credit cards. Parking available on street. **Amenities:** Outdoor pool. *In room:* Wi-Fi (in most), no phone.

Where to Dine

New Orleans restaurant matriarch

Miss Ella Brennan says that whereas in other places, one eats to live, "In New Orleans, we live to eat." Never was that more apparent than when the first high-profile restaurant—as it happens, a Brennan family restaurant called Bacco—reopened in the French Quarter post-Katrina. You can only imagine what that meant for the spirits and souls of the intrepid locals. And the restaurants keep on coming; by nonscientific count, there are more restaurants in the non-flooded, basic tourist areas than there were pre-Katrina.

While it's wonderful that nearly all the high-profile folks have returned, New Orleans cuisine is not just about old-line fancy-pants places. It's also about the corner po' boy shops, and Miss Willie Mae's Scotch House, home to fried chicken so heavenly she was celebrated by a major culinary organization not long before the floodwaters destroyed her restaurant. In one of the shows of grace that emerge from adversity, local restaurateurs and others banded together to help her rebuild, with one vowing he wouldn't rest until that first plate of chicken was served. That's the kind of dedication to food and community that makes New Orleans.

You are going to want to eat a lot here. And then you are going to want to talk about it. After being in New Orleans for just a short amount of time, you will find yourself talking less about the sights and more about the food—if not constantly about the food: what you ate already, what you are going to be eating later, what you wish you had time to eat. We are going to take a stand and say to heck with New York and San Francisco: New Orleans has the best food in the United States. (Some natives will gladly fight you if you say otherwise.)

We have to admit that neither the cuisine nor the cooking of New Orleans is all that innovative, with some exceptions. Many places are variations on either Creole or Italian (or both), and a certain sameness, if you are paying attention, can creep onto menus. Further, there is a long-time citywide tradition wherein on those occasions a new dish does arrive, once it gains enough local credence, it then becomes a "standard"—in other words, you can count on seeing it all over the place. This accounts for the omnipresence of shrimp rémoulade on fried green tomatoes, white-chocolate bread pudding, and a few other new "classics."

This may sound like we are denigrating the food of New Orleans. Believe us. We don't do that. It will take you a while to notice any menu repetition, about the same amount of time it will take you to emerge from a coma that is brought on by equal parts butter sauce and pleasure.

This is the city where the great chefs of the world come to eat—if they don't work here already. Many people love to do nothing more than wax nostalgic about great meals they have had here, describing entrees in practically pornographic detail. It is nearly impossible to have a bad meal in this town; at worst, it will be mediocre, and with proper guidance, you should even be able to avoid that.

Please keep in mind that all times and prices in the following listings are subject to change as restaurants may still have issues with staffing or other economic ups and downs that may cause them to change hours on a whim. You should call in advance to ensure the accuracy of anything significant to you.

While it is true that the New Orleans food scene is dominated by places like Commander's Palace, it is also true that New Orleans food is a classic shrimp or hot sausage po' boy, dressed, of course, and a nectar snoball from a local family that has been making those things for generations. Places like that are brave to make a comeback, so if you see one open, take a chance and stop in. Tell them you are glad they are there. Ask 'em where you ought to eat next.

1 BEST DINING BETS

It's always hard to quantify such things as restaurant comparisons, particularly in a town that has so many wonderful choices. Below is a list to guide you.

Some of you may wonder why there are no "Best Cajun" and "Best Creole" categories. Our feeling was that New Orleans has no exceptional Cajun restaurants (they're adequate at best), and just about everyone has a different definition of Creole cooking, so narrowing it down was nearly impossible. When we consulted with hard-core New Orleans foodies who like nothing more than debates of this nature, loud discussions broke out, names were called, fists were waved in the air. When the dust settled, a compromise was met—"Best Contemporary Creole." But even that caused some to wail, "But those restaurants aren't Creole!" and the whole thing started up again.

- **Best Innovative Restaurant:** In a town full of shrimp rémoulade on top of fried green tomatoes, and fish topped with crabmeat (not that we dislike either dish!), there is **Cuvée,** 322 Magazine St. (© **504/587-9001**), where someone has paid attention to Thomas Keller and then gone off on their own, foie gras crème brûlée direction. See p. 151.
- **Best Neighborhood Restaurant:** (And the winner of Best Breakfasts and Best Dish: the praline bacon) **Elizabeth's,** 601 Gallier St. (© **504/944-9272**), serves monster portions of delicious and curious food and is just flat-out wonderful. See p. 144. A little farther to the north is **Liuzza's by the Track,** 1518 N. Lopez St. (© **504/218-7888**), contender for "City's Best Gumbo" and home to gorgeous salads and fat, perfect po' boys. Everything one could want in a neighborhood joint. See p. 148.
- **Best Neighbahood Restaurant:** You know, the old neighbahood where the locals still ask, "Hey, dahwlin', wheah y'at?" This category is a tossup between the Italian and Creole dishes at **Mandina's,** 3800 Canal St. (© **504/482-9179**), and those found at **Liuzza's,** 3636 Bienville St. (© **504/482-9120**), though the deep-fried dill pickle slices at the latter may tip the scales. See p. 147 and 146.
- **Best Late-Night Choice: Green Goddess,** 307 Exchange Pl. (© **504/301-3347**), the most unusual restaurant in the French Quarter, is a tiny place serving innovative cuisine based on local seasonal ingredients and truly global flavors. You have to experience it to believe it. Because it's open until midnight Thursday through Sunday, it means you can drop in any old time for some divine snacks. See p. 136.
- **Best Wine List:** The wine cellar at **Brennan's,** 417 Royal St. (© **504/525-9711**), was entirely lost in the storm, but they are dedicated to rebuilding and once again reclaiming the title of "unsurpassed in New Orleans." (Prices range $20–$1,000.) See p. 131.

• **Best for Kids:** Take them to **Café du Monde,** 800 Decatur St. (© 504/525-4544), where getting powdered sugar all over yourself is half the fun. It's large and open-air, and street performers are always around. See p. 163.

- **Best Gumbo:** More fighting words, but you can't go wrong at **Dooky Chase,** 2301 Orleans Ave. (© **504/821-0600**), which has reopened for takeout and occasional dine-in, or **Galatoire's,** 209 Bourbon St. (© **504/525-2021**). See p. 146 and 133.

- **Best Barbecued Shrimp:** That's Cajun-style, in a spicy, garlicky butter sauce, and while **Pascal's Manale,** 1838 Napoleon Ave. (© **504/895-4877**), invented it (and has the largest shrimp), we think the sauce at **Bourbon House Seafood,** 144 Bourbon St. (© **504/522-0111**), is sublime. If only the two elements could be combined. And for fans, **Liuzza's by the Track** (see above) does it on a po' boy! See p. 159, 131, and 148, respectively.

- **Best Oysters:** Or "ersters," as the locals would say, and then they would insist that **Felix's Restaurant & Oyster Bar,** 739 Iberville St. (© **504/522-4440**), has the best, unless they insist that **Acme Oyster House,** 724 Iberville St. (© **504/522-5973**), does. We think they are identically good and figure the real winner is **Casamento's,** 4330 Magazine St. (© **504/895-9761**). See p. 140, 139, and 160, respectively.

- **Best Steaks:** They're prime and they're darn near perfect over at **Dickie Brennan's Steakhouse,** 716 Iberville (© **504/522-2467**). See p. 132,

- **Best Contemporary Creole:** We are totally in love with **Café Adelaide,** 300 Poydras St. (© **504/595-3305**), which, pre-Katrina, was a very good restaurant, and is now a great one. See p. 151.

- **Best Italian:** We almost hate to tell you, because there are already too many people ahead of us in line (they don't take reservations), but New Orleans's strong Italian presence is best represented at **Irene's Cuisine,** 539 St. Philip St. (© **504/529-8811**). Get there early or expect a wait. Or don't bother with a wait: **Tommy's Cuisine,** 746 Tchoupitoulas St. (© **504/581-1103**), is owned by one of Irene's original creators, features a nearly identical menu, and takes reservations! See p. 136 and 154.

- **Best Classic New Orleans Restaurant:** Of the three mainstays of New Orleans dining (the others being Galatoire's and Antoine's; p. 133 and 128), **Arnaud's,** 813 Bienville St. (© **504/523-5433**), is the one where you can count on getting a consistently good (and maybe even great) meal in the same way, and in the exact same surroundings, that generations of New Orleanians have done before you. See p. 128.

- **Best Desserts:** Desserts in New Orleans tend to run to the familiar; everyone serves bread pudding or flourless chocolate cake. But there are places (often run by people named Brennan) that stray into more interesting territory with practically Bacchanalian choices. There is the banana cream pie at **Emeril's,** 800 Tchoupitoulas St. (© **504/528-9393**), which reduces grown men to quivering fools. Others are brought to their knees by the white-chocolate bread pudding at the **Palace Café,** 605 Canal St. (© **504/523-1661**). Try 'em all and decide for yourself. See p. 149 and 153, respectively.

- **Best Barbecue:** With an increasing presence in town, the competition is strong, but we say the dry rub and falling-apart meat is the proof that **Bywater Barbeque & Deli,** 3162 Dauphine St. (© **504/944-4445**), is worth searching out. See p. 144.

- **Best Classic Creole Soul Food:** This traditional local cuisine is well represented at **Lil' Dizzy's,** 1500 Esplanade Ave. (© **504/569-8997**), where the lunch specials draw waiting crowds. (They have a branch in the Whitney Wyndham Hotel.) See p. 147.

- **Best Burgers:** Locals swear by **Port of Call,** 838 Esplanade Ave. (© **504/523-0120**), but its cow-size half-pounder might be too much for some. We throw the vote to the more manageable and messy juicy delight at **Stanley,** 457 St. Ann St. (© **504/593-0006**). See p. 138 and 143.

- **Best Bistro:** French and German cuisine crisply conceived and executed at the **Lüke** (in the Hilton St. Charles, 333. St. Charles Ave.; © **504/378-2840**)—we want to go again and again in the hopes of eating our way through the menu.

- **Best Outdoor Dining:** Go to **Bayona,** 430 Dauphine St. (© **504/525-4455**), to eat the fabulous food in the beautiful, quiet, and fairly secluded courtyard. It's especially delightful on starry nights or balmy spring afternoons. See p. 130.

- **Best Po' Boys:** The drippy monster creations at **Mother's,** 401 Poydras St. (© **504/523-9656**), are the bomb and the buttah. But don't overlook the roast beef po' boy at the **Parkway Bakery and Tavern,** 538 Hagan St. (© **504/482-3047**). See p. 154 and 148, respectively.

- **Best Muffulettas:** You really haven't had a sandwich until you've tried a muffuletta, and no one beats **Central Grocery,** 923 Decatur St. (© **504/523-1620**). See p. 142.

- **Best Sazerac:** This famous locally invented cocktail can be found all over the city, but connoisseurs agree that **Arnaud's,** 813 Bienville St. (© **866/230-8892**), tops the pack right now—though as of this writing, the bartenders at **Bayona,** 430 Dauphine St. (© **504/525-4455**), and **Tommy's Cuisine,** 746 Tchoupitoulas St. (© **504/581-1103**), seem to have learned their lessons well. See p. 128, 130, and 154, respectively.

- **Best Original Dessert:** Lilette, 3637 Magazine St. (© **504/895-1636**), serves little rounds of goat-cheese crème fraîche with poached pears, and it's a combo made for the gods. See p. 159.

---

2 A TASTE OF NEW ORLEANS

Boy, does this city love to eat. And boy, does it offer visitors a range of choices. Thanks to influences from French Provincial, Spanish, Italian, West Indian, African, and Native American cuisines, it covers the whole span from down-home Southern cooking to the most creative and artistic gourmet dishes. New Orleans is one of the few cities in America that can justify a visit solely for cooking and cuisine.

Many of the famous dishes here started out as provincial French recipes brought to the New World by early settlers. Native Americans introduced the settlers to native herbs and filé (ground sassafras leaves); the Spanish added saffron and peppers to the mix somewhat later. From the West Indies came new vegetables, spices, and sugar cane, and when slave boats arrived, landing many black women in the kitchens of white slave owners, an African influence was added. Out of all this came the distinctive Creole culinary style unique to New Orleans. Later, Italian immigrants added yet another dimension to the city's tables. In addition, many traditional Old South dishes remain on menus. Keep your eyes peeled for the now rare "Wop salad" (containing olives, shrimp, and asparagus, topped with anchovies), a contribution of the aforementioned Italian population, and a victim of political correctness, even though said Italians didn't mind the name (in this context) a bit.

From this international past, residents of New Orleans have inherited a love of exciting culinary combinations, and from the city's old-world traditions, they've retained an appreciation for fine service in elegant surroundings. There are lots of ironies here, too; you can get gourmet dishes served in the plainest of settings and plain meals (such as boiled crawfish or red beans and rice) in the fanciest of eateries. New Orleanians are

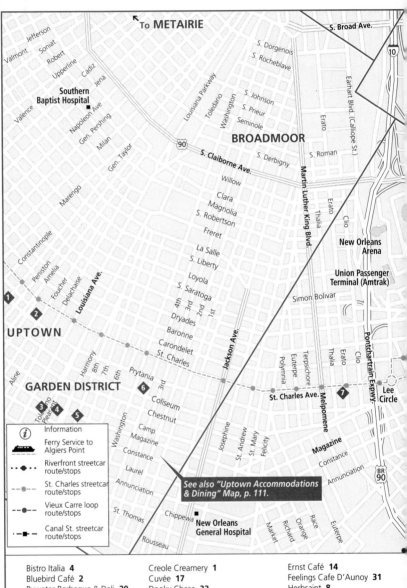

To **METAIRIE**

Jefferson
Valmont Soniat
Robert
Upperline
Cadiz
Jena

Southern
Baptist Hospital

Valence Napoleon Ave
Gen. Pershing
Milan
Gen. Taylor
Marengo

Louisiana Parkway
Toledano
Washington
Seminole

S. Dorgenois
S. Rocheblave

S. Broad Ave.

S. Johnson
S. Prieur

BROADMOOR

Earhart Blvd. (Calliope St.)
Erato

10

S. Claiborne Ave. S. Derbigny
S. Roman
Willow
Clara
Magnolia
S. Robertson
Freret
La Salle
S. Liberty
Loyola
S. Saratoga
4th 3rd 2nd 1st
Dryades
Baronne
Carondelet
St. Charles

Martin Luther King Blvd.
Erato
Thalia
Clio

**New Orleans
Arena**

**Union Passenger
Terminal (Amtrak)**

Simon Bolivar

Constantinople
Peniston
Amelia
Foucher
Delachaise
Louisiana Ave.

UPTOWN

Harmony
Aline 8th 7th 6th
GARDEN DISTRICT

Toledano Prytania
Pleasant 3rd
Coliseum
Chestnut
Camp
Magazine
Constance
Laurel
Annunciation
St. Thomas
Rousseau

1
2

3 **4** **5**

6

Jackson Ave.

Josephine
St. Andrew
St. Mary
Felicity

Polymnia
Euterpe
Terpsichore
Melpomene
Thalia
Erato
Clio

Pontchartrain Expwy.

St. Charles Ave.
7
Lee
Circle

Magazine
Constance
Annunciation

BR
90

Chippewa ■ **New Orleans
General Hospital**

Race
Orange
Richard
Market
Euterpe

*See also "Uptown Accommodations
& Dining" Map, p. 111.*

(i) Information
🚢 Ferry Service to
Algiers Point
•–•–• Riverfront streetcar
route/stops
St. Charles streetcar
route/stops
Vieux Carre loop
route/stops
•–■–• Canal St. streetcar
route/stops

Bistro Italia **4**	Creole Creamery **1**	Ernst Café **14**
Bluebird Café **2**	Cuvée **17**	Feelings Cafe D'Aunoy **31**
Bywater Barbeque & Deli **29**	Dooky Chase **23**	Herbsaint **8**
Café Adelaide **13**	Elizabeth's **32**	Joey K's **5**
The Cake Café **30**	Emeril's **11**	La Côte Brasserie **15**
Cochon **10**	Emeril's Delmonico Restaurant	La Divinia Gelateria **5**
Commander's Palace **6**	and Bar **7**	La Peniche Restaurant **25**

Liborio's Cuban Restaurant **17**
Lil' Dizzy's **24**
Lüke **20**
Marigny Brasserie **28**
MiLa **21**
Mona's Café & Deli **27**
Mother's **18**

Palace Café **19**
P.J.'s Coffee & Tea Company **9**
Praline Connection **26**
Restaurant August **16**
Rue de la Course **5**
Slim Goodies Diner **3**
Sucré **5**

Tommy's Cuisine **12**
Willie Mae's Scotch House **22**

voracious restaurantgoers and are notoriously strict in the qualities they expect from an eating establishment. If a place is below par, it probably won't last very long. And woe to any classic restaurant that dares to remove a beloved dish!

YOU GOT YOUR CAJUN IN MY CREOLE!

Cajun and Creole are the two classic New Orleans cuisines. What's the difference? It lies chiefly in distance between city and countryside.

Cajun cooking came from country folk—the Acadians who left France for Nova Scotia in the 1600s and, after being expelled from Canada by the British in the 1700s, made their way to the swamps and bayous of rural Louisiana. French dishes traveled with them, but along the way recipes were adapted to locally available ingredients. Their cuisine tends to be a lot like their music: spicy and robust. Etouffée, a classic dish, features sausage, duck, poultry, pork, and seafood prepared in a rich roux and served over rice, while jambalaya is rice with many of those same ingredients cooked in it. Both demonstrate how to turn a little into a lot, a necessity for an often-poor people. Creole dishes, on the other hand, were developed by French and Spanish city dwellers and feature delicate sauces and ingredients of fancier quality.

In practice, however, the two cuisines have discovered such a happy marriage in New Orleans that it's often difficult to distinguish between them. Because Creole is already such a hodgepodge—there are so many different ways of defining it that two entirely different restaurants might correctly call themselves Creole—it may soon swallow up Cajun food as just another influence. Paul Prudhomme of K-Paul's Louisiana Kitchen calls the result of Cajun and Creole cross-fertilization "Louisiana food." He goes on to say, "Nowhere else have all the ethnic groups merged to combine all these different tastes, and the only way you'll know the difference, honey, is to live 'em!" No matter how a New Orleans restaurant classifies its culinary offerings, you're bound to find one or two examples of Cajun and Creole cooking on the menu.

OF BEIGNETS, BOUDIN & DIRTY RICE

Many of the foods in New Orleans are unique to the region and consequently may be unfamiliar to first-time visitors. Here's a list that will help you navigate any New Orleans menu:

   andouille (ahn-doo-*we*): A spicy Cajun sausage made with pork.

   bananas Foster: Bananas sautéed in liqueur, brown sugar, cinnamon, and butter, then drenched in rum, set ablaze, and served over vanilla ice cream.

   beignet (bin-*yay*): A big, puffy, deep-fried doughnut (don't look for the hole), liberally sprinkled with powdered sugar—the more sugar, the better.

   boudin (boo-*dan*): A type of Cajun sausage containing onion, spices, pork, and rice.

   café brûlot (cah-*fay* brew-*low*): Coffee mixed with spices and liqueurs and served flaming.

chaurice (cho-*reece*): A hard sausage used chiefly for flavoring beans or soups.
crawfish: A tiny, lobsterlike creature plentiful in the waters around New Orleans and eaten in every conceivable way. When it's served whole and boiled, separate the head from the tail and then remove the first two sections of the tail shell. Squeeze the tail at its base, and the meat should pop right out—you'll get the hang of it.
daube: Beef or sometimes veal.
dirty rice: A popular menu item, it looks dirty because of the spices and other ingredients in which it's cooked—usually chicken livers and gizzards, onions, chopped celery, green bell pepper, cayenne, black and white peppers, and chicken stock.
dressed: Served with the works—used when ordering a sandwich.
eggs hussarde: Poached eggs with hollandaise, *marchand de vin* sauce, tomatoes, and ham. *Marchand de vin* is a wine sauce flavored with onions, shallots, celery, carrots, garlic, red wine, beef broth, and herbs.
eggs Sardou: Legend has it that Antoine Alciatore created this dish especially for French playwright Victorien Sardou (author of *La Tosca*). It includes poached eggs, artichoke bottoms, anchovy filets, hollandaise, and truffles or ham as a garnish.
étouffée (ay-too-*fay*): A Cajun stew (usually containing crawfish) served with rice.
filé (*fee*-lay): A thickener made of ground sassafras leaves. Filé is frequently used to thicken gumbo.
grillades (gree-*yads*): Thin slices of beef or veal smothered in a tomato-and-beef-flavored gravy, often served with grits.
grits: Grains of dried corn that have been ground and hulled. A staple of the Southern breakfast table, grits are most frequently served with butter and salt (not maple syrup or brown sugar) or red-eye gravy.
gumbo: A thick, spicy soup always served with rice and usually containing crab, shrimp, sometimes oysters, and okra in a roux base.
hurricane: A local drink of rum and passion-fruit punch.
hush puppies: Fried balls of cornmeal, often served as a side dish with seafood.
jambalaya (jum-ba-*lie*-ya): A jumble of yellow rice, sausage, seafood, vegetables, and spices.
lagniappe (lan-*yap*): A little something extra you neither paid for nor deserve—like the 13th doughnut when you order a dozen.
muffuletta: A mountainous sandwich made with Italian deli meats, one or two kinds of cheese, olive salad (pickled olives, celery, carrots, cauliflower, and capers), and oil and vinegar, piled onto a round loaf of Italian bread made specially for these incredible sandwiches.
oysters Rockefeller: Oysters on the half shell in a creamy sauce with spinach, so called because Rockefeller was the only name rich enough to match the taste.
pain perdu (pan *pair*-du): Literally "lost bread," this is New Orleans's version of French toast, made with French bread. You'll find a large variety of toppings on *pain perdu* as you make your way around New Orleans.
po' boy: A sandwich on French bread with different fillings (similar to submarine sandwiches and grinders). Most po' boys are filled with fried seafood, but

they can be anything you want, from roast beef to fried eggs to french fries. Yes, french fries.

pralines (*praw*-leens): A very sweet confection made of brown sugar and pecans; they come in "original" and creamy styles.

rémoulade: A spicy sauce, usually over shrimp. The one at Commander's Palace is a concoction of homemade mayonnaise, boiled egg yolks, horseradish, Creole mustard, and lemon juice. But several New Orleans restaurants claim to have invented it, and who can say who is right at this point?

roux: A mixture of flour and fat that's slowly cooked over low heat, used to thicken stews, soups, and sauces.

Sazerac: A cocktail of bourbon or rye (Canadian whiskey) with bitters.

shrimp Creole: Shrimp in a tomato sauce seasoned with what's known around town as "the trinity": onions, garlic, and green bell pepper.

tasso: A local variety of ham. No weak little honey-baked version, this one's smoked and seasoned with red pepper.

3 RESTAURANTS BY CUISINE

American, New American & Regional American

Bluebird Cafe ★★ (Uptown/Garden District, $, p. 159)

Emeril's ★★ (Central Business District, $$$$, p. 149)

Ernst Café (Central Business District, $, p. 154)

Feelings Cafe D'Aunoy ★ (Faubourg Marigny, $$, p. 143)

Nola ★ (French Quarter, $$$, p. 134)

The Pelican Club ★ (French Quarter, $$$, p. 135)

Rémoulade (French Quarter, $, p. 142)

Stanley ★★ (French Quarter, $, p. 143)

Asian

Meauxbar Bistro ★★ (French Quarter, $$, p. 137)

Bakery

EnVie (French Quarter, $, p. 163)

La Boucherie (French Quarter, $, p. 164)

La Boulangerie ★★★ (Uptown, $, p. 164)

La Madeleine ★ (French Quarter, $, p. 164)

Barbecue

Bywater Barbeque & Deli ★★ (Faubourg Marigny, $, p. 144)

Bistro

Café Degas ★★ (Mid-City/Esplanade, $$, p. 146)

Herbsaint ★★ (Central Business District, $$, p. 152)

LaCôte Brasserie ★ (Central Business District, $$$, p. 151)

La Petite Grocery ★★ (Uptown, $$, p. 159)

Lilette ★★ (Uptown/Garden District, $$, p. 159)

Lüke ★★★ (Central Business District, $$, p. 153)

Meauxbar Bistro ★★ (French Quarter, $$, p. 137)

Ralph's on the Park ★★ (Mid-City/Esplanade, $$$, p. 145)

Cafes/Coffee

Café Beignet ★ (French Quarter, $, p. 140)

Café du Monde ★★★ (French Quarter, $, p. 163)

Clover Grill ★ (French Quarter, $, p. 140)

Key to abbreviations: $$$$ = Very Expensive $$$ = Expensive $$ = Moderate $ = Inexpensive

Mandina's ★★ (Mid-City/Esplanade, $$, p. 147)

Napoleon House ★ (French Quarter, $, p. 141)

Pascal's Manale ★ (Uptown/Garden District, $$, p. 159)

Tommy's Cuisine ★★ (Central Business District, $$, p. 154)

Japanese
Sekisui Samurai ★ (French Quarter, $$, p. 139)

Mediterranean
Angeli on Decatur ★★ (French Quarter, $, p. 140)

Mexican
Taqueria Corona ★★ (Uptown/Garden District, $, p. 161)

Middle Eastern
Mona's Café & Deli ★★ (Faubourg Marigny, $, p. 145)

Pizza
Bywater Barbeque & Deli ★★ (Faubourg Marigny, $, p. 144)

Louisiana Pizza Kitchen (French Quarter, $, p. 141)

Sandwiches
Acme Oyster House ★★ (French Quarter, $, p. 139)

Café Maspero ★ (French Quarter, $, p. 140)

The Cake Café ★ (French Quarter, $, p. 144)

Camellia Grill ★★ (Uptown, $, p. 160)

EnVie (French Quarter, $, p. 163)

Johnny's Po' Boys ★★ (French Quarter, $, p. 141)

Liuzza's by the Track ★★ (Mid-City/Esplanade, $, p. 148)

Martin Wine Cellar and Delicatessen ★★★ (Uptown/Garden District, $, p. 162)

Mother's ★★ (Central Business District, $, p. 154)

Parkway Bakery and Tavern ★★ (Mid-City/Esplanade, $, p. 148)

Royal Blend Coffee & Tea House ★ (French Quarter, Central Business District, and Metairie, $, p. 165)

Ye Olde College Inn ★★ (Mid-City/Esplanade, $, p. 149)

Seafood
Acme Oyster House ★★ (French Quarter, $, p. 139)

Bourbon House Seafood ★★ (French Quarter, $$$, p. 131)

Café Maspero ★ (French Quarter, $, p. 140)

Casamento's ★★ (Uptown/Garden District, $, p. 160)

Deanie's Seafood Bucktown USA ★ (Metairie, $$, p. 162)

Felix's Restaurant & Oyster Bar ★★ (French Quarter, $, p. 140)

Franky & Johnny's ★ (Uptown/Garden District, $, p. 160)

Galley Seafood Restaurant ★★ (Metairie, $$, p. 162)

Joey K's ★ (Uptown/Garden District, $, p. 161)

Pascal's Manale ★ (Uptown/Garden District, $$, p. 159)

R&O's ★ (Metairie, $, p. 162)

Red Fish Grill ★ (French Quarter, $$, p. 139)

Rib Room ★ (French Quarter, $$$, p. 135)

Soul Food
Dooky Chase ★ (Mid-City/Esplanade, $$, p. 146)

Jacques-Imo's ★ (Uptown/Garden District, $$, p. 158)

Lil' Dizzy's ★★ (Mid-City/Esplanade, $, p. 147)

Praline Connection (Faubourg Marigny, $, p. 145)

Willie Mae's Scotch House ★★★ (Mid-City/Esplanade, $, p. 149)

Southern

MiLa ★ (Central Business District, $$$, p. 152)

R&O's ★ (Metairie, $, p. 162)

Spanish

Lola's ★★★ (Mid-City/Esplanade, $$, p. 147)

Steak

Dickie Brennan's Steakhouse ★★ (French Quarter, $$$, p. 132)

Pascal's Manale ★ (Uptown/Garden District, $$, p. 159)

Rib Room ★ (French Quarter, $$$, p. 135)

---

4 THE FRENCH QUARTER

EXPENSIVE

Antoine's CREOLE Owned and operated by the same family for an astonishing 160 years, Antoine's sustained some of the most dramatic Katrina damage in the otherwise relatively untouched Quarter. But eventually, all 15(!) of its dining rooms reopened. Because we are sentimental, we have a serious soft spot for Antoine's. We love that Thomas Wolfe said he ate the best meal of his life here, and that author Frances Parkinson Keyes immortalized it in her mystery *Dinner at Antoine's*. We love that we took a friend, a multigeneration New Orleanian, and she reminisced happily about her grandfather's regular visits and favorite dishes.

But we also like to eat, and consequently we can't help but notice that when asked for New Orleans restaurant recommendations, we never think of Antoine's. Not just on the "must-do" list, but even on the "if you can manage five meals a day, here's a bunch of other places you really ought to try" list. The food is as classic New Orleans dining as you can get, but if that were your introduction to same, you may well wonder what all the fuss is about.

Still, it's hard to ignore a legend, and so with some caution you may wish to investigate for yourself. Locals—loyal customers all, mind you—will advise you to focus on starters and dessert and skip the entrees. They're right; at best, the latter are bland but acceptable. You might order a side of creamed spinach, which is classic comfort food. Oysters Rockefeller (served hot in the shell and covered with a mysterious green sauce—Antoine's invented it and still won't give out the recipe) will live up to its rep, and the infamous football-size (and football-shaped) baked Alaska is surely the most frivolous dessert ever. After he won the Nobel Prize for literature, William Faulkner got one inscribed "the Ignoble Prize." Friday lunch features some of the same items that are on the dinner menu, while Sunday brunch offers a different set of dishes.

713 St. Louis St. ✆ **504/581-4422.** www.antoines.com. Reservations not required. No shorts, sandals, or T-shirts, but jackets no longer required. Main courses $24–$40. AE, DC, MC, V. Mon and Thurs–Sat 5:30–9:30pm; lunch Mon–Sat 11:30–2pm; Fri and Sun 11am–2:30pm.

Arnaud's ★★ CREOLE Arnaud's seems to have the lowest profile of all the classic old New Orleans restaurants, but undeservedly so, since it tops them in quality. You need to try at least one venerable, properly New Orleans atmospheric establishment, and that one should be Arnaud's, which is doing some of the best culinary work it has in years. Apart from the signature appetizer, shrimp Arnaud (boiled shrimp topped with a spicy rémoulade sauce), we love the crabmeat Ravigotte (generous amounts of sweet lump crabmeat tossed with a Creole mustard–based sauce, hearts of palm, and other veggies),

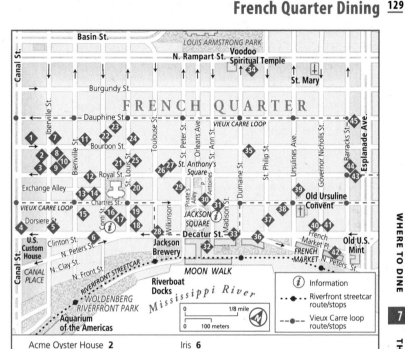

Acme Oyster House **2**

Angeli on Decatur **40**

Antoine's **25**

Arnaud's **10**

Bacco **15**

Bayona **23**

Bourbon House Seafood **3**

Brennan's **21**

Broussard's **22**

Café Beignet **11, 12**

Café du Monde **32**

Cafe Giovanni **4**

Café Maspero **28**

Central Grocery **36**

Clover Grill **35**

Court of Two Sisters **26**

Croissant D'Or **39**

Dickie Brennan's Steakhouse **3**

EnVie **41**

Felix's Restaurant & Oyster Bar **8**

French Quarter Pizza **5**

Galatoire's **7**

Green Goddess **13**

Irene's Cuisine **37**

Iris **6**

Johnny's Po' Boys **18**

K-Paul's Louisiana Kitchen **16**

La Boucherie **14**

La Divinia Gelateria **29**

Louisiana Pizza Kitchen **42**

Meauxbar Bistro **34**

Mona Lisa **43**

Mr. B's Bistro **9**

Muriel's **30**

Napoleon House **19**

Nola **17**

The Pelican Club **13**

Petunia's **24**

Port of Call **45**

Red Fish Grill **1**

Rémoulade **11**

Rib Room **20**

Royal Blend Coffee & Tea House **27**

Sekisui Samurai **5**

Stanley **31**

Stella! **38**

Tujague's **33**

Verdi Marte **44**

and the charbroiled oysters, all smoky and buttery. It's hard to find a better turtle soup. Delicious fish dishes include snapper or trout Pontchartrain (topped with crabmeat), the spicy pompano Duarte, and pompano David and tuna Napoleon, good choices for those watching waistlines. Any filet mignon entree is superb (the meat is often better than what's served in most steakhouses in town), in particular the filet au poivre, while the more daring might want to try the crispy, not gamy, pan-fried sweetbreads. Desserts aren't quite as magnificent, but the bananas Foster are spot on, and one crème brûlée fan said Arnaud's was the best she'd ever had. In addition to the formal (and seriously New Orleans) dining room, there is the more casual jazz bistro, with entertainment (and an extra cover charge) at night.

Arnaud's also operates a less formal, less expensive brasserie, **Rémoulade** (p. 142), right next door.

813 Bienville St. ℂ **866/230-8892** or 504/523-5433. www.arnauds.com. Reservations requested. Business casual. Main courses $23–$50. AE, DC, DISC, MC, V. Sun–Thurs 6–10pm; Fri–Sat 6–10:30pm; Sun brunch 10am–2:30pm.

Bacco ★ ITALIAN/CREOLE   Any affection we already had for Bacco increased exponentially the day, about a month after Katrina, it became the first major Quarter restaurant to reopen. Did it matter the menu was limited to five items, all grilled and served on plastic dinnerware? Heck, no. It was New Orleans food, again, and even taking obvious joyful bias into account, it was delicious. (Former President Bush dined here just a few days later, during his first post-hurricane trip to the city.)

At night it's romantic and candlelit; at lunchtime it's more affordable and casual, with particularly well-priced lunch specials (three courses for around $15). Don't expect spaghetti and marinara sauce here. The menu changes regularly, but our latest trip produced a superior take on New Orleans BBQ shrimp (with a spicy finish) and terrific hickory-smoked redfish. Most of the pasta dishes are probably sure things, but skip the crawfish ravioli. Mr. Ralph's ice-cream sandwich—moist chocolate cake layered with Louisiana strawberry ice cream—made up for the disappointing espresso cupcake.

310 Chartres St. ℂ **504/522-2426.** www.bacco.com. Reservations recommended. Main courses $18–$31. AE, DC, DISC, MC, V. Daily 11:30am–2:30pm; Sun–Thurs 6–9:30pm; Fri–Sat 6–10pm.

Bayona ★★ INTERNATIONAL   A dedicated chef-owner who is a local treasure, superior food, and one of the loveliest courtyards in the restaurant scene—all reasons to eat at Bayona. Be sure to begin with the outstanding cream-of-garlic soup, a perennial favorite. Appetizers include grilled shrimp with cilantro sauce and black-bean cakes, and delicate, flavorful veal sweetbreads sautéed with scallions and diced potatoes in sherry vinaigrette. Knockout entrees have included medallions of lamb loin with a lavender-honey aioli (a mayonnaise-based sauce) and a zinfandel demi-glacé; a perfectly grilled pork chop with a stuffing of fontina cheese, fresh sage, and prosciutto; and yet another lamb dish, this one topped with goat cheese, that may have been the best lamb we've ever tasted. Heaven. Entrees come with a well-balanced selection of sides such as gnocchi, puréed butternut squash, or fresh sweet corn. And lunch brings a smoked-duck (with cashew butter and pepper jelly) sandwich that has been boxed to go on many a plane flight! A light lunch on Saturdays features three courses of *tapas*-like plates you can mix and match for $20. They are offering parking at the nearby Chateau LeMoyne at 301 Dauphine St.

430 Dauphine St. ℂ **504/525-4455.** www.bayona.com. Reservations required at dinner, recommended at lunch. Main courses $10–$15 lunch, $24–$29 dinner. AE, DC, DISC, MC, V. Tues–Thurs 6–9:30pm; Fri–Sat 6–10pm; Wed–Sat 11:30am–2pm.

Impressions

The Louisiana diet will kill a man as surely as the sword.

—King of the Hill

Bourbon House Seafood ★★ SEAFOOD   Sadly, it's easy to overlook this commendable restaurant since it's right on Bourbon Street, but don't. It's a modern take on the classic New Orleans fish house, both aesthetically and gastronomically. The menu's fishy offerings vary, but can feature entrees such as crispy Gulf fish atop crawfish and "rag pasta" or that same Gulf fish stuffed with crabmeat (you can get any fish topped with fresh lump crabmeat for an additional charge, and you should). Our very favorite BBQ shrimp is here—in this city "BBQ shrimp" means shrimp sautéed in a buttery, garlicky spicy sauce (heaven to sop up with bread). This is also the place for some fine seafood appetizers, including versions of oysters Rockefeller, a lovely (and not overly biting) rémoulade sauce, marinated seafood salads, and more. Consider ordering a *fruits de mar* sample platter of all of this, and then get to the cocktail menu, where the chef has collaborated with the bar to come up with some creative drinks, many of which are based on seasonal ingredients and/or fruits the chef preserved especially for later-in-the-year beverages. Check out fresh blueberry mojitos or orange cosmos, not to mention the restaurant's natural deep commitment to all things bourbon. If there is a wait for a table, you can order from the dinner menu at the bar and watch the oyster men shuck away.

144 Bourbon St. ✆ **504/522-0111.** www.bourbonhouse.com. Reservations suggested. Main courses $5.25–$20 breakfast, $8.50–$28 lunch, $16–$32 dinner. AE, DISC, MC, V. Breakfast 6:30–10:30am daily. Dinner 5–11pm daily.

Brennan's ★ FRENCH/CREOLE   For more than 40 years, breakfast at Brennan's has been a New Orleans tradition, a feast that has surely kept many a heart surgeon busy. Reopened in late April 2006 after a lengthy post-K renovation, in time to celebrate their 60th anniversary, Brennan's is a lesson in New Orleans survival, and, of course, diet. Don't expect any California health-conscious fruit-and-granola options here; this multi-course extravaganza is unabashedly sauce- and egg-intensive. It's also costly—it's not hard to drop $50 on breakfast—so you might be better off sticking with the fixed-price meal (though it often limits your choices). Breakfast at Brennan's has changed very little over the years, and that is part of the restaurant's charm, as is the building, constructed by Edgar Degas's great-grandfather and childhood home of tragic chess master Paul Morphy. Dine here and you will find yourself rubbing elbows with loyal locals and tourists in search of a classic. This is Special Event Dining, for Grandma's birthday or to celebrate an engagement, when it seems right to dress up in suits and even hats, and eat classically prepared eggs Benedict or eggs Portuguese (poached on top of a tomato concoction, served in a puff pastry with hollandaise ladled over the whole), very fine turtle soup, and the superb onion soup made with a roux. You can justify the outlay of cash by making this your main meal of the day, though if you do have dinner, have it on the gas-lamp-lined balcony. A weekday three-course lunch special from 11am to 1pm is under $25.

417 Royal St. ✆ **504/525-9711.** www.brennansneworleans.com. Reservations recommended. Main courses $18–$43; fixed-price lunch $36; fixed-price 4-course dinner $48. AE, DC, DISC, MC, V. Thurs–Mon 9am–1pm and 6–9pm. Closed for dinner on Christmas Eve and all day Christmas Day.

Broussard's ★ CREOLE   Unfairly dismissed as a tourist trap (which, in truth, it was for some years), Broussard's is a perfectly fine alternative to some of its similarly well-established peers. And you have to love their post-storm attitude: "We will open up and serve jambalaya if we have to!" vowed owner Gunther Preuss in a CNN interview. "Even if we have to serve frozen fish, I wouldn't mind doing that because we want to open up as soon as possible." You'll be pleased to learn they are back to fresh fish, and even more pleased by the quality of it. What a very fine meal can be had here, especially in the lovely courtyard. "Gunther has a way with crab," claims his press material, and once we stopped giggling over that turn of phrase, we had to admit it was true. We suggest the appetizer of crabmeat Florentine, which includes spinach and is covered in a brie sauce. Another of our favorites is the baked filet of redfish Herbsaint (a local anise-flavored liqueur), clever and delicious in its components, which include impossibly sweet crabmeat and lemon risotto. Pompano Napoleon (grilled, with pepper-crushed scallops and shrimp, puff pastry, and a mustard-caper sauce) is a signature dish, but with phrases such as "pepper-crushed" and "mustard-caper sauce," one would expect a bit more punch. Many of the desserts are happily heavy and creamy.

819 Conti St. ☎ **504/581-3866**. www.broussards.com. Reservations recommended. No jeans, shorts, sneakers, or T-shirts. Main courses $27–$37. AE, MC, V. Daily 5:30–10pm.

Cafe Giovanni ★ ITALIAN   Though Chef Duke LoCicero has been winning culinary awards right and left, Cafe Giovanni is kind of a mixed bag, thanks to a combo of fine food, lackadaisical service even before Katrina, and—of course—the dreaded (or highly enjoyable, depending on your conversational needs during dinner and your love of schmaltz) strolling opera singers (to be found Wed, Fri, and Sat nights, singing with all their might). Though Chef Duke is renowned for his pastas, they are no better than those found over at **Irene's Cuisine** (p. 136).

117 Decatur St. ☎ **504/529-2154**. www.cafegiovanni.com. Main courses $15–$37. AE, DC, DISC, MC, V. Mon–Sat 5:30–10pm.

Court of Two Sisters Overrated CREOLE   This is probably the prettiest restaurant in town (thanks to a huge, foliage-filled courtyard located in a 2-centuries-old building—both spared any storm-related issues), but even major ambience can't obscure the problems with the food. You'll find the only daily jazz brunch in town here (remarkable that they are still doing it, under the circumstances), but it suffers from the typical buffet problem—too many dishes, none of which succeed except maybe the made-to-order items such as eggs Benedict. Avoid the vinegary seviche, but try the seafood slaw (we give it a thumbs up). Dinner may be even worse; apart from a Caesar salad (made in the traditional style, at tableside), there is little, if anything, to recommend. It's a pity, because you can't ask for a better setting.

613 Royal St. ☎ **504/522-7261**. www.courtoftwosisters.com. Reservations recommended for dinner and brunch. Main courses $25–$35; brunch $28. AE, DC, DISC, MC, V. Jazz brunch buffet daily 9am–3pm; dinner nightly 5:30–10pm.

Dickie Brennan's Steakhouse ★★ STEAK   This is one of the few restaurants that received serious physical damage from Katrina, because of both its proximity to the flooded parts of Canal and its own sub-street-level location. Nonetheless, aficionados won't be able to tell the difference in this handsome steakhouse, thanks to a laborious reconstruction. It looks gorgeous, but not as much so as its prime steaks. We are hard-pressed to choose our favorite between the 14-ounce rib-eye, the 16-ounce cast-iron-seared filet, or the house filet topped with béarnaise sauce, flash-fried oysters, and creamed spinach. Each is tender and juicy and seasoned to give it an enhancing kerwallop but not enough to overpower the flavorful meat. Prime rib is less impressive, as it's a bit pallid compared to a hearty aged steak. Finding the steaks a bit costly? Split one (they aren't small), and then you can order plenty of sides and appetizers, all of which are sterling as well. And even fish entrees are entirely successful, particularly the grilled red fish topped with lemon beurre blanc sauce and the terrific crab cake appetizer, which tastes like all crab and no filling. Save room for desserts such as the family's Creole cream-cheese cheesecake (not an ordinary cheesecake by any means), bananas Foster bread pudding (a new twist on an old faithful dish), coconut cake, and a chocolate-café mousse.

716 Iberville St. ℂ 504/522-2467. www.dickiebrennanssteakhouse.com. Reservations recommended. Main courses dinner $29–$40. AE, DISC, MC, V. Daily 5:30–10pm.

Galatoire's ★ FRENCH   The venerable Galatoire's causes heated discussions among local foodies: the best restaurant in New Orleans or past its prime? This conversation was rendered almost irrelevant when it reopened after Katrina. Walking into its classic green-wallpaper interior, exactly as it used to be, complete with favorite waiter John, at his post for 35 years and counting, despite the loss of his home to flooding, was such a relief, such a return to normalcy that any gastronomic inadequacies are easy to overlook. Or even welcomed; really, you don't come to Galatoire's for cutting-edge cuisine. You come here to eat a nice piece of fish, perfectly sautéed or broiled, topped with fresh crabmeat. Or you have a seafood dish with a gloopy white sauce, because that's what you've been eating at your regular Sunday-evening dinners, where all the old waiters know your name, for years. We love it because in *A Streetcar Named Desire*, Stella took Blanche there to escape Stanley's poker game. It was Tennessee Williams's favorite restaurant (his table is the one right behind the word RESTAURANT on the window). And the venerable James Beard Foundation must love it because it honored this restaurant with its Outstanding Restaurant Award in 2005.

Galatoire's has been run by the same family since 1905, and its traditions remain intact. It is New Orleans tradition, and a symbol of everything else we could have lost, and that alone makes it worth the trip. You may not have the same experience as a knowledgeable local unless you get a waiter who can really guide you (ask for John; everyone else does). We love the lump crabmeat appetizer (think coleslaw, only with crab instead of cabbage), the shrimp rémoulade, and the oysters Rockefeller. For an entree, get the red snapper or redfish topped with sautéed crabmeat meunière (a delightful butter sauce)—it will probably be one of the finest fish dishes you'll have during your stay. Don't miss out on the terrific creamed spinach and the puffy potatoes with béarnaise sauce, which will make you swear off regular french fries forever.

209 Bourbon St. ℂ 504/525-2021. www.galatoires.com. Reservations accepted for upstairs. Jackets required after 5pm and all day Sun. Main courses $19–$34. AE, DC, DISC, MC, V. Tues–Sat 11:30am–10pm; Sun 11:30am–10pm. Closed Memorial Day, July 4th, Thanksgiving, and Christmas.

K-Paul's Louisiana Kitchen ★ CAJUN/CREOLE   Paul Prudhomme was at the center of the Cajun revolution of the early 1980s, when Cajun food became known throughout the world. His reputation and his line of spices continue today, while Chef was a culinary hero during the disaster. His establishment cooked for volunteers, firemen, troops, displaced locals, and more, serving tens of thousands of meals. Unfortunately, although the American regional food is still good (our last meal here was really quite good, in fact), it's not spectacular and certainly is not worth the wait (upward of 1½ hr. at its peak, though that's unlikely currently) or the high cost. Different menu items are offered daily, but you can't go wrong with duck *boudin,* blackened beef tenders with debris, or blackened drum with sautéed crabmeat chipotle. A Paul-level of spicy bronzed salmon is just so-so.

416 Chartres St. ⓒ **504/524-7394.** www.kpauls.com. Reservations recommended. Main courses $30–$36. AE, DC, DISC, MC, V. Lunch Thurs–Sat 11am–2pm; dinner Mon–Sat 5:30–9:30pm.

Mr. B's Bistro ★ CONTEMPORARY CREOLE   A favorite among business people for lunch, Mr. B's other claim to fame is its BBQ shrimp, with many a joke being made that the "B" stands for butter. The menu these days is fairly standard, so much so that nothing really stands out—either on it or on the plate. If it's your first introduction to New Orleans restaurants, it's not a bad choice by any means, but if you've been eating pretty well up to this point, it's probably going to be a bit pedestrian. Having said that, those BBQ shrimp *are* plump, though the (yes, buttery) sauce is rather peppery, and you might want to drop by just to split a portion.

201 Royal St. ⓒ **504/523-2078.** www.mrbsbistro.com. Reservations recommended. No shorts or tank tops; business casual. Main courses lunch $14–$20, dinner $23–$38, jazz brunch $18–$32. AE, DC, DISC, MC, V. Mon–Sat 11:30am–2pm and 5:30–9:30pm; Sun jazz brunch 11am–2:30pm.

Muriel's ★★ CREOLE/ECLECTIC   Conventional wisdom would have it that any restaurant this close to tourist-hub Jackson Square—as in, across the street from it—would have to serve overpriced, mediocre food. But then conventional wisdom notes the Gothic-parlor look to the dining rooms in Muriel's (among the pretty touches: a wall covered in antique photos, a dressing table fit for Miss DuBois, a floating doorway leading nowhere) and decides to sit down just to be polite. Then conventional wisdom eats excellent duck confit, a charcuterie plate with chunky pâté, poached oysters in a rosemary cream sauce, and rather sumptuous creamy goat cheese and shrimp crepes—skipping the beet salad, which was a little weird, to be honest—following it up with a perfect double-cut sugar-cane apple-glazed pork chop, and equally good wood-grilled tuna (on top of risotto) and redfish. It then has a "dome" of peanut-butter mousse with a chocolate shell. Sated and fully satisfied, conventional wisdom then floats upstairs, past the table set for the in-house ghosts, and into the Séance Room, which looks like a Gypsy den crossed with a bordello, and has a drink. Possibly a canoodle with its dining companion. Conventional wisdom is reminded that rules are made to be broken and vows to tell everyone to come here.

801 Chartres (at St. Ann). ⓒ **504/568-1885.** Reservations suggested. Main courses $13–$20 lunch, $15–$20 brunch, $15–$37 dinner. AE, DISC, MC, V. Mon–Sat 11:30am–2:30pm; Sun jazz brunch 11am–2pm; Mon–Fri 5:30–10pm; Sat–Sun 5–10pm.

Nola ★ CREOLE/NEW AMERICAN   This modern two-story building with a glass-enclosed elevator is the most casual of Chef Emeril Lagasse's three restaurants, and the most conveniently located for the average tourist. Unlike Lagasse's other restaurants, the dining experience here can be a bit hit-or-miss. It's never less than good (if not excellent) quality, but it can be unmemorable. Whatever variation on duck pizza (confit and fried egg with truffle oil on a recent visit) is always a sure thing, as are soups such as a nearly fork-able thick roasted garlic–Reggiano Parmesan with basil pesto. But while a recent garlic-crusted redfish topped with a bacon and beurre rouge sauce was an excellent combination of flavors (even without the sauce), a pork porterhouse was just a blah hunk of meat, while the shrimp with grits was rather dull compared to other versions around town. It's also a particularly noisy space in a town not known for hushed dining.

The Pelican Club ★ NEW AMERICAN   Just a short stroll from the House of Blues, the Pelican Club is worth investigating. The appetizers are a bit more inventive than the entrees (you could easily make a meal of them), but everything is quite tasty. Escargots come in a tequila garlic-butter sauce (which you will probably find yourself sopping up with bread), topped with tiny puff pastries. Oysters are garnished with apple-smoked bacon—even oysterphobes won't have a problem with these babies. Special salads are served each evening; a recent visit found arugula, Gorgonzola, and apple in balsamic dressing. Tender lamb comes coated in rosemary-flavored bread crumbs with a spicy pepper jelly, and fish is cooked to perfection. Interesting sides such as wild-mushroom bread pudding accompany the entrees. The desserts are certainly standouts. Try the flat (rather than puffy) white-chocolate bread pudding, creamy chocolate pecan pie, or amazing profiteroles filled with coffee ice cream and topped with three sauces.

615 Bienville St., entrance in Exchange Alley. ✆ **504/523-1504.** www.pelicanclub.com. Reservations recommended. Main courses $25–$34. AE, DC, DISC, MC, V. Daily 5:30–10pm. Closed July 4th.

Rib Room ★ SEAFOOD/STEAK   One of the first restaurants in the Quarter to reopen post-Katrina, this is where New Orleanians come to eat beef. And who can fault their choice of surroundings? The solid and cozy Old English feel of this room is complete with natural-brick and open ovens at the back. But while the meat is good, it is not outstanding, and the acclaimed prime rib is just a bit tough and more than lacking in flavor. There are also filets, sirloins, brochettes, *tournedos,* and steak au poivre, plus some seafood dishes. Carnivores, landlubbers, and ichthyophobes will be happier here than at one of the city's Creole restaurants, but it is not the must-do that its reputation would have you believe. Having said that, the old stalwart has added Patrick, the longtime maitre d' of the Bistro at the Maison de Ville, and between his skill and expertise, and that of top maitre d' Joe, who has been at the Rib Room 25 years, you won't ask for better, more charismatic service. Patrick (be sure to say "hi" for us!) is working on bringing his extraordinary wine knowledge to this restaurant's list.

In the Omni Royal Orleans hotel, 621 St. Louis St. ✆ **504/529-7045.** www.omnihotels.com. Reservations recommended. Main courses $24–$38. AE, DC, DISC, MC, V. Daily 6:30–10:30am, 11:30am–2pm, and 6–9pm.

Stella! ★★ INTERNATIONAL   We are now very fond of this charming Quarter restaurant, whose newly redone room glows with real and faux candlelight, making it instantly warm and appealing. The clever, arty food is heavy on design and construction, with some combinations more successful than others. The menu changes daily and it is always interesting to see what Chef might be experimenting with, and a pleasure to participate in something that isn't afraid to depart from the New Orleans culinary norm. A recent foray produced the following: for appetizers, a foie-gras-and-duck-pâté BLT, a decadently stacked, heady combo; shark's fin soup garnished with 24-carat gold leaves, a tricked-out version of an Asian staple that appears as an occasional special. The almond-and-herb-crusted rack of lamb paired with boneless lamb rib-eye is meltingly tender, but the popular duck five ways has some elements that work superbly (the foie-gras wontons) and others that don't quite get there (the lacquered thigh can be dry). There is always an interesting pastry chef at work, and the restaurant always has laudable homemade ice-cream treats. See p. 143 for a review of the owner's excellent inexpensive cafe, Stanley.

1032 Chartres St. (in the Hotel Provincial). ☏ **504/587-0091.** www.restaurantstella.com. Reservations recommended. No shorts or tank tops; business casual. Main courses $28–$36. AE, DC, DISC, MC, V. Thurs–Mon 5:30–10:30pm.

Tujague's ★ CREOLE   Dating back to 1856, Tujague's (pronounced *Two*-jacks) is every bit as venerable and aged as the big-name New Orleans restaurants (heck, the mirror in the bar has been in place for 150 years!), and yet no one ever mentions it—which is a shame. It may not be a knockout, but it's authentic and solid.

Tujague's does not have a menu; instead, each night it offers a set six-course (it seems one course is coffee) meal. You will eat what they cook that night. Don't expect fancy or nouvelle: This is real local food. Meals start with a sinus-clearing shrimp rémoulade (with red or white sauce, or both if you can't make up your mind), heads to a fine gumbo (not as thick as some, but that's not a liability), then on to a sample of a so-tender-you-cut-it-with-a-fork brisket, and then on to whatever is happening for an entree. There's likely to be filet mignon for sure, but skip it (it's ordinary) in favor of items such as stuffed shrimp or perfect fettuccine or Bonne Femme chicken, a baked garlic number from the original owner's recipe (the restaurant has it every night, but you have to ask for it). Finish with a classic—the right-on-the-money bread pudding.

823 Decatur St. ☏ **504/525-8676.** www.tujagues.com. Reservations recommended. 6-course dinner $34–$41. AE, DC, DISC, MC, V. Daily 5pm–"closing."

MODERATE

Green Goddess ★★ ECLECTIC   One of the city's newest restaurants, Green Goddess is sending waves of excitement through local food lovers. Chef Chris DeBarr (formerly of the Delachaise) has a vision of "globetrotting cuisine," inspired by flavors from Spain to India but featuring local seafood, sausage, and produce—it's some of the most creative and exciting food in town. Chef Chris anchors the dinner menu (often serving you himself), while lunch and brunch are handled by Chef Paul Artigues. The menu changes constantly, so just think of the following as an illustration of what you might get. Starters include the signature wedge salad with shrimp, crabmeat, and their eponymous dressing; wonderfully refreshing chilled melon soup; and a terrine of three blue cheeses that had us squealing with delight. For your entree, try the amazing bison and bacon meatloaf; a Creole-Hawaiian dish made with smoked pulled pork seasoned with Hawaiian black lava salt; their version of bangers and mash, with local duck sausage and orangey mashed yams; or the blue corn crêpes with mushrooms and huitlacoche (a wonderful Aztec "truffle" that grows on corn cobs). The array of beverages is astonishing. (Brazilian cashew fruit juice, anyone? It's wonderful.) And now with a new liquor license, they're making some of the most creative cocktails in town (try the amazing Green Fuse, with lime, sugarcane juice, and absinthe; the superb Ginger Mint Julep with mint from the chef's wife's garden; or the house Bloody Mary with roasted Creole tomatoes). The place is tiny (how are they doing all this inventive cooking in there?), so there may be a wait, but they also stay open late, so you've got plenty of time.

307 Exchange Pl. ☏ **504/301-3347.** www.greengoddessnola.com. Reservations not accepted. Main courses $7–$16. AE, DISC, MC, V. Daily 11am–4pm; Thurs–Sun 5pm–midnight.

Irene's Cuisine ★★ FRENCH/ITALIAN   Irene's is somewhat off the regular tourist dining path, and locals would probably prefer to keep it that way—it's hard enough getting into one of their favorite neighborhood bistros. In fact, in a constantly uncertain and changing world, waiting upward of 90 minutes for a table at Irene's is something you can count on. But those same locals feel the French Provincial and Italian food is worth it (you should have seen their faces when Irene's reopened in Oct 2005, wanting to be an oasis in the madness), and you may as well. Once you do enter, after being lured in from a block away by the potent smell of garlic, you will find a dark, cluttered tavern, not unromantic (provided you don't mind a noise level that's a decibel or so above hushed), with ultrafriendly waiters who seem delighted you came and who keep the crowds happy with prompt service.

The menu is heavier on meats and fish than pasta; salads come with a tangy balsamic dressing; and soups can be intriguing combinations, such as the sweet-potato-and-andouille-sausage concoction. On a recent visit, we were thrilled by soft-shell-crab pasta, an entirely successful Italian/New Orleans hybrid consisting of a whole fried crustacean atop a bed of pasta with a cream sauce of garlic, crawfish, tomatoes, and wads of whole basil leaves. The panned oysters and grilled shrimp appetizer can be magnificent, and don't forget the *pollo rosemarino*—five pieces of chicken marinated, partly cooked, marinated again, and then cooked a final time. Desserts, alas, are the usual dull New Orleans suspects (repeat after me: crème brûlée, bread pudding, chocolate torte . . .). *Note:* Irene's longtime partner, Tommy, opened up his own place (aptly named Tommy's Cuisine), which is more or less Irene's all over again, with one crucial detail: It takes reservations. (See review on p. 154.)

539 St. Philip St. ℭ **504/529-8811.** "Limited reservations accepted if space is available." Main courses $17–$28. AE, MC, V. Mon–Sat 5:30–10pm. Closed New Year's Day, July 4th, the week before and including Labor Day to honor the loss caused by Katrina, Thanksgiving, and Christmas.

Iris ★ CONTEMPORARY CREOLE Anyone who opens a restaurant in New Orleans these days is something like a hero, and given that the chef-owner is a talented fellow, we continue to have optimism regarding this small, pretty little place. Having said that, we also wish that the chef (who worked at Lilette before this and clearly learned well from the experience) would be just a little more bold and audacious, since he's currently sticking to some tried-and-true local contemporary formulas—not that one can really blame him. The menu changes daily, but possibilities include hamachi with grilled green garlic, sunchoke and cauliflower soup with sunflower shoots, and a pretty piece of Yukon salmon with a side of English peas and spinach. It's all very pretty, fresh food, meticulously prepared and a delicate contrast to heavier Creole fare around town. Portions are modest compared to other places, and the prices are a bit high for what you get.

321 N. Peters St. (in the Bienville House Hotel). ℭ **504/862-5848.** www.irisneworleans.com. Main courses $23–$29. AE, DISC, MC, V. Mon and Wed–Thurs 6–10pm; Fri–Sat 6–10:30pm; lunch Thurs–Sat 11:30am–2pm.

Meauxbar Bistro ★★ ASIAN/BISTRO Rampart Street needs more places like this: a sweet neighborhood cafe that aspires to serve more than just the usual New Orleans inexpensive fare. Frozen food is rarely used, and all the dressings are made fresh, a touch you appreciate when you try the tart Roquefort onion dressing. The signature starter is ginger crawfish dumplings in a sesame dipping sauce. Entrees include lamb shanks braised for 3 hours, until the meat is falling off the bone; the result is a nongreasy wonder. The salad with poached egg is worth coming back for alone. Coconut shrimp in a red curry sauce is very spicy with just a touch of sweet. Looking for something a little more familiar? Their hamburger is one of the best in the city, topped with goat cheese or Roquefort and bacon, and can be cooked perfectly rare; paired with crispy fries, it's a filling meal for $10. The apple tartin is like no other apple dish in New Orleans. They've even added small plates—half orders of some of their most popular dishes.

942 N. Rampart St. ℭ **504/569-9979.** Main courses $12–$27. AE, MC, V. Tues–Sat 6–10pm.

(Finds) Food on the Fly

Time has a way of disappearing, never again to be accounted for, in New Orleans. This is really not a problem, but still, you gotta eat, if only to keep your strength up for all that, well, whatever it was that you did or will do. So if you find yourself strapped for time, lacking a reservation, or just too exhausted to leave your hotel room, here are some options that deliver. (You might also take note of listings below for the exceptional Martin Wine Cellar, which offers superb takeout choices, the best in the city. Hopefully, it will be delivering again by the time you read this.) Do assume that with staffing problems as they are, deliveries may not be all that prompt, depending on when you call.

The **Verdi Marte,** 1201 Royal St. (© **504/525-4767**), is a favorite with Quarter dwellers (they also deliver to the Faubourg Marigny and claim to have "for 50 years"). It's open 24 hours and has bargain-basement prices for local dishes, plus decent salads and fine barbecue. **Mona Lisa** ★, 1212 Royal St. (© **504/522-6746**), will deliver better-than-fine pizza and Italian dishes to you in the Quarter 7 days a week, though they are closed Tuesdays and Wednesday during the day. **French Quarter Pizza** ★★, 201 Decatur (© **504/948-3287**), won our hearts when they set up a stand on Frenchmen to feed hungry, late-night club hoppers slices. Well located (next to House of Blues and near the aquarium), they deliver to most of the CBD, the Quarter, and Marigny daily, and—get this—are open until midnight Sunday to Wednesday and until 2am Thursday through Saturday.

For those staying uptown or near City Park, there's terrific pizza (try the Mediterranean, which is roasted garlic cloves and bell peppers, or the Sun Pie, with goat cheese and pesto) from **Reginelli's** ★★, 741 State St. (© **504/899-1414**). Better still is **McHardy's** ★★★, 1458 N. Broad St. (© **504/949-0000**), which serves, seriously, the best fried chicken we've ever had—and at under a dollar apiece, it's affordable for all budgets. They don't deliver, but you can get in and out of there, box (or bucket) of chicken (which, along with potato salad and chips, is all they serve) in hand, in under 5 minutes, unless it's really crowded.

Port of Call ★★ HAMBURGERS   Sometimes you just need a burger—particularly when you've been eating many things with sauce. Locals feel strongly that the half-pound monsters served at the cozy (and we mean it) Port of Call are the best in town. We are going to take a stand and say that, yes, they are certainly terrific, but all that meat may be too much of a good thing. The Port of Call is just a half step above a dive, but it's a convivial place with a nice staff that can get justly somewhat harried during busy hours. The brawny hamburgers come with an enormous baked potato (because you might not have gotten enough food), and there also are excellent filet mignon, rib-eye steaks, and New York strip steaks. Because businesspeople come here from all over the city, it's often jammed at regular eating hours, so try it before 7pm, when people who work in the Quarter begin to gather here. Note the helpfully late hours, and that they have their own signature drink, the Monsoon, a citrus-laden rum combo that is refreshing and unexpectedly potent.

838 Esplanade Ave. ✆ **504/523-0120.** www.portofcallneworleans.com. Main courses $10–$25. AE, MC, V. Sun–Thurs 11am–midnight; Fri–Sat 11am–1am.

Red Fish Grill ★ SEAFOOD   Red Fish is far better than anything else in its price range on Bourbon Street, and—surprise!—it's another Brennan restaurant. Ralph Brennan's place (one of the first Quarter restaurants to reopen after Katrina) serves many New Orleans specialties with an emphasis on—surprise again—fish. Skip the dull salads in favor of appetizers like shrimp rémoulade napoleon (layered btw. fried green tomatoes) or grilled shrimp and shiitake-mushroom quesadillas. For your entree, go right to the fish they do so well. Whatever you have will be light and flaky with flavors that complement one another, rich (it *is* New Orleans) but not overly so. The signature dish is a pan-seared catfish topped with sweet-potato crust and an andouille cream drizzle. It's so outstanding, we asked for the recipe so we could try to re-create it at home. (We couldn't really, but it was fun trying.) Also splendid is the grilled Gulf fish with a pecan-butter sauce.

115 Bourbon St. ✆ **504/598-1200.** www.redfishgrill.com. Reservations limited. Main courses $12–$22 lunch, $20–$33 dinner. AE, DC, DISC, MC, V. Daily 11am–3pm; Sun–Thurs 5–10pm; Fri–Sat 5–11pm. Oyster bar Sun–Thurs 11am–10pm, Fri–Sat 11am–11pm.

Sekisui Samurai ★ JAPANESE   Lord knows we love a cream sauce as much as, and probably more than, the next person, to say nothing of our deep commitment to deep-fried anything, but sometimes something's gotta give (like our waistbands), and that's why, if we can't get our hands on a plain green salad, we end up eating sushi. If you find yourself needing a similar break, you could do worse than trying out this French Quarter sushi place, which also delivers both in the Quarter and the Central Business District. While the crawfish-tail sushi is hit-or-miss, the Crunchy Roll (a California roll topped with tempura—see, we always come back to deep-fried) and the spicy tuna roll are worth checking out, as is the enjoyably named Flying Fish Roll. They also have teriyaki and so forth. And it is interesting to see how a town known for fish does it raw. The website often has coupons for discounts and specials.

239 Decatur St. ✆ **504/525-9595.** www.sekisuiusa.com. Sushi $4.50–$10 for pieces/rolls; lunch specials $6.75–$15; dinner $14–$26. AE, DC, DISC, MC, V. Daily 11:30am–10pm.

INEXPENSIVE

Acme Oyster House ★★ SEAFOOD/SANDWICHES   The Quarter's oldest oyster bar needed a $2-million renovation to recover from Katrina, but it looks pretty much as it always did, just spiffier (new floor, new tiling, new bathrooms, and best of all, an expanded kitchen). This joint is always loud, often crowded, and the kind of place where you're likely to run into obnoxious fellow travelers. But if you need an oyster fix or you've never tried oyster shooting (taking a raw oyster, possibly doused in sauce, and letting it slide right down your throat), come here. There's nothing quite like standing at the oyster bar and eating a dozen or so freshly shucked oysters on the half-shell. (You can have them at a table, but somehow they taste better at the bar.) If you can't quite stomach them raw, try the oyster po' boy, with beer, of course. Note that there are people who sincerely prefer Felix's across the street. The two locations are interchangeable to us, but we might be missing something.

724 Iberville St. ✆ **504/522-5973.** www.acmeoyster.com. Oysters $7–$17 per half/whole dozen, respectively; po' boys $8–$12; New Orleans specialties $9–$14; seafood $15–$20. AE, DC, DISC, MC, V. Sun–Thurs 11am–10pm; Fri–Sat 11am–11pm.

Angeli on Decatur ★★ ITALIAN/MEDITERRANEAN   This place features satis-fying (if not particularly New Orleans–specific) food with further praise for its nearly round-the-clock hours and local delivery service (every night until 2am or later)—all things hungry locals and tourists crave. It's conveniently accessible after a day's busy sightseeing or a night's busy club hopping and perfect for a light, actually rather healthy meal—a much-needed alternative to some of the extravaganzas offered by more formal restaurants in town. Portions are substantial—splitting a Greek salad produced two full plates of fresh, lovely veggies and a couple of pieces of garlic bread. Add to that a small but gooey and flavorful pizza (they do them all well, but the Mystical—roasted garlic, goat cheese, onions, sun-dried tomatoes—is a top choice), and you've got a tasty, afford-able meal for two (as long as you have two more or less normal appetites), at almost any hour and even in your hotel room, and a nice palate cleanser if you are a bit tired of local cuisine. It's good enough for occasional Quarter residents Brad and Angelina, after all!

1141 Decatur St. (at Gov. Nicholls St.). ✆ **504/566-0077.** Main courses $7–$21. AE, MC, V. Sun–Thurs 11am–2am; Fri–Sat 11am–4am. Delivery 'til 2am.

Café Beignet ★ CAFE   At breakfast, this full-service bistro-style cafe serves Belgian waffles, an omelet soufflé, bagels and lox, or brioche French toast. Items on the lunch menu include gumbo, vegetable sandwiches, and salads. And, of course, beignets. The latter won't make us forget Café du Monde—nothing will, of course—but if you are here, make the most of it. Their newest location is in the Musical Legends Park on Bour-bon Street.

334B Royal St. ✆ **504/524-5530.** www.cafebeignet.com. Most items under $10. MC, V. Daily 8am–3pm. Other locations: 311 Bourbon St. ✆ **504/525-2611.** Mon–Wed 8am–3pm; Thurs and Sun 8am–10pm; Fri–Sat 8am–midnight.

Café Maspero ★ SEAFOOD/SANDWICHES   Upon hearing complaints about the increasing presence in the Quarter of "foreign" restaurants, such as Subway, one local commented, "Good. That must mean the line will be shorter at Café Maspero." Locals do indeed line up for burgers, deli sandwiches (including a veggie muffuletta!), seafood, grilled marinated chicken, and so on, in some of the largest portions you'll ever run into. And there's an impressive list of wines, beers, and cocktails. Everything is delicious and is sold at low, low prices.

601 Decatur St. ✆ **504/523-6250.** Main courses $4.25–$9. No credit cards. Sun–Thurs 11am–10pm; Fri–Sat 11am–11pm.

Clover Grill ★ COFFEEHOUSE   We are cross with the Clover Grill. Once a place where the irreverent menu ("We're here to serve people and make them feel prettier than they are") competed with the even more outrageous staff for smart-aleck behavior, it has lost its luster. The menu has fewer jokes, and the once charmingly sassy staff is straying lately toward surly. But the burgers are still juicy and perfect and apparently are still cooked under a hubcap (they say it seals in the juices). It seems to work well enough—it's a mighty fine burger. Breakfast is still served round-the-clock, and drag queens still hang out at the tables or counters. But too many times we've come in at night requesting a shake, only to be told "no shakes." Unacceptable for a 24-hour diner. Go—but tell them they are on probation until they reclaim their original *joie de vivre.*

900 Bourbon St. ✆ **504/598-1010.** www.clovergrill.com. All items under $8. AE, MC, V. Daily 24 hr.

Felix's Restaurant & Oyster Bar ★★ SEAFOOD/CREOLE   Like its neighbor the Acme Oyster House, Felix's is a crowded and noisy place, full of locals and tourists taking advantage of the late hours. It's more or less the same as the Acme. Each has its die-hard **141** fans, convinced their particular choice is the superior one. Have your oysters raw, in a stew, in a soup, Rockefeller- or Bienville-style, in spaghetti, or even in an omelet. If oysters aren't your bag, the fried or grilled fish, chicken, steaks, spaghetti, omelets, and Creole cooking are mighty good, too. If you want something blackened, they'll fry it up to order. They usually also have boiled crawfish in season. In addition to this Post-K gussied-up traditional location, they have a newish Uptown location on Prytania Street (definitely open for business) that's well worth checking out!

739 Iberville St. $\textcircled{C}$ **504/522-4440.** Half-dozen oysters $6.25; po' boys under $15; other main courses $10–$26. AE, DISC. Also at 4938 Prytania St. $\textcircled{C}$ **504/895-1330.** Mon–Thurs 10am–10pm; Fri–Sat 10am–midnight; Sun 10am–9pm.

Johnny's Po' Boys ★★ SANDWICHES   For location (right near a busy part of the Quarter) and menu simplicity (po' boys and more po' boys), you can't ask for much more than Johnny's. They put anything you could possibly imagine (and some things you couldn't) on huge hunks of French bread, including the archetypal fried seafood (add some Tabasco, we strongly advise), deli meats, cheese omelets, ham and eggs, and the starch-o-rama that is a french-fry po' boy. You need to try it. *Really.* Johnny boasts that "even my failures are edible," and that says it all. And they deliver!

511 St. Louis St. $\textcircled{C}$ **504/524-8129.** Everything under $13. No credit cards. Mon–Fri 8am–3pm; Sat–Sun 8am–4:30pm.

Louisiana Pizza Kitchen PIZZA   The Louisiana Pizza Kitchen is a local favorite for its creative pies and atmosphere. Pastas have a significant place on the menu, but diners come for the pizzas and Caesar salad. Individual-size pizzas, baked in a wood-fired oven, feature a wide variety of toppings (shrimp and roasted garlic are two of the most popular). The best thing about their pizza is that your toppings won't get lost in an overabundance of cheese and tomato sauce.

95 French Market Place. $\textcircled{C}$ **504/522-9500.** www.louisianapizzakitchen.com. Pizzas $8.25–$13; pastas $10–$16. AE, DC, DISC, MC, V. Daily 11am–10pm. Also at 615 S. Carrollton Ave. $\textcircled{C}$ **504/866-5900.**

Napoleon House ★ CREOLE/ITALIAN   Folklore has it that the name of this place derives from a bit of wishful thinking: Around the time of Napoleon's death, a plot was hatched here to snatch the Little Corporal from his island exile and bring him to live in New Orleans. The third floor was added expressly for the purpose of providing him with a home. Alas, it probably isn't true: The building dates from a couple of years after Napoleon's death. But let's not let the truth get in the way of a good story, or a good hangout, which this is at any time of day, but particularly late at night, when it's dark enough to hatch your own secret plans. Somewhere between tourist-geared and local-friendly, it serves large portions of adequate versions of traditional New Orleans food (po' boys, jambalaya), plus wild-card items like salads with goat cheese and even pita and hummus, plus, most significantly, the only heated muffuletta in town.

500 Chartres St. $\textcircled{C}$ **504/524-9752.** www.napoleonhouse.com. Main courses $6–$8.25. AE, DISC, MC, V. Mon 11am–5:30pm; Tues–Thurs 11am–10pm, Fri–Sat 11am–11pm.

Petunia's ★ CAJUN/CREOLE   Petunia's, located in an 1830s town house, dishes up enormous portions of New Orleans specialties such as shrimp Creole, Cajun pasta with shrimp and andouille, and a variety of fresh seafood. Breakfast and Sunday brunch are popular, with a broad selection of crepes that, at 14 inches, are billed as the world's largest. Options include the St. Marie, a blend of spinach, cheddar, chicken, and hollandaise;

Whole Lotta Muffuletta Goin' On

Muffulettas are sandwiches of (pardon the expression) heroic proportions, enormous concoctions of round Italian bread, Italian cold cuts and cheeses, and olive salad. One person cannot eat a whole one—at least not in one sitting. (And if you can, don't complain to us about your stomachache.) Instead, share; a half makes a good meal, and a quarter is a filling snack. They may not sound like much on paper, but once you try one, you'll be hooked.

Several places in town claim to have invented the muffuletta and also claim to make the best one. (Some fancy restaurants have their own upscale versions—they are often delicious but bear no resemblance to the real McCoy.) Popular opinion, shared by the author, awards the crown to Central Grocery. But why take our word for it? Muffuletta comparison-shopping can be a very rewarding pastime.

Judging from the line that forms at lunchtime, many others agree with us that **Central Grocery ★★★**, 923 Decatur St. (✆ **504/523-1620**), makes the best muffuletta. There are a few seats at the back of this crowded, heavenly smelling Italian grocery, or you can order to go. Best of all, they ship, so once you're hooked—and you will be—you need not wait until your next trip for a muffuletta fix. Take your sandwich across the street and eat it on the banks of the Mississippi for an inexpensive romantic meal (about $14 for a whole sandwich, which feeds two). Central Grocery can make up their sandwiches early in the day, so they are ready to go as the rush hits. This means you can sometimes get a sandwich that is just a bit less fresh. Go early, to get them shortly after they are constructed, or later, if there has been a big rush, forcing production of more later in the day.

Then there are those who swear by the heated muffulettas served at the **Napoleon House ★**, 500 Chartres St. (✆ **504/524-9752**). Others find them blasphemous. We recommend that you start with cold and work up to heated—it's a different taste sensation. Feeling experimental? Go to **Nor-Joe's Importing Co.,** 505 Friscoe, in Metairie (✆ **504/833-9240**), where what many consider outstanding muffulettas are constructed with such iconoclastic ingredients as prosciutto and mortadella. Even bigger than the ones at Central Grocery, these are so good they have been known to make converts to the cult of Nor-Joe!

and the St. Francis, filled with shrimp, crab ratatouille, and Swiss cheese. If you have room for dessert, try the dessert crepes or the peanut-butter pie.

817 St. Louis St. (btw. Bourbon and Dauphine sts.). ✆ **504/522-6440.** Main courses $7–$16. AE, DC, DISC, MC, V. Daily 8am–10pm.

Rémoulade CREOLE/CAJUN/AMERICAN   An informal cafe offshoot of the venerable **Arnaud's** (p. 128), Rémoulade is certainly better than the otherwise exceedingly tourist-trap restaurants on Bourbon Street (Red Fish Grill being the exception), offering average but adequate local food at reasonable prices. You are best off ignoring the undistinguished jambalayas, gumbos, and so forth in favor of trying some of the Arnaud's specialties featured here—particularly the fine turtle soup and shrimp rémoulade. Burgers and pizza fill out the menu. This is one of the few places in town that serves Brocato's Italian ice cream.

309 Bourbon St. ✆ **504/523-0377.** www.remoulade.com. Main courses $9–$20. AE, DISC, MC, V. Daily 11:30am–midnight.

Stanley ★★ AMERICAN Proving the truth of the adage "necessity is the mother of invention," in the days following Katrina, when the Quarter was an isolated island of intrepid survivors determined to carry on regardless, and few, if any, places to eat were open (in New Orleans, that's how you know a disaster has hit), the chef-owner of Stella! began serving sandwiches and grilling burgers on the sidewalk. He ended up serving 3,000 meals in 9 days before shutting down and focusing on opening the cafe properly. The choice of name was obvious. Now it's moved into the old (and nicely renovated) La Madeleine space, right on the corner of Jackson Square, and it's a big boon to dining for tourists and locals alike. Between breakfast all day, cornmeal-crusted oyster po' boys, their drippy burgers (which we think rival Port of Call's naked monsters), and the genuine soda fountain featuring homemade ice cream, there is something for everyone all day long.

457 St. Ann St. (corner of Jackson Square and St. Ann). ✆ **504/578-0093.** www.restaurantstanley.com. Everything under $12. AE, DISC, MC, V. Daily 7am–7pm.

5 THE FAUBOURG MARIGNY

For the restaurants in this section, see the "New Orleans Dining" map on p. 120.

MODERATE

Feelings Cafe D'Aunoy ★ AMERICAN/CREOLE This modest neighborhood joint is a short cab ride away from the French Quarter. Friendly and funky, it serves tasty, solid (if not spectacular) food. It feels like a true local find—because it is—and can be a welcome break from the scene in the Quarter or from more intense dining. Try to get a table in the pretty courtyard or on the balcony overlooking it (particularly delightful on a balmy night), though the dining rooms are perfectly pleasant. Luckily, the courtyard wasn't much affected by Katrina—"The plants are beautiful. I don't know how they do it!" said one admirer. The ambience is even better when the piano bar is up and running (call ahead to see). A typical visit produces oysters *en brochette, pâté de maison,* seafood-stuffed eggplant (shrimp, crabmeat, and crawfish tails in a casserole with spicy sausage and crisp fried eggplant), and a chocolate-mousse/peanut-butter pie for dessert.

2600 Chartres St. ✆ **504/945-2222.** www.feelingscafe.com. Main courses $13–$25. AE, DC, DISC, MC, V. Thurs–Sun 6–9:30pm; Sat until 10pm, bar opens at 5pm; Sun brunch 11am–2pm.

Marigny Brasserie ★ ECLECTIC Originally a neighborhood cafe (and still operating in its original location as such), this is probably our first choice for a nice meal in the Frenchmen/Marigny section of town—not because the food is so outstandingly memorable in retrospect, but it's plenty interesting enough at the time, and everything we tried was pleasing to various degrees. The menu changes, but look for items such as sun-dried tomato braised rabbit, duck breast with hazelnut spaetzle, Abita Amber beer–brined pork chops, and kampachi tartare with watermelon.

640 Frenchmen St. ✆ **504/945-4472.** www.marignybrasserie.com. Reservations suggested. Main courses $10–$16 lunch, $18–$28 dinner, $12–$18 brunch. AE, DC, MC, V. Mon–Thurs 11:30am–2:30pm; Sun–Thurs 5:30–9:30pm; Fri 11:30am–2:30pm and 5:30–10pm; brunch live jazz Sun 11am–3pm.

Bywater Barbeque & Deli ★★ BARBECUE/PIZZA This tiny, charming, popular cafe deep in a residential neighborhood is a great find. As you can guess, it features barbecue, falling-off-the-bone meat properly dry-rubbed, if topped with a too-overwhelming red sauce (perhaps ask for it on the side). Ribs and pulled pork are the best of the meats, which come with sides like solid mac 'n' cheese and mayo-drenched coleslaw. And there is even more to the menu, which is oddly extensive. Weekend brunch specials include biscuits, cheese grits, and elaborate egg dishes, which are just as fab as the barbecue. There is also a lengthy pizza menu, which is where the vegetarians in the group will find relief, plus daily specials including red beans and rice on Monday. Portions are large, so split orders to make matters cheaper still, and save room for desserts like homemade chocolate cake with thick peanut-butter frosting.

3162 Dauphine St. ☎ **504/944-4445.** Main courses $6.50–$18. MC, V. Thurs–Tues 9am–9pm.

The Cake Café ★ SANDWICHES/DESSERT If you are looking for something interesting but not overwhelming in either vision or price, this sweet cafe (about a 10-min. walk from the Esplanade end of the Quarter) should suit the bill. Breakfast and lunch are both served all day, with breads, enormous biscuits (served with homemade jam), and bagels baked on-site. There are sandwiches such as grilled crabmeat with brie, big salads, and, of course, cake—coconut, red velvet, pineapple upside-down, all the down-home flavors. A buck gets you a cupcake with your lunch, and there are other specials as well. If the crowd at Elizabeth's (see below) is too daunting, this makes an adequate substitution.

2440 Chartres St. ☎ **504/943-0010.** Everything under $10. AE, DC, DISC, MC, V. Tues–Sun 7am–3pm.

Elizabeth's ★★★ CREOLE The average tourist may not head over to the Bywater because, well, because it's not the Quarter. That's too bad—not only will they miss a true N'Awlins neighbahood, but they will also miss experiences like Elizabeth's. Forget paying huge sums for average and goopy breakfast food. Here you eat, as they say, "Real Food, Done Real Good"—and, we add, real cheap. Food such as Creole rice calas (sweet rice fritters), a classic breakfast dish that is nearly extinct from menus around town. Food calling for health advisories, such as the praline bacon (topped with sugar and pecans— "pork candy," the shameless chef calls it; you must not miss this, but it's served only at breakfast time); or stuffed French toast (*pain perdu* piled high with cream cheese flavored with strawberries); or the breakfast po' boy, a monster sandwich the size of the Sunday *Picayune* rolled up. Note that the menu changes daily so you might want to call to see what they are offering. Meanwhile, if this wasn't enough, they are now open for dinner, featuring nightly specials like pan-seared salmon with Dijon beurre blanc sauce, Southern fried chicken livers with pepper jelly, and more humble fried shrimp and chicken. We strongly suggest that you not be an average tourist and get yourself down to the Bywater (though it's very, very crowded on the weekends). Out-of-the-way or not, this is one of the city's best restaurants. We'll meet you there—and let's walk back together (it's a hike, but doable) to justify an extra order of praline bacon.

601 Gallier St. ☎ **504/944-9272.** www.elizabeths-restaurant.com. Breakfast and lunch, everything under $10; dinner $8.50–$17. MC, V. Tues–Fri 11am–2:30pm; Sat–Sun 8am–2:30pm; Tues–Sat 6–10pm.

La Peniche Restaurant ★ CREOLE A short walk into the Marigny brings you to this homey (as opposed to "homely") dive; take the walk, because rents in the Quarter are too high for any place that looks like this to be a true bargain. Back to the original menu, if not back to 24 hours (shame, that), expect fried fish, po' boys, burgers, and even quiche. Good brunch options exist as well, which is why it's packed during that time. Come for specials such as the bronzed (with Cajun spices) pork, and be sure to have some chocolate layer cake (like homemade!) and peanut-butter-chocolate-chip pie. If they return to late-night hours, please be careful of the sometimes-dicey neighborhood (though this is often a cop hangout, which helps).

1940 Dauphine St. ℂ **504/943-1460.** Everything under $16, except seafood platter (under $20). AE, MC, V. Thurs–Mon 8am–10pm.

Mona's Café & Deli ★★ MIDDLE EASTERN   This local favorite finally expanded from its original Mid-City location into other parts of the city, with varying results. We like the marinated chicken with basmati rice, but they do credible versions of basic Middle Eastern fare (hummus, kabobs, and so forth). The Mid-City location is probably the best, with the Magazine location impressing us the least, but this is the most convenient for the average tourist.

504 Frenchmen St. ℂ **504/949-4115.** Sandwiches $4–$5.95; main courses $7.95–$15. AE, DC, DISC, MC, V. Mon–Thurs 11am–10pm; Fri–Sat 11am–11pm; Sun noon–9pm. They also have locations at 3901 Banks St.; Uptown, at 1120 S. Carrollton Ave.; and at 4126 Magazine St.

Praline Connection ⓞverrated CREOLE/SOUL FOOD   This might be heresy to some NOLA residents (although we know just as many who will back us up), but we think the Praline Connection is completely overrated and eminently missable. It's probably riding on sentiment and tradition, so if this review helps shake things up and gets it back into shape, well, then, good. This used to be the place to come for solid, reliable, and even—once upon a time—marvelous Creole and soul food. The crowds still come, not noting that what they are getting is sometimes dry and dull. Then again, everyone else has improved their food, so let's hope Praline Connection does, too. And early reports about the superior state of their fried chicken indicate that may well be. And there is always those fried chicken livers with pepper jelly . . .

542 Frenchmen St. ℂ **504/943-3934.** www.pralineconnection.com. Main courses $6.95–$20. AE, DC, DISC, MC, V. Mon–Sat 11am–10pm; Sun 11am–9pm.

6 MID-CITY/ESPLANADE

For a map of the restaurants in this section, see the "Mid-City Accommodations & Dining" map on p. 101.

EXPENSIVE

Ralph's on the Park ★★ BISTRO   You'd be hard-pressed to find a better setting for a New Orleans restaurant than this one, featuring an iconic view of the Spanish moss–draped giant oaks across the street in City Park, and just as likable on the inside as well, albeit a bit more L.A.-fashionable than one might expect. (Well, they can't all be tile floors and tin ceilings.) It's well placed for lunch after a visit to the park and museum, or for an early summer evening dinner, easily reachable from the City Park streetcar line. An excellent alternative to the usual Quarter or Uptown dining choices.

The food consists mostly of reliable variations of local Creole favorites, with a newish chef bringing his own style and dash to the menu. Entrees will change (probably seasonally), but when we were last there we were particularly smitten by an evening special of lamb cheeks in wide, homemade pasta and their BBQ shrimp on gnocchi—a twist on a classic local dish. Desserts are stylish and playful, which is sadly a bit unusual in this city. Right now all the elements are in place to make this restaurant worth your strong consideration.

900 City Park Ave. ✆ **504/488-1000.** www.ralphsonthepark.com. Reservations recommended. Main courses $15–$24 lunch, $18–$35 dinner, $16–$25 brunch. AE, MC, V. Sun–Thurs 5:30–9pm; Fri–Sat 5:30–9:30pm; Fri 11:30am–2pm; Sun 11am–2pm.

MODERATE

Café Degas ★★ BISTRO/FRENCH   Just an adorable, friendly, charming French bistro—a delightful neighborhood restaurant, and one that doesn't emphasize fried food (trust us, that's a combo that's hard to find in this town!). If you want to have a nice meal without the fuss and feathers, Degas should do the trick in terms of both food and atmosphere. The big tree in the dining room is still there, but a lovely outside tree came down in the storm. There are daily dinner and lunch specials—think quiches and real, live salads (always a happy find in this town) and straightforward but flavorful fish and meat dishes, presented in generous portions. You can go light (a salad, a plate of pâtés and cheeses) or heavy (filet of beef tenderloin with a green peppercorn-brandy sauce)—either way, you'll feel as if you ate something worthwhile. Though it's French, this is not France, and this bistro is informal enough that you can go wearing bluejeans.

3127 Esplanade Ave. ✆ **504/945-5635.** www.cafedegas.com. Reservations recommended. Main courses lunch $9–$15, dinner $16–$23. AE, DC, DISC, MC, V. Wed–Sat 11am–2:30pm; Wed–Thurs 6–10pm; Fri–Sat 6–10:30pm; Sun 6–9pm.

Dooky Chase ★ SOUL FOOD/CREOLE   For decades, Leah and husband Dooky Chase have served prominent African-American politicians, musicians, and business-people Chef Leah's classic soul food as gloriously influenced by the city's French, Sicilian, and Italian traditions. This was the place people like Ray Charles (who wrote "Early in the Morning" about it) would come to after local shows and stay up until the wee hours telling stories and eating gumbo—one of the city's best. The restaurant had 2 feet of flooding, not to mention mold issues, and rebuilding has come along very slowly, despite benefits held for the Chases both here and in other cities. (Ms. Leah is pleased she got a new stove out of the deal, though, since she's wanted one for so long. An octogenarian, she says she has to keep going long enough to cook on it!) At press time they were still struggling to open regularly, so call ahead. The Chases lived for over a year in a FEMA trailer outside their restaurant, and they are as wonderful as their cooking. They are everything that is New Orleans, and so make a stop at the restaurant they've worked so hard for, once it comes back. Then you can have shrimp Clemenceau, an unlikely but successful casserole of sautéed shellfish, mushrooms, peas, and potatoes, not to mention exquisite fried chicken, sautéed veal, grits, grillades, and court bouillon. All this, and Dooky and Leah. Long may they cook.

2301 Orleans Ave. ✆ **504/821-0600.** Main courses $9–$20, lower for takeout, slightly higher for dine-in. Tues–Fri takeout 11am–7pm. Dine-in only if staff available Tues–Fri 11am–2pm, so call ahead.

Liuzza's ★★ CREOLE/ITALIAN   Actual moment from a Liuzza's visit: The crusty waitress hands a menu to a customer ("Here you go, Bay-bee") and then abruptly closes it. "Bay-bee," she instructs, gesticulating with a finger, "Numba One, or Numba Two—but *definitely* Numba One." Naturally, the Number One special was ordered (it proved to be a seafood lasagna, dripping with a white cream sauce) and devoured (despite its enormous size).

Yep, this is a neighborhood institution (open since 1947; it's humble, small, and often crowded with regulars), and when the waitress talks, you betcha you listen. You can only imagine the sorrow regulars felt seeing photos of Liuzza's under 8 feet of water (that's over Shaquille O'Neal's head, the owners pointed out) and the joy they felt when, against so many odds, it reopened around Jazz Fest 2006, looking the same as always, if cleaner and newer. Everything is back, all that hearty Italian and other comfort food, including the famous deep-fried dill pickle slices ("You people will batter and deep-fry anything that isn't nailed down!" said yet another astonished visitor) and po' boys. Don't miss having a beer in the massive, frosted mugs that rode out Katrina safely in the fridge!

3636 Bienville St. ℂ **504/482-9120.** www.liuzzas.com. Main courses $9.50–$20. No credit cards. Tues–Thurs 11am–9pm; Fri–Sat 11am–10pm.

Lola's ★★★ SPANISH/INTERNATIONAL "Please, oh please, don't mention Lola's in the book!" beg our local foodie friends. Why? Because this small, special place doesn't take reservations, and the nightly wait is already long as it is. But we are going to spill the beans anyway while assuring you that this is worth waiting for, thanks to incredible Spanish dishes, from various paellas to starters such as garlic shrimp *tapas* and a heck of a garlic soup. Try to arrive 15 to 30 minutes before opening time and wait in line. If you come later and there's a mob, don't be discouraged: Service is attentive and food comes quickly, so your wait shouldn't be too long, though we'd either not bother on the weekends or bring a book. Don't forget to bring cash—and try not to get ahead of our friends in line!

3312 Esplanade Ave. ℂ **504/488-6946.** Main courses $8.75–$16. No credit cards. Sun–Thurs 5:30–9:30pm; Fri–Sat 5:30–10pm.

Mandina's ★★ CREOLE/ITALIAN In a city renowned for its small, funky, local joints as well as its fine-dining establishments, dis is da ultimate neighbahood N'Awlins restaurant. Tommy Mandina's family has owned and operated this restaurant and bar since the late 1800s, and the menu hasn't changed much in the last 50 years or so. This is a good thing. What has changed is the interior; Mandina's got hammered by the storm, and the fourth-generation owners discovered that once you open up a 100-plus-year-old building, especially one that was expanded over the years in a hodgepodge, off-the-cuff manner, you discover all kinds of nifty additional problems. The result is a clean, reconfigured room, with more space—good thing, since relieved regulars are back in droves, as is the longtime staff.

Standouts among the appetizers are the greasy but yummy fried onion rings, the excellent tangy shrimp rémoulade, buttery liberally garlicked bread, and the crawfish cakes. Soups are always fine as well, especially seafood gumbo and turtle soup au sherry. Then go for the wonderful red beans and rice with Italian sausage, the trout meunière, the grilled trout, or our favorite comfort food, the sweet Italian sausage and spaghetti combo—hardly innovative gourmet, but exactly the way we remember it from childhood. Or try the hearty, juicy, oblong cheeseburger po' boy, medium rare.

3800 Canal St. ℂ **504/482-9179.** www.mandinasrestaurant.com. Main courses $10–$25. No credit cards. Mon–Thurs 11am–9:30pm; Fri–Sat 11am–10:30pm; Sun noon–9pm.

INEXPENSIVE

Lil' Dizzy's ★★ CREOLE/SOUL FOOD Not exactly Mid-City—it's on the outskirts of the Treme, on the way to Bayou St. John, so it serves both that neighborhood and the Quarter, which it's actually closer to—this is a quintessential neighborhood restaurant, and understandably so; the owner grew up behind his family's legendary soul food/Creole restaurant. Locals line up here early, so try to time your visit for off hours, though you do run the risk of them running out of certain items by the time you arrive. This is your chance to try authentic regional cooking. Breakfast brings biscuits; waffles; crabmeat and shrimp omelets (among pretty much anything else you can whip up with eggs); grits; homemade hot sausages; and the very popular calves' liver in brown gravy. Lunch brings some terrific fried chicken and more elaborate options like the trout *Baquet* (the fish is topped with garlic-butter sauce and sometimes fresh crabmeat), red beans 'n' rice, and even a T-bone steak. A friendly, lively (if sometimes justly harried) bunch works here, and the owner twinkles above it all. *Note:* Lil' Dizzy's opened a branch in the Wyndham Whitney Hotel in the Central Business District, where prices are a bit higher, but space is considerably greater. It may also be more conveniently located for you.

1500 Esplanade Ave. ℭ **504/569-8997.** Everything under $12 except the Fri $14 seafood platter. AE, DC, DISC, MC, V. Mon–Fri 7am–2:30pm; Sat 7am–2pm.

Liuzza's by the Track ★★ CREOLE/SANDWICHES   Not to be confused with Liuzza's, above, and not to be overlooked, either. This Liuzza's is a near-flawless example of a corner neighborhood hole in the wall. In one visit, you will either get the point or not; by the second visit, the staff will know your name. By the third visit, you might wonder why you would eat anywhere else. It's not just the fact that they serve what may be the best gumbo and red beans 'n' rice in the city, it's the monster perfect po' boys, including a drippy garlic-stuffed roast beef (with a pinch of horseradish in the mayo) and a rare barbecued-shrimp po' boy (about three dozen shrimp in a hollowed-out po' boy loaf, soaked in spicy butter). It's also the surprise of serious daily specials such as "grilled crab cheese" and shish kabobs. It's the salads as well, huge and full of leafy greens (the healthy aspects of which we like to ruin by having ours topped with fried crawfish and green-onion dressing); vegetarians will be thrilled with the portobello mushroom version. Try the sweet-potato and andouille soup. Space is at a premium (they don't have a lot of tables), and it is not out of the question that you could show up and simply never, ever get seated. (Or you could just as easily be the only diner. It's unpredictable.) Call ahead or plan for, say, lunch (the most popular time) at 11:45am instead of noon.

1518 N. Lopez. ℭ **504/218-7888.** Everything under $14. AE, DISC, MC, V. Mon–Sat 11am–7pm.

Parkway Bakery and Tavern ★★ SANDWICHES   A block or so off Bayou St. John, some enterprising folks with a good sense of history resurrected a long-boarded-up and once much-beloved po' boy shop and bakery, founded in 1922. It elicits flashbacks from old customers (though the lovingly renovated and spick-and-span interior bears no relation to the grungy last days of its old incarnation) and deep pleasure in just about everyone. Never was that more evident than the evening the intrepid owner reopened, one of the first businesses in his area to do so. About 1,000 locals came out to sample the (then) limited menu of just one po' boy (roast beef), listen to some music, and rejoice. You won't find any innovations here, just classic po' boys (the falling-apart roast beef, and the *sine non qua* fried oyster have their dedicated fans, while we are believers in the hot sausage and cheese topped with roast beef debris), and many a local-beloved brand name like Barq's and Zapp's. The bar is a good hang as well, lately offering live music many nights, while the bayou remains a pretty walk.

538 Hagan St. ℭ **504/482-3047.** www.parkwaybakeryandtavernnola.com. Everything under $13. AE, DISC, MC, V. Wed–Mon 11am–10pm (closed Tues). Call about live music.

Willie Mae's Scotch House ★★★ SOUL FOOD   This is as much a fairy tale as a restaurant review. Once upon a time, not that many people outside her humble 6th Ward neighborhood thought much about Miss Willie Mae and her chicken shack, which was also part of her home. Until 2005, that is, when the octogenarian and her secret-recipe fried chicken were designated an "American classic" by the James Beard Association. Weeks later, home and restaurant were under 8 feet of water. Weeks after that, a dedicated group of volunteers, including local and regional restaurateurs, banded together to bring back Willie Mae's. (Their Herculean efforts are chronicled on several places on the Web; watch the video at www.neworleanscvb.com and read all about it at www.southern foodways.com.) The place probably didn't look this good before all the work, though as with so many beloved, fully restored dives, it reminds us of how big a role patina of time plays in the appeal of New Orleans. So—the most sublime fried chicken ever? Certainly it's hard to figure out how to improve upon it (other than making it come out of the kitchen sooner—plan on a wait). There is no menu—just let your server recite the day's offerings, and wait as Miss Willie Mae's great-granddaughter, who has the secret recipes, fries you up something great. It's a reward for a beautiful effort of community, and for your stomach.

2401 St. Ann St. ✆ **504/822-9503.** Everything under $15. No credit cards. Mon–Fri 11am–3pm.

Ye Olde College Inn ★★ CREOLE/SANDWICHES   A venerable (since the 1930s) dive/hangout renovated into a really nice space, with a pretty, if simple, interior, now both classy and comfortable, fronted by an excellent and clean bar. The po' boys are mammoth (they brag about 'em on a sign), and include a fried oyster or shrimp topped with bacon and havarti cheese, an option we hope catches on all over the city. More elaborate meals include an appetizer of fried oysters topped with a bleu-cheese oil, a fried soft-shell crab special (seasonal only, of course) on a crouton with sautéed spinach and topped with a green onion aioli and lump crabmeat, and a bacon-wrapped filet topped with sautéed mushrooms. In short, this is a way to try some fancier local cooking for considerably less than the high-profile places in the Quarter. They have live music upstairs some nights.

3016 Carrollton Ave. ✆ **504/866-3683.** Main courses $10–$20. DISC, MC, V. Tues–Sat 4–11pm.

---

7 CENTRAL BUSINESS DISTRICT

For restaurants in this section, see the "New Orleans Dining" map on p. 120. *Note:* Lil' Dizzy's, reviewed above, has a branch in the Wyndham Whitney Hotel. The space is considerably fancier, a bit at odds with the down-home menu, but it's also bigger, and thus less likely to be as crowded as the original.

VERY EXPENSIVE

Emeril's ★★★ CREOLE/NEW AMERICAN   Emeril may be ubiquitous, but we can vouch for his first namesake restaurant. Although it may no longer be trendsetting, it certainly isn't resting on its laurels in terms of quality, a remarkable feat given how long the place has been around. What's more, there are all kinds of interesting chef action going on in the kitchen, and this may be one of the most exciting times to dine here. It remains a popular spot for business lunches.

The menu will change according to the chef, but you can rely on, and should try, the barbecued shrimp, which comes with a heavier sauce than the classic versions of this local

Impressions

New Orleans is one place you can eat and drink the most, and suffer the least.

—William Makepeace Thackeray

dish, and is paired with charming little rosemary biscuits. The amusingly named "salad" of Abita root beer–glazed pork belly consists mostly of large slabs of the soft rich meat and is a must for carnivores in the crowd. Entree standouts include oyster-dressing-crusted salmon with tuna "bacon" and andouille-crusted redfish. There can be some incredible specials on any given evening as well. Try to save part of your generously portioned meal for leftovers, so that you have room for the notable banana cream pie, a behemoth whose fat content doesn't bear thinking about, or perhaps more sanely, some delicate homemade sorbets.

800 Tchoupitoulas St. $\mathcal{C}$ **504/528-9393.** www.emerils.com. Reservations highly recommended at dinner. Main courses lunch $19–$25, dinner $26–$39; menu degustation (tasting menu) only on weekends $65. AE, DC, DISC, MC, V. Dinner daily 6–10pm; lunch Mon–Fri 11:30am–2pm.

Emeril's Delmonico Restaurant and Bar ★★ CREOLE   In theory this is Emeril's more traditionally Creole restaurant, in reality a beautifully renovated space where we've had some mighty fine meals, and where you may or may not eat anything even remotely Creole—but as with Emeril's flagship restaurant (above), such interesting work is going on right now that you will find it hard to care. The menu will also change regularly, but be sure to get a charcuterie plate to start; it will come beautifully laden with all sorts of housemade hams, salamis, and pâté. Entrees can consist of a duo of Moroccan-spiced lamb chops with *merquez* sausage or a confit of duck leg. Get a side of thick buttermilk-battered onion rings and, of course, some of their handsome and interesting desserts.

1300 St. Charles Ave. $\mathcal{C}$ **504/525-4937.** www.emerils.com. Reservations highly recommended. Main courses dinner $25–$39. AE, DC, DISC, MC, V. Sun–Thurs 6–9pm; Fri–Sat 6–10pm.

Restaurant August ★ FRENCH   So there's Chef John Besh, feeding people during the dark days immediately post-Katrina, just hauling out jambalaya and anything else he can cook up in volume, and helping to bring back the venerable Willie Mae's Scotch House, proving he's as much about local indigenous cooking as he is about fancy-pants frivolity. Then he hauls off and wins the 2006 James Beard Award for Best Chef Southeast, plus scads of other gourmet praise, plus near-ubiquity on the Food Channel. And here we are, having eaten here several times . . . never really being all that excited by the experience. We feel like heels, but we just don't get it. Too much use of foam and other nouvelle gimmicks, too dainty and fussy, too many flavors and ingredients crammed on a plate—or the opposite problem, work that is all construction and no flavor. Or the menu is misleading, such as the Moroccan-spiced duck, which was largely enjoyable, but not in the least bit Moroccan, or a dessert that comes out in a form distinctly different from what was described in print. We've never had a bad meal here, but we've never been other than underwhelmed. On the other hand, reliable foodie friends dream about that degustation menu (chef's choice and he varies it from table to table) as one of the highlights of their dining lives, while others say the place is the best the city has to offer. Your mileage may well vary.

courses $28–$46; 5-course tasting menu $75 (with wine pairing $30 extra); 3-hr.-long John Besh degustation menu with wine pairing $170 per person (whole table must participate). AE, DC, MC, V. Daily 5–9pm; Fri lunch 11am–2pm.

EXPENSIVE

Café Adelaide ★★★ CONTEMPORARY CREOLE   From the same branch of the Brennan family that brings you Commander's Palace, and well worth your dining time, given the talented chef, playful menu, and the superb drinks. Come here if you want to sample and taste; those all-the-rage small plates that allow the indecisive to sample a lot, and plates designed specifically for parties to share make up the start of the menu. The menu will change frequently but possibilities include to-die-for duck debris-topped cornbread waffles, shrimp-and-tasso "corn dogs," blue crab pound cake with Port-Salut icing, and fois gras biscuit and gravy. These small plates and apps make it tempting to overlook the culinarily-thoughtful entrees and skip straight to desserts, but those entrees, which also change seasonally, rarely disappoint. At breakfast they offer the classic *pain perdu*, New Orleans's version of French toast. The drinks, especially the sweet and powerful house Swizzle Stick (which can be had on the festive cocktail sampler tree; ask for one!), make this a bar worth investigating as well. As if all that isn't enough to lure you in, they usually have great lunch and dinner multicourse meal deals.

300 Poydras St. (in the Loews Hotel). Ⓒ **504/595-3305.** www.cafeadelaide.com. Reservations suggested. Lunch main courses $14–$19; dinner $26–$36. AE, DC, DISC, MC, V. Mon–Fri 7–10am; Sat–Sun 7am–12:30pm; Mon–Thurs 11:30am–2pm; Fri 11:30am–2:30pm; Sun–Thurs 6–9pm; Fri–Sat 6–9:30pm. "Off hours" menu available at bar 11am–10:30pm.

Cuvée ★★★ CONTEMPORARY CREOLE   Doing its darndest to be considered the best restaurant in town, Cuvée is certainly the most innovative and interesting. Join local raving foodies in a romantic and cozy brick-lined room where you might get to sample—should the seasonally changing menu allow—the foie gras daily special (such as a foie gras mousse with brandy-soaked cherries or—wait for it—in crème brûlée), or shredded duck meat pie with rhubarb, red wine, and Louisiana strawberry jam with a side of strawberry cream soda. Entrees could be sea bass wrapped in parma ham, or a deconstructed *osso buco* with the "bone" made of potato with the marrow whipped into more potato filling the interior. Fittingly, desserts are equally witty (look for their take on the moon pie with dreamsicle ice cream). And then there is the wine list. You might well eat and eat and eat and at the end want to do it all over again.

322 Magazine St. Ⓒ **504/587-9001.** www.restaurantcuvee.com. Reservations highly recommended. Main courses $20–$30 dinner. AE, DC, MC, V. Mon–Thurs 6–9:30pm; Fri–Sat lunch 11:30am–10:30pm.

LaCôte Brasserie ★ BISTRO   A companion restaurant to René Bistrot in the Renaissance Pere Marquette, LaCôte Brasserie has had some chef turnover and its reach sometimes exceeds its grasp, but we would rather a restaurant try and partly miss than rely on old boring standards. The physical space reflects an attempt to create an elegant version of a classic hotel coffeehouse (a poor choice for an upscale restaurant). Every time we review this restaurant, they change their menu (sorry if that sounds cranky!) but at least they always seem to keep the nightly whole-fish presentation; almost no other place in town will dare to serve an entire fish (pompano, pan-roasted, and finished off in the oven, in our case), head intact. For that matter, all fish options seem to fare pretty well here, regardless of who is at the helm or what is presented on your plate.

In the Renaissance Arts Hotel, 700 Tchoupitoulas St. ✆ **504/613-2330.** www.lacotebrasserie.com. Reservations suggested. Entrees $15–$38. AE, DC, DISC, MC, V. Daily 6:30–10am, 11:30am–2:30pm, and 6–10pm.

MiLa ★ NOUVEAU SOUTHERN   Run by a married chef couple (the name reflects their Mississippi and Louisiana roots, respectively), this restaurant was an instant hit, thanks in no small part to the signature appetizer of "deconstructed" oysters Rockefeller. The food (selection will change daily) is oddly delicate—phyllo-crusted redfish, for example, finds the crisp dough a lacy configuration around the fish, while black grouper is porcini dusted and comes with a coffee glaze. White asparagus Veloute is a cloud-light soup. Lunch brings an excellent three-course special for $20 and while it means potentially limiting your options, it is an attractive way to experience the interesting work going on here.

817 Common St. (in the Renaissance Pere Marquette hotel). ✆ **504/412-2580.** www.milaneworleans. com. Reservations suggested. Main courses lunch $15–$22, dinner $19–$30. AE, DC, DISC, MC, V. Mon–Fri 11:30am–2:30pm and 5:30–10pm; Sat 5:30–10pm; Sun 11am–2:30pm and 5:30–10pm.

MODERATE

Cochon ★★ CAJUN   Anyone opening a new restaurant these days is to be lauded, so here's a round of appreciative applause for Chef Donald Link of Herbsaint, and his partner Stephen Stryjewski (who is the one usually in the kitchen), who have not only braved an uncertain market, but also delivered a venture that would be delightful under any circumstances. Influenced by Link's own family background in Acadia, this restaurant features mostly small plates of Cajun-inspired dishes. If we point out that nothing is precisely Cajun, nor is there enough pork, that's not meant to be surly. We just happen to be particular about pig. And it's a compliment; we want more dishes like the garlicky cochon (roasted suckling pig) with cracklins, the pork rillette, the ribs with watermelon pickle, and the oyster-and-bacon sandwich. We also want them bigger (yes, even the "small plates") because the mouthfuls you get are so darn good. Then again, that leaves us room for orange icebox and lemon-buttermilk pie. Order a bunch of plates and mix and match meat to your heart's delight.

930 Tchoupitoulas St. ✆ **504/588-2123.** www.cochonrestaurant.com. Reservations strongly recommended on weekends. Small plates $7–$11; main courses $14–$22. AE, DISC, MC, V. Mon–Fri 11am–10pm; Sat 5:30–10pm.

Herbsaint ★★ BISTRO   Herbsaint would be the locally made pastis found in, among other places, the popular local cocktail, the Sazerac. As a restaurant, it's an alternative to similarly inventive but much higher-priced peers in the Quarter, with thoughtful dishes planned by 2007 James Beard Best Southeast Chef Donald Link. Be sure to try the Herbsaint, tomato, and shrimp bisque—it always sends us into rhapsodies, and we aren't even soup fans—and the "small plate" of fried frogs' legs, because when else are you going to? Fresh, beautiful salads can come delectably decorated with seasonal ingredients or lush extras like burrata cheese. Carnivores might weep over the splendor of the meticulous pork-belly preparations, which can be a 3-day process. The desserts are often simple, but usually standouts. Bistro menu served from 1:30 to 5pm, featuring light entrees from both lunch and dinner menus.

701 St. Charles Ave. ✆ **504/524-4114.** www.herbsaint.com. Reservations suggested for lunch and for 2 or more for dinner. Main courses lunch $12–$14, dinner $24–$32. AE, DC, DISC, MC, V. Mon–Fri 11:30am–1:30pm; Mon–Sat 5:30–10pm.

Liborio's Cuban Restaurant ★ CUBAN   Nicely located in the Central Business
District, this Cuban cafe attracts many local business folk at lunchtime, but despite the
crowds, that might be the best time to go, when prices are very affordable (they do seem
to be needlessly high at dinnertime). Plus, it's a fun space—the chartreuse sponged walls
and pillowy parachute fabric upholstering the ceiling make for a festive and more aesthetically pleasing look than you might think from reading the description. Lazy ceiling
fans and photos from the homeland put you in mind of Hemingway's Havana. Order the
day's special or be like us, partial to Cuban specialties such as the tender, garlicky roast
pork; the flatbread Cuban sandwich; and sweet fried plantains.

321 Magazine St. ℭ **504/581-9680.** Reservations suggested. Main courses $10–$18 lunch, $15–$28
dinner. AE, DC, DISC, MC, V. Mon–Sat 11am–3pm; Thurs–Sat 5:45–9pm.

Lüke ★★★ BISTRO   A fully realized bistro concept from much-lauded local chef
John Besh, and a new dining locale that has hit the ground running. It's hearty and
authentic, but not stodgy French and German brasserie fare. Menu descriptions don't
give the true picture—it really must be seen to be appreciated, so snoop at your neighbor's plate for possibilities. There's so much to try here it's hard to narrow down a choice
for you. *Flamen küche* is an Alsatian tort topped with chunks of bacon and caramelized
onions. The seasonal *Badischer Kalbskopf* is a warm calves' head terrine—a layer of trans-
lucent, gelatinous savory topped by a tart tomato salad, and thus, an entirely new experience in salads. The *choucroûte maison* includes house-made sausages, pork belly, *cochon
de lait* with cherry mustard and is, in short, one fine plate of pig. The big juicy cheeseburger, with caramelized onions and thick-cut bacon on an onion roll, will have you
swear off fast-food imitations forever. The shrimp and grits demolishes other, dry versions around town. The handsome bistro is quite popular at lunch, no doubt in part to
the $15 express lunch special, an entree of the day plus a cup of soup. Save room for the
mini profiteroles filled with warm chocolate custard.

333 St. Charles Ave. ℭ **504/378-2840.** www.lukeneworleans.com. Reservations strongly suggested at
lunch and dinner. Main courses $12–$26 (mostly on lower end for lunch). AE, DC, DISC, MC, V. Daily 7am–
11pm.

Palace Café ★★ CONTEMPORARY CREOLE   This is where to go for low-key
and non-intimidating yet still interesting dining. Housed attractively in the historic
Werlein's for Music building, this popular Brennan family restaurant has the first sidewalk dining on Canal, thanks to some street renovations, which will be a treat on balmy
nights. The menu focuses on evolving Creole cuisine. Be sure to order the crabmeat
cheesecake appetizer (a table-poundingly good dish if ever there was one), and possibly
the escargots as well. As for main courses, they do fish especially well (the andouille-
crusted fish is always spot on). Look for seasonal specials based on what comes from local
farmers and fishermen, including house-made duck pastrami, crusted emu, or multiple
duck preparations. The pork debris potpie is adorable comfort food. For dessert, they
invented the by-now ubiquitous white-chocolate bread pudding, and no matter what
others may claim, they have the best. Of course, we don't much care, because after a long
absence, they brought back one of our favorite desserts of all time—the Mississippi Mud
Pie, which features five layers of chocolate mousse, from lightest to darkest, on a chocolate cookie-crumb crust.

605 Canal St. ℭ **504/523-1661.** www.palacecafe.com. Reservations recommended. Main courses lunch
$14–$26, dinner $17–$32. 3-course meal before 7pm $28. AE, DC, DISC, MC, V. Mon–Sat 11:30am–2:30pm
and 5:30–10pm; Sun brunch 10:30am–2:30pm.

Tommy's Cuisine ★★ FRENCH/ITALIAN   Those of you frustrated by the perennially long lines at Irene's in the Quarter will be delighted to know that Tommy's—the creation of Irene's eponymous co-founder—is more or less exactly the same; it has the same welcome waft of garlic that greets you from a block away, and virtually the same menu. But Tommy's has one important difference: It takes reservations. Don't get us wrong; we love Irene's. But this space is less cramped in feel, if quite dark and chatty. (Forget deep conversations—the noise level is palpable.) And did we mention they take reservations? So you can actually come here and not wait 2 hours before you get to dig into fantastic chicken Rosemarino, chicken marinated in an olive oil, garlic, and rosemary sauce; and duck Tchoupitoulas, which some consider the best duck dish in New Orleans. Both dishes were made famous at Irene's, as is just about the entire menu. The nightly specials are the only real difference we can spot, and even those will seem familiar to those on the New Orleans restaurant scene, because Tommy's chef spent a number of years at Galatoire's and brought along some of their heavy-on-the-béchamel-sauce seafood dishes. Stick to the regular menu, and revel in your ability to do so without having to stand in line.

746 Tchoupitoulas St. ✆ **504/581-1103.** www.tommyscuisine.com. Reservations preferred. Main courses $20–$29. AE, DISC, MC, V. Sun–Thurs 5:30–10pm; Fri–Sat 5:30–11pm.

INEXPENSIVE

Ernst Café AMERICAN   The same family has owned this old brick building since 1902. Located right next to Harrah's casino and featuring live blues music on Friday and Saturday nights, it's a big local scene, understandable given how late they stay open. Sandwiches, hamburgers, fried shrimp, salads, red beans and rice, and po' boys are on offer here.

600 S. Peters St. ✆ **504/525-8544.** www.ernstcafe.net. Main courses $8–$15. AE, DC, DISC, MC, V. Mon–Tues 3pm–"until" (usually 2–6am); Wed–Sun 11am–"until."

Mother's ★★ SANDWICHES/CREOLE   Perhaps the proudest of all restaurants when New Orleans was named Fattest City in the U.S. was Mother's, whose overstuffed, mountain-size po' boys absolutely helped contribute to the results. It has long lines and a most typically New Orleans atmosphere (which is to say, humble, in the best way) and dining room (the "new" dining room is spiffier, if you care about such things), but who cares when faced with a Famous Ferdi Special—a giant roll filled with baked ham (the homemade house specialty), roast beef, gravy, and debris (the bits of beef that fall off when the roast is carved)? There's other food, including one of the best breakfasts in the city, but the po' boys are what New Orleans goes for, and you should, too. Mother's is within walking distance of the Louisiana Superdome and a number of major hotels. Be sure to allow time to stand in line, as there nearly always is one, though it can move quickly.

401 Poydras St. ✆ **504/523-9656.** www.mothersrestaurant.net. Menu items $2.50–$20. AE, MC, V. Mon–Sat 7:30am–10pm.

8 UPTOWN/THE GARDEN DISTRICT

For a map of restaurants in this section, see either the "New Orleans Dining" map on p. 120 or the "Uptown Accommodations & Dining" map on p. 111.

Brigtsen's ★ CAJUN/CREOLE   Nestled in a converted 19th-century house at the Riverbend, Brigtsen's is warm, intimate, and romantic. The individual dining rooms are small and cozy, each sweetly painted with murals, and the menu changes daily. They aren't at the cutting edge of local cuisine, but there is plenty of regular interest. Generous portions make appetizers superfluous but their seasonal salads are so good and the BBQ shrimp with shrimp calas is hard to pass up. Brigtsen has a special touch with rabbit: One of his most mouthwatering dishes is an appetizer of rabbit tenderloin on a tasso-Parmesan grits cake with sautéed spinach and a Creole mustard sauce. You can't miss with any of the soups, especially the lovely butternut squash shrimp bisque, and there's an entree to please everyone. A broiled Gulf fish with crabmeat Parmesan crust and béarnaise sauce is a great piece of seafood. Roast duck with dried cherry sauce is always reliable, with the skin of the duck done to a cracklin' just-rightness. For the indecisive, a seafood platter offers samples of all sorts of fishy goodness, such as artichoke-baked oyster or stuff piquillo pepper with shrimp and crabmeat con queso.

723 Dante St. ℂ **504/861-7610.** www.brigtsens.com. Reservations recommended. Main courses $24–$38. AE, DC, DISC, MC, V. Tues–Sat 5:30–10pm.

Clancy's ★ CREOLE   Your friendly cabdriver may insist that Clancy's is "out of town" because this local favorite is so far uptown, but it's really not that much farther than a trip to the zoo or to Brigtsen's (see above). The food and neighborhood vibe alone should be worth the trip; it's a relief to get off the tourist path. The locals who cram into the smallish, oh-so–New Orleans room nightly are a loyal bunch, as New Orleans diners tend to be, but we have to say our last meal at Clancy's was only average and quite forgettable. We may have hit them on a bad night. But to ensure a better meal, follow the advice of those same locals and order the night's specials rather than sticking to the menu (though the duck dish on the menu is as good as duck gets). You could try the fried oysters with brie appetizer or smoked fried soft-shell crab topped with crabmeat (smoke flavor not overpowering, crab perfectly fried without a drop of grease to taint the dish), and veal topped with crabmeat and béarnaise sauce. Food too heavy? What the heck—make it even more so with desserts such as lemon icebox pie. One local said it was even better than his grandma's!

6100 Annunciation St. ℂ **504/895-1111.** Reservations recommended. Main courses $25–$32. AE, DC, DISC, MC, V. Mon–Sat 5:30–10:30pm; Thurs–Fri 11:30am–2pm.

Commander's Palace ★★★ CREOLE   The much-beloved Commander's is perhaps *the* symbol of the New Orleans dining scene, and for good reason. The building has been a restaurant for a century, it's at the top (more or less) of the multi-branched Brennan family restaurant tree, and its chefs have gone on to their own fame and household-name status (Prudhomme and Emeril ring any bells?), plus they train and produce their own outstanding locals, so the tradition keeps going. Its decor is a subtle wonder—check out the hand-embroidered wallpaper in the entry hall, the display of painted and wooden local birds in the main dining room, and the excellent chandeliers. Dinner here is always good, and often it's superlative (and the same goes for lunch and brunch, lower-price options you may wish to consider depending on the state of your wallet—after all, that's when they serve 25¢ martinis!). The current menu reflects Chef Tory McPhail's constantly working imagination and his commitment to locally grown and locally sourced ingredients. Favorites like the pecan-crusted Gulf fish and the tasso shrimp in pepper jelly appetizer remain, but new dishes reveal all sorts of culinary fun going on in the kitchen.

A standout appetizer is the foie gras "Du Monde," seared foie gras atop a berry-flavored beignet paired with a chicory-flavored foie gras *café*, a rich salute to the venerable Café du Monde. It's one of the most ridiculous and delicious appetizers we've ever had. Chef Tory makes a daily gumbo of relatively unexpected ingredients that might convince even a committed Cajun cook to reconsider his own traditions. The menu changes frequently, but on last visit we were bowled over by the Creole mustard-crusted sliced rack of lamb. Seek out the fresh seafood or the best of the seasonal specialties; we've not been disappointed in either. Your waitperson will tell you to order the bread pudding soufflé. Trust them. If it's strawberry season, don't miss the strawberry shortcake, and if you've never had the Creole cream cheesecake, do, though their signature crème brûlée is a thin sheath of burnt yummy.

1403 Washington Ave. ℂ 504/899-8221. www.commanderspalace.com. Main courses $30–$42. AE, DISC, MC, V. Mon–Fri 11:30am–1:30pm; daily 6–9:30pm; brunch Sat 11:30am–1pm and Sun 10:30am–1:30pm. Closed Christmas Day and Mardi Gras Day.

Gautreau's ★★ FRENCH   Tucked away in a residential uptown neighborhood, with no signage to speak of, is a favorite local hideaway. Those in the know can be observed enjoying the star-level offerings of young chef Sue Zemanick, who was recently named one of the top 10 chefs in America by *Food & Wine* magazine. Gautreau's has long been locally popular for its elegant, understated decor and unimposing service, but now it's once again bringing in the customers through its food. The richly restored apothecary shelves, original to the location and stocked with a classic wine and aperitif selection, are the surrounding *trompe l'oeil* walls a post-Katrina addition by well-known French muralist Grahame Ménage.

Such a talented chef will change the menu regularly, but options include sea scallops with parsley oil, veal glacé, and crisp tender cauliflower. Herbsaint-poached shrimp with fennel, cucumber, jicama, and mint vinaigrette is bright and cheery on a hot tropical summer day. Macadamia-crusted halibut with spaetzle, English peas, and champagne beurre blanc finds four different culinary cultures working harmoniously together, which speaks to the skill of this young chef. The bacon-wrapped pork tenderloin with tomato confit and arugula warmly satisfies while a blood-orange-glazed duck breast with honey-thyme jus was rich and sultry without being too heavy. A welcome departure from the usual New Orleans dessert offerings is a silky cheesecake flan with balsamic and basil macerated strawberries.

1728 Soniat St. ℂ **504/899-7397.** Main courses $22–$32. AE, MC, V. Mon–Sat 6–10pm.

Martinique Bistro ★ FRENCH   This place is just far enough uptown to be off the regular tourist radar. Because it has only 44 seats when the courtyard is not open (100 with), you might have trouble getting a table. This is a sweet little bistro, long a local favorite, but one that hasn't quite survived the transition from its previous, gifted owner. Main-course staple shrimp with sun-dried mango and curry is still solid, as is the salmon, while the flank steak had the tenderness and robust flavor of venison, so much so a diner wondered if it might really be so. But the rest of the menu is hit-or-miss. If the weather permits, be sure to sit in the jasmine-scented courtyard.

5908 Magazine St. ℂ **504/891-8495.** Reservations recommended. Main courses $18–$30. AE, DISC, MC, V. Nov–May Fri–Sun 11am–2:30pm, Tues–Thurs 5:30–9:30pm, Fri–Sat 5:30–10pm, Sun 5:30–9:30pm; June–Oct open for dinner half an hour later.

Patois ★ CONTEMPORARY CREOLE   A very sweet setting, in an old house on an otherwise residential street, and equally sweet, if not culinarily thrilling, food make this

a fine choice for a low-key but pleasurable uptown meal. For brunch, it's delightful. **157**
Braised pork belly comes as toad in the hole, while tuna carpaccio is topped with ginger
and orange-blossom vinaigrette. The grilled hanger steak, with a rich red-wine bone marrow reduction, is really quite excellent, while the roasted duck breast with a bacon-
potato-apple hash is precisely done. Desserts show an interest of working with twists on
standard local offerings; sample one for sure.

6078 Laurel St. (C) **504/895-9441.** www.patoisnola.com. Main courses $21–$27. AE, MC, V. Wed–Thurs
5:30–10pm; Fri 11:30am–2pm and 5:30–10:30pm; Sat 5:30–10:30pm; Sun 10:30am–2:30pm.

Upperline ★★★ ECLECTIC/CREOLE   In a small, charming house in a largely
residential area, the Upperline is more low-key than high-profile places such as Emeril's.
In its own way, though, it's every bit as inventive. It's a great place to try imaginative food
at reasonable (by fancy-restaurant standards) prices. Owner JoAnn Clevenger and her
staff are quite friendly, and their attitude is reflected in the part of the menu where they
actually—gasp!—recommend dishes at *other* restaurants. Perhaps you can afford to be so
generous when your own offerings are so strong. Standout appetizers include fried green
tomatoes with shrimp rémoulade sauce (they invented this dish, which is now featured
just about everywhere in town), spicy shrimp on jalapeño corn bread, seasonal duck
confit, and fried sweetbreads. For entrees, there's moist roast duck with a tingly sauce
(either plum or port wine), cane river country shrimp, and a fall-off-the-bone lamb
shank. If you're lucky, there will be a special menu such as the all-garlic meal, in which
even dessert contains garlic. For dessert, try warm honey-pecan bread pudding or choc-
olate-hazelnut mousse. The award-winning wine list focuses primarily on California
selections.

1413 Upperline St. (C) **504/891-9822.** www.upperline.com. Reservations suggested. Main courses $20–
$29. AE, DC, MC, V. Wed–Sun 5:30–9:30pm.

MODERATE

Bistro Italia ★ (Kids) ITALIAN   Formerly Semolina's (and still owned by same), this
place was long urged upon us by locals—we resisted because it seemed so *ordinary.* But
then we watched a couple of young friends devour generous portions of two solidly made
pastas—a buttery, cheesy, garlicky Alfredo, and shrimp tossed in a light cream and olive-
oil garlic sauce—and we had some hearty, thick lasagna ourselves. And it was all flavorful,
fresh, and good. And we thought, "What's our problem?" Not quite as cheap as it was,
and with a fancier, less immediately family-friendly interior, but still fast, open 7 days a
week, and the menu has enough interest for those who want more than just Italian gloop,
but enough familiars for the slightly timid. Your kids will be happy you aren't forcing
weird fish on them, and you'll be satisfied by the reliable and reasonably priced food. And
it does takeout.

3226 Magazine St. (C) **504/895-4260.** www.semolina.com. They also have a location in Metairie. Pastas
$9–$15; entrees $15–$18. AE, DC, DISC, MC, V. Sun–Thurs 11am–10pm; Fri–Sat 11am–11pm.

Dante's Kitchen ★★ CONTEMPORARY LOUISIANA   Dante's is too easily overlooked thanks to its left-of-center location and relatively low profile, but the reality is that
it's just at the end of the St. Charles streetcar line. Further, its lively take on local cuisine,
with a careful eye toward seasonal and local products, is worthy of greater fame. The bright
and cheerful colors of the interior of its old house setting and the enthusiastic staff make it
a pleasure from the start. At dinner, look for items such as redfish "on the half shell," the
trio of filet mignon topped with pork debris and a Stilton sauce, and a house-made pâté

plate that might include goose riellete with caper berries. Brunch is a strong alternative, especially given their splendid take on eggs Benedict, with tender rosemary-crusted pork taking the place of the traditional Canadian bacon, a hint of honey adding sweetness to the hollandaise sauce, and a caramelized biscuit supporting it all. There's a fat ham-and–runny brie sandwich that is much better than any generic deli version of same, and the grits are perfect. So, too, are their drinks, in particular the seasonal fruit rum punch during watermelon season. Not just another standard-issue New Orleans restaurant.

736 Dante St. ℂ **504/861-3121.** www.danteskitchen.com. Reservations for parties of 6 or more only. Main courses brunch $10–$16, dinner $20–$26. AE, DISC, MC, V. Mon and Wed–Sun 5:30–10pm; Sat–Sun brunch 10:30am–2pm. Closed Tues.

Dick & Jenny's ★★ ECLECTIC/CREOLE   Don't let the out-of-the-way-on-a-depressing-industrial-street location (or, for that matter, a refusal to take reservations) keep you away from this reasonably priced, casual boho-atmosphere restaurant. The room is small, and the wait may still be long, so you might want to time your visit for an off-hour. The menu, which remains very reasonably priced with generous portions, changes a great deal, but recent examples include an excellent summer fruit soup; solidly good spinach, mushroom, and mascarpone ravioli; blackened red fish with crawfish rice; and pan-seared scallops with shrimp and sausage pie and smoked tomato beurre. Each dish is a little busy—just one less layer on everything would help. Desserts include clever variations on classics including an ice-cream-sandwich sundae with real hot fudge.

4501 Tchoupitoulas St. ℂ **504/894-9880.** www.dickandjennys.com. Main courses $19–$35. AE, DISC, MC, V. Tues–Sat 5:30–10pm.

Jacques-Imo's ★ ECLECTIC/CREOLE/SOUL FOOD   We used to be really big fans of this local favorite, a funky, colorful neighborhood joint that the natives love. But the last few times we ate here, the food wasn't worth the wait, which can be absurdly long. So stick to the fried chicken (from a recipe from the late Austin Leslie, of Chez Helene and "Frank's Place" fame), or the catfish stuffed with crabmeat, or the solidly good shrimp Creole. Proceed with caution when it comes to the shrimp and alligator-sausage "cheesecake" (more like a quiche), which has both its fans and detractors, while lovers of chicken livers will certainly want the version here, on toast in a dark brown sauce. Try the three-layer chocolate (white, milk, and dark) mousse pie for dessert. Get there early or you'll have to wait for a table; but that may not be so bad when you're sharing a cold one under a banana tree on a warm Louisiana evening with a bunch of laid-back, like-minded souls.

8324 Oak St. ℂ **504/861-0886.** www.jacquesimoscafe.com. Reservations for 5 or more required. Main courses $14–$25. AE, DC, DISC, MC, V. Mon–Thurs 5:30–10pm; Fri–Sat 5:30–10:30pm.

La Crêpe Nanou ★ FRENCH   La Crêpe Nanou is another not-so-secret local secret. It's always crowded. It's a romantic spot (windows angled into the ceiling let you gaze at the stars) that is simultaneously 19th century and quite modern. You can order crepes wrapped around a variety of stuffings, including crawfish. But you might want to save your crepe consumption for dessert (big and messy, full of chocolate and whipped cream) and concentrate instead on the big healthy salads and moist, flaky fish, particularly the whole grilled fish with herbs. It's big enough for two and is done to perfection. You can usually find knowledgeable locals ordering the mussels and extra bread to sop up the garlic white-wine sauce. Meat dishes come with your choice of sauce (garlic or cognac, for example).

1410 Robert St. ℂ **504/899-2670.** www.lacrepenanou.com. Main courses $12–$23. MC, V. Mon–Thurs 6–10:30pm; Fri–Sat 6–11pm.

La Petite Grocery ★★ BISTRO   This Uptown restaurant, a pretty, renovated room with a sweet atmosphere, generated big buzz when it opened, and thanks to some excellent reviews it quickly became one of the hottest culinary spots in town. But it went through some ups and downs over the years. Happily, it's currently in an "up." The changeable menu isn't always immediately striking—expect options such as braised lamb or pan-seared pork loin—but the preparations absolutely are, while Chef is coming up with exciting appetizers and specials.

4238 Magazine St. ✆ **504/891-3377.** Reservations highly recommended on weekends. Main courses $19–$36. AE, DC, MC, V. Tues–Sat 6–10:30pm.

Lilette ★★ BISTRO   Lilette's chef-owner John Harris trained locally under Bayona's Susan Spicer, who sent him to work in France with Michelin-starred chefs. The result is a menu of more arty playfulness than many other local establishments, served in a space that uses the high ceiling and tile floor to good effect, though the result is a fashionable bistro space that would not look out of place in Tribeca. Full of businesspeople at lunch, and locals at any time, you are probably better off coming here at lunch for the cheaper menu that sufficiently reflects what Harris is up to. Sizzling shrimp bubbles as it arrives, just like the authentic Spanish *tapas* versions. Braised pork belly topped with a poached egg can be heavy rather than satisfyingly rich, but potato gnocchi in a sage brown butter sauce is light and fresh. While sandwiches are only at lunch, at any time of day you can get fancy (sometimes oddly hearty) and nicely composed dishes such as *boudin noir* (dark sausage) with homemade mustard, arugula with white balsamic vinaigrette, and grilled beets with goat cheese. Don't miss the curious signature dessert, little rounds of goat-cheese crème fraîche delicately paired with pears poached in vanilla bean and raisin-flavored liquid, and topped with lavender honey—a marriage made on Mount Olympus.

3637 Magazine St. ✆ **504/895-1636.** www.liletterestaurant.com. Reservations suggested. Main courses $11–$21 lunch, $21–$28 dinner. AE, DISC, MC, V. Tues–Sat 11:30am–2pm; Tues–Thurs 5:30–9:30pm; Fri–Sat 5:30–10:30pm.

Pascal's Manale ★ ITALIAN/STEAK/SEAFOOD   Barbecued shrimp. This restaurant has built its reputation on that one dish, and you should come here if only for that. The place is crowded and noisy and verges on expensive, but it grows on you. It got flooded after Katrina, but extensive renovations restored the interior to just as it always was, down to the photos on the walls. Such a relief to return to hearty, traditional N'Awlins fare, in a hearty, traditional N'Awlins setting. And there's nothing wrong with that, as long as you don't expect anything more. It's still a top-notch place for raw oysters. The spicy barbecued-shrimp sauce may no longer be the best in the city (we are more partial these days to the buttery wonder served over at Mr. B's), but the shrimp within it—plump, sweet, kitten-size—are. Be sure to add sherry to the turtle soup, and be extra sure to skip the dull and even possibly icky desserts. Instead, get another order of shrimp. Just try not to think about your arteries too much; lick your fingers, enjoy, and vow to walk your socks off tomorrow.

1838 Napoleon Ave. ✆ **504/895-4877.** Reservations recommended. Main courses $15–$32. AE, DC, DISC, MC, V. Wed–Fri 11:30am–2pm; Mon–Sat 5pm–"until."

INEXPENSIVE

Bluebird Cafe ★★ AMERICAN   Employees here tell the story of a man who awoke from an extended coma with these two words: Huevos rancheros. As soon as possible, he returned to the Bluebird for his favorite dish. A similar scene repeats each weekend morning when locals wake up with Bluebird on the brain. Why? Because this place consistently offers breakfast and lunch food that can restore and sustain your vital functions. Try the buckwheat pecan waffle, cheese grits, or homemade sausage and corned beef hash. You can also build your own omelet or see why the huevos rancheros enjoys its reputation (if you don't like runny eggs, ask for scrambled huevos). At midmorning on weekends, there is always a wait (up to 30 min.) out front. It's worth it.

3625 Prytania St. ✆ **504/895-7166.** All items under $14. No credit cards. Wed–Fri 7am–2pm; Sat–Sun 8am–2pm.

Camellia Grill ★★ HAMBURGERS/SANDWICHES Even though it's *only* been a part of the city's food culture since 1946, the Camellia Grill seems to have always been there. Consequently, when it wasn't there, for about 18 months after the floods, locals felt off-kilter, and plastered the front door with notes begging the place to return. It did, with a new owner who rehired all the same white-jacketed waiters (some there for 20 years or more) to serve you as you sit on a stool at the counter. There's often a wait because the Camellia serves some of the best breakfasts and big, sloppy burgers (especially their version of a patty melt) in town, but the wait is always worth it. The Camellia is famous for its omelets—heavy and fluffy at the same time and almost as big as a rolled-up newspaper. Notable omelet choices are the chili and cheese, and the potato, onion, and cheese (a personal favorite). Don't forget the pecan waffle, a work of art. If you're feeling really decadent, go with a friend, order omelets, and split a waffle on the side. Wash it all down with one of the famous chocolate freezes and then contemplate a slice of the celebrated pie for dessert. (The chocolate pecan is to die for.)

626 S. Carrollton Ave. ✆ **504/309-2679.** All items under $15. AE, DISC, MC, V. Sun–Thurs 8am–midnight; Fri–Sat 8am–2am.

Casamento's ★★ SEAFOOD When the fatalities attributed to Katrina are tallied, the number will not be accurate, and not just because of post-storm confusion, but because there are many deaths that can, in their way, be blamed on the stress of the storm. Surely the death of Joe Casamento, whose father founded this oyster bar and who was, for 50 years, the best oyster opener in the city, can and should be counted. Joe spent his whole life above the shop, and never took a vacation. Joe suffered from emphysema, and died at age 80, the night he evacuated for Katrina, possibly in a panic over the fate of his city and the store that was his world. So eat here for him.

Not that you shouldn't do so on its own merits, because it probably is the best "erster" joint in the city. The family restaurant takes oysters so seriously that it simply closes down when they're not in season. The oysters are cleanly scrubbed and well selected. You might also take the plunge and order an oyster loaf: a big, fat loaf of bread fried in butter, filled with oysters (or shrimp), and fried again to seal it. Casamento's also has terrific gumbo—perhaps the best in town.

4330 Magazine St. ✆ **504/895-9761.** www.casamentosrestaurant.com. Main courses $4.95–$15. No credit cards. Wed–Sun 11am–2pm; Thurs–Sat 5:30–9pm. Closed June to mid-Sept.

Franky & Johnny's ★ SEAFOOD This is a favorite local hole-in-the-wall neighborhood joint with either zero atmosphere or enough for three restaurants, depending on how you view these things. And by "things" we mean plastic checked tablecloths, a ratty but friendly bar, and locals eating enormous soft-shell-crab po' boys with the crab legs hanging out of the bread and their mouths. You got your po' boys, your boiled or fried seafood platters with two kinds of salad, and, goodness knows, you got your beer. Try that po' boy or the excellent red beans and rice with smoky sausage and other down-home dishes and know you are somewhere that isn't for tourists—and enjoy it all the more.

321 Arabella St. (at Tchoupitoulas St.). ℂ **504/899-9146.** Main courses $6.95–$15. AE, DISC, MC, V. Mon–Sat 11am–9pm.

Joey K's ★ CREOLE/SEAFOOD   This is just a little local corner hangout, though one that savvy tourists have long been hip to. Indeed, it was a tourist who told us to order the trout Tchoupitoulas, and boy, were we happy—lovely pan-fried trout topped with grilled veggies and shrimp. Daily blackboard specials such as brisket, lamb shank, white beans with pork chops, or Creole jambalaya won't fail to please. Order it all to go, and you'll be dining like a real Uptown local.

3001 Magazine St. ℂ **504/891-0997.** Main courses $6.95–$14. DC, MC, V. Mon–Fri 11am–3pm and 5–8:30pm; Sat 11am–4pm and 5–9pm.

Slim Goodies Diner ★ DINER   We were already partial to this place, but when they busted out some heroic culinary moves, as the first restaurant in their neighborhood (if not in the city) to reopen, they won our hearts and loyalty forever. (Seriously, Katrina had barely passed and they dodged anxious health inspectors by serving only fried eggs and other easy-cleanup items on plastic dinnerware.) In the process, they not only became a meeting place for stressed-out hunkered-down locals, but they also demonstrated for other intrepid restaurant owners how they could do likewise. Come for classic diner food with modern diner clever names (not that we mind) like "Low Carbonator" and burgers named after famous folks, though we aren't sure why the Robert Johnson has bacon and bleu cheese, unless it's something to do with the lengths one might go to (such as make a deal with the devil at the crossroads) in order to have such a burger. There are large salads, omelets, and even sweet-potato pancakes and a biscuit topped with étouffée. It's a fine, fun stop while you are shopping, for an Uptown breakfast.

3322 Magazine St. ℂ **504/891-3447.** Everything under $12. No credit cards. Daily 6am–2pm.

Taqueria Corona ★★ MEXICAN   Mexican food has had a low profile in New Orleans, but that appears to be changing with the influx of immigrant workers in town working construction and other jobs. Taco trucks are popping up and more places are likely to follow. In the meantime, Taqueria Corona still rules as the best local Mexican joint. Here you'll find football-size burritos tasting just the right way (and that means not the generic fast-food way, thanks), grilled tacos, combo platters, even gazpacho—and all of it for minimal prices. Be sure to order a side of *cebollitas,* grilled and seasoned green onions.

5932 Magazine St., near Nashville. ℂ **504/897-3974.** Most items under $15. AE, DC, DISC, MC, V. Daily 11:30am–2pm; Sun–Thurs 5–9pm; Fri–Sat 5–9:30pm.

9 METAIRIE

If you got "stuck" with a hotel room down in Metairie, don't despair. You don't have to go all the way to New Orleans to have some terrific food—and you might even get better bargains outside of the "big city." ***Note:*** **Semolina's,** listed above as Bistro Italia, also has two Metairie locations.

Deanie's Seafood Bucktown USA ★ SEAFOOD   The very model of a neighborhood restaurant, Deanie's, with its monster portions and generally high-quality food, is worth making the drive to Metairie for. From the new potatoes (boiled in crab juice) that are plunked on the table when you arrive, to the almost ridiculously high piles of fried seafood that follow, it's one silly and savory experience. Even the salads are large; try the unusual sweet fig and balsamic dressing (made in-house). Opinions differ on whether their barbecued shrimp is the best in town (we think not, but we like it just fine), but note that the portion for two is so large that it's more reasonable (and more affordable) to just split the portion for one—and you may *still* have leftovers!

1713 Lake Ave. 🕐 **504/831-4141.** www.deanies.com. Main courses $11–$35. AE, MC, V. Tues–Sun 11am–10pm. Deanie's also has a location in the French Quarter at 841 Iberville. 🕐 **504/581-1316.**

Galley Seafood Restaurant ★★ SEAFOOD   An easy drive from Mid-City and City Park (and a pretty one, down Old Metairie Rd.), this classic seafood joint is one of our favorite reliable spots. Don't expect ambience, apart from that of a busy family restaurant, but do expect terrific fried and boiled shrimp and crabs. You can get creamy pastas topped with crab cakes (the latter too bready for our tastes, though), or lump crabmeat on an enormous bed of fresh spinach, a fine option if you are trying desperately to still fit into your clothes when you leave town. They have daily specials that are always worth investigating, such as grilled lemon fish stuffed with crabmeat bordelaise and wild cards like blackened tuna Caesar wraps.

2535 Metairie Rd. 🕐 **504/832-0955.** Main courses $11–$25; po' boys $8–$12. AE, DISC, MC, V. Tues–Fri 11am–9pm; Sat noon–8:30pm.

INEXPENSIVE

Martin Wine Cellar and Delicatessen ★★★ SANDWICHES   A gourmet liquor and food store that also has a full-service deli counter, Martin's is one of our favorite fallback reliable places to eat in the city. Unfortunately, ongoing issues require that the original building in Uptown be razed and rebuilt, so it won't be open again for an undetermined amount of time. In the meantime, they have a temporary location on Magazine Street, emphasizing wine with some cheese, and better still, a full location here in Metairie, perfect for a stop as you head to the airport. In addition to the usual deli suspects, they offer about two dozen specialty sandwiches, elaborate concoctions such as the Dave's Special: rare roast beef, coleslaw, pâté de Campagne, and special mustard on rye. Weekdays feature daily specials, gorgeous entire meals that we always regret trying because we are so consistently seduced by the sandwiches.

714 Elmeer, in the 1200 block of Veterans Memorial Blvd. 🕐 **504/896-7300.** www.martinwine.com. Everything under $14. AE, DC, DISC, MC, V. Mon–Wed 9am–7pm (bistro/deli closes at 5pm); Thurs–Sat 9am–7pm (bistro/deli closes 6:30pm); Sun 10am–4pm (bistro/deli closes 3pm). New Orleans location: 3500 Magazine St. 🕐 **504/899-7411.**

R&O's ★ SEAFOOD/SOUTHERN   Sometimes we forget to spend time rhapsodizing about genuine New Orleans neighborhood family restaurants, with sawdust on the floor, a menu heavy on the po' boys and the fried seafood (not to mention the fried-seafood po' boys), and light on the wallet. You can get a big Italian salad here, one of the better ones around, and quite credible pizza, all in a noisy, friendly, low-ambience, utterly without-pretense dining room. You really can't go wrong with any of the fried seafood platters—the oysters and shrimp are superb—and the mixed platter can probably serve four. Of course, you will need that car we swore you could do without to get here.

10 COFFEE, TEA & SWEETS

Angelo Brocato's Ice Cream & Confectionary ★★★ ICE CREAM/SWEETS   In
a constant stream of heartbreak, the sight of this sweet, genuine ice-cream parlor, which
was celebrating its 100th birthday (run by the same family the entire time), under 5 feet
of water, its classic sign askew, was particularly painful. By that same token, the news that
the Brocato family (originally from Palermo; this establishment was a replica of ones
found there) would be back was particularly joyful and inspiring. And that's even before
you get to the goods. They make rich Italian ice cream (made fresh daily), cookies, and
candy in the kind of atmosphere that is slowly being lost in this age of strip malls and
superstores. The chocolate ice cream is one of our all-time favorites, but the fresh lemon
ice and pana-cotta custard have brought us to our knees. The fresh cannolis are also
inspired.

214 N. Carrollton Ave. ⓒ **504/486-0078.** www.angelobrocatoicecream.com. Everything under $10. AE,
DC, DISC, MC, V. Tues–Thurs 10am–10pm; Fri–Sat 10am–10:30pm; Sun 10am–9pm; closed Mon.

Café du Monde ★★★ ⓜ Moments COFFEE   Excuse us while we wax rhapsodic. Since
1862 Café du Monde has been selling café au lait and beignets (and nothing but) on the
edge of Jackson Square. A New Orleans landmark, it's *the* place for people-watching. Not
only is it a must-stop on any trip to New Orleans, but you also may find yourself wandering back several times a day. What's a beignet? (Say ben-*yay*, by the way.) A square French
doughnut–type object, hot and covered in powdered sugar. You might be tempted to
shake off some of the sugar. Don't. Trust us. Pour more on, even. You'll be glad you did.
At three for about $1.75, they're a hell of a deal. Wash them down with chicory coffee.

In the French Market, 800 Decatur St. ⓒ **504/525-4544.** www.cafedumonde.com. 3 beignets for $2. No
credit cards. Daily 24 hr. Closed Christmas. Additional location at Riverwalk Mall.

Creole Creamery ★★★ ICE CREAM   Locals were already justly fond of this local
ice-cream parlor, where innovative flavors are made fresh every day, but when it reopened
about 3 weeks after Katrina, in a neighborhood (and city) where little else was available
commercially, it earned a near-fanatic loyal following. Thick, luscious ice cream with a
rotating list of flavors from lavender-honey to red velvet cake, with stops at tiramisu,
chocolate with hot pepper, and more along the way. Completely refreshing, maybe even
mandatory on a hot day with late enough hours to make it an option for a snack on the
way to or from a club or bar uptown.

4924 Prytania St. ⓒ **504/894-8680.** Everything under $10. No credit cards. Sun–Thurs noon–10pm;
Fri–Sat noon–11pm.

Croissant D'Or ★ COFFEE   A quiet and calm place with the same snacks you might
find in a French-leaning coffeehouse, and you can almost always find an open table. Are
the croissants made of gold? The prices feel like it sometimes, but they are credibly
French.

617 Ursulines St. ⓒ **504/524-4663.** Pastries under $7. AE, MC, V. Wed–Mon 6am–2pm.

EnVie COFFEE/BAKERY/SANDWICHES   A Euro-style coffeehouse, very handsome, with a nice selection of drinks and pastries, some bagels and cream cheese, and

even free Wi-Fi access. The location is excellent if you are waiting for the clubs on Frenchmen to get cranking.

1241 Decatur St. ✆ **504/524-3689.** Everything under $10. MC, V. Daily 7am–midnight.

La Boucherie COFFEE/BAKERY   A handsome interior makes this a good-to-know-about stop on a chilly or (more likely) hot day. They have a large coffee-drink menu with plenty of frothy/frosty/icy options, though they aren't quite as good as one might hope, plus pretty good pastries and cookies.

339 Chartres St. ✆ **504/581-6868.** Everything under $8. AE, MC, V. Daily 7:30am–4pm.

La Boulangerie ★★★ BAKERY   This bakery would be a jewel even if it were in a major bread city. Perhaps the only authentic baguettes in the city (the owners are from France, so they are particular about their bread, as you might guess), the loaves are crusty on the outside, soft and flavorful on the inside. But we forget about the baguettes, perfect though they may be, because of the olive bread, an oval loaf studded with olives, and just slightly greasy (in a good way) with olive oil. Heaven. They also do marvelous croissants, chocolate-filled croissants, and other pastries, and even have savory sandwiches. No coffee, though.

4600 Magazine St. (Uptown). ✆ **504/269-3777.** Loaf of bread $3–$7. No credit cards. Mon–Sat 6:30am–5pm; Sun 7am–1pm.

La Divinia Gelateria ★★ GELATO/ICE CREAM   A superb gelato place. This one has the best selection and the richest, most wonderful ice cream, but its interior needs work to make it more inviting a place to dawdle. All dairy is made from Louisiana cows, plus they are a big part of the local sustainable and local food movement. Look for seasonal fruits and flavors, plus a daily rotation of options like dark chocolate with cayenne, or the honey sesame goat's milk, or sorbet made with local Abita Turbodog beer. They also serve nice light lunches.

621 St. Peter (French Quarter). ✆ **504/302-2692.** Scoops $3.25–$5.45. AE, MC, V. Sun–Thurs 8:30am–10pm; Fri–Sat 8:30am–11pm. Also at 3005 Magazine. ✆ **504/342-2634.** Sun–Thurs 11am–10pm; Fri–Sat 11am–11pm.

La Madeleine ★ BAKERY/COFFEE   One of a chain of French bakeries, it has a wood-burning brick oven that turns out a wide variety of breads, croissants, and brioches—and claims that the skills for making these treats come right from France, so it's all authentic. We like their thick-chunk chocolate chip cookie, even if they don't serve milk to wash it down with. Don't order their main dishes—stick with their wonderful baked goods.

601 S. Carrollton Ave. ✆ **504/861-8662.** www.lamadeleine.com. Pastries $1.50–$3; main courses $4–$12. AE, DISC, MC, V. Daily 7am–9pm.

P.J.'s Coffee & Tea Company ★ COFFEE   P.J.'s is a local institution, with a lot of locations around town. It offers a great variety of teas and coffees, and it roasts its own coffee beans. The iced coffee is made by a cold-water process that requires 12 hours of preparation. P.J.'s also serves mochas, cappuccinos, and lattes. The granita is prepared with P.J.'s Espresso Dolce iced coffee concentrate, frozen with milk and sugar, and served as a coffee "slushee"—great on hot, muggy days.

5432 Magazine St. ✆ **504/895-2202.** www.pjscoffee.com. 95¢–$4. AE, DC, MC, V. Daily 6am–9pm, sometimes later on weekends. P.J.'s has branches at Tulane University, ✆ **504/865-5705;** 644 Camp St., ✆ **504/529-3658;** and 7624 Maple St., ✆ **504/866-7031,** among other locations.

A Snoball's Chance

While towns across the U.S. enjoy ice cream (and New Orleans is no exception), New Orleans does have another iced dessert that is especially popular among the locals: the snoball. These mouthwatering concoctions are made with only the best-quality shaved ice, sometimes so fine that skiers envy the powder. And the flavors—including exotic ones such as wedding cake (almond, mostly), nectar (think cream soda, only much better), and even orchid cream vanilla (bright purple and must be seen to be believed)—are absolutely delectable. You can order them with condensed or evaporated milk if you prefer your refreshing drinks on the more creamy side. At any time of the day during the hot New Orleans summers, lines at local snoball establishments can be out the door. You should stop in at any snoball stand you see, but the following locations are tops and worth the drive uptown for, though you should call for hours because they vary, especially during the winter when they might be closed entirely. Go with a sweet tooth and get plenty of napkins.

Hansen's Sno-Bliz ★★★, 4801 Tchoupitoulas (© **504/891-9788**), is a city tradition after decades of service, still provided with a smile by the third-generation owner Ashley Hansen, who officially took over after her grandparents died in the months after Katrina. Her grandparents invented the particular shaved-ice machine in use here and their own special syrups. Their snoballs come in a souvenir cup. Try the bubble-gum-flavored Sno-bliz. **Plum St. Snoballs** ★★, 1300 Burdette (© **504/866-7996**), has been cooling New Orleanians for over 70 years. Local favorites include the chocolate and cream vanilla-flavored snoballs. Served in a Chinese food container, the way it ought to be.

Royal Blend Coffee & Tea House ★ COFFEE/SANDWICHES   This place is set back off the street; to reach it, you walk through a courtyard. Order a sandwich, quiche, or salad at the counter and take it out into the courtyard. On Saturday afternoons, weather permitting, a guitarist serenades diners. (You can also eat inside, but it's not as much fun.) If you're just in the mood for coffee and pastry, they have plenty of that, too, and the pastry menu changes daily.

621 Royal St. © **504/523-2716.** www.royalblendcoffee.com. Pastries 85¢–$2.95; lunch items $5.25–$8.50. AE, MC, V. Daily 8am–6pm. Royal Blend has a branch at 204 Metairie Rd. in Metairie, © **504/835-7779.**

Rue de la Course ★ COFFEE   This is your basic comfy boho coffeehouse: cavernous in appearance, thanks to a very tall ceiling; manned by cool, friendly college kids; and full of locals seeking a quick pick-me-up, lingering over the paper, or poring over their journals. In addition to prepared coffee and tea, Rue de la Course sells decent sandwiches as well as a few newspapers and local magazines.

3121 Magazine St. © **504/899-0242.** Coffee $2–$4.50; pastries $2–$4; sandwiches $7. No credit cards. Mon–Fri 6:30am–midnight; Sat–Sun 7am–midnight. 2nd location: 1140 S. Carrollton Ave., © **504/861-4343.**

166 Sucré ★ SWEETS/ICE CREAM This high-end confectionaire is heavy on style but a little disappointing in terms of culinary results. The gelato is solid but not nearly as interesting as La Divina's next door. But aesthetically, it beats all its closest competitors, a candy-colored, eye-popping work of modern design, sweets for the sweet, and much inclining visitors to linger. And they actually have near-superb daily lunches and are probably worth stopping off just for that, with maybe a little chocolate to go. We just wish we found that their picture-perfect pastries and candy tasted as good as they—and their setting—look.

3025 Magazine St. © **504/520-8311.** www.shopsucre.com. AE, DC, MC, V. Sun–Thurs 9am–10pm; Fri–Sat 9am–midnight.

Sights to See & Places to Be

A common sentiment voiced in the days immediately following Katrina was "I wish I had gotten to New Orleans again/for the first time before this happened." The implication is that New Orleans is no longer that place the speaker wished to visit. And that's sort of true—and yet absolutely not. By some act of grace, the most notable—from a visitor's perspective—and historic portions of New Orleans, the French Quarter and the Garden District (along with much of the rest of Uptown), were not flooded and escaped serious storm damage. With few exceptions, one is hard-pressed to find any major Katrina damage to a noteworthy (or even minor) attraction in these areas. Within the two most prominent neighborhoods, all but a few significant sights have reopened, including several fine museums and the city's world-class aquarium and sweet zoo, though ongoing budget problems have prevented others from reopening. While it is true that a geographical majority of New Orleans remains either in uneasy flux, in ruins, or in stasis, these areas were never on the ordinary visitor's path. Virtually all of what the average tourist would want to see not only survived the disaster, but also—4-plus years later—doesn't look as though anything happened to it at all. Its very existence makes it all the more precious. So go see it.

Still, our favorite New Orleans activities involve walking, eating, listening to music, and dancing. If instead of sightseeing, that's all you do while you're visiting the town, we won't complain. At least you are here, and it is still here, and that may be enough for now.

But some people feel guilty if they don't take in some culture or history while they're on vacation. And all the local attractions do need the visitors in order to stay open. Besides, there will be occasions when you'll need to escape the rain or heat!

Frankly, New Orleans itself is one big sight—it's one of the most unusual-looking cities in America, and being nice and flat, it's just made for exploring on foot. So get out there and do it. (See the walking tours in chapter 9, "City Strolls," if you'd like some structure.)

Don't confine yourself to the French Quarter. Yes, it certainly is a seductive place, but to go to New Orleans and never leave the Quarter is like going to New York, remaining in Greenwich Village, and believing you've seen Manhattan. Make sure you also take time to stroll the lush Garden District, marvel at the oaks in City Park, ride the streetcar down St.

Impressions

Yet to all men whose desire only is to live a short life, but a merry one, I have no hesitation in recommending New Orleans.

—Henry Fearon, "Sketches of America," 1817

SIGHTS TO SEE & PLACES TO BE

8

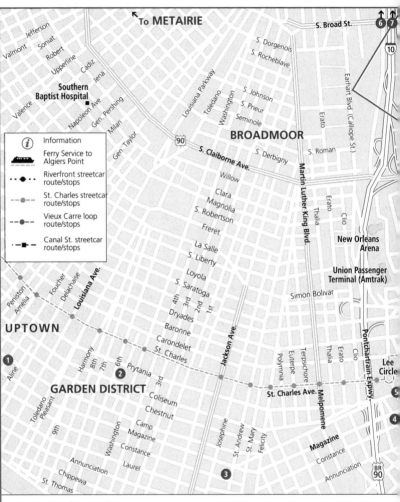

Audubon Park & Audubon Zoo **1**
Backstreet Cultural Museum **15**
Blaine Kern's Mardi Gras World **23**
Canal Place **27**
Chalmette Battlefield/Jean Lafitte National
   Historical Park & Preserve **10**
City Park **8**
Confederate Memorial Museum **5**
Contemporary Arts Center **18**
Creole Queen **22**

Cypress Grove and Greenwood Cemeteries **7**
Degas House **9**
Gallier Hall **16**
Harrah's Casino **26**
John James Audubon (boat to Audubon Zoo) **28**
Lafayette No. 1 Cemetery **2**
Louisiana Children's Museum **20**
Metairie Cemetery **6**
National World War II Museum **4**
New Orleans Botanical Gardens & Train Garden **8**

N. Broad St.

N. Dorgenois
N. Rocheblave
N. Tonti
N. Miro
N. Galvez
N. Johnson
N. Prieur
N. Roman
Derbigny

Tulane Ave.

MID-CITY

LaFitte Ave.

Orleans Ave.
St. Ann
Dumaine
St. Phillip
Ursulines Ave.

Bayou Rd.

St. Bernard Ave.

See "Mid-City Attractions & Nightlife" Map, p. 183.

N. Claiborne Ave.

ST. LOUIS CEMETERY NO. 2

N. Villere

See "French Quarter Attractions" Map, p. 171.

uperdome

Poydras

La Salle St.

Duncan Plaza

ST. LOUIS CEMETERY NO. 1

LOUIS ARMSTRONG PARK

Basin St.

Univ. Pl.

Conti
St. Louis
Toulouse
N. Rampart
St. Ann
Dumaine
Burgundy

Dauphine
Bourbon
Royal
Chartres
Decatur

Ursulines
Gov. Nichols
Barracks
Esplanade

FAUBOURG MARIGNY

McShane Pl.
Touro
Frenchmen
Elysian Fields Ave.
Marigny
Mandeville

Loyola Ave.
S. Rampart
O'Keefe St.
Gravier
Common
Union
Perdido

THE FRENCH QUARTER

Iberville
Bienville

French Market

CENTRAL BUSINESS DISTRICT

St. Charles Ave.
Lafayette Square

Carondelet
Camp
Julia
Girod
Poydras

Magazine St.

Tchoupitoulas
Commerce
S. Peters
Fulton

St. Joseph
Conv. Ctr. Blvd.

Howard Ave.
allipe

RIVERFRONT

World Trade Center

Canal St. Ferry (Toll)

Morgan

ALGIERS

Mississippi River

Lake Pontchartrain

CITY PARK

10
610
10

Area of detail

Superdome

SIGHTS TO SEE & PLACES TO BE

8

Charles Avenue and gape with jealousy at the gorgeous homes, or go visit some gators on a swamp tour. And yes, if you like, go and see the ruined neighborhoods; it's the only way to comprehend the extent of the disaster.

But if you leave the Quarter only to visit clubs and restaurants, we won't blame you a bit.

1 THE FRENCH QUARTER

Those who have been to Disneyland might be forgiven if they experience some déjà vu upon first seeing the French Quarter. It's somewhat more worn, of course, and, in spots, a whole lot smellier. But it's also real. However, thanks perhaps in part to Disney, many tourists treat the Quarter like a theme park, going from bar to bar instead of ride to ride, broadcasting their every move with rowdy shrieks of merriment.

Fine—except, it isn't an amusement park constructed just for the delight of out-of-towners. It's an actual neighborhood, one of the most visually interesting in America, and one that has existed for more than 200 years. (Some of the people living in the Quarter are the fifth generation of their family to do so.) That it was spared any flooding and relatively little storm damage after Hurricane Katrina was a tremendous gift to the city.

There's a great deal to the French Quarter—history, architecture, cultural oddities—and to overlook all that in favor of T-shirt shops and the ubiquitous bars is a darn shame, which is not to say we don't understand, and rather enjoy, the lure of the more playful angle of the area. And as much as we find **Bourbon Street** tacky and often disgusting, we walk down it at least every once in a while. We just don't want you to end up like some tourists who never even get *off* Bourbon. (And regardless of where you go in the Quarter, please remember that you are walking by people's homes. You wouldn't like it if someone did something biologically disgusting on your doorstep, so please afford French Quarter dwellers the same courtesy.)

A French engineer named Adrien de Pauger laid out the Quarter in 1718, and today it's a great anomaly in America. Almost all other American cities have torn down or gutted their historic centers, but thanks to a strict preservation policy, the area looks exactly as it always has and is still the center of town.

Aside from Bourbon Street, you will find the most bustling activity at **Jackson Square,** where musicians, artists, fortunetellers, jugglers, and those peculiar "living statue" performance artists gather to sell their wares or entertain for change. Pay attention to that seeming ad-hoc jazz band that plays right in front of the Cabildo—it's about as good jazz music as you will hear, and notable locals occasionally sit in. **Royal Street** is home to numerous pricey antiques shops, with other interesting stores on **Chartres and Decatur streets** and the cross streets between.

The closer you get to **Esplanade Avenue** and toward **Rampart Street,** the more residential the Quarter becomes, and buildings are entirely homes (in the business sections, the ground floors are commercial and the stories above apartments). Walk through these areas, and peep in through any open gate; surprises await in the form of graceful brick-and flagstone-lined courtyards filled with foliage and bubbling fountains. Follow the French Quarter stroll in chapter 9, "City Strolls," and you'll see a few of the nicest courtyards in the Quarter.

The Vieux Carré Commission is ever vigilant about balancing contemporary economic interests in the Quarter with concerns for historical preservation. Not only has the

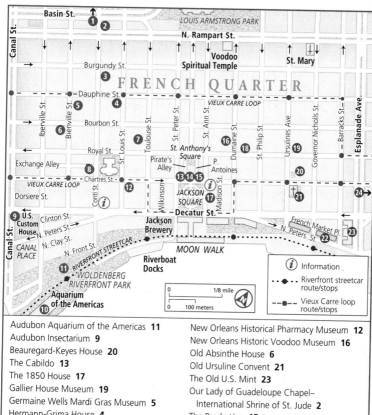

Audubon Aquarium of the Americas **11**
Audubon Insectarium **9**
Beauregard-Keyes House **20**
The Cabildo **13**
The 1850 House **17**
Gallier House Museum **19**
Germaine Wells Mardi Gras Museum **5**
Hermann-Grima House **4**
The Historic French Market **22**
Historic New Orleans Collection **7**
Island of Salvation Botanica **24**
Madame John's Legacy **18**
Musée Conti Wax Museum **3**

New Orleans Historical Pharmacy Museum **12**
New Orleans Historic Voodoo Museum **16**
Old Absinthe House **6**
Old Ursuline Convent **21**
The Old U.S. Mint **23**
Our Lady of Guadeloupe Chapel–
    International Shrine of St. Jude **2**
The Presbytère **15**
St. Louis Cathedral **14**
St Louis Cemetery No. 1 **1**
Williams Research Center **8**
Woldenberg Riverfront Park **10**

commission encouraged restoration, but it has also joined in the battle to hold back certain would-be intruders of the modern world. There's not a traffic light in the whole of the French Quarter—they're relegated to fringe streets—and streetlights are of the old gaslight style. In 1996 large city buses were banned from the neighborhood. During a good part of each day, Royal and Bourbon streets are pedestrian malls, and no vehicles are *ever* allowed in the area around Jackson Square. We also applaud the hard-drawn lines that have mostly kept out the generic chain stores that populate most city centers these days.

Though much of New Orleans is made for walking, the Quarter is particularly pedestrian-friendly. The streets are laid out in an almost perfect rectangle, so it's nearly impossible to get lost. It's also so well traveled that it is nearly always safe, particularly in the central parts. Again, as you get toward the fringes (especially near Rampart) and as night falls, you should exercise caution; stay in the more bustling parts and try not to walk alone.

The French Quarter walking tour in chapter 9 will give you the best overview of the historic buildings in the area and of the city's history. Many other attractions that aren't in the walking tour are listed in this chapter, so make sure to cross-reference as you go along. For attractions in this section, see the "French Quarter Attractions" map on p. 171.

MAJOR ATTRACTIONS

Audubon Aquarium of the Americas ★★★ (Kids)

The world-class Audubon Institute's Aquarium of the Americas was one of the saddest of so many terrible Katrina stories. The facility had superb hurricane contingency plans, not to mention engineering that one only wishes was shared by the levee system, and consequently both building and fishy residents came through the initial storm beautifully. But as the days following the evacuation stretched out, and the staff was forced to leave so that government relief efforts could use the building as a staging area, generators failed, and most of its 10,000 fish died, breaking the hearts not only of the staff who worked so hard to keep their charges healthy and alive, but of just about anyone who had ever visited this lovely place. Survivors included the popular otter pair, the penguins, the leafy and weedy sea dragons, and Midas, the 250-pound sea turtle. The facility's reopening in May 2006 was a cause for rejoicing, not least because those penguins, who memorably were marched out of the aquarium during the post-storm days to take a flight to Oakland for a temporary stay, were flown home from their vacation via a specially designated FedEx flight.

Enough time has passed that this is once again a world-class aquarium, highly entertaining and painlessly educational, with beautifully constructed exhibits. Kids love it, even those too impatient to read the graphics, but adults shouldn't overlook it, if for no other reason than it's a handy refuge from the heat or rain.

The aquarium is on the banks of the Mississippi River, a very easy walk from the main Quarter action. Five major exhibit areas and dozens of smaller aquariums hold a veritable ocean of aquatic life native to the region (especially the Mississippi River and Gulf of Mexico) and to North, Central, and South Americas. You can walk through the underwater tunnel in the Caribbean Reef exhibit and wave to finny friends swimming all around you, view a shark-filled re-creation of the Gulf of Mexico, or drop in to see the penguin exhibit. We particularly like the walk-through Waters of the Americas, where you wander in rainforests (complete with birds and piranhas) and see what goes on below the surface of swamps; one look will quash any thoughts of a dip in a bayou. Not to be missed are a fine exhibit on frogs, the impossibly cute giant sea otters, and the ongoing drama of the sea-horse exhibit. There is also an excellent interactive play zone for kids.

The **IMAX theater** ★★ shows two or three films at regular intervals. Look for an astonishing Katrina documentary, showing the flooding and the rest of the devastation. The Audubon Institute also runs the city's zoo (p. 195) at Audubon Park uptown. **Combination tickets** for the aquarium, the IMAX theater, the Insectarium and the zoo via air-conditioned shuttle to the zoo are $31 for adults, $22 for seniors, $21 for children. Zoo and Aquarium combo tickets including shuttle ride are $25 for adults, $14 for children, $9 for seniors. You can also buy tickets for different combinations of the attractions.

1 Canal St., at the river. ℂ **800/774-7394** or 504/581-4629. www.auduboninstitute.org. Aquarium $18 adults, $14 seniors, $11 children 2–12. IMAX $9 adults, $8 seniors, $6 children. Combination aquarium/ IMAX tickets $31 adults, $22 seniors, $21 children. Aquarium and IMAX Tues–Sun 10am–5pm. Call for showtimes; advance tickets recommended. Closed Mardi Gras and Christmas.

Audubon Insectarium ★★ (Kids) This long-anticipated museum is dedicated to all things bug (okay, and arachnid. Don't get picky), specifically 900,000 species of critters that creep, crawl, and flutter. Located in the old U.S. Customs House, it's the largest free-standing museum in the world dedicated to its multi-legged, winged subjects. Don't like insects? You might well be surprised; you might not only find your attitude changed considerably, you may even muster the courage to "pet" an Australian Prickly Stick bug or a giant beetle.

The journey through ickiness (kidding! Bugs are great!) begins in the Prehistoric hallway with insect replicas some 30 inches wide. A gallery that simulates the experience of being underground exposes the tiny world living in our soil. Beetles sparkle like emeralds and sapphires in the "Hall of Fame," while termites tear through a house frame before your very eyes, reminding you to keep your termite contract up-to-date. Don't miss the short, surprise-filled movie. In the Tiny Termite Café, each glass-topped table has an insect colony living in it (watch silkworms spin their fibers while you dine). You may even watch a chef prepare some bug delicacies on a TV monitor while you dine, and if that inspires you, there are a few creepy-crawler-based snacks available for your own daring munching. Finally, the Japanese-inspired butterfly gallery, full of living, fluttering beauty, is a peaceful departure from the hustle of Canal Street. Clearly certain kids will love it here, but only the most bug-phobic of any size should skip this incredible facility. And we don't care what they tell us; those ginormous thingies that locals insist on calling palmetto bugs are really just fancy roaches.

423 Canal St. ℂ **800/774-7394** or 504/581-4629. www.auduboninstitute.org. Admission $15 adults, $12 seniors, $10 children 2–12. Insectarium, aquarium, and IMAX tickets $34 adults, $25 seniors, $20 children. Tues–Sun 10am–6pm (last entry at 5pm).

The Historic French Market ★★ (Kids) Legend has it that the site of the French Market was originally used by Native Americans as a bartering market. It began to grow into an official market in 1812. From around 1840 to 1870, it was part of Gallatin Street, an impossibly rough area so full of bars, drunken sailors, and criminals of every shape and size that it made Bourbon Street look like Disneyland. Today it's a mixed bag, and not nearly as colorful as its past. Still, both sections have been spiffed up with an extensive renovation that was completed in late 2007. The farmers market makes a fun amble as you admire everything from fresh produce and fish to more tourist-oriented items like hot sauces and Cajun and Creole mixes. (*Tip:* Don't buy that stuff here. The markups are absurd. If you have the time, get someone to take you to a proper supermarket, like the Winn-Dixie, and buy it all there.) Snacks like gator on a stick (when was the last time you had that?) will amuse the kids. The flea market, a bit farther down from the Farmers Market, is considered a must-shop place, but the reality is that many of the goods are kind of junky: T-shirts, jewelry, hats, purses, toys, sunglasses, and so on. Still, some good deals can be had (even better if you are up for bargaining), so the savvy often find it the right place for souvenir shopping. This is a great place to shop for New Orleans–related jewelry—there is a vast array of fleur-de-lis earrings, necklaces, and bracelets, plus the rapidly increasing in popularity water meters, all for prices better than in nearby conventional shops. (Though we can't vouch for the quality of the metal.) The flea market is open daily.

On Decatur St., toward Esplanade Ave. from Jackson Sq. ℂ **504/522-2621.** www.frenchmarket.org. Daily roughly 9am–6pm (tends to start shutting down about an hour before closing).

St. Louis Cathedral ★   The St. Louis Cathedral prides itself on being the oldest continuously active cathedral in the United States. What usually doesn't get mentioned is that it is also one of the ugliest. The outside is all right, but the rather grim interior wouldn't give even a minor European church a run for its money.

Still, its history is impressive and somewhat dramatic. The cathedral formed the center of the original settlement, and it is still the major landmark of the French Quarter. This is the third building to stand on this spot. A hurricane destroyed the first in 1722. On Good Friday 1788, the bells of its replacement were kept silent for religious reasons rather than ringing out the alarm for a fire—which eventually went out of control and burned down more than 850 buildings, including the cathedral itself.

Rebuilt in 1794, the structure was remodeled and enlarged between 1845 and 1851 by J. N. B. de Pouilly. The brick used in its construction was taken from the original town cemetery and was covered with stucco to protect the mortar from dampness. And just when you think that's all, along comes Katrina. The roof leaked, ruining the $1-million organ; subsequently, it's been rebuilt and returned. Outside, two magnificent, ancient live oaks fell down, narrowly missing the statue of Jesus that stood between them. Jesus' thumbs were amputated, and Archbishop Hughes, in his first post-Katrina sermon in the cathedral, vowed not to replace them until the rest of New Orleans is healed. The stately oaks were a painful loss, but plans are in the works to restore the garden to the design of the late 1800s. It's worth going inside to catch one of the free docent tours; the knowledgeable guides are full of fun facts about all of the above, plus the windows and murals and how the building nearly collapsed once from water table sinkage. Be sure to look at the slope of the floor: Clever architectural design somehow keeps the building upright even as it continues to sink. Outside is a plaque marking the visit by Pope John Paul II in 1987, plus an additional large commemorative marker set into the flagstones of Jackson Square, renaming that area for the late Pontiff.

615 Pere Antoine Alley. ✆ **504/525-9585.** Fax 504/525-9583. www.stlouiscathedral.org. Free admission. Mon–Sat 9am–4pm; Sun 9am–2pm. Free tours usually given in the afternoon, pending docent availability.

HISTORIC BUILDINGS

Beauregard-Keyes House ★   This "raised cottage," with its Doric columns and handsome twin staircases, was built as a residence by a wealthy New Orleans auctioneer, Joseph Le Carpentier, in 1826. Confederate Gen. P. G. T. Beauregard lived in the house with several members of his family for 18 months between 1865 and 1867, and from 1944 until 1970, it was the residence of Frances Parkinson Keyes (pronounced *Cause*), who wrote many novels about the region. One of them, *Madame Castel's Lodger,* concerns the general's stay in this house. *Dinner at Antoine's,* perhaps her most famous novel, was also written here. Mrs. Keyes left her home to a foundation, and the house, rear buildings, and garden are open to the public. The gift shop has a wide selection of her novels.

1113 Chartres St., at Ursulines St. ✆ **504/523-7257.** Admission $5 adults; $4 seniors, students, and AAA members; $2 children 6–13; free for children 5 and under. Mon–Sat 10am–3pm. Tours on the hour. Closed Sun and holidays.

The 1850 House ★   James Gallier, Sr., and his son designed the historic Pontalba Buildings for the Baroness Micaela Almonester de Pontalba (see box below), who had them built in 1849 (see stop no. 32 of "Walking Tour 1: The French Quarter" in chapter 9, "City Strolls") in an effort to combat the deterioration of the older part of the city. The rows of town houses on either side of Jackson Square were the largest private buildings in the country at the time. Legend has it that the baroness, miffed that her friend Andrew Jackson wouldn't tip his hat to her, had his statue erected in the square, where to this day he continues to doff his chapeau toward her apartment on the top floor of the Upper Pontalba. It's probably not true, but we never stand in the way of a good story.

In this house, the Louisiana State Museum presents a demonstration of life in 1850, when the buildings opened for residential use. The self-guided tour uses a fact-filled sheet that explains in detail the history of the interior and the uses of the rooms, which are filled with period furnishings arranged to show how the rooms were typically used. It vividly illustrates the difference between the "upstairs" portion of the house, where the upper-middle-class family lived in comfort (and the children were largely confined to a nursery and raised by servants), and the "downstairs," where the staff toiled in considerable drudgery to make their bosses comfortable. It's a surprisingly enjoyable look at life in the "good old days"; it might have you reconsidering just how good they were.

Lower Pontalba Bldg., 523 St. Ann St., Jackson Sq. ✆ **800/568-6968** or 504/568-6968. Fax 504/568-4995. http://lsm.crt.state.la.us/1850ex.htm. Admission $3 adults; $2 students, seniors, and active military; children 11 and under free. Tues–Sun 9am–5pm. Closed all legal holidays.

Old Absinthe House The Old Absinthe House was built in 1806 and now houses the Old Absinthe House bar and two restaurants. The drink for which the building and bar were named is now outlawed in this country (it caused blindness and madness), but you can sip a legal libation in the bar and feel at one with the famous types who came before you, listed on a plaque outside: William Thackeray, Oscar Wilde, Sarah Bernhardt, and Walt Whitman. Andrew Jackson and the Lafitte brothers plotted their desperate defense of New Orleans here in 1815.

The house was a speak-easy during Prohibition, and when federal officers closed it in 1924, the interior was mysteriously stripped of its antique fixtures—including the long marble-topped bar and the old water dripper that was used to infuse water into the absinthe. Just as mysteriously, they all reappeared down the street at a corner establishment called, oddly enough, the Old Absinthe House Bar (400 Bourbon St.). The latter has closed, and a neon-bedecked daiquiri shack opened in its stead. The fixtures have since turned up in one of the restaurants on this site! The bar is covered with business cards (and drunks), so don't come here looking to recapture old-timey and classy atmosphere, but it's still a genuinely fun hangout.

240 Bourbon St., btw. Iberville and Bienville sts. ✆ **504/523-3181.** www.oldabsinthehouse.com. Free admission. Sun–Thurs 9am–2am; Fri–Sat 9am–4am.

Old Ursuline Convent ★★ Forget tales of America being founded by brawny, brave, tough guys in buckskin and beards. The real pioneers—at least, in Louisiana— were well-educated Frenchwomen clad in 40 pounds of black wool robes. That's right; you don't know tough until you know the Ursuline nuns, and this city would have been a very different place without them.

The Sisters of Ursula came to the mudhole that was New Orleans in 1727 after a journey that several times nearly saw them lost at sea or to pirates or disease. Once in town, they provided the first decent medical care (saving countless lives) and later founded the first local school and orphanage for girls. They also helped raise girls shipped over from France as marriage material for local men, teaching the girls everything from languages to homemaking of the most exacting sort (laying the foundation for who knows how many local families).

Lady Bountiful: Baroness de Pontalba

New Orleans owes a great debt to Baroness Micaela Almonester de Pontalba and her family—without them, Jackson Square would be a mudhole. Her father, Don Almonester, used his money and influence to have the St. Louis Cathedral, Cabildo, and Presbytère built. The baroness was responsible for the two long brick apartment buildings that flank Jackson Square and for the renovation that turned the center of the square into what it is today.

Born in 1795 into the most influential family in New Orleans, she married her cousin, who subsequently stole her inheritance. When she wanted a separation at a time when such things were unheard of, her father-in-law shot her several times and then shot himself. She survived, though some of her fingers did not. In subsequent portraits, she would hide the wounded hand in her dress. In the end, she got her money back—she used it for those French Quarter improvements—and also ended up taking care of her (eventually) slightly nutty husband for the rest of his life. She died in Paris in 1874, and her home there is now the residence of the American ambassador. The book *Intimate Enemies,* by Christina Vella (Louisiana State University Press, 1997), has all the details about this remarkable woman.

The convent dates from 1752 (the sisters themselves moved uptown in 1824, where they remain to this day), and it is the oldest building in the Mississippi River valley and the only surviving building from the French colonial period in the United States. It also houses Catholic archives dating back to 1718.

1110 Chartres St., at Ursulines St. © **877/529-2242.** Admission $5 adults, $4 seniors, $3 students, children 11 and under free. Mon–Sat 10am–4pm. (Last tour begins at 4pm.)

The Old U.S. Mint ★★ **Kids** The Old U.S. Mint (the only building in America to have served as both a U.S. and a Confederate Mint) got hammered by Katrina. The roof peeled off, and part of it flew down the street, landing on the French Market, leaving giant pieces of copper dangling over that structure, and requiring a forklift to remove them. Luckily, nothing important inside got wet, but the organization still needed to move everything out, thanks to a month without climate control, to reevaluate the state of the collection. Because they needed to redesign exhibits, not to mention renovate pretty much everything, though they have now reopened, the Mint will not have its superb collection on display again until probably 2010. Until then, expect terrific and sweeping temporary exhibits showcasing art and artifacts related to New Orleans and Louisiana.

And what can you look forward to returning? A comprehensive collection of pictures, musical instruments, and other artifacts connected with jazz greats—Louis Armstrong's first trumpet among them. A stunning array of Carnival mementos from New Orleans and other communities across Louisiana—from ornate Mardi Gras costumes (currently over in the Presbytère) to a street scene complete with maskers and a parade float. We can't wait for this stuff to return, but the temporary exhibits will be well worth your time. ***Note:*** At press time, the Mint was temporarily closed for the mentioned renovation.

400 Esplanade Ave., at N. Peters St. (enter on Esplanade Ave. or Barracks St.). ℂ **800/568-6968** or 504/ 568-6968. Fax 504/568-4995. Admission $6 adults; $5 students, seniors, and active military; children 11 and under free. Tues–Sun 9am–5pm. Closed all legal holidays.

Our Lady of Guadalupe Chapel—International Shrine of St. Jude ★ This is known as the "funeral chapel." It was erected (in 1826) conveniently near St. Louis Cemetery No. 1, specifically for funeral services, so as not to spread disease through the Quarter. We like it for three reasons: the catacomb-like devotional chapel with plaques thanking the Virgin Mary for favors granted, the gift shop full of religious medals including a number of obscure saints, and the statue of St. Expedite. He got his name, according to legend, when his crate arrived with no identification other than the word EXPEDITE stamped on the outside. Now he's the "saint" you pray to when you want things in a hurry. (We are not making this up.) Expedite has his cults in France and Spain and is also popular among the voodoo folks. He's just inside the door on the right. There is also a pretty great religious gift shop in case you want to pick up an Expedite prayer card.

411 N. Rampart St., at Conti St. parish office. ℂ **504/525-1551.** www.saintjudeshrine.com. Mon–Sat 9am–5pm; Sun 7am–6pm.

MUSEUMS

In addition to the destinations listed here, you might be interested in the **Germaine Wells Mardi Gras Museum** at 813 Bienville St., on the second floor of Arnaud's restaurant (ℂ **504/523-5433;** fax 504/581-7908), where you'll find a private collection of Mardi Gras costumes and ball gowns dating from around 1910 to 1960. Admission is free, and the museum is open during restaurant hours.

The Cabildo ★★★ Constructed from 1795 to 1799 as the Spanish government seat in New Orleans, the Cabildo was the site of the signing of the Louisiana Purchase transfer. It was severely damaged by fire in 1988 (it lost only some roof shingles and a couple of shutters in Katrina) and closed for 5 years for reconstruction, which included total restoration of the roof by French artisans using 600-year-old timber-framing techniques. It is now the center of the Louisiana State Museum's facilities in the French Quarter.

The Cabildo is conveniently located right on Jackson Square and is quite worth your time. A multiroom exhibition informatively, entertainingly, and exhaustively traces the history of Louisiana from exploration through Reconstruction from a multicultural perspective. It covers all aspects of life, not just the obvious discussions of slavery and the battle for statehood. Topics include antebellum music, mourning and burial customs (a big deal when much of your population is succumbing to yellow fever), immigrants and how they fared here, and the changing roles of women in the South (which occupies a large space). As you wander through the exhibits, each room seems more interesting than the last. Throughout are portraits of nearly all the prominent figures from Louisiana history plus other fabulous artifacts, including Napoleon's death mask.

701 Chartres St. ℂ **800/568-6968** or 504/568-6968. Fax 504/568-4995. http://lsm.crt.state.la.us/cabildo/ cabildo.htm. Admission $6 adults, $5 students and seniors, free for children 11 and under. Tues–Sun 9am–5pm.

Gallier House Museum ★ James Gallier, Jr. (it's pronounced *Gaul*-ee-er, by the way; he was Irish, not French), designed and built the Gallier House Museum as his residence in 1857. Anne Rice fans will want to at least walk by—this is the house she was thinking of when she described Louis and Lestat's New Orleans residence in *Interview with the Vampire*. Gallier and his father were leading New Orleans architects—they also designed the old French Opera House, the original St. Charles Exchange Hotel, Municipality Hall (now Gallier Hall), and the Pontalba Buildings. This carefully restored town house contains an early working bathroom, a passive ventilation system, and furnishings of the period. Leaders of local ghost tours swear that Gallier haunts the place. Inquire about seasonal special programs. Combination tickets with the Hermann-Grima House are available for an additional $4.

1118 and 1132 Royal St., btw. Gov. Nicholls and Ursulines sts. © **504/525-5661**. www.hgghh.org. Admission $10 adults; $8 seniors, students, AAA members, and children 8–18; free for children 7 and under. Mon–Fri (Wed by appt. only) with tours at 10, 11am, noon, 2, and 3pm. Sat tours at noon, 1, 2, and 3pm.

Hermann-Grima House ★ Brought to you by the same folks who run the Gallier House (see above), the 1831 Hermann-Grima House is a symmetrical Federal-style building (perhaps the first in the Quarter) that's very different from its French surroundings. The knowledgeable docents who give the regular tours make this a satisfactory stop at any time, but keep an eye out for the frequent special tours. At Halloween, for example, the house is draped in typical 1800s mourning, and the docents explain mourning customs. The house, which stretches from St. Louis Street to Conti Street, passed through two different families before becoming a boardinghouse in the 1920s. It has been meticulously restored and researched, and the tour is one of the city's more historically accurate offerings. On Thursdays from October through May, cooking demonstrations should take place in the authentic 1830s kitchen, using methods of the era. (Alas, health rules prevent those on the tour from sampling the results.) The house also contains one of the Quarter's last surviving stables, complete with stalls.

820 St. Louis St. © **504/525-5661**. www.hgghh.org. Admission $10 adults; $8 seniors, students, AAA members, and children 8–18; free for children 7 and under. Mon–Fri 10am–4pm. Tours offered at 10, 11am, noon, 2, and 3pm.

Historic New Orleans Collection—Museum/Research Center ★★ The Historic New Orleans Collection's museum of local and regional history is almost hidden away within a complex of historic French Quarter buildings. The oldest, constructed in the late 18th century, was one of the few structures to escape the disastrous fire of 1794. These buildings were owned by the collection's founders, Gen. and Mrs. L. Kemper Williams. Their former residence, behind the courtyard, is open to the public for tours. There are also excellent tours of the Louisiana history galleries, which feature choice items from the collection—expertly preserved and displayed art, maps, and original documents like the transfer papers for the Louisiana Purchase (1803). The collection is owned and managed by a private foundation, not a governmental organization, and therefore offers more historical perspective and artifacts than boosterism. The Williams Gallery, also on the site, is free to the public and presents changing exhibitions that focus on Louisiana's history and culture, including a terrific Katrina-related one. They also have the best gift shop in town.

If you want to see another grandly restored French Quarter building (and a researcher's dream), visit the **Williams Research Center,** 410 Chartres St., near Conti Street (© **504/598-7171**), which houses and displays the bulk of the collection's many thousands of items. Admission is free.

533 Royal St., btw. St. Louis and Toulouse sts. © **504/523-4662**. Fax 504/598-7108. www.hnoc.org. Free admission; tours $5. Tues–Sat 9:30am–4:30pm; Sun 10:30am–4:30pm. Tours Tues–Sat 10 and 11am and 2 and 3pm. Closed major holidays and Mardi Gras.

Madame John's Legacy ★ The second-oldest building in the Mississippi Valley (after the Ursuline Convent) and a rare example of Creole architecture that miraculously survived the 1794 fire. Drop in to appreciate its historic—and long-lived—status and get a glimpse of life back in the very earliest days of the Vieux Carré.

Built around 1788 on the foundations of an earlier home that was destroyed in the fire of that year, the house has had a number of owners and renters (including the son of Gov. Claiborne), but none of them were named John (or even Madame!). It acquired its moniker courtesy of author George Washington Cable, who used the house as a setting for his short story *Tite Poulette.* The protagonist was a quadroon named Madame John after her lover, who willed this house to her. Visitors can view the interior of the house, though there isn't much in the way of furniture and other artifacts in there at press time.

632 Dumaine St. ℂ **504/568-6968.** http://lsm.crt.state.la.us. Admission $3 adults; $2 students, seniors, and active military; children 11 and under free. Tues–Sun 9am–5pm. Closed all legal holidays.

Musée Conti Wax Museum ★ (**Kids**) You might wonder about the advisability of a wax museum in a place as hot as New Orleans, but the Musée Conti holds up fine. This place is pretty neat—and downright spooky in spots. (And, of course, when it is hot, this is a good place to cool off!) A large section is devoted to a sketch of Louisiana legends (Andrew Jackson, Napoleon, Jean Lafitte, Marie Laveau, Huey Long, a Mardi Gras Indian, Louis Armstrong, and Pete Fountain) and historical episodes. Whether or not these figures are the exact reproductions touted and prized by so many other wax museums is highly dubious, but the descriptions, especially of the historical scenes, are surprisingly informative and witty.

917 Conti St. ℂ **504/525-2605.** www.get-waxed.com. Admission $7 adults $7, $6 children 11 and under. Mon, Fri, Sat 10am–4pm, or by appt.

New Orleans Historical Pharmacy Museum ★ Founded in 1950, the New Orleans Historical Pharmacy Museum is just what the name implies. In 1823, the first licensed pharmacist in the United States, Louis J. Dufilho, Jr., opened an apothecary shop here. The Creole-style town house doubled as his home, and he cultivated the herbs he needed for his medicines in the interior courtyard. Inside you'll find old apothecary bottles, voodoo potions, pill tile, and suppository molds as well as the old glass cosmetics counter (pharmacists of the 1800s also manufactured makeup and perfumes), plus 19th-century surgical instruments and questionable medical devices such as blood-letting gizmos, and a whole slew of opium products. As alternative medicine gains acceptance, it's fascinating to look back at a time when medicine was barely more than snake-oil potions.

514 Chartres St., at St. Louis St. ℂ **504/565-8027.** www.pharmacymuseum.org. Admission $5 adults, $4 students and seniors, children 5 and under free. Tues–Fri 11:30am–5pm; Sat 10am–5pm; call for tours at other times of day.

New Orleans Historic Voodoo Museum Some of the hard-core voodoo practitioners in town might scoff at the Voodoo Museum, and perhaps rightly so. It is largely designed for tourists, but it is also really the only opportunity for tourists to get acquainted with the history and culture of voodoo. Don't expect high-quality, comprehensive exhibits—the place is dark, dusty, and musty. It's such a wasted opportunity, given the potential. There are occult objects from all over the globe plus some articles that allegedly belonged to the legendary Marie Laveau. Unless someone on staff talks you through it (which they will, if you ask), you might come away with more confusion than facts. Still, it's an adequate introduction. Who wouldn't want to bring home a voodoo doll from here? The people who run the museum are involved in voodoo, and there is generally a voodoo priestess on-site, giving readings and making personal gris-gris bags. Again, it's voodoo for tourists, but for most tourists, it's probably the right amount. (Don't confuse this place with the Marie Laveau House of Voodoo on Bourbon St.)

The museum can arrange psychic readings and visits to voodoo rituals if you want to delve deeper into the subject.

724 Dumaine St., at Bourbon St. ℭ **504/680-0128.** www.voodoomuseum.com. Admission $7 adults; $5 students, seniors, and military; $4.50 high-school students; $3.50 grade-school students. Cemetery tour $19. Daily 10am–6pm.

The Presbytère ★★★ The Presbytère was planned as housing for clergy but was never used for that purpose. It's part of the Louisiana State Museum, which has turned the entire building into a smashing Mardi Gras museum, one that puts all other efforts in town to shame. (Blaine Kern's Mardi Gras World in Algiers Point is also a cool experience, and it wouldn't be overkill to do both if you're interested. At Mardi Gras World, you'll see floats being made, but the tour experience could be a bit better, and it's out-of-the-way.)

Five major themes (History, Masking, Parades, Balls, and the Courir du Mardi Gras) trace the history of this high-profile but frankly little-understood (outside of New Orleans) annual event. It does an excellent job of summing up to outsiders the complex history of the city's major holiday, which is so much more than just rowdy college kids displaying nekkid body parts. The exhibits are stunning and the attention to detail is startling, with everything from elaborate Mardi Gras Indian costumes to Rex Queen jewelry from the turn of the 20th century. A re-creation of a float allows you to pretend you are throwing beads to a crowd on a screen in front of you. Heck, even some of the restrooms masquerade (appropriately) as the ubiquitous Fat Tuesday port-a-potties! There is almost too much to see (and if you are sincerely interested, you will want to read most of the detailed graphics), so allow a couple of hours to take it all in properly.

751 Chartres St., Jackson Sq. ℭ **800/568-6968** or 504/568-6968. Fax 504/568-4995. http://lsm.crt.state. la.us. Admission $6 adults, $5 seniors and students, free for children 12 and under. Tues–Sun 9am–5pm.

Woldenberg Riverfront Park ★ Made up of just under 20 acres of green space, Woldenberg Riverfront Park has historically been the city's promenade; now it's an oasis of greenery in the heart of the city with numerous works by popular local artists scattered throughout. (Make a point of finding the unusual Holocaust memorial, which uses a rainbow to unexpected symbolic effect.) The park includes a large lawn with a brick promenade leading to the Mississippi, and it's home to hundreds of trees—oaks, magnolias, willows, and crape myrtles—and thousands of shrubs.

The **Moonwalk** ★★★ is a paved pedestrian thoroughfare along the river, a wonderful walk on a pretty New Orleans day but really a must-do for any weather other than pouring rain. It has steps that allow you to get right down to Old Muddy—on foggy nights, you feel as if you are floating above the water. There are many benches from which to view the city's main industry: its busy port (second in the world only to Amsterdam in annual tonnage). To your right, you'll see the Greater New Orleans Bridge and the World Trade Center of New Orleans (formerly the International Trade Mart) skyscraper as well as the Toulouse Street wharf, the departure point for excursion steamboats. This is also an excellent spot to watch full moons rise over the river.

Along the Mississippi from the Moonwalk at the old Gov. Nicholls St. wharf to the Aquarium of the Americas at Canal St. ℭ **504/861-2537.** Daily dawn–dusk.

UPTOWN & THE GARDEN DISTRICT

If you can see just one thing outside the French Quarter, make it the Garden District. These two neighborhoods are the first places that come to mind when one hears the words "New Orleans," and like the Quarter, it is part of the "sliver by the river" that did not flood after Katrina. It has no significant historic buildings or important museums—it's simply beautiful. In some ways, even more so than the Quarter, this is New Orleans. Authors as diverse as Truman Capote and Anne Rice have been enchanted by its spell. Gorgeous homes stand quietly amid lush foliage, elegant but ever so slightly (or more) decayed. You can see why this is the setting for so many novels; it's hard to imagine that anything real actually happens here.

But it does. Like the Quarter, this is a neighborhood, so please be courteous as you wander around. Seeing the sights consists mostly of looking at the exteriors of nice houses, so we suggest that you see "Walking Tour 2: The Garden District" (see chapter 9, "City Strolls"), which will help guide you to the Garden District's treasures and explain a little of its history. Use the listings in chapter 10, "Shopping," to find the best shops, galleries, and bookstores on **Magazine Street,** the main shopping strip that bounds the Garden District.

Meanwhile, a little background: Across Canal Street from the Quarter, "American" New Orleans begins. After the Louisiana Purchase of 1803, an essentially French-Creole city came under the auspices of a government determined to develop it as an American city. As American citizens moved in, tensions between Creole society and the newcomers began to increase. Some historians lay this at the feet of Creole snobbery; others blame the naive and uncultured Americans. In any case, Creole society succeeded in maintaining a relatively distinct social world, deflecting American settlement upriver of Canal Street (Uptown); the Americans in turn came to dominate the city with sheer numbers of immigrants. Newcomers bought up land in what had been the old Gravier Plantation (now the Uptown area) and began to build a parallel city. Very soon, Americans came to dominate the local business scene, centered along Canal Street. In 1833 the American enclave that we now know as the Garden District was incorporated as Lafayette City, and—thanks in large part to the New Orleans–Carrollton Railroad, which covered the route of today's St. Charles Avenue streetcar—the Americans kept right on expanding until they reached the tiny resort town of Carrollton. It wasn't until 1852 that the various sections came together officially as a united New Orleans.

Again, as with the Quarter, it was great good fortune for the crucial economy generated by tourism that the Garden District was essentially undamaged from Katrina and Rita (wind and rain damage here and there, no worse than after even a tropical storm, and no flooding at all), and its beauty remains as intoxicating as ever.

TROLLING ST. JOHN'S BAYOU & LAKE PONTCHARTRAIN ★★★

St. John's Bayou is a body of water that originally extended from the outskirts of New Orleans to Lake Pontchartrain, and it's one of the most important reasons New Orleans is where it is today. Jean Baptiste Le Moyne, Sieur de Bienville, was commissioned to establish a settlement in Louisiana that would both make money and protect French holdings in the New World from British expansion. Bienville chose the spot where New

Orleans now sits because he recognized the strategic importance of "back-door" access to the Gulf of Mexico provided by the bayou's linkage to the lake. Boats could enter the lake from the Gulf and then follow the bayou until they were within easy portage distance of the mouth of the Mississippi River. Area Native American tribes had used this route for years.

The early path from the city to the bayou is today's Bayou Road, an extension of Governor Nicholls Street in the French Quarter. Modern-day Gentilly Boulevard, which crosses the bayou, was another Native American trail—it led around the lake and on to settlements in Florida.

As New Orleans grew and prospered, the bayou became a suburb as planters moved out along its shores. In the early 1800s, a canal was dug to connect the waterway with the city, reaching a basin at the edge of Congo Square. The bayou became a popular recreation area with fine restaurants and dance halls (as well as meeting places for voodoo practitioners, who held secret ceremonies along its shores). Gradually, New Orleans reached beyond the French Quarter and enveloped the whole area—overtaking farmland, plantation homes, and resorts.

The canal is gone, filled in long ago, and the bayou is a meek re-creation of itself. It is no longer navigable (even if it were, bridges were built too low to permit the passage of boats of any size), but residents still prize their waterfront sites, and rowboats and sailboats sometimes make use of the bayou's surface. This is one of the prettiest areas of New Orleans—full of the old houses tourists love to marvel at without the hustle, bustle, and confusion of more high-profile locations.

There was some flooding here following Katrina, particularly on the lakeside bank, near City Park, but for the most part, residents in the immediate area did well, thanks to just enough elevation in both land and house construction. The bayou was on the news when a U.S. Coast Guard helicopter crashed along its banks in the early days following the disaster. Despite all this, and the loss of a few trees, it remains picturesque. A walk along the banks and through the nearby neighborhoods is one of our favorite things to do on a nice afternoon.

GETTING THERE   The simplest way to reach St. John's Bayou from the French Quarter is to drive straight up Esplanade Avenue about 20 blocks (you can also grab the bus that says ESPLANADE at any of the bus stops along the avenue). Or take the Esplanade Ridge walking tour in chapter 9, "City Strolls." Right before you reach the bayou, you'll pass **St. Louis Cemetery No. 3** (just past Leda St.). It's the final resting place of many prominent New Orleanians, among them Father Adrien Rouquette, who lived and worked among the Choctaw; Storyville photographer E. J. Bellocq; and Thomy Lafon, the black philanthropist who bought the old Orleans Ballroom as an orphanage for African-American children and put an end to its infamous "quadroon balls," where well-bred women of mixed color would socialize with and become the mistresses of white men. Walking just past the cemetery, turn left onto Moss Street, which runs along the banks of St. John's Bayou. If you want to see an example of an 18th-century West Indies–style plantation house, stop at the **Pitot House,** 1440 Moss St. (p. 190).

To continue, drive along Wisner Boulevard, on the opposite bank of St. John's Bayou from Moss Street, and you'll pass some of New Orleans's grandest modern homes—a sharp contrast to those on Moss Street. At this point, you can make a Katrina-damage tour that takes you through the once-flooded neighborhood of Gentilly, all the way to Lake Pontchartrain.

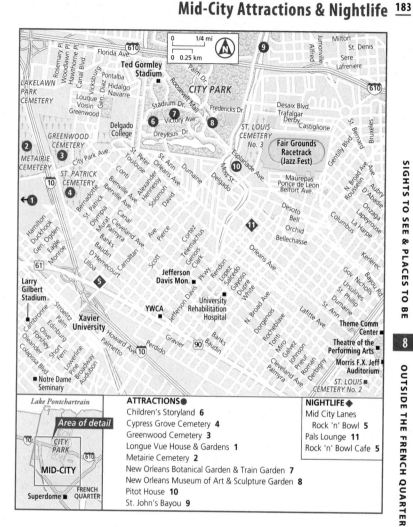

SIGHTS TO SEE & PLACES TO BE

8

OUTSIDE THE FRENCH QUARTER

ATTRACTIONS●
Children's Storyland **6**
Cypress Grove Cemetery **4**
Greenwood Cemetery **3**
Longue Vue House & Gardens **1**
Metairie Cemetery **2**
New Orleans Botanical Garden & Train Garden **7**
New Orleans Museum of Art & Sculpture Garden **8**
Pitot House **10**
St. John's Bayou **9**

NIGHTLIFE◆
Mid City Lanes
 Rock 'n' Bowl **5**
Pals Lounge **11**
Rock 'n' Bowl Cafe **5**

Stay on Wisner to Robert E. Lee Boulevard, turn right, drive to Elysian Fields Avenue, and then turn left. That's the University of New Orleans campus on your left, which didn't have as much flooding as some of the other major campuses in the city (such as Dillard), though it did have a great deal of wind damage, and underground electrical systems took on water. Classes have resumed and the campus is coming back to life. At any point, you can take a street off to the left or the right if you wish to go through the neighborhoods in more detail, though by the time you read this, there may be less to see, depending on what sort of plans have been made for reconstruction. Regardless, please remember these are neighborhoods, not sights, and treat whatever you see, even if it's abandoned desolation, with respect.

Turn left onto the broad concrete highway, Lake Shore Drive. It runs for 5½ miles along the lake, and normally in the summer, the parkway alongside its sea wall is swarming with swimmers and picnickers. On the other side are more luxurious, modern residences. Thanks to higher ground, these and other houses nearby did not flood, though they did sustain incredible wind damage. Further, the road buckled. About 2 miles down the road to the west is the fishing-oriented Bucktown neighborhood, which was totally devastated by the 17th Street Canal breech, including the marina, where expensive yachts were piled on top of each other by the power of the storm. Commercial fishing fleets (terribly hard hit by the storm) of some kind have been working out of Bucktown since the late 1800s (some local families have been living and working here just about that long). But as engineers need to reclaim some of the area for a temporary floodgate for the canal, fishermen, some of whom have been working this area for decades, may need to move elsewhere. The beloved Sid-Mar's restaurant is gone for good.

As you return, you can drive through the Lakeview neighborhood, south of Robert E. Lee, between Canal and City Park. Here, houses look fine on the outside, but watch for the now-fading telltale water marks demonstrating that these homes sat in anywhere from 6 to 10 feet of water. By the time you visit, presumably the majority will have been renovated or destroyed.

Lake Pontchartrain is some 40 miles long and 25 miles wide. Native Americans once lived along both sides, and it was a major waterway long before white people were seen in this hemisphere. You can drive across it over the 24-mile Greater New Orleans Causeway, the longest bridge in the world.

MUSEUMS & GALLERIES

Backstreet Cultural Museum ★ Part private obsession, part cultural jewel, this small facility is off the beaten path but a must-stop for anyone interested in the true history and culture of New Orleans. The city would be nothing without the rhythms of such rituals as brass bands, second lines, social clubs, jazz funerals, and the wholly unique Mardi Gras Indians, and this collection gathers remarkable examples and explanations for all of them in one place. It's not as slick as similar efforts at the Presbytère, but it contains even more special examples of such art as the feathered and sequined wonders that are Mardi Gras Indians' handmade suits. It's also located right in the heart of the Treme, the neighborhood that spawned so much of what is celebrated here. The owner, Sylvester, is an eccentric trip, but not only has he carefully documented this vital culture, but he's also the real New Orleans, so spend some time with him.

1116 St. Claude Ave. ✆ **504/303-9058.** www.backstreetmuseum.org. Admission $8. Tues–Sat 10am–5pm.

Confederate Memorial Museum ★★ Not far from the French Quarter, the Confederate Museum was established in 1891 (giving it claim to being the oldest surviving museum in Louisiana; it made it through a takeover bid for its lovely brick facility by the Ogden Museum of Southern Art next door) and currently houses the second-largest collection of Confederate memorabilia in the country. It opened so soon after the end of the war that many of the donated items are in excellent condition. Among these are guns, swords, photographs, oil paintings, 125 battle flags, and 50 Confederate uniforms. You'll see personal effects of Confederate Gen. P. G. T. Beauregard and Confederate President Jefferson Davis (including his evening clothes), part of Robert E. Lee's silver camp service, and many portraits of Confederate military and civilian personalities. For the most part, though, only buffs will find much of interest here, though they can have remarkable temporary exhibitions like a most moving one on Jefferson Davis's youngest daughter, Winnie.

929 Camp St., at St. Joseph's. ✆ **504/523-4522.** www.confederatemuseum.com. Admission $7 adults; $5 students, active military, and seniors; $2 children 11 and under. Wed–Sat 10am–4pm.

Contemporary Arts Center ★★ Redesigned in the early 1990s to much critical applause, the Contemporary Arts Center (CAC) is a main anchor of the city's young arts district (once the city's old Warehouse District, it's now home to a handful of leading local galleries). Over the past 2 decades, the center has consistently exhibited influential and groundbreaking work by regional, national, and international artists in various mediums. The CAC staggers its shows, so there should always be something worth seeing hanging on the walls; it also presents theater, performance art, and music concerts. Individual exhibitions hang for 6 to 8 weeks, and performances are weekly.

900 Camp St. ✆ **504/528-3805.** Fax 504/528-3828. www.cacno.org. Gallery admission $5, $3 seniors, free for members. (Sometimes exhibits are free, even for non-members!) Performance and event tickets $7–$60. Thurs–Sun 11am–4pm.

National World War II Museum ★★★ Opened on the anniversary of D-day, June 6, 2000, this is the creation of the late best-selling author (and *Saving Private Ryan* consultant) Stephen Ambrose, and it is the only museum of its kind in the country. The official designation as the national World War II museum expanded its scope and prestige. It tells the story of all 19 U.S. amphibious operations worldwide on that fateful day of June 6, 1944 (Normandy may have been the subject of a Spielberg movie, but many other battles were waged and won). A rich collection of artifacts (including some British Spitfire airplanes) coupled with top-of-the-line educational materials (including an oral-history station) makes this one of the highlights of New Orleans. An expansion to be completed in phases will triple the museum's size and cover all the theaters and services in World War II (the Pacific Theater exhibit, including a short and choking film, silent but for carefully chosen classical music, on the atomic bomb, is already in place, but is in spots too gruesome and intense for children), turning this already world-class facility into one of the major museums of the world.

Many of the exhibits emphasize personal stories, including audio exhibits featuring civilians and soldiers alike relating their own experiences. Artifacts from both home and former soldiers help give the sort of specific detail that pulls history off the pages of books. A panorama allows visitors to see just what it was like on those notorious beaches. There is also a copy of Eisenhower's contingency speech, in which he planned to apologize to the country for the failure of D-day—thankfully, it was a speech that was never needed nor delivered. Volunteers who served on D-day are often around, ready to tell their own history in vivid and riveting detail. The entire place is deeply moving, even for those with only minimal interest in matters military.

945 Magazine St., in the Historic Warehouse District. ✆ **504/527-6012.** www.ddaymuseum.org. Admission $14 adults, $8 seniors, $6 active or retired military with ID and children 5–17, free for military in uniform and children 4 and under. Daily 9am–5pm. Closed holidays.

New Orleans Museum of Art ★★ Often called NOMA, this museum is located in an idyllic section of City Park. The front portion of the museum is the original large, imposing neoclassical building ("sufficiently modified to give a subtropical appearance," said the architect Samuel Marx); the rear portion is a striking contrast of curves and contemporary styles.

The museum opened in 1911 after a gift to the City Park Commission from Isaac Delgado, a sugar broker and Jamaican immigrant. Today it houses a 40,000-piece collection including pre-Columbian and Native American ethnographic art; 16th- through 20th-century European paintings, drawings, sculptures, and prints; early American art; Asian art; a gallery entirely devoted to Fabergé; and one of the six largest decorative glass collections in the United States. Exhibits in 2010 will include an exhibition on African America in collaboration with Tulane University's Amistad Research Center, a retrospective on the porcelain works of Jacob Petit, and an exhibition on Pueblo and Navajo Native American culture, all leading up to the museum's centennial celebration in 2011. A great addition to the city's artistic offerings came when the museum opened the **Besthoff Sculpture Garden** ★★★, 5 acres of gardens, grass, and walkways that spotlight 50 modern sculptures by artists such as Henry Moore, Gaston Lachaise, Elizabeth Frink, George Segal, and others, including a version of the famous pop-art *LOVE* sculpture. The garden, which lost only one piece to the storm (and the artist had it repaired by the beginning of 2006!), has quickly become a New Orleans cultural highlight and is open Wednesday to Sunday from 10am to 5pm, with free admission.

1 Collins Diboll Circle, at City Park and Esplanade. ✆ **504/658-4100.** www.noma.org. Admission $8 adults, $7 seniors (over 64) and students, $4 children 3–17, free to Louisiana residents. Wed noon–8pm, Thurs–Sun 10am–5pm. Closed most major holidays.

The Ogden Museum of Southern Art ★★★

The premier collection of Southern art in the United States. Though the building is dazzling, it is built around an atrium that takes up a great deal of space that could be devoted to still more displays. It does make for a dramatic interior, but given such a marvelous collection, one is greedy for more art rather than more architecture. But the facility is wonderful, the artists are impressive, and the graphics are well designed, informative, and often humorous. Just the permanent exhibit of self-taught/outsider art alone makes this worth a visit. Special exhibits are thoughtfully constructed, often containing enriching details—for example, a blues soundtrack for a display of Delta musicians, a video documentary on the late Benny Andrews.

A newer annex, the splendid Patrick F. Taylor library, originally designed by native Southerner Henry Hobson Richardson in the late 1800s, is an incredible salvation and use of an existing structure—don't miss whatever temporary exhibit is currently on display. It bodes well for the institute's planned upcoming expansions. Consider coming during Thursdays' delightful Ogden After Hours, which includes a live band (anything from 1930s country to old Delta blues guys to the New Orleans Klezmer All-Stars) playing in the atrium, adding a soundtrack to your visit. These evenings are one of the special delights of New Orleans.

925 Camp St. ✆ **504/539-9600.** www.ogdenmuseum.org. Admission $10 adults, $8 seniors and students, $5 children 5–17. Wed–Sun 10am–5pm; Thurs 6–8pm for evening shows.

Southern Food and Beverage Museum & Museum of the American Cocktail ★★

Enough with these museums about the history of New Orleans, interesting though it may be, you may be saying. What about the food? And the booze? Your cries have been heard. Local restaurateur Dickie Brennan, Liz Williams, and a host of other committed NOLA foodies have opened the South's first food-and-beverage museum. It's an informative assemblage of Southern food and drink history, from farmers to cooks and all between, represented by all kinds of goodies. Ultimately, this is probably more for food or history buffs than a general audience. The location is in the Riverwalk Marketplace at the far west end—be prepared for a potentially long walk to get there but enjoy the river views along the way.

The main hall houses a comprehensive collection of artifacts illustrating how different ethnic groups (it's not just the usual French, Spanish, and African suspects, but also Germans, Italians, and Irish), geography, and time have contributed to the local cuisine. Exhibits will rotate, but SOFAB opened with one that explored the various aspects of White House culinaria through photos, menus, and tableware. White House customs were exposed for all to see, even offering a sneak peek into the refrigerator of the official capital kitchens. Another room housed the provocative photography of noted Cuban-American artist Jorge Otero. In addition to the expected museum fare, free samples of local chicory-roasted coffee and sweet tea were available to patrons expected to cast a vote for "people's choice." As if your appetite wasn't whetted enough, get a load of those delicious smells from the food court—a little l'eau de red beans 'n' rice and crawfish étouffée adds to the atmosphere.

Included in your admission fee is a museum within the food museum—the Museum of the American Cocktail. It's a stumble through 200 years of cocktail history and New Orleans's own vital role in same. (So the Sazerac may not have been the first cocktail after all. It was one of the first!) Curator Ted "Dr. Cocktail" Haigh is passionate about his impressive collection and offers an original and lively glimpse into the colorful history of our favorite "poison." Historical artifacts include bottles from defunct products, menus, and photos with displays on subjects such as Prohibition and what it did to the cocktail. (We love the bottles of commercially sold gin, rye, and bourbon flavoring that one would put into whatever rot gut you produced at home to make it palatable.) Like with the main SOFAB, not only will exhibits rotate, but there will be regular seminars, demonstrations, and tastings.

Further, SOFAB has collaborated with existing institutions like Tulane University to collect and archive various items that are available for research purposes, while a cookbook library is in the works. If that weren't enough, Chef Emeril Lagasse offers a culinary camp for children during the summer months. And do hit the gift shop on your way out for cookbooks and cutting-edge kitchen and beverage ware.

1 Poydras St. (in the Riverwalk Marketplace Mall). ⓒ **504/569-0405**. www.southernfood.org and www. museumoftheamericancocktail.org. Admission $10 adults, $5 seniors and students with ID. Mon–Sat 10am–7pm; Sun noon–6pm.

The UCM Museum ★★ (Finds) Now you know we don't tell you to leave town lightly. There's so much to see in New Orleans, and you probably have too short a time (any period other than "endless years" is too short). But still, consider making the 45-minute drive across the Causeway to Abita Springs, to this classic folk-art roadside attraction. It's pronounced "You-see-em," by the way, and there's probably nothing here you can trust with your own eyes. For starters, it only looks like it's been around forever. In reality, that's part of the master plan by Louisiana artist/inventor John Preble, who started this project up just a few years ago. You'll be smitten with the mini-dioramas that come to life in unexpected ways, illustrating local scenes such as a jazz funeral, a Mardi Gras parade, a haunted Southern plantation, and more. How about the preserved (and cheerfully fake) freaks such as Darrell the Dogigator (half-dog, half-alligator), Buford the Bassigator (half-fish, half-gator), and the Quackigator (you get the idea)? Or the 1950s Airstream trailer that was struck by a UFO? Is this place the best roadside attraction ever or one heck of a piece of conceptual art? No matter. It's all great fun, and at such an affordable price, you can breeze through it or spend hours marveling at the sort of minds that can create such a place, not to mention continuing to add more stuff all the time. Only in New Orleans, we would say, except it's not. But that shouldn't stop you from buying all your NOLA souvenirs at the excellent gift shop.

22275 Hwy. 36, Abita Springs. © **985/892-2624.** www.ucmmuseum.com. Admission $3. Daily 10am–5pm.

HISTORIC NEW ORLEANS CHURCHES

Church and religion are not likely to be the first things that jump to mind in a city known for its debauchery. But New Orleans remains a very Catholic city—don't forget that Mardi Gras is a pre-Lenten celebration. In fact, religion of one form or another directed much of the city's early history and molded its culture in countless ways.

For a detailed review of the St. Louis Cathedral, see "Major Attractions," earlier in this chapter.

St. Alphonsus Church ★   The interior of this church is probably the most beautiful of any church in the city, right up there with some of the lusher ones in Italy. The Irish built St. Alphonsus Church in 1855 because they refused to worship at St. Mary's (see below) with their German-speaking neighbors. The gallery, columns, and sharply curving staircases that lead to balconies where the paint and plaster are peeling off in chunks are spooky and atmospheric. That's probably why portions of Anne Rice's *The Witching Hour* take place here.

The church no longer holds Mass. Ironically, when St. Mary's was restored, St. Alphonsus was closed, and the congregation moved across the street. Hopes for similar restoration here are high but may have to be put off some; the church's exterior didn't fare that well in the storm. Dramatically, the downriver bell tower was blown across the street, while the upriver one was moved 15 degrees. It also lost several stained-glass windows and ultimately incurred over half a million dollars in damage.

Currently, the church operates an Arts and Cultural Center, which includes an Irish art museum. You can tour the still fabulous-looking interior and the museum with a self-guided audiotape, or take the tour conducted by Anne Rice's raconteur cousin, Billy Murphy, an option we highly recommend. Tour times are more than contingent these days (Tues, Thurs, and Sat as we went to press), so call for information.

2030 Constance St., at St. Andrew St. © **504/524-8116.** For information, call the Friends of St. Alphonsus at © **504/482-0008.**

St. Augustine Church ★★   One of the great cultural landmarks of New Orleans's black history, St. Augustine's has been a center of community life in the troubled but striving Treme neighborhood since the mid-1800s. This church was founded by "free people of color," who also purchased pews for the exclusive use by slaves (frustrating their white masters!). This was a first in the history of slavery in the U.S., and resulted in one of the most integrated churches in the country. In the modern era, under the direction of its visionary and charismatic pastor, Fr. Jerome LeDoux, St. Augustine's continued to celebrate its history by integrating traditional African and New Orleans elements into its services. Homer Plessy, Sidney Bechet, and Big Chief Tootie Montana all called this their home church. In late 2005 the archdiocese decided to close St. Augustine's thanks to diminished membership, but a major public outcry bought it a reprieve and it seems safe now, though Fr. LeDoux is no longer its full-time priest. Nonetheless, services here remain remarkable, especially when the church has one of its frequent jazz Masses, which can feature performers like Troy Andrews, John Boutte, and others, and can be the best free concert in town. (There is excellent music at pretty much every Sun 10am Mass.)

Frequent art exhibits celebrating the neighborhood, and the deeply moving Tomb of the Unknown Slave outside, make this worth a stop even if it's not a Sunday (though you should call ahead to make sure it's open). Combine it with a trip to the Backstreet Cultural Museum across the street. And give them a donation; let's try to keep them going another couple centuries.

1210 Gov. Nicholls St. ℭ **504/525-5934.** www.staugustinecatholicchurch-neworleans.org.

St. Mary's Assumption ★   Built in 1860 by the German Catholics, this is an even more baroque and grand church than its Irish neighbor across the street (see St. Alphonsus Church, above), complete with dozens of life-size saints' statues. The two churches make an interesting contrast to each other. Also inside the church is the national shrine for the hero of the 1867 yellow-fever epidemic, Blessed Fr. Francis Xavier Seelos, who was beatified (one step away from sainthood) in 2000. Here you can see his original coffin, a portrait, some of his personal belongings, a display containing newly discovered locks of his hair, and the centerpiece of the shrine, a reliquary containing his bodily remains. Should he become a saint, expect this shrine to be an even bigger deal and place of pilgrimage than it already is. Still more of Anne Rice's action in *The Witching Hour* takes place here, including Rowan and Michael's wedding. The church had over $1 million worth of damage (though Seelos's reliquary came through fine), but with a new roof, hopes are high for the interior work necessary.

2030 Constance St., at Josephine St. ℭ **504/522-6748.** Tours of the Fr. Seelos shrine are offered Mon–Sat; call ℭ **504/525-2495** to arrange a tour.

St. Patrick's Church   The original St. Patrick's was a tiny wooden building founded to serve the spiritual needs of Irish Catholics. The present building, begun in 1838, was constructed around the old one, which was then dismantled. The distinguished architect James Gallier, Sr., designed much of the interior, including the altar. It opened in 1840, proudly proclaiming itself as the "American" Catholics' answer to the St. Louis Cathedral in the French Quarter (where, according to the Americans, God spoke only in French).

724 Camp St., at Girod St. ℭ **504/525-4413.**

St. Roch and the Campo Santo ★ (Finds)   St. Roch is the patron saint of plague victims; a local priest prayed to him to keep his flock safe during an epidemic in 1867. When everyone came through all right, the priest made good on his promise to build St. Roch a chapel. The Gothic result is fine enough, but what is best is the small room just off the altar, where successful supplicants to St. Roch leave gifts, usually in the form of plaster anatomical parts or medical supplies, to represent what the saint healed for them. The resulting collection of bizarre artifacts (everything from eyeballs and crutches to organs and false limbs) is either deeply moving or the greatest creepy spontaneous folk-art installation you've ever seen. The chapel is not always open, so call first.

1725 St. Roch Ave., at N. Derbigny St. ℭ **504/945-5961.**

A FEW MORE INTERESTING NEW ORLEANS BUILDINGS

Degas House ★   Legendary French Impressionist Edgar Degas felt very tender toward New Orleans; his mother and grandmother were born here, and he spent several months in 1872 and 1873 visiting his brother at this house. It was a trip that resulted in a number of paintings, and this is the only residence or studio associated with Degas anywhere in the world that is open to the public. One of his paintings showed the garden of the house behind his brother's. His brother liked that view, too; he later ran off with the wife of the judge who lived there. His wife and children later took back her maiden name, Musson. The Musson home, as it is formally known, was erected in 1854 and has since been sliced in two and redone in an Italianate manner. Both buildings have been restored and are open to the public via a tour. There is also a very nice (though fairly humble) B&B setup.

2306 Esplanade Ave., north of the Quarter, before you reach N. Broad Ave. ✆ **504/821-5009.** www. degashouse.com. Admission $10 adults, $8 seniors. Daily 9am–3pm by advance appt. only.

Gallier Hall   This impressive Greek Revival building was the inspiration of James Gallier, Sr. Erected between 1845 and 1853, it served as City Hall for just over a century and has been the site of many important events in the city's history—especially during the Reconstruction and Huey Long eras. Several important figures in Louisiana history lay in state in Gallier Hall, including Jefferson Davis and General Beauregard. Of late, it was local music legends Ernie K-Doe and Earl King who were so honored. Both received big send-offs: More than 5,000 mourners came to Gallier Hall on July 14, 2001, to pay their respects to the flamboyant K-Doe, who was laid out in a white costume and a silver crown and scepter before being delivered to his final resting place in the company of a big, brassy jazz procession. Wearing a vivid purple suit, King also was honored with a jazz funeral, with twirling umbrellas and rock royalty in attendance at his service on May 1, 2003.

545 St. Charles Ave. Not usually open to the public.

Pitot House ★   The Pitot House is a typical West Indies–style plantation home, restored and furnished with early-19th-century Louisiana and American antiques. Dating from 1799, it originally stood where the nearby modern Catholic school is. In 1810 it became the home of James Pitot, the first mayor of incorporated New Orleans (he served 1804–05). Fortunately, despite overlooking the bayou, the house didn't take on any water after Katrina. It did have some storm damage, such as a column and some shutters that needed to be replaced, not to mention the loss of some plants, but nothing that affects the visitor's experience. Tours here are usually given by a most knowledgeable docent and are surprisingly interesting and informative.

1440 Moss St., near Esplanade Ave. ✆ **504/482-0312.** Fax 504/482-0363. www.pitothouse.org. Admission $7 adults, $5 seniors and students, free for children 7 and under, parties of 10 or more $5 each. Wed–Fri 10am–3pm (last tour at 2:15pm); or by appt.

The Superdome ★   Completed in 1975 (at a cost of around $180 million), the Superdome is a landmark civic structure that the world will never look at the same again. When it was proposed as a shelter during Katrina, that suggestion was intended as the last resort for those who simply had no other evacuation choice. As such, adequate plans were not in place, and when tens of thousands of refugees came or were brought there, within 24 hours it turned into hell on earth. Along with the Convention Center, it became a symbol of suffering, neglect, and despair, as people were trapped without sufficient food, water, medical care, or, it seemed, hope.

As it happened, the New Orleans Saints reopened the Superdome in 2006 with much hoopla for their first home game, against the Atlanta Falcons on Monday Night Football. The halftime show was anchored by a special blend of Green Day and U2, singing their charity cover of an old punk song. Over and over, regulars and even those who had taken refuge here remarked on the gleaming success of the $118-million renovation that wiped out any physical trace of the misery the Dome hosted during the dark Katrina days. As

(Finds) The Healing Powers of Beer

The little town of Abita Springs, on the opposite side of Lake Pontchartrain from New Orleans, was a big destination for elite New Orleanians in the 19th century, who were drawn to its artesian springs of ozone water, for years considered to have restorative or healing powers. Today the town attracts visitors who want to hike through the Piney Woods along the Tammany Trace, those who are on their way to the Honey Island Swamp, and those who are looking to take a deep draft of its famous liquid—and we don't mean the water. The **Abita Brewing Company** ★★, at 21084 Hwy. 36, Covington (℗ **800/737-2311** or 985/893-3143; www.abita.com), brews up one of the most successful regional microbrew brands in the country, served in bars and sold in convenience stores throughout Louisiana and across the South. In 1994 the brewery moved down the road, and its original building was converted into the Abita Brewpub, a restaurant and Abita-product central store. Despite the much larger scale of the overall brewing operation, the beer is still made in small batches. Free tours of the brewery are held on Wednesday, Thursday, and Friday at 2pm and Saturday at 1 and 2:30pm; they are closed Sundays.

The town itself is quite small—it has one traffic light—but charming, with a couple of small but commendable po' boy–type places to eat, plus a small history museum that has rotating exhibits such as a fine Smithsonian-organized look at American music from gospel and the blues to zydeco and protest songs. You can see nearly everything in the morning and still make it back to New Orleans by early afternoon. See p. 187 for our review of Abita Springs's **UCM Museum,** which alone is worth the trip. Abita Springs is about 45 minutes out of town. Take I-10 west from New Orleans to the causeway (a spectacular drive thanks to the seemingly endless miles of water on either side of the roadway), go east on I-12 toward Slidell (3 miles), take the Abita Springs exit (65), and drive north along Hwy. 59 (4 miles).

if that wasn't enough, the Saints won! And they went on to a winning season and playoff berths, for once! We won't comment on hopes for their 2009–10 season, as we don't want to jinx it, but do join us locals in a chant of "WHO DAT?!"

Here are the Superdome's stats: It's a 27-story windowless building with a seating capacity of 76,000 and a computerized climate-control system that uses more than 9,000 tons of equipment. It's one of the largest buildings in the world in diameter (680 ft.), and its grounds cover some 13 acres. Inside, no posts obstruct the spectator's view of sporting events, be they football, baseball, or basketball, while movable partitions and seats allow the building to be configured for almost any event. Most people think of the Superdome as a sports center only (the Super Bowl has been held here numerous times, and the Sugar Bowl is back), but this flying saucer of a building has played host to conventions, balls, and big theatrical and musical productions.

1500 block of Poydras St., near Rampart St. ℗ **504/587-3663.** www.superdome.com.

Algiers, annexed by New Orleans in 1870, stretches across the Mississippi River from New Orleans. Generally ignored because of its location, it became a sort of God's country after the hurricane because it did not flood at all, and many services, such as mail delivery, were restored quite quickly. It is easily accessible via the free ferry that runs from the base of Canal Street. *Note:* This ferry is one of New Orleans's best-kept secrets—it's a great way to get out onto the river and see the skyline. With such easy access (a ferry leaves every 15–20 min.), who knows why the point hasn't been better assimilated into the larger city, but it hasn't. Though it's only about ¼ mile across the river from downtown and the French Quarter, it still has the feel of an undisturbed turn-of-the-20th-century suburb, albeit a little bit beaten up by the storm. Strolling around here is a delightfully low-key way to spend an hour or two.

The last ferry returns at around 11:15pm, but be sure to check the schedule before you set out, just in case. While you're over there, you might want to stop in at:

Blaine Kern's Mardi Gras World ★★ (Kids) Few cities can boast a thriving float-making industry. New Orleans can, and no float maker thrives more than Blaine Kern, who makes more than three-quarters of the floats used by the various krewes every Carnival season. Blaine Kern's Mardi Gras World offers tours of its collection of float sculptures and its studios, where you can see floats being made year-round. Yes, they were back at work on the 2006 Mardi Gras, despite losing many already-completed floats, shortly after Katrina. (Nothing can stop the party!) Visitors see sculptors at work, doing everything from making small "sketches" of the figures to creating and painting the enormous sculptures that adorn Mardi Gras floats each year. You can even try on some heavily bejeweled and dazzling costumes (definitely bring your camera!). Although they could do more with this tour, the entire package does add up to a most enjoyable experience, and it is rather nifty to see the floats up close. Since they moved across the river from Algiers to New Orleans proper, a visit here is a little less of an adventure than it used to be—but on the other hand it's more convenient. All tours include King Cake and coffee.

1380 Port of New Orleans Place. (C) **800/362-8213** or 504/362-8211. www.mardigrasworld.com. Admission $18 adults, $14 seniors (over 65), $11 children 3–11, free for children 2 and under. Daily 9am–5pm. Last tour at 4:30pm. Closed Mardi Gras, Easter, Thanksgiving, Christmas.

3 PARKS & GARDENS

One of the many unsettling details following weeks of Katrina flooding was how normally verdant New Orleans had turned to shades of gray and brown. The vegetation had drowned. Regular rainfall has restored New Orleans's lushness, though the loss of some centuries-old oaks is hard to get past. With enough funds and TLC, all but the most badly damaged buildings can be repaired, but a massive old oak cannot be replaced in our lifetime.

PARKS
Audubon Park ★★ (Kids) Across from Loyola and Tulane universities, Audubon Park and the adjacent Audubon Zoo (see "A Day at the Zoo," below) sprawl over 340 acres, extending from St. Charles Avenue all the way to the Mississippi River. This tract once belonged to city founder Jean-Baptiste Le Moyne and later was part of the Etienne de Boré plantation, where sugar was granulated for the first time in 1794. Although John

James Audubon, the country's best-known ornithologist, lived only briefly in New Orleans (in a cottage on Dauphine St. in the French Quarter), the city has honored him by naming both the park and the zoo after him. There is no historical evidence to suggest that Audubon was much of a golfer; nevertheless, a golf course now fills the middle of the park that bears his name.

The park was briefly used as a campground for the National Guard, but was soon restored post-hurricane to its recreational purposes. The huge trees with black bark are live oaks; some go back to plantation days, and more than 200 additional ones were recently planted here, though any number of young and old oaks did not survive Hurricane Katrina. Still, there is a gratifyingly large number left, which is good, because with the exception of the trees, it's not the most visually interesting park in the world—it's just pretty and a nice place to be. Visitors can enjoy a picnic in the shade of the trees, feed ducks in a lagoon, and pretend they're Thoreau. Or they can look with envy at the lovely old houses whose backyards literally bump up against the park. The park includes the Ogden Entrance Pavilion and Garden (at St. Charles Ave.) and a smattering of gazebos, shelters, fountains, and statuary.

Without question, the most utilized feature of the park is the 1¾-mile paved, traffic-free road that loops around the lagoon and golf course. It was estimated a few years ago that between 2,000 and 3,000 joggers use the track each day, joined by cyclists, walkers, and in-line skaters. Along the track are 18 exercise stations; tennis courts and horseback-riding facilities can be found elsewhere in the park. Check out the pavilion on the riverbank for one of the most pleasant views of the Mississippi you'll find. The Audubon Zoo is toward the back of the park, across Magazine Street.

6500 Magazine St., btw. Broadway and Exposition Blvd. ⓒ **504/581-4629.** www.auduboninstitute.org. Daily 6am–10pm.

Chalmette Battlefield/Jean Lafitte National Historical Park & Preserve ★★

On the grounds of what is now Chalmette National Historical Park, the bloody **Battle of New Orleans** was waged on January 14, 1815. Ironically, the battle should never have been fought because a treaty signed 2 weeks before in Ghent, Belgium, had ended the War of 1812. But word had not yet reached Congress, the commander of the British forces, or Andrew Jackson, who stood with American forces to defend New Orleans and the mouth of the Mississippi River. The battle did, however, succeed in uniting Americans and Creoles in New Orleans and in making Jackson a hero in this city.

After Katrina, 5 feet of water flooded the battlefield, the visitor station (which had to be destroyed; there is currently a double-wide trailer in its place, with some nice displays), and the Beauregard House plantation house. The latter was "built to be flooded," said a justly impressed employee, out of materials that let the building breathe, and so it actually fared pretty well, and has since reopened. A new visitor center is under construction, with work scheduled to be completed in mid-2010. And you can once again visit the battlefield with markers that allow you to follow the course of the battle. There's a national cemetery in the park, established in 1864. It holds only two American veterans from the Battle of New Orleans, but some 14,000 Union soldiers who fell in the Civil War are buried here. For a terrific view of the Mississippi River, climb the levee in back of the Beauregard House. To reach the park, take St. Claude Avenue southeast from the French Quarter until it becomes St. Bernard Highway, in approximately 7 miles. Note that this drive will take you through the hard-hit Lower 9th Ward and the similarly devastated towns of Arabi and Chalmette.

8606 W. St. Bernard Hwy. © **504/589-3882.** www.nps.gov/jela. Free admission. Grounds and restrooms daily 9am–4:30pm. Closed Mardi Gras and Dec 25.

City Park ★★★ Once part of the Louis Allard plantation, City Park has been here a long time and has seen it all—including that favorite pastime among 18th-century New Orleans gentry: dueling. At the entrance, you'll see a statue of General P. G. T. Beauregard, whose order to fire on Fort Sumter opened the Civil War and who New Orleanians fondly refer to as "the Great Creole." The extensive, once-beautifully landscaped grounds were, unlike Audubon Park, Katrina-ized, enduring serious flooding. Given what it went through (devastating photos can be viewed at their website), it looks pretty good, and is a charming place for a walk and bird-watching. It holds botanical gardens and a conservatory, four golf courses, picnic areas, lagoons for boating and fishing, tennis courts, a bandstand (which has resumed summertime concerts; check the website for scheduled events), two miniature trains, and **Children's Storyland,** an amusement area, including fairy-tale figures upon which one can climb and carouse, and an antique carousel (see "Especially for Kids," later in this chapter). At Christmastime, the mighty oaks (too many of which fell during the storm, though a large number are standing tough), already dripping with Spanish moss, are strung with lights—quite a magical sight—and during Halloween there is a fabulous haunted house.

You'll also find the **New Orleans Museum of Art** (p. 185) at Collins Diboll Circle, on Lelong Avenue, in a building that is itself a work of art. Also in City Park are the **New Orleans Botanical Gardens,** which are pretty much like any good version of same, though given the heartache of 3 feet of flooding, which destroyed most of their collection, you have to admire the efforts needed to restore them after the storm. More significantly, it's here you'll find tucked away one of the oddest and most charming attractions in this odd and charming city, the **Train Garden.** Imagine a massive train set, the kind every 9-year-old kid (or kid at heart) would kill for. Now imagine that it's located in Dr. Seuss's basement, if Dr. Seuss was obsessed with both New Orleans and organic materials. Along 1,300 feet of track are replicas of 1890s streetcars and ornately detailed, slightly off-perspective, bizarrely beautiful representations of actual New Orleans neighborhoods and landmarks (the miniature buildings are based on very specific addresses)—all made from organic plant material! In a town of must-see attractions, this is just one more.

The Train Garden is open during normal Botanical Garden hours (year-round Tues–Sun 10am–4:30pm), but the trains only run on Saturday and Sunday from 10am to 2pm, weather permitting. Admission to the gardens is $5 adults, $2 children 5 to 12, and free for children 4 and under. The gardens are located in the Pavilions of Two Sisters on Victory Avenue in the park. Storyland admission is $3. Carousel Gardens is $3, with additional prices varying on the rides; a $15 "bracelet" allows you unlimited rides.

1 Palm Dr. © **504/482-4888.** www.neworleanscitypark.com. Daily sunrise–10pm.

GARDENS
Longue Vue House & Gardens ★★ One of many remarkable things about New Orleans is all the little pockets of the unexpected. Here it is, a relatively big city, with some typical big-city landscape, but also the Garden District and the Marigny. And also the Longue Vue mansion. Just about at the point when you cross over into the good (which is to say, the interesting) part of the suburb of Metairie, no more than 20 minutes from the center city (depending on traffic, of course) is a unique expression of Greek

Revival architecture set on an 8-acre estate. It's like stumbling across a British country-house estate. You expect plantations (it never was one, but you will be forgiven for having brief Tara flashbacks) in these here parts, but not just a few minutes from a Home Depot. Add it to your list of "nice places to ramble on a pretty day."

Constructed from 1939 to 1942, Longue Vue House & Gardens is listed on the National Register of Historic Places and is accredited by the American Association of Museums. The mansion was designed to foster a close rapport between indoors and outdoors, with vistas of formal terraces and pastoral woods. We think that if you've seen one big fancy house you've seen them all, so you may not want to bother timing your visit with one of the house tours. Leaks caused some (though not as much as initially feared) damage to the collections, while flooding destroyed the electrical system, now repaired. The charming gardens, some inspired by the Generalife, the former summer-house of the sultans in Granada, Spain, naturally, got pounded by the storm and flooding, requiring extensive restoration. From a garden standpoint, this is both depressing and exciting; years and years of hard work are gone, but then again, the possibilities for the future are many. And the future is now; replanting is ongoing (salt content in the soil has made some of this process drag on), but it's already looking pretty good. Look also for fountains and a colonnaded loggia.

It goes without saying that this is a must for garden enthusiasts, but you might be surprised what a nice time you could have regardless. We are completely smitten with the delightful Discovery Garden, fully back up and running. Once again, kids can play (and maybe even learn) from various clever and amusing exhibits. It costs more than a park, and there is nothing that goes beep (though there might be exhibits on insects, which will buzz!), but it's something to keep in mind for an alternate kid-friendly activity.

7 Bamboo Rd., New Orleans, near Metairie. (C) **504/488-5488.** www.longuevue.com. Admission $10 adults, $5 children and students. Mon–Sat 10am–4:30pm; Sun 1–5pm. Hourly tours start at 10am. Closed Jan 1, Mardi Gras, Easter Sunday, July 4th, Labor Day, Thanksgiving, and Dec 24–25.

A DAY AT THE ZOO

Audubon Zoo ★★★ (**Kids**) It's been about 30 years since the Audubon Zoo underwent a total renovation that turned it from one of the worst zoos in the country into one of the best. The achievement is still worth noting, and the result is a place of justifiable civic pride that delights even non-zoo fans. While a terrific destination for visitors with children, this small and sweet attraction offers a good change of pace for anyone. Note that on hot and humid days, you should plan your visit for early or late in the day; otherwise, the animals will be sleeping off the heat.

Here, in a setting of subtropical plants, waterfalls, and lagoons, some 1,800 animals (including rare and endangered species) live in natural habitats rather than cages. Don't miss the replica of a Louisiana swamp (complete with a rare white gator). Keep your eyes peeled for wry, post-disaster additions like a few Katrina-victim fridges!

A memorable way to visit the zoo is to arrive on the stern-wheeler *John James Audubon* (see "Audubon Aquarium of the Americas," p. 172) and depart on the St. Charles Avenue streetcar. You can reach the streetcar by walking through Audubon Park or by taking the free shuttle bus.

During your visit to the zoo, look for the bronze statue of naturalist John James Audubon standing in a grove of trees with a notebook and pencil in hand. Also, look for a funny-looking mound near the river: Monkey Hill was constructed so that the children of this flatland city could see what a hill looked like.

6500 Magazine St. ✆ **504/581-4629.** www.auduboninstitute.org. Admission $13 adults, $9.50 seniors (65 and over), $7.50 children 2–12. Tues–Sun 10am–5pm. Last ticket sold 1 hr. before closing. Closed Mardi Gras Day, Thanksgiving, and Christmas.

---

4 NEW ORLEANS CEMETERIES ★★★

Along with Spanish moss and lacy iron balconies, the cities of the dead are part of the indelible landscape of New Orleans. Their ghostly and inscrutable presence enthralls visitors, who are used to traditional methods of burial—in the ground or in mausoleums.

Why are bodies here buried aboveground? Well, it rains in New Orleans—a lot—and then it floods. Soon after New Orleans was settled, it became apparent that Uncle Etienne had an unpleasant habit of bobbing back to the surface (doubtless no longer looking his best). Add to that cholera and yellow-fever epidemics, which helped increase not only the number of bodies but also the infection possibility, and given that the cemetery of the time was inside the Vieux Carré, it's all pretty disgusting to think about.

So in 1789 the city opened St. Louis No. 1, right outside the city walls (which no longer exist) on what is now Rampart Street. The "condo crypt" look—the dead are placed in vaults that look like miniature buildings—was inspired to a certain extent by the famous Père Lachaise cemetery in Paris. Crypts were laid out haphazardly in St. Louis No. 1, which quickly filled up even as the city outgrew the Vieux Carré and expanded around the cemetery. Other cemeteries soon followed and eventually were incorporated into the city proper. They have designated lanes, making for a more orderly appearance. The rows of tombs look like nothing so much as a city—a city where the dead inhabitants peer over the shoulders of the living.

These little houses of the dead, in addition to solving the problem of below-ground burial, are even more functional. There are two types of crypts: the aforementioned "family vaults" and the "oven crypts"—so called because of their resemblance to bread ovens in a wall. A coffin is slid inside, and the combination of heat and humidity acts like a slow form of cremation. In a year or so, the occupant is reduced to bone. As the space is needed, the bones are pushed to the back, coffin pieces are removed, and another coffin is inserted. In the larger family vaults (made of whitewashed brick), there are a couple of shelves and the same thing happens. As family members die, the bones are swept off the shelves into a pit below, and everyone eventually lies jumbled together. The result is sometimes dozens of names, going back generations, on a single spot. It's a very efficient use of cemetery space, far more so than conventional sweeping expanses of graveyard landscaping.

For many years, New Orleans cemeteries were in shambles. Crypts lay open, exposing their pitiful contents—if they weren't robbed of them—bricks lay everywhere, marble tablets were shattered, and visitors might even trip over stray bones. Thanks to local civic efforts, several of the worst eyesores have been cleaned up, though some remain in deplorable shape. A faux voodoo practice continues in some of the St. Louis cemeteries, where visitors are encouraged to scrawl Xs on the tombs. Please don't do this; not only is it a made-up voodoo ritual, but it also destroys the fragile tombs.

Though it may seem silly, concerns were high for the fate of the cemeteries during the disaster days, because they are such an important part of the New Orleans landscape. But "the system worked," as one local expert said; the tombs sailed through with no problem and with only the same high-water marks on their sides borne by any other structure in the flooded areas.

Tips Safety First

You will be warned against going to the cemeteries alone and urged to go with a scheduled tour group (see "Organized Tours," later in this chapter). Thanks to their location and layout—some are in dicey neighborhoods, and the crypts obscure threats to your safety—some cemeteries can be quite risky, making visitors prime pickings for muggers and so forth. Other cemeteries, those with better security and in better neighborhoods, not to mention with layouts that permit driving, are probably safe. Ironically, two of the most hazardous, St. Louis No. 1 and Lafayette No. 1, are often so full of tour groups that you could actually go there without one and be fairly safe. On the other hand, a good tour is fun and informative, so why not take the precaution?

If you're going to make a day of the cemeteries, you should also think about renting a car. You won't be driving through horrendous downtown traffic, you can visit tombs at your own pace, and you'll feel safer.

For more information, we highly recommend Robert Florence's *New Orleans Cemeteries: Life in the Cities of the Dead* (Batture Press, 1997). It's full of photos, facts, and human-interest stories and is available at bookstores throughout the city.

THREE CEMETERIES YOU SHOULD SEE WITH A TOUR

St. Louis No. 1   This is the oldest extant cemetery (1789) and the most iconic. Here lie Marie Laveau, Bernard Marigny, and assorted other New Orleans characters. Louis the vampire from Anne Rice's *Vampire Chronicles* even has his (empty) tomb here. Also, the acid-dropping scene from *Easy Rider* was shot here.

Basin St. btw. Conti and St. Louis sts.

St. Louis No. 2   Established in 1823, the city's next-oldest cemetery, unfortunately, is in such a terrible neighborhood (next to the so-called Storyville Projects) that regular cemetery tours don't usually bother with it. If there is a tour running when you are in town, go—it's worth it. The Emperor of the Universe, R&B legend Ernie K-Doe, was laid to rest here in 2001, with bluesman extraordinaire Earl King joining him in the same tomb in 2003. Their neighbors include Marie Laveau II, some Storyville characters, and others who lie within its 3 blocks.

Note: As of this writing, there is no regular tour of St. Louis No. 2, which is absolutely unsafe. Do not go there, even in a large group, without an official tour.

N. Claiborne Ave. btw. Iberville and St. Louis sts.

Lafayette No. 1   Right across the street from Commander's Palace restaurant, this is the lush uptown cemetery. Once in horrible condition, it's been beautifully restored. Anne Rice's Mayfair witches have their family tomb here.

1427 Sixth St.

SOME CEMETERIES YOU COULD SEE ON YOUR OWN

If you decide to visit the cemeteries below on your own, please exercise caution. Take a cab to and from or consider renting a car for the day. Most of these cemeteries (such as St. Louis No. 3 and Metairie) have offices that can sometimes provide maps; if they run out, they will give you directions to any grave location you like. All have sort-of-regular hours—figure from 9am to 4pm as a safe bet.

Cypress Grove and Greenwood Cemeteries   Located across the street from each other, both were founded in the mid-1800s by the Firemen's Charitable and Benevolent Association. Each has some highly original tombs; keep your eyes open for the ones made entirely of iron. These two cemeteries are an easy streetcar ride up Canal Street from the Quarter.

120 City Park Ave. and 5242 Canal Blvd. By car, take Esplanade north to City Park Ave., turn left until it becomes Metairie Ave.

Metairie Cemetery   Don't be fooled by the slightly more modern look—some of the most amazing tombs in New Orleans are here. Not to be missed is the pyramid-and-Sphinx Brunswig mausoleum and the "ruined castle" Egan family tomb, not to mention the former resting place of Storyville madam Josie Arlington. Her mortified family had her body moved when her crypt became a tourist attraction, but the tomb remains exactly the same, including the statue of a young woman knocking on the door. Legend had it that it was Josie herself, being turned away from her father's house, or a virgin being denied entrance to Josie's brothel—she claimed never to despoil anyone. The reality is that it's just a copy of a statue Josie liked. Other famous residents include Confederate General P. G. T. Beauregard and jazz greats Louis Prima and Al Hirt. Ruth of Ruth's Chris Steakhouse was entombed here in 2002 in a marble edifice that looks remarkably like one of her famous pieces of beef.

5100 Pontchartrain Blvd. ℰ **504/486-6331.** By car, take Esplanade north to City Park Ave., turn left until it becomes Metairie Ave.

St. Louis No. 3   Conveniently located next to the Fair Grounds racetrack (home of the Jazz Fest), St. Louis No. 3 was built on top of a former graveyard for lepers. Storyville photographer E. J. Bellocq lies here. The Esplanade Avenue bus will take you there.

3421 Esplanade Ave.

---

5 VOODOO

Voodoo's mystical presence is one of the most common motifs in New Orleans. The problem is that the presence is mostly reduced to a tourist gimmick. Every gift shop seems to have voodoo dolls for sale, there is a **Voodoo Museum** (p. 179), and Marie Laveau, the famous voodoo queen, comes off as the town's patron saint. But lost among the kitsch is a very real religion with a serious past and considerable cultural importance.

Voodoo's roots can be traced in part back to the African **Yoruba** religion, which incorporates the worship of several different spiritual forces that include a supreme being, deities, and the spirits of ancestors. When Africans were kidnapped, enslaved, and brought to Brazil—and, ultimately, Haiti—beginning in the 1500s, they brought their religion with them.

By the 1700s, 30,000 slaves a year were brought to Haiti. Voodoo began to emerge at this time as different African religions met and melded. (The word *voodoo* comes from an African word meaning "god" or "spirit.") Slaves were forced to convert to Catholicism, but they found it easy to practice both religions. Voodoo gods were given saints' names, and voodoo worship more or less continued, appropriating certain Catholic rituals and beliefs. Rituals involved participants dancing in a frenzy to increasingly wild drumbeats

That Voodoo That You Do

Voodoo is a nature-based traditional African religion. It is the religion that the slaves brought here when they were taken from Africa. The word literally means "spirit deity and God, the creator of the universe," but it was taken out of context.

African people were not brought to the New World to have themselves or their culture glorified. Anything that was not white and Protestant or Catholic was looked upon as demonic. And it was not. We are all worshipping God in our own ways. And it is every culture's prerogative to do so.

People confuse negative magic with voodoo. It is not. That is not dealing with the religion of voodoo but the intent to harm. That is hoodoo. And it is not voodoo.

I was drawn to it by my family. My mother used to do candles, and she was very psychic, and she would tell me about spirits and ghosts and how to protect myself from spirits. And I grew up in a neighborhood where people would hoodoo each other. Being born on Halloween, I've always been drawn to spiritual things. I started becoming actively involved in traditional African religions over 25 years ago, but it was always part of my culture.

I had to go through levels of study and initiation with elders here and in Haiti. My Yoruba/Santeria initiation was in Atlanta. Additionally, I am a priestess of Oya, the goddess of hurricanes, the queen of the spirit world, and the queen of the marketplace. I did her initiation about 12 years ago.

Voodoo is a viable religion because people feel that by using the rituals and the prayers and all of the implements, they can do things and have power and control over their own lives. People lack something in their lives, and there is a void that traditional religions do not seem to fill—at least, the way they practice it. Voodoo a lot of times fills that void, helps a person get more in touch with their spiritual self.

The voodoo dolls are greatly overrated. They are used to help you focus, and you can use them in healing. I do not sell pins with my dolls. In Haiti I've seen the dolls, and they are never with pins. It's Hollywood to think that. People will use them that way, but it's black magic. The focal point can be positive or negative, but negative work will come back to you.

You can definitely be another religion along with voodoo—any religion. I have a lot of Jewish people who work with me and also go to synagogue. I am Catholic, I go to church, I take communion, I sing in the choir for midnight Mass. Everyone in my church knows I'm very Catholic, but also I'm a voodoo and Yoruba priestess.

—Ava Kay Jones

Ava Kay Jones has a law degree from Loyola University and is a practicing voodoo and Yoruba priestess. She also heads the Voodoo Macumba dance troupe. She is available for readings, gris-gris bags, and other items of voodoo interest at © 504/412-0202 by appointment only.

and eventually falling into a trancelike state, during which a *loa* (a spirit and/or lower-level deity intermediary btw. humans and gods) would take possession of themVoodoo didn't immediately take root in New Orleans, thanks to repressive slaveholders and an edict banning its practice. But the edict was repealed after the Louisiana Purchase in 1803, and in 1804, when slaves in Haiti revolted and overthrew the government, free blacks came to New Orleans in great numbers, as did fleeing plantation owners with their own slaves, all bringing a fresh infusion of voodoo.

Napoleonic law forced slave owners to give their slaves Sundays off and to provide them with a gathering place. **Congo Square** on Rampart Street, part of what is now Louis Armstrong Park, became the place for slaves to gather for voodoo or drumming rituals. Voodoo then was a way for slaves to have their own community and a certain amount of freedom. The religion emphasized knowledge of family and gave power to ancestors. Further, women were usually the powerful forces in voodoo—priestesses ran matters more often than priests—and this appealed to women in a time when women simply didn't have that kind of authority and power.

These gatherings naturally attracted white onlookers, as did the rituals held (often by free people of color) along St. John's Bayou. The local papers of the 1800s are full of lurid accounts of voodoo "orgies" and of whites being possessed by spirits, otherwise losing control, or being arrested after being caught in a naked pose. Thanks to the white scrutiny, the Congo Square gatherings became more like performance pieces, emphasizing drumming and music rather than religious rituals. Because of the square's proximity to what became Storyville, legend has it that madams from the houses would come down to the Sunday gatherings and hire some of the performers to entertain at their houses.

It was during the 1800s that the famous voodoo priestesses came to some prominence. Mostly free women of color, they were devout religious practitioners and very good businesswomen who had a steady clientele of whites secretly coming to them for help in love or money matters. During the 1900s, voodoo largely went back underground.

It is estimated that today as much as 15% of the population of New Orleans practices voodoo. The most common public perception of voodoo involves casting spells or sticking pins in voodoo dolls. Most of that is Hollywood nonsense. Voodoo dolls do exist, as do gris-gris bags—little packets of herbs, stones, and other bits and pieces designed to bring luck, love, health, or what have you (*gris* means "gray," to symbolize a magic somewhere btw. white and black). Other rituals more or less incorporate magic, but most of it is done for good, not for evil. Ask a real practitioner about helping you with the latter, and you will probably get some nasty looks.

Most of the stores and places in New Orleans that advertise voodoo are set up strictly for tourism. This is not to say that some facts can't be found there or that you shouldn't buy a mass-produced gris-gris bag or voodoo doll as a souvenir. For an introduction to voodoo, check out the New Orleans Historic Voodoo Museum (p. 179). If you want to know about true voodoo, however, you need to seek out real voodoo temples or practitioners, of which there are several in New Orleans (you can find them at the temples listed below or by calling Ava Kay, who works on her own—see "That Voodoo That You Do" box, above). If you want to know still more, check out Robert Tallant's book *Voodoo in New Orleans* (Pelican Pocket, 1983).

VOODOO TEMPLES ★★

Here are two authentic voodoo temples, attached to two botanicas selling everything you might need for potions and spells. The public is welcome, and the employees are happy to educate the honestly curious.

The **Island of Salvation Botanica** and the **Temple Simbi-sen Jak,** 835 Piety St. (© **504/948-9961**), are run by Sallie Glassman, voodoo priestess and author of a deck of voodoo tarot cards. The staff at the well-stocked botanica is very interested in educating the public. If you demonstrate the right enthusiasm, they might show you the temple, or you might get invited to their Saturday-night ceremony—but be aware that you will be required to participate: It is not something to observe as a performance. The botanica is open Wednesday through Saturday from 10:30am to 5pm, but due to morning readings, browsers are usually not allowed in until noon. Glassman observes that hers was the only house on her block that did not have any flooding "and I think this is pretty significant."

Located right in the French Quarter, the **Voodoo Spiritual Temple,** 828 N. Rampart St. (© **504/522-9627**), is the real McCoy—interested tourists are welcome, but please be respectful. Priestess Miriam belonged to the Spiritual Church in Chicago before setting up this spiritual house, which has a store attached. The main room is a temple, full of fascinating altars. There are both personal and open rituals. The staff wants to increase others' knowledge of voodoo and sweep away myths and ignorance, so the honestly inquisitive are quite welcome. You can also purchase a haunting CD of Priestess Miriam's voodoo chants and rituals. It's open with irregular hours. For a slightly slicker, but still authentic, voodoo experience, visit **Voodoo Authentica** (612 Dumaine; © **504/522-2111**), which, though primarily a store, also has working altars for all the *loa* and for Maria Laveau. Mama Lola, subject of the sociological voodoo study *Mama Lola: Haitian Voodou Priestess in Brooklyn,* is often in attendance, reading cards and performing cleansings.

VISITING MARIE LAVEAU

Marie Laveau is the most famous New Orleans voodoo queen. Though she was a real woman, her life has been so mythologized that it is nearly impossible to separate fact from fiction. But who really wants to? Certainly we know that she was born a free woman of color in 1794 and married Jacques Paris in 1819. Paris disappeared about 4 years later, and Marie later took up with Christophe Glapion.

Along the way, Marie, a hairdresser by trade, became known for her psychic abilities and powerful gris-gris. It didn't hurt that her day job allowed her into the best houses, where she heard all the good gossip and could apply it to her other clientele. In one famous story, a young woman about to be forced into a marriage with a much older, wealthy man approached Marie. She wanted to marry her young lover instead. Marie counseled patience. The marriage went forward, and the happy groom died from a heart attack while dancing with his bride at the reception. After a respectable time, the wealthy widow was free to marry her lover.

Marie wholeheartedly believed in voodoo and turned it into a good business, too. Her home at what is now 1020 St. Ann St. (you can now see only the building itself) was purportedly a gift from a grateful client. A devout Catholic, Marie continued to attend daily Mass and was publicly noted for her charity work that included regular visits to inmates awaiting execution.

Her death in 1881 was noted by the *Times-Picayune,* though voodoo was not mentioned. Her look-alike daughter, Marie II, took over her work, leading some to believe (mistakenly) that Marie I lived a very long time, looking quite well indeed—which only added to her legend. But Marie II allegedly worked more for the darker side than her mother. Her eventual reward, the story goes, was death by poison (delivered by whom is unknown). Today visitors can bring Marie tokens (candles, Mardi Gras beads, change) and ask her for favors—she's buried in **St. Louis Cemetery No. 1.**

Love her or loathe her, Anne Rice is one of New Orleans's biggest boosters. Though Rice tourist interest seems to have passed its peak, a good number of visitors still come here just because they have read her books; she writes seductive descriptions of her hometown that are actually quite accurate—minus the vampires, witches, and ghosts, of course. Rice uses many real locales; the Gallier House, for example, was the inspiration for the home of vampires Lestat and Louis in *Interview with the Vampire*. Her own childhood homes and former Garden District dwelling turn up in *Violin* and *The Witching Hour*. Even her nonhorror novel *Exit to Eden* sent its protagonists on a romantic trip to New Orleans, exulting in the sensual tropical air and gorging on barbecued shrimp at **Pascal's Manale** (p. 159).

Anne Rice (née O'Brien) was born on October 4, 1941, in New Orleans to Irish parents. When she was 16, her family moved to Texas, where she met her husband, the late Stan Rice. They married in 1961 and moved to California a few years later, living for years in the San Francisco area. *Interview with the Vampire* was published in 1976, and in the 1980s, the Rices and their son packed up and moved back to New Orleans. As her fortunes grew, she bought a number of significant buildings from her youth. Stan Rice died at the end of 2002, and this prompted Anne to eventually put her beloved Garden District home (along with her childhood home and most of her other New Orleans holdings) on the market, and move first to the Kenner suburbs and eventually to Southern California. Rice continues to publish regularly. You can find signed copies of her books at the **Garden District Book Shop,** 2727 Prytania St. (p. 238).

ANNE RICE IN THE FRENCH QUARTER

The romance of the French Quarter seems to attract vampires, who found easy pickin's in its dark corners in the days before electricity.

St. Louis Cemetery No. 1, 400 Basin St.: A tomb (empty, of course) with Louis the vampire's name is located here in the "Vampire Chronicle" books, and Louis occasionally goes to sit on it and brood. Rumor has it that Rice has purchased a tomb here for her eventual use. *Note:* Keep your wits about you here—not because of vampires but because this isn't the safest neighborhood. See p. 197 for more on cemetery tours.

Gallier House, 1132 Royal St.: This famously preserved museum is said by Rice scholars to be the model for the house on Rue Royal that was home to vampires Lestat and Louis in *Interview with the Vampire*. Also see p. 177.

The stretch of 700 to 900 Royal St.: Quite a few of the exteriors for the *Interview with the Vampire* movie were filmed along this stretch—though the set decorators had to labor long and hard to erase all traces of the 20th century. Try to imagine the streets covered in mud. Then try to imagine how folks who live around here felt about it.

Madame John's Legacy, 632 Dumaine St.: In the *Interview with the Vampire* movie, this is the house from which the caskets are being carried as Brad Pitt's voice-over describes Lestat and the little vampire Claudia going out on the town: "An infant prodigy with a lust for killing that matched his own. Together, they finished off whole families." Also see p. 179.

Café du Monde, 800 Decatur St.: Lestat visits this restaurant in *The Tale of the Body Thief,* and Michael and Rowan snack here in *The Witching Hour*. Also see p. 163.

Jackson Square: It's here that Claudia makes an important decision regarding Lestat's fate in *Interview with the Vampire* and that Raglan James meets Lestat in *The Tale of the Body Thief.*

Omni Royal Orleans hotel, at 621 St. Louis St.: Katherine and Julien Mayfair stay here—it's still the St. Louis Hotel—in *The Witching Hour.* Also see p. 93.

Court of Two Sisters, 613 Royal St.: Characters in *The Witching Hour* dine here. Also see p. 132.

Galatoire's, 209 Bourbon St.: Characters from several books, including *The Witching Hour,* dine here as well. Also see p. 133.

Hotel Monteleone, 214 Royal St.: This was Aaron Lightner's house in *The Witching Hour.*

Boyer Antiques Doll & Toy Museum, 241 Chartres St.: In the *Interview with the Vampire* movie, this is the shop where Claudia admires a doll and then deals with the patronizing shopkeeper in typical vampire fashion.

Marsoudet-Caruso House, 1519 Esplanade Ave.: A few blocks north of the French Quarter at the intersection of Esplanade and Claiborne avenues, this is the house where Louis smells the scent of old death in the *Interview with the Vampire* movie and finds the moldering Lestat shrinking from helicopters in a musty chair.

Jackson Barracks, south of the French Quarter along the Mississippi: This area was used for numerous exteriors in the *Interview with the Vampire* movie, including the scene where Louis and Claudia run for their ship after setting Lestat on fire.

ANNE RICE IN THE GARDEN DISTRICT

Rice's books increasingly have featured the Garden District and the area around it, perhaps because she and her family used to live in and own a number of properties there.

Coliseum Theater, 1233 Coliseum St.: In the film version of *Interview with the Vampire,* this is the theater where Louis sees *Tequila Sunrise.*

The property at 1515–17 St. Charles Ave.: For a long time, rumor had it Rice was going to open a Lestat-themed cafe. It's probably just as well that never came to pass.

Pontchartrain Hotel, 2031 St. Charles St.: This upscale hotel and its restaurant, the Caribbean Room (now closed), appear in *The Witching Hour.*

The old Mercedes dealership (now a different property), 2001 St. Charles Ave.: This building was at the center of a dispute that amused the city for months. The vampire Lestat disappeared from this world through an image of himself in the window of this building. When Straya (as it was then) opened, Rice (who rumor had it wanted to open her own cafe on the site) criticized owner Al Copeland with a full-page ad in the daily newspaper. Lestat (wink, wink—word on the street was that it was Copeland himself) then mysteriously returned to this realm and bought an ad of his own, congratulating Copeland for his "stroke of genius."

St. Alphonsus Church, 2030 Constance St.: This is a small (now deconsecrated) church with a stunning interior (p. 188). It was the O'Brien family church—Anne's parents married here, and she was baptized and received communion here. She also took Alphonsus as her confirmation name. Readers will recognize this as a setting in *The Witching Hour.*

1239 First St.: This historic property (see "Walking Tour 2: The Garden District" in chapter 9, "City Strolls") was for many years Anne Rice's primary residence. The Mayfair house in *The Witching Hour* matches her home in almost every detail, including address.

2301 St. Charles Ave.: This spacious, two-story white house was Rice's childhood home.

2524 St. Charles Ave.: Rice's family moved into this traditional-style raised villa when Anne was 14. It's prominently featured in her novel *Violin*.

Commander's Palace, 1403 Washington Ave.: Rice readers will recognize this restaurant as a favorite of the Mayfair family (p. 155).

Lafayette No. 1: This centerpiece of the Garden District is also a frequent setting in Rice's work, especially as a roaming ground for Lestat and Claudia in *Interview with the Vampire* and as the graveyard for the Mayfairs in *The Witching Hour.*

7 ORGANIZED TOURS

There are some advantages to taking tours. Though many are touristy (by definition), someone else does the planning, it's an easy way to get to outlying areas, and if the tour guide is good, you should learn a lot in a fairly entertaining way. Any of the following will be adding details about Katrina, to varying degrees, to their lectures, but don't look for that to be the focus. New Orleans had, in case you haven't figured out, a long rich history well before it, a history that covers a couple of near city-devastating disasters prior to the most recent one, and hearing all of that provides excellent perspective, not to mention optimism for what is possible for the city's future.

Be warned: Though we can't vouch for the accuracy of this information, we have heard reports that some hotel concierges take kickbacks from the tour companies they recommend—a widespread practice around the world. Obviously, not every concierge is on the take, and some may have honest opinions about the merits of one company over another. The way to avoid this problem is to cut out the middleman; no matter how you learned about it, pay the fee directly to the company, not to your concierge. No reputable firm will insist you pay someone else first. In addition, except for the outstanding **Historic New Orleans Tours,** most tour companies seem to be hit-or-miss, depending on the guide you get.

For information on organized and self-guided tours of the plantation houses outside New Orleans, see chapter 12, "Plantation Homes & Cajun Country: Side Trips from New Orleans."

IN THE FRENCH QUARTER

Note: Chapter 9, "City Strolls," includes a French Quarter walking tour you can do on your own.

Historic New Orleans Tours ★★★ (© 504/947-2120; www.tourneworleans.com) is the place to go for authenticity rather than sensationalism. Here, the tour guides are carefully chosen for their combination of knowledge and entertaining manner, and we cannot recommend the guides or the tours highly enough. The daily French Quarter tours are the best straightforward, nonspecialized walking tours of this neighborhood. They also offer a Voodoo tour and a Haunted tour and a Garden District tour. All of their tours are $20 for adults while students and seniors with ID are $15; children 6 to 12 are $7 and those 5 and under go free.

The nonprofit volunteer group **Friends of the Cabildo** (© 504/523-3939) also offers an excellent 2-hour walking tour of the Quarter. It leaves from in front of the 1850 House Museum Store, at 523 St. Ann St., on Jackson Square. The fee is $15 per adult; it's free for children 12 and under accompanied by an adult. Tours leave Tuesday through Sunday at 10am and 1:30pm, except holidays. Reservations aren't necessary—just show

up, about 15 minutes early. Stop by the **Jean Lafitte National Park and Preserve's**
Folklife and Visitor Center, 419 Decatur St., near Conti Street (© **504/589-2636**), for
details on its excellent free walking tour conducted by National Park Service rangers. The
History of New Orleans tour covers about a mile in the French Quarter and brings to
life the city's history and the ethnic roots of its unique cultural mix. No reservations are
required for this tour, but only 25 people are taken in a group. The tour starts at 9:30am
daily (except for Mardi Gras and Christmas); the office opens at 9am, and it's strongly
suggested that you get there then to ensure that you get a ticket.

The **Bienville Foundation** ★★★, run by Roberts Batson (© **504/945-6789;** info@
decafest.org; www.decafest.org), offers a live-on-stage Scandal Tour titled "Amazing
Place, This New Orleans," and a highly popular and recommended Gay Heritage Tour.
The tours last roughly 2½ hours and generally cost $20 per person. Times and departure
locations also change seasonally, so call or e-mail to find out what's happening when.

Inez Douglas gives **Heritage Literary Tours** ★★ (© **504/949-9805**). In addition to
a general tour about the considerable literary legacy of the French Quarter—with stops
at spots where the greats and the pretty-goods lived, played, wrote and caroused, tours
can be designed around a specific author such as John Kennedy Toole or Tennessee Williams. Group tours (2½-hr. walking tour, $20 per person for adults, 3 people minimum.)
scheduled by appointment only.

Le Monde Creole ★★★ (© **504/568-1801**) offers a unique tour that uses the
dramatic lives of one classic Creole family as a microcosm of the Creole world of the 19th
century. This is the sister operation of **Laura Plantation** (p. 284). At the city location,
you can learn about Creole city life and the extraordinary story of Laura's family, off the
plantation and in the Vieux Carré, while viewing French Quarter courtyards associated
with the family. This is probably the only operation that also offers tours in French. (And
also in German and Italian, but that needs to be arranged further in advance.) Currently,
there are tours (which include a visit to St. Louis No. 1 and the voodoo temple on Rampart) daily at 10:30am in English and 10am daily in French. All tours are reservation
only, so call in advance. Prices are $20 adults, $16 for students, $10 for children 4 to 10,
and free for kids 3 and under. E-mail: creolwrld@aol.com.

BEYOND THE FRENCH QUARTER

Author Robert Florence (who has written two excellent books about New Orleans cemeteries as well as our Garden District walking tour in chapter 9, "City Strolls") loves his
work, and his **Historic New Orleans Tours** ★★★ (© **504/947-2120**) are full of
meticulously researched facts and more than a few good stories. A very thorough tour of
the Garden District and Lafayette Cemetery (a section of town not many of the other
companies go into) leaves daily at 11am and 1:45pm from the Garden District Book
Shop (in the Rink, corner of Washington Ave. and Prytania St.); you are advised to arrive
about 15 minutes before departure. Rates are $20 for adults, $13 for students with ID
and seniors, $7 for children 7 to 12, and free for children 6 and under.

Tours by Isabelle ★★ (© **504/398-0365;** (www.toursbyisabelle.com) offers eight
different tours for small groups in passenger vans. Most of their business is currently
coming from the Post-Katrina City Tour ($60; which is the only way they still show the
city apart from what is listed below and in walking tours). It is 70 miles long and takes
3 hours and 20 minutes. It still shows French Quarter, City Park, and other places that
date from the beginning of the city's history, but otherwise is highly geared toward post-
Katrina damage and sights, and is comprehensive. This may seem exploitative, but most

of the drivers are from that impacted area, and this gives them work. Prices and departure times vary. Make reservations as far in advance as possible. For $65, you can join Isabelle's afternoon Combo Tour, which begins at 1pm and adds Longue Vue House and Gardens to a tour of the French Quarter, St. Louis Cemetery No. 3, Bayou St. John, the shores of Lake Pontchartrain, and the Uptown and Downtown neighborhoods. Many more tours are available; contact them for more information.

Gray Line ★★, 2 Canal St., Ste. 1300 (© 800/535-7786 or 504/569-1401; www.graylineneworleans.com), like all businesses around town, took a hard hit, between severely reduced staff (most of whom, including the head of the local company, lost their homes), and, of course, being a business that involves sightseeing. Consequently, they took the controversial move of adding Katrina disaster tours to their menu. Initially, locals thought the tours a bad idea, but upon reflection, the majority agreed: These sights need to be seen, so that this disaster, and its victims, are not forgotten. Certainly, the company has gone to great lengths to operate these tours with respect. Guides are locals with their own storm stories to tell, tourists are not allowed to exit the vans while in the damaged neighborhoods, a portion of the ticket price goes to Katrina relief (and passengers can choose which organization, out of a selection, their money will go to), and petitions to various government agencies are sent around for voluntary signatures. Gray Line also offers tours of the entire city in comfortable coaches, with the exception of the French Quarter tour. And it has a tour that includes a 2-hour cruise on the **steamboat Natchez** (www.steamboatnatchez.com), plus plantation tours, swamp tours, and a number of walking tours, including nighttime and ghost tours.

SWAMP TOURS

In addition to the tour providers listed below, Jean Lafitte and Gray Line (see above) both offer **swamp tours,** which can be a hoot, particularly if you get a guide who calls alligators to your boat for a little snack of chicken (please keep your hands inside the boat—they tend to look a lot like chicken to a gator). On all of the following tours, you're likely to see alligators, bald eagles, waterfowl, egrets, owls, herons, ospreys, feral hogs, otters, beavers, frogs, turtles, raccoons, deer, and nutria (maybe even a black bear or a mink)—and a morning spent floating on the bayou can be mighty pleasant.

Dr. Wagner's Honey Island Swamp Tours ★★ (© 985/641-1769 or 504/242-5877; www.honeyislandswamp.com), located at 41490 Crawford Landing Rd. in Slidell about 30 miles outside of New Orleans, takes you by boat into the interior of Honey Island Swamp to view wildlife with native professional naturalist guides. The tour guides provide a solid educational experience to go with the purer swamp excitement. Tours last approximately 2 hours. Prices are $23 for adults, $15 for children 11 and under, if you drive to the launch site yourself; the rates are $45 and $32 for children if you want a hotel pickup in New Orleans.

Jean Lafitte Swamp Tours (© 800/445-4109; www.jeanlafitteswamptour.com) in Marerro offers "native Cajun" tour guides replete with lore about the flora, fauna, and legends—as well as proximity to New Orleans. Speedy airboat tours are also available for the more adventurous. It includes transportation from most downtown hotels for an additional fee. Prices for the hour and 45 minute tour are $25 for adults and $13 for children 3 to 12 for drive-ups; with transportation prices are $49 for adults and $24 for children. Kids 2 and under free with paid adult.

Pearl River Eco-Tours ★★, 55050 Hwy. 90, Slidell, LA 70461 (© 866/59-SWAMP [597-9267] or 504/581-3395; www.pearlriverecotours.com), is built on Southern hospitality. The boat captain, Neil, has been doing tours of Honey Island Swamp for over 10

years. The swamp is beautiful, even during the months the gators are in hibernation. If
you have a car, you can drive over there and tour for $23 (children 4–12 go for $15). Tours run at 10am and 2:30pm. If they provide transportation from New Orleans, the cost is $49 for adults, $33 for children ages 4 to 12.

MYSTICAL & MYSTERIOUS TOURS

Interest in the supernatural, ghostly side of New Orleans—let's go right ahead and blame Anne Rice and subsequent stories of sparkly vampires—has meant an increased number of tours catering to the vampire set. It has also resulted in some rather humorous infighting as rival tour operators have accused each other of stealing their shtick—and customers. We enjoy a good nighttime ghost tour of the Quarter as much as anyone, but we also have to admit that what's available is really hit-or-miss in presentation (it depends on who conducts your particular tour) and more miss than hit with regard to facts. Go for the entertainment value, not for the education (with some exceptions—see below). But just remember this: There was no New Orleans vampire tradition until Ms. Rice created one.

While most of the ghost tours are a bunch of hooey hokum (many using bullhorns during nighttime tours, disturbing neighborhood peace and quiet), we are pleased that there is one we can send you to with a clear conscience: **Historic New Orleans Tours** ★★★ (© 504/947-2120). They offer a Cemetery and Voodoo Tour, the only one that is fact- and not sensation-based, though it is no less entertaining for it. The trip goes through St. Louis Cemetery No. 1, Congo Square, and an active voodoo temple. It leaves Monday through Saturday at 10am and 1pm, Sunday at 10am only, from the courtyard at 334-B Royal St. Rates are $20 for adults, $13 for students and seniors, and free for children 11 and under. They are also offering a nighttime haunted tour, perhaps the only one in town where well-researched guides will offer genuine thrills and chills. It leaves at 7:30pm from Snooks, at the corner of Bourbon and Orleans.

Magic Walking Tours ★, 714 N. Rampart (© **504/588-9693;** www.magictoursnola.com), was apparently the first to up the ante on the evening tours, offering a bit of theatrical spectacle along with the tours. When others copied the concept, they toned down the gimmicks, emphasizing the history and folklore along with ghost stories. The guides are generally good—all, per the owner (who has a Ph.D. in history), scholars and journalists. Several guided walking tours are offered daily: St. Louis Cemetery No. 1 (which is probably the only voodoo-free cemetery tour out there), Courtyards, the French Quarter, the Garden District, and the Ghost-Hunt and Voodoo Walking Tour. Reservations are required, but call ahead for tour schedules. Meeting places vary according to the tour. Tours cost $20 for adults; $17 for students, seniors, and military; and are free for children 5 and under.

Haunted History Tours ★, 97 Fontainebleau Dr. (© **888/6-GHOSTS** [644-6787] or 504/861-2727; www.hauntedhistorytours.com), is the Magic Walking Tours' big rival and the place to go if you want mild theatrics along with facts (and we use the term "facts" very loosely). Expect fake snakes and blood, costumes, and gizmos. They offer everything from a voodoo/cemetery tour to a nocturnal vampire tour of the Quarter. Prices are $20 for adults, $17 for seniors and students, $10 for children; meeting places and departure times vary with the offerings. Plan to arrive 30 minutes before the tour is scheduled.

BOAT TOURS

For those interested in doing the Mark Twain thing, a number of operators offer riverboat cruises; some cruises have specific destinations like the zoo or Chalmette, while

Creole Cooking Vacations

For visitors who want to take their New Orleans culinary experience one big step further, the **New Orleans Cooking Experience** (℗ **504/945-9104;** www.new orleanscookingexperience.com) offers personalized cooking classes, from half-day courses to special-events demonstrations to 2- or 4-day complete vacations. The latter includes classes, dining out, and most meals. Classes are taught at the House on Bayou Road (p. 100), a charming 18th-century inn. Celebrated New Orleans chef Frank Brigtsen has created the course curriculum, which will feature classic New Orleans Creole dishes such as filé gumbo, crabmeat ravigote, barbe-cued shrimp, jambalaya, crawfish étouffée, and bananas Foster. Look for classes and special series taught by local culinary legend Leah Chase, and other high-profile local chefs. Regular classes are limited to no more than 10 people. **Single classes** are $150 per person and include recipes, a multicourse meal, and wines. **Classes-only series** are priced at four classes for $560 and three classes for $420. **Complete vacation classes** are $290 and $385 for 2 and 4 days. **Private classes** and **customized group rates** are available by reservation.

others just cruise the river and harbor without stopping. They're touristy, but they can be fun if you're in the right mood, and they are good for families. Docks are at the foot of Toulouse and Canal streets, and there's ample parking. Call for reservations, which are required for all these tours, and to confirm prices and schedules.

The steamboat *Natchez,* 2 Canal St., Ste. 1300 (℗ **800/233-BOAT** [233-2628] or 504/586-8777; www.steamboatnatchez.com), a marvelous three-deck stern-wheeler docked at the wharf behind the Jackson Brewery, offers at least one 2-hour daytime cruise Wednesday through Sunday, and a jazz dinner cruise Thursday through Sunday. The narration is by professional guides, and there are a cocktail bar, live jazz, an optional lunch ($10 extra for ages 5 and up; 4 and under the meal is $8), and a gift shop. Daytime fares are $25 for adults and $13 for children; for evening cruises (not including dinner) they are $40 for adults, $20 for children. Children 2 and under ride free. The cruise with dinner runs $65 for adults, $33 for children 6 to 12, and $12 for children 2 to 5.

The paddle-wheeler *Creole Queen,* Riverwalk Dock (℗ **800/445-4109** or 504/529-4567; www.neworleanspaddlewheels.com), departs from the Poydras Street Wharf adjacent to the Riverwalk on Friday and Saturday afternoon for a 1½-hour narrated excursion to the port and to the historic site of the Battle of New Orleans. There is also a 7pm jazz dinner cruise. The boat has a covered promenade deck, and its inner lounges are air-conditioned or heated as needed. Snacks are available on daytime cruises. Daytime fares are $20 for adults, $12 for children; the nighttime jazz cruise is $59 for adults, $20 for children. Children 2 and under ride free. They also offer swamp tours and harbor cruises; prices vary.

CARRIAGE TOURS

Corny it may be, but there is a sheepish romantic lure to the old horse-drawn carriages that pick up passengers at Jackson Square and take them for day- and nighttime tours of the Quarter. (They are actually mule-drawn because mules can take heat and humidity while horses can't.) The mules are decked out with ribbons, flowers, or even hats, and the drivers seem to be in a fierce competition to win the "most unusual city story" award. Once again, the "facts" presented are probably dubious but should be most entertaining. Carriages wait at the Decatur Street end of Jackson Square from 9am to midnight in good weather; the charges are $8 per adult and $5 for kids 11 and under for a ride that lasts roughly half an hour.

Private horse-and-carriage tours offered by **Good Old Days Buggies** (© 504/523-0804) include hotel or restaurant pickup and cost $150 an hour.

ANTIQUING TOURS

Antiquing in New Orleans can be an overwhelming experience, especially if you have your heart set on something in particular. For that, you might need a little expert help, and that's why Macon Riddle founded **Let's Go Antiquing!**, 1412 Fourth St. (© 504/899-3027). She'll organize and customize antiques-shopping tours to fit your needs. Hotel pickup is included, and she will even make lunch reservations for you. If you find something and need to ship it home, she'll take care of that, too. Prices vary.

8 ESPECIALLY FOR KIDS

New Orleans is one of those destinations that may be more fun *sans enfants.* Don't get us wrong—there are plenty of unusual things to do during daylight hours that will wear out everyone under 12 or over 40, but any adult confined to his or her hotel room past 9pm has entirely missed the point of vacationing here. Still, we suppose it's in everyone's best interest to introduce the little tykes to the land of big food and big music so that they'll beg to return when they're old enough to go clubbing with Mom and Dad. In the meantime, you can entertain them with a combination of conventional and unconventional, only-in-New-Orleans activities.

The **French Quarter** in and of itself is fascinating to children over 7. A walkabout with a rest stop for beignets at **Café du Monde** (p. 163) will while away a pleasant morning and give you an opportunity to see the architecture and peek into the shops. Continue (or begin) their roots-music education with a visit to the Presbytère (p. 180) for some colorful Mardi Gras history and later to **Preservation Hall** (p. 258) for a show. For those progeny who aren't terrifically self-conscious, a **horse-and-buggy ride** (see "Carriage Tours," above) around the Quarter is very appealing—but save it for later when they start getting tired and you need a tiny bribe to keep them going. (If you happen to be in New Orleans in Dec, be sure to take a **ride** through City Park, when thousands of lights turn the landscape and trees into fairy-tale scenery.)

The **Musée Conti Wax Museum** (p. 179), which features effigies of local historical figures, is an acceptable pick, though you need to call in advance to tour it. **Riverwalk Marketplace** (p. 232), the glass-enclosed shopping center on the edge of the Quarter on Canal Street, also appeals to kids with its relaxed atmosphere and food vendors, though for adults, it's a rather basic and, apart from the river views, dull mall (well, if you can sneak away, the **Museum of the American Cocktail** is inside!). The **Canal Street ferry** (p. 53), which crosses the Mississippi River to Algiers, is free to pedestrians and offers views of the harbor and skyline. Shuttle service is then available from the Algiers ferry landing to **Blaine Kern's Mardi Gras World** (p. 192), where the floats and costumes alone should intrigue even adolescents—whether they'll admit it or not. The slices of King Cake at the end may appease them.

Returning to Canal Street, you'll find the **Audubon Aquarium of the Americas** (p. 172) with lots of jellyfish, sea horses, and other creatures from the deep and the not-so-deep. Every boy is going to want to go to the **Insectarium,** you just know it, but let's not be sexist and exclusive; all of you should go, because it's swell. The *John James Audubon* riverboat chugs from the aquarium to lovely **Audubon Park** (p. 192) and the highly regarded **Audubon Zoo** (see "A Day at the Zoo," earlier in this chapter). The park is fronted by magnificent old oak trees. The **Audubon Louisiana Nature Center** offers several short walks through various Louisiana environments, including a swamp via a wooden walkway. Kids love getting up close with the baby gators. The center also has the **Discovery Loft,** a 1,000-square-foot hollow "tree" filled with all kinds of hands-on exhibits. The following destinations are also particularly well suited for younger children.

Children's Storyland ★★ (**Kids**) The under-8 set will be delighted with this playground (rated one of the 10 best in the country by *Child* magazine), where well-known children's stories and rhymes have inspired the charming decor. It offers plenty to slide down and climb on, and generally get juvenile ya-yas out.

Kids and adults will enjoy the carousel, two Ferris wheels (one big, one small), bumper cars, some miniature trains, a lady-bug-shaped roller coaster, and other rides at the **Carousel Gardens,** also in City Park. Delighting local families since 1906, the carousel (or "da flying horses," as real locals call it) is one of only 100 all-wood merry-go-rounds in the country, and the only one in the state.

City Park at Victory Ave. ✆ **504/483-9356.** Admission $3, ride prices vary; unlimited rides with $15 armband. Carousel Gardens amusement park Fri–Sun 11am–6pm; Storyland Sat–Sun 11am–6pm.

Louisiana Children's Museum ★★★ (**Kids**) This popular two-story interactive museum is really a playground in disguise that will keep kids occupied for a good couple of hours. Along with changing exhibits, the museum offers an art shop with regularly scheduled projects, a mini-grocery store, a chance to be a "star anchor" at a simulated television studio, and lots of activities exploring music, fitness, water, and life itself. If you belong to your local science museum, check your membership card for reciprocal entry privileges. Children 15 and under must be accompanied by a parent.

420 Julia St., at Tchoupitoulas St. ✆ **504/523-1357.** Fax 504/529-3666. www.lcm.org. Admission $7, children 16 and under free. Tues–Sat 9:30am–4:30pm; Sun noon–4:30pm.

9 GAMBLING

After years of political and legal wrangling—much of which is still an ongoing source of fun in the daily paper—**Harrah's Casino** opened. "Oh, goody," we said, along with other even more sarcastic things, as we experienced severe disorientation stepping inside for the first time. Then again, post-Katrina, the Harrah's company was financially generous to all their hurricane-affected employees and has been similarly generous with Katrina-relief benefits. So what the hey; come here and spend your money, if you like. Acting as the staging area for the police after the storm, it only needed a bit of brushing up to restore it. It's exactly like a Vegas casino (100,000 sq. ft. of nearly 3,000 slot machines and 120 tables plus buffet and twice-nightly live "Mardi Gras parade" shows), which is mighty shocking to the system and also a bit peculiar because like many a Vegas casino, it is Mardi Gras/New Orleans–themed—but exactly like a Vegas casino interpretation of same, which means it's almost exactly *not* like the real thing. It can be found on Canal Street at the river (*©* **504/533-6000;** www.harrahs.com).

There's also riverboat gambling in the area. Outside the city, you can find the **Boomtown Casino** (*©* **504/366-7711** for information and directions; www.boomtown neworleans.com) on the West Bank and the **Treasure Chest Casino** (*©* **504/443-8000;** www.treasurechest.com) docked on Lake Pontchartrain in Kenner.

10 WEDDINGS IN NEW ORLEANS

While it is true that Vegas remains the top place for weddings—as well it should, with no waiting period and a ceremony perhaps as short as 10 minutes from start (obtaining license) to finish (kiss the bride!)—New Orleans is becoming nearly as popular a nuptial destination. The city has seen a big boom in wedding business post-Katrina. Potential happy couples should be aware, however, that Louisiana requires a 72-hour waiting period (unless you know the right judge to waive it—don't laugh, we did) once you have the marriage license. In addition to the nearly endless number of romantic spots from which to choose, you can get hitched at the **French Quarter Wedding Chapel,** 333 Burgundy St. (*©* **504/598-6808;** www.frenchquarterwedding.com). This 24-hour chapel will officiate for traditional and civil ceremonies as well as "alternative lifestyle" unions. A voodoo priestess is on call to oversee commitment ceremonies.

A quick ferry ride to Algiers Point to see Judge Mary "KK" Norman (*©* **504/368-4099**) is for the no-frills justice-of-the-peace approach; her office can issue the license as well for a one-stop wedding. If you prefer a standard service in a big St. Charles Avenue mansion, the **House of Broel** (*©* **800/827-4325** or 504/525-1000; www.houseofbroel. com) offers packages for 2 to 200 people.

11 SPORTING EVENTS

In addition to the pro teams listed below, don't forget that this is a college town, with plenty of sports action available. And the city continues to draw big-time sporting events—most recently hosting the NBA All-Star Game in 2008 while the post–New Year's Sugar Bowl is, along with the Rose Bowl and Orange Bowl, at the top of college bowl games, frequently decisive in the national championship standings.

New Orleans Hornets ★★ Two words: Chris Paul. The young star didn't just make the Hornets good—leading the team to the 2008 semifinals and finishing second to Kobe Bryant in MVP voting (he was robbed, ask any New Orleanian)—he made them a real attraction. That's no small feat in a city that forgot to care about pro basketball (the Jazz residency lasted just 4 years before that team moved to Salt Lake City in 1979). Even before Katrina, the 2002 move of the team from Charlotte to the New Orleans Arena seemed a doomed experiment. And frankly, the flood may have stopped an otherwise inevitable move, as it would have been bad PR to abandon the city, even after it played most of the 2005–06 and 2006–07 seasons in Oklahoma City in front of crowds much more into it than the Crescent City folks. But with that league commitment, 2007–08 became a magical year with the Hornets fully home in NOLA, hosting the All-Star Game spectacle with typical party aplomb and seeing Paul become a true force in the game.

After a follow-up playoff appearance in the 2008–09 season, you might even have trouble getting tickets to their games in the renovated Arena now. A few years ago that was not an issue.

1501 Girod St. Ticket info ☏ **504/525-HOOP** [525-4667]. Fax 504/301-4121. www.hornets.com. Tickets $10–$350.

New Orleans Saints ★★ Owner Tom Benson, long in dispute with the city about finding a new home to replace the long-decaying Superdome, didn't make any local friends when he started talking up San Antonio as more than merely a temporary location for the team after the flood. Sure, for much of the time since the team entered the NFL in 1967, it's been known to frustrated (but intensely loyal) fans as the Ain'ts. But that doesn't mean the love part of the love-hate equation wasn't the strongest. Ultimately (a shamed?) Benson agreed to put the team back in a refurbished (if severely tainted by recent events) dome. And new love was won with the spring 2006 drafting of two-time Heisman Trophy–winning running back Reggie Bush. Indeed, the revitalized team came heartbreakingly close to their first Super Bowl appearance ever, losing the NFC championship in 2007 to the Chicago Bears. Hopes are high for the 2009–10 season, but only time will tell if Bush will lead the Saints to glory at last—or join the storied legacy of such colorful but failed figures as former coach Mike Ditka, former quarterback Archie Manning, and former running back Ricky Williams. A game here means time spent with amped-up fans chanting "WHO DAT?" as they equate hope for their city with the fate of their beloved Saints.

Superdome, 1500 block of Poydras. Saints home office: 5800 Airline Dr., Metairie. ☏ **504/733-0255.** Ticket info ☏ **504/731-1700.** www.neworleanssaints.com. Tickets $40–$160.

New Orleans Zephyrs ★★ Many maintain that there's no better entertainment value in pro sports than minor-league baseball, and an afternoon or evening at Zephyr Field out near the airport affirms that. Though the facility had some post-Katrina flooding and served as a staging area for rescue efforts, the Zephyrs stepped up to the plate on schedule for the 2006 season, accompanied by mascots Boudreaux D. and Clotile Nutria and their four kids. As that implied, family fun is foremost, with various promotions and fan-participation activities, plus a pool area behind right field (rentable for groups or parties), and a general-admission grass "levee" back of center field. Since moving from Denver in 1993, the team has served as the AAA team first for the Milwaukee Brewers, then the Houston Astros, and more recently the Washington Nationals. Among the stars-to-be that played here have been Bobby Abreu and Lance Berkman. (For baseball history buffs, the city has a strong minor-league legacy with the New Orleans Pelicans playing in various Mid-City locations 1887–1959.) It's a charming way to spend an evening—plus the snacks are great!

Zephyr Field, 6000 Airline Dr., Metairie. ☏ **504/734-5155.** www.zephyrsbaseball.com. Tickets $6–$10.

City Strolls

We've said it before, and we will keep saying it: This town was made for walking. Except maybe at the height of the summer months when heat and humidity—especially humidity—make you not want to do much of anything except sit gasping in the nearest shade, sipping cool drinks.

This unique-looking city is one of the most beautiful in the country—yes, still—and to not stroll through it and marvel at it is a huge loss. Everywhere, you will find gorgeous buildings, each more interesting than the last. The French Quarter and the Garden District have their own distinct appearances, and both are easily manageable on foot.

Forget those reports about Katrina destruction and how the city was "destroyed" or "wiped off the map." Don't get us wrong; the damage was intense and severe. But by some great grace, most of it bypassed the prettiest and more tourist-accessible neighborhoods. We were hard-pressed to find any storm-related damage to the following tours. And now it's hard to believe anything happened at all.

So put on some good walking shoes, breathe in that river wind and tropical breeze, and take a walk. Go slow—there's a reason New Orleans is called the Big Easy. Admire the iron lacework on one building and see how it differs from another's. Peek through gateways, particularly in the French Quarter, where simple facades hide exquisite secrets in the form of surprising courtyards with fountains, brickwork, and thick foliage. Gawk at the mighty oaks, some with swaying Spanish moss dripping from their branches, lining the streets. Don't just look at the stops on each tour below; if you're doing things right, there should be plenty to see in between the stops we detail.

Take a stroll along St. John's Bayou, turning at any corner that strikes your fancy. Admittedly, parts of this less-touristed neighborhood did flood, but locals love it here, and the area is blooming again. If you're lucky or if you walk at the right time of day (especially early in the morning), you might have a street or two to yourself. Imagine taking this walk 100 years ago; it would have looked almost exactly the way it does now. At certain times, ghosts seem to flit just out of sight around every corner. But don't get so carried away with daydreams and fantasies that you forget to be aware of your surroundings; these areas should be safe, but be careful all the same.

The following walking tours will give you a nice overview and are perfect for answering the "That looks interesting—what the heck *is* it?" kind of questions that arise during a casual stroll. Formal professional walking tours (such as the ones offered by **Historic New Orleans Tours;** ✆ **504/947-2120;** www.tourneworleans. com) cover more ground and go into considerably more detail, though they tend to deal only with the French Quarter and the Garden District. Below you will find our personalized walking tours of the French Quarter and the Garden District, as well as a stroll along a less traveled route (Esplanade Ridge) that should prove no less rewarding.

START:	The intersection of Royal and Bienville streets.
FINISH:	Jackson Square.
TIME:	Allow approximately 1½ hours, not including time spent in shops or historic homes.
BEST TIMES:	Any day before 8am (when it's still quiet and deserted), up to 10am (when the day begins in the French Quarter).
WORST TIME:	At night. Some attractions won't be open, and you won't be able to get a good look at the architecture.

Even if it's the only recreational time you spend in New Orleans, you owe it to yourself to experience the French Quarter, also known by the French name *Vieux Carré*, or "old square." The area is made up of just over 80 city blocks, and it's a living monument to history. Here, the colonial empires of France, Spain, and, to a lesser extent, Britain, intersected with the emerging American nation. Still, somehow the place seems timeless, at once recognizably old and vibrantly alive. Today's residents and merchants are stewards of a rich tradition of individuality, creativity, and disregard for many of the concerns of the world beyond. This tour is designed to acquaint you with a bit of the style and history of this place and its important landmarks and to lead you through some of its more picturesque regions.

From the corner of Royal and Bienville streets, head into the Quarter (away from Canal St.). As you walk along Royal, imagine that streetcar named *Desire* rattling along its tracks. It traveled along Royal and Bourbon streets until 1948. (It was replaced by the bus named *Desire*. Really.) You can also imagine how noisy these narrow streets were when the streetcars were in place. Your first stop is:

① 339–343 Royal St.

Also known as the Rillieux-Waldhorn House, this is now the home of Waldhorn Antiques (est. 1881). The building was built between 1795 and 1800 for Vincent Rillieux, the great-grandfather of the French Impressionist artist Edgar Degas. Offices of the (second) Bank of the United States occupied the building from 1820 until 1836 when, thanks to President Andrew Jackson's famous veto, its charter expired. Note the wrought-iron balconies—an example of excellent Spanish colonial workmanship.

② The Bank of Louisiana

Across the street, this old bank was erected in 1826 at 334 Royal St. by Philip Hamblet and Tobias Bickle, after the designs of Benjamin Fox. Its Greek Revival edifice was erected in the early 1860s, and the bank was liquidated in 1867. The building has suffered a number of fires (in 1840, 1861, and 1931) and has served as the Louisiana State Capitol, an auction exchange, a criminal court, a juvenile court, and a social hall for the American Legion. It now houses the police station for the Vieux Carré.

Cross Conti Street to:

③ 403 Royal St.

Benjamin H. B. Latrobe died of yellow fever shortly after completing designs for the Louisiana State Bank, which opened in this building in 1821. At the time of his death, Latrobe was one of the nation's most eminent architects, having designed the Bank of Pennsylvania in Philadelphia (1796) and contributed to the design of the U.S. Capitol. You can see the monogram "LSB" on the Creole-style iron balcony railing.

④ Brennan's Restaurant

Brennan's (p. 131) opened in this building at 417 Royal St., also built by Vincent Rillieux, in 1855. The structure was erected

Walking Tour: The French Quarter

339–343 Royal St.
The Bank of Louisiana
403 Royal Street
Brennan's Restaurant
437 Royal St.
New Orleans Court Building
The Brulatour Court
The Merieult House
The Court of Two Sisters
627 Royal St.
Le Monnier Mansion
The LaBranche House
714 St. Peter St.
Pat O'Brien's
Preservation Hall
Plique-LaBranche House
623 Bourbon St.
Bourbon Orleans Hotel
Le Pretre Mansion
707 Dumaine St.
Madame John's Legacy
Lafitte's Blacksmith Shop
The Thierry House
618–630 Governor Nicholls St.
The Lalaurie Home
The Gallier House Museum
The Beauregard-Keyes House
The Archbishop Antoine Blanc Memorial
The Old U.S. Mint
The Historic French Market
Decatur Street
The Pontalba Buildings
The Presbytère
St. Louis Cathedral
Faulkner House Books
The Cabildo

9

THE FRENCH QUARTER

after the fire of 1794 destroyed more than 200 of the original buildings along this street. (This is why we are so confident New Orleans will rise again. It's happened before!) From 1805 to 1841, it was home to the Banque de la Louisiane. The world-famous chess champion Paul Charles Morphy moved here as a child in 1841. The parents of Edgar Degas also lived here.

❺ 437 Royal St.

Masonic lodge meetings were held regularly in a drugstore here in the early 1800s, but that's not what made the place famous. What did? Proprietor and druggist Antoine A. Peychaud served after-meeting drinks of bitters and cognac to lodge members in small egg cups, whose French name *(coquetier)* was Americanized to "cocktail."

⑥ New Orleans Court Building

Built in 1909, this courthouse at 400 Royal St. covers the length of the block across from Brennan's. The baroque edifice, made of Georgia marble, certainly seems out of place in the French Quarter—especially considering that many Spanish-era structures were demolished to make way for it. Originally home to parish and state courts, the building was laboriously renovated over many years and is now the home of the Louisiana Supreme Court and the Fourth Circuit Court of Appeals.

Cross St. Louis Street to:

⑦ The Brulatour Court

This structure at 520 Royal St. was built in 1816 as a home for François Seignouret, a furniture maker and wine importer from Bordeaux—his furniture, with a signature "S" carved into each piece, still commands the respect of collectors. From 1870 to 1887, wine importer Pierre Brulatour occupied the building. WDSU-TV no longer maintains offices there, but during business hours you should still be welcome to walk into the courtyard—it's one of the few four-walled courtyards in the French Quarter and among the more exotic. Also, from the street, notice the elaborate, fan-shaped guard screen (garde de frise) on the right end of the third-floor balcony—look closely for Seignouret's "S" carved into the screen.

⑧ The Merieult House

Built for the merchant Jean François Merieult in 1792, this house at 533 Royal St. was the only building in the area left standing after the fire of 1794. Legend has it that Napoleon repeatedly offered Madame Merieult great riches in exchange for her hair. (He wanted it for a wig to present to a Turkish sultan.) She refused. Nowadays, it's home to the Historic New Orleans Collection—Museum/Research Center. (See p. 178 for tour times and more information.)

Cross Toulouse Street to:

⑨ The Court of Two Sisters

This structure at 613 Royal St. was built in 1832 for a local bank president on the site of the 18th-century home of a French governor. The two sisters were Emma and Bertha Camors (whose father owned the building); from 1886 to 1906, they ran a curio store here.

⑩ 627 Royal St.

Walk through the entrance of the Horizon Gallery to the back to see another of the French Quarter's magnificent courtyards. This 1777 building, the former home of the Old Town Praline Shop, is where opera singer Adelina Patti first came for a visit and then lived after becoming something of a local heroine in 1860. The 17-year-old girl's popularity as a last-minute stand-in lead soprano in Lucia di Lammermoor saved the local opera company from financial ruin.

⑪ Le Monnier Mansion

This 640 Royal St. structure, currently towering above every other French Quarter building as the city's first "skyscraper," was all of three stories high when it was built in 1811. A fourth story was added in 1876. George W. Cable, the celebrated author of Old Creole Days, chose this building as the residence of his fictional hero, Sieur George.

Cross St. Peter Street to:

⑫ The LaBranche House

This building at 700 Royal St. is probably the most photographed building in the Quarter—and no wonder. Take a look at the lacy cast-iron grillwork, with its delicate oak leaf and acorn design that fairly drips from all three floors. There are actually 11 LaBranche buildings (three-story brick row houses built 1835–1840 for the widow of wealthy sugar planter Jean Baptiste LaBranche). Eight face St. Peter Street, one faces Royal, and two face Pirates Alley.

Turn left at St. Peter Street and continue to:

⑬ 714 St. Peter St.

Built in 1829 by a prominent physician, this was a boardinghouse run by Antoine Alciatore for several years during the 1860s. His cooking became so popular with the locals that he eventually gave up catering to open the famous Antoine's restaurant, still operated today by his descendants.

⑭ Pat O'Brien's

You've probably heard of this famous New Orleans nightspot at 718 St. Peter St. (p. 267). The building was completed in 1790 for a wealthy planter and was known as the Maison de Flechier. Later, Louis Tabary put on popular plays here. It's said that the first grand opera in America was performed within these walls. The courtyard is open to visitors and is well worth a look—if you can see it past the crowds consuming the Hurricane drinks for which the place is famous.

⑮ Preservation Hall

Scores of people descend on this spot, at 726 St. Peter St. (p. 258), nightly to hear traditional New Orleans jazz. A daytime stop affords a glimpse, through the big, ornate iron gate, of a lush tropical courtyard in back. Erle Stanley Gardner, the author who brought us Perry Mason, lived in an apartment above the Hall.

⑯ Plique-LaBranche House

This house, at 730 St. Peter St., was built in 1825, sold to Giraud M. Plique in 1827, and sold to Jean Baptiste LaBranche in 1829. The wrought-iron balcony dates from the 1820s. This is believed to be the site of New Orleans's first theater, which burned in the fire of 1816, but that is the subject of some debate.

Continue up St. Peter Street until you reach Bourbon Street. Turn left onto Bourbon Street.

⑰ 623 Bourbon St.

Tennessee Williams and Truman Capote lived in this house, though not together

(get your mind out of the gutter!). It's owned by Lindy Boggs, a much-beloved local politician (and mother of NPR and ABC commentator Cokie Roberts), who took over her husband's congressional seat after his death. After her last political appointment (U.S. special envoy to the Vatican), Boggs now lends her name and support to various causes around town, including the Lindy Boggs National Center for Community Literacy and the Lindy Boggs Medical Center. (The latter has been closed since Katrina.)

Turn around and head the other way down Bourbon Street. At the corner of Bourbon and Orleans streets, look down Orleans Street, toward the river, at:

⑱ Bourbon Orleans Hotel

This building at 717 Orleans St. was the site of the famous quadroon balls, where wealthy white men would come to form alliances (read: acquire a mistress) with free women of color, who were one-eighth to one-fourth black. Look at the balcony and imagine the assignations that went on there while the balls were in session. The building later became a convent, home to the Sisters of the Holy Family, the second-oldest order of black nuns in the country. Their founder (whose mother was a quadroon mistress!), Henriette Delille, has been presented to the Vatican for consideration for sainthood.

Turn left onto Orleans and follow it a block to Dauphine (pronounced Daw-*feen*) Street. On the corner is:

⑲ Le Pretre Mansion

In 1839 Jean Baptiste Le Pretre bought this 1836 Greek Revival house at 716 Dauphine St. and added the romantic cast-iron galleries. The house is the subject of a real-life horror story: Sometime in the 19th century, a Turk, supposedly the brother of a sultan, arrived in New Orleans and rented the Le Pretre house. He was conspicuously wealthy, and his entourage included many servants and more than a few beautiful young girls—all thought to have been stolen from the sultan.

Rumors quickly spread about the situation, even as the home became the scene of lavish entertainment with guest lists that included the cream of society. One night shrieks came from inside the house; the next morning, neighbors entered and found the tenant's body lying in a pool of blood surrounded by the bodies of the young beauties. The mystery remains unsolved. Local ghost experts say you can hear exotic music and shrieks on the right night.

Turn right on Dauphine Street and go 2 blocks to Dumaine Street and then turn right. You'll find an interesting little cottage at:

⑳ 707 Dumaine St.

After the 1794 fire, all houses in the French Quarter were required by law to have flat tile roofs. Most have since been covered with conventional roofs, but this Spanish colonial cottage is still in compliance with the flat-roof rule.

㉑ Madame John's Legacy

This structure, at 632 Dumaine St., was once thought to be the oldest building on the Mississippi River. Recent research suggests, however, that only a few parts of the original building survived the 1788 fire and were used in its reconstruction. The house was originally erected in 1726, 8 years after the founding of New Orleans. Its first owner was a ship captain who died in the 1729 *Natchez* Massacre; upon his death, the house passed to the captain of a Lafitte-era smuggling ship.

It has had no fewer than 21 owners since. The present structure is a fine example of a French "raised cottage." The aboveground basement is of brick-between-posts construction (locally made bricks were too soft to be the primary building material), covered with boards laid horizontally. The hipped, dormered roof extends out over the veranda. Its name, incidentally, comes from George W. Cable's fictional character that was bequeathed the house in the short story *Tite Poulette*. Now a part of the Louisiana State Museum complex, it's open for tours (p. 179).

Take a left at the corner of Dumaine and Chartres streets and follow Chartres to the next corner; make a left onto St. Philip Street and continue to the corner of St. Philip and Bourbon streets to:

㉒ Lafitte's Blacksmith Shop

For many years, this structure, at 941 Bourbon St., has been a bar (for the full story, see chapter 11, "New Orleans After Dark"), but the legend is that Jean Lafitte and his pirates posed as blacksmiths here while using it as headquarters for selling goods they'd plundered on the high seas. It has survived in its original condition, reflecting the architectural influence of French colonials who escaped St. Domingue in the late 1700s.

It may be the oldest building in the Mississippi Valley, but that has not been documented. Unfortunately, the exterior has been redone to replicate the original brick and plaster, which makes it look fake when it's actually not. Thus far, the modern-day owners of the building have resisted interior invasions of chrome and plastic, which makes this an excellent place to imagine life in the Quarter in the 19th century.

Turn right onto Bourbon Street and follow it 2 blocks to Governor Nicholls Street. Turn right to:

㉓ The Thierry House

The structure at 721 Governor Nicholls St. was built in 1814 and announced the arrival of the Greek Revival style of architecture in New Orleans. It was designed in part by architect Henry S. Boneval Latrobe, son of Benjamin H. B. Latrobe, when he was 19 years old.

Cross Royal Street to:

㉔ 618–630 Governor Nicholls St.

Henry Clay's brother, John, built a house for his wife here in 1828, and in 1871 a two-story building was added at the rear of its garden. In the rear building Frances Xavier Cabrini (now a Catholic saint) ran a school.

Backtrack to the corner of Royal and Governor Nicholls streets. Take a left onto Royal and look for:

㉕ The Lalaurie Home

Many people simply refer to this place, at 1140 Royal St., as "the haunted house."

Here's why: When Madame Delphine Macarty de Lopez Blanque wed Dr. Louis Lalaurie, it was her third marriage—she'd already been widowed twice. The Lalauries moved into this residence in 1832, and they soon were impressing the city with extravagant parties. One night in 1834, however, fire broke out and neighbors crashed through a locked door to find seven starving slaves chained in painful positions, unable to move. The sight, combined with Delphine's stories of past slaves having "committed suicide," enraged her neighbors. Madame Lalaurie and her family escaped a mob's wrath and fled to Paris. Several years later she died in Europe, and her body was returned to New Orleans—and even then she had to be buried in secrecy.

The building was a Union headquarters during the Civil War and later was a gambling house. Through the years, stories have circulated of ghosts inhabiting the building, especially that of one young slave child who fell from the roof trying to escape Delphine's cruelties.

26 Gallier House Museum

This house, at 1132 Royal St., was built in 1857 by James Gallier, Jr., as his residence. Gallier and his father were two of the city's leading architects (p. 177). Anne Rice was thinking of this house when she described where Lestat and Louis lived in *Interview with the Vampire*.

Turn left onto Ursulines Street, toward the river.

TAKE A BREAK
If you need a little rest or sustenance at this point, you can stop in the popular **Croissant D'Or,** 617 Ursulines St. (© **504/524-4663;** p. 163). The croissants and pastries here are very good, and the ambience—inside or out on the patio—even better.

At the corner of Ursulines and Chartres streets is the:

27 Beauregard-Keyes House

This "raised cottage" at 1113 Chartres St. was built as a residence in 1826 by Joseph Le Carpentier, though it has several other claims to fame (p. 174). Notice the Doric columns and handsome twin staircases.

28 The Archbishop Antoine Blanc Memorial

Across the street, the complex at 1112–1114 Chartres St., which was completed in 1752, includes the Old Ursuline Convent (p. 175) and the Archiepiscopal Residence.

Turn left on to Chartres Street and continue walking until you get to Esplanade (pronounced Es-pla-*nade*) Avenue, which served as the parade ground for troops quartered on Barracks Street. Along with St. Charles Avenue, it is one of the city's most picturesque historic thoroughfares. Some of the grandest town houses built in the late 1800s grace this wide, tree-lined avenue. (If you're interested in viewing some of these houses, Walking Tour 3, later in this chapter, concentrates on the architecture of Esplanade Ridge.) The entire 400 block of Esplanade is occupied by:

29 The Old U.S. Mint

This was once the site of Fort St. Charles, one of the defenses built to protect New Orleans in 1792. It was here that Andrew Jackson reviewed the "troops"—pirates, volunteers, and a nucleus of trained soldiers—he later led in the Battle of New Orleans (p. 176).

Follow Esplanade toward the river and turn right at the corner of North Peters Street. Follow North Peters until it intersects with Decatur Street. This is the back end of:

30 The Historic French Market

This European-style market (p. 173) has been here for well over 200 years, and today it has a farmers market and stalls featuring everything from gator on a stick to somewhat tacky souvenir items. On most days the Esplanade end of the market houses a "flea market," which is really just a collection of stalls of jewelry, T-shirts, and knockoff purses, though more than one excellent souvenir or bargain has been found therein.

When you leave the French Market, exit on the side away from the river onto:

31 Decatur Street

Not long ago, this section of Decatur—from Jackson Square all the way over to Esplanade—was a seedy, run-down area of wild bars and cheap rooming houses. Fortunately, few of either remain. Instead, this portion of the strip has fallen into step with the rest of the Quarter, sporting a number of restaurants and noisy bars. (The stretch of Decatur btw. Ursulines and Esplanade sts. has retained more of the run-down aesthetic, with secondhand shops that are worth taking a browse through and smaller, darker bars.)

As you walk toward St. Ann Street along Decatur, you'll pass 923 and 919 Decatur St., where the Café de Refugies and Hôtel de la Marine were located in the 1700s and early 1800s. These were reputed to be gathering places for pirates, smugglers, and European refugees (some of them outlaws)—a far cry from today's scene.

TAKE A BREAK
If you're walking in the area of 923 Decatur St. around lunchtime, pop into the **Central Grocery,** 923 Decatur St. (☏ **504/523-1620;** p. 142), and pick up a muffuletta sandwich. You can eat inside at little tables, or you can take your food and sit outside, maybe right on the riverbank.

Decatur Street will take you to Jackson Square. Turn right onto St. Ann Street; the twin four-story, red-brick buildings here and on the St. Peter Street side of the square are:

32 The Pontalba Buildings

These buildings sport some of the most impressive cast-iron balcony railings in the French Quarter. They also represent one of the first eras of revitalization in the Quarter. In the mid-1800s, Baroness Micaela

Almonester Pontalba inherited rows of buildings along both sides of the Place d'Armes from her father, Don Almonester (who had been responsible for rebuilding the St. Louis Cathedral; p. 174). In an effort to counteract the emerging preeminence of the American sector across Canal Street, she decided to raze the structures and, in their place, build high-end apartments and commercial space.

The Pontalba Buildings were begun in 1849 under her very direct supervision; you can see her mark today in the entwined initials A.P. in the ironwork. The buildings were designed in a traditional Creole-European style, with commercial space on the street level, housing above, and a courtyard in the rear. The row houses on St. Ann Street, now owned by the state of Louisiana, were completed in 1851.

Baroness Pontalba is also responsible for the current design of Jackson Square, including the cast-iron fence and the equestrian statue of Andrew Jackson. (See p. 174 and 176 for more on the statue and Baroness Pontalba, respectively.)

At the corner of St. Ann and Chartres streets, turn left and continue around Jackson Square; you will see:

33 The Presbytère

This, the Cabildo, and the St. Louis Cathedral (see later stops on this walk for both of the latter)—all designed by Gilberto Guillemard—were the first major public buildings in the Louisiana Territory. The Presbytère, at 751 Chartres St., was originally designed to be the rectory of the cathedral. Baroness Pontalba's father financed the building's beginnings, but he died in 1798, leaving only the first floor done. The building was finally completed in 1813. It was never used as a rectory, however, but was rented and then purchased (in 1853) by the city to be used as a courthouse. It now houses wonderful exhibits on the history of Mardi Gras (p. 180).

Next you'll come to:

34 St. Louis Cathedral

The building standing here today is the third erected on this spot—the first was destroyed by a hurricane in 1722, the second by fire in 1788. The cathedral was rebuilt in 1794; the central tower was later designed by Henry S. Boneval Latrobe, and the building was remodeled and enlarged between 1845 and 1851 (p. 174).

On the other side of the cathedral, you'll come to Pirates Alley. Go right down Pirates Alley to:

35 Faulkner House Books

In 1925 William Faulkner lived at 624 Pirates Alley and worked on his first novels, *Mosquitoes* and *Soldiers' Pay*. While here, he contributed to the *Times-Picayune* and to a literary magazine called the *Double Dealer*. This is a great stop for Faulkner lovers and collectors of literature (p. 237).

To the left of the bookstore is a small alley that takes you to St. Peter Street, which is behind and parallel to Pirate's Alley.

36 Tennessee Williams House

Have a sudden urge to scream "Stella!!!" at that second-story wrought-iron balcony at 632 St. Peter? No wonder. That's because this is where Tennessee Williams wrote *A Streetcar Named Desire,* one of the greatest pieces of American theater. He said he could hear "that rattle trap streetcar named Desire running along Royal and the one named Cemeteries running along Canal and it seemed the perfect metaphor for the human condition."

Return to Jackson Square. On the left side of the cathedral on the corner of Chartres and St. Peter streets (with your back to the Mississippi River and Jackson Square) is:

37 The Cabildo

In the 1750s this was the site of a French police station and guardhouse. Part of that building was incorporated into the original Cabildo, statehouse of the Spanish governing body (the "Very Illustrious Cabildo"). The Cabildo was still under reconstruction when the transfer papers for the Louisiana Purchase were signed in a room on the second floor in 1803. Since then, it has served as New Orleans's City Hall, the Louisiana State Supreme Court, and, since 1911, a facility of the Louisiana State Museum (p. 177).

One further note: If you think those old Civil War cannons out front look pitifully small and ineffective by modern standards, think again. In 1921, in a near-deadly prank, one was loaded with powder, an iron ball was rammed down its muzzle, and it was fired in the dead of night. That missile traveled from the Cabildo's portico across the wide expanse of the Mississippi and some 6 blocks inland before landing in a house in Algiers, narrowly missing its occupants.

> **WINDING DOWN**
> You've finished! Now go back across Jackson Square and Decatur Street to **Café du Monde,** 813 Decatur St. (© **504/525-4544;** p. 163), in the French Market—no trip to New Orleans is complete without a leisurely stop here for beignets and coffee. Be sure to hike up the levee and relax on a bench. Too many visitors come to New Orleans and never even look at the river!

CITY STROLLS

9

THE GARDEN DISTRICT

WALKING TOUR 2   **THE GARDEN DISTRICT**

START:	Prytania Street and Washington Avenue.
FINISH:	Lafayette Cemetery.
TIME:	45 minutes to 1½ hours.
BEST TIME:	Daylight.
WORST TIME:	Night, when you won't be able to get a good look at the architecture.

Walking through the architecturally phenomenal Garden District, you could get the impression that you've entered an entirely separate city from New Orleans as defined by the French Quarter—or, perhaps more specifically, entered a different time period. Although the Garden District was indeed once a separate city (Lafayette) from the Vieux Carré and was established during a later period, the fact that this neighborhood was created by a different group of people most profoundly distinguishes it from the old section, the French Quarter.

The French Quarter was initially established by Creoles during the French and Spanish colonial periods, and the Garden District was created by Americans after the 1803 Louisiana Purchase. Antebellum New Orleans's lucrative combination of Mississippi River commerce, regional abundance of cash crops, slave trade, and national banks fueled the local economy, resulting in a remarkable building boom that extended for several square miles through Uptown.

Although very few people from the United States lived in New Orleans during its colonial era, after the Louisiana Purchase, thousands of Americans flooded the city and clashed with the Creoles. Friction arose between the two groups due to mutual snobbery, a language barrier, religious division, and, most significantly, competition over burgeoning commerce. Americans were arriving at the brink of a boom time to make fortunes. With inferior business experience, education, and organizational skills, the Creoles worried that *les Americains* would work them out of business. Americans were, therefore, kept out of the already overcrowded French Quarter. Feeling snubbed, the Americans moved upriver to create a residential district of astounding opulence. The Garden District is, therefore, a study of a cultural clash reflected through architecture, with Americans creating an identity by boldly introducing styles and forms familiar to them and previously unknown in colonial Louisiana.

Note: The houses described on this tour are not open to the public.

To reach the Garden District, take the St. Charles streetcar to Washington Avenue (stop no. 16) and walk 1 block toward the river to:

❶ The Garden District Book Shop

Inside the historic property known as the Rink, you will find this store at 2727 Prytania St. (p. 238), an excellent starting point for a Garden District tour. Built in 1884 as the Crescent City Skating Rink, the building subsequently acted as a livery stable, mortuary facility, grocery store, and gas station. You probably will not view the interiors of any private homes, but the bookshop's stellar collection of regional titles allows you a revealing glimpse into the neighborhood's majestic homes.

This is Anne Rice's favorite bookstore, and she usually holds her first book signing here when a new book is released. (The shop stocks a supply of her signed first editions.) Owner Britton Trice schedules signings by many regionally and nationally acclaimed authors. The Rink also offers a coffee shop, restrooms, and air-conditioning (crucial in the summer).

Across Prytania Street, you'll find:

❷ Colonel Short's Villa

This house, at 1448 Fourth St., was built by architect Henry Howard for Kentucky Colonel Robert Short. The story goes that Short's wife complained of missing the cornfields in her native Iowa, so he bought her the cornstalk fence. A revisionist explanation supplied by a recent owner is that the wife saw that it was the most expensive fence in the building catalog and requested it. Second Civil War occupational governor Nathaniel Banks was quartered here.

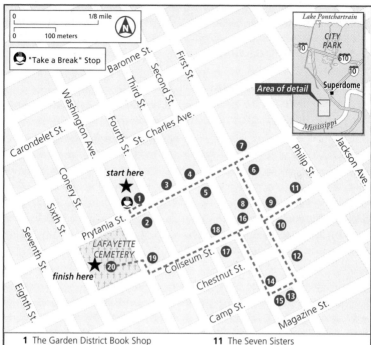

1 The Garden District Book Shop
2 Colonel Short's Villa
3 Briggs-Staub House
4 Our Mother of Perpetual Help Chapel
5 Women's Opera Guild House
6 Toby's Corner
7 Bradish Johnson House and
   Louise S. McGehee Schools
8 Archie Manning House
9 Pritchard-Pigott House
10 Morris-Israel House
11 The Seven Sisters
12 Brevard-Mahat-Rice House
13 Payne-Strachan House
14 Warwick Manor
15 1137 Second St.
16 Joseph Merrick Jones House
17 Musson-Bell House
18 Robinson House
19 Commander's Palace Restaurant
20 Lafayette Cemetery

Continuing down Prytania, you'll find the:

❸ Briggs-Staub House

Located at 2605 Prytania St., this is the Garden District's only example of Gothic Revival architecture. Because this style reminded the Protestant Americans of the Roman Catholicism of their Creole antagonists, it did not become popular. Original owner Charles Briggs did not hold African slaves but did employ Irish servants, for whom he built the relatively large adjacent servant quarters. Irish immigration was then starting to create the Irish Channel neighborhood across Magazine Street from the Garden District.

❹ Our Mother of Perpetual Help Chapel

Once an active Catholic chapel, this site, at 2523 Prytania St., was owned by Anne

Rice, as was the Marigny-Claiborne House (built for the daughter-in-law of Bernard Marigny) on the other side of the block at 2524 St. Charles Ave. It's the setting for her novel *Violin*. The author's childhood home is down the street at 2301 St. Charles Ave.

❺ Women's Opera Guild House

Some of the Garden District's most memorable homes incorporate more than one style. Designed by William Freret in 1858, this building, at 2504 Prytania St., combines Greek Revival and Queen Anne styles. Now owned by the Women's Opera Guild, the home can be toured by special arrangement (✆ **504/899-1945**).

❻ Toby's Corner

Located at 2340 Prytania St., the Garden District's oldest known home dates to at least 1838. Built for Philadelphia wheelwright Thomas Toby, it is in Greek Revival style, which was then very popular throughout the United States. Although the home represents an American attempt at creating a non-Creole architectural identity, this Anglicized style required Creole building techniques such as raising the house up on brick piers to combat flooding and encourage air circulation.

❼ Bradish Johnson House and Louise S. McGehee School

Paris-trained architect James Freret designed this French Second Empire–style mansion at 2343 Prytania St., which was built for sugar factor Bradish Johnson in 1872 at a cost of $100,000 (that's more than $1.6 million today). Contrast this house's awesome detail with the stark classical simplicity of Toby's Corner (see above) across the street—a visual indication of the effect that one generation of outrageous fortune had on Garden District architecture. Since 1929 the building has been the private Louise S. McGehee School for girls.

Turn down First Street (away from St. Charles) and it's less than a block to the:

❽ Archie Manning House

This house, at 1420 First St., is the home of former New Orleans Saints superstar quarterback Archie Manning and the childhood home of his sons, who football fans may have heard something about as well: Peyton, the quarterback for the Indianapolis Colts; and Eli, the quarterback for the New York Giants.

❾ Pritchard-Pigott House

This Greek Revival double-galleried town house is located at 1407 First St. As fortunes compounded, the typical Garden District house size grew. Americans introduced two house forms: the cottage (as in Toby's Corner; see above) and the grander town house (seen here).

❿ Morris-Israel House

As time passed, Garden District homes moved away from the simplicity of Greek Revival and became more playful with design. By the 1860s the Italianate style was popular, as seen in this double-galleried town house at 1331 First St. Architect Samuel Jamison designed this house and the **Carroll-Crawford House** on the next corner (1315 First St.); note the identical ornate cast-iron galleries. The Morris-Israel House is reputedly haunted.

Follow Coliseum Street to the left less than half a block to:

⓫ The Seven Sisters

This row of "shotgun" houses at 2329–2305 Coliseum St. gets its nickname from a story that a 19th-century Garden District resident had seven daughters whom he wanted to keep close to home, so he built these homes as wedding gifts. That story is not true. If you count the "Seven Sisters," you will find eight. (They were actually built on speculation.)

An explanation for the name "shotgun" is that if you fire a gun through the front door, the bullet will go right out the back.

Also, a West African word for this native African house form sounds something like "shotgun." The shotgun house effectively circulates air and is commonly found in hot climates. Its relatively small size makes the shotgun house a rarity along the imposing streets of the Garden District, but it is extremely popular throughout the rest of New Orleans.

Now turn around and go back to First Street and turn left. At the corner of First and Chestnut, you'll see the:

⑫ Brevard-Mahat-Rice House

Designed in 1857 as a Greek Revival town house and later augmented with an Italianate bay, this house, at 1239 First St., is a fine example of "transitional" architecture. It was historically called Rosegate for the rosette pattern on the fence. (The fence's woven diamond pattern is believed to be the precursor to the chain-link fence.) This was the home of novelist Anne Rice and the setting for her *Witching Hour* novels.

⑬ Payne-Strachan House

Jefferson Davis, president of the Confederate States of America, died at this house at 1134 First St. Davis fell ill while traveling and was taken here, the home of his friend Judge Charles Fenner (son-in-law of owner Jacob Payne). A stone marker in front of the house bears the date of Davis's death, December 6, 1889. (Davis was buried in magnificent Metairie Cemetery for 2 years and then was disinterred and moved to Virginia.) This house is a classic antebellum Greek Revival home. Note the sky-blue ceiling of the gallery—the color is believed to keep winged insects from nesting there and to ward off evil spirits. Many Garden District homes adhere to this tradition.

Turn right on Camp and go less than a block to:

⑭ Warwick Manor

An example of Georgian architecture, this house, at 2427 Camp St., is one of the few homes in the vicinity that's not a single-family residence. Note the buzzers, which indicate rented apartments.

⑮ 1137 Second St.

This house is an example of the type of Victorian architecture popularized in uptown New Orleans toward the end of the 19th century. Many who built such homes were from the Northeast and left New Orleans in the summer; otherwise, it would be odd to see this kind of claustrophobic house, normally intended for cool climates, in New Orleans. Note the exquisite stained glass and rounded railing on the gallery.

Turn right onto Second Street and go 2 blocks to the corner of Coliseum, where you'll see the:

⑯ Joseph Merrick Jones House

This house, at 2425 Coliseum St., was the home of Nine Inch Nails singer Trent Reznor. When he moved in, more anti-noise ordinances began being introduced into city council proceedings. Could it be a coincidence that his next-door neighbor was City Councilwoman Peggy Wilson? The house is now the home of actor John Goodman.

Turn left onto Coliseum Street and go 1 block to Third Street. Turn left to get to the:

⑰ Musson-Bell House

This house, at 1331 Third St., is the 1853 home of Michel Musson, one of the few French Creoles then living in the Garden District. Musson was the uncle of French Impressionist artist Edgar Degas, who once lived with Musson on Esplanade Avenue during a visit to New Orleans. On the Coliseum Street side of the house is the foundation of a cistern. These water tanks were so common in the Garden District that Mark Twain once commented that it looked as if everybody in the neighborhood had a private brewery. Cisterns were destroyed at the turn of the 20th century when mosquitoes, which breed in standing water, were found to be carriers of yellow fever and malaria.

⓲ Robinson House

Built between 1859 and 1865 by architect Henry Howard for tobacco grower and merchant Walter Robinson, this house, at 1415 Third St., is one of the Garden District's most striking and unusual homes. Walk past the house to appreciate its scale—the outbuildings, visible from the front, are actually connected to the side of the main house. The entire roof is a large vat that once collected water and acted as a cistern. Gravity provided water pressure and the Garden District's earliest indoor plumbing.

Continue down Coliseum Street 2 blocks to the corner of Washington Avenue. There you'll find:

⓳ Commander's Palace Restaurant

Established in 1883 by Emile Commander, this turreted Victorian structure (a bordello back in the 1920s), at 1403 Washington Ave., is now the pride of the Brennan family, the most visible and successful restaurateurs in New Orleans. Commander's is perennially rated one of the nation's top restaurants (p. 155), and the jazz brunch—a tradition that originated here—is extremely popular. Commander's had enough rain damage within

its walls to require a to-the-studs stripping, both inside and out, but it looks once again as it always did!

⓴ Lafayette Cemetery

Established in 1833, this "city of the dead," on Washington Avenue between Prytania and Coliseum streets, is one of New Orleans's oldest cemeteries. It has examples of all the classic aboveground, multiple-burial techniques and features a number of interesting Anne Rice–related sites (the Mayfair witches' family tomb is here, for example). Although the cemetery gates display New Orleans Police Department signs that say PATROLLED, that is not true. Be careful in this and all cemeteries, as predatory crime is a possibility. A guided tour is an alternative.

Walk to St. Charles Avenue to pick up the streetcar (there is a stop right there) or flag down a cab to return to the French Quarter.

WINDING DOWN
Now go back to your first stop, the Rink, where you can enjoy a cup of coffee and some light refreshments at an outlet of the local **P.J.'s** coffee shop chain.

WALKING TOUR 3	ESPLANADE RIDGE

START:	Esplanade Avenue and Johnson Street.
FINISH:	City Park.
TIME:	Allow approximately 1½ hours, not including museum, cemetery, and shopping stops.
BEST TIMES:	Monday through Saturday, early or late morning.
WORST TIMES:	Sunday, when attractions are closed. Also, you certainly don't want to walk in this area after dark; if you decide to stay in City Park or in the upper Esplanade area until early evening, plan to return on the bus or by taxi.

This is another region of New Orleans that many visitors overlook—even when they drive through it on the way to City Park, the New Orleans Museum of Art, or the Jazz & Heritage Festival. If you're heading to those attractions, consider taking this stroll or leaving enough time for sightseeing from your car. We particularly enjoy the stretch along St. John's Bayou—mostly as slow and quiet as the sluggish water itself. Historically, the Esplanade Ridge area is Creole society's answer to St. Charles Avenue—it's an equally lush boulevard with stately homes and seemingly ancient trees stretching overhead. Originally it was the site of homes of the descendants of the earliest settlers. The avenue had its finest days toward the end of the 19th century, and some of the neighborhoods along its path, especially the Faubourg Treme, are visibly suffering. If it is a little worn compared with St. Charles Avenue, Esplanade Avenue is still closer to the soul of the city (read: Regular people live here, whereas St. Charles always was for the well-heeled and is that way now more than ever). While parts of this street did flood, the area demonstrated why it is locally known as the "Esplanade Ridge"; the land is relatively high ground (for New Orleans!) and most of the water was in the street itself, sparing the houses alongside it.

You can catch a bus on Esplanade Avenue at the French Quarter, headed toward the park to your starting point. Otherwise, stroll (about 15 min.) up Esplanade Avenue to:

❶ 2023 Esplanade Ave.

Originally a plantation home, this was designed in 1861 for A. B. Charpentier. The building is now operating as Ashtons Bed & Breakfast (p. 101).

❷ Widow Castanedo's House

Juan Rodriguez purchased this land in the 1780s, and his granddaughter, Widow Castanedo, lived in this home at 2033–2035 Esplanade Ave. until her death in 1861. At that time the house was a smaller, Spanish colonial–style plantation home. Before Esplanade Avenue extended this far from the river, the house was located in what is now the middle of the street. The widow tried and failed to block the extension of the street. The house was moved to its present site and was enlarged sometime around the 1890s. It has a late-Italianate appearance, and is split down the middle and inhabited today by two sisters.

❸ 2139 Esplanade Ave.

This building is a great example of the typical Esplanade Ridge style. Note the Ionic columns on the upper level.

On the opposite side of the street is:

❹ 2176 Esplanade Ave.

A simple, classic-style town house, this was the second Bayou Road home built by Hubert Gerard, who also built the 1861 structure that now houses Ashton's Bed & Breakfast at no. 2023 (see above).

After you cross North Miro Street, Esplanade Avenue crosses the diagonal Bayou Road, which was the route to the French-Canadian settlements at St. John's Bayou in the late 17th century. Veer left at the fork to stay on Esplanade Avenue and look for:

❺ Goddess of History—Genius of Peace Statue

This victory monument stands on the triangular piece of land at the intersection of Bayou Road, Esplanade Avenue, and Miro Street. In 1886 the land, known to earlier generations as Gayarre Place, was given to the city by Charles Gayarre. George H. Dunbar donated the statue to be placed there. The original terra-cotta statue was destroyed in 1938, and the present one, made of cement and marble, is a replacement.

❻ Degas House

The Musson family rented this house, at 2306 Esplanade Ave., for many years. Estelle Musson married René Degas, brother of Edgar Degas, the French Impressionist artist. (She and her descendants dropped his last name after he ran off with a neighbor's wife.) Degas is said to have painted the portrait of Estelle that is now in the New Orleans Museum of Art, as well as many other works, during the time he spent living at no. 2306.

The house was built in 1854, and the Italianate decorations were added later when it was split into two buildings. Both have been restored and include a B&B. This is the only studio or residence of Degas open to the public in the world, so do come poke around, but know that in general it's a good idea to set up an appointment in advance to get in (p. 189).

❼ Reuther House

The current resident of this house, at 2326 Esplanade Ave., has a collection of small metal houses, cinder-block sculptures, and a beautiful metal-crafted marlin on display on the front porch, which is readily visible from the street. The house is known as the Reuther House because it was owned by Joseph Reuther, a baker, in 1913.

In passing, take a look at nos. 2325, 2329, and 2331—all are interesting examples of Creole cottages. Then, continue to:

❽ 2337 and 2341 Esplanade Ave.

These houses were identical structures when they were built in 1862 for John Budd Slawson, owner of a horse-drawn-streetcar company that operated along Bayou Road in the 19th century. Back then, they were both single-story shotgun-style houses. Notice the unusual ironwork underneath the front roof overhang.

Cross North Dorgenois Street to:

❾ 2453 Esplanade Ave.

Until the other was demolished, this house was one of a pair at the corner of Dorgenois Street. Though its architecture has been changed extensively, it's one of the few remaining mansard-roofed homes on Esplanade Ridge.

Cross North Broad Avenue to:

❿ 2623 Esplanade Ave.

Here is a classical revival Victorian home built in 1896 by Louis A. Jung. Note the Corinthian columns. The Jungs donated the triangular piece of land at Esplanade Avenue, Broad Street, and Crete Street to the city on the condition that it remain public property. It is officially known as DeSoto Park and is graced by a fence in the Art Nouveau style.

⓫ 2809 Esplanade Ave.

This is one of the more decorative Victorian Queen Anne center-hall houses on Esplanade Ridge.

⓬ 2936 Esplanade Ave.

A nice example of what's known as a Gothic villa.

TAKE A BREAK At the intersection of Mystery Street and Esplanade Avenue, you'll find a little grouping of shops and restaurants. If you're in the area at lunchtime, you might want to stop at **Café Degas**, 3127 Esplanade Ave. (✆ **504/945-5635;** p. 146), for a leisurely meal—if the weather is nice, the semi-outdoor setting is exceedingly pleasant. If you just want a snack or some picnic food for City Park, you can get cold cuts, ice cream, and other snacks at the family-run Italian grocery **Terranova**, 3308 Esplanade Ave. (✆ **504/482-4131**), across the street. You can also opt for a break at the excellent **Fair Grinds** coffeehouse just off Esplanade at 3133 Ponce De Leon (✆ **504/913-9072**).

Continue to:

⓭ 3330 Esplanade Ave.

A galleried frame home built in the Creole-cottage style.

On your right is:

⓮ St. Louis Cemetery No. 3

This was the site of the public Bayou Cemetery, established in 1835. It was purchased by the St. Louis diocese in 1856 and contains the burial monuments of many of the diocese's priests. If you've been putting off going into the cemeteries because of concerns over safety, this is one you can explore on your own—though you should still keep your wits about you and be aware of your surroundings. You can pick up brochures in the office, which is right inside the gate.

1 2023 Esplanade Ave.
2 Widow Castanedo's House
3 2139 Esplanade Ave.
4 2176 Esplanade Ave.
5 "Goddess of History–
   Genius of Peace" Statue
6 Musson-Degas House
7 Reuther House
8 2337 and 2341 Esplanade
   Ave.
9 2453 Esplanade Ave.
10 2623 Esplanade Ave.
11 2809 Esplanade Ave.
12 2936 Esplanade Ave.
13 3330 Esplanade Ave.
14 St. Louis Cemetery No. 3
15 Pitot House
16 City Park

From the cemetery, head back out to Esplanade Avenue and continue walking toward City Park. When you get to the bridge, go left, following the signs, along St. John's Bayou (one of the nicest and least touristy areas of the city), to:

⑮ Pitot House
This house, at 1440 Moss St., is open for public viewing (p. 190).

Head back to Esplanade Avenue, turn left, cross the bridge, and walk straight into:

⑯ City Park
Here you can explore the amphitheater, museum, and gardens (p. 194).

10

Shopping

Shopping in New Orleans is a highly evolved leisure activity, with a shop for every strategy and a fix for every shopaholic—and every budget. Don't assume those endless T-shirt shops on Bourbon Street or even the costly antiques stores on Royal Street are all that New Orleans has to offer. The range of shopping here is as good as it gets—many a clever person has come to New Orleans just to open up a quaint boutique filled with strange items gathered from all parts of the globe or produced by local, somewhat twisted, folk artists.

Want to totally redecorate your house? You can do that here whether you want a complete Victorian look or top-to-bottom folk art. Want to double your record or CD collection? This town is made of music. Want to bring home the perfect souvenir? From an antique sofa that costs about as much as a year at a private college to 50¢ Mardi Gras beads, you'll have plenty of options. Even now, post-Katrina, with some shops necessarily shuttering, new ones are popping up constantly.

Searching for these treasures will be part of what contributes to your calorie-burning walks. Many a well-spent day, or even days, can be had strolling the Quarter window-shopping. But don't forget the many options on Magazine Street. Antiques aficionados eschew exorbitant Royal Street for Magazine because they know the best buys are found there. That's not as true as it has been in the past—the Magazine Street merchants have caught on—but the prices are definitely lower. We also love Magazine for its range of adorable shops with trendy clothes and unique gifts. For more specific information on said shops, call ℂ **866/679-4764** or try **www.magazinestreet.com**.

New Orleans has always been a place for fine homes and fine furnishings, and as people trade up, they leave some great antiques for the rest of us. Many came from Europe in the early days, while others were crafted right in the city by cabinetmakers internationally known for their exquisite pieces. Antiquing has become so popular in New Orleans that there are even people who will take you on a personalized guided tour of city shops (p. 209).

You'll also notice below that the city's art galleries are clustered around the antiques shops and on Julia Street as well. Over the past 20-plus years (notice that's about as long as the Contemporary Arts Center has been open), New Orleans has grown to be an important regional and national market for contemporary fine arts.

Of course, if you're just looking for some souvenirs, whole colonies of shops in the French Quarter sell postcards, posters, sunglasses, and T-shirts. Most of them are cheap and ghastly, if not in flamingly bad taste. You might also consider bringing home Cajun spices, pralines, a jazz CD or two, some chicory coffee, or a box of beignet mix; these are the things that truly say you've been to New Orleans. If you can get to the local Winn-Dixie or other supermarket, however, the food items will be considerably cheaper than if you buy them at a souvenir shop in the Quarter.

General hours for the stores in New Orleans are from 10am to 5pm, but call ahead to make sure. In these post-Katrina days, operating hours can change abruptly, and many that have rather limited hours listed below may have been able to expand their hours since we went to press, while, conversely, some may have had to reduce hours further.

1 MAJOR HUNTING GROUNDS

CANAL PLACE At the foot of Canal Street (365 Canal St.), where the street reaches the Mississippi River, this shopping center holds more than 50 shops, many of them branches of some of this country's most elegant retailers. Stores in this sophisticated setting include Brooks Brothers, Saks Fifth Avenue, Gucci, Williams-Sonoma, Coach, and a branch of local jeweler Mignon Faget (reviewed later in this chapter). If you want classy mall shopping, this is the place. Open Monday to Saturday from 10am to 6pm, Sunday from noon to 6pm (www.theshopsatcanalplace.com).

THE FRENCH MARKET Shops within the market begin on Decatur Street across from Jackson Square; offerings include candy, cookware, fashion, crafts, toys, New Orleans memorabilia, and jewelry. It's open from 10am to 6pm (and Café du Monde, next to the Farmers Market, is open 24 hr.). Quite honestly, you'll find a lot of junk here, but there are some very good buys mixed in, and it's always fun to stroll through—and grab a nibble. Be sure to walk all the way to the "flea market" in the back (near Esplanade), where you can find jewelry; designer-knockoff handbags; pretty, flowing dresses; and more. Just about every dealer in back will bargain with you, so don't take the first price offered, just in case. Despite the mix of quality, this is a must-start place for souvenirs or other sorts of New Orleans shopping. Drop into the actual farmers market portion for some excellent fruit and veggies. Please note that portions of the French Market will be closed at varying times through the shelf life of this book, as the entire structure gets renovated (www.frenchmarket.org).

JACKSON BREWERY Just across from Jackson Square at 600–620 Decatur St., the old brewery building has been transformed into a jumble of shops, cafes, delicatessens, restaurants, and entertainment. Keep in mind that many shops in the Brewery close at 5:30 or 6pm, before the brewery itself. Open daily from 10am to 6pm.

JULIA STREET From Camp Street down to the river on Julia Street, you'll find some of the city's best contemporary-art galleries (many are listed below, under "Art Galleries"). Some of the works are a bit pricey, but there are good deals to be had if you're collecting and fine art to be seen if you're not.

MAGAZINE STREET This is the Garden District's premier shopping street. More than 140 shops (some of which are listed below) line the street in 19th-century brick storefronts and quaint cottagelike buildings. Among the offerings are antiques, art galleries, boutiques, crafts, and dolls. If you're so inclined, you could shop all the way from Washington Street to Audubon Park. We haven't listed as many shops as we would like below, because those sorts of stores—with adorable clothes and fun gift ideas—are so subject to economic vagaries that they may well be out of business by the time you get there, replaced with something else altogether (of equal appeal). Just poke around for yourself. The most likely section goes, roughly, from the 3500 to 4200 blocks (from about Aline St. to Milan St., with the odd block or so of nothing). Other good groupings can be found in the 1800 to 2100, 2800 to 3300, and 5400 to 5700 blocks. Be sure to pick up a copy of *Visit Magazine Street: For a Shopper's Dream,* a free guide and map to most (if not all) of the stores on the 6 miles of Magazine Street, which is available all along the street.

RIVERBEND To reach this district (in the Carrollton area), ride the St. Charles Avenue streetcar to stop no. 44, then walk down Maple Street 1 block to Dublin Park, the site of an old public market that was once lined with open stalls. Nowadays a variety of renovated shops inhabit the old general store, a produce warehouse made of barge board, and the town surveyor's raised-cottage home.

RIVERWALK MARKETPLACE   A mall is a mall is a mall, unless it has picture windows offering a Mississippi River panorama. Even though you almost certainly have a mall at home, this one, at 1 Poydras St., is worth visiting. Besides, if you packed wrong and need T-shirts instead of sweaters or vice versa, this is the closest Gap to the Quarter. Note that the best river views are in the upper section of the mall closest to the convention center. The better knickknack and souvenir shops are up there as well. Stop by the Fudgery, a candy store that offers regular and highly entertaining musical fudge-making demos. There is also a branch of Café du Monde for beignet fixes. The Southern Food and Beverage Museum (p. 186) is also located here, which does add considerable motivation for a trip. Otherwise, it's the usual mall suspects. Open daily from 10am to 6pm. Validated parking with any purchase of $10 or more (www.riverwalkmarketplace.com).

2 SHOPPING A TO Z

ANTIQUES

Note: The majority of the listings below are true antiques shops, and in many cases, the sort of establishments that have objects in the six-figure range. For those of us without jet-set budgets, we have listed, and made note of, less stratospherically priced places.

Aesthetics & Antiques ★★   The shop calls itself a "Baby Boomer's Gumbo," which seems to translate as all the stuff that's too good, quirky, or collectible to let go at a yard sale. Prices are already reasonable but they will bargain if you buy enough. On a typical visit, we bought old sheet music, a piece of Sputnik incased in Lucite, and a collie figurine from the 1940s, while passing up a menu from Antoine's 75th anniversary, a series of black-and-white photos taken from an old album that included a shot from a family funeral, and a decanter shaped like the pope. Throw in some china, boxes of vintage postcards, some better prices on the increasingly costly vintage Mardi Gras beads, a collection of local antique doorknobs, vintage jewelry, and you begin to get the idea. The set decorators shooting locally tend to regularly clean them out. 3122 Magazine St. ✆ **504/895-7011.** Mon–Tues and Thurs–Sat 11am–6pm; Sun 1–5:30pm. Closed Wed.

Collectible Antiques ★★   One of our favorites of the several little, dusty, crammed, and eclectic antiques/junk stores on the Esplanade end of Decatur, for no reason other than we bought old Gibson girl cartoons, a cookie jar shaped like a monk, and a garish chalk religious statue all at once, and all for prices that didn't deplete our meal budget. The large and jumbled shop includes lighting fixtures and stock runs from Art Deco to the 1960s. 1232 Decatur St. ✆ **504/566-0399.** Daily noon–6pm.

Ida Manheim Antiques   At this gallery you'll find an enormous collection of Continental, English, and Oriental furnishings along with porcelains, jade, silver, and fine paintings, and sometimes attitude to match. The store is also the agent for Boehm Birds. 409 Royal St. ✆ **888/627-5969** or 504/620-4114. www.idamanheimantiques.com. Mon–Sat 9am–5pm.

Keil's Antiques ★★★   Keil's was established in 1899 and is currently run by the fourth generation of the founding family. The shop has a considerable collection of 18th- and 19th-century French and English furniture, chandeliers, jewelry, and decorative items. This is our choice for antiques browsing, because somewhere on these three crowded floors (and more in a warehouse), there is something for almost every budget, from a $2,000 chest of drawers to six-figure items. Try to talk to one of the members of the family, and hear tales of the doorman who worked his spot for 78 years and whatever other stories you can coax out of them. 325 Royal St. ℂ **504/522-4552.** www.keilsantiques. com. Mon–Sat 9am–5pm.

Lucullus ★★★ An unusual shop, Lucullus has a wonderful collection of culinary antiques as well as 17th-, 18th-, and 19th-century furnishings to "complement the grand pursuits of cooking, dining, and imbibing," not just silverware and china (if you can call a French platter, ca. 1820, something so simple as "china"), but coffee grinders, dining room furniture, fixtures such as mirrors and lights, and even absinthe glasses and spoons. The owner has added Art Deco flatware and table decorations. "Basically," said the store owner, "anything for gracious dining." They have a terrific second shop at 107 N. Main St. in Beaux Bridge (ℂ **337/332-2625;** daily 10am–5pm). 610 Chartres St. ℂ **504/528-9620.** Mon–Sat 9am–5pm; closed Sun–Mon in the summer.

Miss Edna's Antiques ★ Miss Edna's carries eclectic antiques—furniture, specialty items, curios—and paintings, with a focus on 19th-century works. Miss Edna recently moved a few feet up Magazine, doubling her inventory and expanding her art collection. 2035 Magazine St. ℂ **504/524-1897.** Mon–Sat 10am–5pm. Closed Mon–Tues during summer.

Rare Finds ★★ Unusual for a shop on Decatur Street, this establishment is beautifully organized by subject, theme, or sometimes color. It makes browsing among the vintage jewelry, dolls, books, dishware, and other collectibles so much easier. 1231 Decatur St. ℂ **504/568-1004.** Thurs–Mon noon–5pm.

Rothschild's Antiques ★ Rothschild's is a fourth-generation furniture merchandiser. Some of the most interesting things you'll find here are antique, estate, and custom-made jewelry. They have a dreamy display of antique pieces, though they sadly had to stop their jewelry manufacturing and repair business because their factory was lost to post-storm damage. There's a fine selection of antique silver, marble mantels, porcelains, and English and French furnishings including chandeliers. 321 Royal St. ℂ **504/523-5816.** Mon–Sat 9:30am–5pm; Sun and any day by appointment.

Whisnant Galleries ★ The quantity and variety of merchandise in this shop is mind-boggling. You'll find all sorts of unusual and unique antique collectibles, including items from Ethiopia, Russia, Greece, South America, Morocco, and other parts of North Africa and the Middle East. 222 Chartres St. ℂ **504/524-9766.** Mon–Sat 9:30am–5:30pm; Sun 10am–5pm.

ART GALLERIES

With one major exception, galleries in New Orleans follow the landscape of antiques shops: **Royal and Magazine streets.**

Since the opening of the Contemporary Arts Center (p. 185), however, galleries also keep popping up around **Julia Street** and the **Warehouse District.** Some are listed below, but there are many others. All are strong contemporary fine-art galleries, but it can be hard to tell them apart. If you're contemplating a gallery-hopping jaunt, start at Julia Street.

Angela King Gallery Angela King Gallery shows paintings and sculptures by contemporary artists such as Peter Max, Frederick Hart, Charles Thysell, Joanna Zjawinska, Mark Erickson, LeRoy Neiman, Andrew Baird, Ryahmond Douillert, Richard Currier, and Michelle Gagaliano. 241 Royal St. ℂ **504/524-8211.** www.angelakinggallery.com. Mon–Sat 10am–5pm; Sun 11am–5pm.

Ariodante   A contemporary-craft gallery, Ariodante features handcrafted furniture, glass, ceramics, jewelry, and decorative accessories by nationally acclaimed artists. Rotating shows offer a detailed look at works by various artists. If visiting during the summer, be sure to call ahead, as they close for a lengthy vacation. 535 Julia St. ℂ **504/524-3233.** Daily 11am–5pm.

Arthur Roger Gallery ★★   Arthur Roger sets the pace for the city's fine-art galleries. Since opening in New Orleans more than 30 years ago, Roger has played a major role in developing the art community and in tying it to the art world in New York. Time and again, he has taken chances—moving early into the Warehouse District and briefly opening a second gallery in New York—and he continues to do so, scheduling shows that range from strongly regional work to the far-flung. The gallery represents many artists including Francis Pavy (who did the 1997 and 2007 Jazz Fest posters), Ida Kohlmeyer, Douglas Bourgeois, Paul Lucas, Clyde Connell, Willie Birch, Gene Koss, and George Dureau. 432 Julia St. ℂ **504/522-1000.** www.arthurrogergallery.com. Tues–Sat 11am–5pm.

Berta's and Mina's Antiquities ★★   In years past, this was just another place that bought and sold antiques and secondhand furniture and art. That all ended on the day in 1993 that Nilo Lanzas (Berta's husband and Mina's dad) began painting. Now you can barely see the furniture in the shop for all the new art. Dubbed "folk art" or "outsider art," Lanzas's works (which he paints right near the counter—for about 10–12 hr. a day!) are colorful scenes from life in New Orleans or his native Latin America, stories out of the Bible, or images sprung from his imagination. His paintings are on wood with titles or commentaries painted on the frames; he also makes some tin sculptures and woodcarvings. Mina has brought in her work as well—she started painting before Nilo—and her joyful celebrations of local life and landscapes are attracting their own following. 4138 Magazine St. ℂ **504/895-6201.** Mon–Sat 10am–6pm; Sun 11am–5pm.

Bryant Galleries   This gallery represents renowned artists Ed Dwight, Fritzner Lamour, and Leonardo Nierman as well as other American, European, and Haitian artists. The varied work on display here may include jazz bronzes, glasswork, and graphics. The staff is very friendly and helpful. 316 Royal St. ℂ **800/844-1994** or 504/525-5584. www.bryantgalleries.com. Sun–Wed 10am–5pm; Thurs–Sat 10am–8pm.

Cole Pratt Gallery, Ltd. ★   This gallery showcases the work of Southern artists whose creations include abstract and realist paintings, sculptures, and ceramics. The art is of the highest quality and the prices are surprisingly reasonable. 3800 Magazine St. ℂ **504/891-6789.** www.coleprattgallery.com. Tues–Sat 10am–5pm.

Davis Galleries ★★★   One of two world-class galleries in New Orleans (the other being A Gallery for Fine Photography; see below), this may be the best place in the world for Central and West African traditional art. The owner makes regular trips to Africa for collecting. Works on display might include sculpture, costuming, basketry, textiles, weapons, and/or jewelry. 904 Louisiana Ave. ℂ **504/895-5206.** www.davisafricanart.com. By appointment only. Call to see if regular hours have returned.

Galerie Royale ★★   This gallery's collection is built around the works of William Tolliver, an African-American artist from Mississippi whose untimely death at the age of 48 in 2000 received national coverage. Tolliver came to painting relatively late in his life and without formal training. Despite this, he quickly became an internationally recognized contemporary Impressionist painter. (He was chosen to create the official poster for the 1996 Summer Olympics.) At Galerie Royale you can find a selection of Tolliver's museum-quality pieces as well as work by other artists including Salvador Dalí, Bonny Stanglmaier, and Verna Hart. 3648 Magazine St. ℂ **504/894-1588.** www.galerieroyale.com. Wed–Sat 11am–5pm, or by appointment.

A Gallery for Fine Photography ★★★ It would be a mistake to skip this incredibly well-stocked photography gallery (one of two world-class galleries in New Orleans—the other is the Davis Galleries; p. 234). Even if you aren't in the market, it's worth looking around. Owner Joshua Mann Pailet calls this "the only museum in the world that's for sale." It really is like a museum of photography, with just about every period and style represented and frequent shows of contemporary artists. When they aren't swamped, the staff is more than happy to show you some of the many photos in the files (Pailet remained in New Orleans during the storm and flood, documenting the events with his camera). The gallery emphasizes New Orleans and Southern history and contemporary culture (you can buy Ernest Bellocq's legendary Storyville photos) as well as black culture and music. There is something in just about every price range as well as a terrific collection of photography books if that better fits your budget. Do ask for them to open the cabinets, where more art is cleverly hung inside. 241 Chartres St. ℂ **504/568-1313.** www.agallery.com. Thurs–Mon 10am–5pm.

Great Artists' Collective ★★ Over 40 local artists take turns manning this shop, which stocks their work. Covering two sides of a Creole cottage is a colorful hodgepodge of paints, prints, ceramics, glasswork, earrings by "the Earring Lady" (who calls them "costume jewelry that lasts"), photos, hand-tinted clothing, and more. Some of the work is locally themed, some of it not, but the artists are all quite good. (One has work featured in both the New Orleans Museum of Art and the Ogden.) By going, you support local artists, the local economy, and the collective spirit! 815 Royal St. ℂ **504/525-8190.** www.greatartistscollective.com. Daily 10:30am–6pm.

Kurt E. Schon, Ltd. ★★ Here you'll find the country's largest inventory of 19th-century European paintings. Works include French and British Impressionist and post-Impressionist paintings as well as art from the Royal Academy and the French Salon. 510 St. Louis St. ℂ **504/524-5462.** www.kurteschonltd.com. Mon–Fri 10am–5pm; Sat 10am–3pm.

LeMieux Galleries ★ LeMieux represents contemporary artists and fine craftspeople from Louisiana and the Gulf Coast. They include Leslie Staub, Charles Barbier, Pat Bernard, Mary Lee Eggart, Leslie Elliottsmith, JoAnn Greenberg, David Lambert, Deedra Ludwig, Shirley Rabe Masinter, Evelyn Menge, Paul Ninas, Billy Solitario, and Kate Trepagnier. 332 Julia St. ℂ **504/522-5988.** Fax 504/522-5682. www.lemieuxgalleries.com. Mon–Sat 10am–6pm.

New Orleans School of GlassWorks and Printmaking Studio ★★★ This institution serves multiple purposes. Here, within 25,000 square feet of studio space, are a 550-pound tank of hot molten glass and a pre–Civil War press. At GlassWorks, the sister school to the Louvre Museum of Decorative Arts, established glasswork artists and master printmakers display their work in the on-site gallery and teach classes in glass blowing, kiln-fired glass, hand-engraved printmaking, papermaking, and bookbinding. Absolutely unique to the area, the place is worth a visit during gallery hours. Daily glassblowing and fusing demonstrations are open for viewing. Beginning in October, visitors may design their holiday ornaments. 727 Magazine St. ℂ **504/529-7277.** www.neworleansglassworks.com. Mon–Fri 10am–5pm.

Photo Works ★★ Photographer Louis Sahuc's family has been in New Orleans "since day One," and so it's no wonder his life's work has been documenting his city. This gallery is devoted to his photos. Come here for iconic images (such as Jackson Sq. swathed in fog, or fragments of the ironwork and other architecture that gives New Orleans its distinct look), both black-and-white and color. 839 Chartres St. ℂ **504/593-9090.** www.photoworksneworleans.com. Thurs–Mon 10am–5pm and by appointment.

Rodrigue Studio New Orleans Blue Dog is the Freddie Krueger of New Orleans; once you've seen Cajun artist George Rodrigue's creation, it invades your consciousness and torments your life. Oh, the staring, otherworldly, bordering-on-kitsch canine has its fans, but it scares us. This gallery is the source for all your Blue Dog needs. 721 Royal St. ℂ 504/581-4244. www.georgerodrigue.com. Mon–Sat 10am–6pm; Sun noon–5pm.

Shadyside Pottery ★ If you want to see a master potter at work, Shadyside Pottery is an excellent place to stop. Charlie Bohn, who apprenticed in Japan, can be seen at his wheel pretty much all the time. He specializes in the Japanese tradition of raku, a type of pottery that has a "cracked" look. Open most days, though if it's important that you see him, you might call ahead to make sure he hasn't taken a rare day off. 3823 Magazine St. ℂ **504/897-1710.** www.shadysidepottery.com. Mon–Sat 10am–5pm.

Studio Inferno ★★ A longtime seller at the Jazz Fest crafts booths where they also demonstrate the art of glass blowing, Studio Inferno is known for its clever NOLA-related designs, such as glass reproductions of the local water meters (seriously stylish, which is why they turn up in designs all the time); chili pepper necklaces; and large-size milagros, flaming hearts, torsos, and other "miraculous" shapes. Everything from good stemware to paperweights. Excellent for unique gifts, if a bit off the beaten path. 3000 Royal St. ℂ **504/945-1878.** Mon–Sat 10am–4pm.

BATH & BEAUTY PRODUCTS & DAY SPAS

Note: Kevin Wu, co-owner of the Courtyards B&B, does in-room on-call massages to any hotel in town (ℂ **504/945-9418**). Old-fashioned gentlemen should consider the barbershop at the Hotel Monteleone, where one can receive a proper hot towel, straight razor shave. Call for appointment at ℂ **504/523-6700.**

Aidan Gill for Men ★★ Why should only the women be represented in this section? This is old-fashioned men's grooming, from the days when a guy could be a dandy with no fear, and the barbershop was your local hangout. Look for old-fashioned shave brushes, hand-held razors, hot towels, and cigar smoke—all of it adding up to the blissful experience they call "The Shave at the End of the Universe." That scruffy grunge look was so '90s. You know you want to be a sharp-dressed man, and you can start here. Or buy that man of yours some good grooming implements (they have a fine selection of such items), and for the love of mike, teach him to shave with the grain. Aidan Gill never closed during the storm and its aftermath, and that ought to count for something. 2026 Magazine St. ℂ **504/587-9090.** www.aidangillformen.com. Mon–Fri 10am–6pm; Sat 9am–5pm. Also at 550 Fulton St. ℂ **504/566-4903.** Daily 10am–8pm.

Belladonna Day Spa ★ A very nice, oasis-like, Asian/Zen–themed day spa in Uptown, offering a variety of spa services. If you can't afford the Ritz, this is undoubtedly your best bet for a detoxing, revivifying afternoon of relaxation. 2900 Magazine St. ℂ **504/891-4393.** www.belladonnadayspa.com. Mon–Tues and Fri–Sat 9am–6pm; Wed–Thurs 9am–8pm.

Hove ★★★ Founded in 1931, Hove is the oldest perfumery in the city. It features all-natural scents (except the musk, which is synthetic), and the selection is almost overwhelming. Strips with various options, for both men and women, are laid out to help you. They have some original creations ("Kiss in the Dark") and some very Southern smells, such as vetiver and tea olive, and have expanded their line to include bath salts. This store is a good choice for unique presents for people back home. Literature buffs will be amused by the letter from author Tom Robbins, confirming that the shop in his *Jitterbug Perfume* was more or less based on Hove's appearance. 824 Royal St. ℂ **504/525-7827.** www.hoveparfumeur.com. Mon–Sat 10am–5pm.

Ritz-Carlton Spa ★★★ The finest spa in just about any town, the Ritz spa is tranquil, majestic, classy, lush—and costly. But who cares? With this kind of atmosphere, not to mention the new Prada treatment line, it's all about the pampering. After all, you stayed up late last night, and you danced hard. You earned this! In addition to a wide range of exotic scrubs and rubs, plus wraps, water treatments, and more, they have a luxe sauna and relaxation areas, and a full-service salon for beauty treatments. 921 Canal St. ℂ **504/524-1331.** www.ritzcarlton.com. Daily 8am–6pm.

BOOKS

Literary enthusiasts will find many destinations in New Orleans. **Maple Street Book Shop,** 7523 Maple St. (ℂ **504/866-4916**), is an uptown mecca for bookworms; the **Maple Street Children's Book Shop** is next door at 7529 Maple St. (ℂ **504/861-2105**).

Beckham's Bookshop ★ Beckham's has two entire floors of old editions, rare secondhand books, and thousands of classical LPs that will tie up your whole afternoon or morning if you don't tear yourself away. The owners also operate **Librairie Bookshop,** 823 Chartres St. (ℂ **504/525-4837**), which has a sizable collection of secondhand books. 228 Decatur St. ℂ **504/522-9875.** Daily 10am–5pm.

Crescent City Books ★ Two floors of dusty treasures (the emphasis is on history, social history, literary criticism, philosophy, and art) and a staff that ranges from nonchalant to quite sweet and helpful. 204 Chartres St. ℂ **800/546-4013** or 504/524-4997. www.crescentcitybooks.com. Mon–Sat 10am–7pm; Sun 10am–5pm.

FAB, Faubourg Marigny Art & Books ★ This well-stocked gay and lesbian bookstore also carries some local titles. It has a used section, CDs, posters, cards, and gifts (all with a more or less gay or lesbian slant) and holds regular readings and signings. The staff makes this a fine resource center—you can call them for local gay and lesbian info. They also have a selection of gay- and lesbian-themed figurative art on display and available for sale. They are open quite late every day, right on Frenchmen Street, providing an incongruous contrast to the club hopping around them. 600 Frenchmen St. ℂ **504/947-3700.** www.fabonfrenchman.com. Daily noon–10pm.

Faulkner House Books ★★★ This shop is on a lot of walking tours of the French Quarter because it's where Nobel prize–winner William Faulkner lived while he was writing his early works *Mosquitoes* and *Soldiers' Pay.* Those who step inside instead of just snapping a photo and walking on will find something remarkable: possibly the best selection per square foot of any bookstore in the whole wide world, with every bit of shelf space occupied by a book that's both highly collectible and of literary value. The shop holds a large collection of Faulkner first editions and rare and first-edition classics by many other authors, and it has a particularly comprehensive collection of New Orleans–related work. Taking up one room and a hallway, Faulkner House feels like a portion of somebody's private home—which it is—but the selection of books here shows the art that is in bookselling. 624 Pirates Alley. © **504/524-2940.** www.faulknerhousebooks.net. Daily 10am–6pm.

Garden District Book Shop ★★★   Owner Britton Trice has stocked his medium-size shop with just about every regional book you can think of; if you want a New Orleans–or Louisiana-specific book, no matter what the exact focus (interiors, exteriors, food, Creoles, you name it), you should be able to find it here. This is also where Anne Rice does book signings whenever she has a new release. They usually have autographed copies of her books plus fancy special editions of Rice titles that they publish themselves and a large selection of signed books by local (such as Poppy Z. Brite) and nonlocal authors (from Clive Barker to James Lee Burke). 2727 Prytania St. (in the Rink). © **504/895-2266.** Fax 504/895-0111. www.gardendistrictbookshop.com. Mon–Sat 10am–6pm; Sun 10am–4pm.

Octavia Books ★   We do love our independent bookstores, and although this may be a bit far uptown, a sweet, tiny patio, complete with waterfall, is the customer's reward—what better way to linger over a purchase from stock that is chosen with obvious literary care? Book signings and other literary events are common. 513 Octavia St. (at Laurel St.). © **504/899-7323.** www.octaviabooks.com. Mon–Sat 10am–6pm; Sun noon–5pm.

CANDIES & PRALINES

Aunt Sally's Praline Shop ★   At Aunt Sally's you can watch skilled workers perform the 150-year-old process of cooking the original Creole pecan pralines right before your eyes. You'll know they're fresh. The large store also has a broad selection of regional cookbooks, books on the history of New Orleans and its environs, Creole and Cajun foods, folk and souvenir dolls, and local memorabilia. In addition, Aunt Sally's has a collection of zydeco, Cajun, R&B, and jazz CDs and cassettes. They'll ship any purchase. In the French Market, 810 Decatur St. © **800/642-7257** or 504/944-6090. www.auntsallys.com. Mon–Tues 9am–6pm; Wed–Fri 9am–8pm; Sat 9am–8pm; Sun 8am–6pm.

Blue Frog Chocolates ★★   If you've noticed our chocolate bias, you know how happy we are at this store, which has the finest chocolate and candy collection in the city. Just for starters is Belgium liquor-filled chocolate; Michel Cluizel fresh butter creams from France; Joseph Schmidt's (often referred to as the "Nipples of Venus"), which are plump and dense; Jordan almonds (good ones are difficult to find); Dulce de Leche (Argentina) served over ice cream—or as Ann Streiffer, owner with husband Rick, suggested, "Eat it with a spoon from the jar." We could go on about the 21 different colors of M&Ms or the chocolate film for your camera. 5707 Magazine St. © **504/269-5707.** www.bluefrogchocolates.com. Sept–June Mon–Fri 10am–6pm, Sat 10am–4pm; July–Aug Tues–Fri 11am–5:30pm, Sat 11am–4pm.

Laura's Candies ★   Laura's is said to be the city's oldest candy store, established in 1913. It has fabulous pralines, but it also has rich, delectable golf ball-size truffles—our personal favorite indulgence, although they've gotten a bit pricey as of late. 331 Chartres St. © **504/525-3880.** www.laurascandies.com. Daily 11am–6pm.

Leah's Candy Kitchen ★★   After you've tried all of the city's Creole candy shops, you might very well come to the conclusion that Leah's tops the list. Everything here, from the candy fillings to the chocolate-covered pecan brittle, is made from scratch by second- and third-generation members of Leah Johnson's praline-cookin' family, who

have been confecting confections since 1944. 714 St. Louis St. ✆ **888/523-5324** or 504/523-
5662. www.leahspralines.com. Mon–Sat 10am–6pm.

Southern Candymakers ★   Here is yet another place to taste-test pralines. Our group of experts found these a bit nontraditional but quite good—that they are often making the candy on the spot at their newer address probably doesn't hurt. Their confections send people into swoons. They've recently opened a location at 1010 Decatur St. with the same phone number, but different hours, 9am to 6pm daily. 334 Decatur St. ✆ **800/344-9773** or 504/523-5544. www.southerncandymakers.com. Daily 10am–7pm.

Sucré ★   Usually lumped in with the many other gelato places that have popped up post-Katrina, the emphasis of this charming modern-stylish shop is really more on high-end confectionery. Their French pastries and gourmet candies look as picture-perfect as their interior, but opinions vary from bland to brilliant as far as quality. 3025 Magazine St. ✆ **504/520-8311.** www.shopsucre.com. Sun–Thurs 9am–10pm; Fri–Sat 9am–midnight.

COSTUMES & MASKS

Costumery is big business in New Orleans, and not just in the days before Lent. In this city you never know *when* you're going to want or need a costume. A number of shops in New Orleans specialize in props for Mardi Gras, Halloween, and other occasions. *Tip:* New Orleanians often sell their costumes back to these shops after Ash Wednesday, and you can sometimes pick up an outfit that's only been worn once at a small fraction of its original cost.

Uptown Costume & Dance Company ★   The walls of this small store are covered with spooky monster masks, goofy arrow-through-the-head-type tricks, hats, wigs, makeup, and all other manner of playfulness. It draws a steady, yearlong stream of loyal customers: kids going to parties, dancers, clowns, actors, and so forth. Conventioneers come here for rental disguises. At Mardi Gras, though, things really get cooking. The shop designs party uniforms for a number of Mardi Gras krewe members. Owner Cheryll Berlier also creates a limited number of wacky Mardi Gras tuxedo jackets, which get gobbled up quickly. 4326 Magazine St. ✆ **504/895-7969.** Mon–Sat 10am–7pm; Sun noon–5pm during Halloween and Mardi Gras.

FASHION & VINTAGE CLOTHING

All About Me ★★   A clothing venture at the Canal end of Decatur, this shop is well stocked with not only good-looking, well-priced sundresses but also T-shirts, purses, masks, and jewelry. Not sure if those terrific hours will hold, but we hope so; who doesn't want to break up the evening with a little late-night shopping? 401 Decatur. **504/599-3092.** Daily 9am–10:30pm.

Dirty Coast ★★   On one hand, this shop is producing some of the most eye-catching and original T-shirt designs in a town full of humor, graphic artists, and cotton garments. ("Ruffins for Mayor" has a silhouette of the local beloved musician, while "Onward, Upward, Ninth Ward" says it all.) Plus, all the shirts are painted in the city. On the other hand, this is a very far uptown location, and we are the ones who told you that you don't need a car to get around. Plus, the shirts, wonderful though they are, are not cheap. But they are so much better than the crap in those French Quarter shops! 5704 Magazine St. ✆ **504/324-3745.** www.dirtycoast.com. Mon–Sat 11am–6pm.

Fleur de Paris ★★★   Remember when a woman was simply not dressed unless she wore a hat? Help bring back those times by patronizing this shop, which makes hand-blocked, stylishly trimmed hats. Think you aren't a hat person? The experts here can take one look at any head and face and find the right style to fit it. Expensive, but works of art often are. They will also stay open late and even bring in champagne for special parties! Additionally, you can find decades' worth of experience in their ever-changing collection of vintage gowns. The 1920s and 1930s elegance on display constantly brings us to our knees with covetousness. 523 Royal St. ✆ **504/525-1899.** Daily 10am–6pm.

House of Lounge ★★   If you want to be a couch potato, you might as well be a well-dressed one. Or do you want to treat your humble bedroom more like a boudoir? House of Lounge offers all sorts of silky robes and impressive "hostess gowns," plus sexy lingerie (and admittedly, there isn't much difference btw. the categories). 2044 Magazine St. ✆ **504/671-8300.** www.houseoflounge.com. Mon–Sat 11am–6pm; Sun noon–5pm.

Jeantherapy ★   No fashion-conscious teenage girl will want to miss this store, which sells just about every single trendy brand of bluejeans, from Seven to Juicy to True Religion and back again, none of which has a zipper that rises more than 4 inches or looks good on anyone over 17 or 105 pounds. Perhaps it was just the day we went. Or all the meals we had eaten. There is also a good selection of lovely soft cotton fashion T-shirts. 5505 Magazine St. ✆ **504/897-5535.** www.jeantherapy.com. Mon–Sat 10am–6pm; Sun noon–5pm.

Metro Three ★★   They were the first ones to come up with the design for the ubiquitous "Make Levees, Not War" shirts, and their soft, vintage-feeling tees are a lot better than the rip-offs on Bourbon Street. Other local slogans include neighborhood-representing options (show your support for the 9th Ward, the Lower Garden District, and the rest), "Katrina and Rita: Girls Gone Wild," and more. Everyone in New Orleans has at least one of their shirts, and you should, too. 2032 Magazine St. ✆ **504/558-0212.** www. metrothree.com. Mon–Sat 11am–6pm; Sun noon–5pm.

Tomato ★   Kicky-cute women's clothes geared toward the season. A nice place for fresh frock. Sometimes a little high priced, but there is a better-priced sales rack in the back to make up for it. 3318 Magazine St. ✆ **504/895-0444.** Mon–Fri 11am–6pm; Sun noon–4pm.

Trashy Diva ★★   Despite the name, there is nothing trashy about the vintage clothes found here. The heyday of women's garments—in the sense of designs that know how to flatter curves—is present in these floaty and velvety numbers that will please everyone from the hat-and-gloves-wearing crowds to the inner flappers to the Goth teens. Dresses can be a bit dear, but there is often a sales rack in the back that's full of incredible bargains. They also have vintage-inspired shoes and accessories. 2048 Magazine St. ✆ **888/818-DIVA** (818-3482) or 504/299-8777. www.trashydiva.com. Mon–Fri noon–6pm; Sat 11am–5pm; Sun 1–5pm.

UAL ★★★   Once one of the secrets of the well-informed—and really well-dressed—local fashionistas, it was a cause for both rejoicing and mourning when United Apparel Liquidators moved from their obscure Metairie location to a central one right in the middle of the Quarter. Advantage—easier to get to. Disadvantage—now we have even *more* competition for UAL's incredible deals. The shop gets discontinued or leftover items from designers of all levels and sells them at ridiculous markdowns—a $1,500 garment going for $350. As if that wasn't enough, they often have hourly sales (20% off all accessories, for example). The problem is that average sizes go fast, and there often isn't more than one of anything. (We still angst about the darling Jimmy Choos that were one size too small.) Consequently, a trip here can be hit-or-miss. But when you do hit, you will be the envy of bargain lovers everywhere. 518 Chartres St. ✆ **504/301-4437.** Sun–Wed 10am–6pm; Thurs–Sat 11am–8pm.

Violet's ★★ This is our greatest temptation among French Quarter shops, given how we feel about romantic, Edwardian, and '20s-inspired clothes in lush velvets and satins. There are some dazzling creations here with appropriate accessories (jewelry, hats, scarves) as well. 808 Chartres St. © **504/569-0088.** Sun–Thurs 11am–7pm; Fri–Sat 10am–8pm.

Voluptuous Vixens ★ Catering to "real-size women"—that would be figures from size 10 to size 28—this shop covers everything from dresses and pants to fancy T-shirts and lingerie and nightwear. All of it is cute and/or elegant, rather than condescending to the demographic. 818 Chartres St. © **504/529-3588.** Mon–Thurs 10am–6pm; Fri–Sat 10am–7pm; Sun noon–6pm.

Yvonne LaFleur—New Orleans ★ Yvonne LaFleur, a confessed incurable romantic, is the creator of beautifully feminine original designs. Her custom millinery, silk dresses, evening gowns, lingerie, and sportswear, are surprisingly affordable, and all are enhanced by her signature perfume. Her store is in the Riverbend district. 8131 Hampson St. © **504/866-9666.** www.yvonnelafleur.com. Mon–Wed and Fri–Sat 10am–6pm; Thurs 10am–8pm.

FOOD & DRINK

Martin Wine Cellar If you're a wine lover or connoisseur—or if you want to become one—Martin Wine Cellar may be your most significant find in New Orleans. It carries an eye-popping selection of wines, spirits, and champagnes at surprisingly reasonable prices. It's not rare to find a $10 wine recommended and described in baffling detail. The store has an extensive selection of preserves, coffees, teas, crackers, biscotti, cookies, cheeses, and even cigars that are a perfect accompaniment to drinks (and that are often imported and hard to find elsewhere). A bigger location is at 714 Elmeer Ave. (in the 1200 block of Veterans Memorial Blvd.) in Metairie (© **888/407-7496** or 504/896-7300). 3500 Magazine St. © **504/899-7411.** www.martinwine.com. Tues–Sat 10am–7pm.

GIFTS

If you're in town on the third Saturday of any month, consider a trip to the **Bywater Art Market** (Royal St. at Piety; © **504/944-7900;** www.art-restoration.com/bam; 9am–4pm). Paintings, pottery, glass mosaic, jewelry, handmade frames from old wood, and more, with the quality assured, as only juried artists are permitted to participate. It's all original, it's all local and regional, and much of it is surprisingly affordable. Also look at the listings earlier for **Studio Inferno** and the **Great Artists Collective,** both of which carry items more than suitable for this category.

The Artists' Market ★★ A collective overseen by four local artists, who display their own work alongside that of up to 65 others working on consignment. Local themes are reflected in the pottery, plates, paintings, photos, ironwork, and more. There is also glasswork and custom beads. The shop extends all the way through the block to the French Market behind, which makes for easy souvenir shopping. 1228 Decatur. © **504/561-0046.** Mon–Fri 10am–5pm; Sat–Sun 10am–6pm.

Aux Belles Choses ★★ This shop feels as though it could be located at a lonely crossroads in rural France. Maybe it's all the pretty dried plants and flowers. If you like creamy French soaps, especially with exotic scents, you'll probably leave with a handful—this place has many that are hard to find on this side of the Atlantic. The shop has everything from beautiful linens to old English pudding pots—terrific wedding and other special-occasion gifts. 3912 Magazine St. © **504/891-1009.** www.abcneworleans.com. Wed–Sat 10am–5pm.

Belladonna Retail Therapy ★★   If you've booked a treatment at the day spa, allow yourself extra time to browse through the shop—you are going to need it. Between the jewelry lines, including those whose simple silver work is etched with wee inscriptions of quotes from Shakespeare and others, the selection of gorgeous home wares, the cute clothes, and the clever gift items, there is a lot to coo over. 2900 Magazine St. ℭ 504/891-4393. www.belladonnadayspa.com. Mon–Tues and Fri–Sat 9am–6pm; Wed–Thurs 9am–8pm.

Bellanoche ★   Bellanoche is one more ultrafine shop, dripping with comfort and luxury, from the proprietor of the Belladonna (p. 236), Kim Dudek. Bellanoche carries the best in bed linens, with lines such as Bella Notte (washable embroidered satin) and Matteo & Co., as well as accessories such as dreamy pouf slipper/shoes by both Olivia Rose Tal and Amy Jo Gladstone. 3632 Magazine St. ℭ 504/891-6483. www.belladonnadayspa.com. Mon–Tues and Fri–Sat 9am–6pm; Wed–Thurs 9am–8pm.

The Black Butterfly ★★   The Black Butterfly is a place for any collector or admirer of miniatures. This fourth-generation shop (in business since 1894) is filled with porcelain, brass, wood, and pewter figures as well as dollhouse furniture and accessories. The store also has a collection of miniature soldiers and a selection of trains and cars. 727 Royal St. ℭ 504/524-6464. www.blackbutterfly.com. Mon–Sat 11am–5pm.

Funrock'n ★   They advertise as "the stuff you want," and, sure, why not? Provided that stuff is pop culture–based retro toys, both reissued and collectible, lunchboxes, brightly colored novelty items, T-shirts with sayings like "New Orleans is for Levees," and much, much more. Overstuffed like a Decatur Street junk shop and as over-stimulated as a kid hopped up on sugar and cartoons, the place surely doesn't lack for fun—or options. 1128 Decatur St. ℭ 504/524-1122. www.funrockn.com. Sun–Thurs 11am–6pm; Fri–Sat 11am–7pm.

Hoi Polloi Boutique ★★   Feeling a little underdressed compared to those well-put-together Southern ladies? Forgot to pack that little extra something needed to pull your outfit together? Here's your solution. A feminine boutique with stylish quality hats, scarves, purses, jewelry, and more. It's fun to poke around in, because the products are all interesting and playful. 434 Chartres St. ℭ 504/561-7585. www.hoipolloiboutique.com. Daily 10am–6pm.

Scriptura ★★   This store has everything related to the elegant art of scribbling. You can get designer stationery, glass fountain pens, sealing wax, and all types of generic or specific (travel, cigar, wine, restaurant) journals. This is the kind of place where you can find a gift for that impossible-to-shop-for person in your life. They have a second location at 3301 Veterans, Ste. 137. 5423 Magazine St. ℭ 504/897-1555. www.scriptura.com. Mon–Sat 10:30am–5pm.

Shop of the Two Sisters ★   This shop has upscale "girly" items such as throw pillows, lamps, sconces, accessories, unique accent pieces (with an emphasis on florals and fruits), and upholstery. Here you'll find consumerism at its most beautiful, but be prepared to pay for it. 1800 Magazine St. ℭ 504/525-2747. www.shopofthetwosisters.com. Mon–Sat 10am–5pm.

Simon of New Orleans/Antiques on Jackson ★★   Folk artist Simon, whose brightly painted signs are seen throughout New Orleans in homes and businesses, will paint-to-order your own personal sign and ship it to you. This gallery and shop is shared with Simon and his wife, Maria, who has particularly good taste in primitive furniture, antiques, and hodgepodgery. Visit them at this relatively new location in a larger space that shows off the eclectic collections. 1028 Jackson Ave. ℓ **504/524-8201.** Mon by appoint- ment; Tues–Sat 10am–5pm.

Vintage 429 ★ "Fun. Funky. Fabulous," is how they bill themselves, and it is a pretty jocular place, full of autographed memorabilia. It's all eye-catching, though a little too pricey for impulse buys. 429 Royal St. ℓ **866/846-8429** or 504/529-2288. www.vintage429. com. Daily 10am–5:30pm.

HATS
See also the superb Fleur de Paris millinery, p. 239.

Meyer the Hatter ★★★ Meyer's opened more than 100 years ago and has been in the same family ever since. Today the haberdashery has one of the largest selections of fine hats and caps in the South. Men will find distinguished international labels such as Stetson, Kangol, Akubra, Dobbs, and Borsalino (and there are some hats for women as well). Half the fun is having the owner and his son fuss over you—let them pick out the proper feather to go in your new chapeau! Go outfit yourself like a proper gentleman caller. 120 St. Charles Ave. ℓ **800/882-4287** or 504/525-1048. www.meyerthehatter.com. Mon–Sat 10am–5:45pm.

JEWELRY
Katy Beh Contemporary Jewelry ★ The modern design of the store's structure sets the stage for what is housed within. Katy Beh, herself a jewelry artist, personally selects pieces made by celebrated designers and fresh new talent from across the U.S. Bring in your own stones to be remade into a distinctive piece or choose a new luxurious gold, silver, or gemstone item. 3708 Magazine St. ℓ **504/896-9600.** www.katybeh.com. Mon–Sat 10am–5pm.

Mignon Faget, Ltd. ★★ Mignon Faget is one of the biggest personalities in New Orleans's jewelry universe, and a piece from here is as much a must for a New Orleans lady as a Tiffany piece is for an NYC one. The designer is a New Orleans native; in fact, some of her ancestors moved here to escape the French Revolution, while others were longtime plantation owners. Today, in her main studio display room, you can see some of her signature styles—gold, silver, and bronze d'oré fashioned into pendants, bracelets, rings, earrings, shirt studs, and cuff links. Their New Orleans–specific pieces make superb presents for yourself or anyone back home. There's an uptown location at 3801 Magazine St. (ℓ **504/891-2005**). Canal Place, Level 1. ℓ **800/375-7557** or 504/524-2973. www.mignonfaget.com. Mon–Sat 10am–6pm.

Rumors ★★ This longtime local jewelry and gift store moved to a larger location just up the block, and double the space means double the number of items. They are chock-ablock full of all kinds of glittery earrings, necklaces, masks, and more, many the work of local artists. Don't be turned off by the gaudy nature of some of the contents. Excellent buys are abundant, particularly their own silver fleur-de-lis necklaces, which stand up proudly to the ones offered at Mignon Faget. Also check out the gorgeous "do you know what it means" crescent design medallions, which make poignant and stylish souvenirs. 537 Royal St. ℓ **504/525-0292.** www.rumorsno.com. Daily 10am–6pm.

Sabai Jewelry Gallery ★ This store offers a unique array of Asian and handcrafted jewelry. The stones and settings are displayed on antique wooden block prints (some on flat stones embedded in rice). But the best part is when one discovers the lack of designer prices that usually tag along with incredible designs. 3115 Magazine St. ℓ **504/899-9555.** Second location at 924 Royal St. ℓ **504/525-6211.** Daily 10:30am–6pm.

Thomas Mann Designs/Gallery I/O ★★   Local jewelry designer Thomas Mann is known for his "techno-romantic" work with metal and found objects, creating curious pieces of highly original jewelry that straddle a line between classic and contemporary. For example, even though we favor Deco and Victorian, every time we wear his sterling-silver heart with the glass front, we get compliments. 1804 Magazine St. ℂ **504/581-2113.** Mon–Sat 11am–6pm.

MUSIC

Beckham's Bookshop ★   It's better known for its fine collection of used books (see "Books," earlier in this chapter), but Beckham's also has a large selection of secondhand classical LPs. 228 Decatur St. ℂ **504/522-9875.** Daily 10am–5pm.

Louisiana Music Factory ★★★   This popular and terrific store carries a large selection of regional music—including Cajun, zydeco, R&B, jazz, blues, and gospel—plus books, posters, and T-shirts. It also has frequent live music and beer bashes—shop while you bop! It's the place to get yourself informed about New Orleans music. 210 Decatur St. ℂ **504/586-1094.** www.louisianamusicfactory.com. Mon–Sat 10am–7pm; Sun noon–6pm.

Peaches Records   This family-owned indie shop moved boldly into the French Quarter space vacated by Tower Records and stocked the place with a broad swath of locally focused CDs, vinyl, books, DVDs, T-shirts, and art. Peaches' New Orleans roots go back to 1975 when their first store opened and became a stop-off for R&B royalty like Stevie Wonder. Later they made a mark supporting local rap and hip-hop artists like Juvenile and Lil Wayne. Nowadays the selection spans those genres as well as rock, jazz, and all manner of New Orleans tuneage. If you tire from perusing the 10,000-square-foot behemoth, find sustenance in a cuppa joe from their cafe. And while we can't promise you'll see Mr. Wonder, on weekend afternoons check out the free in-store shows. 408 N. Peters. ℂ **504/282-3322.** www.peachesrecordsneworleans.com. Mon–Fri 10am–8pm; Sat–Sun 11am–7pm.

THE OCCULT

Bottom of the Cup Tearoom ★   It's been open since 1929 and bills itself as the "oldest tearoom in the United States." In addition to having a psychic consultation, you can also purchase teas, books, jewelry, crystal balls, tarot cards, crystals, and healing wands. 327 Chartres. ℂ **504/524-1997.** www.bottomofthecup.com. Daily 10am–6pm.

Esoterica Occult Goods ★   This is the hip witch store for all your occult needs. Well, maybe not all, but they cover both pagan witch and voodoo rituals with their potions, herbs, gris-gris bags, and selection of related books plus similar magical and death-oriented jewelry. 541 Dumaine St. ℂ **504/581-7711.** www.onewitch.com. Daily noon–6pm.

Marie Laveau's House of Voodoo   This is the place for voodoo dolls and gris-gris bags. It's tourist voodoo, to be sure, but such items make great souvenirs for the right friends, and it's a fun store to poke around in. Their hours are somewhat flexible—don't be surprised if they come in a little later or close a little earlier. 739 Bourbon St. ℂ **504/581-3751.** Mon–Thurs 1:30–11:30pm; Fri–Sun 11am–1am.

Voodoo Authentica ★   It's about time someone established a shop specializing in voodoo paraphernalia that doesn't feel like someone's dusty shack, but like a real retail establishment. Two big rooms with a range of voodoo dolls, from cheap to costly, from an easy souvenir to serious works of art, plus a similar array of potions, spell candles, and daubs. 612 Dumaine St. ℂ **504/522-2111.** www.voodooshop.com. Daily 11am–7pm.

New Orleans After Dark

New Orleans is one of the most beautiful cities in the United States, possibly the world, but we won't mind if you never see the sights—provided, however, that the omission is because you are spending the daylight hours recovering from the equally extraordinary nightlife.

This is a city of music and rhythm. It is impossible to imagine New Orleans without a soundtrack of jazz, brass bands, R&B, and even Cajun and zydeco. Music streams from every doorway, and sometimes it seems people are dancing down the street. Sometimes they really are. (After all, this is the town that sends you to your grave with music and then dances back from the cemetery.) You walk along Bourbon Street, for example, and with every step you hear music of all varieties. Maybe none of it is world-class, but that doesn't matter too much. It's just that it's there and in such variety. Plus, it's darn infectious. And even Katrina barely put a dent in the nightlife; at least a couple of intrepid bars on Bourbon Street never closed, while residents cranked up boomboxes when they couldn't get live music, which itself returned in some form or another in a matter of weeks, if not days.

This is also the city of decadence and good times rolling. Not to mention really loose liquor laws and drinks in "go" cups (plastic containers you can take with you—many bars and clubs even have walk-up windows for easy refills). And all this increases at night. We aren't just talking about the open-air frat party that is Bourbon Street some (okay, most) evenings. In fact, we prefer not to talk about that at all.

Most important is that virtually every night, dozens of clubs all over town offer music that can range from average to extraordinary but is never less than danceable. In most places, cover prices vary from night to night and performer to performer, but rarely will you have to pay more than $10—and then only for more high-falutin' places such as the House of Blues.

When the clubs get too full, no matter: The crowd spills into the street, talking, drinking, and still dancing right there on the sidewalk (the music is often plenty audible out there). Sometimes the action outside is even more fun than inside, not to mention less hot and sweaty.

Club hopping is easy, though with some exceptions some of the better choices will require leaving the Quarter by cab or some other vehicle. Don't worry—most are an easy taxi ride away, and many are within an additional, even easier, cab ride, if not walking distance, of each other. We strongly urge you to leave the Quarter at night to visit some of the town's better joints.

However, if you aren't up to that, don't fret. Some of the best jazz and brass-band clubs are right in the Quarter. And only steps away is the excellent scene in the Frenchmen section of the Faubourg Marigny, where at least a dozen clubs and bars are going at once within 3 blocks of each other. People wander from one to the other, sometimes never bothering to pay the cover price and go inside. If you do your evening right, those calories you consumed all day long will be gone by morning.

Or, yes, you could spend your night running from bar to bar. There is no lack. With such great music available, that seems a waste of time, however; if all you wanted to do was drink, you could have stayed home and enjoyed yourself just as much. Still, it is New Orleans, and some of these places are as convivial and atmospheric as you will ever find; ducking into a few isn't a bad idea at all. And, of course, everything only gets livelier and wilder as the evening goes on.

Speaking of which, don't be fooled by the times given in local listings for band performances. If it says 10pm, the band will probably go on closer to midnight and keep playing until late. Really late. This isn't always true—once in a blue moon, an act will go on when billed and finish up rather early—but chances are good that if you come late, even really late, you will still catch quite a bit of the act you came to see.

However you decide to do it, don't miss it. New Orleans at night is not New Orleans during the day, and not to take advantage of it is to miss out. You could

stay in your hotel room with the covers pulled over your head, but if that's what you want, you came to the wrong city: Just tell yourself you'll sleep when you get home.

For up-to-date information on what's happening around town, look for current editions of **Gambit, Offbeat,** and **WhereY'at,** all distributed free in many hotels and all record stores. You can also check out *Offbeat* on the Internet (www.nola.com; once you get to the NOLA home page, go to "Music" in the "Entertainment" section) and *Gambit* at www.bestofneworleans.com. Other sources include the **Times-Picayune**'s daily entertainment calendar and Friday's **"Lagniappe"** section of the newspaper. Additionally, **WWOZ** (90.7 FM) broadcasts the local music schedule several times throughout the day.

For the nightlife listings in this chapter, see the "New Orleans Nightlife," "French Quarter Nightlife," or "Uptown Nightlife" maps in this chapter or the "Mid-City Attractions & Nightlife" map on p. 183 of chapter 8, "Sights to See & Places to Be."

1 THE RHYTHMS OF NEW ORLEANS

The late New Orleans R&B legend Ernie K-Doe was once quoted as saying, "I'm not sure, but I think all music came from New Orleans." What might be a more accurate account—and relatively hyperbole-free—is that all music came *to* New Orleans. Any style you can name, from African field hollers to industrial techno-rock, has found its way to the Crescent City, where it's been blended, shaken, and stirred into a new, distinctive, and usually frothy concoction that, it seems, could have come from nowhere else.

"Yeah," you scoff, "but what about classical music?" Well, maybe you've never heard how pianist James Booker, an eye-patched eccentric even by New Orleans standards, could make a Bach chorale strut like a second-line umbrella twirler. Or maybe you're forgetting that Wynton Marsalis has Grammy Awards for both jazz and classical recordings, not to mention a 1997 Pulitzer Prize for his slavery-themed jazz oratorio *Blood on the Fields.*

On the other side of the spectrum, don't forget that Trent Reznor, the man behind the brutal sounds and imagery of the industrial act Nine Inch Nails, chose to live and record in New Orleans—not because of the good property values, but because the aesthetics and atmosphere suit him. (His now-former studio is in a former funeral home, natch.)

Even more unusual is the New Orleans Klezmer All Stars ensemble, a group of musicians that plays the lively music of eastern European Jewish troubadours with a few New Orleans embellishments. You're not required to dance at their performances, but you'll probably find it impossible not to.

Of course, what you're most likely to experience is somewhere in the middle, music more truly rooted in the Crescent City—the Storyville jazz descended from Louis Armstrong and Jelly Roll Morton, the bubbly R&B transmitted via Fats Domino and Professor Longhair, the Mardi Gras Indians, and the brass bands of the second lines that recently added exuberant, youthful infusions of funk and hip-hop.

Finding music in New Orleans is no trick. Walk anywhere in the vicinity of Bourbon Street and your ears will be assaulted by a variety of sounds. If you're really interested, it's worth a little effort to seek out the good stuff and avoid the tourist-oriented caricatures that will be thrust at you. Consult the free monthly *Offbeat,* available at many businesses in the French Quarter and elsewhere around town, for what's playing at such clubs as the Howlin' Wolf, Donna's, the Maple Leaf, Tipitina's, the clubs on Frenchmen Street, or the gotta-see-it-to-believe-it Mid City Lanes bowling alley, home of the famed Rock 'n' Bowl. Listen to public radio station WWOZ-FM (90.7 FM), which plays the best of New Orleans music and gives concert info.

THE JAZZ LIFE OF NEW ORLEANS

by George Hocutt

Jazz historian and executive producer of the Grammy Award–winning album
Doc Cheatham & Nicholas Payton

New Orleans did not invent jazz, but the crescents in the Mississippi River became the crucible in which jazz evolved. The city's French Catholic background has always inspired a more tolerant attitude toward the simple pleasures of the world than did the Puritan fathers from Plymouth Rock. Melodic sounds of all kinds were one of those pleasures.

Music was of great importance to the Louisiana settlers and their Creole offspring, and the city early on had a fascination with marching bands and parades. As early as 1787, Governor Miro entertained a gathering of Indian leaders with a parade. Eventually, bands were required for nearly every occasion—Mardi Gras, dedications, religious holidays, cornerstone laying, weddings, funerals, ad infinitum. With this plethora of musical activities, one major ingredient was in great need: musicians.

The musicians of early New Orleans were expected to do just what the word implied—provide music. They were not categorized or labeled by any brand or style of music. They were considered tradesmen just like other skilled craftsmen such as carpenters, shoemakers, and what-have-you. From an afternoon parade, they might be required to play at the opera and then possibly a late dance. At the dance the program would call for waltzes, galops, gavottes, and quadrilles, among others. (The jazz song "Tiger Rag" derived from a quadrille.) Obviously, these 19th-century instrumentalists were quite accomplished and versatile.

In the early 19th century, slaves were allowed to congregate in the area known as **Congo Square** for dancing to the rhythms of their homelands' drums and other percussive instruments. With the passing of time, many slaves, former slaves, and free men of color became accomplished instrumentalists. There were Negro marching bands in New Orleans before the Civil War, and many continued playing during the city's occupation by simply trading their gray uniforms for the Union blue.

Some of these musicians, possibly graduates of the Congo Square gatherings, brought to their playing a native rhythm that was likely a primitive syncopation. In an evolutionary way, many of New Orleans's musicians began absorbing this amalgam of European and African influences. Then came the addition of the very personal statements of the blues, work songs, hollers, and spirituals. The music was changing and was taking on a certain American and distinctly New Orleanian aura.

In the 1870s two men were born who were to have a profound effect on the music. **"Papa" Jack Laine** was born in 1873 and **Charles "Buddy" Bolden** in 1878, both in New Orleans.

Bolden, a cornetist who would later be known as the First Man of Jazz, began playing dances and parties around 1895. By 1897 he had put together the band that most old-timers remember. They also remember that when Bolden put his cornet up and blew loud from Johnson Park in uptown New Orleans, he could be heard for miles around. Fans said, "Buddy's callin' his chickens home." Unfortunately, Bolden was committed to an institution for the insane in 1907, where he died in 1931, never having recorded.

At approximately the same time, Papa Jack, primarily a drummer, formed several groups simultaneously, all called the Reliance Band. They played all over the Gulf Coast and in New Orleans and were extremely popular. Almost all the early white New Orleans jazzmen played in one of Laine's groups. He withdrew from the music business around the time of World War I, but his legacy lived on through the many greats he fostered, later known as Papa Jack's children.

Much of what we know of these two pioneers we have learned from taped interviews with men who were already old at the time they were interviewed—but not old enough to remember the music scene before Bolden and Laine. Names that have emerged, though dimly, include the legendary Mass Quamba, William Martin, Picayune Butler, and a performer known as Old Corn Meal. All of them likely added their own touches to the evolution of New Orleans music.

Concurrent with Bolden and Laine's contributions to the musical life of the city, another event that would affect the spread of jazz everywhere was unfolding. **Storyville,** the only prescribed district for legalized prostitution ever attempted in this country, operated from 1897 to 1917. The most elegant houses were along the lake side of Rampart Street between Iberville and Conti streets. Among them were the Arlington and Lulu White's Mahogany Hall.

No documentation or mention in the taped oral histories of early New Orleans jazzmen (contained in the jazz archives at Tulane Univ.) tells us of an orchestra ever playing in any of the houses, but most of them did have a piano player in the parlor. Among those entertainers were Spencer Williams, later a very successful songwriter; Tony Jackson, who wrote *Pretty Baby;* and the immortal **Jelly Roll Morton.**

Born Ferdinand Joseph Lamothe (his actual name, established by jazz researcher Lawrence Gushee from Jelly's baptismal certificate) in 1890, Morton was the first true jazz composer and, next to Louis Armstrong, the most important figure in early jazz. His compositions were recorded well into the swing era and are still performed today. He was inducted into the Rock and Roll Hall of Fame in the Early Influence category.

Although the houses did not use bands for entertainment, there were many playing opportunities in the bars and clubs that dotted Storyville and the adjacent areas. These clubs—the Arlington Annex, the Cadillac, Frank Early's, 101 Ranch, the Frenchmen's, and Pete Lala's, among others—all featured bands. The great musicians of New Orleans all played in the clubs and doubled during the day in the multitude of brass bands that were always in demand. All the prominent names of early New Orleans jazz served this apprenticeship, including Freddy Keppard, King Oliver, Kid Ory, Sidney Bechet, Papa Celestin, "Big Eye" Louis Nelson, Buddy Petit, Bunk Johnson, Johnny and Baby Dodds, Alphonse Picou, Achille Baquet, Lorenzo Tio, and Tommy Ladnier. The list could go on and on.

As early as 1916, some New Orleans bands that included many of Papa Jack's children decided to try the musical climate in Chicago. Freddy Keppard and the Original Creole Band had been spreading music from New Orleans throughout the country in concerts and on vaudeville stages, but the groups going to Chicago made extended stays at specified clubs. The most successful group was the **Original Dixieland Jazz Band,** led by Nick LaRocca. The ODJB moved on from Chicago to open at Reisenweber's Cafe in New York City in 1917. They were a smash. Everybody loved the new music from New Orleans. After an abortive attempt by Columbia Records, they cut the first jazz record ever, released by Victor Records on February 16, 1917. The record, coupling "Livery Stable Blues" and "Dixie Jazz Band One Step," was an instant hit and was soon topping whatever hit parade existed at that time. The jazz flood had started.

In October 1917 the houses of Storyville were completely shut down by order of the U.S. Navy, and a great many jobs for entertainers and musicians started drying up. The performers began to look elsewhere for work. Apparently, word was filtering back to the city of the success the former New Orleanians were enjoying up north. Many decided to follow that example.

Kid Ory headed to California, where he made the first black jazz record. King Oliver traveled to Chicago in 1919, taking Johnny Dodds and other New Orleans musicians with him. After a brief sojourn in California, he returned to Chicago, and in 1922 he sent for **Louis Armstrong** to come up and join King Oliver's Creole Jazz Band—arguably the greatest collection of jazz musicians ever assembled (and all but one were natives of New Orleans). A young Emmett Hardy, the legendary white cornetist, went on tour with Bea Palmer and, while playing in Davenport, Iowa, was reportedly an influence on the great Bix Beiderbecke. Bix got his earliest musical experience by playing along with Nick LaRocca records. The New Orleans Rhythm Kings, all New Orleans musicians, opened at the Friars Inn in Chicago in 1922; cornetist Paul Mares certainly influenced Beiderbecke, who was attending school nearby and often sat in with the band. Jazz was spreading rapidly, and New Orleans musicians were in great demand by other groups around the country. Every other leader wanted to bring that something special to his music.

After leaving Oliver, Louis Armstrong, already the greatest soloist in jazz, went on to become one of the greatest entertainers and stars we have ever known. At one time his were probably the most identifiable face and voice in the world. More than 30 years after his death, his records are still bestsellers. He transcended New Orleans and became a national treasure.

Sidney Bechet settled in France after World War II and became a huge star performer and prolific composer. On his wedding day, a total holiday was declared in Antibes, and the entire city participated in a massive wedding party, dancing to music he had written.

New Orleans is still producing jazz greats. There is Harry Connick, Jr., who is making his mark in Hollywood as well as in music. **Ellis Marsalis** has fathered a group of jazz-playing sons, including trumpeter Wynton, who won a 1997 Pulitzer Prize for his composition *Blood on the Fields,* the first such award for a jazz composer. **Nicholas Payton** is another rising trumpet player from New Orleans. In 1998 Payton and Doc Cheatham shared the Grammy Award for best instrumental recording for their performance of "Stardust" on the album *Doc Cheatham & Nicholas Payton.* Obviously, the city still abounds with creativity.

Much remains in New Orleans for the adventurous jazz fan and explorer. Morton's home still stands on Frenchmen Street. Buddy Bolden's house is on First Street in Uptown, and a monument to him stands in Holt Cemetery, where he was buried in an unmarked grave. A plaque marks the house on Chartres Street where Danny Barker was born. At Rampart and Conti streets, one of Lulu White's buildings remains standing. Down the street is Frank Early's saloon (now a neighborhood convenience store). There is more, but that should give you an idea. Search them out. You can get six free pamphlets detailing different jazz-history walking tours, sponsored by the New Orleans Jazz Commission, by contacting the New Orleans Jazz National Historical Park, 916 N. Peters (© **504/589-4841;** www.nps.gov/jazz), or by visiting the **Louisiana Music Factory** store (p. 244). Alternatively, look at some of the books about music we've recommended on p. 17.

Music still resounds around the town. Although many of the originals are gone, **Preservation Hall** continues to showcase younger players. The **Palm Court Jazz Cafe** offers good jazz many nights a week. **Donna's** books great local music with a heavy emphasis on jazz. **Snug Harbor** on Frenchmen Street presents a broad spectrum of jazz from traditional to modern. **Fritzel's** on Bourbon Street hosts weekend jam sessions. Bands also appear on the steamboat excursions.

So certainly there is life in the old gal yet. Whether it's in the water, the air, or that good Creole cooking, jazz continues to grow in the fertile soil that settles on the banks of the curves of the Mississippi River.

BRASS BANDS

If your idea of New Orleans brass bands is merely the post-funeral "second line" parade of "When the Saints Go Marching In," you're in for some joyous surprises. In recent years young African-American kids have picked up the tradition and given it new life while also stimulating renewed interest in some of the veteran practitioners. At its roots it's primal jazz nonpareil, with group improvisations, unexpected turns, and spirit to burn.

The key act of the current revival was the **ReBirth Brass Band,** a gaggle of teens and preteens who in the late 1980s and early 1990s tossed pop-funk tunes like "Grazin' in the Grass" and the Doobie Brothers' "Takin' It to the Streets" into their mix of New Orleans standards. They even had a local hit with "Do Whatcha Wanna." The group's still around, though trumpeter **Kermit Ruffins,** who as a preteen Louis Armstrong look- and sound-alike was the centerpiece, left several years ago to form his own versatile jazz band, the **Barbecue Swingers.** Others working today in the same vein include **New Birth** and **Olympia,** while such newer arrivals as the **Soul Rebels** (perhaps the best of the new crop) and **Hot 8** have explored hip-hop, reggae, and funk styles in the brass context, often with terrific results. And brothers **Troy "Trombone Shorty"** and **James "Satchmo of the Ghetto" Andrews** demonstrate their knowledge of and reverence for the past as well as their intent for the future, as they fall between traditional jazz, brass bands (they both have and continue to play with various combos), and new directions with funk and jazz, such as Troy's own **Orleans Avenue.**

At the same time, older ensembles like the **Olympia Brass Band** have gained from the interest, as well as the **Treme Brass Band,** headed by the venerable and supremely dapper still plays every Tuesday night at the Maple Leaf, while the Soul Rebels have a regular weekly gig at Le Bon Temps Roulez and do regular weekend club gigs.

CAJUN & ZYDECO

Two of the music styles often associated with New Orleans are technically not from here at all. Both Cajun and zydeco really originated in the bayous of southwest Louisiana, a good 3 hours away. And while it's customary for the two to be named in the same breath, they are not the same thing—though they are arguably two sides of the same coin.

The foundations of the two styles lie in the arrival of two different French-speaking peoples in the swamp country: the Acadians (French migrants who were booted out of Nova Scotia by the English in 1755) and the Creole people (who were jettisoned by or escaped from the Caribbean slave trade of the same era). Entwined by the pervasive poverty and hardship of the region and by their common status as underclass peoples— the white Acadians, or Cajuns, as the name was eventually corrupted, were beaten by schoolteachers for speaking French well into the 20th century, while the Creoles suffered the same oppression as blacks elsewhere—the cultures blended in many ways, nowhere more evidently than in their music.

Introduction of the button accordion and its folksy, diatonic scale was a key development. It added a richness and power to what had largely been fiddle and guitar music. Early recordings of such seminal figures as Joe Falcon (a white man) and Amede Ardoin

---

(Tips) **Using the Listings**

Most clubs in New Orleans feature an eclectic lineup that reflects the town's music scene; the ReBirth Brass Band, for example, attracts as many rock fans as it does brass-band fans. Consequently, while we have broken down the clubs into musical genres, that's somewhat misleading: The bulk of the club scene escapes categorization (and, of course, booking policies are often subject to change)—even the local papers refer to club lineups as "mixed bags." Brass bands, old-timey-sounding bands, jazz bands—they cross-pollinate throughout the local club scene. Rock 'n' Bowl is listed under "Zydeco" but you can find brass and jazz bands there as well, and pretty much every kind of music goes through the doors of d.b.a. If you want a specific sound, you have to look at listings (in *Offbeat* and *Gambit* magazines, for example) night by night. Some places are generally good fun on their own regardless of who is playing; any night at the **Maple Leaf** (see later in this chapter) is going to be a good one, while wandering from spot to spot in the Frenchmen section is a well-spent, must-do evening. Be sure to check to see who is playing at the Ogden Museum of Southern Art ((𝄌 **504/539-9600**) on Thursday nights, lest you think all the good music in the city happens only in humid bars.

Really, in New Orleans, you can't go too wrong going just about anywhere simply to hang out. And in the process, you might get exposed to a new, wonderful genre of music or an incredible band.

Tips **A Night on the Town**

If you only have a night or two in New Orleans, you should try your best to hear some incredible live local music. But how to choose? Here is a guide to some of the best regular performers doing their best to keep their city's musical traditions alive. Okay, it would take a whole bunch of nights to hear them all, but you can't go wrong with any one—or two, or three—of the following.

Bob French, a drummer and second-generation powerhouse, is the keeper of the flame of traditional New Orleans jazz both on the bandstand and on the air at WWOZ. **Hot Club of New Orleans** brings acoustic swing and Gypsy jazz with New Orleans twists. **Hot Eight** means nonstop booty shaking from one of the top of the current crop of brass bands. **Soul Rebels Brass Band** is perhaps the most inventive of the young brass bands, subtly integrating some hip-hop energy to become a major local favorite. **John Boutte** is one of *the* voices of New Orleans these days and a national treasure, not just for his thrilling singing but for his ability to turn a wide range of songs, old and new, topical and pointed. Boutte's one of the finest singers in the country, and not to be missed. After reenergizing the brass-band revival as teenagers 2 decades ago, **ReBirth Brass Band**'s Tuesday-night gigs at the Maple Leaf remain must-do marathons. Like Louis Armstrong, a major musical role model, the former ReBirth trumpeter **Kermit Ruffins** has become a New Orleans music ambassador, even though he rarely plays outside the city these days. **Troy ("Trombone Shorty") Andrews** has been playing more with his funk band Orleans Avenue lately, with older brother **James ("12")** sticking a bit more to the traditional, but both of the former prodigies have matured into leaders on the scene. **New Orleans Jazz Vipers** is the best, and least precious, traditional jazz band in town. **Va va voom** is a Vipers spinoff taking the Gypsy jazz route. **Linnzi Zaorski** plays speak-easy jazz in a voice that sounds like it's coming straight off a 78 through

(a Creole) reveal a rough-hewed music tied to ancient tunes rooted in France and elsewhere, with hints of influence from the sounds starting to arrive through the radio and recordings of popular tunes. Such acts as the **Hackberry Ramblers,** who up until recently continued to perform with a couple of more or less original members, played the dance-hall circuits from New Orleans into Texas through the 1930s. Many added drums and amplifiers and steel guitars as they became available to fill out the sound.

In the postwar era, the styles began to separate more, with the Cajuns gravitating toward country-and-western swing and Creole musicians heavily influenced by the urban blues. The purer music of the region was suppressed and nearly lost in the 1950s, though such figures as **D. L. Menard** (the Cajun Hank Williams) and **Clifton Chenier** (the King of Zydeco) pioneered exciting new strains in their respective directions. Chenier, at first performing with just his brother Cleveland on washboard percussion, was among those who took up the chromatic "piano"-style accordion, which suited the blues in ways the button accordion could not. Menard, as his nickname indicates, melded Cajun with the style of the country balladeer he a gramophone horn. **Tom McDermott** takes audiences on a tour of Caribbean, southern, and South American piano styles that fed into the music of Jelly Roll Morton and others. He's always a wonder, in particular in his shows with clarinetist Evan Christopher. **New Birth Brass Band** is carrying on family legacies going back through several generations of great brass bands, with James and Troy Andrews often among the members. **New Orleans Klezmer All Stars**— yes, there are Jewish traditions in NOLA, too—give exciting life through this adventurous music. Their reeds man **Rob Wagner**'s solo gigs veer more toward free jazz. Great stuff, but for specific tastes.

Big Sam and Funky Nation: Descended from Buddy Bolden, so he claims, trombonist Sam Williams ain't lying about the "funky" part. Formerly of popular party band Cowboy Mouth, **Paul Sanchez** may be the top singer-songwriter in town. Catch him on a double bill with **Susan Cowsill**—yes, that Cowsill! Susan, who co-fronted the Continental Drifters for years as well, covers a lot of ground in her terrific solo shows, literally in her "Covered in Vinyl" nights when she and friends re-create such entire classic albums as Fleetwood Mac's *Rumours* and U2's *The Joshua Tree.* Sax man **Donald Harrison, Jr.,** mixes his top-flight modern jazz with the spirit of his role as chief of the Congo Nation Mardi Gras Indian tribe, a role he inherited from his father.

Henry Butler is an heir to the piano crown of Professor Longhair. Butler can also bring in some modern styles with dazzling keyboard skills. **Bonerama** is a brass band, sure, but with funk-rock variations heard on versions of such songs as "Helter Skelter" and "Frankenstein." **Irvin Mayfield** has become a central educator and ambassador of a wide range of New Orleans jazz, on top of being a star trumpeter and bandleader.

idolized (and met once, providing a tale he's joyously told countless times). In 1959 Menard wrote "La Porte Den Arriere" (The Back Door), which, along with the traditional "Jolie Blon," is certainly the most-performed song in the Cajun repertoire.

The great folk music boom of the early 1960s spilled over to Cajun music, and such figures as the **Balfa Brothers** and fiddler **Dennis McGee** suddenly had the opportunity to perform at such folk festivals as the famed Newport gathering. A turning point came when a Cajun group received a standing ovation at the 1964 Newport Festival. It was a real boost for the form and for Cajun pride, both of which seemed on the verge of extinction. With such younger musicians as **Marc Savoy,** who had begun producing homemade accordions of fine quality, providing new energy and commitment, and such entrepreneurs as Floyd Soileau recording the styles of the region, Cajun music gained new life.

This spawned a new generation, proud of their Cajun musical legacy but also fueled by rock 'n' roll. Leading the way are fiddler **Michael Doucet** and his band, **Beausoleil,** now Cajun music's best-known band. Even if he hasn't always delighted the purists,

Doucet has been a tireless ambassador for his heritage. And Marc's family continues his tradition, with son Wilson anchoring the critically acclaimed and Grammy-nominated **Pine Leaf Boys.**

In zydeco, Clifton Chenier led the way from the 1950s on, with a handful of others (the late Boozoo Chavis, John Delafose, Rockin' Sydney) adding their own embellishments. Chenier, recorded by Ville Platte's Floyd Soileau and Berkeley-based Chris Strackwitz's Arhoolie Records, became internationally famous, even playing the esteemed Montreaux Jazz Festival in Switzerland. His name loomed so large over the field that at his death in the mid-1980s, there seemed to be no one ready to step into his royal shoes.

But after a little drifting, zydeco has, arguably, grown stronger than ever. A new generation, including Chenier's son **C. J.** and Delafose's son **Geno,** is updating the old traditions, while such figures as **Keith Frank, Nathan Williams,** and the late **Beau Jocque** have added their own variations of funk, hip-hop, and blues.

RHYTHM & BLUES

Technically, the blues is not a New Orleans form, belonging more to the rural delta and, in its urban forms, Texas and Chicago. But rhythm and blues, with its gospel and African-Caribbean bloodlines, carries a Crescent City heartbeat. In the 1950s **Fats Domino,** along with his great producer-collaborator Dave Bartholomew, fused those elements into such seminal songs as "Blueberry Hill" and "Walkin' to New Orleans"—music that still fuels much of the New Orleans R&B sound today. At the same time, such then-unheralded figures as **Professor Longhair** and **"Champion" Jack Dupree** developed earthier variations of the piano-based sound, contrasting mournful woe with party-time spirit.

The keepers of the flame today are the **Neville Brothers,** who in their various combinations and incarnations (the Meters, Aaron Neville's solo projects, and so on) have explored and expanded just about every direction of this music.

And if the Nevilles are the royal family of New Orleans music, **Irma Thomas** is its duchess of soul. (The Rolling Stones version of "Time Is on My Side" is note-for-note taken from Irma's!) Though she had only one national hit ("Wish Somebody Would Care"), her feel for a song and her magnanimous spirit have led devotees to make regular pilgrimages to her club, the Lion's Den, to hear her perform. Her club got swamped after Hurricane Katrina, but Miss Thomas has returned to the city she loves. Go see her if you have the lucky opportunity.

2 JAZZ & BLUES CLUBS

This being New Orleans, jazz and blues are everywhere—though not all of it is worth hearing. Not that any of it is bad, per se. It's just that there is world-class stuff out there competing with tourist traps for your ears, so don't just settle for the first sight (or sound) of brass instruments you find. Seek out the really good stuff and you'll be rewarded. It's hard to predict opening/closing hours of New Orleans's nightlife. Many bars are open all the time, and because many clubs are in many bars (bars that have stages on which live bands play), there are no set opening and closing hours. In general, know that most clubs' hours both start and end late, if they ever end at all.

Of note is Irvin Mayfield's Jazz Playhouse at the Royal Sonesta Hotel. One of the city's premier musicians and a cultural ambassador for his hometown, his new venue features excellent jazz from up-and-comers and established artists, as well as not infrequent shows by Mayfield himself.

Blue Nile ★★   A terrific medium-size two-story venue—upstairs is generally reserved for smaller shows and DJs while downstairs has the regulation stage and better-than-average sightlines despite some pillars near the bar that can block views of said stage. Admire the mural on the left-hand wall—it is the plywood that was covering the windows post-storm, and a local artist painted on it. This venue has gone through some name changes, some identity swaps, and now a hurricane. It's taken a long while for the dedicated owner to get it back in order following the storm damage and insurance tussles, but his victory is complete with a well-scrubbed new facility. Grit like that, plus loyalty to the city, should be rewarded, which is easy, since the Nile is smack in the center of the thriving Frenchmen club scene, and so is easily added to your list of stops with at least four shows a week by a wide variety of locals plus late-night DJs. 532 Frenchmen St. ℭ 504/948-BLUE (948-2583). www.bluenilelive.com. Cover varies.

Donna's ★★★   A corner bar at the very northern edge of the Quarter, Donna's has become one of the top spots for great local music, including the revival of the brass-band experience and a variety of jazz and blues traditions. (The booking emphasis lately is on jazz.) But the main asset may be Donna herself, often monitoring the door to make sure you don't bring in drinks from outside and making sure you do order something inside. She's been one of the true boosters of new generations of New Orleans music (she's managed both the hip-hop-edged brass band Soul Rebels and the new-funk ensemble Galactic) and has helped promote awareness of veteran brass bands like Treme and Olympia. As with most real New Orleans hangouts, atmosphere is minimal, but spirits (liquid and otherwise) are high. The cover charge for performances is usually no more than the cost of a good mixed drink. Donna's must be included during an evening of club hopping. *Note:* Donna's is in a transitional neighborhood, so be careful upon entering and leaving. 800 N. Rampart St. ℭ 504/596-6914. www.donnasbarandgrill.com. Closed Tues–Wed. Cover varies.

The Famous Door   John Wehner no longer owns the club, so it's up to you to see how famous it still is. Open since 1934, the Famous Door is the oldest music club on Bourbon Street. Many local jazz, pop, and rock musicians have passed through here. One of them, Harry Connick, Jr., played his first gigs here at the age of 13. So far, it seems the club is similar to its old identity, but that may have changed by the time you read this. An in-house band now jams nightly. 339 Bourbon St. ℭ 504/598-4334.

Fritzel's European Jazz Pub ★★★   You might walk right past this small establishment, but that would be a big mistake because the 1831 building brings some fine traditional jazz musicians to play on its tiny stage. In addition to the regular nightly programs there can be special musical guests from Europe, and if you're lucky, jam sessions in the wee hours during the week when performers end their stints elsewhere and gather to play "musicians' music." Sets are short, but if Tom McDermott or Tim Laughlin are playing, don't miss them. The full bar also stocks a variety of schnapps (served ice-cold) and German beers. 733 Bourbon St. ℭ 504/586-4800. 1-drink minimum per set.

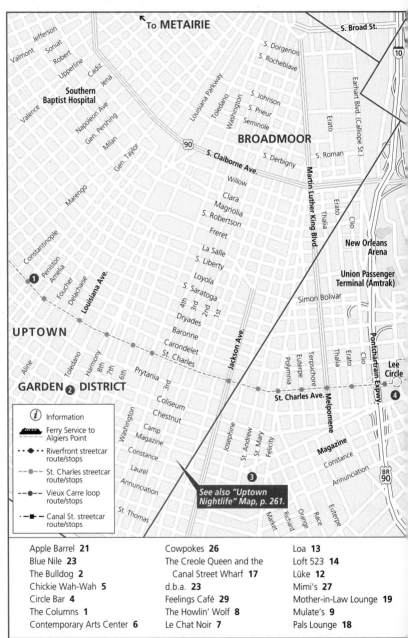

See also "Uptown Nightlife" Map, p. 261.

NEW ORLEANS AFTER DARK

11

JAZZ & BLUES CLUBS

Apple Barrel **21**	Cowpokes **26**	Loa **13**
Blue Nile **23**	The Creole Queen and the	Loft 523 **14**
The Bulldog **2**	Canal Street Wharf **17**	Lüke **12**
Chickie Wah-Wah **5**	d.b.a. **23**	Mimi's **27**
Circle Bar **4**	Feelings Café **29**	Mother-in-Law Lounge **19**
The Columns **1**	The Howlin' Wolf **8**	Mulate's **9**
Contemporary Arts Center **6**	Le Chat Noir **7**	Pals Lounge **18**

Map labels: To METAIRIE, S. Broad St., Jefferson, Valmont, Soniat, Robert, Upperline, Cadiz, Jena, Valence, Southern Baptist Hospital, Napoleon Ave., Gen. Pershing, Milan, Gen. Taylor, Marengo, Constantinople, Peniston, Amelia, Foucher, Delachaise, Louisiana Ave., S. Dorgenois, S. Rocheblave, Louisiana Parkway, Toledano, Washington, S. Johnson, S. Prieur, Seminole, BROADMOOR, S. Claiborne Ave., S. Derbigny, S. Roman, Willow, Clara, Magnolia, S. Robertson, Freret, La Salle, S. Liberty, Loyola, S. Saratoga, 4th, 3rd, 2nd, 1st, Dryades, Baronne, Carondelet, St. Charles, Prytania, Jackson Ave., UPTOWN, Aline, Toledano, Harmony, 8th, 7th, 6th, GARDEN DISTRICT, Coliseum, Chestnut, Camp, Magazine, Washington, Constance, Laurel, Annunciation, St. Thomas, Josephine, St. Andrew, St. Mary, Felicity, 3rd, St. Charles Ave., Melpomene, Terpsichore, Euterpe, Polymnia, Thalia, Clio, Erato, Simon Bolivar, Martin Luther King Blvd., Earhart Blvd. (Calliope St.), New Orleans Arena, Union Passenger Terminal (Amtrak), Lee Circle, Pontchartrain Expwy., Magazine, Constance, Annunciation, Richard, Orange, Race, Euterpe, Market

Legend:
- Information
- Ferry Service to Algiers Point
- Riverfront streetcar route/stops
- St. Charles streetcar route/stops
- Vieux Carre loop route/stops
- Canal St. streetcar route/stops

The Polo Lounge **15**
Ray's Boom Boom Room **24**
R Bar and Royal Street Inn **20**
The Saint **3**
Saturn Bar **25**
Snug Harbor **22**
Southern Repertory Theatre **16**

Swizzle Stick Bar **11**
Vaughan's Lounge **28**
Vic's Kangaroo Café **10**

Funky Pirate   Decorated to resemble a pirate's lair, the Funky Pirate lives up to its name—especially the "funky" part. The Pirate is as far from urbane modern jazz as you can get, so there's no chance you'll confuse it with the Funky Butt, should the latter ever return. The place seems to be perpetually full of loud beer drinkers, and at night it can get jampacked. "Big" Al Carson and the Blues Masters hold court here playing live blues, and Big Al lives up to his name—especially the "big" part. 727 Bourbon St. ✆ **504/523-1960.** www.tropicalisle.com. 1-drink minimum per set.

Irvin Mayfield's Jazz Playhouse ★★   The hyphenated Mayfield (trumpeter-bandleader-composer-cultural ambassador) recently opened this draperied, mid-sized room and outdoor patio in the venerable Royal Sonesta Hotel. It's the standing locale for the New Orleans Jazz Orchestra and also showcases established and up-and-coming jazz practitioners spanning the genre's spectrum, with occasional forays into cabaret and even burlesque. Mixing spangly chandeliers with comfy sofas, they're going for swank but not stuffy in bringing a fine addition to and a comfortable retreat from Bourbon Street. And if you didn't think milk and cookies went with clarinets, well, think again. They're served in cocktail glasses here. We'll take our Tollhouse straight, no chaser, please. 300 Bourbon St. ✆ **504/553-2299.** www.thenojo.com/jazz-playhouse.htm.

Maison Bourbon ★★   Despite its location and the sign saying the building is "dedicated to the preservation of jazz" (which seems a clear attempt to confuse tourists into thinking this is the legendary Preservation Hall), Maison Bourbon is not a tourist trap. The music is very authentic, and often superb, jazz. Stepping into the brick-lined room, or even just peering in from the street, takes you away from the mayhem outside. From about midafternoon until the wee hours, Dixieland and traditional jazz hold forth, often at loud and lively volume. Players include Wallace Davenport, Steve Slocum, and Tommy Yetta. Patrons must be at least 18 with ID. 641 Bourbon St. ✆ **504/522-8818.** 1-drink minimum.

Palm Court Jazz Cafe ★★   This is one of the most stylish jazz haunts in the Quarter. It's an elegant setting in which to catch top-notch jazz groups Wednesday through Sunday. The music varies nightly but is generally traditional or classic jazz. If you collect jazz records, peek at the records for sale in a back alcove. *Tip:* You should make reservations—it's that kind of place. 1204 Decatur St. ✆ **504/525-0200.** www.palmcourtjazzcafe.com. Cover $5 per person at tables; no cover at bar.

Preservation Hall ★★★   The gray, bombed-out building that looks as if it were erected just shortly after the dawn of time (or at least the dawn of New Orleans) doesn't seem like much, but it's a mecca for traditional-jazz fans. This is an essential spot for anyone coming to New Orleans. No amplification, no air-conditioning—it doesn't get any more authentic than this. It's not quite as dirt-cheap as it used to be, but it still is one of your must-do stops on your trip. After all, this place is so awesome, U2's Edge sat in for a set when in town working on his New Orleans music charity.

With no seats, terrible sightlines, and constant crowds, you won't be able to see much, but you won't care because you will be having too fun and cheerfully sweaty a time. Even if you don't consider yourself interested in jazz, there is a seriously good time to be had here, and you very probably will come away with a new appreciation for the music. Patrons start lining up at 6:15pm—the doors open at 8pm, so the trick to avoid the line is to get here either just as the doors open or later in the evening. The band plays until midnight, and the first audience usually empties out around 10pm.

The Abbey **38**

Apple Barrel **36**

Balcony Music Club **37**

Blue Nile **36**

The Bombay Club **3**

Bourbon House Seafood and
Oyster Bar **2**

The Bourbon Pub–Parade Disco **31**

Café Lafitte in Exile **28**

Carousel Bar & Lounge **8**

Chart Room **9**

Checkpoint Charlie's **35**

The Corner Pocket **14**

Coyote Ugly **12**

Crescent City Brewhouse **20**

Dickie Brennan's Steakhouse **7**

Donna's **18**

Fahy's Irish Pub **15**

The Famous Door **5**

French 75 Bar **4**

Fritzel's European Jazz Pub **31**

Funky Pirate **30**

Golden Lantern **33**

Good Friends Bar & Queens Head Pub **29**

House of Blues **11**

Irvin Mayfield's Jazz Playhouse **6**

Jimmy Buffett's Margaritaville
Cafe & Storyville Tavern **40**

Kerry Irish Pub **10**

Lafitte's Blacksmith Shop **32**

Le Petit Théâtre du Vieux Carré **26**

LeRoundup **16**

Mahalia Jackson Theater for
the Performing Arts **17**

Maison Bourbon **21**

Molly's on the Market **42**

Napoleon House Bar & Café **19**

One Eyed Jacks **25**

Orleans Grapevine Wine Bar & Bistro **24**

Oz **27**

Palm Court Jazz Café **41**

Pat O'Brien's **23**

Pravda **39**

Preservation Hall **22**

R Bar and Royal Street Inn **34**

Rawhide 2010 **13**

Saenger Theatre **1**

Snug Harbor **36**

A sign on the wall gives prices for requests—figure on $10 for "Saints Go Marchin' In," $5 for everything else. (One night some big spenders tossed seven $100 bills for seven rounds of "Saints.") Or just offer something. Thanks to the casual atmosphere, not to mention the inexpensive cover, Preservation Hall is one of the few nightspots where it's appropriate to take kids. Early in the evening you'll notice a number of local families doing just that. Call ahead for current open hours. 726 St. Peter St. & 888/946-JAZZ (946-5299) or 504/522-2841. www.preservationhall.com. Cover $8.

Snug Harbor ★★   If your idea of jazz extends beyond Dixieland and if you prefer a concert-type setting over a messy nightclub, get your hands on Snug Harbor's monthly schedule. On the fringes of the French Quarter (1 block beyond Esplanade Ave.), Snug Harbor is the city's premier showcase for contemporary jazz, with a few blues and R&B combos thrown in for good measure. Here, jazz is presented as it should be: part entertainment, part art, and often, part intellectual stimulation. It's all due to the late owner (who died suddenly in mid-2007), who never missed a show at the place to which he dedicated his life. His family vows to continue the place as he did, as a legacy. This is the surest place to find Ellis Marsalis (patriarch of the Marsalis dynasty) and Charmaine Neville (of the Neville family).

Not only does Snug offer good music, but the two-level seating also provides generally good viewing of the bandstand. (Beware the pillars upstairs, especially if you don't get seats along the rail and have to sit a way back, though.) You should buy tickets in advance, but be warned: Waiting for a show usually means hanging in the crowded, low-ceilinged bar, where personal space is at a minimum—not recommended for claustrophobes. 626 Frenchmen St. & 504/949-0696. www.snugjazz.com. Cover $12–$20, depending on performer. Doors open at 7pm; sets start at 8 and 10pm.

ELSEWHERE AROUND THE CITY

Worth keeping in mind is the unreliable but well-booked **Chickie Wah-Wah** (2828 Canal St.; ✆ **504/304-4714**). The owner seems to open only when he feels like it (though he has promised to turn his club into a po' boy shop during the day), which is both good—he only books acts of some significance, like Jazz Fest 2008's Sousapolooza, the first all-sousaphone jam session ever (at least that any of the big horn players could recall)—and bad—it means this small but excellent facility is only open erratically. It also tends to have high cover charges (around $20, though the later you go, the more likely it is you could get a discount). It's an easy streetcar ride from the Quarter, so if something is cooking there, consider attending.

Vaughan's Lounge   Tucked deep in the Bywater section of New Orleans, Vaughan's Lounge is way down-home—as in, it's in a residential neighborhood and feels almost as though you're in someone's house. The long bar takes up so much room that people almost fall over the band at the end of the room. Thursday—Kermit Ruffins's night—is the night to go to Vaughan's. Go early and get some of the barbecue Kermit is often cooking up before a show—he likes to barbecue as much as he likes to play, and he tends to bring his grill along with him wherever he is playing; you should call ahead and check. When he isn't playing and helping out with the eats, you might catch a Mardi Gras Indian practice. Thanks to the many post-Katrina volunteers around the Bywater area, Vaughan's has become a major scene even beyond its original NOLA role. Be sure to call ahead to see if there will be live music on—and be sure to take a taxi. 4229 Dauphine St. ✆ 504/947-5562. Cover varies, usually $8–$10.

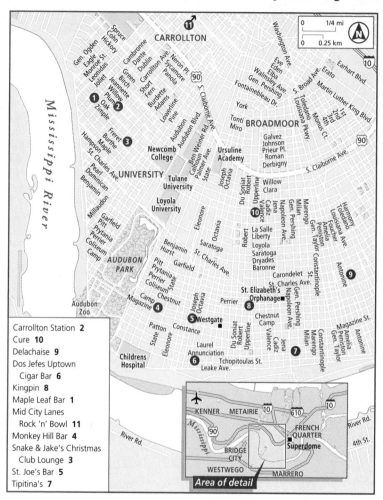

Carrollton Station **2**
Cure **10**
Delachaise **9**
Dos Jefes Uptown
  Cigar Bar **6**
Kingpin **8**
Maple Leaf Bar **1**
Mid City Lanes
  Rock 'n' Bowl **11**
Monkey Hill Bar **4**
Snake & Jake's Christmas
  Club Lounge **3**
St. Joe's Bar **5**
Tipitina's **7**

NEW ORLEANS AFTER DARK

11

CAJUN & ZYDECO JOINTS

3 CAJUN & ZYDECO JOINTS

Most of the so-called Cajun joints in New Orleans are really Cajun for tourists, in both sound and setting. If you want the real thing, you are better off going out to bayou country. Which is not to say some of the finest Cajun bands don't play in New Orleans—it's just that you are likely to find, say, the world-renowned Beausoleil at the Maple Leaf, or the up-and-coming Pine Leaf Boys at Tipitina's, neither of which is a Cajun club. None of this should be taken to mean that terrific and authentic Cajun bands don't play at the places listed below—it's just that it's hit-or-miss in terms of true quality. What these spots do offer, however, is a place to learn to Cajun dance, which is not only a skill that comes in handy in New Orleans (trust us, when crowds start to two-step, you'll want to join in) and a dandy way to burn off calories, but it's also just darn fun.

Mid City Lanes Rock 'n' Bowl ★★★   The spiffy, spacious new Rock 'n' Bowl—still in Mid-City but now located a few blocks less mid—no longer has the rough-hewn, er, patina of its former, circa 1941 locale. But if you like your lanes sans potholes and your dance floor big enough to seriously swing, you'll be happy as a split pick-up here. The combination of bowling, dancing, a full bar, and stellar live music—from zydeco to rockabilly to salsa and beyond—is an utter hoot and an unbeatable experience that draws all ages and ranks (though most evening shows are for the 21-and-older crowd). If it's cool enough for Keith Richards, it's cool enough for us. And if you're lucky enough to be there for one of their legendary Zydeco Wars—when the audience votes on whether, say, Geno Delafose or C.J. Chenier should wear the crown—you must abide and attend. We might have had to give up some of the fine funk of the old locale, but an improved menu, effective air-conditioning, and no restroom lines make for a fine trade-off, and if legendary proprietor John Blancher shows off his singular dance moves, more's the better. Consider splurging on a custom-embroidered bowling shirt—a splendid souvenir. 3000 S. Carrollton Ave. ✆ 504/861-1700. www.rockandbowl.com. Tues–Sat 5pm until "the party closes down." Bowling $20 per hour and a $1 shoe-rental fee; show admission $5–$20.

Mulate's ★   A not-unlikely place to find authentic, and decent, Cajun bands. The stage and dance area are relatively spacious, and the food isn't bad. During Jazz Fest 2006, when Beausoleil played, none other than Bob Dylan dropped by to listen! 201 Julia St., at Convention Center Blvd. ✆ 800/854-9149 or 504/522-1492. www.mulates.com.

4 RHYTHM, ROCK, BLUES & MORE

THE FRENCH QUARTER & THE FAUBOURG MARIGNY

Balcony Music Club ★   Might as well start your Frenchmen Street club hopping here, since it's right on your way (if you are walking from the Quarter) at the corner of Esplanade and Decatur, gateway to all things live. It's a good-size room for a corner bar and club, the booking policy includes DJs as well as local acts, and it makes for a tasty appetizer to your evening's multicourse musical feast. Live bands Wednesday through Sunday. 1331 Decatur St. ✆ 504/599-7770. Cover varies.

Checkpoint Charlie's   Somewhere between a biker bar and a college hangout, the dark Checkpoint Charlie's only *seems* intimidating—an effect that's helped by the hard-rock sounds usually blaring from the stage. It's easy to overlook straight rock with all the other New Orleans sounds around, but this would be the place to start trying to find it. R&B and blues also sneak into the mix as well as the occasional acoustic open-mic night. A full bar, food, and pool tables help soften the ambience for the easily intimidated, and it's open 24 hours, making it a less touristy place for a quick drink during the day. Plus, there's a coin laundry, so a dusty traveler can clean up while enjoying the music. And right across the street is a fire station known for its hunky firemen, who, on sultry nights, sit outside and admire the views. Admire them right back. 501 Esplanade Ave. ✆ 504/281-4847.

d.b.a. ★★★   It's been around long enough that its prefab yuppie patina has worn off, aging it into another excellent New Orleans bar. Better still, their live bookings are increasing in profile, with a wide variety of excellent local acts, including magnificent crooner John Boutte as a frequent performer, and a regular Tuesday night gig by the highly recommended New Orleans Jazz Vipers. It helps that when they say an act goes on at 7pm, it usually does. Early shows are often free, but get to the later shows early if you want to see the band, because the stage is set fairly low and the talkers at the bar can be loud. The list of 160 beers (best selection in the city), wines, and other drinks is most impressive. 618 Frenchmen St. (✆ **504/942-3731.** www.drinkgoodstuff.com/no. Cover varies.

House of Blues ★ New Orleans was a natural place for this franchise to set up shop, but its presence in the French Quarter seems rather unnatural. With all the great, funky, authentic music clubs in town, why build one with ersatz "authenticity" that wouldn't be out of place in Disneyland's Pirates of the Caribbean? And while it's noble that they've patronized many deserving Southern "primitive" artists to line the walls with colorful works, there's a certain Hearst Castle grab-bag element to that, too, which diminishes the value and cultural context of the individual works. That isn't to say the facility is without its good points. The music room has adequate sightlines and good sound, and the chain's financial muscle assures first-rate bookings, from local legends such as the Neville Brothers to such ace out-of-towners as Mos Def, Los Lobos, Marcia Ball, and Nanci Griffith. The nouvelle Orleans menu in the bustling restaurant also is high-quality, from a piquant jambalaya to fancy-schmancy pizzas. But patronizing this club rather than the real thing, like Tipitina's (which lost considerable business after the HOB opened), is akin to eating at McDonald's rather than Mother's. Having said all of that, a smaller room, the **House of Blues Parish,** features both local and national acts, and on any given day, probably offers more (for a cheaper price) than the big room. Checking the listings for the Parish along with the other recommended clubs is essential. 225 Decatur St. (✆ **504/529-2583.** www. hob.com. Cover varies.

Jimmy Buffett's Margaritaville Cafe & Storyville Tavern Yeah, Jimmy Buffett occasionally plays here, and yeah, they serve margaritas. Don't mind us if we sound grumpy; Buffett means well (isn't that practically his whole shtick as an artist?), but he took over a perfectly nice little jazz club (the Storyville Tavern, and by the way, it is not in or even all that near Storyville) and made it part of the brand-name takeover of the Quarter. Lineups are solid if unimaginative. There's no cover—they'll try to sell you food and merchandise instead. It's not as bad as, say, the Hard Rock Cafe, but still. 1104 Decatur St. (✆ **504/592-2565.** www.margaritaville.com.

One Eyed Jacks ★★ Still bearing the decor of its previous incarnation as the burlesque Shim-Sham Club (the flocked wallpaper looks straight out of *Pretty Baby*), Jack's seems at once hip nightspot and funky club, with its tiered main level, proscenium stage, and a crowded bar in the middle of the whole thing—all overlooked by a cozy balcony. The stepped setting and easy alcohol access pretty much invite people to fall on top of each other. Not that that's a bad thing. Bookings favor rock, alternative, and world music (such as Femi Kuti), with national and international touring acts in addition to eclectic and eccentric local faves, and, of course, '80s dance night and "rock 'n' roll karaoke," plus a fancy old-time burlesque show that tickles the locals. 615 Toulouse St. (✆ **504/569-8361.** www.oneeyedjacks.net. Cover varies.

Ray's Boom Boom Room ★★ A fine addition to the already terrific Frenchmen club scene, this long two-story room is the epitome of New Orleans style. Music covers the gamut, with acts on both the small stage near the street-facing window and on the larger stage at the back. Food is served all day long, everything from raw oysters to BBQ, though that's not the reason to go there. That there is no phone is frustrating, but it's still a good place to see a show and it's all part of the Frenchmen Street musical buffet. 508 Frenchmen St. No phone at press time. Daily 11am–"until." Cover varies.

ELSEWHERE AROUND THE CITY

Throughout this book, we keep nagging you to leave the Quarter. This advice is most important at night. It's not that there aren't some worthwhile, memorable clubs in the Quarter or at the fringes. It's just that there are so many terrific (and, in some cases, outright better) ones elsewhere. They aren't hard to find—any cabdriver knows where they are. And not only do they feature some of the best music in town (if not, on some nights, in the country), they also aren't designed as tourist destinations, so your experience will be that much more legitimate.

Carrollton Station ★★   Way uptown in the Riverbend area, Carrollton Station is a gourmet beer house that, thanks to some renovations to the room and the stage, is a prime folk, acoustic, and local rock venue in town. A long, narrow space means that folks at the back won't get to see much of what's up onstage, but hey, that puts them closer to the bar, so everyone wins. (Okay, not really. If you really want to see a band, come early to nab a spot near the front.) The crowd is a good mix of college students, music aficionados, and fans of whatever act is appearing on a given night. Bar opens 3pm daily; shows start usually around 10:30pm. 8140 Willow St. ℂ 504/865-9190. www.carrolltonstation. com. Cover varies on weekends. No cover weekdays.

The Howlin' Wolf ★   Pre-Katrina this was arguably the premier club in town in terms of the quality and fame of its bookings. The House of Blues might be sneaking back in place, but the Wolf's October 2005 move down the block and across the street has put it into an even better space, and great things should be on the horizon. The move was in the works during summer 2006, and given that the building next to their old one collapsed, the timing worked out in their favor. And with 10,000 square feet (quite a bit more than they used to have), including more restrooms, a wide but shallow room (which means great sightlines from about anywhere; sightlines are a problem in most New Orleans clubs), a bar that came from Al Capone's hotel in Chicago, and bookings that range from local acts to midlevel national touring rock bands, it's a good place to see a show. If you feel like a drive, they just opened another branch on the Northshore, in Mandeville, at 1623 Montgomery St. Doors at 9pm, shows at 10pm. 907 S. Peters St., in the Warehouse District. ℂ 504/522-WOLF (522-9653). www.thehowlinwolf.com. Cover varies.

Maple Leaf Bar ★★★   This is what a New Orleans club is all about, and its reputation was only furthered when it became the very first live music venue to reopen, just weeks after Katrina, with an emotional, generator-powered performance by Walter "Wolfman" Washington. It's medium-size but feels smaller when a crowd is packed in, and by 11pm on most nights, it is, with personal space at times becoming something you can only wistfully remember. But that's no problem. The stage is against the window facing the street, so more often than not, the crowd spills onto the sidewalk and into the street to dance and drink (and escape the heat and sweat, which are prodigious despite a high ceiling). You can hear the music just as well, watch the musicians' rear ends, and then dance some more. With a party atmosphere like this, outside is almost more fun than in. But inside is mighty fine. A good bar and a rather pretty patio out back (the other place to escape the crush) make the Maple Leaf worth hanging out at even if you don't care about the music on a particular night. But if the ReBirth Brass Band is playing, do not miss it; go and dance until you drop. 8316 Oak St. ℂ 504/866-9359. Cover varies.

Sunday School at Tipitina's

Besides its pedigree as one of the city's premier live music venues, Tipitina's also actively supports and enhances the local scene through its foundation and educational activities. At their Sunday afternoon music workshops, for example, music students can play and study with leading names such as Stanton Moore, Johnny Vidacovich, Kirk Joseph, and Theresa Andersson. This low-key scene, open to the public, offers a pretty cool opportunity to watch and listen as traditions are literally passed down.

Tipitina's ★★★   Dedicated to the late piano master Professor Longhair and featured in the movie *The Big Easy,* Tip's was long *the* New Orleans club. But due to circumstances both external (increased competition from House of Blues and others as well as the club's capacity being cut in half by city authorities) and internal (some gripes about pre-Katrina booking quality), its star has faded some. It remains a reliable place for top local bands, though, and if you can catch Troy Andrews or especially Dr. John on one of his excursions back to his city, it's a must.

The place is nothing fancy—just four walls, a wraparound balcony, and a stage, all of it overseen by a giant drawing of 'Fess his own self. Oh, and a couple of bars, of course, including one that serves the people milling outside the club, which as at other top locales is as much a part of the atmosphere as what's inside. Bookings range from top indigenous acts (a brass-bands blowout and a jazz piano night are the perennial highlights of Jazz Fest week) to touring alt-rock and roots acts, both U.S.-based and international. It's uptown and a bit out-of-the-way, but it's definitely worth the cab ride on the right night. A stop can make for a memorable experience. 501 Napoleon Ave. & 504/895-8477 or 897-3943 for concert line. www.tipitinas.com. Cover varies.

5 THE BAR SCENE

You won't have any trouble finding a place to drink in New Orleans. Heck, thanks to "go" (or *geaux*) cups, you won't have to spend a minute without a drink in your hand. (It's legal to have liquor outside as long as it's in a plastic cup. Actually, given the number of people who take advantage of this law, it almost seems illegal *not* to have such a cup in your hand.)

Bourbon Street comes off like a blocks-long bar—and smells like it, too. It's sort of pointless to single out any one drinking establishment there; not only are they ultimately all more or less similar, but their clientele also hardly varies. The crowd is simply moving down the street from one locale to the next. If we sound a bit scornful about drinking in New Orleans, it's because so many seem to treat a visit as nothing more than a license to get blotto, and the streets as one big place to regurgitate. Not only is this obnoxious, but there's also a lot more to this town.

Which is not to entirely dismiss drinking as a recreational activity (or, better still, as a sociological study). Certainly, New Orleans provides some of the most convivial, quaint, or downright eccentric spots to do so; in many cases, the places are worth going to even if you plan to imbibe nothing stronger than a soda.

Note that many of the clubs listed above are terrific spots to hoist a few (or a dozen), while some of the bars below also provide music—but that is strictly background for their real design. Many bars stay open all the time or have varying hours depending upon the night or the season. If you have your heart set on a particular place, it's always best to call and make sure what their hours will be for that day. Unless noted, none of the places listed below has a cover charge.

THE FRENCH QUARTER & THE FAUBOURG MARIGNY

In addition to the places below, you might consider the clubby bar at **Dickie Brennan's Steakhouse,** 716 Iberville St. (℃ 504/522-2467; p. 132), a place where manly men go to drink strong drinks inside, smoke smelly cigars outside on the street (they have a vast selection for sale, but don't allow smoking in the establishment), and chat up girlie girls. Or you could enjoy the low-key sophistication found at **Begue's at the Royal Sonesta,** 300 Bourbon St. (℃ 504/586-0300), where a jazz trio is usually playing.

The Abbey   Despite the name, this place is more basement rumpus room (walls covered with stickers and old album covers) than Gothic church (well, there are some motley stained-glass windows). But it's been a bar since the 1930s, the jukebox plays the Cramps and Iggy Pop and the Stooges' "I Wanna Be Your Dog," and the clientele is very David Lynchian (maybe still left over from the place's heyday 20-plus years ago!). Still, you might find this a scary dump rather than a cool dump. 1123 Decatur St. ℃ **504/523-7177.** Open 24 hr.

Apple Barrel   A small, dusty, wooden-floored watering hole complete with jukebox and darts (of course). You can find refuge here from the hectic Frenchmen scene (catch your breath and have a beer)—or gear up to join in, as they have live music (tending toward local blues acts like Coco Robicheaux) most nights. 609 Frenchmen St. ℃ **504/949-9399.**

The Bombay Club   This posh piano bar features jazz nightly. It's also a restaurant (the food is not great) and a martini bar—the drink has been a specialty here for years, so don't accuse the club of trying to ride the current martini trend. In fact, the Bombay's martinis are hailed by some as the best in town; they serve 125 different versions. The bar bills itself as casually elegant—a polite way of saying don't wear jeans or shorts. 830 Conti St. ℃ **800/699-7711** or 504/586-0972. www.thebombayclub.com.

Bourbon House Seafood and Oyster Bar ★★   Step up to this clean and convivial horseshoe-shaped bar not just for raw seafood but also house specialty drinks (some listed as "new-fashioneds"!) and the rest of its creative and clever cocktail menu. To cocktail purists, such beverages as an orange cosmo might seem like blasphemy, but we enjoyed the chef's thoughtful introduction of seasonal fruits into concoctions such as a delicious blueberry mojito. Naturally, they are deeply interested in bourbon (even if the street is named for the French royal family, not the liquor), whether straight up or in a frozen bourbon milk punch, and by the time you finish here, you might be, too. 144 Bourbon St. ℃ **504/522-0111.** www.bourbonhouse.com.

Carousel Bar & Lounge ★★   Piano music is featured here Wednesday through Saturday, but the real attraction is the bar itself—it really is a carousel, and it really does revolve ("and has been since 1949!" said a justly proud employee). The music goes on until 2am (or simply "until" these days). But don't think of this as a cheesy place: It's really a great spot to step back in time and have a cocktail—not a beer, of course, but a grown-up drink (with, unfortunately, grown-up prices, comparable to those found in New York City). A top choice for those not interested in Bourbon frat-party fun or even the young and the frenzied on Frenchmen Street. And if the bartender isn't busy or indifferent, they make a fine Sazerac, as well as their signature drink, the Vierre Carre Cocktail, created in the 1930s by the hotel's then-head bartender. In the Monteleone Hotel, 214 Royal St. © 504/523-3341.

Chart Room ★ One of the only bars on Chartres Street in the French Quarter. Dark and mysterious, this sometimes-seedy place is the perfect place to be left alone and escape the hustle and bustle of Bourbon Street. This place is popular with the local Quarter crowd. 300 Chartres St. © 504/522-1708.

Coyote Ugly The bar made famous by the movie (or at least the soundtrack to the movie), where comely female bartenders dance on the bar and hose down the rowdy patrons with water and liquid, has set up shop in the French Quarter. Like it needed another rowdy bar . . . like this kind of scene hasn't been happening (with boys) over at **the Corner Pocket** (p. 274), where they are at least honest that they are parading around for the dough. 225 N. Peters St. © 504/561-0003. www.coyoteuglysaloon.com/orleans.

Crescent City Brewhouse When this place opened in 1991, it was the first new brewery in New Orleans in more than 70 years, and now it's the place to go for microbrewery desires, including live jazz. 527 Decatur St. © 504/522-0571. www.crescentcitybrew house.com.

Pat O'Brien's & the Mighty Hurricane

Pat O'Brien's, 718 St. Peter St. (© 504/525-4823; www.patobriens.com), is world-famous for the gigantic, rum-based drink with the big-wind name. The formula (according to legend) was stumbled upon by bar owners Charlie Cantrell and George Oechsner while they were experimenting with Caribbean rum during World War II. The drink is served in signature 29-ounce hurricane lamp-style glasses. The bar now offers a 3-gallon Magnum Hurricane that stands taller than many small children. It's served with a handful of straws and takes a group to finish (we profoundly hope)—all of whom must drink standing up. Naturally, the offerings and reputation attract the tourists and college yahoos in droves. Some nights the line can stretch out the door and down the street, which seems quite silly given how many other drinking options there are mere feet away.

Which is not to say that Pat's isn't worth a stop—it's a reliable, rowdy, friendly introduction to New Orleans. Just don't expect to be the only person who thinks so. Fortunately, it's large enough to accommodate nearly everyone—in three different bars, including a large lounge that usually offers entertainment (an emcee and alternating piano players)—with the highlight, on nonrainy days at least, being the attractive tropical patio. Don't look there for quiet, though. The party-hearty atmosphere thrives in that section, and on pretty days, tables can be hard to come by.

Even if it is a gimmick, what trip to New Orleans is complete without sampling the famous Hurricane? There's no minimum and no cover, but if you buy a drink and it comes in a glass, you'll be paying for the glass until you turn it in at the register for a $3 refund.

Fahy's Irish Pub   One night we went looking for a bar with pool tables and you know what? New Orleans (or at least the Quarter) doesn't have a lot of 'em. So it was with relief we found Fahy's, a corner neighborhood pub (which attracts a pool-playin' crowd) that keeps its two tables in good condition. 540 Burgundy St. ℂ **504/586-9806.**

Feelings Cafe ★   Here's a funky, low-key neighborhood restaurant and hangout set around a classic New Orleans courtyard, which is where most folks drink—unless they are hanging out with the piano player, a currently every-other-Friday performer, with the occasional guest hitting the keys on other nights. (See p. 143 for the restaurant listing.) It's authentic in the right ways but is also more cheerful than some of the darker, hole-in-the-wall spots that deserve that adjective. Though it's a bit out-of-the-way in the Faubourg Marigny, everyone who goes there comes back raving about it. *Note:* The bar is open only Thursday through Sunday at 5pm; the balcony, with a pianist taking request, is open Fridays only. 2600 Chartres St. ℂ **504/945-2222.** www.feelingscafe.com.

French 75 Bar ★★   A beautiful bar space in one of the Quarter's most venerable restaurants, it feels like drinking in New Orleans should, in terms of classy presentation and atmosphere. Any dedicated cocktailian should come by to test the bartenders on their knowledge or to experiment with curious beverages. It's a great place to get a Sazerac or a Ramos Gin Fizz. In Arnaud's restaurant, 813 Bienville St. ℂ **504/523-5433.**

Kerry Irish Pub ★   This traditional Irish pub has a variety of beers and other spirits but is most proud of its properly poured pints of Guinness and hard cider. The pub is a good bet for live Irish and "alternative" folk music; it's also a place to throw darts and shoot pool. In case you want one last nightcap on your way back through the Quarter, you should know that Kerry specializes in very-late-night drinking. 331 Decatur St. ℂ **504/527-5954.** www.kerryirishpub.com.

Lafitte's Blacksmith Shop ★★   It's some steps away from the main action on Bourbon, but you'll know Lafitte's when you see it. Dating from the 1770s, it's the oldest building in the Quarter—possibly in the Mississippi Valley (though that's not documented)—and it looks it. Legend has it that the privateer brothers Pierre and Jean Lafitte used the smithy as a "blind" for their lucrative trade in contraband (and, some say, slaves they'd captured on the high seas). Like all legends, that's probably not true.

The owner managed to maintain the exposed-brick interior when he rescued the building from deterioration in the 1940s. At night when you step inside and it's entirely lit by candles (*Offbeat* magazine claims Lafitte's patented the word *dank*), the past of the Lafitte brothers doesn't seem so distant. (Unfortunately, the owner's penchant for treating good friends such as Tennessee Williams and Lucius Beebe to refreshments was stronger than his business acumen, and he eventually lost the building.) In other towns, this would be a tourist trap. Here, it feels authentic, though a renovation on the outside ended up falsifying the previous genuine plaster-and-exposed-brick look, turning it into something rather plastic in appearance. We still don't understand why. And for some reason, it's almost always easy to get into, even on a crowded Mardi Gras day. Definitely worth swinging by for atmosphere, but drink only beer; their mixed drinks appall cocktail aficionados. 941 Bourbon St. & 504/593-9761.

Mimi's   It looks and feels a bit like an L.A. club impresario's idea of a Marigny bar (that is, very clean, perfectly lit, not out of place in a New York hipster hotel that wanted a New Orleans–themed club). Then again, it's also what everyone wished would exist in the Marigny, a well-thought-out version of the (slightly divey, even if we do love it) R Bar. Having said that, for all the trends on parade (dreads, funny hats, and some attitude), the bar and employees are welcoming. And if you find our favorite New Orleans bars too shabby and run-down for comfort, we won't mind if you spend your time here. 2601 Royal St. ✆ **504/872-9865.**

Molly's on the Market ★★★   *The* hangout for boho and literary locals, who chew over the state of their world and their city, and who will get mad at us for broadcasting the location of their clubhouse. They consider it the best bar in the French Quarter. It's noted especially for being one of the only bars to remain open during Hurricane Katrina. Part eccentric English bar, and yet accessible enough to make it popular with firefighters and policemen, this place has a cool, East Village feel. Molly's also serves as the starting point for the French Quarter Halloween parade, a must-see should you happen to land in New Orleans during what many locals hail as the Second Biggest Party of the year. 1107 Decatur St. ✆ **504/525-5169.**

Napoleon House Bar & Café ★★★   Set in a landmark building, the Napoleon House is one of the best barrooms in the country, a must-do and just the place to go to have a quiet drink (as opposed to the very loud drinks found elsewhere in the Quarter) and maybe hatch some schemes. (See p. 141 for the restaurant listing.) Like Lafitte's (see above), it's dark, dark, dark, with walls you really wish could talk. Also like Lafitte's, it seems too perfect to be real—surely this must be constructed just for the tourists. It's not. Even locals like it here. You really should come here, and Lafitte's, too, for your token (if that's all it will be) New Orleans drink. Unless you need lights with your drinks as part of the fun. Be sure to try the Pimm's Cup. You might check their website for summer hours and vacation closures. 500 Chartres St. ✆ **504/524-9752.** www.napoleonhouse.com.

Orleans Grapevine Wine Bar & Bistro ★★   Now that *Sideways* has shown us all what a great big metaphor for life wine can be, come sample the possibilities off the staggering list at this quiet little refuge. 720 Orleans Ave. ✆ **504/523-1930.**

Pravda ★   Almost too high-concept and hip to tolerate, with its Soviet-era kitsch decor, it still is worth visiting, especially if you are curious about the return of absinthe. While other bars in town stock this once-banned liquor, this has a good selection of decent varieties, plus all the correct paraphernalia for drinking it. Just don't let them set it on fire, a silly party trick that was developed in the 1990s in Eastern Europe. 1113 Decatur. No phone at press time. www.myspace.com/pravdaofnola.

R Bar and Royal Street Inn ★★★   The R (short for Royal St.) Bar is a little taste of New York's East Village in the Faubourg Marigny. It is a quintessential neighborhood bar in a neighborhood full of artists, wannabe artists, punk-rock intellectuals, urban gentrifiers, and well-rounded hipsters. It's a talkers' bar (crowds tend to gather in layers along the bar) and a haven for strutting, overconfident pool players. On Mardi Gras Day this is also the headquarters for the locals described above—it's their designated meeting place and watering hole on Fat Tuesday. The R Bar has a large selection of imported beers and one of the best alternative and art-rock jukeboxes in the city. Thanks to all this (or perhaps in spite of some of it), it's just a cool little local bar. You'll see a sign behind the bar for the Royal Street Inn & R Bar, otherwise known as the R Bar Inn, a B&B (bed-and-beverage, that is). If you like the bar, you'll probably love the accommodations, too (p. 100). 1431 Royal St. ✆ **504/948-7499.** www.royalstreetinn.com.

ELSEWHERE AROUND THE CITY

In addition to those listed below, hang with the local beautiful people at any of the following (not one of which is particularly New Orleans–like, but that might come as a relief for Los Angeles refugees): **Loa,** the bar at the International House hotel, 221 Camp St., in the Central Business District (hotel review p. 106) is a hip and happening hangout with a very non–New Orleans (and yet, deeply attractive) atmosphere; it's a good place to meet a date, though bring a full wallet—it's not cheap. Hot on its heels for hipness and with a slightly higher energy level is the bar at **Loft 523,** a gorgeous and not particularly crowded space that beautifully shows off the old timbers that hold up this former warehouse. It often features terrific live music; for information on the hotel, see p. 104. Also, the bar at **Lüke** (333 St. Charles Ave.; © **504/378-2840**) is excellent, with an inspired cocktail list, but it's often hard to find a seat since it's part of the very busy restaurant (p.153).

The Bulldog ★ Don't let the name fool you. This local haunt has an incredible beer selection, and some of the best bar food in the city. Want a souvenir from New Orleans that is not from the French Quarter? Wednesday is Free Pint night. Both locations now have outdoor patios for sippin' your libations in the hot, muggy New Orleans evenings. 2 locations Uptown: 3236 Magazine St., © **504/891-1516;** and Old Metairie, 5135 Canal Blvd., © **504/488-4191.**

Circle Bar ★★ This tiny bar is among the most bohemian-hip in town, courtesy of the slightly twisted folks behind Snake & Jake's. Ambience is the key; it's got the ever-popular "elegant decay" look, from peeling wallpaper to a neon glow from an old K&B drugstore sign on the ceiling. The jukebox keeps the quirky romantic mood going, thanks to bewitching, mood-enhancing selections from the Velvet Underground, Dusty Springfield, and Curtis Mayfield. The clientele is laid-back. Live music includes mostly local acts. Bet you'll see us there. Bet we will be complaining about how late the acts come on, again. 1032 St. Charles Ave., in the CBD at Lee Circle. © **504/588-2616.** www.circle barnola.com.

The Columns ★★ Here's a local favorite for drinks on the white-columned porch under spreading oak trees. Why? Well, aside from the Old South setting, beers at happy hour are a measly $2, and mixed drinks are not much more, though the latter are only middling in quality. Watching a downpour from the safety of that classic veranda is rather on the awesome side. Inside, you will think you've stumbled onto the set of *Pretty Baby*—because, in fact, you have. The interiors were shot here, though it's gotten pretty worn since then. All that perfect New Orleans atmosphere may not make up for how one can be engulfed in cigarette smoke in the dark interior bar. 3811 St. Charles Ave., Uptown. © **504/899-9308.** www.thecolumns.com.

Cure ★★★ For a city that has played such a serious role in the history of the cocktail, it's frustratingly easy to get a bad drink in New Orleans. But this is changing rapidly, thanks to places like Cure. Located in a beautifully converted firehouse Uptown, it's one of the top destinations for serious cocktail enthusiasts, but don't let that intimidate you. The staff is friendly, very knowledgeable, and extremely enthusiastic about what they do, and will be more than happy to guide you through their menu, which ranges from their twists on the classics to refreshing originals to drinks that'll truly challenge what you've come to expect from a cocktail. Let them work their magic, and your palate will be slapped (in the best possible way). The food menu isn't to be missed—you can snack on a lovely plate of Spanish cured meats or devour the intensely delicious duck liver mousse crostini, or have a meal of *cochon de lait* panini or crab rolls. Thursday through Saturday evenings, Cure revives a New Orleans tradition we sorely miss: the dress code. Leave your shorts, sandals, and baseball caps at home. Come early Sunday through Wednesday to

commune with the bartenders, beat the bar-scene crowd, and enjoy what Neal Boden-
heimer and his talented crew have wrought—it's a gem in the city's drinking scene. 4905 Freret St., Uptown. ☎ 504/302-2357. www.curenola.com.

Delachaise ★★   A rare free-standing bar on its own little island on St. Charles, it's become best known for its terrific bar-food menu. But it's still first and foremost a bar—a long, lean, tin-ceilinged one, with a fine selection of whiskeys, gins, tequilas, rums, and vodkas, as well as an excellent beer and wine list and not a lot of seating for its size. 3442 St. Charles Ave. ☎ **504/895-0858.** www.thedelachaise.com.

Dos Jefes Uptown Cigar Bar   Dos Jefes has a post-college, young, yuppie-ish clientele (mostly men, it seems). The patio outside has banana trees and iron chairs, and it's nicer than inside—carpet and cigars are a bad combination. The bar has a good selection of beer on tap and piano music until midnight-ish Monday through Saturday. 5535 Tchoupitoulas St., Uptown. ☎ **504/891-8500.**

Kingpin ★★   For those who want that *Barfly* experience without the smelly drunks and in the company of other like-minded folks of a certain (20-something) age. Nominally Elvis-themed (though expect bashes on key dates in the timeline of Himself), this absurdly small space is increasingly popular among hipster/rocker/Dave Navarro types—when they can find it, that is. (***Hint:*** It's across from the Upperline restaurant and behind the market.) 1307 Lyons St., Uptown. ☎ **504/891-2373.**

Monkey Hill Bar ★   Sleaze is fun, but there are limits. This bar is part of a trend to convert seedy old taverns into places where you won't feel as if you have to wash your hands after you touch anything inside. Monkey Hill used to be an establishment called Sticky Fingers, which tells you a lot about the hand-washing requirements back then. It was also once a frat-boy bar, the mention of which sends many a local dreamily back to the time when they threw up here. Now it's really quite nice on the inside, and while we can do without the yuppie meat-market weekend scene, the rest of the time it has the best happy hour in town (though the drinks are only so-so in quality), which you can enjoy from comfy sofas and chairs. If you aren't a yuppie, you probably will wish it was still sleazy, but we've got other options for you. 6100 Magazine St. ☎ **504/899-4800.**

Mother-in-Law Lounge ★★   The sudden death of Ernie K-Doe's much-beloved widow, Antoinette, was a great loss to a city that cherishes its characters. Her relatives have vowed to keep her beloved bar going, as a tribute, but one never knows. We sure hope so. Named after K-Doe's biggest hit, a rousing 1961 number-one pop/R&B novelty, this is a true neighborhood dive bar, weird and wonderful, distinguished by the K-Doe memorabilia that lines the walls. K-Doe himself, in the form of a startlingly life-like mannequin, which has become a celebrity of sorts around town, still holds court among a cast that is straight out of a Fellini movie. You may want to be careful in the neighborhood, but once you're there, be sure to play one of K-Doe's songs on the jukebox and drink a toast to the man who billed himself as "Emperor of the Universe." And while you are at it, hoist one for Antoinette, a great and much-missed lady. Call first—hours are erratic (and often early). 1500 N. Claiborne Ave., northeast of the Quarter. ☎ **504/947-1078.** www.kdoe.com.

Pals Lounge ★★   This used to be a nondescript corner neighborhood bar called Yvonne's that was only open for a couple of hours in the afternoon. Now, well-heeled backers (including Rio Hackford, son of director Taylor) have turned it into a retro hipster bar, and are offering an alternative watering hole for the increasingly gentrified

St. John's Bayou neighborhood. As compensation to the working-class clientele who lost their old hangout, it sells Pabst Blue Ribbon for two bucks a can. Now you have vintage barflies mingling with the neighborhood bohos who come with their dogs or riding their bikes. It's too smoky for some, and it can be hard to find a seat. Then again, the place still flies below the tourist radar—which is part of the reason Jude Law and Sean Penn went here to drink while in town shooting *All the King's Men*. 949 N. Rendon St., Bayou St. John. ✆ **504/488-PALS** (488-7257).

The Polo Lounge ★★   The **Windsor Court** is probably the city's finest hotel (p. 104), and the Polo Lounge is the place to go if you're feeling particularly stylish. Sazeracs and cigars are popular here. Don't expect to find any kids; if you like to seal your deals with a drink, this is likely to be your first choice. But don't wear jeans lest you are turned away from the door. In the Windsor Court hotel, 300 Gravier St., in the CBD. ✆ **504/523-6000.**

The Saint ★   This dim, smoky (though sometimes so much so that one reluctant patron describes it as "like rolling around in an ashtray") spot is favored by local indie-rockers, or people with trust funds who like to imagine themselves as indie rockers. Having now snickered at the clientele, we can add that this former cruddy old tavern has been nicely cleaned up and is quite large for its genre. As such, it should satisfy your desire to hang out at a cool New Orleans bar. They can answer the phone, "Your wife's not here." 961 St. Mary St., Lower Garden District. ✆ **504/523-0050.**

St. Joe's Bar ★★   An agreeably dark (but not pretentious), nonseedy corner bar, this is a very typical New Orleans friendly, but not overbearing, place. Its Upper Magazine location means it's more neighborhood- than business-oriented. This may be the best typical New Orleans bar going right now; it has the right vibe without trying for the vibe at all, and it's not in the direct path of most tourists. Folk-art crosses hang from the (apparently) hammered tin ceiling, and the place is often seasonally decorated. At Halloween the cobwebs look as if they should be permanent. It has a sweet patio, a pool table, and a well-stocked jukebox with the likes of Ray Charles and the Grateful Dead. 5535 Magazine St., Uptown. ✆ **504/899-3744.**

Saturn Bar ★   Genuine barflies or just slumming celebs? It's so hard to tell when they are passed out in the crumbling (and we mean it) booths or blending in with the pack-rat collection that passes as decor. The Saturn Bar is among the hipster set's most beloved dives, but it's hard to decide if the love is genuine or comes from a postmodern, ironic appreciation of the grubby, art-project (we can only hope) interior. It must be seen to be believed. The irascible owner, already in failing health, died shortly after Katrina, but his family has vowed to carry on, even adding live bands a couple of times a week. Given the vibe, said bands are usually fairly wacky. They maybe even cleaned up the place a little, which, truth be told, it really did need. The neighborhood demands that caution be exercised—get someone to walk you to and from your car, especially if you are a woman alone. 3067 St. Claude Ave., in the Bywater. ✆ **504/949-7532.**

Snake & Jake's Christmas Club Lounge ★★   Though admittedly off the beaten path, this tiny, friendly dive is the perfect place for those looking for an authentic neighborhood bar. Co-owned by local musician Dave Clements, decorated (sort of) with Christmas lights, and featuring a great jukebox heavy on soul and R&B, this is the kind of place where everybody not only knows your name, but also your dog's name, 'cause you can bring the dog, too. There is almost no light at all, so make friends and be prepared to be surprised. Naturally, Snake & Jake's can get really hot, crowded, and sweaty—if you're lucky. 7612 Oak St., Uptown. ✆ **504/861-2802.** www.snakeandjakes.com.

Swizzle Stick Bar ★★   Part of Café Adelaide, in the Loews Hotel, this is a grown-up place to drink, but in the way that recognizes "grown-up" is not synonymous with "boring." It's a good place for a date, but also a place where you won't feel on display if you don't have a partner. This classy, busy bar jumps at night with locals and others who know that manager and bartender Lu is an increasingly famed mixologist. Try the bar's own Swizzle Stick cocktail (a playful cocktail made of New Orleans silver rum, bitters, and a "special ingredient"), or a perfect Sazerac, Sidecar, or even the infamous Corpse Reviver #2. There are also some rare pre-Prohibition classics on the menu. Can't decide? Get the "Trouble Tree," a metal holder containing various shots of everything. Bar is open from 7am usually until midnight and has its own special menu. 300 Poydras St., in the CBD. ⓒ **504/595-3305.**

Vic's Kangaroo Cafe   Really missing the brief Australia craze of the mid-'80s? Actually remember *Crocodile Dundee?* Drop by Vic's for a fix (or call; the last four digits of the phone number spell "g'day"). Despite the perplexing gimmick (how did Australian Vic land in New Orleans?), this is a friendly bar (and now with air-conditioning!) that caters to the local after-work crowd. Enjoy some shepherd's pie, wash it down with a sample of the nice selection of beers on tap, play a round of pool or darts, and generally have a—oh dear, we are going to say it—g'day. 636 Tchoupitoulas St., in the CBD. ⓒ **504/524-4329.**

6 GAY NIGHTLIFE

The gay and lesbian community is quite strong and visible in New Orleans, and the gay bars are some of the most bustling places in town—full of action nearly 24 hours a day. Though there are no strictly lesbian clubs in New Orleans, all gay bars are lesbian-friendly. Below you'll find listings of New Orleans's most popular gay nightspots.

For more information, you can check **Ambush,** 828-A Bourbon St. (ⓒ **504/522-8047;** www.ambushmag.com), a great source for the gay community in New Orleans and for visitors. Once you're in New Orleans, you can call the office or pick up a copy at Faubourg Marigny Art and Books (600 Frenchmen St.; ⓒ **504/947-3700**) or at any gay bar in the Quarter.

BARS

In addition to those listed below, you might also try the **Golden Lantern,** 1239 Royal St. (ⓒ **504/529-2860**), a nice neighborhood spot where the bartender knows the patrons by name. It's the second-oldest gay bar in town, and one longtime patron said that "it used to look like one half of Noah's Ark—with one of everything, one drag queen, one leather boy, one guy in a suit." If Levi's and leather is your scene, then **Rawhide 2010,** 740 Burgundy St. (ⓒ **504/525-8106;** www.rawhide2010.com), is your best bet; during Mardi Gras, it hosts a great gay costume contest that's not to be missed. The rest of the year, it's a hustler bar.

The Bourbon Pub–Parade Disco   This is more or less the most centrally located of the gay bars, with many of the other popular gay bars nearby. The downstairs pub offers a video bar and is the calmer of the two; it's open 24 hours daily and usually gets most crowded in the hour just before the Parade Disco opens. (***Note:*** Sun nights the cover charge gets you all the draft beer you can drink 5–9pm.) The Parade Disco is upstairs and features a high-tech dance floor complete with lasers and smoke. It usually opens around 9pm, except on Sunday, when it gets going in the afternoon. 801 Bourbon St. ℂ 504/529-2107. www.bourbonpub.com.

Café Lafitte in Exile This place is one of the oldest gay bars in the United States, having been around since 1953. There's a bar downstairs, and upstairs you'll find a pool table and a balcony that overlooks Bourbon Street. The whole shebang is open 24 hours. This is a cruise bar, but it doesn't attract a teeny-bopper or twinkie crowd. Monday nights they've started a campy movie event. 901 Bourbon St. ℂ 504/522-8397. www.lafittes.com.

The Corner Pocket While the boast that they have the hottest male strippers in town may be perhaps too generous, you can decide for yourself by checking out this bar nightly after 9pm. The bar itself is none too special (and despite the name, the only draw for the pool table is that players might not be especially clothed). The average age of the clientele is around 70. 940 St. Louis St. ℂ 504/568-9829. www.cornerpocket.net.

Cowpokes Looking for a gay country bar? Never let it be said that Frommer's lets you down. This is a particularly nice gay country bar, though it resides in a transitional neighborhood, so do let a cab bring you out for some of the weekly activities, including Saturday-night country line dancing and Fleur de Lis Divas Revue, the Sunday-afternoon drag revue. 2240 St. Claude. ℂ 504/947-0505. www.cowpokesno.biz.

Good Friends Bar & Queens Head Pub This bar and pub is very friendly to visitors and often wins the Gay Achievement Award for Best Neighborhood Gay Bar. The local clientele is happy to offer suggestions about where you might find the type of entertainment you're looking for. Downstairs is a mahogany bar and a pool table. Upstairs is the quiet Queens Head Pub, which was recently decorated in the style of a Victorian English pub. The bar is open 24 hours. 740 Dauphine St. ℂ 504/566-7191. www.goodfriendsbar.com.

LeRoundup LeRoundup attracts the most diverse crowd around. You'll find transsexuals lining up at the bar with drag queens and well-groomed men in khakis and Levi's. Expect encounters with working boys. It's open 24 hours. 819 St. Louis St. ℂ 504/561-8340.

DANCE CLUBS

Oz Oz is the place to see and be seen, with a primarily young crowd. It was ranked the city's best dance club by *Gambit* magazine, and *Details* magazine named it one of the top 50 clubs in the country. The music is great, there's an incredible laser-light show, and from time to time there are go-go boys atop the bar. 800 Bourbon St. ℂ 504/593-9491. www.ozneworleans.com. Cover varies.

7 THE PERFORMING ARTS

PERFORMING ARTS COMPANIES
Opera

It wasn't until 1943 that the **New Orleans Opera Association** (ℂ 504/529-2278; www.neworleansopera.org) was formed. They present several operas a season. Stars from New York's Metropolitan Opera Company frequently appear in leading roles, supported by talented local voices. The Met's touring company occasionally performs here, too. For most performances, seats start at $30.

The **New Orleans Ballet Association** (© 504/522-0996; www.nobadance.com) presents excellent dance programs and runs a much-lauded educational program. Visiting dance companies, including some top names, perform regularly. Check the newspapers for current performances. The ballet's season generally runs from September through April, though offerings have been more limited since Katrina.

Classical Music

The **Louisiana Philharmonic Orchestra** (© 504/523-6530; www.lpomusic.com) plays a subscription series of concerts during the fall-to-spring season and offers pops concerts on weekends in June and July; tickets start at $11. Performances take place at various locales ranging from a church to halls at Loyola and Tulane to the convention center.

THEATERS

Contemporary Arts Center   Located in the Warehouse District, the Contemporary Arts Center is best known for its changing exhibitions of contemporary art. Also on the premises are two theaters that frequently feature dance performances and concerts as well as experimental works by local playwrights. Call for the current schedule. 900 Camp St. © 504/528-3805. www.cacno.org.

Le Chat Noir ★★   This cool-cat, swanky, cabaret-style theater in the Warehouse District (with tables and candles) features rotating performances of a variety of entertainment: jazz, cabaret shows (think Broadway tunes), musical revues, and plays. They usually, but not exclusively, feature local talent (Thurs–Sun). They also have live piano music in their Bar Noir Tuesday through Sunday from 6pm. Prices run $5 to $21, depending on the act featured, and reservations are suggested. 715 St. Charles Ave. © 504/581-5812. www.cabaretlechatnoir.com.

Le Petit Théâtre du Vieux Carré ★ (Kids)   You may hear this place referred to as "The Little Theater in the French Quarter." It's home to one of the oldest nonprofessional theater troupes in the country. Throughout its season (early fall to late spring), the theater puts on a series of well-chosen and familiar musicals and plays. It's a community theater, but it might provide an appropriate family nighttime activity. 616 St. Peter St. © 504/522-2081. www.lepetittheatre.com.

Mahalia Jackson Theater for the Performing Arts   This cultural hub located in Armstrong Park bordering the French Quarter is home to the Louisiana Philharmonic Orchestra, the New Orleans Opera Association, and the New Orleans Ballet Association. Following a post-flood rehab with close attention paid to acoustics and lighting, the 2,100-seat theater's 2009 reopening gala featured performances by Itzhak Perlman, the New York City Ballet, and Placido Domingo. The handsome, bi-level theater also hosts Broadway touring companies, dance troupes, rock concerts, and other live acts. If you're considering mixing some highbrow into your visit, check the website to find out what's playing. 801 N. Rampart St. © 504/525-1052. www.mahaliajacksontheater.com.

Southern Repertory Theatre ★   The Southern Rep Theatre focuses on the works of Southern playwrights and actors. Located near the Canal Place movie theater, the Southern Rep is comfortable, intimate, and easily accessible from all downtown and French Quarter hotels. Expect to find productions by or (occasionally) about famous Southern playwrights (though not exclusively), projects by local playwrights, and even world premieres. Ample parking is available in the shopping center garage. Canal Place

8 AN EVENING CRUISE

The *Creole Queen* (ℂ **800/445-4109** or 504/524-0814; www.neworleanspaddlewheels. com), riverboat cruisers built in the tradition of their forebears, host lovely (if a bit touristy) Creole dinners and jazz cruises nightly. Departures are at 8pm (boarding at 7pm) from the Canal Street Wharf. The fare of $65 per person includes a sumptuous Creole buffet (it's $40 without the meal), and there's bar service as well as live jazz and dancing against a backdrop of the city's sparkling skyline. Schedules are subject to change, so call ahead to confirm days and times.

12

Plantation Homes & Cajun Country: Side Trips from New Orleans

If you have time (to us, that means an overall trip lasting more than 3 days), you should strongly consider a sojourn into the countryside around the city. Not only does it make for an interesting cultural and visual contrast, but all the areas discussed below are also hurting for tourism as much as New Orleans is. This chapter starts off by following the River Road and the plantation homes that line the banks of the Mississippi, heading upriver from New Orleans; the second part will take you a little more than 100 miles west of New Orleans to the heart of Acadiana, or Cajun Country.

How much time you devote to these trips depends on your schedule. On the River Road trip, you can see many of the highlights in a day trip, but it's quite possible to keep rambling north to visit the plantation homes in the St. Francisville area, an exploration that will call for an overnight stay. The Cajun Country trip requires an overnight, and you'll have no trouble filling the time if you can spend a few more days in the region.

1 PLANTATIONS ALONG THE GREAT RIVER ROAD

If your image of plantations comes strictly from repeated viewings of *Gone With the Wind,* you may well be disappointed when you go plantation hopping. That particular Tara was a Hollywood creation—indeed, in Margaret Mitchell's novel, Tara was quite different, a rambling structure of no particular style.

Plantation houses, at least the ones that are extant and open to public tours, are often more humble in scale (it wasn't until after 1850 that the houses got bigger, and most of these predate that). They also come in two models: the Creole style, which tends to be a low-slung, simple affair (Creoles preferring to keep the goodies on the inside where they can actually be enjoyed), and the American style, which is closer to classic antebellum grandeur. Nevertheless, these houses run smaller than you might think; even the "big" ones feel a bit cramped compared with certain lavish mansions built by turn-of-the-20th-century oil barons and today's nouveau riche. If your fantasies would be dashed without pillars and porticos, consider sticking to Destrehan, San Francisco, Oak Alley, and Madewood (see their listings under "Plantations Between New Orleans & Baton Rouge," below). Katrina had little to no impact on this area and it remains as picturesque as ever.

In the beginning the Creole planters of Louisiana were rugged frontier people. As they spread out along the Mississippi from New Orleans, they cleared swamplands with a mighty energy. Indigo, the area's first cash crop, had to be transported downriver to New

Orleans. Even as you drive on the modern highways that course through some of the bayous, you can easily imagine the challenges those early settlers faced.

In spite of all the obstacles, however, fields were cleared, swamps were drained, and crops were planted. Rough flatboats and keelboats were able to get the produce to market in New Orleans—if they weren't capsized by rapids, snags, sandbars, and floating debris, and if their cargoes weren't captured by bands of river pirates. These farming men (and a few extraordinary women) poled their boats to New Orleans, collected their pay for the journey, and then went on wild sprees of drinking, gambling, and brawling—behavior that gave the Creoles of the French Quarter their first (and lasting) impression of Americans as barbarians.

By the 1800s, Louisiana planters had introduced farming on a large scale, based primarily on their use of (and dependence on) slave labor. With cheap labor available, more and more acres went under cultivation. King Cotton, which proved to be a most profitable crop, arrived on the scene around this time. So did sugar cane, which brought huge monetary returns, especially after Etienne de Boré discovered the secret of successful granulation. Rice also became a secondary crop. But natural dangers risked disaster for planters: A hurricane could wipe out a whole year's work, and a swift change in the capricious Mississippi's course could inundate entire plantations. So, there were always small fortunes to be made in the area—and then lost.

THE RIVERBOATS   After 1812 the planters turned to a newly invented water vessel for speedier and safer transportation of their crops to the market. When the first of the steamboats (the *New Orleans,* built in Pittsburgh) chugged downriver belching sooty smoke, it was so dirty, dangerous, and potentially explosive that it was dubbed a "floating volcano."

Over a 30-year period, however, as vast improvements were made, the steamboats came to be viewed as veritable floating pleasure palaces. The need to move goods to market may have floated the boat, so to speak, but the lavish staterooms and ornate "grand salons" put a whole new face on river travel and made a profound change in plantation life. A planter and his wife, children, and slaves could now travel the river with ease and comfort; many set up dual residences and spent the winters in elegant town houses in New Orleans. After months of isolation in the country, where visitors were few, the sociability of the city—with its grand balls, theatrical performances, elaborate banquets, and other entertainment—was a welcome relief. Also, it became possible to ship fine furnishings upriver to plantation homes, allowing the planters to enjoy a more comfortable and elegant lifestyle in the fields.

The riverboats did have a darker side, however. Along with families, merchants, peddlers, and European visitors, the boats were the realm of some cunning and colorful characters: the riverboat gambler and "confidence" (or "con") man. Plantation owners were drawn like magnets to the sharp-witted, silver-tongued professional gamers, crooks, and cranks. Huge fortunes were won and lost on the river, and more than a few deeds to plantations changed hands at the table on a river steamboat.

BUILDING THE PLANTATION HOUSES   During this period of prosperity, from the 1820s until the beginning of the Civil War, most of the impressive plantation homes were built. It was also during this time that many of the grand town houses in cities like New Orleans and Natchez were erected.

The plantation home was the focal point of a self-sustaining community and generally was located near the riverfront; it may have been graced with a wide, oak-lined avenue

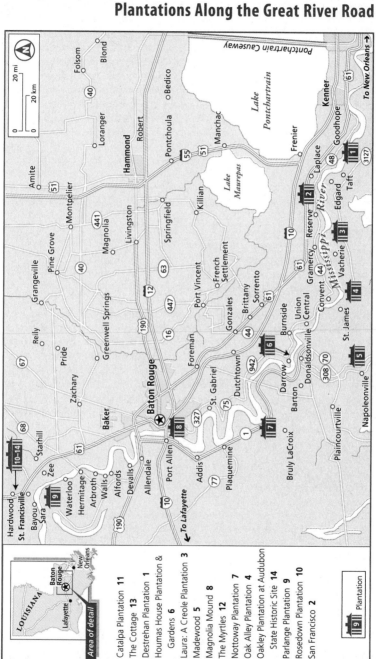

Catalpa Plantation 11
The Cottage 13
Destrehan Plantation 1
Houmas House Plantation & Gardens 6
Laura: A Creole Plantation 3
Madewood 5
Magnolia Mound 8
The Myrtles 12
Nottoway Plantation 7
Oak Alley Plantation 4
Oakley Plantation at Audubon State Historic Site 14
Parlange Plantation 9
Rosedown Plantation 10
San Francisco 2

leading from its entrance to a wharf (though some were much more modest). On either side of the avenue would frequently be *garçonnieres* (much smaller houses, sometimes used to give adolescent sons and their friends privacy or as guesthouses for travelers who stopped for a night's lodging). Behind the main house the kitchen was often separate from the house because of the danger of fire, and the overseer's office was almost always close enough for convenience. Some plantations had, behind these two structures, pigeon houses or dovecotes—and all had the inevitable slave quarters, usually in twin lines bordering a lane leading to cotton or sugar-cane fields. When cotton gins and sugar mills came along, they were generally built across the fields, out of sight of the main house.

When the main houses were first raised, they were much like the simple "raised cottage" known as Madame John's Legacy on Dumaine Street in New Orleans (p. 179)—with long, sloping roofs; cement-covered brick walls on the ground floor; and wood-and-brick (brick between posts) construction in the living quarters on the second floor. These structures suited the sultry Louisiana climate and swampy building sites and made use of native materials. Houses of the colonial period in this region were distinctly influenced by styles from the West Indies, very different from the grander revival styles that followed in the 1800s.

In the 1820s, homes that combined traces of the West Indian style with some Greek Revival and Georgian influences—a style that has been dubbed Louisiana Classic—began to appear. Large, rounded columns usually surrounded the main body of the house, wide galleries reaching from the columns to the walls encircled upper floors, and the roof was dormered. The upper and lower floors consisted of four large rooms (two on either side) flanking a wide central hall. They were constructed of native materials, with a few imported interior details such as fireplace mantels. There were no stone quarries in Louisiana; if stone was used (which wasn't very often), it had to be shipped by sea from New England and transported up the Mississippi River from New Orleans. Because the river flowed through banks of clay, however, bricks could be made on the spot. Cypress, too, was plentiful, and it did well in the hot, humid climate, which could quickly rot other woods. To protect the homemade bricks from dampness, they were plastered or covered with cement. Sometimes the outer coating was tinted, although more often it was left to mellow to a soft off-white. The columns were almost always of plastered brick and very occasionally of cypress wood; the capitals were of these materials or, rarely, of iron.

GRAND & GRANDER By the 1850s many planters were quite prosperous, and their homes became more grandiose. Many embraced extravagant Victorian architecture and gave it a unique Louisiana flavor; others tended to borrow from the features of northern Italian villas, and some plantation homes followed Gothic lines (notably the fantastic San Francisco plantation, sometimes called "steamboat Gothic"; p. 283). Planters and their families traveled to Europe more frequently during this period, and they brought back ornate furnishings. European masters were imported for fine woodworking until Louisiana artisans such as Mallard and Seignouret developed skills that rivaled or surpassed the Europeans. Ceilings were adorned with elaborate medallions from which glittering crystal chandeliers hung, and on wooden mantels and wainscoting, the art of *faux marbre* (false marble) began to appear. The wealthiest plantation owners were determined to make their country homes every bit as elegant as their New Orleans town houses.

Plantation houses also expanded in size over time, with some coming to have as many as 30 or 40 rooms. Families were quite large, and social life in the country consisted of visits from neighbors or friends who might stay several days or weeks. After all, travel was difficult; there was very little dropping by or popping in during those times. And certainly a Louisiana version of keeping up with the Joneses had its place as well: The Madewood house on Bayou Lafourche was built for no other reason than to outshine Woodlawn, the beautiful home of the builder's brother (unfortunately, not open to the public).

The planters' enormous wealth stemmed from an economy based on human servitude. The injustice and frequent cruelty of slavery, however, were the seeds of its own demise. Whether or not the issue of slavery caused the Civil War, it soon became a central target of the Union effort. When emancipation came, it had an inestimable effect on plantations all across the South. Farming as it had been practiced on the plantations was impossible without that large, cheap labor base. During Reconstruction, lands were often confiscated and turned over intact to people who later proved unable to run the large-scale operations; many were broken up into smaller, more manageable farms. Increasing international competition began to erode the cotton and sugar markets that had built the planters' large fortunes. The culture represented by the few houses that remain today emerged and died away in a span of less than 100 years.

THE PLANTATION HOUSES TODAY   Where dozens of grand homes once dotted the landscape along and around the river, relatively few now remain. Several houses that survived the Civil War have since fallen victim to fires or floods, and some have been torn down to make way for other things such as industrial plants. Others, too costly to be maintained, have been left to the ravages of dampness and decay. A few, however, have been saved, preserved, and treated to the installation of modern conveniences such as plumbing and electricity. Most of the old houses are private residences, but you can visit others for an admission fee (which, in some instances, supplements the owner's own resources to keep up the old house).

Tours of plantations are a hit-or-miss affair—much depends on your guide—and if you visit several, you'll begin to hear many of the same facts about plantation life after a while. The problem is that often the history of the house in question is lost in time, or it never had a particularly good story to begin with; consequently, other details, like the practicalities of plantation living, have to be thrown in to fill out a tour. The exceptions are mostly noted below.

PLANNING YOUR TRIP

All the plantation homes shown on the map on p. 279 are within easy driving distance of New Orleans. How many you can tour in a day will depend on your endurance behind the wheel, your walking stamina (you'll cover a lot of ground touring the houses), how early you set out, how many of the same details you can stand to hear repeated, and how late you want to return (the small highways get a little intimidating after dark). You'll be driving through some ravaged countryside—this is oil- and chemical-company country now—though you will probably see more sugar cane than you've seen in your entire life. Also, don't expect to enjoy broad river views as you drive along the Great River Road (the name of the roadway on *both* sides of the Mississippi); you'll have to drive up on the levee for that. You will, however, pass through little towns that date from plantation days, and you'll have the luxury of turning off to inspect interesting old churches or aboveground cemeteries.

If you have minimal time, we suggest viewing just the Laura and Oak Alley plantations (see below); they are just a mile apart, and each offers a different perspective on plantation life (Laura being classic understated Creole, while Tara-esque Oak Alley represents the showy Americans) and the tourism industry (Oak Alley is slick and glitzy, while Laura is more low-key but a superb presentation). Both are approximately an hour's drive from New Orleans.

If you're in New Orleans on **Christmas Eve,** consider driving along the River Road to see the huge bonfires residents build on the levees to light the way for the Christ Child and Papa Noël (who rides in a sleigh drawn by—what else?—eight alligators!). They spend weeks collecting wood, trash, and anything else flammable to make the fires blaze brightly—and often explode with fireworks.

Not all Louisiana plantations actually bordered the Mississippi River (many were on bayous that also provided water transportation), and some of the grand old homes are too far away from New Orleans to be visited in a single day. These are listed separately with the recommendation that you try to stay overnight at one that offers the option. There are also listings for lodgings in St. Francisville, later in this chapter, which can serve as a convenient plantation-tour base.

ORGANIZED TOURS

A plantation-house bus tour is a stress-free way to visit the River Road region from New Orleans (someone else does the planning and deals with directions and tricky turns), though most of the tours visit only one or two of the houses described below. In general, tour guides are well informed, and the buses are an easy, comfortable way to get around in unfamiliar territory. Almost every New Orleans tour company operates a River Road plantation tour.

The 4½-hour tours offered by **Gray Line** (*©* **800/535-7786** or 504/569-1401; www.graylineneworleans.com) are a reliable choice. The tours (available by appt.) visit either of two plantations, Oak Alley or Laura. The $49 price ($21 for children 6–12) includes admission fees. Tours depart at noon on Monday, Wednesday, Friday, and Saturday from June to September, and at 12:30pm the rest of the year.

If you prefer a smaller tour group, **Tours by Isabelle** (*©* **888/223-2093** or 504/391-3544; www.toursbyisabelle.com) takes up to 13 people in a comfortable van on an 8-hour expedition to visit Oak Alley and Laura plantations. The cost ($136) includes lunch at Oak Alley's restaurant. The tour runs only when six or more people request it, so you might have to wait a day or two for a large enough group. Other tours by Isabelle, which are also subject to such a restriction, include a 4½-hour Cajun Bayou Tour for $65 (the boat tour is 1½ hr.), the 5½-hour Westbank Plantation Tour for $76 (which includes guided tours of Oak Alley and Laura Plantation and stops in front of Whitney, Josephine, and Evergreen plantations), and the Ultimate Combination Tour ($175 per person), which takes visitors to the Cajun village of Lafitee for a ride on a high-speed airboat, followed by a guided tour of Houmas House Plantation, a Greek Revival antebellum mansion lovingly restored. Lunch is included in this tour, and is followed by a drive along the levee to view three other plantations.

PLANTATIONS BETWEEN NEW ORLEANS & BATON ROUGE

The plantations below are listed in the order in which they appear on the map, running along the Mississippi north, out of New Orleans. Many people choose one or two homes—Oak Alley, Nottoway, Laura, and Madewood are popular ones—and find the quickest route (get a good map). If you choose to follow the route along the riverbanks, know that you will have to cross the Mississippi a few times to see every plantation; there is a bridge just downriver from Destrehan, and one between San Francisco and Laura plantations. The river does wind, so distances along it are deceiving; give yourself more time than you think you'll need to arrive at your destination. All the plantations discussed in this section are roughly 1 hour from New Orleans and approximately 15 minutes from each other.

Note: Unfortunately, **Tezcuco Plantation** was completely destroyed by fire in May 2002. The 147-year-old plantation home was built by Benjamin Tureaud in 1855 and was named after a lake not far from Mexico City. The word *tezcuco* means "resting place." For more information, go to www.cr.nps.gov/nr/travel/louisiana/tez.htm.

Destrehan Plantation ★★   An appearance in *Interview with the Vampire,* not to mention its proximity to New Orleans (perhaps 30 min. away), has made Destrehan Manor a popular plantation jaunt. It's also the oldest intact plantation home in the lower Mississippi Valley open to the public. It was built in 1787 by a free person of color for a wealthy Frenchman and was modified between 1830 and 1840 from its already dated French colonial style to Greek Revival. Its warmly colored, graceful lines should please nearly everyone's aesthetic sensibilities. In addition to playing the role of Louis's ancestral home in *Interview,* it also supplied some later interiors.

The tour, led by costumed guides who stay in character (it's better than it sounds), is worth taking. The house stayed in the original family's possession until 1910 (some female descendants are still on the board that oversees the place), so a fair amount is documented, and some of the furnishings (including a table used by Lafayette) are original. One of the rooms has been left deliberately unrenovated, and its messy deconstructed state shows you the humble rawness under the usual public grandeur. *Important note:* This is perhaps the only plantation that is truly accessible for those with disabilities; there is an elevator to take wheelchairs up to the second floor (where the true living spaces are located).

Destrehan Plantation holds a fall festival each November featuring arts and crafts vendors, antiques dealers, Cajun Creole food, and live music, along with tours of the plantation house.

13034 River Rd., La. 48 (P.O. Box 5), Destrehan, LA 70047. ⓒ **877/453-2095** or 985/764-8758. www. destrehanplantation.org. Admission $15 adults, $5 children 6–16, free for children 5 and under. Daily 9am–4pm. Closed New Year's Day, Mardi Gras, Easter, Thanksgiving, and Dec 24–25.

San Francisco ★   This fanciful mansion, a brightly colored creation known as steamboat Gothic, is a farther schlep from Destrehan (its closest neighbor) than it seems on the map. But it's worth the trip if you want to see something other than a cookie-cutter plantation home. Located 2 miles north of Reserve, the house was built between 1853 and 1856 by Edmond B. Marmillion. Unfortunately, Marmillion died shortly after its completion and never occupied the home, which was willed to his sons, Valsin and Charles. In 1855, while on a grand tour of Europe, Valsin met and married Louise Seybold. Valsin and Louise undertook decorating the home in high style, and when they were finished, Valsin jokingly declared to his friends that he was *sans fruscin,* or "without a cent" to his name. This is how the plantation home gained its first name, St. Frusquin. When Achille Bougère bought the estate, the name was changed to San Francisco.

The three-story Gothic house has broad galleries that look for all the world like a ship's double decks, and twin stairs lead to a broad main portal much like one that leads to a steamboat's grand salon. Novelist Frances Parkinson Keyes visited the house and used it as the setting for her novel *Steamboat Gothic.* Inside, the owner created beauty in every room through the use of carved woodwork and paintings alive with flowers, birds, nymphs, and cherubs on walls and ceilings of cypress tongue-and-groove boards.

2646 Hwy. 44, Garyville, LA 70051. © **888/509-1756** or 985/535-2341. www.sanfranciscoplantation.org. Admission $15 adults, $14 military with ID and AAA members, $7 children 7–17, free for children 6 and under. Daily Apr–Oct 9:30am–5pm, tours start at 9:40am and last tour at 4:40pm; Nov–Mar 9am–5pm, tours start at 10am and last tour at 4pm. Closed New Year's Day, Mardi Gras, Easter, Thanksgiving Day, and Dec 24–25.

Laura: A Creole Plantation ★★★

If you see only one plantation, make it this one. Laura is the very model of a modern plantation—that is, when you figure that today's crop is tourism, not sugar cane or indigo. And it's all thanks to the vision of developer and general manager Norman Marmillion, who was determined to make this property rise above the average antebellum mansion. The hoop-skirted tours found elsewhere are banished in favor of a comprehensive view of daily life on an 18th- and 19th-century plantation, a cultural history of Louisiana's Creole population, and a dramatic, entertaining, in-depth look at one extended Creole family.

This is a classic Creole house, simple on the outside but with real magic within. Unlike many other plantation homes, much is known about this house and the family that lived here, thanks to extensive records (more than 5,000 documents researched in France), particularly the detailed memoirs of Laura Locoul (for whom the plantation is named). On display are more than 375 original artifacts, making this the largest collection in the region of items belonging to one plantation family. They cover a 200-year period and include household items like clothes and jewelry. The property itself is a labor of love, as all of the outbuildings are slowly being renovated (next up, the slave quarters).

Sadly, a huge fire hit the plantation on August 8, 2004. Employees worked hard and saved many artifacts, and a significant portion of the original house survived. Tours continued the very next morning, and renovation ultimately turned a disaster into opportunity. During the restoration, which was completed last year, they returned the house to the 1805 period, with new accurate details. They also added Louisiana-made furniture to replace lost dining room furniture and other destroyed fixtures. But they've also been able to acquire more original contents of the house. Naturally, all of this is detailed in the tour. Basic tours of the freshly gorgeous main building and the property start every 20 minutes and last about 70 minutes and are organized around true (albeit spiced-up) stories from the history of the home and its residents. (*Of special note:* The stories that eventually became the beloved B'rer Rabbit were first collected here by a folklorist in the 1870s.) Special tours are available on subjects including Creole architecture, Creole women, children, slaves, and the "Americanization of Louisiana." The special tours last about 1½ hours and must be scheduled in advance. They offer tours in both English and French (Tues and Sat only) and have handouts in several additional languages. *Note:* To learn about Laura's family's life in the big city of New Orleans, go on the **Le Monde Creole** tours (p. 205).

2247 La. 18, Vacherie, LA 70090. © **888/799-7690** or 225/265-7690. www.lauraplantation.com. Admission $15 adults, $13 for military and AAA members, $5 children 6–17, free for children 5 and under. Daily 10am–4pm. Last tour begins at 4pm. Closed Jan 1, Mardi Gras, Easter, Thanksgiving, and Dec 25.

Oak Alley Plantation ★★★

This is precisely what comes to mind when most people think "plantation." A splendid white house, its porch lined with giant columns, approached by a magnificent drive lined with stately oak trees—yep, it's all here. Consequently, this is the most famous (and probably most photographed) plantation house in Louisiana. (Parts of *Interview with the Vampire* and *Primary Colors* were shot here.) It's also the slickest operation, with a large parking lot, an expensive lunch buffet (bring your own picnic), hoop-skirted guides, and golf carts traversing the blacktopped lanes around the property. It's an interesting contrast with Laura (see above), and they are just a mile apart, so we highly recommend that you visit both.

The house was built in 1839 by Jacques Telesphore Roman III and was named Bon Séjour—but if you walk out to the levee and look back at the ¼-mile avenue of 300-year-old live oaks, you'll see why steamboat passengers quickly dubbed it "Oak Alley." Roman was so enamored of the trees that he planned his house to have exactly as many columns—28 in all. The fluted Doric columns completely surround the Greek Revival house and support a broad second-story gallery. Oak Alley lay disintegrating until 1914, when Mr. and Mrs. Jefferson Hardin of New Orleans bought it. Then, in 1925, it passed to Mr. and Mrs. Andrew Stewart, whose loving restoration is responsible for its National Historic Landmark designation.

Little is known about the families who lived here; consequently, tours focus on more general plantation facts. Over the last few years, renovations have given the rooms and furnishings a face-lift, returning the house to its 1830s roots, and though the furnishings are not original, they are strict to the time period and mostly correspond to the Romans' actual inventory. The plantation hosts two arts and crafts fairs annually, one in April, the other in October, as well as a bonfire party in December.

Overnight accommodations are available in five really nice century-old Creole cottages (complete with sitting rooms, porches, and air-conditioning). Rates are $130 to $175 and include breakfast but not a tour. The overpriced restaurant is open for breakfast and lunch daily from 8:30am to 3pm.

3645 La. 18 (60 miles from New Orleans), Vacherie, LA 70090. ⓒ **800/44-ALLEY** (442-5539) or 225/265-2151. www.oakalleyplantation.com. Admission $15 adults, $7.50 students 13–18, $4.50 children 6–12, free for children 5 and under. Mon–Fri grounds open daily at 9am; tours begin every half-hour at 10am; Mon–Fri last tour at 4pm, Sat–Sun tours until 5pm. Closed Jan 1, Thanksgiving, and Dec 25.

Madewood ★★ This imposing house, a two-story Greek Revival on Bayou Lafourche, just below Napoleonville, is one of the best-preserved plantation mansions and is the place to fulfill your own plantation dreams—literally. The overnight accommodations, unlike those offered by other plantation homes, are in the main house, allowing you and the other guests a chance to run around the 20 rooms at night, pretending it's yours, all yours. When you hear the recent history, however, you might be rather glad it's not.

A youngest brother originally built Madewood for the sole purpose of outdoing his older brother's elegant mansion, Woodlawn. Four years were spent cutting lumber and making bricks, and another four were spent in actual construction. It was finally completed in 1848, but the owner never got to gloat over his brother—he died of yellow fever just before it was finished. As with many of the grand plantation homes, Madewood fell into disrepair and stood empty for a while until it was bought in 1964 by the parents of the present owner, Keith Marshall. When you hear the stories and see the photos of the laborious renovation (done in large part by the Marshalls and their friends), you realize how much work it is to save, and then continue to keep up, these glorious houses.

If you do **stay overnight,** you'll get the run of the place in the evening as well as grand canopied or half-tester (curtains at the head end) beds, wine and cheese in the library, a multicourse dinner of Southern specialties (served by a charming woman whose family has worked at Madewood for seven generations; be sure to chat with her), brandy in the parlor, and coffee in bed the next morning followed by a full plantation breakfast. Now that's gracious Southern living. If you're lucky, Marshall and his wife, Millie Ball, will join you and share their stories. Rates are $259 for two Sunday through Thursday, $289 Friday and Saturday. Rooms in the elegant 1820s raised cottage are more secluded with fewer formal furnishings. A bronze plaque in one tells you that Brad Pitt slept there while filming *Interview with the Vampire*. Other celebrities make this a getaway spot.

4250 La. 308, Napoleonville, LA 70390. ✆ **800/375-7151** or 985/369-7151. Fax 985/369-9848. www. madewood.com. Admission $10 adults, $6 students and children 11 and under. Daily 10am–4pm. Closed Dec 31, Jan 1, Thanksgiving, and Dec 25.

Houmas House Plantation & Gardens ★★
This is a different sort of plantation house in that it is actually two houses joined together. The original structure was a mere four rooms built in 1775. In 1828 a larger, Greek Revival–style house was built next to it, and some time over the subsequent years a roof was put over both, joining them together. The property, a former sugar plantation, has had multiple owners and little is known about them. The late Dr. George Crozat of New Orleans purchased the house some years ago and restored it as a comfortable home for himself and his mother, bringing in authentic period furnishings. Two of his nieces lived until 2003 on the third floor. Recent owner Kevin Kelly now lives there, and the place reflects the feel of an active home, which makes a difference.

Live oaks, magnolias, and beautifully landscaped formal gardens frame Houmas House in a way that is precisely what comes to mind when most of us think "plantation house." It so closely fits this image that its exterior was used in the film *Hush . . . Hush, Sweet Charlotte*. The inside has been lovingly brought back to early 1800s detail from when the house was completed, including period-accurate touches such as paint colors, 19th-century paintings, antique rugs, and several unexpected exquisite touches. Costumed guides deliver stories from the house's busy past. Because scenes from *All My Children* were shot here, be sure to ask for those Susan Lucci stories (they've got 'em). There is also a cafe, and a restaurant touted by *Esquire* magazine as one of the best in the country.

40136 La. 942, Burnside (58 miles from New Orleans; mailing address: 40136 Hwy. 942, Darrow, LA 70725). ✆ **888/323-8314** or 225/473-9830. Fax 225/473-7891. www.houmashouse.com. Admission (including guided tour) $20 adults, $15 children ages 13–18, $10 children ages 6–12, free for children 5 and under; gardens and grounds only $10. Year-round Mon–Tues 9am–5pm, Wed–Sun 9am–8pm. Closed Dec 25 and Jan 1. Take I-10 from New Orleans or Baton Rouge. Exit on La. 44 to Burnside and turn right on La. 942.

Nottoway Plantation ★★
There are two reasons to come to this particular plantation. The first is the house itself, dating from 1858, the largest existing plantation house in the South, a mammoth structure with 64 rooms (covering 53,000 sq. ft.), an opening (window or door) for every day in the year, and pillars that could challenge those holding up the White House. It was saved from Civil War destruction by a northern gunboat officer who had once been a guest here, and kindness still blesses it. With handsome interiors featuring marvelous curlicue plasterwork, hand-carved Corinthian columns of cypress wood in the ballroom, beautiful archways, original crystal chandeliers, and other details, it's been lovingly restored over the years by a series of owners. This is everything you want in a dazzling Old South mansion.

You can stay at the plantation in rooms running from $160 to $303 per night, and with perhaps greater motivation than in the past, as extensive renovations throughout the summer of 2008 brought in amenities such as period furnishings, luxurious bathrooms, flatscreen TVs, Wi-Fi, room service, and breakfast for each room. You should still check to see if the more costly rooms require late check-ins and early checkouts because they are on the daily tours.

Mississippi River Rd. (P.O. Box 160), White Castle, LA 70788. ✆ **866/LASOUTH** (527-6884) or 225/545-2730. Fax 225/545-8632. www.nottoway.com. Admission $15 adults, $6 children ages 6–12, free for children 5 and under. Daily 9am–4pm, tours begin on the hour. Closed Dec 25. From New Orleans, follow I-10 west to La. 22 exit, then turn left on La. 70 across Sunshine Bridge. Exit onto La. 1 and drive 14 miles north through Donaldsonville. From Baton Rouge, take I-10 west to Plaquemine exit and then La. 1 south for 18 miles.

Dining

Note that many of the plantations operate their own restaurants, but most of them aren't very good.

In Vacherie

B&C Seafood Market & Cajun Restaurant ★ CAJUN/SEAFOOD We believe in "when in Rome," so if you are out scouting plantations, join the locals and stop off at this decidedly low-atmosphere family operation for some fresh seafood (the house specialty—boiled or fried), gumbo, jambalaya, po' boys, and our favorite, fried *boudin* (sausage) balls (they make a great car snack). Their seafood buffet is every Friday beginning at 5:30pm.

2155 Hwy. 18. ✆ **225/265-8356.** All items $5–$24. AE, DISC, MC, V. Sun–Thurs 9am–6pm; Fri–Sat 9am–11pm.

ST. FRANCISVILLE & SURROUNDING PLANTATIONS

St. Francisville, 30 miles northwest of Baton Rouge, doesn't look like much on approach, but by the time you get to the center of town, you are utterly charmed. Many of the plantations described below are clustered around St. Francisville, which is a roughly 2-hour drive from New Orleans and pretty much requires an overnight stay. You can get into the spirit of things and plan to stay at one of the plantations described below, or you may choose to stay in St. Francisville (they have several options there; see below for listings in St. Francisville). We strongly suggest staying here (if not *at* one of said plantations) overnight rather than going back and forth from Baton Rouge, where there is very little of interest aside from one plantation home. Contact the **St. Francisville tourism information office** for more information (✆ **800/789-4221** or 225/635-4224; www.stfrancisville.us; 9am–5pm daily). It's worth pointing out that this is *not* Cajun Country; the area has English plantations only and no French history at all.

If you do, however, decide to stay in Baton Rouge, which is 77 miles northwest of New Orleans, contact the **Baton Rouge Area Convention and Visitors Bureau,** 730 North Blvd., Baton Rouge, LA 70802 (✆ **800/LA-ROUGE** [527-6843]; www.visitbaton rogue.com), and ask for its useful *Baton Rouge Visitors Guide,* which contains maps of attractions in the city and surrounding area.

Magnolia Mound ★ This home was built in the late 1700s as a small settler's house. As prosperity came to the lower Mississippi Valley, the house was enlarged and renovated, eventually becoming the center of a 900-acre plantation. Its single story is nearly 5 feet off the ground and has a front porch 80 feet across. The hand-carved woodwork and the ceiling in the parlor are authentically restored. Magnolia Mound takes its name from its setting within a grove of trees on a bluff overlooking the Mississippi. One of the oldest wooden structures in the state, it is typical French Creole in architecture and is furnished in Louisiana and early Federal styles. Costumed guides take you through. Magnolia Mound also has renovations of slave cabins on the site.

2161 Nicholson Dr., Baton Rouge, LA 70802. ✆ **225/343-4955.** Fax 225/343-6739. www.magnolia mound.org. Admission $8 adults, $6 seniors and students 18–22, $3 children 5–17, free for children 4 and under. Mon–Sat 10am–4pm; Sun 1–4pm. Last tour begins at 3:15pm.

Parlange Plantation ★   This plantation is one of the few that still functions as a working farm. Built in 1750 by Marquis Vincent de Ternant, the house is one of the oldest in the state, and its two stories rise above a raised brick basement. Galleries encircle the house, which is flanked by two brick *pigeonniers* (large houses for pigeons). Indigo was planted here at first; in the 1800s, sugar cane became the plantation's main crop. Today the plantation grows sugar cane, corn, and soybeans and also supports its own cattle. During the Civil War this house was host to generals from both sides (Gen. Nathaniel Banks of the Union and Gen. Dick Taylor of the Confederacy)—not, of course, at the same time. Parlange is a National Historic Landmark and is owned by relatives of the original builders.

8211 False River Rd., New Roads, LA 70760. ✆ **225/638-8410.** www.nps.gov/history/nr/travel/louisiana/ par.htm. Admission $10 adults, $5 children 6–12. By appt. only. From Baton Rouge, take U.S. 190 19 miles west and then La. Hwy. 1 another 8 miles north.

Oakley Plantation at Audubon State Historic Site ★   Oakley Plantation, 3 miles east of U.S. 61, features the old house where John James Audubon came to study and paint the wildlife of this part of Louisiana. Built in 1799, it is a three-story frame house with the raised basement typical of that era. A curved stairway joins the two galleries, and the whole house has a simplicity that bespeaks its age. When Audubon was here, he tutored a daughter of the family and painted some 32 of his *Birds of America* series. When you visit the house today, you will see some original prints from Audubon's portfolio and many fine antiques. A walk through the gardens and nature trails will explain why this location had such appeal for Audubon. Oakley is part of the 100-acre Audubon State Commemorative Area, a wildlife sanctuary that would have gladdened the naturalist's heart. There's a gift shop in the kitchen building, but you can still see the huge old fireplace where the family's meals were cooked.

La. 965 (P.O. Box 546), St. Francisville, LA 70775. ✆ **888/677-2838** or 225/635-3739. Fax 225/784-0578. Admission $2 adults, free for seniors (over 62) and children 12 and under. Daily 9am–5pm. Guided tours of the house 10am–4pm. Closed Jan 1, Thanksgiving, and Dec 25.

Rosedown Plantation ★★   By far the most impressive and historic of the more far-flung plantations, Rosedown is notable for its dramatic gardens and a tour stuffed with intriguing bits of facts and trivia, courtesy of more than 8,000 documents in their archives. Just east of St. Francisville, Rosedown was completed in 1834 for Daniel Turnbull (whose son, William, married Martha Washington's great-great-granddaughter) on land granted by the Spanish in 1789 to a founder of the Port of Bayou Sara on the Mississippi River. The two-story house, flanked by one-story wings, combines classic and indigenous Louisiana styles. It has the typical columns and wide galleries across the front, and it's made of cement-covered brick. A wide avenue of ancient oaks, their branches meeting overhead, leads up to the house. The 28 acres of historic gardens were begun in 1835 and came to be one of the great horticultural collections of the 19th century as well as one of the nation's most significant historical gardens in the 20th century. Fittingly, marble statues of gods and goddesses (brought back from trips to Europe by the family) dot the winding pathways. Unfortunately, ownership of Rosedown has changed a couple of times, finally landing in the hands of the state of Louisiana. In the process, many of its wonderful family treasures have been lost (well, sold, but don't get anyone started on *that* scandal), so what you see will depend on an ongoing process. Still, you can easily spend 2 hours wandering through house and gardens.

12501 Hwy. 10 (at La. 10 and U.S. 61), St. Francisville, LA 70775. (C) **225/635-3332.** Fax 225/784-1382. Admission (house tour and historic gardens) $10 adults, $8 seniors, $4 students 6–17, free for children 5 and under. Daily 9am–5pm; tours begin at 10am. Closed Jan 1, Thanksgiving, and Dec 25.

Catalpa Plantation   Unless you are just a die-hard plantation buff, this relatively humble Victorian home is probably not worth going out of your way for. It's not all that historic or notable architecturally. On the other hand, it is still owned by the original family, which is practically unheard of among plantations these days. The oaks that line the drive up to the house grew from acorns planted by the present owner's great-great-great-grandfather, and tours do feature all sorts of curious stories about the family heirlooms that still lie within its walls. The slightly dented silver tea service, for example, lay buried in a pond during the Civil War; the lovely hand-painted china was done by none other than John James Audubon. This sense of family history and direct connection with the past is rare, so that alone may make your visit worthwhile.

Off U.S. 61 (P.O. Box 131), St. Francisville, LA 70775. (C) **225/635-3372.** Admission $6 adults, $3 children 6–12, free for children 5 and under. By appt.

The Myrtles ★   A little over 1 mile north of the intersection with Louisiana Highway 10, along U.S. Highway 61, is this beautiful, if a tad dull, house built in 1795. Its gallery is 110 feet long, and the elaborate iron grillwork is reminiscent of the French Quarter. The Myrtles is in an astonishingly good state of preservation, especially inside, where the intricate plaster moldings in each room are intact. The house is set in a grove of great old live oaks; the grounds are not as big as at Rosedown (well, nothing else really is) but are still worth a ramble through. Too bad it's all set right on the noisy highway, which helps dispel any fantasy about drifting back to another era.

Overnight accommodations are available. They have finished some badly needed renovations to the guest rooms, and while the suites (apart from the charming Judge Clark) still aren't anything to shout about, apart from size (we hate the carpeting but do love the bedsteads), regular rooms, particularly those in the main house, look much better, with lavish linens, fresh paint, and eye-catching canopy beds, all of which goes prettily with the fireplaces and wide-plank floors. Some rooms have bathrooms in the hall, which are actually better than the in-room bathrooms, which are usually dinky and motel-like. Floral garden rooms are less interesting but do have better bathrooms. The whole setting feels quite rural, and the newly relandscaped grounds are nice for strolling.

They offer "mystery" tours Friday and Saturday nights, wherein guides tell tales of various ghosts haunting the place; these tend to be kitschy fun, which is just fine if that's what you're looking for (we say that because we once heard, in an occult shop, a woman sincerely complaining that no real ghosts turned up when she stayed here). The Carriage House (on the property) serves fancy dinners and simple lunches and is a worthwhile place to eat.

7747 U.S. 61 (P.O. Box 1100), St. Francisville, LA 70775. (C) **225/635-6277.** Fax 225/635-5837. www.myrtlesplantation.com. Admission $8 adults, $4 children; mystery tours $10. Private, personalized tours available; rates vary. Daily 9am–5pm. Closed major holidays.

The Cottage ★   This rambling country home, 5 miles north of St. Francisville, is really a series of buildings constructed between 1795 and 1859. It's not that much to see, inside or out, and the accommodations pale when compared to what's offered at Madewood. Still,

> ### (Finds) Grandmother's Buttons
>
> Once in St. Francisville, do stop by **Grandmother's Buttons** ★, at 9814 Royal St. (**℃ 800/580-6941** or 225/635-4107; www.grandmothersbuttons.com). The owner makes jewelry from antique and vintage buttons (from Victorian brass picture buttons to 1940s Bakelite)—one-of-a-kind, amazing creations. We've bought more earrings, brooches, and other gewgaws from here than we could ever possibly wear. Don't overlook their much-more-interesting-than-you-might-think Button Museum. Hours are Monday through Saturday from 10am to 5:30pm, Sunday from 11am to 5pm.

the low, two-story house has a long gallery out front, a nice place to sit and relax for an evening, perhaps joined by the owners' sociable dogs.

The first house was built entirely of virgin cypress taken from the grounds. Many of the outbuildings date from 1811, when Judge Thomas Butler (of the "Fighting Butlers," prominent in American history) acquired the property. After his victory in the Battle of New Orleans, Gen. Andrew Jackson, along with a troop of officers that included no fewer than *eight* butlers, stopped off here for a 3-week stay on his way from New Orleans to Natchez. The Cottage's interior looks very much as it did when the Butlers lived here, with hand-screened wallpaper, a 19th-century love seat (with space for a chaperone), and needlepoint fire screens made by the ladies of the family. This is a working family farm of some 360 acres.

The six **guest rooms** ($115–$150 double, including breakfast) are a mix of elegant (huge four-poster canopy beds) and funky (icky motel room carpeting) and are not available January, February, or major holidays. But there is a small pool, and you do have breakfast in the elegant dining room of the main house.

10528 Cottage Lane (at U.S. 61), St. Francisville, LA 70775. ℃ **225/635-3674.** www.cottageplantation. com. Admission $7. Daily for tours 10am–4pm. Closed major holidays.

Accommodations in St. Francisville

In addition to the establishments listed below, you might consider spending the night at Madewood or Nottoway Plantation, described in the previous section. All should be booked well in advance.

If the accommodations listed below are booked up, call the St. Francisville **tourism information office** for a list of (and suggestions regarding) local B&Bs (℃ **225/635-4220**).

Barrow House Inn ★★   The Barrow House Inn is actually two guesthouses: the Barrow House and the Printer's House. Both are listed on the National Register of Historic Places and are located in the heart of St. Francisville's charming historic district. The Printer's House, dating from the 1780s, is the oldest in town and was built and occupied by the monks for whom St. Francisville is named. Across the street is the New England saltbox–style Barrow House (ca. 1809). Owned and operated by Shirley Dittloff and her son Christopher, the houses have been restored and furnished with 1840s-to-1880s antiques. Each room has its own fine furniture, and most have claw-foot tubs. The Empire Suite is the most popular, but we'd go for the Peach Suite just to try the authentic Spanish-moss mattress—the only one in the country! Upstairs are two tiny but much cheaper rooms, including one that lost its roof thanks to a poorly placed Civil War cannonball (you can still see the repair work on the exposed joists). The kitchen is well stocked with drinks and munchy snacks, while the Dittloffs offer a choice of continental or full breakfast in the historic dining room. In addition to numerous pampering touches, guests also have access to a mini space exploration museum dedicated to Shirley's father, Jim Chamberlin, a pioneer in American space history.

9779 Royal St. (P.O. Box 2550), St. Francisville, LA 70775. © **225/635-4791.** Fax 225/635-1863. www. topteninn.com. 8 units, all with private bathroom. $115–$135 double; $160 suite. Extra person $30. AE, DISC, MC, V. **Amenities:** Complimentary wine; continental or full breakfast; gift shop; horseshoes; designated smoking areas; audio walking tour. *In room:* A/C, TV, DVD player (w/more than 400 movies!), canopy beds, Wi-Fi.

Butler Greenwood Plantation B&B ★★

This is a dynamite place to stay (as a plantation tour, it's nothing you won't see elsewhere—though it is one of few that is still owned and occupied by the original family, and still a full-time family home), starting with the setting: extensive grounds full of tangled oak trees, plus a pond with resident ducks. The front main house (a tour can be arranged for $5) is full of original family furnishings. The guest quarters are seven cottages, each with its own personality, from the **Old Kitchen** (with a working fireplace and the original 150-ft. well, covered by glass so guests can peer down it) to the **Gazebo,** with old church windows, to the storybook-cunning three-story **Dovecot.** Each unit has been set in such a way that it has its own bit of privacy and is decorated with a mix of old and new furnishings. Some have ugly kitchen units, and some have decks overlooking a minigorge. Continental breakfasts are brought to the cottages in the morning. It all adds up to a splendid romantic private retreat. Be sure to ask the owner about her true-crime book, which just happens to detail a true crime she herself survived.

8345 U.S. Hwy. 61, St. Francisville, LA 70775. © **225/635-6312.** Fax 225/635-6370. www.butlergreenwood. com. 8 units, all with private bathroom. $135 double. Rates include continental breakfast. AE, MC, V. **Amenities:** Pool; nature walks. *In room:* A/C, cable TV, Jacuzzi, kitchen, porch or deck, 4-poster bed, working fireplace (in some).

St. Francisville Inn ★

Formerly the Wolf-Schlesinger House, this is a budget alternative to local B&Bs. Rooms are motel-comfortable (the top-end choice is the queen with the Jacuzzi tub) and plain (though there are some antiques tossed into the mix), but the owners inject plenty of family-friendly hospitality, and that makes anything pretty. They certainly go all-out for the breakfast buffet, which they've had to open up for locals; it's small but top-heavy with choices (bacon, grits, filled crepes, plus a bunch of breakfast pastries). There is a pool, plus an antiques shop. If you are traveling with a large party, the inn can accommodate more than a small B&B (and is potentially more interesting than just a chain hotel, with a great vibe), and the owners can also do rather tasty group dinners in the various dining rooms. Guests can also enjoy a "wine parlor" with a wine of the week, red and white served by the glass.

5720 Commerce St., St. Francisville, LA 70775. © **800/488-6502** or 225/635-6502. Fax 225/635-6421. www.stfrancisvilleinn.com. 10 units. $90–$115 double. Full buffet breakfast included in rates. AE, DC, DISC, MC, V. **Amenities:** Pool; shop. *In room:* A/C, TV, Wi-Fi.

3 V Tourist Court ★★★ (Finds)

The best accommodations value in the area if you don't require a lot of space. This is a genuine 1930s tourist court consisting of wee cottages, many of which have been turned into shops, art studios, and cafes as part of a whole, unexpected artist colony. But five of the cottages are still dedicated to guests, and they are adorable. Each has its own color scheme, with sweet bed linens topping excellent double mattresses (which nearly take up the whole room), teeny kitchenettes, and nice basic bathrooms. There's also a pair of two-bedroom cabins with full kitchens. And look at those prices! It's a great deal for a weekend jaunt, which puts you right in the middle of the local fun scene at the Magnolia Cafe. Note that the reservation number is a mobile phone.

5689 Commerce St., St. Francisville, LA 70775. ☎ **225/721-7003.** 9 units. $75 double, $125 cabins. AE, MC, V. *In room:* A/C, TV, fridge, microwave, Wi-Fi.

Dining in St. Francisville

Also consider, for a light snack or drink, **Bird Man Coffee & Books** (5687 E. Commerce St.; ☎ **225/635-3665**), on the same grounds as the 3 V Tourist Court and Magnolia Cafe. "The best espresso around," a visiting Polish man told us, and who are we to disagree with such a coffee authority? A small bookstore-cum-coffeehouse, open daily from 7am to 6pm on weekdays and 8am to 6pm on Saturdays, closing 2 hours earlier on Sundays, offers excellent drinks and decent pastries.

Magnolia Cafe ★★★ (Finds) CAFE   Relocated (just a shift to the left, more or less) after a bad fire and even better than ever, this sweet cafe has become the center of a local scene thanks to a newish bar and airy patio that features live music on Friday nights. Those who have to eat étouffée and jambalaya may be disappointed by the less-than-local-centric menu, but everyone else should be thoroughly pleased by this excellent cafe. Don't be deceived by the seemingly ordinary nature of the menu, which is heavy on salads and sandwiches—even a humble roast turkey on pita is fresh and striking. Look also for a spicy shrimp po' boy (shrimp in garlic butter with pepper jack cheese), muffulettas, and even enchiladas and nachos. Dinner brings additional entrees such as steaks, fish, and even fancier appetizers.

5687 E. Commerce St. ☎ **225/635-6528.** Fax 225/635-2463. Everything under $25. MC, V. Sun–Wed 10am–4pm; Thurs–Sat 10am–10pm. Bar opens and closes with restaurant usually.

2 CAJUN COUNTRY

The official name of this area is Acadiana, and it consists of a rough triangle of Louisiana made up of 22 parishes (counties), from St. Landry Parish at the top of the triangle to the Gulf of Mexico at its base. Lafayette is Acadiana's "capital," and it's dotted with such towns as St. Martinville, New Iberia, Abbeville, and Eunice. You won't find its boundaries on any map, nor the name "Acadiana" stamped across it. But those 22 parishes are Cajun Country, and its history and culture are unique in America.

MEET THE CAJUNS

The Cajun history is a sad one, but it produced a people and a culture well worth getting to know.

THE ACADIAN ODYSSEY   In the early 1600s colonists from France began settling the southeastern coast of Canada in a region of Nova Scotia they named Acadia. They developed a peaceful agricultural society based on the values of a strong Catholic faith, deep love of family, and respect for their relatively small landholdings. The community was isolated from the mainstream of European culture for nearly 150 years. Life was defined by the company of families and friends. This pastoral existence was maintained until

> **(Fun Facts)** **The Real Evangeline**
>
> You may know Henry Wadsworth Longfellow's epic poem *Evangeline*—the story of Evangeline and Gabriel, Acadian lovers who spent their lives wandering this land searching for each other after being wrenched from their homeland. In real life, Evangeline was Emmeline Labiche, and her sweetheart was Louis Pierre Arceneaux. Their story has a different ending from the poet's—Emmeline found Louis Pierre, after years of searching, in Cajun Country, in St. Martinville. The real-life tragedy was that, by then, Louis had given up hope of finding her and was pledged to another. She died of a broken heart in Louisiana, not Philadelphia. (**Note:** Not to be read by romantics; probably none of the above is true at all. But who cares? It's a good story!)

1713 when Acadia became the property of the British under the Treaty of Utrecht. Though the Acadians were determined to keep to their peaceful existence under the new rulers, it became clear that it would not be possible. For more than 40 years, they were harassed by the king's representatives, who tried to force them to pledge allegiance to the British Crown and renounce Catholicism and embrace the king's Protestant religion. This was so abhorrent to Acadians and they were so steadfast in their refusal that, in 1755, the British governor of the region sent troops to seize their farms and deport them. Villages were burned; husbands, wives, and children were separated as ships were loaded; and a 10-year odyssey began.

Some Acadians were returned to France, some went to England, many were put ashore along America's East Coast, and some wound up in the West Indies. The deportation voyages, made on poorly equipped, overcrowded ships, took a huge toll, and hundreds of lives were lost. Many of the survivors who were sent to France and England returned to America as much as 20 years later.

Louisiana, with its strong French background, was a natural destination for Acadians hoping to reestablish a permanent home, and those who were transported to the West Indies were probably the first to head there. In 1765 Bernard Andry brought a band of 231 men, women, and children to the region now known as Acadiana.

The land on which they settled differed greatly from what they had left in Nova Scotia. The swampy terrain was low-lying and boggy; interlaced with bayous and lakes; forested with live oak, willow, ash, and gum; and teeming with wildlife. Given land that mostly bounded the bayous, the Acadians built small levees (or dikes) along the banks and drained fields for small farms and pastures.

A NEW PRIDE After many decades during which Cajuns shied away from their roots (children were beaten in school for speaking French, which was considered a sign of ignorance; Cajun music was considered primitive or hokey; and so forth), the Cajun culture is experiencing a resurgence of popularity and respect as well as a new sense of community pride.

CAJUN LANGUAGE

This essay was provided by Ann Allen Savoy, who is, along with her husband, Marc, a musician in the Savoy-Doucet Cajun Band and in her own group, the Magnolia Sisters. Both groups have released CDs on the Arhoolie label. Ann is also the author of **Cajun Music Vol.**

1 (*Bluebird Press, 1984*), *an excellent and definitive work that combines oral history with a songbook.* Evangeline Made (*Vanguard*), *a collection of Cajun tunes covered by artists such as Linda Ronstadt, John Fogerty, and Maria McKee (which Ann produced and performed on), was released in 2002 to great critical acclaim and earned a Grammy nomination for Savoy. Her Grammy-nominated collaboration with Linda Ronstadt,* **Adieu False Heart** (*Vanguard*), *is a critical smash. You can see her and son Joel playing musicians in the film* Divine Secrets of the Ya-Ya Sisterhood, *and she performs three songs on the soundtrack. She also worked on the soundtrack for the remake of* All the King's Men.

The French influence in Louisiana is one of the things that sets the state apart from the rest of the United States. As soon as you get west of Baton Rouge, you can cruise down the Louisiana highways listening on your radio to French news, church services, music, and talk shows. The accent is sharp and bright with occasional English words thrown in (*"On va revenir right back"*—"We'll be right back"), so it is fun to see how much even Anglophones can follow the French story lines.

Though French is spoken by most of the older Cajuns (ages 60 and up), most middle-aged and young Louisianans don't speak the language. This is partially because the knowledge of the French language, from the 1930s on, became associated with a lack of business success or a lack of education, so a stigma became attached to it. Today, however, there is a resurgence in pride at being bilingual, particularly in larger towns and metropolitan areas. French emergence programs are cropping up here and there, and educated musicians and teachers ages 30 to 50 are learning to speak French.

CAJUN FRENCH   Where can you hear the language spoken? I recommend wandering through old grocery stores, dance halls, and feed stores, where you will hear many "natives" speaking French. This French is peppered with beautiful old words dating from Louis XIV. These words, no longer used in France, are historically intriguing. Cajun French is not a dialect of the French language, nor are there actual dialects of Cajun French from town to town in southwest Louisiana. The impression that there are various dialects could come from the fact that many words refer to particular items, and certain areas prefer particular words over others. For example, a mosquito can be called a *marougouin, moustique,* or *cousin.* One area might use only one of the words and never use the others. Remember that Cajun French is not a written language (it's only spoken), so certain words that were originally mispronounced have become part of the language. Similarly, some English words are part of the language today because when the Acadians first came to Louisiana, there were no such things as pickup trucks, typewriters, and other modern inventions, so the English words are used.

THE CREOLE LANGUAGE   Parallel to the Cajun French language, the fascinating Creole language is still spoken by many black Louisianans. The language is a compilation of African dialects and French and is quite different from standard French. However, Cajuns and black Creoles can speak and understand both languages.

At the weekly broadcast at the Liberty Theater in Eunice, you can listen to Cajun and zydeco music and enjoy the beauty of the unique Cajun language.

CAJUN MUSIC

It's hard to decide which is more important to a Cajun: food or music. Cajuns love music so much that, even in the early days when instruments were scarce, they held dances, with a cappella voices providing the accompaniment. With roots probably found in medieval France, traditional Cajun music is largely an orally transmitted art form. The strains usually come in the form of a brisk two-step or a waltz. The more traditional groups still play mostly acoustic instruments—a fiddle, an accordion, a triangle, and maybe a guitar.

The best place to hear real Cajun music is on someone's back porch, the time-honored spot for gathering to eat some gumbo and listening to several generations of musicians jamming together all night long. If you don't know a Cajun and don't have access to a back-porch gathering, don't fret. Throughout Cajun Country there are dance halls with something going on just about every weekend. Locals come to dance, and so should you. Don't know how to Cajun dance? Many people will be delighted to show you. Worried everyone will be watching you because you dance so badly? Observe the couples out on the dance floor. Who are you watching? That's right—the really good couples who fly in complex, almost jitterbug patterns. You aren't looking at the mediocre couples, and neither is anyone else. So don't be shy. And talk to the people around you. This is a social gathering, and Cajuns love to visit, telling stories and jokes.

Restaurants such as **Mulate's, Randol's,** and **D.I.'s** (see listings later in this chapter) offer regular live music and Cajun dancing. The regular Saturday morning jam session at the **Savoy Music Center** (p. 302) in Eunice is not to be missed—it's the closest you will get to that back-porch experience, and it is a sheer delight.

In your search for Cajun music, please don't forget zydeco, which also thrives in this region. Zydeco bands share the bill at the weekly live show at Eunice's **Liberty Theater,** and they are the house specialty at such clubs as **Slim's Y Ki-Ki** in Opelousas, the **Zydeco Hall of Fame** in Lawtell, and **El Sido's** in Lafayette. (You can find more information on these venues later in this chapter.)

PLANNING YOUR TRIP

A circular drive will allow you to take in one or two of the plantation homes en route to Baton Rouge (if you take the River Rd. instead of I-10) before turning west on I-10 to reach Lafayette and the land of the Cajuns. Go north of Lafayette on I-49 to reach Opelousas; Eunice is about 20 minutes west of there on Highway 190. A return to New Orleans on U.S. 90 is a trip through the history, legend, and romance of this region. There is more than a day's worth of interest in this area, so you'll probably want to plan at least an overnight stay. On I-10 the distance from New Orleans to Lafayette is 134 miles; Lafayette to New Orleans on U.S. 90 is 167 miles. Listed below (in alphabetical order) are some of the places you should not miss, but you will find scores of other Cajun Country attractions on your own. Also listed are some places to stay overnight as well as some of the outstanding Cajun restaurants (rest assured, bad restaurants do not last long) in the area.

Contact the excellent **Lafayette Convention and Visitors Commission,** 1400 NW Evangeline Thruway (P.O. Box 52066), Lafayette, LA 70505 (*©* **800/346-1958** in the U.S., 800/543-5340 in Canada, or 337/232-3737; fax 337/232-0161; www.lafayette travel.com). It will send you tons of detailed information to make your trip even more fun. The office is open weekdays from 8:30am to 5pm and weekends from 9am to 5pm. (See the "Lafayette" section, later in this chapter, for driving directions.)

Hands down, the best time to visit Acadiana is during festival time (p. 37). You'll have a terrific time along with native Cajuns, who celebrate with real gusto. If you miss this, however, every weekend seems to bring a smaller festival somewhere else in the area—and plenty of music at any time of the year.

Growing Up Cajun

Growing up immersed in Cajun culture was rewarding but alienating. My heroes weren't football jocks or rock-'n'-roll stars but rather my old neighbors who spoke French, farmed for a living, and played the accordion or fiddle. When fiddler Dennis McGee farmed for my grandpa, I didn't play with his children, even though they were my age—I hung around Dennis. I followed him in the fields while he plowed with his mule team. I wanted to hear his stories.

Needless to say, none of my classmates shared my love for what these old-timers had to offer. On my best days, my peers' attitude toward me was indifference. I remember a beautiful girl who sat near my desk all during grade school. I would fantasize about being her boyfriend, which was, of course, impossible. She was very heavy into sports and cheerleading and the mainstream, and I wasn't. Recently this same girl came into my store to purchase some Cajun CDs to send to her daughter, who was out of state and expressed a love for Cajun music. I recognized her immediately when she came in, even though 40 years had passed. We talked awhile, and when she was leaving she asked, "Where are you from?"

Even though it was difficult being Cajun in the '40s and '50s, I never felt any anger toward the negativity of the non-Cajuns or by those Cajuns who had given up their heritage. My feelings at this time were frustration and disappointment toward those people. To me, the choice they were making was bad for themselves. They were turning away from this wonderful heritage in pursuit of the mainstream. They were turning their backs on a delicious bowl of gumbo in favor of an American hot dog. I think my ulterior motive in 1966 in opening up a music store that specialized in Cajun music, rather than country or rock, was that I had an ax to grind. I wanted to destroy the stigma of being Cajun. I wanted to prove to the locals that heritage and success could coexist, that being Cajun and speaking French was okay. I wanted to tell outsiders how good our food was and about all these wonderful, warm, friendly, and sincere people who were called Cajuns.

The year was a turning point—Cajun music was first presented to the outside world. It happened at the Newport Folk Festival. A three-piece group of old Cajuns was up against names such as Bob Dylan and Joan Baez. The Cajuns played their first simple tune, "Grand Mamou," and before they were halfway through, an audience of 10,000 gave them a standing ovation.

This experience did two things. First, it reinforced the passion that had kept the fire burning in the musicians' hearts. They came home with newspaper clippings and stories about the reception at Newport that surprised even the local non-Cajuns. Second, it called outsiders to come to Louisiana to search out all things Cajun. And this had a legitimizing effect on the people down here. The outsiders came down in droves, not for things they could see or hear back home but for the things the Cajuns had not allowed the Americanization process to destroy. What was once considered a stigma was now considered an asset—to be Cajun.

The Americanization process has not been completely successful down here; it has taken its toll, influencing many people who have become a caricature of Cajun. I find what is passed off as Cajun culture in major metropolitan areas rather yuppified. In the rural areas there are a lot of snake farms hawking the Hollywood version. But in isolated rural areas, there is also a very viable culture that exists without the slickness of the modern-day mainstream. These places can be found by getting off the interstate highways and searching out the small villages through the prairie.

It is important for the tourist to know that Cajun music is localized and is never found in the forested bayou or salt marshes but in the flat prairie region. Look at the old-timers, the first people to record—they were from Crowley. Dennis McGee and Amede Ardoin were from Eunice. Musicians didn't live in the bayous or the marshes. Cajuns lived there, but the music came from the prairie. Where you find rice planted in Louisiana, you will find Cajun accordion music. The Germans brought the button accordion from their homeland, and some say they brought rice as well. My theory is this: Prosperity equals permanence, and permanence equals roots. Having been raised on a rice farm, I know the topsoil in some places is 6 feet deep. The first settlers who came into this region could sustain themselves very easily in one spot and didn't have to move after the first spot was depleted. We also don't have big rivers. Big rivers bring in big industry and masses of people diluting the existing culture.

I don't think modern Cajuns are much different than they were in the past. Being a Cajun, a Mexican, a Native American, or any other ethnic group—it's not about one certain aspect of that culture. It's not about whether or not you play music, or eat spicy food, or speak a certain language. You can be a mute and still be an example of that culture. It isn't the person who wears costumes consisting of red bandannas, white rubber boots, and big straw hats with a plucked rubber chicken hanging from his belt. That isn't Cajun either. It's about having roots or a foundation. It's about having roots that were cultivated in good times and bad times. And because of devotion and love, those roots sink deep, deep, deep and produce a strong, strong, strong tree, which gives protection and comfort to all those who come into its embrace. It's a matter of vision, being from a certain ethnic minority. It's about how you see yourself in your environment and how you relate and function in that environment. It's about having a deep sense of the past in order to know your direction. It's about having respect and love for the things that make you who you are and prevent you from being someone else. It's not about being crowd-pleasers. It's about being natural.

—Marc Savoy

Marc Savoy supports his Cajun heritage through the craftsmanship of accordions, as a musician with the highly acclaimed Savoy-Doucet Cajun Band and the Savoy Family Band, and by keeping Cajun community traditions alive.

If you can't find time for an extended visit to Cajun Country, a 1-day guided tour can provide an introduction to the area. **Tours by Isabelle** (© 888/223-2093 or 504/391-3544; www.toursbyisabelle.com) specializes in small tours in comfortable, air-conditioned passenger vans. You'll cross the Mississippi to visit Cajun Country and then take a 1½-hour narrated swamp tour. The Cajun Bayou Tour ($65) leaves New Orleans at 1pm and returns around 5:30pm. Isabelle's Grand Tour ($136) includes the Cajun Bayou Tour, a guided tour and lunch at Oak Alley Plantation, and a guided tour of Laura: A Creole Plantation.

For other Cajun Country tours, see the "Organized Tours" section of chapter 8, "Sights to See & Places to Be," beginning on p. 204.

A CAJUN WEEKEND

For music lovers, a trip out of New Orleans to the source of Cajun and zydeco music is practically a must. Though it's especially tempting to go during an organized event such as Lafayette's Festival International or Breaux Bridge's Crawfish Festival, there is always plenty of music happening—so much that you can easily fill a couple of days. Here are our suggestions for a good Cajun Country weekend itinerary (all specifics can be found in more detail later in this chapter):

FRIDAY   Drive out from New Orleans (avoid rush hour, when it can take a very long time to get through Baton Rouge). Stay in Lafayette, Eunice, or Washington, pretty towns with nice B&Bs (and some basic chain hotels). That night, drive into Lafayette and hear whatever's going on at the **Blue Moon Saloon** or check out Opelousas's **Slim's Y Ki-Ki** for the best in zydeco.

SATURDAY   Get up early and head to the **Savoy Music Center** in Eunice for the weekly jam session. Leave before noon and drive to Mamou, where **Fred's Lounge** should be jampacked. The action at Fred's stops at 1pm, but the bar next door picks up the slack. Then head to Ville Platte and **Floyd's Record Shop** to buy some of what you've heard. Have a bite at the **Pig Stand** or back in Eunice. That night, go to Eunice's **Liberty Theater** for the live radio broadcast featuring Cajun and zydeco groups—plus plenty of Cajun folk tales and jokes. Consider dinner at **D.I.'s,** which also has live music.

SUNDAY   Spend the morning checking out picturesque Washington, strolling the wonderful gardens at **Magnolia Ridge,** or combing the many antiques shops before heading back to New Orleans.

BREAUX BRIDGE ★

Just off I-10 on La. 31, this little town, founded in 1859, prides itself on being the Crawfish Capital of the World. Its Crawfish Festival and Fair has drawn as many as 100,000 to the town of 4,500, and it's quite the event, with music, a unique parade, crawfish races, crawfish-eating contests, and lots more. It's held the first week in May. Some locals actually dislike the Crawfish Festival and feel that their town is at its best the rest of the year. Consider taking them up on this challenge—the town is pretty and offers some of the nicest options in the area. Many little antiques shops of varying price and charm line the main drag. (We notice they tend to close early on Tues afternoons.) The standout is **Lucullus** (107 N. Main St.; © 337/332-2625), a branch of the culinary and dining oriented shop in New Orleans, one of the best and most carefully stocked shops around. Poke around for special items like absinthe spoons.

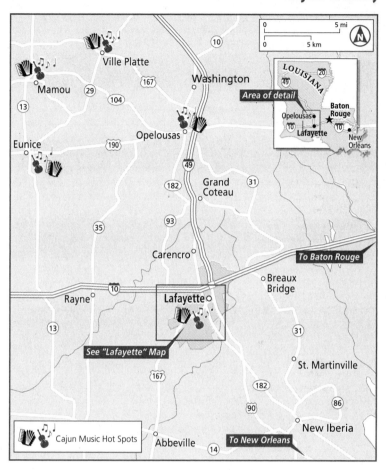

Accommodations

Note: If the B&B listed below is full, you may be directed to the also charming Bayou Teche B&B, next door.

Maison Des Amis ★★ The winner of a national preservation award, this one-story Creole-Caribbean cabin (ca. 1860) is one of the best B&Bs we've ever stayed in, for sheer comfort and style. We can't decide which we like best: the front room, with the towering half-canopy bed; the middle room with the nearly 300-year-old four-poster; or the small room with the mosquito-net-draped plantation bed. The two front rooms have private bathrooms and the biggest windows. One room has a DVD player, but all rooms have premium cable. A fine bonus, housekeeping will do your laundry on-site. Best of all, guests get breakfast at the near-perfect **Café Des Amis** (see below) or, on the mornings the former is closed for breakfast, at the still lovely Chez Jacqueline. There is also a nicely painted gazebo down by the bayou.

111 Washington St., Breaux Bridge, LA 70517. ✆ **337/507-3399.** Fax 337/332-2227. www.maisondes amis.com. 4 units, all with private bathroom. $100–$125 double. Rates include full-service breakfast. AE, DISC, MC, V. **Amenities:** Restaurant; complimentary beverages; gardens; gazebo. *In room:* A/C, TV, Wi-Fi.

Dining

For less formal dining, head to **Poche's Market Restaurant & Smokehouse** (3015 Main Hwy. #A, 70517—call **800/3-POCHES** [376-2437] or 337/332-2108 for directions!) for excellent spicy *boudin,* cracklins (fresher earlier in the day), weekend barbecue plates, and other regional meaty delicacies. They also ship tasso, sausages, and more, in case you want to cook like a Cajun at home.

Café Des Amis ★★★ CAJUN   Not even a devastating fire could keep down the pride and joy of Breaux Bridge, a charming cafe that features local art and often live music in addition to meals so good at least one recent customer thought his breakfast (eggs Begnaud—eggs on a grilled biscuit topped with crawfish étouffée) was worth driving up from New Orleans for. (And don't forget the *crielle de couchon*—fried dough in the shape of pigs' ears! You can get them stuffed with *boudin,* or the omelets stuffed with tasso, with a side of andouille-cheese grits.) At dinner try the crabmeat Napoleon or the crawfish corn bread topped with shrimp, and be sure to order the drum with andouille sausage and shrimp topped with garlic shrimp sauce (you have to order it this way, but the combination is perfect). Save room for the superb creamy white-chocolate bread pudding. This restaurant is hugely popular with locals, so expect a wait on the weekends (among a bunch of older Creole men nursing full glasses of whiskey on the rocks—for breakfast). Weekends they start seating at 7:30am, and the band goes on at 8:30am Saturday.

140 E. Bridge St. ✆ **337/332-5273.** Fax 337/332-2227. www.cafedesamis.com. Main courses $8.95–$26. AE, DISC, MC, V. Tues 11am–2pm; Wed–Thurs 11am–9pm; Fri–Sat 7:30am–9:30pm; Sun 8am–2:30pm.

Chez Jacqueline ★★ CAJUN/FRENCH   After you've had breakfast and one other meal at Café Des Amis (above), save room for a bite at this cafe, just steps away from its higher-profile neighbor. This is a small, unfussy restaurant, where the chef is also the bartender; eat here only when you can linger. The menu is divided into two parts, Cajun (for the tourists) and French (for the locals, who want to eat something different when they go out!). Order the Coquille St. Jacques (scallops, shrimp, and crab in a seasoned, buttery, creamy house sauce) or Les Huitres au gratin (oysters baked with garlic, butter, and Parmesan cheese) to start. Entrees include a filet medallion sautéed with a pepper-corn-and-cognac cream sauce, and veal *cordon bleu,* a golden, perfectly crispy version of this classic. Banana cake is moist and not overly sweet. If you plan ahead, call the cafe and ask to be put on the bouillabaisse list; the owner calls the list a few weeks ahead of time when she's planning on making one, so listed patrons can reserve a table. They also serve a zydeco breakfast on weekends.

114 E. Bridge St. ✆ **337/507-3320** or owner's cellphone, 337/277-4938. Reservations suggested. Main courses $11–$30. DC, DISC, MC, V. Sun–Mon and Wed–Sat 7:30am–2pm and 5–9pm. Zydeco breakfast Sat 10am–2pm.

Crawfish Town USA ★★ SEAFOOD/CAJUN   See if you can guess what the house specialty is here. The food is as pleasant as the heavily decorated dining room and is prepared to your taste: mild, strong, or extra hot. The staff says they serve the biggest crawfish in the world—and who are we to challenge them? The steaming platters of boiled crawfish that come out of the kitchen by the hundreds look almost like small lobsters. The crawfish étouffée and the gumbo are delicious. You shouldn't miss the bread pudding here, either. And if you just can't decide what you want, take a deep breath and go for the Seafood Festival Platter: a cup of gumbo plus jambalaya, crawfish étouffée, grilled catfish, shrimp, seafood pie, frogs' legs, crawfish, and a crawfish patty—all served with grilled potatoes, vegetables, and garlic bread.

The second Saturday of the month they throw a *fais-do-do* with a $5 admission; children under 6 get in free.

2815 Grand Point Hwy. ☏ **337/667-6148.** www.crawfishtown.com. Reservations recommended. Main courses $6.95–$25. AE, DISC, MC, V. Sun–Thurs 11am–9pm; Fri–Sat 11am–10pm. From Lafayette, take I-10 to Henderson (exit 115). Go north ½ mile and follow the signs; you can't miss it.

Mulate's the Original Cajun Restaurant ★★ (Kids) CAJUN   Skip the no-longer-affiliated Mulate's in New Orleans, and come here instead. It's gotten a bit touristy, but the food is solid (and the prices reasonable) and so is the music—Mulate's is definitely a good introduction to Cajun music and food. Stuffed crab or the catfish are the specialties here. Live Cajun music is offered nightly and at noon on Sundays.

325 Mills Ave. ☏ **800/422-2586** or 337/332-4648. Fax 337/323-4013. Reservations recommended for parties of 6 or more. Main courses $16–$20. AE, DC, DISC, MC, V. Daily 11am–10pm.

EUNICE ★★★

Founded in 1894 by C. C. Duson, who named the town for his wife, Eunice, is a prairie town, not as picturesque as, say, Opelousas or Washington. But some of the most significant Cajun cultural happenings come out of this friendly town, including the Saturday-morning jam sessions at the Savoy Music Center, the Liberty Theater's live radio broadcasts, and the exhibits and crafts demonstrations at the Prairie Acadian Cultural Center, all of which will greatly enrich your understanding of Cajun traditions and modern life. That is, if you aren't having too much fun to notice that you're also getting an education.

Liberty Theater ★★★ (Moments)   This classic 1927 theater has been lovingly restored and turned into a showcase for Cajun music. There's live music most nights, but Saturday attracts the big crowds for the *Rendezvous des Cajuns* radio show. From 6 to 7:30pm, Cajun historian and folklorist Barry Ancelet hosts a live program—simulcast on local radio—that features Cajun and zydeco bands. It includes anything from up-and-comers to some of the biggest names as well as folk tales and jokes. Oh, and it's all in French. Locals and tourists alike pack the seats and aisles, with dancing on the sloped floor by the stage. Don't understand what's being said? As Barry points out, turn to your neighbors—they will be happy to translate. This is the right way (actually, *the* way) to begin your Saturday night of music in Cajun Country.

Second St. and Park Ave. ☏ **337/457-7389.** www.eunice-la.com. Admission $5 adults, $3 children, free for children 5 and under. Tickets on sale at 4pm daily, doors open at 4pm; show runs 6–7:30pm.

Prairie Acadian Cultural Center ★★★ (Finds)   A terrific small museum, the Acadian Cultural Center is devoted to Cajun life and culture. Exhibits explain everything from the history of the Cajuns to how they worked, played, and got married. The graphics are lively and very readable and are well combined with the objects on display (most were acquired from local families who have owned them for generations). It's all quite informative and enjoyable. In other parts of the building, there might be quilting or

other crafts demonstrations going on. The center has a collection of videos about Cajun life and will show any and all of them in the small theater (just ask). Anything by Les Blanc is a good choice, but you might also check out *Anything I Can Catch*, a documentary about the nearly lost art of hand-fishing. (You *need* to see someone catch a giant catfish with his bare hands!)

250 W. Park. ✆ **337/457-8490.** www.lsue.edu/acadgate/lafitte.htm. Free admission; donations accepted. Tues–Fri 8am–5pm; Sat 8am–6pm. Closed Christmas.

Savoy Music Center ★★★ (Moments) On weekdays this is a working music store with instruments, accessories, and a small but essential selection of Cajun and zydeco CDs and tapes. In the back is the workshop where musician Marc Savoy (see the "Growing Up Cajun" box, earlier in this chapter) lovingly crafts his Acadian accordions—not just fine musical instruments but works of art—amid cabinets bearing his observations and aphorisms.

On most Saturday mornings, though, this nondescript faded-green building on the outskirts of Eunice is the spiritual center of Cajun music. Keeping alive a tradition that dates from way before electricity, Marc and his wife, Ann (or one of their sons, who are now thriving musicians in their own right), host a jam session where you can hear some of the region's finest music and watch the tunes being passed down from generation to generation. Here, the older musicians are given their due respect, with octogenarians often leading the sessions while players as young as those in their preteens glean all they can—if they can keep up. Meanwhile, guests munch on hunks of *boudin* sausage and sip beer while listening or socializing. All comers are welcome; if they're properly respectful, they can get a member of the Savoy family or shop associate Tina Pillone to show them around. But don't come empty-handed—a pound of *boudin* or a six-pack of something is appropriate. And if you play guitar, fiddle, accordion, or triangle, bring one along and join in—well, actually, they request no more than one triangle player at a time. Don't try to show off. Simply follow along with the locals, or you're sure to get a cold shoulder.

Hwy. 190 E. (3 miles east of Eunice). ✆ **337/457-9563.** www.savoymusiccenter.com. Tues–Fri 9am–5pm (closed for lunch noon–1:30pm); jams Sat 9am–noon.

Accommodations

Unfortunately, there is a dearth of interesting hotels or B&Bs in town, so you will have to make due with the clean and basic **Best Western** (1531 W. Laurel Ave.; ✆ 337/457-2800); the newly opened **Holiday Inn Express,** in our experience, a very reliable chain that includes a free breakfast bar (1698 Hwy. 190; ✆ 337/517-7791); or the **Days Inn and Suites** (1251 E. Laurel Ave. [Hwy. 190 E.]; ✆ 337/457-3040).

Dining

D.I.'s Cajun Restaurant ★★ CAJUN Even when you follow the directions to D.I.'s Cajun Restaurant, you will think you are about to drive off the face of the earth, particularly if you're driving there in the dark. You'll know you're there—and that you are not alone—when you see all the cars in the gravel parking lot. Located on a back highway, D.I.'s is more or less what Mulate's was before the tourists found it: a homey family restaurant full of locals dancing to live music (Tues–Sat) and stuffing themselves with crawfish and catfish. Some items are not fried, but most are—or they're stuffed or topped with a sauce—and it's all good.

6561 Evangeline Thruway, Basile. ✆ **337/432-5141.** www.discajunrestaurant.biz. Main courses $7.95–$26. AE, DISC, MC, V. Mon–Fri 10:30am–1:30pm; Tues–Sat 5–10pm. Take Hwy. 190 to Hwy. 97, then drive 8 miles south.

(Finds) Boudin Joints

Boudin is Cajun sausage made of pork, usually mixed with rice, onions, and spices, and stuffed inside a chewy casing. If it's done right, it's spicy and sublime. You can get *boudin* (warm) at just about any grocery store or gas station, and we've spent many a day driving through Cajun Country taste-testing. Of course, disputes rage about who makes the best. Visit **www.boudinlink.com** for hard-core ratings and listings of dozens of *boudin* shops in the area. Try several to compare for yourself—it's a cheap (just over $2 per lb.), filling snack. For the less intrepid, we recommend the following, relatively easy places to locate:

Superette Slaughterhouse ★, 1044 Hwy. 91, Eunice ((℅ **337/546-6041**), is open Monday through Friday from 6am to 5:30pm, and Saturday from 6am to noon. The name is a little unnerving to some of us urbanites, but the locals swear this is the best *boudin* around.

Poche's, 3015-A Main Hwy., Breaux Bridge ((℅ **337/332-2108**), has not only pork but also crawfish *boudin* plus tasso and other local tidbits—and they ship, too. Open Monday through Saturday from 5am to 8pm, and Sunday from 5am to 6pm.

Ray's Grocery, 904 Shortvine (off Hwy. 190, across from Town Center), Opelousas ((℅ **337/942-9150**), has the advantage of a drive-through window. Place your order with little interruption in your road trip. Hours are Monday through Friday from 7:30am to 6pm, Saturday from 8am to 5pm, and Sunday from 8am to 2pm.

Shopping

Lejeune's Sausage Kitchen   Look for the signs or just ask, but do find your way to the Sausage Kitchen for a delicious, if perishable, souvenir. In addition to tasso (Cajun ham) and pounce (stuffed pig stomach), Lejeune's sells a variety of sausages, including a memorable garlic pork. It all freezes well, but alas, they don't ship. Old Crowley Rd. 108 Tasso Circle. (℅ 337/457-8491. Mon–Fri 7am–5:30pm.

GRAND COTEAU ★

Grand Coteau seems like just a wide spot in the road, but it's worth exploring (it won't take you long). First see the beautiful, 180+-year-old **Academy of the Sacred Heart,** 1821 Academy Rd. ((℅ **337/662-5494;** tours by appt. only), and its gardens. Then there are two places to eat (one where you can also shop) that are surprising in this land of Cajun cooking.

Dining

Catahoula's ★ CLASSIC & NOUVELLE LOUISIANA CUISINE   Named for the Louisiana state dog (a hound with startling blue eyes), Catahoula's is in a 1920s general store. It's a pretty, simple place with subdued lighting that at night virtually requires candles. It serves surprisingly modern fare, but unfortunately goes through ups and downs with regard to the quality of its food. On a recent visit, we had a savory cheesecake starter that alone was fine, but it came drenched in a tomato-based sauce that clashed with the creaminess of the cheesecake (and contained what appeared to be canned ingredients). Most chefs who prepare this dish either realize it's rich enough without a sauce or that a butter-based one should be used. A "house specialty," a cold seafood sampler platter, had stingy portions of uninspiring, mostly boiled seafood that showed off neither special cooking nor particularly fine specimens of fish. It's really too bad, because it's such a pretty place. Our advice: Stick to pastas and salads. Owner John Slaughter is also a photographer, and his photos line the walls.

234 Martin Luther King Dr. (Hwy. 93). ✆ 337/662-2275. Reservations recommended. Main courses $16–$34; specials somewhat higher. AE, DISC, MC, V. Wed–Thurs 5–9pm; Fri–Sat 5–10pm; Sun 11am–2pm.

Kitchen Shop ★ CAFE   The name is misleading because this is actually a well-stocked, cute gift store that features kitchen, cooking, and nice food items as well as having a much larger room stuffed with local books, upscale knickknacks, jewelry (including Grandmother's Buttons [p. 290], a line made from antique buttons), and vintage-looking clothes. There is also a tiny cafe with a sweet little patio. The owner is a New York–trained pastry chef who serves quiches, delicious pastries (the specialty is Gateau Nana), and terrific café au lait. It's all packed into an 1840 building that used to be a stagecoach stop.

296 Martin Luther King Dr. ✆ 337/662-3500. Entrees $7.50–$9.50; desserts $5–$7; coffee and tea $1.50–$3. DISC, MC, V. Tues–Sat 10am–5pm; Sun 1–5pm.

LAFAYETTE ★★

Stop by the **Lafayette Convention and Visitors Center,** 1400 NW Evangeline Thruway (✆ **800/346-1958** in the U.S., 800/543-5340 in Canada, or 337/232-3808; www.lafayettetravel.com). The helpful staff will tell you everything you could possibly want to know about the region and will send you out loaded with informative materials. Turn off I-10 at exit 103A, go south for about a mile, and you'll find the office in the center of the median. It's open weekdays from 8:30am to 5pm and weekends from 9am to 5pm. Near the intersection of Willow Street and the thruway, the attractive offices are in Cajun-style homes set on landscaped grounds that hold a pond and benches. It is a restful spot to sit and plan your Cajun Country excursion.

We also highly recommend the **Festival International de Louisiane** ★, a 6-day music-and-art festival that many find to be a good alternative to New Orleans's increasingly crowded Jazz Fest. Although the scope of the bands, naturally, is nothing like the big deal in New Orleans, there's an interesting lineup each year, with an emphasis on music from other French-speaking lands. The festival takes place in the center of town with streets blocked off to allow easy movement from one stage to another. In contrast to Jazz Fest, it's low-key and a manageable size. Best of all, it's free! Festival International is held at the end of April; for dates, call or write the Festival International de Louisiane, 735 Jefferson St., Lafayette, LA 70501 (✆ **337/232-8086;** www.festivalinternational.com).

Music can be found year-round at the **Blue Moon Saloon** ★★★ (215 E. Convent St.; ✆ **337/234-2422;** www.bluemoonpresents.com), which is filled pretty much every night with cool people who know a good hangout when they see one. Some of the best local bands, Cajun and otherwise, play here Wednesdays through Saturdays and sometimes on Sundays (look for members of the talented and critically celebrated Savoys in various band incarnations). The Blue Moon also operates cheap (but likeable) hostel-style lodgings, as well as four private bedrooms. The zydeco hot spot is **El Sido's,** 1523 N.

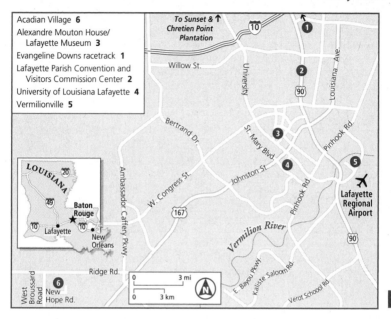

Acadian Village **6**
Alexandre Mouton House/
  Lafayette Museum **3**
Evangeline Downs racetrack **1**
Lafayette Parish Convention and
  Visitors Commission Center **2**
University of Louisiana Lafayette **4**
Vermilionville **5**

To Sunset & ↑
Chretien Point
Plantation

Willow St.

University

Bertrand Dr.

St. Mary Blvd

Pinhook Rd.

LOUISIANA

Baton
Rouge

Lafayette

New
Orleans

Ambassador Caffery Pkwy.

W. Congress St.

Johnston St.

Pinhook Rd.

Lafayette
Regional
Airport

Vermilion River

E. Bayou Pkwy.

Kaliste Saloom Rd.

Verot School Rd.

Ridge Rd.

West
Broussard
Road

New
Hope Rd.

0   3 mi
0   3 km

PLANTATION HOMES & CAJUN COUNTRY

12

CAJUN COUNTRY

Martin Luther King St. (© **337/235-0647**), where combos such as Nathan & the Zydeco Cha Chas hold sway. Hours are irregular so call ahead (or just ask a local), but when it jumps, it jumps high.

Seeing the Sights

You shouldn't leave this area without exploring its bayous and swamps. Gliding through misty bayous dotted with gnarled cypress trees that drip Spanish moss, seeing native water creatures and birds in their natural habitat, and learning how Cajuns harvest their beloved crawfish is an experience not to be missed.

To arrange a voyage, contact **McGee's Landing Atchafalaya Basin Swamp Tours** (1337 Henderson Levee Rd., Henderson; © **337/228-2384;** www.mcgeeslanding.com; $20 adults, $18 seniors, $15 children ages 4–12, free for children 3 and under). Tours last 90 minutes and go to Henderson Lake in the Atchafalaya Basin, with "extreme" private airboat tours also available ($50 for adults, $35 children, these last 2 hr.). You can also talk to someone at the helpful and friendly Breaux Bridge Tourism Board (© **337/332-8500**) for further suggestions.

If you're in Cajun Country between the first week in April and Labor Day and happen to be a devotee of the sport of kings, you can enjoy an evening of horse racing at **Evangeline Downs** (© **866/472-2466** or 337/594-3000; www.evangelinedowns.com), 3 miles north of town on I-49. Post time and racing days change periodically, so call before setting out. Don't bring the kids, though—no minors are allowed.

There's a lovely natural swamp environment in the very heart of Lafayette on the grounds of the University of Louisiana at Lafayette. Although it's small, it gives the effect of being in the wild, and during the warm months you can see alligators. Several varieties of water birds, as well as turtles, are almost always on hand, and in April the swamp is abloom with Louisiana irises. If you want to know more about the lake and how it is used as a teaching tool, contact the **Communications and Marketing Department,** University of Louisiana at Lafayette, Lafayette, LA 70504 (✆ **337/482-6397**). If you just want to get closer to the sort of swampland seen most often from highways, you'll like **Cypress Lake,** next to the Student Union on the ULL campus, between St. Mary Boulevard and University Avenue and Hebrard Boulevard and McKinley Street.

Acadian Village ★

Just south of La. 342, you'll find a reconstructed (actually, reassembled) Cajun bayou community. It looks a little prefab at first, but it grows more alluring as you wander through. Houses have been moved from their original locations to this site beside a sleepy bayou, and a footpath on its banks takes you past the historic structures. There is a dear small church, and a proper Cajun dance hall that periodically features bands playing the sort of music played 200 years ago, in a setting that isn't radically different from 200 years ago. The buildings hold a representative collection of Cajun furnishings. This is also the site of the up-and-coming Black Pot Festival, a cook-off and music event held in early November.

200 Greenleaf Dr. ✆ **800/962-9133** or 337/981-2364. www.acadianvillage.org. Admission $8 adults, $7 seniors, $5 children 7–14, free for children 6 and under. Group rates available. Daily 10am–4pm. Closed major holidays. Take I-10 to exit 97. Go south on La. 93 to Ridge Rd., turn right, and then turn left on W. Broussard.

Alexandre Mouton House/Lafayette Museum ★

Louisiana's first Democratic governor, Alexandre Mouton, once lived in this antebellum town house with square columns and two galleries. Today it is home to the Lafayette Museum. The main house was built in the early 1800s, and the cupola, attic, and second floor were added in 1849. Inside, in addition to the antiques, paintings, and historical documents, there's a colorful collection of Mardi Gras costumes that were worn by Lafayette's krewe kings and queens.

1122 Lafayette St. ✆ **337/234-2208.** Admission $3 adults, $2 seniors, $1 students. Tues–Sat 9am–4:30pm; Sun 1–4pm. Closed major holidays.

Vermilionville ★★

An addition to the Lafayette scene is this reconstruction of a Cajun-Creole settlement from the 1765-to-1890 era. Vermilionville sits on the banks of the brooding Bayou Vermilion, adjacent to the airport on U.S. 90. While it may sound like a "Cajunland" theme park, it's actually quite a valid operation. Hundreds of skilled artisans labored to restore original Cajun homes and to reconstruct others that were typical of such a village. Homes of every level in society are represented, from the humblest to the most well-to-do. (It *must* be authentic: One Cajun we know refuses to go, not because he dislikes the place or finds it offensive but because "I already *live* in Vermilionville!") The costumed staff in each gives a vivid demonstration of daily life back then, and craftspeople ply their traditional crafts. In the performance center, there are plays, music, dancing, and storytelling. Vermilionville is both bigger and better than Acadian Village (see above).

300 Fisher Rd., off Surrey St. ✆ **866/99-BAYOU** (992-2968) or 337/233-4077. www.vermilionville.org. Admission $8 adults, $6.50 seniors, $5 students, free for children 5 and under. Tues–Sun 10am–4pm; admission desk closes at 3pm. Closed New Year's Eve, New Year's Day, Martin Luther King Day, Mardi Gras, Thanksgiving, and Dec 24–25. Take I-10 to exit 103A. Take Evangeline Thruway south to Surrey St. and then follow signs.

As always, we tend toward directing you to stay at local B&Bs—mainly because they are more interesting than the alternative, which is simply a chain hotel. However, we can't deny that prices and even the preference for what a standardized hotel has to offer can make said chain hotels even more attractive than an antique bed. Lafayette has several such options, including the **Holiday Inn Lafayette–Central,** 2032 NE Evangeline Thruway (*C* **800/942-4868** or 337/233-6815), and the **Lafayette Hilton & Towers,** 1521 W. Pinhook Rd. (*C* **800/33-CAJUN** [332-2586] or 337/235-6111).

Aaah! T'Frere's Bed & Breakfast ★★★

Everything about this place cracks us up, from the name (it's so they're first in any alphabetical listing) to the evening "T'Juleps" to the owners' gorgeous son who cooked us breakfast but swore he was really a super-model (did you hear us argue?) to the cheerful owners themselves, Pat and Maugie Pastor—the latter would be adorable even if she didn't preside over breakfast in red silk pajamas every day. (She and Pat used to operate restaurants, and after years in chef's whites, she wanted as radical a change as possible.) Oh, wait, did we mention the goofily named breakfasts? Daily extravaganzas, easily the best around, like the "Ooh-La-La, Mardi Gras" breakfast—eggs in white sauce on ham-topped biscuits, cheese and garlic grits, tomato grille, sweet potatoes, and chocolate muffins? Did we mention Maugie used to be a chef? And apparently still is? The rooms (and grounds) are gorgeous (okay, the public areas are a bit Grandma-cluttered for our tastes, but maybe not for yours), though the ones in the Garconniere in the back are a bit more Country Plain than Victorian Fancy. We particularly like Mary's Room, with its priceless antique wood canopy bed and working fireplace. Look, they've been in business for years; they know how to do this right—just stay here, okay?

1905 Verot School Rd., Lafayette, LA 70508. *C* **800/984-9347** or 337/984-9347. Fax 337/984-9347. www.tfreres.com. 8 units, all with private bathroom. $100–$135 double; extra person $35. Rates include full breakfast. AE, DC, DISC, MC, V. **Amenities:** Welcome drinks and Cajun canapés (hors d'oeuvres). *In room:* A/C, TV, terry-cloth robes, Wi-Fi.

Bois des Chênes Inn ★

Three rooms at the Bois des Chênes Inn are in the carriage house, and two rooms, one with an open fireplace, are in the 1820s Acadian-style plantation home known as the Charles Mouton House. Now listed on the National Register of Historical Houses, Bois des Chênes was once the center of a 3,000-acre cattle and sugar plantation. Rooms are plain if you are used to the more lavish offerings splashed out in travel magazines. There are fireplaces in some rooms, and Wi-Fi in two rooms, as well as in the main public areas. The third-floor room with its long skinny bathroom and clawfoot tub is the most appealing. The grounds are quite pretty. The rates include a Louisiana-style breakfast, a bottle of wine, and a tour of the house. The owner, a geologist, can conduct nature and birding trips into the Atchafalaya Swamp on the weekend; the tours have been featured on over 40 television programs nationally and internationally. Note that at press time, the facility was for sale and may have different owners by now.

338 N. Sterling (at Mudd Ave.), Lafayette, LA 70501. *C* **337/233-7816.** Fax 337/233-7816. www.boisdechenes.com. 5 units. $110–$150 double. Rates include breakfast. Extra person $30. AE, MC, V. *In room:* A/C, TV, fridge, Wi-Fi (in 2 rooms).

La Maison de Belle ★★

This 1898 house sits on a large and pretty piece of property near the university, having been moved from its original location over 5 years ago. It's been lovingly restored to the point that it's one of the best-looking B&Bs in the city. The downstairs suite in particular is a knockout, with its own parlor and a bathroom that is practically an additional sitting room itself. It's just right for a honeymooning couple. The upstairs rooms have garret ceilings and double beds, and one has the original dinky cast-iron tub. The coolest thing is the cottage in back: a two-bedroom, dark cypress wood-paneled dwelling that author John Kennedy Toole called home during the 1960s and 1970s. Yes, he wrote part of *A Confederacy of Dunces* here, and now you can sleep where the (troubled) genius did. Given that it also has a full kitchen, it's a good choice for families, though it can be a little dark. (The effect is cozy at night.) The talented chef-owner lives in the house next door, and makes a tasty breakfast each morning.

610 Girard Park Dr., Lafayette, LA 70503 *C* **337/235-2520.** 5 units. $100–$125 (and sometimes up) double. Rates include breakfast. No credit cards. **Amenities:** Afternoon wine and hors d'oeuvres. *In room:* A/C, TV, hair dryer, iron/ironing board, Wi-Fi.

Dining in & Around Lafayette

Café Vermilionville INTERNATIONAL/CAJUN   Though it's highly touted locally, and a very pretty place to dine (it's in a beautifully restored old Acadian cypress house that dates back to 1799), we find it to be a bit disappointing. The food is extremely fussy, with layer upon layer of ingredients (as they recite specials, an entree will start out sounding lovely, but then they keep going and going describing everything that's on it, until you want to yell, "Stop!"), many of which are cream-sauce intensive. Having said that, the crawfish beignets are a perfect appetizer, and the pecan tilapia with a garlic-and-herb beurre blanc sauce comes with the sauce on the side, so the fish (crusted with pistachios and peppercorns) stays crunchy and relatively plain. Service can be inexplicably slow.

1304 W. Pinhook Rd. *C* **337/237-0100.** Fax 337/233-5599. www.cafev.com. Reservations and appropriate attire recommended. Main courses lunch $10–$18, dinner $27–$32. AE, DC, DISC, MC, V. Mon–Fri 11am–2pm; Mon–Sat 5:30–9:30pm. Closed major holidays.

Dean-o's ★ Kids PIZZA   Yeah, yeah, you're supposed to be eating jambalaya and red beans and rice, to say nothing of *boudin,* but let's pretend you have already, or that you've got a kid who just won't touch fish or something spicy. We know, it happens, and you can't send 'em back after they are born. Anyway, to this end, Dean-o's offers up the best pizza in Lafayette, with homemade olive oil crust and several homemade sauces. Even a small pizza is big enough for two to share, and they offer a sampler—up to four of their elaborate specialty combos on one pizza, perfect for the indecisive. Stuff your kid with the T. Rex (the "ultimate meat eaters") while you try the Marie Laveau, which has blue-point crab. But next meal, have some étouffée, *cher,* okay?

305 Bertrand (at Johnston St.). *C* **337/233-5446.** Takeout but no delivery. Main courses $5.25–$25 (for a giant specialty pizza). AE, DC, DISC, MC, V. Mon–Thurs 11am–11pm; Fri–Sat 11am–midnight; Sun 11am–9pm.

Edie's Express ★★ CAJUN   This is Lafayette's favorite breakfast place, and for good reason. Things will be smothered, but they will also be melt-in-your-mouth. And the biscuits? All you can ask for in baked dough.

1400 W. Pinhook Rd. *C* **337/234-2485.** All main courses under $9. AE, MC, V. Mon–Fri 5:30am–11am.

Prejean's ★★ CAJUN   An unpretentious family restaurant, this likeable place has live Cajun music every night. Their glory days may or may not be behind them, but the hearty meals at Prejean's still make this worth a drop-in. Their smoked duck and andouille gumbo (sans pheasant) is a Fest favorite, and justly, as are the crawfish enchiladas, which made one taster swear off the usual sort forever. There are lots of recognizable Cajun dishes, but with elaborate flourishes, perhaps sometimes erring on the gloppy side. Look for fried crawfish *boudin* balls and the seafood-stuffed mushrooms (think a sort of mini crab cake stuffed into a 'shroom) for appetizers, and shrimp stuffed with tasso and jack cheese, and then wrapped in bacon, or a more traditional, more staid blackened fish on top of crawfish étouffée for an entree. Matters are cheaper and lighter at lunch when the menu includes a BBQ shrimp po' boy and less expensive versions of the dinner menu. If the menu still lists the "fresh" Louisiana strawberry shortcake, insist on knowing for sure that they mean it before you order it, as the one we had featured a hideous gelatinous syrup instead of actual fruit.

3480 I-49 N. 337/896-3247. Fax 337/896-3278. www.prejeans.com. Reservations recommended for 15 or more. Children's menu $3.50–$8.95; main courses $17–$27; breakfast $5.50 and up. AE, DC, DISC, MC, V. Sun–Thurs 7am–10pm; Fri–Sat 7am–11pm. Take I-10 to exit 103B and then I-49 north to exit 2/ Gloria Switch.

Randol's Restaurant and Cajun Dance Hall ★ CAJUN

In addition to better-than-average Cajun food, Randol's offers a good-size, popular dance floor where dancers are likely to be locals enjoying their own *fais-do-do*. In fact, they eagerly volunteer when owner Frank Randol needs dancers for his traveling Cajun food-and-dance show. Back home, the star of the menu is seafood, all fresh from bayou or Gulf waters, and served fried, steamed, blackened, or grilled. (Given how often fried is the only option at most Cajun restaurants, the other alternatives alone make Randol's an attractive stop.) A house specialty is the seafood platter, which includes a cup of seafood gumbo, fried shrimp, fried oysters, fried catfish, stuffed crab, crawfish étouffée, French bread, and coleslaw. Randol's chef won the gold medal at the 22nd annual World's Championship Crawfish Etouffe Cookoff.

2320 Kaliste Saloom Rd. 800/YO-CAJUN (962-2586) or 337/981-7080. www.randols.com. Reservations accepted only for parties of 8 or more. Main courses $14–$27. MC, V. Sun–Thurs 5–10pm; Fri–Sat 5–11pm. Closed major holidays. From New Orleans, take I-10 west to exit 103A. Follow Evangeline Thruway to Pinhook Rd., turn right, and follow Pinhook to Kaliste Saloom Rd. (on the right). Randol's will be on your right.

MAMOU ★

There is one reason to come to Mamou and that's **Fred's Lounge** ★, 420 Sixth St. (337/468-5411)—and it's a darn good reason, too. At the other end of the Cajun music scale from the Savoy Music Center (p. 302), this small-town bar nonetheless offers just as essential an Acadiana Saturday-morning experience. For half a century, Fred's has been the site of Saturday daytime dances, for many years with Donald Thibodeaux & Cajun Fever playing from a "bandstand" that's really no more than a roped-off area in the middle of the floor. Couples waltz and two-step in the remaining space, and the whole thing airs from 8am to noon on radio station KVPI (1050 AM). While Savoy honors the folksy "house music" tradition, this is pure dance-hall stuff, a place for hardworking people to blow off steam and let loose. The music leans toward the country-western side of Cajun, with the band featuring steel guitar and drums along with accordion and fiddle. Everyone's welcome as long as you dive right in—though it might be a good idea to practice dancing with a drink in one hand before you give it a try here.

OPELOUSAS ★

Opelousas, the third-oldest city in Louisiana, is the seat (and heart) of St. Landry Parish; the courthouse is there, but for the average tourist, there isn't that much to see. It's such a pretty town, though—particularly the main drag, Landry Street—that passers-through often find themselves pulling over to have a look around. Opelousas has several chain hotels, so accommodations are easy to come by.

The **Tourist Center,** 828 E. Landry St. (© **800/424-5442** or 337/948-6263), is open Monday to Friday from 8am to 5pm, Saturday and Sunday 8am to 4pm. Famed frontiersman Jim Bowie lived in the building for a (really) short time as a child, and there is a small collection of ephemera devoted to him. Don't go out of your way for that, but do drop in for other tourist and lodging advice. You can also call the **St. Landry Parish Tourist Commission** (© **877/948-8004;** www.cajuntravel.com) for more info. Particularly during the spring and fall, they have frequent live music events so do check the website. Show up and go have a two-step. And in passing, admire the 300-year-old oak across the street from City Hall; its branches have gotten so heavy that in spots they not only touch the ground but are buried beneath the sod.

If you feel lost without proper tourist and museum-going experiences, you may drop by the **Opelousas Museum and Interpretive Center,** 329 N. Main St. (© **337/948-2589;** www.cityofopelousas.com; Mon–Sat 9am–5pm). The last weekend in October, Opelousas features its annual long-lived and delightfully named **Yambilee Festival,** a salute to everyone's favorite Thanksgiving side dish.

As for music, two of the best clubs in Cajun Country are here. The ultimate spot for zydeco, **Slim's Y Ki-Ki** (© **337/942-6242**) is located at 8393 Hwy. 182 in Opelousas. Most weekends, Slim's fills up to hot and sweaty capacity with some darn fine music. And just down the highway in Lawtell, the **Zydeco Hall of Fame** (formerly Richard's) is keeping the dance hall traditions of its legendary predecessor going strong (11154 Hwy. 190, Lawtell; © **337/349-8827;** www.thezydecohalloffame.com).

Accommodations

Unfortunately, the two nicest B&Bs in town (one of which was perhaps the finest in the entire region) have closed. Opelousas still has a **Super 8,** 5791 I-49 Service Rd. S. (© **337/942-6250**); a **Days Inn,** 5761 1-49 Service Rd. S. (© **337/407-0004**); and a **Holiday Inn,** 5696 I-49 Service Rd. N. (© **337/948-3300**), but if you are looking for less generic comfort, either stay up the road in Washington (p. 315), or call the Tourist Center or Tourist Commission (above) to see if any new and worthy establishments have opened up. Meanwhile, we list the only remaining B&B below.

Country Ridge Bed and Breakfast   This place is a throwback to the classic B&B, in which nice people rented you a room in their house. Which is precisely what this feels like—or even is. The house in question is a 1980s-style contemporary, and guest rooms are up-to-date with wireless Internet access, broadband, and fax and copy machines. The Southern Belle room (more feminine) and the Southwest Room (more masculine) have their own private bathrooms and also share a Jacuzzi tub for an extra fee. The economical "Study" is slightly smaller and has a bathroom across the hall. The Acadiana Suite is significantly larger, with access to a patio, washer and dryer, sound system, and Jacuzzi tub. All rooms have queen-size beds with high-thread-count sheets. A large living room has a DVD player and stereo. Don't miss the homemade banana-nut muffins, which the owners make with their homegrown ingredients! The pool area backs up to a thoroughbred horse farm. The entire property is nonsmoking. It's a bit like staying with nice relatives, in a very comfortable environment.

169 Country Ridge Rd., Opelousas, LA 70570. © **337/948-1678.** 4 units. $85–$165 double. Rates include continental breakfast. DISC, MC, V. Free parking. No children. No pets. **Amenities:** Jacuzzi; pool; Wi-Fi. *In room:* A/C, TV, hair dryer, robes.

Dining

Back in Time ★★ SANDWICHES/SALADS   This cafe and gift store is run by Wanda Juneau, only the second owner of the building since 1921. The first, shoe repairman Mr. Grecco, may still be haunting the place; ask Wanda to tell you her ghost stories. The cafe has homemade diner-type selections: sandwiches (including muffulettas with Back in Time's own olive dressing) and salads (with not-terribly Cajun dressings like honey-raspberry-walnut vinaigrette). The gooey desserts include Wanda's justly award-winning brownies. Admire the picture from a local bar from the 1920s—the man who bought the picture drank the last cup of coffee at that bar.

123 W. Landry St. ✆ **337/942-2413.** All items under $14. AE, MC, V. Mon–Fri 11:30am–4pm (lunch stops at 2:30pm); Sat 11:30am–2:30pm.

Palace Cafe ★★ CAJUN/GREEK   Owned by the same family since 1927, the Palace Cafe is the place to sate your crawfish cravings—it serves a heck of an étouffée, not to mention textbook versions of other local favorites. If the tradition doesn't bring you into this no-frills place, the location (right on the main drag) surely will. There are daily lunch specials.

135 W. Landry St. ✆ **337/942-2142.** Main courses $5.95–$14. AE, DISC, MC, V. Mon–Sat 6am–9pm.

ST. MARTINVILLE ★

This historic town dates from 1765 when it was a military station known as the Poste des Attakapas. It is also the last home of Emmeline Labiche, Henry Wadsworth Longfellow's Evangeline (see "The Real Evangeline" box on p. 293). There was a time when it was known as la Petite Paris—many French aristocrats fled their homeland during the Revolution and settled here, bringing with them such traditions as fancy balls, lavish banquets, and other forms of high living.

Seeing the Sights

Three of St. Martinville's main attractions revolve around Longfellow's epic poem *Evangeline.* Understandably, over time it was adopted with great pride by local Cajuns as part of their heritage. Too bad the poem's contents—including its heroine and her lover—are entirely fictitious, with only a vague connection to any historical personage. To read more about the evolution of the local folklore that has sprung up around the poem, look at the informative site www.lafayettetravel.com/culture/history/legendofevangeline.

The **Evangeline Monument,** on Main Street, is a statue to the side and slightly to the rear of St. Martin's Church. It was donated to the town in 1929 by a movie company that came here to film the epic. The star of that movie, Dolores del Rio, supposedly posed for the statue. This also reportedly marks the spot of the grave of the "real-life" Evangeline, Emmeline Labiche, herself a work of fiction by a local author in the early 20th century. (Don't say that out loud, though!)

At Port Street and Bayou Teche is the ancient **Evangeline Oak,** where self-proclaimed descendants say Emmeline's boat landed at the end of her long trip from Nova Scotia. Legend has it that it was here, too, that she learned of her lover's betrothal to another. As far as a sight goes, it's just a big tree, plus it's also possibly the third such oak so designated. But we like it. And it is right on the bayou, which makes for a pretty sight indeed. If you make a left at the tree, you will soon come upon a very nice memorial to the original Cajun settlers, a mural depicting their arrival after expulsion from Nova Scotia.

Also on the banks of Bayou Teche, just north of St. Martinville on La. Highway. 31 at 1200 N. Main St., is the **Longfellow-Evangeline State Historic Site** (✆ **888/677-2900** or 337/394-3754). The 157 acres that make up the park purportedly once belonged to Louis Pierre Arceneaux, allegedly Emmeline's real-life Gabriel, but we know how valid that story is. The **Olivier Plantation House** on the grounds, dating from about 1765, is typical of larger Acadian homes, with bricks made by hand and baked in the sun, a cypress frame and pegs (instead of nails), and bousillage construction on the upper floor. You can also see the *cuisine* (outdoor kitchen) and *magazin* (storehouse) out back. Admission to the park and house is $2 for adults, free for children 12 and under, school groups, and seniors. It's open daily from 9am to 5pm. Tours start every hour on the hour from 9am to 4pm. Questions about the tour can be directed to the Longfellow-Evangeline State Historic Site.

African-American Museum and Museum of the Acadian Memorial ★   Just down the block from the Acadian Memorial (where an eternal flame commemorates the expulsion of French immigrants from Canada, the same ones who eventually made their way to Louisiana and became Cajuns) is a small but well-designed exhibit discussing the various roles of African Americans within the local Cajun communities (both as slaves and free people), while the other side of the building does the same with the story and history of the Cajun people. Both are simple but exceedingly well done. *A sweet note:* The museum has a copy of the first recorded act of the local St. Martin de Tours church, the baptism and marriage of a woman from Senegal. A local contingent took a copy of this back to a village there and presented it to the locals, symbolically returning her to her people.

123 S. New Market St. (337/394-2258. Fax 337/394-2265. www.acadianmemorial.org/english/area. html#african. Free (but do make a donation). Daily 10am–4pm, closed major holidays.

St. Martin de Tours Church ★   This is the mother church of the Acadians, 201 Evangeline Blvd. ((337/394-6021); the building was constructed in 1836 on the site of a previous church building. It is the fourth-oldest Roman Catholic church in Louisiana. Father George Murphy, an Irish priest, was the first to associate it with its patron saint, St. Martin, in the 1790s, and there's a noteworthy portrait of the saint behind the main altar. You'll also see the original box pews, an ornate baptismal font (which some say was a gift from King Louis XVI of France), and the lovely old altar. Outside is a cemetery that purportedly holds the grave of Evangeline herself. Open daily 8:30am to 5pm.

The **Petit Paris Museum,** 103 S. Main St. ((337/394-7334), next to the church, often has some unexpectedly interesting displays—a recent visit found a terrific St. Martinville Mardi Gras exhibit with some splendiferous costumes and the extraordinary local story that inspired the theme that year. Guided tours of the church, antebellum rectory, and museum are available; call for details.

Admission $1. Thurs–Sat 10am–4pm.

Accommodations

Old Castillo Bed & Breakfast ★★   This place reminds us of a rooming house—it used to be a Catholic girls' school—though the rooms, with four-poster beds topped with pretty quilts, are quite a bit nicer than boarding school accommodations. They aren't lavish, but they are appealing, and the rates can be cheaper than at some local B&Bs. It's right next to the town square, though in a teeming metropolis like St. Martinville, that's not saying much. The rooms are generously sized—no. 3 is positively cavernous—but they can have food smells from the restaurant. Bathrooms (though private) are dinky. Four of the five rooms have tubs. All rooms and public areas have free Wi-Fi. The hot breakfast in the morning is most satisfying.

www.oldcastillo.com. 5 units. $80–$150 double. Rates include breakfast. AE, DISC, MC, V. Free parking. *In room:* A/C, Wi-Fi.

NEW IBERIA ★

This town dates from 1779, when a group of 300 immigrants from the Spanish province of Málaga came up Bayou Teche and settled here. It was incorporated in 1813, and its history changed drastically after the arrival of the steamboat *Plowboy* in 1836. New Iberia then became the terminal for steamboats traveling up the bayou from New Orleans, and it promptly developed the rambunctious character of a frontier town. In 1839, however, yellow fever traveled up the bayou with the steamboats and killed more than a quarter of the population. Many residents were saved, though, through the heroic nursing of a black woman called Tante Félicité, who had come here from Santo Domingo; she went tirelessly from family to family, carrying food and medicine. (She had had the fever many years before and was immune.)

During the Civil War, New Iberia was a Confederate training center and was attacked again and again. Some say that Confederate and Union soldiers alike plundered the land to such an extent that local Acadians threatened to declare war on *both* sides if any more of their chickens, cattle, and produce were appropriated. The steamboats continued coming up the bayou until 1947. (We bet you didn't know the steamboat era lasted that long anywhere in the U.S.) Today New Iberia, known as the Queen City of the Teche, continues to grow.

Seeing the Sights

"Alligator" Annie Miller has gone to the Big Swamp in the sky (and we miss her), but her son is continuing her legacy with **Annie Miller's Son's Swamp and Marsh Tours** ★ (ℂ **800/341-5441** or 985/868-4758; www.annie-miller.com). Come here (year-round, with evening tours that they swear aren't troubled by bugs in the summer) for a close-up look at the bayou and its wildlife. In a comfortable, Coast Guard licensed boat, you'll visit a rookery of nesting egrets and herons and can say hello to the gators who come when they are called ("*Bah*-bee! *Tone*-y! *Ti*-gar!") by the friendly operators of the very personal and delightful cruises. Tours cost $15 for adults, $10 for children 4 to 12, free for children under 3. Be sure to call for current schedules, to find out which location (there are several) is nearest you, and to make reservations.

Note: This is also worth the drive from New Orleans. Take U.S. 90 west through Houma (about 57 miles), exit right at the tourist office on St. Charles Street, turn left at the stoplight onto Southdown/Mandalay Road, and proceed to Miller's Landing on Big Bayou Black.

Jungle Gardens ★ Across the street from the Tabasco factory (but not affiliated with it), these gardens cover more than 200 acres with something in bloom November through June. On a self-guided driving or walking tour, you'll see a 1,000-year-old Buddha in the Chinese Garden, sunken gardens, a bird sanctuary (with egrets and herons), and tropical plants. There is a $1 car fee to drive onto Avery Island.

La. 329, Avery Island. ℂ **337/369-6243.** Admission $6.25 adults, $4.50 children 6–12, free for children 5 and under. Daily 9am–5:30pm.

Rip Van Winkle Gardens ★★ On the shores of Lake Peigneur, this is a place of huge oak trees, 350 years old or more, draped with Spanish moss. Originally known as Jefferson Island, it isn't a proper island, but a piece of land held up higher than its surroundings.

Actor Joseph Jefferson, who gained national fame for his portrayal of Rip Van Winkle, purchased the land in 1869 and erected an extravagant three-story home, much of which he designed himself. Although Jefferson did more than a little landscaping and gardening on the grounds, the Bayless family, which bought the estate in 1917, was responsible for the colorful panorama you see today.

The gardens were well developed when disaster struck in 1980—the lake disappeared after an oil company drilled into the salt mine, creating a gigantic whirlpool so powerful that it sucked in all the waters of the lake and huge portions of the adjacent gardens. The gardens have been rebuilt but have been reduced from their original 65 acres to a mere 25. Of course, that was before Hurricane Lily ripped through, damaging both house and gardens. But it's all restored, after a closure of 2½ years. A tour takes you through Jefferson's old home and gives you an idea of (wealthy) life 100 years ago. Pirate Jean Lafitte's brother-in-law was rumored to have owned this land before Jefferson, a bit of folklore that may have been proven when three pots of very old silver coins were unearthed here.

Admire the 550-year-old oak tree Grover Cleveland snoozed under, while walking around and pretending this land is yours, which you sort of can, thanks to B&B accommodations. This smashing setup may be the best bargain in all of Cajun Country. The guests are handed the keys (figuratively speaking) to this plantation when the place closes for the day. Accommodations consist of just three rooms, a stand-alone cottage plus two rooms in old servants' quarters behind the main house. Rooms are prettily decorated (we prefer the cottage) and include a sweet little minikitchen, four-poster beds, good linens, and great mattresses. Look for a nice gift basket of amenities in the modern gleaming bathrooms ($104 per night Sun–Thurs and $156 Fri–Sat; includes continental breakfast, and wine and cheese).

5505 Rip Van Winkle Rd., New Iberia, LA 70560. ℰ **337/359-8525.** www.ripvanwinklegardens.com. Admission $10 adults, $8 seniors and children 8–12, free for children 7 and under. Daily 9am–5pm.

Shadows-on-the-Teche Plantation ★★ This beautifully preserved 1834 Greek Revival home was only owned by one family (who had a nearby sugar plantation). Eighty-five percent of the contents are original to the house, and its history is well documented, which is unusual for plantation and old-home tours around here. The informative and practical tour gives a lot of specific detail about the family and their lives, particularly about life back during the heyday of such places, and what it took to support such a place. They even have photos of the property dating from 1870. The well-done visitor center has even more belongings on display.

317 E. Main St., New Iberia, LA 70560. ℰ **877/200-4924** or 337/369-6446. Fax 337/365-5213. www.shadows onthetreche.org. Admission $10 adults, $8 seniors, $6.50 children ages 6–11, free for children 5 and under. Mon–Sat 9am–4:30pm; Sun noon–4:30pm. From New Orleans (approx. 3 hr.), take U.S. 90 to La. 14 and follow La. 14 east to the intersection with La. 182.

Tabasco Sauce Factory ★★ Avery Island, south of New Iberia, sits atop a gigantic salt dome and the oldest salt-rock mine in the Western Hemisphere. However, it's not salt but pepper—fiery-hot peppers that grow especially well here—that's brought Avery Island its greatest fame. Tabasco brand pepper sauce, loved all over the world, is made by a close-knit family and equally close workers who grow the peppers and then nurse them through the fermentation process developed by Edmund McIlhenny, founder of the McIlhenny Company. Tour the Tabasco factory and visitor center, which includes an old-fashioned Tabasco Country Store. Expect to spend less than an hour. There is a $1 car fee to drive onto Avery Island.

La. 329, Avery Island. ✆ **337/365-8173.** www.tabasco.com. Free admission. Parking $1. Tours available daily 9am–4pm (no production Fri–Sun). From Lafayette, take Hwy. 90 to Hwy. 14, turn left to Hwy. 329, and turn right; it's about 7 miles down.

VILLE PLATTE ★

If you've fallen in love with Cajun music and want to take some home with you, you have a good reason to detour to the town of Ville Platte.

Floyd's Record Shop ★★   Long before Cajun and zydeco were known outside the region, Floyd Soileau was recording and releasing the music on three labels: Swallow for Cajun, Maison de Soul for zydeco, and Jin (named after his charming wife) for swamp pop, the regional offshoot of 1950s and early 1960s pop and soul styles. Eventually, he built a whole operation of recording, pressing (his plant was pressing vinyl well into the CD age), and selling records, by mail order and at this store. For fans of the music, this is a must-stop locale with a fine selection of Floyd's releases by such great artists as D. L. Menard (the Cajun Hank Williams) and Clifton Chenier (the King of Zydeco), as well as other releases that may be hard to find anywhere else. Current best sellers are available too—might as well get them here and help support an institution.

434 E. Main St. ✆ **800/738-8668** or 337/363-2138. Fax 337/363-5622. www.floydsrecords.com. DISC, MC, V. Mon–Sat 8:30am–5pm.

Dining

The Pig Stand ★★ PIG   As you might guess, the Pig Stand serves pig—oh, and such pig! It's a little dump of a local hangout (and we mean that in the best way possible) that also serves divine barbecued chicken and other Southern specialties for cheap prices. New owners are adding New Orleans po' boy, soft-shell crab, and other dishes from the big city to their menu. It's a real treat, so don't miss it. And it's just down the street from Floyd's in case you worked up an appetite buying music.

318 E. Main St. ✆ **337/363-2883.** Main courses $14 and under. AE, DISC, MC, V. Tues–Thurs 6:30am–9pm; Fri–Sat 6:30am–10pm; Sun 6:30am–2pm.

WASHINGTON ★

This is a very small town—10 minutes will get you all the highlights—but even non-residents will urge you to take the quick detour from Opelousas simply because it's so pretty. This is thanks in large part to an abundance of graceful old homes (of which there are even more than in other towns in the area) and trees. The many antiques stores are also a draw. At least seven of the old homes have been converted to B&Bs; staying here is an interesting, and more attractive, experience than a night in some other towns in Cajun Country.

If you plan only to drive through, it is worth getting out of the car for **Magnolia Ridge,** ½ mile north of town on Highway 103 (✆ **337/826-3027**). This 1820s house is not open to the public, but its 63 acres of gardens and paths, some winding down to the bayou, are.

You'll also find a few old **cemeteries** in Washington. All B&Bs in Washington will refer callers to others in the area if they're full on a particular night. We particularly liked **Camellia Cove,** 211 W. Hill St. (✆ **337/826-7362**), with double rooms (all air-conditioned but none with TV) starting at $135, including breakfast. The nicely restored old house has its original furniture from 1905. There are three bedrooms, two with private bathrooms—the large blue bedroom with the ornate wood bedstead is probably the best. The large front porch is perfect for sitting and rocking. *Note:* Camellia Cove does not accept credit cards. An alternative to B&B Land is the **Steamboat Cottages** (525 N. Main St.; ✆ **337/826-1009**), cute little cottages furnished with cypress, set right by the muddy bayou. The more-country setting, plus the opportunity to sit on your patio and listen to cicadas or old-time music played outside the restaurant next door, makes this an attractive option (though the price—$90 a night—has gone up a bit from what was a more economical fee).

The **Steamboat Warehouse Restaurant** ★★ (525 N. Main; ✆ **337/826-7227**) has solidly accurate takes on local cooking. Look for excellent versions of the usual étouffée, or better still, the deeply pleasurable catfish palmetto, pan-fried and topped with a crawfish cream sauce on a bed of wild rice. Open for dinner Tuesday to Saturday for dinner from 5 to 10pm and lunch on Sundays from 11am to 2pm.

Fast Facts

1 FAST FACTS: NEW ORLEANS

AMERICAN EXPRESS The local office is in the Central Business District at 201 St. Charles Ave. (℃ **800/508-0274**). It's open weekdays from 9am to 5pm.

AREA CODES The area code for New Orleans is 504.

ATM NETWORKS/CASHPOINTS See "Money & Costs," p. 54.

AUTOMOBILE ORGANIZATIONS Motor clubs will supply maps, suggested routes, guidebooks, accident and bail-bond insurance, and emergency road service. The **American Automobile Association (AAA)** is the major auto club in the United States. If you belong to a motor club in your home country, inquire about AAA reciprocity before you leave. You may be able to join AAA even if you're not a member of a reciprocal club; to inquire, call AAA (℃ **800/222-4357**; www.aaa.com). AAA is actually an organization of regional motor clubs, so look under "AAA Automobile Club" in the White Pages of the telephone directory. AAA has a nationwide emergency road service telephone number (℃ 800/AAA-HELP).

BABY SITTERS It's best to ask at your hotel about babysitting services. If your hotel doesn't offer help finding child care, try calling **Accent on Children's Arrangements** (℃ **504/524-1227**) or **Dependable Kid Care** (℃ **504/486-4001**).

BUSINESS HOURS Most stores are open 10am to 6pm; bars can stay open until the wee hours, and restaurants' hours vary depending on the types of meals they serve. Expect breakfast to start around 8am, lunch around 11am, and dinner at 6pm.

CAR RENTALS See "Getting There & Getting Around," in chapter 4, and "Airline, Hotel & Car Rental Websites," later in this chapter.

DRINKING LAWS The legal age for purchase and consumption of alcoholic beverages is 21; proof of age is required and often requested at bars, nightclubs, and restaurants, so it's always a good idea to bring ID when you go out. Bars can stay open all night in New Orleans, and liquor is sold in markets and liquor stores.

Do not carry open containers of alcohol in your car or any public area that isn't zoned for alcohol consumption. The police can fine you on the spot. And nothing will ruin your trip faster than getting a citation for DUI ("driving under the influence"), so don't even think about driving while intoxicated.

DRIVING RULES See "Getting There & Getting Around," in chapter 4.

ELECTRICITY Like Canada, the United States uses 110 to 120 volts AC (60 cycles), compared to 220 to 240 volts AC (50 cycles) in most of Europe, Australia, and New Zealand. Downward converters that change 220–240 volts to 110–120 volts are difficult to find in the United States, so bring one with you.

Wherever you go, bring a **connection kit** of the right power and phone adapters, a spare phone cord, and a spare Ethernet network cable—or find out whether your hotel supplies them to guests.

EMBASSIES & CONSULATES All embassies are located in the nation's capital, Washington, D.C. Some consulates are located in major U.S. cities, and most nations have a mission to the United Nations in New York City. If your country isn't listed below, call for directory information in Washington, D.C. (© 202/555-1212), or check **www.embassy.org/embassies**.

The embassy of **Australia** is at 1601 Massachusetts Ave. NW, Washington, DC 20036 (© **202/797-3000;** www.usa. embassy.gov.au). There are consulates in New York, Honolulu, Houston, Los Angeles, and San Francisco.

The embassy of **Canada** is at 501 Pennsylvania Ave. NW, Washington, DC 20001 (© **202/682-1740;** www.canadian embassy.org). Other Canadian consulates are in Buffalo (New York), Detroit, Los Angeles, New York, and Seattle.

The embassy of **Ireland** is at 2234 Massachusetts Ave. NW, Washington, DC 20008 (© **202/462-3939;** www.ireland emb.org). Irish consulates are in Boston, Chicago, New York, San Francisco, and other cities. See website for complete listing.

The embassy of **New Zealand** is at 37 Observatory Circle NW, Washington, DC 20008 (© **202/328-4800;** www.nz embassy.com). New Zealand consulates are in Los Angeles, Salt Lake City, San Francisco, and Seattle.

The embassy of the **United Kingdom** is at 3100 Massachusetts Ave. NW, Washington, DC 20008 (© **202/588-7800;** www.britainusa.com). Other British consulates are in Atlanta, Boston, Chicago, Cleveland, Houston, Los Angeles, New York, San Francisco, and Seattle.

EMERGENCIES For fire, ambulance, and police, dial © **911.** This is a free call from pay phones.

GASOLINE (PETROL) At press time, in the U.S., the cost of gasoline (also known as gas, but never petrol), is high, about $3 a gallon. Taxes are already included in the printed price. One U.S. gallon equals 3.8 liters or .85 imperial gallons. Fill-up locations are known as gas or service stations.

HOLIDAYS Banks, government offices, post offices, and many stores, restaurants, and museums are closed on the following legal national holidays: January 1 (New Year's Day), the third Monday in January (Martin Luther King, Jr., Day), the third Monday in February (Presidents' Day), the last Monday in May (Memorial Day), July 4 (Independence Day), the first Monday in September (Labor Day), the second Monday in October (Columbus Day), November 11 (Veterans' Day/Armistice Day), the fourth Thursday in November (Thanksgiving Day), and December 25 (Christmas). The Tuesday after the first Monday in November is Election Day, a federal government holiday in presidential-election years (held every 4 years, and next in 2012).

For more information on holidays see "Calendar of Events," in chapter 4.

HOSPITALS Because so many residents, including medical personnel, have been displaced by the hurricane, and their offices or hospitals remain closed, medical care in New Orleans is far more limited than it should be. If you have an ongoing problem or condition that may require very specific medical care, please take the time to find out what the current situation is before planning your trip. Should you become ill, call or go to the emergency room at **Ochsner Medical Center,** 1514 Jefferson Hwy. (© **504/842-3460**), or the **Tulane University Medical Center,** 1415 Tulane Ave. (© **504/588-5800**).

INSURANCE Medical Insurance Although it's not required of travelers, health insurance is highly recommended. Most health insurance policies cover you if you get sick away from home—but check your coverage before you leave.

International visitors to the U.S. should note that unlike many European countries, the United States does not usually offer free or low-cost medical care to its citizens or visitors. Doctors and hospitals are expensive, and in most cases will require advance payment or proof of coverage before they render their services. Good policies will cover the costs of an accident, repatriation, or death. Packages such as **Europ Assistance's "Worldwide Healthcare Plan"** are sold by European automobile clubs and travel agencies at attractive rates. **Worldwide Assistance Services, Inc.** (© 800/777-8710; www. worldwideassistance.com) is the agent for Europ Assistance in the United States. Though lack of health insurance may prevent you from being admitted to a hospital in nonemergencies, don't worry about being left on a street corner to die: The American way is to fix you now and bill the daylights out of you later.

If you're ever hospitalized more than 150 miles from home, **MedjetAssist** (© 800/527-7478; www.medjetassistance. com) will pick you up and fly you to the hospital of your choice in a medically equipped and staffed aircraft 24 hours day, 7 days a week. Annual memberships are $225 individual, $350 family; you can also purchase short-term memberships.

Canadians should check with their provincial health plan offices or call **Health Canada** (© 866/225-0709; www. hc-sc.gc.ca) to find out the extent of their coverage and what documentation and receipts they must take home in case they are treated in the United States.

Travelers from the U.K. should carry their European Health Insurance Card (EHIC), which replaced the E111 form as proof of entitlement to free/reduced cost medical treatment abroad (© 0845-606-2030; www.ehic.org.uk). Note, however, that the EHIC only covers "necessary medical treatment," and for repatriation costs, lost money, baggage, or cancellation, travel insurance from a reputable company should always be sought (www.travelinsuranceweb.com).

Travel Insurance The cost of travel insurance varies widely, depending on the destination, the cost and length of your trip, your age and health, and the type of trip you're taking, but expect to pay between 5% and 8% of the vacation itself. You can get estimates from various providers through **InsureMyTrip.com.** Enter your trip cost and dates, your age, and other information, for prices from more than a dozen companies.

U.K. citizens and their families who make more than one trip abroad per year may find an annual travel insurance policy works out cheaper. Check **www.money supermarket.com**, which compares prices across a wide range of providers for single- and multi-trip policies.

Most big travel agents offer their own insurance and will probably try to sell you their package when you book a holiday. Think before you sign. **Britain's Consumers' Association** recommends that you insist on seeing the policy and reading the fine print before buying travel insurance. **The Association of British Insurers** (© 020/ 7600-3333; www.abi.org.uk) gives advice by phone and publishes Holiday Insurance, a free guide to policy provisions and prices. You might also shop around for better deals: Try **Columbus Direct** (© 0870/033-9988; www.columbusdirect.net).

Trip-Cancellation Insurance Trip-cancellation insurance will help retrieve your money if you have to back out of a trip or depart early, or if your travel supplier goes bankrupt. Trip cancellation traditionally covers such events as sickness, natural disasters, and State Department advisories. The latest news in trip-cancellation insurance is the availability of **expanded hurricane coverage** and the **"any-reason"** cancellation coverage—which costs more but covers cancellations made for any reason. You won't get back 100% of your prepaid trip cost, but you'll be refunded a substantial portion. **TravelSafe** (© 888/ 885-7233; www.travelsafe.com) offers both types of coverage. Expedia also offers any-reason cancellation coverage for its air-hotel packages. For details, contact one of the following recommended insurers: **Access America** (✆ 866/807-3982; www.accessamerica.com); **Travel Guard International** (✆ 800/826-4919; www.travelguard.com); **Travel Insured International** (✆ 800/243-3174; www.travelinsured.com); or **Travelex Insurance Services** (✆ 888/457-4602; www.travelex-insurance.com).

INTERNET ACCESS Most of New Orleans is Wi-Fi accessible. Check out copy shops like **FedEx Office** (formerly, FedEx Kinko's), which offers computer stations with fully loaded software (as well as Wi-Fi).

LAUNDROMATS The family-owned and -operated Washing Well (841 Bourbon St.; ✆ **504/525-3983;** Mon–Sat 7:30am–5pm) has been in business since 1949, so they must know what they are doing. Services include self-laundry, but also reasonably priced 1-hour washing and drying, plus regular dry cleaning. They pick up and deliver, and are conveniently located on Bourbon Street, so you can have a quick quaff while waiting for your clothes.

LEGAL AID If you are "pulled over" for a minor infraction (such as speeding), never attempt to pay the fine directly to a police officer; this could be construed as attempted bribery, a much more serious crime. Pay fines by mail, or directly into the hands of the clerk of the court. If accused of a more serious offense, say and do nothing before consulting a lawyer. Here the burden is on the state to prove a person's guilt beyond a reasonable doubt, and everyone has the right to remain silent, whether he or she is suspected of a crime or actually arrested. Once arrested, a person can make one telephone call to a party of his or her choice. International visitors should call your embassy or consulate.

LIQUOR LAWS The legal drinking age in Louisiana is 21, but don't be surprised if people much younger take a seat next to you at the bar. Alcoholic beverages are available round-the-clock, 7 days a week. You're allowed to drink on the street but not from a glass or bottle. Bars will often provide a plastic "go cup" that you can transfer your drink to as you leave (and some have walk-up windows for quick and easy refills).

A warning: Although the police may look the other way if they see a pedestrian who's had a few too many (as long as he or she is peaceful and is not bothering anyone), they have no tolerance at all for those who are intoxicated behind the wheel.

LOST & FOUND Be sure to tell all of your credit card companies the minute you discover your wallet has been lost or stolen and file a report at the nearest police precinct. Your credit card company or insurer may require a police report number or record of the loss. Most credit card companies have an emergency toll-free number to call if your card is lost or stolen; they may be able to wire you a cash advance immediately or deliver an emergency credit card in a day or two. Visa's U.S. emergency number is ✆ **800/847-2911** or 410/581-9994. American Express cardholders and traveler's check holders should call ✆ **800/221-7282.** MasterCard holders should call ✆ **800/307-7309** or 636/722-7111. For other credit cards, call the toll-free number directory at ✆ **800/555-1212.**

If you need emergency cash over the weekend when all banks and American Express offices are closed, you can have money wired to you via **Western Union** (✆ **800/325-6000;** www.westernunion.com).

MAIL At press time, domestic postage rates were 28¢ for a postcard and 44¢ for a letter. For international mail, a first-class letter of up to 1 ounce costs 98¢ (75¢ to Canada and 79¢ to Mexico); a first-class postcard costs the same as a letter. For more information go to **www.usps.com.**

If you aren't sure what your address will be in the United States, mail can be sent to you, in your name, c/o General Delivery at the main post office of the city or region where you expect to be. (Call ✆ **800/275-8777** for information on the nearest post office.) The addressee must pick up mail in person and must produce proof of identity (driver's license, passport, and so on). Most post offices will hold your mail for up to 1 month, and are open Monday to Friday from 8am to 6pm, and Saturday from 9am to 3pm.

The main post office in New Orleans is at 701 Loyola Ave. In the Quarter, there is one at 1022 Iberville. If you have something large or fragile to send home and don't feel like hunting around for packing materials, go to **Royal Mail Service,** 828 Royal St., near St. Ann Street (✆ **504/522-8523**) in the Quarter.

Always include zip codes when mailing items in the U.S. If you don't know your zip code, visit www.usps.com/zip4.

MEDICAL CONDITIONS If you have a medical condition that requires **syringe-administered medications,** carry a valid signed prescription from your physician; syringes in carry-on baggage will be inspected. Insulin in any form should have the proper pharmaceutical documentation. If you have a disease that requires treatment with **narcotics,** you should also carry documented proof with you—smuggling narcotics aboard a plane carries severe penalties in the U.S.

For **HIV-positive visitors,** requirements for entering the United States are somewhat vague and change frequently. For up-to-the-minute information, contact **AIDSinfo** (✆ **800/448-0440** or 301/519-6616 outside the U.S.; www.aidsinfo.nih.gov) or the **Gay Men's Health Crisis** (✆ **212/367-1000;** www.gmhc.org).

NEWSPAPERS & MAGAZINES To find out what's going on around town, you might want to pick up a copy of the daily *Times-Picayune* (www.nola.com) or *Offbeat*

(www.offbeat.com), a monthly guide (probably the most extensive one available) to the city's evening entertainment, art galleries, and special events. It can be found in most hotels, though it's often hard to locate toward the end of the month. The *Gambit Weekly* (www.bestofneworleans.com) is the city's free alternative paper and has a good mix of news and entertainment information. It comes out every Sunday. The paper conducts an annual **"Best of New Orleans"** readers' poll; check their website for the results.

PASSPORTS The websites listed provide downloadable passport applications as well as the current fees for processing applications. For an up-to-date, country-by-country listing of passport requirements around the world, go to the "International Travel" tab of the U.S. State Department at **http://travel.state.gov.** International visitors to the U.S. can obtain a visa application at the same website. *Note:* Children are required to present a passport when entering the United States at airports. More information on obtaining a passport for a minor can be found at http://travel.state.gov. Allow plenty of time before your trip to apply for a passport; processing normally takes 4–6 weeks (3 weeks for expedited service) but can take longer during busy periods (especially spring). And keep in mind that if you need a passport in a hurry, you'll pay a higher processing fee.

For Residents of Australia You can pick up an application from your local post office or any branch of Passports Australia, but you must schedule an interview at the passport office to present your application materials. Call the **Australian Passport Information Service** at ✆ **131-232,** or visit the government website at www.passports.gov.au.

For Residents of Canada Passport applications are available at travel agencies throughout Canada or from the central **Passport Office,** Department of Foreign

Affairs and International Trade, Ottawa, ON K1A 0G3 (© **800/567-6868;** www. ppt.gc.ca). *Note:* Canadian children who travel must have their own passport.

For Residents of Ireland   You can apply for a 10-year passport at the **Passport Office,** Setanta Centre, Molesworth Street, Dublin 2 (© **01/671-1633;** www.irlgov.ie/ iveagh). Those under age 18 and over 65 must apply for a 3-year passport. You can also apply at 1A South Mall, Cork (© **21/ 494-4700**) or at most main post offices.

For Residents of New Zealand   You can pick up a passport application at any New Zealand Passports Office or download it from their website. Contact the **Passports Office** at © **0800/225-050** in New Zealand or 04/474-8100, or log on to www. passports.govt.nz.

For Residents of the United Kingdom   To pick up an application for a standard 10-year passport (5-yr. passport for children under 16), visit your nearest passport office, major post office, or travel agency or contact the **United Kingdom Passport Service** at © **0870/521-0410** or search its website at www.ukpa.gov.uk.

For Residents of the United States: Whether you're applying in person or by mail, you can download passport applications from the U.S. State Department website at **http://travel.state.gov.** To find your regional passport office, either check the U.S. State Department website or call the **National Passport Information Center** toll-free number (© **877/487-2778**) for automated information.

PHARMACIES   Drugstores still aren't back in the numbers they were pre-Katrina. While there is a Walgreens located on the corner of Iberville and Royal (© **504/525-2180**), the closest 24-hour pharmacy to the Quarter is Walgreens at 1801 St. Charles (© **504/561-8458**). There is also a 24-hour **Rite Aid** at 3401 St. Charles Ave., at Louisiana Avenue (© **504/ 896-4575**), which is more convenient if

you're staying Uptown or in the Garden District.

POLICE   Dial © **911** for emergencies. This is a free call from pay phones.

POST OFFICE   The main post office is at 701 Loyola Ave. In the Quarter, there is one at 1022 Iberville. If you have something large or fragile to send home and don't feel like hunting around for packing materials, go to **Royal Mail Service,** 828 Royal St., near St. Ann Street (© **504/ 522-8523**) in the Quarter.

RADIO   **WWOZ** (90.7 FM) is *the* New Orleans radio station. They say they are the best in the world, and we aren't inclined to disagree. New Orleans jazz, R&B, brass bands, Mardi Gras Indians, gospel, Cajun, zydeco—it's all here. It's such a vital part of the city's soundtrack that during the days the station was off the air, another public radio station took to broadcasting old OZ tapes on the Internet, to help keep it alive. Its studio in Armstrong Park was damaged, so it's temporarily located near the French Market. Tune in, feel the beat, and support it. The city's NPR station is **WWNO** (89.9 FM). Also, Tulane's station, **WTUL** (91.5 FM), plays very interesting, eclectic, art-rock, college-radio-station music.

SMOKING   Smoking is allowed in free-standing bars, but not in establishments serving food.

TAXES   The United States has no value-added tax (VAT) or other indirect tax at the national level. Every state, county, and city may levy its own local tax on all purchases, including hotel and restaurant checks and airline tickets. These taxes will not appear on price tags. The sales tax in New Orleans is 9%. An additional 4% tax is added to hotel bills for a total of 13%. There is also a nightly tax of 50¢ to $2 based on the number of rooms a hotel has.

TELEPHONES   Many convenience groceries and packaging services sell **prepaid calling cards** in denominations up to $50;

for international visitors these can be the least expensive way to call home. Many public pay phones at airports now accept American Express, MasterCard, and Visa credit cards. **Local calls** made from pay phones in most locales cost either 25¢ or 35¢ (no pennies, please). Most long-distance and international calls can be dialed directly from any phone. **For calls within the United States and to Canada,** dial 1 followed by the area code and the seven-digit number. **For other international calls,** dial 011 followed by the country code, city code, and the number you are calling.

Calls to area codes **800, 888, 877,** and **866** are toll-free. However, calls to area codes **700** and **900** (chat lines, bulletin boards, "dating" services, and so on) can be very expensive—usually a charge of 95¢ to $3 or more per minute, and they sometimes have minimum charges that can run as high as $15 or more.

For **reversed-charge or collect calls,** and for person-to-person calls, dial the number 0 then the area code and number; an operator will come on the line, and you should specify whether you are calling collect, person-to-person, or both. If your operator-assisted call is international, ask for the overseas operator.

For **local directory assistance** ("information"), dial $\mathcal{O}$ 411; for long-distance information, dial 1, then the appropriate area code and 555-1212.

TELEGRAPH, TELEX & FAX Telegraph and telex services are provided primarily by **Western Union** ($\mathcal{O}$ **800/325-6000;** www.westernunion.com). You can telegraph (wire) money, or have it telegraphed to you, very quickly over the Western Union system, but this service can cost as much as 15% to 20% of the amount sent.

Most hotels have **fax machines** available for guest use (be sure to ask about the charge to use it). Many hotel rooms are wired for guests' fax machines. A less expensive way to send and receive faxes may be at stores such as the **UPS Store.**

TIME New Orleans is located in the Central Time zone. The continental United States is divided into **four time zones:** Eastern Standard Time (EST), Central Standard Time (CST), Mountain Standard Time (MST), and Pacific Standard Time (PST). Alaska and Hawaii have their own zones. For example, when it's 9am in Los Angeles (PST), it's 7am in Honolulu (HST), 10am in Denver (MST), 11am in Chicago (CST), noon in New York City (EST), 5pm in London (GMT), and 2am the next day in Sydney.

Daylight saving time is in effect from 1am on the second Sunday in March to 1am on the first Sunday in November, except in Arizona, Hawaii, the U.S. Virgin Islands, and Puerto Rico. Daylight saving time moves the clock 1 hour ahead of standard time.

TIPPING Tips are a very important part of certain workers' income, and gratuities are the standard way of showing appreciation for services provided. (Tipping is certainly not compulsory if the service is poor!) In hotels, tip **bellhops** at least $1 per bag ($2–$3 if you have a lot of luggage) and tip the **chamber staff** $1 to $2 per day (more if you've left a disaster area for him or her to clean up). Tip the **doorman** or **concierge** only if he or she has provided you with some specific service (for example, calling a cab for you or obtaining difficult-to-get theater tickets). Tip the **valet-parking attendant** $1 every time you get your car.

In restaurants, bars, and nightclubs, tip **service staff** 15% to 20% of the check, tip **bartenders** 10% to 15%, tip **checkroom attendants** $1 per garment, and tip **valet-parking attendants** $1 per vehicle.

As for other service personnel, tip **cab drivers** 15% of the fare; tip **skycaps** at airports at least $1 per bag ($2–$3 if you have a lot of luggage); and tip **hairdressers** and **barbers** 15% to 20%.

TOILETS You won't find public toilets or "restrooms" on the streets in most U.S. cities but they can be found in hotel lobbies, bars, restaurants, museums, department stores, railway and bus stations, and service stations. Large hotels and fast-food restaurants are often the best bet for clean facilities. Restaurants and bars in resorts or heavily visited areas may reserve their restrooms for patrons.

TRANSIT INFORMATION Local bus routes and schedules can be obtained from the **RTA Ride Line** (✆ **504/248-3900;** www.norta.org). **Union Passenger Terminal,** 1001 Loyola Ave., provides bus information (✆ **504/524-7571**) and train information (✆ **504/528-1610;** www.amtrak.com) and is the place where trains and buses deliver and pick up their passengers who are traveling away from or into New Orleans.

USEFUL PHONE NUMBERS U.S. Dept. of State Travel Advisory: ✆ 202/647-5225 (manned 24 hrs.).

U.S. Passport Agency: ✆ 202/647-0518.

U.S. Centers for Disease Control International Traveler's Hotline: ✆ 404/332-4559.

VISAS For information about U.S. Visas, go to **http://travel.state.gov** and click on "Visas." Or go to one of the following websites:

Australian citizens can obtain up-to-date visa information from the **U.S. Embassy Canberra,** Moonah Place, Yarralumla, ACT 2600 (✆ **02/6214-5600**) or by checking the U.S. Diplomatic Mission's website at **http://usembassy-australia. state.gov/consular**.

British subjects can obtain up-to-date visa information by calling the **U.S. Embassy Visa Information Line** (✆ **0891/ 200-290**) or by visiting the "Visas to the U.S." section of the American Embassy London's website at **www.usembassy.org.uk**.

Irish citizens can obtain up-to-date visa information through the **Embassy of the USA Dublin,** 42 Elgin Rd., Dublin 4, Ireland (✆ **353/1-668-8777**) or by checking the "Consular Services" section of the website at **http://dublin.usembassy.gov**.

Citizens of **New Zealand** can obtain up-to-date visa information by contacting the **U.S. Embassy New Zealand,** 29 Fitzherbert Terrace, Thorndon, Wellington (✆ **644/472-2068**), or get the information directly from the website at **http:// wellington.usembassy.gov**.

2 AIRLINE, HOTEL & CAR-RENTAL WEBSITES

MAJOR AIRLINES

Aeroméxico
✆ 800/237-6639
www.aeromexico.com

Air Canada
✆ 888/247-2262 (in U.S. or Canada)
✆ 0871/220-1111 (in U.K.)
www.aircanada.com

Air France
✆ 800/237-2747 (in U.S.)
✆ 800/667-2747 (in Canada)
✆ 0871/663-3777 (in U.K.)
www.airfrance.com

Air New Zealand
✆ 800/262-1234 (in U.S.)
✆ 800/663-5494 (in Canada)
✆ 0800/028-4149 (in U.K.)
www.airnewzealand.com

American Airlines
✆ 800/433-7300 (in U.S. or Canada)
✆ 020/7365-0777 (in U.K.)
www.aa.com

British Airways
✆ 800/247-9297 (in U.S. and Canada)
✆ 0870/850-9850 (in U.K.)
www.british-airways.com

Continental Airlines
☎ 800/523-3273 (in U.S. or Canada)
☎ 0845/607-6760 (in U.K.)
www.continental.com

Delta Air Lines
☎ 800/221-1212 (in U.S. or Canada)
☎ 0845/600-0950 (in U.K.)
www.delta.com

Northwest Airlines
☎ 800/225-2525 (in U.S. or Canada)
☎ 0871/231-0000 (in U.K.)
www.nwa.com

United Airlines
☎ 800/864-8331 (in U.S. and Canada)
☎ 084/5844-4777 (in U.K.)
www.united.com

US Airways
☎ 800/428-4322
www.usairways.com

BUDGET AIRLINES

AirTran Airways
☎ 800/247-8726
www.airtran.com

JetBlue Airways
☎ 800/538-2583
www.jetblue.com

Southwest Airlines
☎ 800/435-9792
www.southwest.com

MAJOR HOTEL & MOTEL CHAINS

Best Western International
☎ 800/780-7234 (in U.S. or Canada)
☎ 0800/393-130 (in U.K.)
www.bestwestern.com

Clarion Hotels
☎ 877/424-6423 (in U.S. or Canada)
☎ 0800/444-444 (in U.K.)
www.choicehotels.com

Comfort Inns
☎ 877/424-6423 (in U.S. or Canada)
☎ 0800/444-444 (in U.K.)
www.comfortinn.com

Courtyard by Marriott
☎ 888/236-2427 (in U.S. or Canada)
☎ 0800/221-222 (in U.K.)
www.marriott.com/courtyard

Crowne Plaza Hotels
☎ 800/227-6963 (in U.S. or Canada)
☎ 0800/8222-8222 (in U.K.)
www.ichotelsgroup.com/crowneplaza

Days Inn
☎ 800/329-7466 (in U.S. or Canada)
☎ 0800/0280-400 (in U.K.)
www.daysinn.com

Doubletree Hotels
☎ 800/445-8667 (in U.S. or Canada)
☎ 0800/4445-8667 (in U.K.)
www.doubletree.com

Econo Lodges
☎ 877/424-6423 (in U.S. or Canada)
☎ 0800/444-444 (in U.K.)
www.choicehotels.com

Embassy Suites
☎ 800/445-8667 (in U.S. or Canada)
☎ 0800/4445-8667 (in U.K.)
www.embassysuites.com

Fairfield Inn by Marriott
☎ 888/236-2427 (in U.S. or Canada)
☎ 0800/221-222 (in U.K.)
www.fairfieldinn.com

Four Points by Sheraton
☎ 800/368-7764 (in U.S. or Canada)
☎ 021/493-0493 (in U.K.)
www.starwoodhotels.com/fourpoints

Hampton Inn
☎ 800/445-8667 (in U.S. or Canada)
☎ 0800/4445-8667 (in U.K.)
www.hamptoninn1.hilton.com

Hilton Garden Inn
✆ 800/445-8667 (in U.S. or Canada)
✆ 0800/4445-8667 (in U.K.)
http://hiltongardeninn1.hilton.com

Hilton Hotels
✆ 800/445-8667 (in U.S. or Canada)
✆ 0800/4445-8667 (in U.K.)
www.hilton.com

Holiday Inn
✆ 800/465-4329 (in U.S. or Canada)
✆ 0800/405-060 (in U.K.)
www.holidayinn.com

Homewood Suites
✆ 800/445-8667 (in U.S. or Canada)
✆ 0800/4445-8667 (in U.K.)
http://homewoodsuites1.hilton.com

Hyatt
✆ 888/591-1234 (in U.S. or Canada)
✆ 0845/888-1234 (in U.K.)
www.hyatt.com

InterContinental Hotels & Resorts
✆ 800/424-6835 (in U.S. or Canada)
✆ 0800/1800-1800 (in U.K.)
www.ichotelsgroup.com

La Quinta Inns and Suites
✆ 800/753-3757
www.lq.com

Loews Hotels
✆ 866/563-9792
www.loewshotels.com

Marriott
✆ 888/236-2427 (in U.S. or Canada)
✆ 0800/221-222 (in U.K.)
www.marriott.com

Motel 6
✆ 800/466-8356
www.motel6.com

Omni Hotels
✆ 800/843-6664
www.omnihotels.com

Quality
✆ 877/424-6423 (in U.S. or Canada)
✆ 0800/444-444 (in U.K.)
www.qualityinn.choicehotels.com

Radisson Hotels & Resorts
✆ 800/395-7046 (in U.S. or Canada)
✆ 0800/374-411 (in U.K.)
www.radisson.com

Ramada Worldwide
✆ 800/272-6232 (in U.S. or Canada)
✆ 0808/1000-783 (in U.K.)
www.ramada.com

Red Carpet Inns
✆ 800/251-1962
www.bookroomsnow.com

Renaissance
✆ 888/236-2427 (in U.S. or Canada)
✆ 0800/221-222 (in U.K.)
www.renaissancehotels.com

Residence Inn by Marriott
✆ 888/236-2427 (in U.S. or Canada)
✆ 0800/221-222 (in U.K.)
www.marriott.com/residenceinn

Sheraton Hotels & Resorts
✆ 800/325-2525 (in U.S. or Canada)
✆ 0800/3253-5353 (in U.K.)
www.starwoodhotels.com/sheraton

Staybridge Suites
✆ 800/238-8000 (in U.S. or Canada)
✆ 0800/988-4663 (in U.K.)
www.staybridge.com

Super 8 Motels
✆ 800/800-8000
www.super8.com

Travelodge
✆ 800/578-7878
www.travelodge.com

Westin Hotels & Resorts
✆ 800/937-8461 (in U.S. or Canada)
✆ 0800/3259-5959 (in U.K.)
www.starwoodhotels.com/westin

W Hotels Worldwide
✆ 877/946-8357 (in U.S. or Canada)
✆ 0800/3252-5252 (in U.K.)
www.starwoodhotels.com/whotels

Wyndham Hotels & Resorts
✆ 800/996-3426
www.wyndham.com

CAR-RENTAL AGENCIES

Advantage
℃ 800/654-3131
www.advantage.com

Alamo
℃ 877/222-9075
www.alamo.com

Avis
℃ 800/331-1212 (in U.S. or Canada)
℃ 0870/010-0287 (in U.K.)
www.avis.com

Budget
℃ 800/527-0700 (in U.S.)
℃ 800/268-8900 (in Canada)
℃ 0870/156-5656 (in U.K.)
www.budget.com

Dollar
℃ 800/800-3665
www.dollar.com

Enterprise
℃ 800/261-7331
www.enterprise.com

Hertz
℃ 800/654-3131 (in U.S. or Canada)
℃ 0870/844-8844 (in U.K.)
www.hertz.com

National
℃ 877/222-9058
www.nationalcar.com

Thrifty
℃ 800/847-4389
www.thrifty.com

FAST FACTS

13

AIRLINE, HOTEL & CAR-RENTAL WEBSITES

INDEX

See also Accommodations and Restaurant indexes, below.